Praise for
The Prevention of Crime

The Prevention of Crime is scholarly, comprehensive, and accessible—three essential criteria for making a text ideal for classroom use. But two insights, integrated across its pages, allow this volume to provide a special learning experience. First, it shows that crime can be prevented in diverse ways, whether across the life course or across social contexts. And second, it shows that evidence matters, playing a crucial role in telling us which interventions are most likely to save offenders from a life in crime and to make communities safer.

Francis T. Cullen, *University of Cincinnati*

This is the first text on evidence-based crime prevention that provides a comprehensive overview of how to identify effective programs, what they offer, what is required to implement them, and their current utilization. Both authors played leading roles in identifying and promoting evidence-based programs, and in making them more accessible to public officials and practitioners.

Peter Greenwood, *Association for the Advancement of Evidence-Based Practice*

The Prevention of Crime is an indispensable resource for prevention researchers, instructors, and students. This tour de force combines in one source up-to-date research on all aspects relevant to the prevention of crime. It provides definitions of crime and prevention, relates the history of crime prevention, summarizes theories about the causes of crime and research on the causes and consequences of crime, and discusses crime measurement and standards for intervention research. It provides a comprehensive framework for thinking about different prevention approaches and summarizes what is known about each approach generally as well as about specific examples of policies and practices within each approach. It discusses challenges to translating research on effective programs into usual practice. This book is a valuable reference for prevention researchers and will quickly become the main text used for teaching about prevention.

Denise C. Gottfredson, *University of Maryland*

The Prevention of Crime

Delbert Elliott and Abigail Fagan

WILEY Blackwell

This edition first published 2017
© 2017 John Wiley & Sons, Inc.

Registered Office
John Wiley & Sons, Ltd, The Atrium, Southern Gate, Chichester, West Sussex, PO19 8SQ, UK

Editorial Offices
350 Main Street, Malden, MA 02148-5020, USA
9600 Garsington Road, Oxford, OX4 2DQ, UK
The Atrium, Southern Gate, Chichester, West Sussex, PO19 8SQ, UK

For details of our global editorial offices, for customer services, and for information about how to apply for permission to reuse the copyright material in this book please see our website at www.wiley.com/wiley-blackwell.

The right of Delbert Elliott and Abigail Fagan to be identified as the authors of this work has been asserted in accordance with the UK Copyright, Designs and Patents Act 1988.

Library of Congress Cataloging-in-Publication data applied for.

Paperback: 9781118843598

A catalogue record for this book is available from the British Library.

Cover image: Security camera © Blazej Lyjak/Shutterstock

Set in 10.5/13pt Bembo by SPi Global, Pondicherry, India
Printed in Singapore by C.O.S. Printers Pte Ltd

1   2017

Contents

Preface

Our aim with this text is to present a fresh, up to date, comprehensive, and first-hand account of what is currently known about crime prevention. The content includes the theoretical foundation of crime prevention, new strategies and methods for evaluating the effectiveness of prevention programs, the identification of interventions that have been proven to work, and issues involved in getting these programs adopted and well implemented on a national or state-wide scale. As you may or may not know prior to reading this book, there are also programs that have been proven ineffective and in some cases even harmful. We will identify these interventions as well. It is as critical to know what does not work as what does work, especially since most interventions used in the past were ineffective, and even today, interventions shown to *increase* crime are being used.

An updated approach to crime prevention is needed because in the past decade, there has been a paradigm shift in theoretical thinking about the causes of crime. This shift in thinking about the causes of crime has led to new research findings and new approaches to the design, evaluation, and implementation of crime prevention and rehabilitation programs. It also involves the emergence of the life course developmental paradigm which views crime as a response to social, emotional, and physical barriers to a positive course of child and adolescent development. A new field of prevention science based on the public health approach to prevention and involving a new classification of types of prevention programs has also emerged. In addition, we now have improved measures of criminal behavior based upon the National Research Council's (1986) study of criminal careers that improve our understanding about different dimensions of involvement in criminal activity. These are relatively recent developments which have reshaped criminological thinking about crime prevention, and we draw from these advances with the goal of stimulating your interest in prevention science and providing you with scientifically proven methods for significantly reducing rates of criminal behavior.

We are now in what has been called "the golden age" of evidence-based interventions. Evidence-based interventions are prevention programs, practices, and policies that have been proven effective in experimental evaluations, primarily in randomized controlled trials (RCTs) like those used to evaluate the effectiveness and safety of new medical drugs. National task forces have been created to review the scientific standards that should be used to certify interventions as evidence-based, and many federal justice, health, and human service agencies, as well as a number of related professional organizations, have established registries with lists of interventions shown to be evidence-based in order to promote their increased use. In the United States, federal legislation has funded large-scale initiatives to increase the dissemination of specific evidence-based programs, including those that claim to prevent delinquency, like the $1.5 billion initiative (2010–2014) funding evidence-based home visitation programs and a $109 million (FY 2014) initiative for evidence-based teen pregnancy prevention programs. Recent legislation (in 2016) has established a federal bipartisan Commission on Evidence-Based Policymaking. And there is now strong public and private support for RCT evaluations as the preferred standard for certifying evidence-based interventions. All of these developments will be described in this book with particular attention to their significance for the prevention of crime.

We have chosen to write this book because we have been on the front lines of current research on crime prevention. Dr Elliott's research includes directing one of the few national longitudinal studies of crime, substance use, and mental health problems. The National Youth Survey involved a representative panel of American youth followed into their middle adult years, allowing identification of the major risk factors and barriers to a successful course of child and adolescent development that predicted later involvement in criminal behavior. Dr Elliott also directs one of the current evidence-based registries of effective prevention programs, Blueprints for Healthy Youth Development, a Consumers Reports type initiative which reviews all the evidence for a program's effectiveness and certifies those programs proven to work. Both authors have conducted many evaluations of delinquency, drug and crime prevention programs, including RCTs of individual programs and evaluations of community-based systems and national crime prevention initiatives designed to increase the dissemination of evidence-based initiatives. Dr Fagan has provided one-on-one training and consultation to numerous schools, community coalitions, and other groups to improve the implementation of evidence-based interventions. We are intimately aware of the issues surrounding the identification of evidence-based crime prevention programs, practices, and policies, and why so few of these interventions are being well implemented in communities and at a scale necessary to have some impact on national rates of crime. We believe this text represents the cutting edge of knowledge about crime prevention and provides insight into what is known about crime prevention, what is controversial, and the direction of future work on the prevention of crime.

Finally, we have tried to present this information in an engaging, forthright manner. If you find it boring, we will have failed. We think that understanding why persons come to engage in criminal behavior and how we can intervene to prevent this type of behavior are among the most exciting tasks we can engage in as scientists and practitioners of crime prevention. These topics should not be boring. They are complex and will require some study and diligence on your part, but if the information you learn in this textbook leads to a deeper understanding and/or to a career in some aspect of crime prevention, we will have realized our goal. In any event, we thank you for reading the text and welcome your comments and suggestions.

Delbert Elliott and Abigail Fagan
August 2016

Acknowledgments

This book discusses findings generated by passionate, dedicated, and forward-thinking scientists too numerous to count. We want to offer a general acknowledgment of all those working to increase our understanding of how to effectively prevent crime. Without your insights, we could not have written this textbook.

More personally, Del's acknowledgment's are as follows: I would like to acknowledge Dr Clarence Schrag, the person who introduced me to the study of criminal behavior in graduate school, made this an exciting field of inquiry, and supported and encouraged me during my early research career in criminology. When invited to write this text, the first person I thought of as a co-author was Dr Abby Fagan, a brilliant young criminologist I had the pleasure of mentoring in graduate school. Abby's early career also involved working with me on the Blueprints for Violence Prevention initiative, a kind of Consumer's Report website identifying crime prevention programs that have been proven to work. So it was only natural we should co-author this text. My career in criminology now spans over 55 years and no one has been more supportive and encouraging over these many years than my wife, Mary Grace Elliott.

Abby's acknowledgments are as follows: I would like to acknowledge my appreciation for the opportunity to collaborate on this book with Dr Del Elliott, my first mentor in the field of crime prevention. Del has had a tremendous impact on my knowledge and attitudes regarding the causes and prevention of youth delinquency. Similarly, my understanding of community-based crime prevention could not have been gained without the mentoring of Drs David Hawkins and Richard Catalano at the University of Washington. I am honored to follow in the footsteps of these three prevention giants! I would also like to acknowledge and thank the undergraduate and graduate students who assisted me in conducting literature review searches, proofreading chapters, and preparing materials for the book: Molly Buchanan, Andrea Lindsey, Stephanie Mintz, Danielle Rapapport, Mary Ann Thursh, and Kathryn Zambrana.

About the Companion Website

Don't forget to visit the companion website for this book:

www.wiley.com/go/elliott/prevention_of_crime

There you will find valuable material designed to enhance your learning, including:

- More than 600 sample exam questions, including multiple choice, true/false, and short essay questions
- 434 PowerPoint slides summarizing key points, available to download
- Chapter outlines
- Sample syllabus

Section I
Introduction to Crime Prevention

1

The Goals and Logic of Crime Prevention

Learning Objectives

Upon finishing this chapter, students should be able to:
- Understand the goals and logic of crime prevention
- Identify the personal and social costs of crime
- Distinguish between criminal behavior and other types of antisocial behavior
- Understand how crimes are classified
- Identify the primary measures of crime and how they differ
- Understand the objectives of prevention science.

Introduction

Consider the following three scenarios:

Scenario 1   *On January 5, 2012 in Chicago, a woman was awakened late at night and saw a man going through the jewelry box on her bedroom dresser. She screamed. Startled, the man attacked her: covering her mouth, tying her up and raping her. When he left shortly before daybreak, he took all of her expensive jewelry.*

If this violent crime happened to your mother or sister, you would almost certainly want this man found, arrested, convicted, and sent to prison for a long time. You would want justice. But wouldn't it be better, for your mother or sister, for yourself and for the whole community, if this crime never happened in the first place? If the personal, social, or environmental factors that led this man to commit this violent crime had been recognized earlier in his life and some action taken that would

The Prevention of Crime, First Edition. Delbert Elliott and Abigail Fagan.
© 2017 John Wiley & Sons, Inc. Published 2017 by John Wiley & Sons, Inc.
Companion website: www.wiley.com/go/elliott/prevention_of_crime

change his and the victim's future? If this event could have been *prevented*, and this victim never assaulted, wouldn't it be even better than having to seek justice after the fact?

Scenario 2 *The young man who committed the rape and burglary was caught two weeks following this event, was convicted and sentenced to 12 years in prison. After serving 8 years, he was released back into the community on parole. Twenty days after being released, he was involved in a car-jacking which left the car owner with a serious head injury requiring hospitalization. The perpetrator was apprehended by police, convicted and sentenced back to the same state prison that previously hosted him.*

When the victim of the first crime found out that her attacker was released from prison and committed another serious violent crime, she was outraged. Do you agree with her? Wasn't justice served, given that the man was caught and punished for the first crime and served eight years in prison? Would you be satisfied with his punishment if you knew that there were treatment options available in his prison that had been shown to rehabilitate nearly half of their participants so that they did not re-offend once out of prison, but that he never received such programming? Wouldn't requiring that the offender receive treatment be a better option than releasing him back to the community with no help in addressing the problems and conditions that led him to commit another crime?

Scenario 3 *In 1967, the manager of public safety in Denver, Colorado was reviewing a report of yet another robbery of a city bus driver that happened the night before. She was angry about how many similar robberies had occurred in the past several years and the recent increase in such crimes in the past year. Bus drivers were often targets for robbery, as they carried relatively large sums of money towards the end of their shift, after cash fares had accumulated. Not only was the city losing a significant amount of money, but in an increasing number of cases, bus drivers were injured in these robberies.*

Although the city manager did not realize it at the time, a relatively simple prevention strategy was available that had been shown to greatly reduce bus and transportation robberies. In the late 1960s, locked bus fare boxes, similar to safes in homes, were introduced in order to reduce bus drivers' and would-be offenders' access to cash. As a result of this innovation, opportunities for successful bus robberies were significantly lowered. Moreover, these reductions resulted in savings that far exceeded the cost of installing the boxes. Unlike crime prevention strategies that try to change an individual's behavior, which can be difficult, this and other types of situational crime prevention efforts try to affect the circumstances or opportunities that make it easier or less risky to commit a crime.

As these examples show, criminal behavior, no matter what form it takes, can result in significant financial costs to society and much pain and suffering for victims and their families. One of the first questions asked after events like those described above is: *Why did this happen?* This question is often followed by another: *How could we have stopped this from happening?* Then we might ask: *What was going on in these offenders' minds? What happened to them at school, work, or in their homes that led them to even consider, let alone carry out, these crimes? Why was this particular person or place targeted? How can we make places and persons less vulnerable to crime?*

The implication is that if we knew more about what caused a crime, we could do something to prevent it from ever happening. *The goal of crime prevention is to reduce the number of persons or groups committing criminal acts in society, to reduce the number of offenses they commit, and to reduce the overall number of criminal acts committed in a school, community, or society.*

It is generally accepted that the causes which lead a person or group to initially engage in a crime might be psychological or biological (e.g., a mental health disorder, genetic predisposition, or some type of physical illness); found in the offender's childhood upbringing; or related to the conditions, situations, or experiences the person or group encountered while at school, in their family,

> *Intellectuals solve problems.*
> *Geniuses prevent them.*
> Albert Einstein

at work, or in their neighborhood. While it may not be possible to change or fix some of these factors, others can be successfully modified using carefully designed and well-implemented prevention programs. As we will emphasize throughout this book, *the key to crime prevention is successfully identifying the cause(s) of crime*. The logic of crime prevention is to then do something about these causes. Doing so may involve changing the conditions, situations, personal characteristics, and experiences which influence offending by individuals or groups.

Different types of crimes may require different types of crime prevention programs or policies. Recall the scenarios discussed at the beginning of this chapter. To prevent the rape and burglary described in the first example, we would use what is called a **universal** or **selective** prevention program. This type of intervention involves working with an individual or group *before* any criminal behavior has occurred; the goal is to reduce the likelihood of future criminal behavior. The type of prevention program that would address the crimes of the offender in the second scenario is called an **indicated** prevention program. This type of intervention is aimed at individuals who have already committed an illegal offense; the goal is to end or at least reduce their further involvement in criminal activity. The third scenario described an **environmental** or **situational** prevention strategy to reduce bus robberies. Rather than trying to change individuals, these types of prevention try to alter social or physical environments that facilitate or provide opportunities for crime, making it harder to carry out crimes and/or increasing the likelihood offenders will be caught. In some cases, they might involve creating legal statutes and policies to deter criminal activity among the general population.

We will provide more details about these and other types of strategies that can be used to prevent crime in the following chapters. The goal of this textbook is to share with you exactly what criminologists know about crime prevention, including the types of actions highlighted above as well as many other crime prevention strategies. Even if you do not think you have been directly affected by crime, it is likely that you have felt its impact in some way. For example, have you ever been afraid to walk down a dark alley or gone back to your car or house to make sure it is locked? If so, you have been affected by crime. The main point to realize right now, and what we will emphasize throughout this book, is that *crime can be prevented*. This is very good news!

Also encouraging is that, in the past 30 years, major advances have been made in crime prevention. Since the mid-1990s, the national crime rate in the United States (USA) has declined and it is generally believed that the development of better crime prevention programs played a role in facilitating this decline. We now know a lot more than we used to about the many causes of crime, how to change many of these factors and conditions, and how to design and test different types of preventive interventions. We have also learned a lot about what works and what does not work to prevent crime, how to increase the use of effective prevention strategies, and how to ensure that these programs and practices are well implemented. This body of knowledge is what the emerging field of study called **prevention science**, which is described in more detail in Chapter 3, is all about, and our textbook will show how this information is being used in crime prevention efforts today.

So that you can properly appreciate the need for crime prevention, we will first describe the financial and emotional impact that crime has on society. We then discuss how crime is measured, an important component of prevention given that successful crime prevention efforts must show that crime has actually been reduced. While this seems obvious, prevention strategies may claim to be effective but may not actually measure or have any impact on rates of crime. For example, various prevention strategies may increase

New York City paid $167,732 to feed, house and guard each inmate in its jails in 2012.

Marc Santora (2013), reporter, *The New York Times*

citizen satisfaction with police or reduce fear of crime, but if rates of illegal behavior are not affected, we would not classify them as effective crime prevention strategies.

The Financial Costs of Crime

Estimating the costs of crime is a complex task and different economists include different figures in their estimations, making it difficult to precisely determine the cost of illegal behavior (for a discussion, see: McCollister, French, and Fang, 2010). For example, in the early 1990s, the total costs of crime in the USA were estimated to range from $425 billion (Mandel and Magnusson, 1993) to $1.7 trillion per year (Anderson, 1999). The trillion dollar figure included $603 billion in losses to the economy from fraud and unpaid taxes; $450 billion in medical bills, lost earnings, and lost quality of life; $45 billion in insurance payments to crime victims; and $15 billion in stolen property. Overall, the average cost per person in the USA was estimated to be $4,118. More recent estimates indicate a cost of $312 billion for the most serious index offenses alone, representing about 2% of the US Gross Domestic Product (GDP) in 2012. The majority of this cost, $250 billion, was for violent offenses, primarily murder and aggravated assault (Chalfin, 2015). In the United Kingdom (UK), violent crime was estimated to cost £124 billion in 2012, an amount which equates to €4,700 per household and 7.7% of the country's GDP (Institute for Economics and Peace, 2013).

Although there is variation in how costs are estimated, most studies will consider: (i) costs associated with the operation of the criminal justice system, such as costs of police, courts, and prisons; (ii) costs experienced by victims including medical expenses, lost productivity, and loss of property; (iii) costs that occur because individuals have chosen to commit crimes rather than work in legitimate occupations; and (iv) intangible costs such as those related to the pain and suffering of victims or the fear of crime experienced by the public when crimes occur (McCollister *et al.*, 2010). You will not be surprised to learn that the costs included under the first category are staggering. According to the Bureau of Justice Statistics (www.bjs.gov/index.cfm?ty=pbdetail&iid=5049), it cost the USA $270 billion dollars in 2010 to operate correctional facilities such as jails, prisons, and detention centers. The Pew Charitable Trusts (2008) estimates that states spend roughly about the same amount of money on corrections as they do on higher education. In addition, the amount of money spent on corrections is increasing rapidly, in part due to the escalating costs of providing health care to a growing population of elderly prisoners (The Pew Charitable Trusts, 2013). With limited budgets, spending more on offenders means spending less on education and other public services.

In addition to estimating the total costs of crime, some studies have reported costs associated with particular offenses and/or particular types of offenders. Figure 1.1 displays the costs of various violent and property offenses committed in the USA. Again, these figures show that violent crimes result in the largest costs to society, with the average, estimated cost of each murder being nearly $9 million (in 2008 dollars), each rape or sexual assault costing $241,000, each aggravated assault costing over $100,000, and each robbery costing about $42,000 (McCollister *et al.*, 2010). The **tangible costs** included in these figures are those that we commonly think about: the costs to victims related to medical bills and lost productivity at work, costs for police and court processing, and the expenses of incarcerating offenders in jails, prisons, and detention centers. **Intangible costs** may be less familiar, but these make up the majority of the total costs of violent crimes. Intangible costs are related the physical and emotional pain and suffering of victims and, although this type of cost can be difficult to quantify, they are often estimated by considering how juries might award compensation to victims.

A study based on following individuals from Philadelphia, PA from birth to age 26 also found that serious, violent offenses accounted for most of the total costs of crime (Cohen, Piquero, and Jennings, 2010). This study reported that a small proportion of individuals, those committing the most serious crimes, generate substantial costs to society. More specifically, the authors found that about 3% of all

Total (tangible plus intangible) per-offense cost for different crimes in 2008 dollars.

Type of offense	Tangible cost	Intangible cost	Total cost[a]
Murder	$1,285,146	$8,442,000	$8,982,907
Rape/sexual assault	$41,252	$199,642	$240,776
Aggravated assault	$19,472	$95,023	$107,020
Robbery	$21,373	$22,575	$42,310
Arson	$16,429	$5,133	$21,103
Motor vehicle theft	$10,534	$262	$10,772
Stolen property	$7,974	N/A	$7,974
Household burglary	$6,169	$321	$6,462
Embezzlement	$5,480	N/A	$5,480
Forgery and counterfeiting	$5,265	N/A	$5,265
Fraud	$5,032	N/A	$5,032
Vandalism	$4,860	N/A	$4,860
Larceny/theft	$3,523	$10	$3,532

N/A: not available or not applicable.

[a] Total per-offense cost calculated as the sum of tangible cost (excluding the uncorrected risk-of-homicide cost from crime victim cost, when applicable) and intangible cost.

Figure 1.1 Costs of crime in the United States. Source: McCollister *et al.*, 2010. Reproduced with permission of Elsevier.

individuals followed in the study were "high-rate, chronic offenders" who steadily committed crimes from adolescence to early adulthood. As a whole, this group accounted for 40% of all estimated costs, and each individual in the group was estimated to cost society about $1 million!

Recent research has begun to focus on the costs of **cyber crime**, or crimes committed via the Internet such as theft of intellectual property; virus attacks that insert malicious code into computers to disrupt work and destroy documents; theft of funds from bank accounts; and posting of fraudulent information. Based on reports from 56 companies across the USA, the Ponemon Institute (2012) estimated that cyber crimes cost companies an average of almost $9 million per year. Such crimes are becoming commonplace, with businesses reporting an average of 94 successful attacks per year in 2012. In December, 2013, a particularly devastating notable cyber crime occurred in the USA, with "malware" leading to a security breach that compromised the credit cards of over 110 million shoppers at the Target and Neiman Marcus stores.

Some international research indicates that US companies may be victimized more often, suffer more costly forms of attacks, and lose more money overall to cyber crime compared to other countries. The overall costs of cyber crime in the USA and in six other industrialized countries are shown in Figure 1.2. Costs in the USA are about double those in Germany, Japan, and the UK, at over 15 million dollars, four times higher than those in Brazil and Australia, and seven times as large as Russia's (Ponemon Institute, 2015).

It is important to be aware that drug use and abuse also have significant financial costs to society, especially when taking into account the number of crimes committed by those under the influence of both legal and illegal substances. One report estimated that drug use and drug-related crimes cost American taxpayers $193 billion in 2007 due to lost productivity, health care and criminal justice

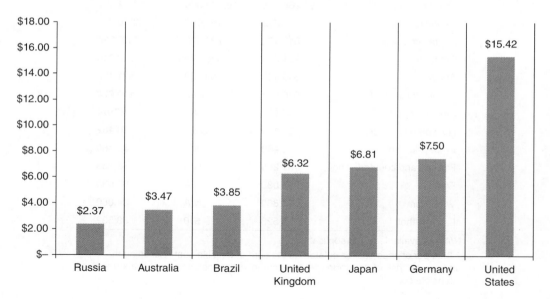

Figure 1.2 Costs of cyber crime in seven countries, in millions of US dollars. Source: Ponemon Institute, 2015. Reproduced with permission of Ponemon Institute.

costs (https://www.whitehouse.gov/blog/2013/04/10/president-s-fy-2014-budget-supporting-21st-century-drug-policy).

It is obvious from this information that even a modest reduction in the level of crime can have a significant effect on the public's health and welfare and strongly benefit the economy. As we will show in later chapters, prevention science has demonstrated that prevention programs can be effective, can achieve significant reductions in criminal behavior, and can reduce the costs of crime.

Fear of Crime

As we mentioned earlier, in addition to economic costs, there are intangible and difficult to quantify costs associated with crime. For example, the **fear of crime** is a psychological and emotional cost brought about when you worry that you or someone you care about might become a victim of crime. Many criminological studies have investigated fear of crime, including who is most likely to fear crime, how fear relates to the chances of actually being victimized, and the consequences of being fearful on one's lifestyle and activities, physical health and emotional well-being. We summarize this research in this section of the chapter and discuss how fear of crime is related to crime prevention.

How widespread is fear of crime? Such fears likely affect most people in society in some way or another. Just consider the number of times you may have experienced some fear or anxiety about potential victimization, such as worrying about being attacked, that your new smart phone might be stolen, or that your car or home might be broken into. Surveys of the public have shown that, when specifically asked to report their fear of crime, about 40% to 50% of individuals express a general worry that they may be victimized in some way. On average, about 40% of participants in such surveys indicate that there are neighborhoods or places near their homes where they would be afraid to walk at night (Saad, 2010). In some countries, rates are even higher. Over 50% of respondents in 31 of 135 countries polled by Gallup in 2012 and about 75% of adult residents in Venezuela and South Africa reported being afraid to walk alone at night (Crabtree, 2013). This particular concern represents a significant impact of crime on people's lifestyle choices and behavior patterns.

> Lethal violence is the most frightening threat in every modern industrial nation.
>
> Zimring and Hawkins, 1997: 9

Although we might think that violent crimes generate the most fear, in fact, property crimes may produce more worry. The greatest worry, reported by two-thirds of respondents in a 2009 Gallup poll (Saad, 2009), was being a victim of identity theft, while slightly less than half worried about auto theft and burglary (see Figure 1.3). Of the violent crimes, being the victim of terrorism was the most feared, reported by 35% of the sample. Less than one in five people worried about being sexually assaulted, murdered, or being the target of a hate crime.

Crimes are likely to generate fear and anger among victims, but such feelings can extend to victims' family members and acquaintances, as well as to neighborhood residents and even the larger community (Brunton-Smith and Jackson, 2012). Research shows that even those who do not know a victim but hear about a crime perpetrated against someone else will often experience some personal

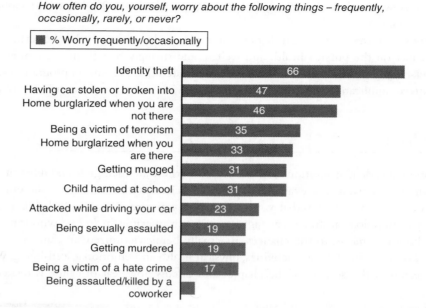

How often do you, yourself, worry about the following things – frequently, occasionally, rarely, or never?

■ % Worry frequently/occasionally

Identity theft	66
Having car stolen or broken into	47
Home burglarized when you are not there	46
Being a victim of terrorism	35
Home burglarized when you are there	33
Getting mugged	31
Child harmed at school	31
Attacked while driving your car	23
Being sexually assaulted	19
Getting murdered	19
Being a victim of a hate crime	17
Being assaulted/killed by a coworker	

Figure 1.3   Fear of crime in the United States. Source: Saad, 2009.

fear that it could happen to them or those they care about (Brunton-Smith and Jackson, 2012; Hough, 1995). Local crime events can even spark national and international anxiety and fear. For example, in a 2006 Gallup poll conducted shortly after an attack in the USA at a one-room Amish schoolhouse that killed six people including the shooter, 35% of parents reported they feared for their child's safety at school, an increase from 25% reported in the prior year (Jones, 2006). Likewise, following the murder of 20 children and six adults at the Sandy Hook Elementary School in Newtown, CT, in 2012, which dominated the news for weeks, parents across the nation worried about sending their children to school. Over half (52%) of American adults surveyed in a Gallup poll following this incident reported fearing that similar events could happen where they lived (Saad, 2012). This crime also sparked a contentious national debate over gun control, demands for better identification and services for the mentally ill (given that the shooter was known to have such problems), and calls for the placement of armed police officers and/or teachers in schools. Many schools reported lockdowns in response to reports of suspicious persons around their schools, and many brought in counselors to meet with children and staff to help them deal with their emotional responses to this event.

While some events can inspire widespread anxiety, it is also true that fear of crime varies by gender, age, income, race/ethnicity, and neighborhood/city. In a 2003 Gallup poll (Saad, 2003), women were eight times as likely as men to report anxiety over being a sexual assault victim (39% vs 5%). Women were also more likely than men to report worrying about other violent crimes such as muggings and terrorism and were much more likely to report being afraid to walk alone at night. This gender difference is found globally. Women around the world are nearly twice as likely as men to report being afraid to walk alone (Saad, 2010). Polls also show that fear of crime, specifically the fear of walking alone at night, is more common among those over age 65 compared to younger individuals and is twice as likely among those earning low incomes compared to higher income earners (Saad, 2003). Fear of crime has also been shown to be higher among ethnic minorities than non-Hispanic Caucasians (Chiricos, Hogan, and Gertz, 1997). Finally, those who live in urban areas have been shown to be twice as likely as those living in rural areas to worry about safety in their neighborhoods (Chiricos *et al.*, 1997; Saad, 2003).

The relationship between fear of crime and rates of crime

Presumably, a major benefit of preventing or reducing crime is to lessen the public's fear of crime. But how closely connected are fear of crime and crime rates? Lab (2010: 17) claims that "… it would be naïve to claim that changes in the crime rate have no influence on reported fear." While this seems reasonable, the bulk of research indicates that fear of crime is not closely related to the actual probability of being a victim of crime. Instead, the relationship between levels of fear and officially reported levels of crime is weak and inconsistent (Rountree, 1998; Saad, 2003). For example, American's fear of crime remained fairly stable between 1989 and 2003, while violent and property crime rates reported by the FBI dropped by about 50% (Saad, 2003). As another example, elderly women have very low risks of victimization but studies show that they report very high levels of fear (LaGrange and Ferraro, 1989; Warr, 1984).

A number of explanations for the discrepancy between actual rates of crime and individuals' reported fear of crime have been proposed. *First*, as already mentioned, one does not have to actually experience a criminal event to fear the possibility of becoming a victim (Hough, 1995). The fact that a single crime can generate fear among a larger network of acquaintances, friends, and family members suggests that actual crime rates can be low, but fear of crime high. Relatedly, perceptions of the risk of victimization, and resulting fear of crime, are likely to be influenced by the mass media and its coverage of violent crimes (Williams and Dickinson, 1993). The news slogan "*if it bleeds, it leads*" indicates the priority given by the media to crime, and this attention may well distort perceptions about the actual levels of crime occurring locally or in other parts of the country (Warr, 2000). With the explosion of social media, such stories can easily "go viral," with images and stories spreading quickly across the world. Surveys have shown that levels of fear typically spike after major, dramatic events that are highly publicized, like the Columbine school shooting in 1999, the Washington DC-area sniper shootings in 2002 and the more recent Amish and Newtown Sandy Hook school shootings (Jones, 2006; Saad, 2006). It is also true, however, that research has not shown a consistent relationship between fear of crime and exposure to media reports of crime (Warr, 2000).

Second, as already noted, some groups are more likely to report fear of crime even if they do not have a strong likelihood of being victimized, which can also lead to a discrepancy between rates of fear and rates of crime. The perceived risk of victimization is influenced both by the anticipated level of harm associated with victimization and with the level of control over the conditions and situations that are related to victimization (Warr, 1984). For example, the elderly and many females are likely to face a physical disadvantage in violent encounters, which are often committed by young males, and this knowledge could cause these groups to fear the possibility of these interactions even if their actual risk of victimization is low (Bennett and Flavin, 1994; Smith and Torstensson, 1997).

For property crimes, the economic impact of burglary or theft is greater for the poor and for many elderly living on fixed incomes, which can affect their anticipated fear of crime (Warr, 1984). All in all, differences in reported fears may be due more to differences in one's vulnerability to potential victimization than to the actual chances of becoming a victim.

Third, there is evidence that fear is linked to one's neighborhood. Anxiety and worry about crime tends to be highest in areas with high levels of social disorder or incivilities such as public drunkenness, panhandling/begging, homelessness, gangs, and drug sales, and in areas with physical disorder and deterioration like trash, graffiti, and rundown and abandoned buildings (LaGrange, Ferraro, and Supancic, 1992; McGarrell, Giacomazzi, and Thurman, 1997; Skogan, 1986). These neighborhood conditions are relatively stable over time and slower to change compared to actual crime rates. Such patterns account for at least some of the discrepancy between levels of fear and official levels of crime.

The personal consequences of fear of crime

Whether or not it is a true reflection of crime rates and the actual risk of victimization, fear of crime can have serious effects on personal well-being, health, and lifestyles. High levels of fear can restrict the number of places one is willing to travel to, the times of day one feels comfortable outside, and the number of people one trusts (Stafford, Chandola, and Marmot, 2007). The end result is often social isolation. Studies have also shown a relationship between fear of crime and poor mental health, reduced physical functioning and a lower quality of life (Jackson and Stafford, 2009; Stafford *et al.*, 2007). For example, a long-term study of British men and women (Stafford *et al.*, 2007) showed that those reporting greater fear were, on average, nearly twice as likely to be depressed and had worse mental health than respondents reporting lower levels of fear. Fear of crime was also related to exercising less frequently, visiting friends less often, and being involved in fewer social activities.

Although the exact relationship between fear of crime and rates of crime is difficult to determine, the prevention of property and violent crimes should result in numerous positive effects for society. If rates are reduced, fewer individuals will be victimized, neighborhoods should feel and look safer, and the financial burdens of crime will be lessened. In turn, fear of crime could be reduced. Of course, these benefits can only be realized if effective prevention programs are widely implemented. To that end, the goal of this text is to increase knowledge regarding effective crime prevention efforts and to greatly expand the use of these strategies.

Measuring Crime

The goal of crime prevention is to reduce crime rates, and documenting success in reaching this goal requires good measures of crime. Thus, good measurement is critical when planning and evaluating prevention programs. As we will discuss in this section, prevention researchers have a range of options for measuring crime. The three types of measures used most often to evaluate the effectiveness of prevention efforts are: (i) arrest records obtained from law enforcement agencies; (ii) victimization reports obtained from individuals; and (iii) offender reports obtained from individuals.[1] The first type of measure is referred to as an **official** measure, while the last two are often referred to as **self-report** measures of crime. Each of the three measures has advantages and limitations, and the preferred measure for assessing rates of crime depends on the type of intervention being tested and the specific criminal behaviors of interest to the researcher. In this section, we will describe each of these types, summarize their accuracy and validity in measuring crime and provide some recommendations for appropriately using each type of measure. But first, let us actually define what we mean by **crime** and describe how particular offenses are typically categorized and classified by criminologists.

From the fight against polio to fixing education, what's missing is often good measurement and a commitment to follow the data.

Bill Gates (2013), Developer and CEO of Microsoft

What makes a crime a crime? This may seem like a lead-in to a bad joke, but determining what actually "counts" as a crime is very important … and rather challenging. For example, is smoking marijuana a criminal behavior? The answer to this question is not straightforward because whether or not marijuana use is illegal varies by country, state/region and, in some cases, according to an individual's medical history. In addition, not all harmful, immoral, or scandalous behaviors are crimes. Lying to your spouse or friend, cheating on an exam, and committing adultery may be "wrong," but they are not crimes. The most basic, and hopefully most simplistic, definition of a crime is *behavior that violates the criminal law*. In the USA, a criminal statute is a law passed by Congress, a state or a local legislative body. Statutes describe a specific behavior or class of behaviors that are prohibited, prescribe a specific punishment for the perpetration of these behaviors, and allow law enforcement to enforce these statutes and apply these penalties. In the USA we also make a distinction between **crime** and **delinquency**, the latter being behavior committed by minors (those less than age 18) that violates the law. For simplicity, in this textbook we will generally refer to illegal behaviors by adults and minors/juveniles as crime.

In a classic illustration of the problems of defining crime, the 1963 assassination of President John F. Kennedy in Dallas resulted in a "Texas standoff" between the US Secret Service and the Dallas police over who had jurisdiction over the murder. In 1963, there was no federal law prohibiting the killing of a US president. As a result, the murder of President Kennedy was not a federal crime. There was a Texas state law prohibiting murder, and this technically gave the Dallas police, not the Federal government, jurisdiction over the investigation of the assassination of the president.

So, only specific behaviors prohibited by the criminal law can be considered crimes. It is the prevention of these behaviors that concern us in this book. The prevention of other problem behaviors – for example, dropping out of school, teenage pregnancy, adult tobacco or alcohol use, obesity, chronic unemployment, depression and other mental health disorders – is worthwhile but outside the scope of this text. However, keep in mind that some crime prevention strategies have been shown to reduce some of these negative outcomes as well as illegal behavior, making crime prevention efforts all the more noteworthy.

Offense classifications

Felonies, misdemeanors, and infractions

Criminal law categorizes crimes into three general types depending on their seriousness: felonies, misdemeanors, and infractions. **Felonies** are the most serious crimes and carry a punishment of confinement for more than a year in a state or federal prison. Homicide, robbery, rape, burglary, and auto theft are examples of felony crimes. **Misdemeanors** are less serious and typically involve sentences of up to a year in a county jail and/or monetary fines or community service. Examples include shoplifting, minor assault, and possession of an illicit drug. **Infractions** are less serious than misdemeanors and typically involve monetary fines. Violations of traffic laws are an example of an infraction. Those charged with infractions are not entitled to a jury trial or a public defender, while those charged with felonies and misdemeanors are entitled to both.

There is one other type of crime that may be familiar to you. **Ordinances** are laws passed by a particular city or county and identify behaviors that are illegal in that particular location; that is, these laws are limited in jurisdiction to the local area. Examples are laws prohibiting overnight parking or parking in a red zone, smoking in public buildings, and failing to have a leash on your dog. Like infractions, violation of an ordinance usually results in a monetary fine, and those charged with ordinance violations are not entitled to a jury trial or public defender.

Personal and property offenses

Criminal offenses are further classified as personal or property crimes. **Personal crimes** are offenses that involve physical or mental harm to an individual. Examples include homicide, assault, kidnapping, and sexual assault. **Property crimes** are those that interfere with another person's right to use or enjoy their property. They typically involve the theft, destruction or damage of another's property. More specific examples include larceny, burglary, and vandalism. Some personal and property offenses are felonies and others are misdemeanors, depending on their seriousness.

Official (law enforcement) measures

Official measures of crime, sometimes referred to as **law enforcement measures**, include crimes known to police, arrests, court convictions, and crimes that are cleared or "closed," either because an arrest has been made or some other event has occurred, such as the death of the suspect. Official measures also include court filings and dispositions, but such records are rarely used in evaluations of prevention programs and policies. National and state law enforcement agencies usually report statistics about crime as "rates" of the number of crimes per 100,000 persons in the population. Local city and county agencies may report the actual numbers of offenses committed or crime rates for different populations (e.g., for males and females).

The **Uniform Crime Reports (UCR)** is the best-known and most comprehensive official measure of crime in the USA (see: http://www.fbi.gov/about-us/cjis/ucr). The UCR provide a count of crimes known to the police, crimes cleared (i.e., closed by arrest or other means), and arrest rates. Information on crime is provided voluntarily every year by over 18,000 federal, state and local law enforcement agencies. As such, UCR statistics do not capture crimes that go unreported to the police and thus represent a lesser number of crimes than are actually committed. These data are reported as counts of the total number of offenses reported or as rates of crime per 100,000 persons in the nation. Crime rates can also be reported for smaller areas, like regions of the country, states, counties, cities, universities and colleges, and tribal areas.

Each year, UCR rates are made available in the publication: *Crime in the United States* (http://www.fbi.gov/about-us/cjis/ucr/ucr-publications#Crime). The most comprehensive descriptions are reported for **Part I offenses** representing certain serious person and property offenses. For these

Table 1.1 Part I and Part II offenses in the Uniform Crime Reports (UCR).

Part I Offenses

1. Criminal Homicide	5. Burglary
2. Forcible Rape	6. Larceny-theft (except motor vehicle theft)
3. Robbery	7. Motor vehicle Theft
4. Aggravated Assault	8. Arson

Part II Offenses

9. Other Assaults	20. Offenses Against the Family and Children
10. Forgery and Counterfeiting	21. Driving Under the Influence
11. Fraud	22. Liquor Laws
12. Embezzlement	23. Drunkenness
13. Buying or Receiving Stolen Property	24. Disorderly Conduct
14. Vandalism	25. Vagrancy (e.g. Homelessness)
15. Weapons Carrying or Possession	26. All Other Offenses
16. Prostitution and Commercialized Vice	27. Suspicion
17. Sex Offenses	28. Curfew and Loitering (for persons under 18)
18. Drug Abuse Violations	29. Runaways (persons under 18)
19. Gambling	

Source: Federal Bureau of Investigations (2004), Uniform Crime Reporting (UCR) Program, US Department of Justice.

crimes, the FBI reports the number and rates of crimes known to the police, number of arrests and number of crimes that are cleared. In addition, information may be provided regarding the location of the offense, the time the crime occurred, whether or not and what type of weapon was used during the offense, and the type of value or property stolen if applicable. For homicide only, the age, sex and race/ethnicity of the victim and offender, the type of weapon used, the relationship between the offender and victim and information about the circumstances of the offense are all reported. **Part II** crimes include less serious crimes. Only arrest data are reported for these crimes. The types of offenses classified as Part I and Part II offenses are shown in Table 1.1.

A second official measure of crime associated with the UCR and reported by local, state, and federal law enforcement agencies is the **National Incident-Based Reporting System (NIBRS)**. This is an incident-based reporting system, meaning that detailed information is recorded for every crime incident known to police, as well as on arrests for these incidents. Data are reported for 22 offense categories encompassing 46 specific crimes. For each offense, law enforcement agencies provide information about where and when the offense occurred, the type of weapon or force used, property lost, characteristics of the victim(s) like age, sex, race, injury, and relationship to offender as well as offender characteristics like age, sex, and race. Information about arrests only is reported for an additional 10 offenses. In 2012, 6,115 law enforcement agencies voluntarily submitted NIBRS data.

NIBRS differs from the UCR data reported in *Crime in the United States* in many ways. First, it provides information on *all* the offenses (up to 10) occurring during or related to a single criminal event, as well as details on the offenders and victims involved in those offenses. The UCR reports information only on the single most serious offense that occurred. For example, if during the commission of a bank robbery, the offenders also murdered the bank manager, stole property from three bank customers, and kidnapped a family during the getaway, only detailed information regarding the murder would be published in the UCR, whereas details of the other offenses would be included in NIBRS. A second difference is that NIBRS provides added information about more crimes than the UCR. Third, NIBRS differentiates between crimes that were only attempted and those that were completed, while the UCR describes only the latter. Fourth, NIBRS involves an expanded definition of rape which includes male victims; in the UCR, sexual attacks on males are counted as aggravated assaults or sex offenses, not as rapes.

In addition to the NIBRS and *Crime in the United States* publications, as part of the UCR, the FBI publishes two other annual reports on crimes in the United States: *Law Enforcement Officers Killed or Assaulted* and *Hate Crime Statistics*. Data from these reports are rarely used in evaluations of crime prevention programs or policies. However, the data would be appropriate if one were evaluating an intervention designed to prevent these specific types of crimes; for example, programs designed to reduce violent crimes targeting police officers or hate crimes motivated by bias towards certain groups.

Official measures of crimes occurring in other countries, especially those in the United Nations, are also available. For example, the United Nations reports on crimes known to the police for selected years and offenses, primarily offenses similar to the UCR's Part I offenses (Harrendorf, Heiskanen, and Malby, 2010). The *European Crime Prevention Monitor* publishes a report on crime rates and trends for selected years for most of the UCR Part I offenses, with a special focus on the 27 European Union member states (Klima and Wijckmans, 2012). This is a new series and also includes rates of self-reported victimization and self-reported offending for selected years. These data sources could be useful when evaluating the effectiveness of interventions taking place outside of the USA.

Of the official measures described, arrest is the most frequently used to document the effectiveness of prevention programs. Evaluations of very large-scale programs or policies intended to affect large numbers of people could rely on annual arrest rates when determining the success of the intervention. For example, research investigating the impact of a new law restricting gun sales could assess the degree to which arrests for certain violent offenses were reduced following the legislation. Or, if all law enforcement agencies in a particular county began using **hot spots policing** to reduce crime (see Chapter 6 for more detail on this prevention practice), county-level arrest rates could be used to evaluate effectiveness. For smaller, more localized interventions, the UCR database could be searched to determine the arrest rates for individuals participating in evaluations. Since most local police agencies collect information on arrests for Part I and II offenses, evaluators can also request arrest data of adult participants from these agencies, rather than searching the UCR data. Individual arrest records of juveniles are confidential and require special permission to obtain, usually a court order or parent/guardian permission, but many local police departments provide anonymous information on numbers or rates of juvenile arrests upon request.

Self-reported victimization measures

Another crime measure involves asking persons in a written survey or in-person interview if they have been victims of specific crimes. These **self-reported measures** provide a more complete assessment of criminal behavior compared to arrest data, since not all crimes are detected by or reported to the police, and not all crimes known to the police result in an arrest. Self-reports also avoid the potential **bias** associated with official arrest data. We know that particular types of crimes, like sexual assaults and child abuse, are under-reported to law enforcement, and that certain types of individuals may be subject to increased surveillance by law enforcement. For example, police officers may more closely monitor the behavior of individuals known to have extensive criminal histories and may more frequently patrol neighborhoods with high rates of crime. These practices can bias or distort crime statistics. Self-reported data from victims, or offenders, as discussed in the next section, should be subject to less bias, particularly when survey participants understand that the information they provide will be confidential and anonymous.

There are a number of sources for obtaining self-reported measures of criminal victimization. The **National Crime Victimization Survey** (http://www.bjs.gov/index.cfm?ty=dcdetail&iid=245) is the largest and probably best-known victimization survey in the USA. This survey has been administered by the Bureau of Justice Statistics and US Census Bureau every six months since 1973. These agencies collect data from over 100,000 individuals aged 10 and older living in 50,000 to 90,000 households across the USA. Even individuals living in dormitories and on cargo ships are included to ensure the sample represents American citizens as a whole. Participants are asked to report on most of the UCR Part I offenses, including assault, domestic violence, robbery, rape, burglary, auto theft, personal larceny (e.g., pickpocketing and purse snatching), and theft. Homicides are obviously excluded as it would be hard for the victim to report them.

NCVS surveys are conducted in-person and over the telephone. After collecting demographic characteristics of the participants such as sex, age, race/ethnicity, marital status, level of education, and income, trained interviewers ask a series of questions about crimes the respondent might have experienced in the past six months. For example, to measure violent assaults, the interviewer asks: "*Has anyone attacked or threatened you in any of these ways*"

1. *With any weapon, for instance, a gun or knife*
2. *By something thrown, such as a rock or bottle*
3. *With anything like a baseball bat, frying pan, scissors, or stick*
4. *By anything thrown, such as a rock or bottle*
5. *Any rape, attempted rape or other type of sexual attack*
6. *Any face-to-face threats*
7. *Any attack or threat or use of force by anyone at all?*

If the answer is yes to any of these crimes, respondents are asked, "*How many times?*" They are also asked to provide details of each incident, including the date and location of the event, damage or loss of property, injury from the assault, weapon used, characteristics of the offender, their relationship to the offender, and whether or not the crime was reported to the police. This information is then compiled to produce national, regional, and urban/suburban/rural rates of each of the specific crimes included in the survey.

The NCVS is the only regularly occurring, comprehensive and national victimization survey. The **Monitoring the Future (MTF)** study (www.monitoringthefuture.org) provides annual victimization data on a limited number of offenses (theft, assault, and property damage) reported by

8th, 10th, and 12th grade students, but it does not ask detailed information about each incident. A few other national-level victimization surveys provide data for specific years and specific age groups. For example, the **National Youth Survey** (Elliott, Huizinga, and Menard, 1989) asks adolescent and young adult participants to describe whether or not they experienced certain UCR Part I offenses and to provide detailed information about each victimization. The **National Survey of Children's Exposure to Violence** (Finkelhor *et al.*, 2014) has been conducted in the USA in 2008 and 2011 to measure the degree to which youth aged 0–17 were violently victimized in their homes, schools, and/or neighborhoods in the past year and in their lifetime. It also asked respondents to provide some details about the offender, use of weapon, and injuries sustained. It is unclear if this survey will be repeated in future years. There are also many smaller scale victimization surveys that ask particular groups to report on their experiences as victims of crime.

Some international victimization surveys also use self-reported methodology for measuring crime. They include the **British Crime Survey** in the UK and the annual **Crime Victimization Survey** in Australia. Reports for countries in the European Union are also available for selected years between 1989 and 2010 from the European Crime Prevention Network (Klima and Wijckmans, 2012).

Self-reported offending measures

The other common self-reported measure asks respondents about criminal offending; that is, whether or not and how often they have committed certain criminal acts during the past year or some other designated period of time. As with victimization measures, **self-reported measures** of offending are intended to capture crimes unknown to the police as well as those that have been reported or detected. Because individuals are asked to incriminate themselves by admitting to illegal behaviors, respondents are almost always guaranteed anonymity and/or confidentiality when asked to participate in these types of surveys. Self-reported offending measures have been available for many decades, pre-dating victimization surveys, but early examples tended to focus heavily on the least serious types of criminal behaviors (Hindelang, Hirschi, and Weis, 1979; Thornberry and Krohn, 2000). More recent measures assess a wider range of crimes and typically include most of the serious Part I and Part II offenses (Elliott and Ageton, 1980).

There is no ongoing, comprehensive, national effort to measure offending in the USA using self-reports comparable to the NCVS measure of victimization. Also, unlike the NCVS, most self-reported sources of offending behavior focus on youth populations; offender surveys of adults are relatively rare. One well-known youth survey is the **Youth Risk Behavior Survey** (**YRBS**) (https://www.cdc.gov/healthyyouth/data/yrbs/overview.htm), which has been conducted by the Centers for Disease Control and Prevention (CDC) every two years since 1991. Students in Grades 9–12 in public and private schools across the USA are asked to report their participation in two types of offenses, carrying a gun or other weapon and participating in a physical fight, and to report use of various illegal substances.

The **Monitoring the Future (MTF)** study (www.monitoringthefuture.org) also provides ongoing, national self-reported offender rates, with a broader range of offenses than the YRBS. However, only high school seniors report on the full range of crimes, whereas 8th, 10th, and 12th grade students report on use of tobacco, alcohol, and other drugs. The YRBS and MTF studies are the best available measures to assess the effectiveness of large-scale national crime prevention programs or policies. The **National Youth Survey** (NYS, www.colorado.edu/ibs/NYSFS) has collected self-reported offending information from a group of adolescents aged 11–17 in 1976 and followed until middle adulthood, aged 38–44 (Elliott and Huizinga, 1985; Knight, Menard, and Simmons, 2014). However, because the last data collection effort for the NYS was in 2004, its usefulness for evaluating newly developed crime prevention efforts is limited. Similarly, the **National Longitudinal Study of Adolescent Health** (www.cpc.unc.edu/projects/addhealth) has tracked delinquent behaviors among a group of individuals followed over time, but data are currently available at only four time points, from 1994 to 2008.

The **International Self Report Delinquency Study (ISRD)** (Junger-Tas and Marshall, 2012) has used the self-report methodology to collect national-level information on adolescent offending in the USA and other countries. The study has been repeated twice, in 1992 and 2007, with the second survey conducted across 31 countries with students aged 12–15 years. They were asked to report the involvement in Part I offenses and some less serious illegal behaviors.

Many smaller scale criminological studies have used self-reported measures to assess rates of offending among adolescents or adults. As we will describe later, the self-report methodology is viewed as a valid method for measuring the extent of illegal behaviors. As a result, evaluators are likely to utilize self-reported offending measures to investigate the impact of particular crime prevention programs. In most cases, they will collect data directly from study participants, rather than trying to utilize publically available rates of offending which are not likely to correspond to their population of interest or match the timeline of the study.

Comparison of crime measures

Of the three measures of crime we have discussed, arrests and self-reported criminal behavior measures are used more frequently than self-reported victimization measures to evaluate crime prevention programs, practices, and policies. Nonetheless, all three can be selected with confidence, so long as the evaluator understands that they capture different dimensions of crime and that they have different strengths and weaknesses. The type of measure that is chosen should depend on the particular criminal behavior(s) the preventive intervention is trying to change, how well that behavior is assessed with the crime measure and the degree to which the strengths of the measure outweigh its limitations. Throughout this section, we will provide some recommendations for which measures should be selected to evaluate particular prevention strategies. We also review the extensive body of research assessing the advantages and disadvantages of the measures. These strengths and limitations are summarized in Table 1.2. Because the strengths and limitations of self-reported victimization and self-reported offending measures are very similar, we combine them in the table.

An obvious but important point to keep in mind is that official crime measures capture *law enforcement responses to crimes* reported to the police by victims and other citizens, or, in a relatively small number of cases, directly observed by police. As a result, official measures are largely an indirect rather than direct (observed or experienced) measure of criminal behavior. These measures are heavily influenced by the specific policies, attitudes, and biases of individual law enforcement agencies. Even when crimes are reported to police, agencies can decide whether or not to file

Table 1.2   Strengths and limitations of crime measures.

	Official measures	*Self-reported measures (victimization and offending)*
Strengths	Provides national, regional, and local estimates of crimes known to police, primarily arrests	Provides a more complete count of criminal behavior, as it includes crimes committed but not known to law enforcement as well as those known to police
	Easily accessible	Can provide details about the offenses, victims, and offenders
	Provides information on trends over time	Direct measure of crime
Limitations	Under-estimates crime levels, as it does not measure crimes that are unknown to police	May over- or under-estimate crime due to reluctance to report an offense or an inability to recall criminal behaviors
	Measurement error related to discrepancies and bias in how different agencies respond to and record crime	Few large-scale, national or ongoing studies
	For most offenses, does not provide much detail about the crime, victim, or offender	
	Rates may depend as much on law enforcement practices as on actual criminal behavior	
	Indirect measure of crime	

charges and which charges should be filed. At different times and for different reasons, law enforcement can decide to "crack down" on certain crimes or be more lenient. For example, political pressures, economic circumstances and the attitudes or characteristics of particular officers can affect how law enforcement agencies respond to and record crime. As a result, changes in arrest and clearance rates may reflect changes in law enforcement practices rather than changes in criminal behavior. This discrepancy can reduce the **validity** of official measures of crime, or their ability to accurately estimate the number of crimes that are actually committed. Their **reliability** can also be questioned, given that the same behavior may not be recorded as a crime by all law enforcement agencies or even in the same agency at different points in time.

When compared to self-reported victimization or self-reported offending measures, *arrests capture a relatively small proportion of all crimes committed*, which also reduces their validity in measuring crime. According to the NCVS, nearly half of all self-reported violent victimizations, including rapes, sexual assaults, robberies, and aggravated assaults, are not reported to law enforcement agencies, and only about one-third of property crimes are reported (Langton *et al.*, 2012; Truman, Langton, and Planty, 2013). Interviews with victims indicate that many fail to report offenses to the police because they consider the event to be a personal matter and may feel embarrassed, ashamed, or responsible; they do not feel the offense is important enough to report; they do not believe the police would or could help them; they are afraid of the offender; and/or they do not want to get the offender in trouble (Langton *et al.*, 2012). Obviously, crimes that are never reported or detected have no chance of ending up in official statistics. Many offenses go undetected for other reasons; for example, because there are no victims or no witnesses to the crime. As a result, many offenders do not come into contact with the police and are never arrested for their crimes. Self-reported offending studies have indicated that less than 10% of self-reported UCR Part I offenses result in an arrest and only about 1% of more minor offenses end in an arrest (Elliott, 1995; Farrington *et al.*, 2003). For all of these reasons, arrest measures capture a very small proportion of crimes committed. Although UCR statistics documenting **crimes known to the police** capture a larger proportion of crimes compared to arrests, neither measure captures the majority of crimes reported by victims or offenders.

While the severe under-reporting of crime is the most frequently cited and serious limitation of official measures, there are other sources of error. For example, a proportion of arrests eventually end up being unjustified or unwarranted, and the criminal charges are later modified or dropped. However, police departments rarely report this information to the FBI or correct their own official records to reflect these changes, which results in measurement error (Elliott, 1995).

A second problem, mentioned briefly earlier in this chapter, is that of **bias**, meaning that the types of offenses and characteristics of offenders who come to the attention of law enforcement are not truly representative of all offenses that occur or of all individuals who break the law. Instead, reported crimes and arrest rates are influenced by: (i) offense type, with serious offenses more likely to be reported than minor offenses; (ii) characteristics of the offender, with those from racial and ethnic minorities more likely to be reported to the police and formally arrested compared to non–Hispanic Caucasians; (iii) sex, with males more likely than females to be arrested for most offenses; and (iv) residence, with persons living in high-poverty, high-crime neighborhoods more likely to be reported, apprehended, and arrested than persons from more affluent neighborhoods (Krohn *et al.*, 2010).

Although you may automatically assume that bias in reporting crimes is related to discrimination of certain groups, this is not true in all cases. Victims are likely to report the perpetration of more serious crimes, no matter who commits them, because they want help and justice for these offenses; they believe the police are more likely to take action on these offenses; and they more often involve other parties or organizations, such as paramedics or insurance agencies, who require that a report be made to the police. The higher risk of arrest for minorities, males, and those living in disadvantaged neighborhoods is a result of several factors. Minority offenders, especially those from high-risk neighborhoods, typically have fewer resources than those from more affluent backgrounds and thus are less able to avoid detection and capture by police. Victims may perceive such offenders, especially if they are male, as more dangerous and more likely to break the law, and will then be more likely to report them to the police; such actions would be a form of reporting discrimination. Finally, offenders from minority racial/ethnic groups may be disrespectful to police when apprehended, which will increase their probability of arrest. All of these factors mean that the characteristics of offenses and persons captured in arrest data are substantially different from those reflected in self-reported victimization and offending studies.

While most criminologists would agree that official measures do not provide "true," valid, and reliable estimates of the number of illegal activities committed, arrests could be a valid measure of *change* in criminal behavior over time if levels of under-reporting and bias remained steady over time. However, the evidence suggests that the factors influencing under-reporting and bias can change abruptly. For example, a new police chief determined to "get tough on crime" may be hired to replace an administrator more concerned with giving the impression that his/her city is a safe place to live. An upswing in arrest rates would be expected to follow. Similarly, new policies can be implemented following dramatic crime events, such as increased surveillance of citizens following 9/11 and **zero-tolerance policies** adopted in response to heavily publicized school shootings that apply severe and certain penalties for offenses. Implementation of these new practices could cause crime rates to increase or decrease.

Given their limitations, our view is that arrest rates are *not* the preferred measure to use in evaluations of prevention programs or policies designed to change rates of criminal behavior. However, arrest rates are preferable when evaluating prevention efforts that try to change law enforcement practices. For example, a crime prevention program designed to increase police efficiency in clearing reported burglaries or a new policy designed to increase the use of arrest in domestic disputes should be evaluated using arrest statistics. The NCVS could also be used to assess changes in domestic violence victimization following the new law. Installing and publicizing the use of surveillance cameras in shopping malls should reduce shoplifting, as individuals will be reluctant to risk being caught. At the same time, cameras could increase the likelihood that shoplifters are apprehended and arrested, leading to an increase in arrest rates. In this case, self-reported offending rates would be a better choice than arrest rates to determine if shoplifting behaviors drop following use of cameras.

In contrast to official measures, self-reported measures more directly measure criminal behavior and capture more of those crimes actually committed. However, they also have limitations and potential biases. When first introduced, there was much skepticism that an individual would willingly, honestly, and fully disclose his/her own victimization or involvement in criminal behavior, particularly when surveying individuals known to lie, cheat, and steal. In fact, there is some evidence that respondents may deliberately fail to report their victimization or criminal behavior. This may be because they are ashamed or because they fear retaliation from those they harmed or who harmed them. They may also be afraid of damage to their reputation or possible legal action if their answers to the survey were to become known to police (Langton *et al.*, 2012). It is also true that some respondents may not remember their victimization or involvement in a crime, especially if the event(s) happened in the distant past. Studies indicate significant under-reporting of criminal events when participants are asked to recall events that happened over a year prior to the survey (Bachman, Johnston, and O'Malley, 1996; Elliott and Huizinga, 1989). Finally, participants may not correctly understand the type of behavior described in the question, which could lead them to under-estimate its occurrence. All of these biases would lead to under-reporting of crime. When using self-reports to evaluate crime prevention programs, this bias could result in the perception that individuals committed fewer offenses than actually occurred.

Comparisons of self-reported offending with known arrest records of the same individuals have shown that levels of under-reporting range from 5% to 20% (Huizinga and Elliott, 1986). While some early studies indicated that under-reporting varied by race/ethnicity, with African American males more likely to under-estimate crimes compared to Caucasian males (Elliott and Huizinga, 1989; Hindelang, Hirschi, and Weis, 1981), more recent research has not shown consistent evidence for this claim (Krohn *et al.*, 2010).[2] Surprisingly, research has also indicated that levels of over-reporting can be as great as under-reporting (Gibbons, 1976; Gold and Reimer, 1974). Over-reporting is most likely due to individuals admitting offenses that would be considered trivial by the police, such as smoking or stealing a pack of gum, and so not subject to official intervention (Elliott and Huizinga, 1989; Gold and Reimer, 1974). Overall, it is likely that the problems of over- and under-reporting balance each other out (Maxfield, Weiler, and Widom, 2000), or, if anything, that self-reports slightly overstate actual levels of criminal behavior (Elliott and Huizinga, 1989).

Given these concerns, researchers have identified and implemented many strategies to improve the reliability and validity of self-report measures of offending and victimization. For example, the quality of data can be improved by asking for detailed information about each offense reported, ensuring that a range of less and more serious offenses is included and excluding reports of trivial offenses (Elliott and Ageton, 1980; Thornberry and Krohn, 2000). It may also be important to assure participants that their responses will be confidential and anonymous (Bachman, Johnston, and O'Malley, 1996); for example, by physically separating multiple respondents in a home or classroom or using web-based or computer-assisted data collection techniques (Krohn *et al.*, 2010). Advanced statistical techniques can also be used to test the reliability and validity of self-reported data (Krohn *et al.*, 2010; Osgood, McMorris, and Potenza, 2002; Raudenbush, Johnson, and Sampson, 2003). If careful procedures are used, self-reported measures are more likely to live up to the conclusion reached by Hindelang and colleagues (1981: 212):

> The self-report method easily demonstrates that people will report crimes, that they will report crimes not known to officials, that they are highly likely to report those crimes known to officials, and that their reports of crimes are internally consistent.

Given the limitations of official measures and improvements in the validity and reliability of self-reported measures, the latter have become a core foundation of criminology and are commonly used in evaluations of crime prevention programs and policies. As they provide more direct measures of individual offending compared to arrest rates, self-reported offending measures are most appropriate for evaluations of prevention programs and practices targeting changes in individuals' criminal behavior. Self-reported victimization measures are rarely used in evaluations and would not be appropriate when trying to determine changes in individuals' criminal behavior given that victims do not identify offenders by name. However, they could be used to assess the effectiveness of some environmental and situational prevention programs and policies. For example, the degree to which installing more street lighting or increasing police patrols in certain areas of a city reduces crime could be assessed using victimization surveys. In Table 1.3, we provide some additional examples of the types of measures that are appropriate for evaluating different types of crime prevention programs and practices.

Summary

The goal of this textbook is to describe what works to reduce crime. We will describe what is currently known about what works to prevent persons or groups from first becoming involved in crime; what works to reduce offending among those actively engaging in crime; and how to change features of our social and physical environments, law enforcement practices and government policies to successfully deter crime and reduce levels or rates of criminal activity.

Until quite recently, we had no good answers to the basic questions about how to prevent crime. Fortunately, in the past few decades, the discipline of **prevention science**, devoted to studying the

Table 1.3 Recommended measures for evaluating the effectiveness of crime prevention programs, practices, or policies.

Type of crime prevention	Recommended measure
Installation of electronic alarm systems by all car manufacturers	National arrest rates for motor vehicle theft (UCR) *OR* Victimization rates of motor vehicle theft (NCVS)
Evaluation of "three strikes" laws	State-level victimization rates (NCVS)
Therapeutic intervention for juvenile offenders and their families	Self-report of offending *OR* Individual arrest rates from participants (if trying to reduce formal contact with law enforcement)
Afterschool mentoring program implemented in one neighborhood in Chicago	Self-report of offending from participants

prevention of social problems such as crime, has emerged and provided some critical answers to these questions. The result is that we can now identify a number of programs, practices, and policies that have demonstrated effectiveness in preventing crime. We now know a substantial amount about the causes of crime and we have good evidence that crime can be prevented. Unfortunately, despite these improvements, this newfound knowledge has not had much of an impact on current crime prevention efforts. Our knowledge of what works is not consistently informing public decision-making about how to deal with crime and criminals. But we are in a much better position now to make changes that will have an effect. If we can communicate and draw upon the knowledge generated in prevention science, there is a strong potential for significantly reducing crime.

In this chapter, we began to set the stage for thinking about why crime prevention is important and how to evaluate crime prevention efforts. We described the cost of crime in both financial terms and according to how fear of crime can negatively affect lifestyles and behaviors. The implication is that there is a huge payoff associated with preventing crime: we can save potentially billions of dollars, thereby improving the economy; we can reduce the relatively high levels of fear reported by many citizens; and we can ensure more positive, productive, and healthy lifestyles. We also reviewed the basic measures used to determine crime levels and identified those that are most useful when assessing the effectiveness of crime prevention programs. Special attention was given to the two measures most frequently used in evaluation studies: official arrest data and self-reported information on individuals' offending behaviors. The strengths and weaknesses of each type of measure were described. It will be helpful to remember these strengths and limitations when reading about the effectiveness of particular crime prevention programs and policies in Section III of this book.

Overview of the Textbook

A number of issues related to the study of crime prevention will be reviewed in this text. To provide additional perspective on how the field of crime prevention has developed, **Chapter 2** describes criminologists' earliest attempts to prevent crime. The present success in knowing what works depends in part on lessons learned in the early attempts to design, implement, and evaluate the effectiveness of prevention programs, practices, and policies. This chapter also provides an overview of the major criminological theories that guide the development of crime prevention efforts. In **Chapter 3**, we describe how the disciplines of public health and prevention science have guided the most recent crime prevention programs, practices, and policies based on recent progress in: (i) identifying the major causes of crime, (ii) identifying the causes which are most amenable to change, and (iii) considering how these causes can be used to develop interventions to prevent and reduce crime. We will also describe the criminal career and life-course developmental frameworks that help define and explain criminal behavior and review how contemporary criminological theories have been integrated into these perspectives. **Chapter 4** provides a basic review of the principles of research methodology as they apply to the evaluation of crime prevention programs, practices, and policies. We describe methods for assessing whether or not interventions are effective and determining how large effects need to be to produce meaningful reductions in crime. It should not come as a surprise to know that there are differences of opinion among criminologists about the scientific methods and standards that should be used to make the determination that a program or policy is effective; that it is "evidence-based" or that it "works." These controversies are discussed in **Chapter 5**. The major governmental and private agency lists of effective prevention programs, practices, and policies, and their standards for determining effectiveness, are also identified and compared.

We are still standing on the bank of the river, rescuing people who are drowning. We have not gone to the head of the river to keep them from falling in. That is the 21st century task.

Gloria Steinem

Chapters 6 through 9 in **Section III** provide the foundation of this textbook and the information you are probably most interested in learning. These chapters describe what has been proven effective in preventing crime: the different types of interventions that "work" and are considered to be "evidence-based." Strategies that have been evaluated and found not to work or to be harmful are also described in these chapters. Yes, sometimes programs designed to prevent crime actually *increase* the likelihood of offending and some of these practices are widely used! It is as important to know what does not work as to know what does, so as not to waste valuable resources, raise false hopes, and avoid doing more harm than good. We will describe the effectiveness of situational and deterrence-based law enforcement prevention approaches (**Chapter 6**); contextual interventions, including programs that try to change the family, school, peer, and community contexts (**Chapter 7**); individual-level programs to prevent the initiation or onset of criminal behavior (**Chapter 8**); and individual-level programs to prevent the continuation of criminal activity of those already involved in crime (**Chapter 9**).

Given a list of effective programs, practices, and policies, how do we ensure their widespread and appropriate use? We discuss these issues in **Section IV**. **Chapter 10** describes methods used by communities to select the "right" prevention program; that is, the intervention that is considered most feasible and cost effective to implement, best able to address local crime needs and most likely to be supported by participants and the larger community. We will also describe factors shown to affect how well interventions are implemented and methods for ensuring high-quality implementation. In **Chapter 11**, we discuss emerging research on how to implement evidence-based programs on a large scale (i.e., across states and nations) and with the rigor, care, and sustainability required to achieve substantial reductions in criminal behavior. Finally, in **Chapter 12**, we summarize what we currently know about effective crime prevention and what needs further investigation and provide a few more recommendations for advancing crime prevention and increasing our ability to significantly reduce rates of crime.

Critical Thinking Questions and Practice Activities

1. Re-read Scenario #1 at the start of the chapter. Suppose the offender in this example participated in an effective prevention program while serving his prison term. Based on what you know about prevention at this point, what type of intervention do you think he should receive? What measure of crime should be used to evaluate this program? Explain.
2. Identify the difference between tangible and intangible costs of crime. Which type is typically larger? Which type do you think is more likely to be related to the fear of crime?
3. Talk to someone you know who has been the victim of a crime. Ask them: (a) how this experience changed their perceived risk of being a victim again in the future; (b) what, if anything, they did or are doing now to reduce their risk of future victimization; and (c) whether or not they reported their victimization experience to the police. Be sure to ask why they reported or decided not to report the victimization.
4. Go to the UCR and NCVS websites shown in the Helpful Websites and compare the arrest and victimization rates for 1980, 1990, and 2000 for aggravated assaults, robbery, and burglary offenses. Describe the similarities and differences in the rates of crime across the two sources of information. What do you think accounts for these differences?
5. Imagine that you are asked to participate in a survey that asks you to self-report your involvement as a perpetrator of the UCR Part I and Part II Offenses shown in Table 1.1. To what extent do you think you would answer questions about these offenses honestly? Are there some crimes that you would be more or less likely to report? Why or why not? Is there anything the researcher could do to increase the likelihood that you would provide accurate and honest answers?

Endnotes

1. There are several other possible measures that can be used to assess rates of crime. For example, researchers may: (i) directly observe and record crimes; (ii) compile detailed "life histories" of offenders, which involves the systematic recording of crimes, usually over an extended period of time, using self-reported and/or official records; or (iii) conduct detailed case studies of offenders based on in-depth interviews of individuals. While these methodologies have some strengths, they are rarely used in prevention research because they tend to be impractical, unsystematic, and limited to small local samples.
2. To briefly summarize some of the research that has examined racial differences in under-reporting, Hindelang and colleagues (1981) found that African American males reported significantly fewer offenses known to the police than did Caucasian males. Hirschi (1969) and Maxfield *et al.* (2000) reported similar

findings, while Elliott and Huizinga (1989) found no race or ethnic differences in the reporting of relatively trivial offenses, but they did find a higher level of under-reporting of known arrests among African American males compared to Caucasian males. Farrington *et al.* (1996), Gold (1970), Rojek (1983), and Hardt and Peterson-Hardt (1977) reported no differences in the under-reporting of arrests by race. Although the evidence is mixed, Hindelang *et al.* (1981) and Huizinga and Elliott (1986) consider the potential for African American males to under-report arrests to be at least partly a result of a higher number of invalid (unfounded) arrests for African American males and confusion about whether or not any encounter with police "counts" as an arrest.

Helpful Websites (last accessed July 27, 2016)

- Uniform Crime Report: https://ucr.fbi.gov/ucr-publications
- National Crime Victimization Survey: http://www.bjs.gov/index.cfm?ty=dcdetail&iid=245 and www.icpsr.umich.edu/icpsrweb/NACJD/NCVS
- Youth Risk Behavior Survey: https://www.cdc.gov/healthyyouth/data/yrbs/data.htm
- Monitoring the Future: www.monitoringthefuture.org

Further Reading

- Truman, J. L., Langton, L., and Planty, M. 2013. Criminal Victimization, 2012. Washington, DC: US Department of Justice, Bureau of Justice Statistics.
  Summarizes findings from the National Crime Victimization Survey (NCVS) on rates and levels of serious crimes in the United States in 2012 and trends in these statistics from 2003 to 2012. It also includes information on the characteristics of victims and offenders.
- US Department of Health and Human Services. 2001. Youth violence: A report of the Surgeon General. Rockville, MD: US Department of Health and Human Services.
  Chapter 2 ("The Magnitude of Youth Violence") provides a comprehensive review of official and self-reported measures of criminal behavior of adolescents in the United States.
- Warr, M. 2000. Fear of crime in the United States: Avenues for research and policy. In: D. Duffee, D. McDowall, L. Green Mazerolle, and S. D. Mastrofski (eds), *Measurement and Analysis of Crime and Justice*, pp. 451–489. Washington, DC: US Department of Justice, Office of Justice Programs.
  Summarizes current research regarding the study of the fear of crime and provides suggestions for how to improve this research.

References

Anderson, D. A. 1999. The aggregate burden of crime. *Journal of Law and Economics*, 42(2):611–642.

Bachman, J. G., Johnston, L. D., and O'Malley, P. M. 1996. The Monitoring the Future project after twenty-two years: Design and procedures. In: *Monitoring the Future Occasional Paper 38*. Ann Arbor, MI: Institute for Social Research, The University of Michigan.

Bennett, R. R., and Flavin, J. M. 1994. Determinants of fear of crime: The effect of cultural setting. *Justice Quarterly*, 11(3):357–382.

Brunton-Smith, I., and Jackson, J. 2012. Urban fear and its roots in place. In: V. Ceccato (ed.), *Urban Fabric of Crime and Fear*, pp. 55–84. New York, NY: Springer.

Chalfin, A. 2015. The economic costs of crime. In: W. G. Jennings (ed.), *The Encyclopedia of Crime and Punishment*. Malden, MA: Wiley-Blackwell.

Chiricos, T., Hogan, M., and Gertz, M. 1997. Racial composition of neighborhood and fear of crime. *Criminology*, 35(1):107–132.

Cohen, M. A., Piquero, A. R., and Jennings, W. G. 2010. Studying the costs of crime across offender trajectories. *Criminology and Public Policy*, 9(2):279–305.

Crabtree, S. 2013. Venezuelans, South Africans least likely to feel safe. In: *Gallop News Service*.

Elliott, D. 1995. Lies, damn lies, and arrest statistics: The Sutherland Award Presentation. Paper read at The American Society of Criminology Annual Meeting, at Boston, MA.

Elliott, D. S., and Ageton, S. 1980. Reconciling race and class differences in self-reported and official estimates of delinquency. *American Sociological Review*, 45(1):95–110.

Elliott, D. S., and Huizinga, D. 1985. Self-reported incidence and prevalence rates. In: E. F. McGarrell and T. J. Flanagan (eds), *Sourcebook of Criminal Justice Statistics, 1984*, pp. 363–379. Washington, DC: Government Printing Office: Bureau of Justice Statistics, US Department of Justice.

Elliott, D. S., and Huizinga, D. 1989. Improving self-reported measures of delinquency. In: M. W. Klein (ed.), *Cross-National Research in Self-Reported Crime and Delinquency*, pp. 155–186. Boston, MA: Kluwer Academic Publishers.

Elliott, D. S., Huizinga, D., and Menard, S. 1989. *Multiple Problem Youth*. New York, NY: Springer-Verlag.

Farrington, D. P., Hawkins, J. D., Catalano, R. F., Hill, K. G., and Kosterman, R. 2003. Comparing delinquency careers in court records and self-reports. *Criminology*, 41:933–958.

Farrington, D. P., Loeber, R., Stouthamer-Loeber, M., Van Kammen, W. B., and Schmidt, L. C. 1996. Self-reported delinquency and a combined delinquency seriousness scale based on boys, mothers, and teachers: Concurrent and predictive validity for African-Americans and Caucasians. *Criminology*, 34(4):493–517.

Finkelhor, D., Shattuck, A., Turner, H. A., and Hamby, S. 2014. Trends in children's exposure to violence, 2003 to 2011. *JAMA Pediatrics*, 168(6):540–546.

Gates, B. 2013. My plan to fix the world's biggest problems – measure them! *The Wall Street Journal*.

Gibbons, D. C. 1976. *Delinquent Behavior,* 2nd ed. Englewood Cliffs, NJ: Prentice Hall.

Gold, M. 1970. *Delinquent Behavior in an American City*. Belmont, CA: Wadsworth.

Gold, M., and Reimer, D. J. 1974. Changing patterns of delinquent behavior among Americans 13 to 16 years old: 1967–1972. Ann Arbor, MI: Institute for Social Research, The University of Michigan.

Hardt, R. H., and Peterson-Hardt, S. 1977. On determining the quality of the delinquency self-report method. *Journal of Research in Crime and Delinquency*, 14:247–259.

Harrendorf, S., Heiskanen, M., and Malby, S. 2010. International Statistics on Crime and Justice. Helsinki, Finland: European Institute for Crime Prevention and Control and United Nations Office on Drugs and Crime.

Hindelang, M. J., Hirschi, T., and Weis, J. G. 1979. Correlates of delinquency: The illusion of discrepancy between self-report and official measures. *American Sociological Review*, 44(6):995–1014.

Hindelang, M. J., Hirschi, T., and Weis, J. G. 1981. *Measuring Delinquency*. Beverly Hills, CA: Sage.

Hirschi, T. 1969. *Causes of Delinquency*. Berkeley, CA: University of California Press.

Hough, M. 1995. *Anxiety about Crime: Findings from the 1994 British Crime Survey*. London, UK: The Home Office.

Huizinga, D., and Elliott, D. S. 1986. Reassessing the reliability and validity of self-reported delinquent measures. *Journal of Quantitative Criminology*, 2(4):293–327.

Institute for Economics and Peace. 2013. UK Peace Index: Exploring the fabric of peace in the UK from 2003 to 2012. New York, NY: Institute for Economics and Peace.

Jackson, J., and Stafford, M. 2009. Public health and fear of crime: A prospective cohort study. *British Journal of Criminology*, 49(6):832–847.

Jones, J. M. 2006. Parent concern about children's safety at school on the rise. *Gallop News Service*; http://www.gallop.com/poll/25021/Parent-Concern-About-Childrens-Safety-School-Rise.aspx (accessed July 14, 2016).

Junger-Tas, J., and Marshall, I. H. 2012. Introduction to the International Self-report Study of Delinquency (ISRD-2). In: J. Junger-Tas, I. H. Marshall, D. Enzmann, *et al.* (eds), *The Many Faces of Youth Crime: Contrasting Theoretical Perspectives on Juvenile Delinquency Across Countries and Cultures*, pp. 3–20. New York, NY: Springer.

Klima, N., and Wijckmans, B. 2012. European cross-country crime statistics, surveys and reports. Brussels, Belgium: European Crime Prevention Network.

Knight, K. E., Menard, S., and Simmons, S. B. 2014. Intergenerational continuity of substance use. *Substance Use and Misuse*, 49:221–233.

Krohn, M. D., Thornberry, T. P., Gibson, C. L., and Baldwin, J. M. 2010. The development and impact of self-report measures of crime and delinquency. *Journal of Quantitative Criminology*, 26:509–525.

Lab, S. P. 2010. *Crime Prevention: Approaches, Practices, and Evaluations*. New Providence, NJ: Anderson Publishing Company.

LaGrange, R. L., and Ferraro, K. F. 1989. Assessing age and gender differences in perceived risk and fear of crime. *Criminology*, 27(4):697–719.

LaGrange, R. L., Ferraro, K. F., and Supancic, M. 1992. Perceived risk and fear of crime: Role of social and physical incivilities. *Journal of Research in Crime and Delinquency*, 29(3):311–334.

Langton, L., Berzofsky, M., Krebs, C., and Smiley-McDonald, H. 2012. Victimizations Not Reported to the Police, 2006–2010. Washington, DC: US Department of Justice, Bureau of Justice Statistics.

Mandel, M. J., and Magnusson, P. 1993. The economics of crime. *Business Week*, December 12.

Maxfield, M. G., Weiler, B. L., and Widom, C. S. 2000. Comparing self-reports and official records of arrests. *Journal of Quantitative Criminology*, 16(1):87–110.

McCollister, K. E., French, M. T., and Fang, H. 2010. The cost of crime to society: New crime-specific estimates for policy and program evaluation. *Drug and Alcohol Dependence*, 108(1–2):98–109.

McGarrell, E. F., Giacomazzi, A. L., and Thurman, Q. C. 1997. Neighborhood disorder, integration, and the fear of crime. *Justice Quarterly*, 14(3):479–500.

Osgood, D. W., McMorris, B. J., and Potenza, M. T. 2002. Analyzing multiple-item measures of crime and delinquency I: Item response theory scaling. *Journal of Quantitative Criminology*, 18(3):267–296.

Ponemon Institute. 2012. 2012 Cost of Cyber Crime Study: United States. Traverse City, MI: Ponemon Institute.

Ponemon Institute. 2015. 2015 Cost of Cyber Crime Study: United States. Traverse City, MI: Ponemon Institute.

Raudenbush, S. W., Johnson, C., and Sampson, R. J. 2003. A multivariate, multilevel Rasch model with application to self-reported criminal behavior. *Sociological Methodology*, 33:169–211.

Rojek, D. G. 1983. Social status and delinquency: Do self-reports and official reports match? In: G. P. Waldo (ed.), *Measurement Issues in Criminal Justice*. Beverly Hills, CA: Sage.

Rountree, P. W. 1998. A reexamination of the crime-fear linkage. *Journal of Research in Crime and Delinquency*, 35(3):341–372.

Saad, L. 2003. Pessimism about crime is up, despite declining crime rate. *Gallup Poll* [Online], October 23.

Saad, L. 2006. Worry about crime remains at last year's elevated levels. *Gallup Poll* [Online], October 19.

Saad, L. 2009. Two in three Americans worry about identity theft. *Gallup Poll* [Online], October 16.

Saad, L. 2010. Nearly 4 in 10 Americans still fear walking alone at night. *Gallop Poll* [Online], November 5.

Saad, L. 2012. Parent's fear for children's safety at school rises slightly. *Gallop Poll* [Online], December 28.

Santora, M. 2013. City's Annual Cost Per Inmate Is $168,000, Study Finds. *The New York Times*.

Skogan, W. G. 1986. Fear of crime and neighborhood change. In: A. J. Reiss and M. Tonry (eds), *Communities and Crime*, pp. 203–229. Chicago, IL: University of Chicago Press.

Smith, W. R., and Torstensson, M. 1997. Gender differences in risk perception and neutralizing fear of crime. *British Journal of Criminology*, 37(4):608–634.

Stafford, M., Chandola, T., and Marmot, M. 2007. Association between fear of crime and mental health and physical functioning. *American Journal of Public Health*, 97:2076–2081.

The Pew Charitable Trusts. 2008. One in 100: Behind Bars in America 2008. Washington, DC: The Pew Charitable Trusts.

The Pew Charitable Trusts. 2013. Managing Prison Health Care Spending. Washington, DC: The Pew Charitable Trusts and John D. and Catherine T. MacArthur Foundation.

Thornberry, T. P., and Krohn, M. D. 2000. The self-report method for measuring delinquency and crime. In: D. Duffee, D. McDowall, L. Green Mazerolle, and S. D. Mastrofski (eds), *Measurement and Analysis of Crime and Justice*, pp. 33–83. Washington, DC: US Department of Justice, Office of Justice Programs.

Truman, J. L., Langton, L., and Planty, M. 2013. Criminal victimization, 2012. Washington, DC: US Department of Justice, Bureau of Justice Statistics.

Warr, M. 1984. Fear of victimization: Why are women and the elderly more afraid? *Social Science Quarterly*, 65:681–702.

Warr, M. 2000. Fear of crime in the United States: Avenues for research and policy. In: D. Duffee, D. McDowall, L. Green Mazerolle, and S. D. Mastrofski (eds), *Measurement and Analysis of Crime and Justice*, pp. 451–489. Washington, DC: US Department of Justice, Office of Justice Programs.

Williams, P., and Dickinson, J. 1993. Fear of crime: Read all about it? *British Journal of Criminology*, 33(1):33–56.

Zimring, F. E., and Hawkins, G. 1997. *Crime is Not the Problem*. New York, NY: Oxford University Press.

2

A Brief History of Crime Prevention

Learning Objectives

Upon finishing this chapter, students should be able to:
- Understand the origins of current crime prevention theories and strategies
- Be able to identify the types of crime prevention strategies used through history and the theories upon which they have been based
- Explain the difference between micro and macro theories of crime and prevention strategies
- Describe the principles of positivism and its significance for crime prevention research
- Summarize the reasons for and consequences of the "nothing works" period of crime prevention.

Introduction: Why Study the History of Crime Prevention?

Crime is an ancient problem, dating back to Cain's murder of his brother Abel in the Biblical account of the argument between the first two humans born on Earth. Through the centuries, many explanations for criminal behavior have been proposed and remedies for preventing crime tried. Most of these early explanations and their associated prevention strategies have been disproved or rejected on ethical or moral grounds, but some have persisted into modern criminology without any major changes to their original

He who knows only his own generation remains forever a child

Inscription over Norlin Library at the University of Colorado, Boulder

The Prevention of Crime, First Edition. Delbert Elliott and Abigail Fagan.
© 2017 John Wiley & Sons, Inc. Published 2017 by John Wiley & Sons, Inc.
Companion website: www.wiley.com/go/elliott/prevention_of_crime

Prevention theories and strategies

21st century BC	18th century BC	12th century BC	451 BC	18th century AD	19th century AD	20th century AD
Deterrence Retribution	Deterrence Retribution	Deterrence Retribution Cities of refuge	Deterrence Prisons	Deterrence Prisons	Deterrence Prisons Insane asylum	Deterrence Strengthening social controls Increased opportunities Community reorganization Mental institutions
Code of Ur-Nammu	Code of Hammurabi	Mosaic law Ten Commandments	Roman 12 Tablets	Enlightenment Classical school of criminology	Positivism Social structural theory	The first juvenile court First presidential Crime Commission The Chicago Area Project Mobilization for Youth

Crime-related historical events

Figure 2.1   Historical events in crime prevention.

design or intentions even in the face of evidence indicating that they may not be successful in reducing crime.

Knowing the history of crime prevention is critical if we are to understand how our current ideas about the causes of crime and its prevention originated, and if we want to avoid repeating or reinventing the invalid theories, false leads, and ineffective interventions of the past. In Figure 2.1, we identify some of the major events and periods that influenced the development of ideas regarding the causes of crime and strategies used to prevent crime up to the twentieth century. In the following sections, we discuss these ideas, identify some of the most important philosophers and theorists associated with these views on crime and provide examples of strategies used throughout history to punish offenders and prevent crime.

Early Attempts at Crime Prevention

The earliest written definitions of crime and proposed sanctions for criminal behavior that we know of date back to a code created by Ur-Nammu, a Sumarian ruler from the city of Ur in the twenty-first century BC. Other ancient codes that have had a significant influence on current legal systems in the Western world include the code of the Babylonian ruler Hammurabi (written in eighteenth century BC), the Hebrew Mosaic Law (twelfth century BC), and the Twelve Tables of Roman Law (451 BC). The first of these, the **Code of Hammurabi**, defined conduct that was prohibited and established specific punishments for violations of these laws. From a crime prevention perspective, these punishments were intended to serve as a deterrent to crime. They are considered a **lex talionis**, which calls for "an eye for an eye" in retribution or retaliation for wrongdoing. For example, if a man knocked out the teeth or broke a bone of another man, his teeth were to be knocked out or his same bone broken. Punishments for law violations were to be carried out by the ruling elders of the city or the family or clan of the victim.

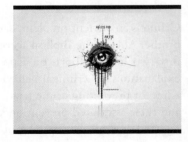

The 284 laws in the Code of Hammurabi specified some very brutal punishments for illegal behavior. For example, if a son hit his father, the Code dictated that the son's hands be "hewn off." If someone was guilty of incest with his mother or her father, both parties were to be burned. The severity of these punishments was designed to offset any potential gain or benefit from the criminal act and to create a fear of punishment which would deter any rational person from committing a crime. As we will explain later in this chapter, these ideas are consistent with deterrence theory.

The Code also included other principles found in our present laws. For example, a minimum wage for workers was present in the Code, with field workers and herdsmen guaranteed "eight gur of corn" as an annual salary. The Code also made a presumption of innocence for the accused offender and imposed a severe penalty for making false accusations against another. For example, the Code stipulated that if one brought an accusation of a capital crime before the elders and did not prove what s/he had charged, s/he would be put to death.

The **Mosaic Law** was both similar to and different from the Code of Hammurabi. Like the latter, it involved an "eye for an eye" retribution system with some very harsh punishments, as well as a presumption of innocence and regulations for wages paid to workers. New elements not found in the prior Code included an attempt to deter crime through appealing to individual morality with prescriptions such as: *"Honor your father and mother," Do not covet your neighbor's house … or anything that belongs to your neighbor," "Love your neighbor as yourself"* (Deuteronomy 5:16, 22; Leviticus 19:18). The Mosaic Law also provided a right of asylum and protection for certain wrong-doers. For example, it established "cities of refuge" where individuals who accidentally or unintentionally killed others could find protection from the family or other appointed avenger of the death(s). From a crime prevention perspective, the Mosaic Law included both specific deterrents to crime in the form of anticipated punishments for offenders and general deterrents for reducing the motivation of all individuals to engage in criminal behavior.

The goal of the **Roman Twelve Tables** was to specify laws that would apply to both privileged (e.g., wealthy) and common citizens. The first version included 10 tablets, each of which covered a different domain of law, such as court and trial procedures, debt, rights of fathers over the family, inheritance, and injury. Apparently, this set of laws was not adequate in the eyes of the commoners, and a new commission was appointed and two additional tables of law were created around 450 BC. These Twelve Tables, like the earlier codes of law, continued to endorse the "eye for an eye" principle. For example, Table 8.2 stated: *"If a person has maimed another's limb, let there be retaliation in kind, unless he agrees to make compensation with him."* The brutality of sanctions is also reflected, as seen in Law 8.1: *"If any person has sung or composed against another person a song such as was causing slander or insult … he shall be clubbed to death"* and Law 8.21: *"If a patron shall defraud his client, he must be solemnly forfeited (killed)"* (Livy, 2002).

Several new principles, which are found in current US law, were also found in the Twelve Tables. For example, they provided for due process of law, grace periods for payment of debt, extenuating circumstances that could help explain a criminal act, common law marriage, and a legally binding, word-of-mouth agreement. A broader range of sanctions was also proposed for violations of these laws compared to that found in earlier codes, including monetary fines, fetters/chains, flogging, banishment, and slavery. Various forms of punishment leading to death were also specified. From a prevention perspective, the Twelve Tables, like the earlier codes, again assumed that fear of punishment (i.e., deterrence) was the basic and best strategy for preventing crime.

The focus on punishment as the primary deterrent to crime continued to influence thinking about prevention during the Middle Ages (500–1500 AD), also known as the Dark Ages, when satanic possession, witchcraft, and biological inferiority or depravity came to be viewed as causes of crime. Correspondingly, prevention strategies now included the identification and treatment or elimination of demon-possessed, biologically deficient and depraved persons. Evidence of possession or depravity/wickedness included observation of "unusual" behavior, especially indecent and obscene acts, as well as having a "strange" personality; bodily deformities, especially of the face; supernatural strength; unexplained knowledge of the future; and the possession of tools or materials associated with witchcraft. Those displaying such signs were subject to various "tests" and sometimes trials to determine if they were, in fact, involved in witchcraft or possessed. For those who failed the test or who were convicted at trial of witchcraft, the typical sentence was a public burning at the stake. Exorcism was used for those who were possessed to cast out the demon(s). For the biologically inferior and depraved, treatments often involved confinement in an insane asylum. It is estimated that approximately 100,000 persons were prosecuted for demon possession and witchcraft during the sixteenth and seventeenth centuries in Europe (Weber, 1971).

Are these causal explanations of crime still used today? Witchcraft, demon possession, and biological inferiority have been rejected by most criminologists and the general public, and the proposed treatment strategies are considered misguided, ineffective, and overly cruel. We are horrified by the witch trials, burning at the stake, and brutal forms of exorcism used in the past, as well as the incarceration of persons with physical deformities or unusual personalities who posed no threat of serious criminal behavior.

Despite these views, these causal explanations of criminal behavior and suggested prevention techniques are not entirely dead; some live on in a somewhat revised form. Many of the behaviors considered evidence of demon possession are now considered rare forms of insanity or mental disorders, and the recommended remedy typically involves some form of psychiatric treatment (a type of exorcism) and/or confinement in a mental institution (i.e., modern day insane asylums). In addition, brain damage and some genetic characteristics representing biological inferiority or vulnerability to certain conditions are considered viable explanations for crime today (Boardman et al., 2014). While the methods used to identify individuals with these criminal characteristics are very different now than they were in the Dark Ages, the basic prevention and intervention strategies are actually somewhat similar.

The dominant and most consistent crime prevention strategy used in history to this point was **deterrence**. *Deterrence is a crime prevention strategy that relies on a perceived threat of punishment that is severe enough to outweigh any profit or gain that would follow from committing the crime.* As a prevention strategy, it is designed to deter both those who have not yet committed an offense and to prevent offenders from committing another offense. The first strategy is called **general deterrence**. It calls for a public awareness that committing a crime will result in punishment, and the punishment must be severe enough to prevent a rational person who might consider committing a crime from actually doing it. The second strategy, **specific deterrence**, involves a punishment inflicted on offenders for their crimes that is severe enough to prevent a rational offender from re-offending. The severity of the punishment is emphasized in deterrence strategies, and the early sanctions imposed on criminals were very severe.

While there is little current support for the brutal punishments used previously, deterrence remains one of the major crime prevention strategies used in the twenty-first century, although, as noted later in this chapter, it has been extended in several important ways. To preview that discussion, we should note that some criminologist do not consider specific deterrence to be a crime *prevention* strategy (Lejins, 1967; Weis and Hawkins, 1981). They refer to interventions that occur *after* persons have committed an initial offense as **crime control** rather than **crime prevention**. Crime control is also sometimes viewed as punishments imposed upon offenders by the justice system and/or interventions mandated by the justice system to be delivered in correctional or community settings (Welsh and Pfeffer, 2013). Still others refer to crime control as the use of punishment to deter crime, via general and specific deterrence.

These different uses of the term "crime control" and "crime prevention" are confusing. In this text, we consider both specific and general deterrence to be crime prevention strategies as they have the same objective: to prevent crime, whether it be the first, second, or twentieth crime. We also consider interventions designed to reduce offending to be crime prevention whether they are implemented by the justice system or by a private or public agency outside of the justice system. Nonetheless, it is important to distinguish between interventions that occur before an individual's first offense and those that occur after the first offense. We will discuss this distinction more in the following chapter, and we describe these interventions types separately in Chapters 8 and 9.

Crime Prevention in the Eighteenth-century Enlightenment Period

In the eighteenth-century period of Enlightenment, some scholars began to question the explanations for crime and the laws and crime prevention policies and practices that had occurred in Europe since the Dark Ages. They protested the use of cruel and brutal punishments and the often arbitrary and biased decision-making of the courts that imposed these sanctions. They called for reforms in Europe's criminal laws, courts, and penal systems. Specifically, they argued for more just and reasonable criminal sanctions, which they believed would also be more effective in deterring crime because the public would view these punishments as more legitimate and fair. The most influential of these reformers, who are often referred to as **utilitarian social philosophers,** and as the founders of the **classical school of criminology**, were Cesare Beccaria (1738–1794) and Jeremy Bentham (1748–1832). While their primary concern was making changes to the judicial process, their theories about the causes of crime and refinements to the earlier deterrence strategies have had a profound influence on crime prevention.

> *Nature has placed mankind under the governance of two sovereign masters, pain and pleasure. It is for them alone to point out what we ought to do, as well as determine what we shall do.*
>
> Jeremy Bentham

Beccaria was an Italian philosopher, politician, and economist. He was strongly influenced by the English philosopher Thomas Hobbes' writings on the **social contract.** This philosophy stated that, to maintain the social order, avoid conflict and prevent crime, people enter into an agreement with the government to enforce laws as needed to protect them and insure their well-being. Beccaria argued in his book, *On Crimes and Punishments* (1764/1983), that the legitimacy of criminal sanctions must be based on the social contract and that punishment is unjust when its severity exceeds what is necessary to deter a rational person from engaging in crime. He also stated that excessively severe punishments will actually increase crime as they will undermine the perceived legitimacy of government. He proposed the following basic principles of deterrence: (i) laws should have specific, prescribed punishments; (ii) laws should be published, known and understood by the public; (iii) the severity of sanctions should be proportionate to the offense involved; and (iv) punishment should be swift and certain.

Bentham, an English contemporary of Beccaria, was also concerned about the arbitrary and excessive use of cruel and brutal punishments in the English courts and penal systems. In his book, *An Introduction to the Principles of Morals and Legislation* (1789/1970), he defined morality as that which promotes "the greatest happiness of the greatest number" and asserted that the duty of government was to promote the happiness of a society by punishing poor behaviors and rewarding positive behavior. He also argued that using punishments that were more severe than required to deter a rational person from committing crime was immoral and unjustified.

Beccaria and Bentham were clearly deterrence theorists, and their writings provide the foundation for modern deterrence theory, especially the view that criminal behavior is the result of free will and rational choice. Their recommendations for crime prevention also involved deterrence, but with several important revisions and extensions compared to prior beliefs. *First*, in reaction to the historical use of arbitrary and often brutal punishment for relatively minor offenses, they argued that the severity of punishment should be proportionate to the crime committed. Moreover, they provided a rationale for determining a proportionate severity of punishment, one that was consistent with the social contract movement of the Enlightenment and its corresponding emphasis on citizen participation in government and democratic processes. How to judge the severity of punishment continues in modern versions of deterrence theory and in legal views about what constitutes "cruel and unusual" punishment. *Second*, they proposed additional ways in which punishment could be administered – it should be certain and swift – so as to make it a more effective deterrent. The *certainty* of punishment for a crime refers to one's perceived risk of apprehension, conviction, and punishment. The greater the expectation that an offender will be caught and punished, the greater the deterrent effect. Beccaria stated that punishments should be administered *quickly*, and as close to the criminal act as possible, because the shorter the time interval between the crime and the resulting punishment, the stronger and more lasting the association between crime and punishment. When punishment is severe enough, swift and certain, people can rationally determine that the personal cost of engaging in crime exceeds the expected benefit.

The principles of deterrence articulated by Beccaria and Bentham are the foundation for modern deterrence theory and many of the laws and justice policies used in the Western world to deter crime. Can you think of any examples? How about: doubling fines for speeding in construction zones? Placing surveillance cameras in public places? The right to a speedy trial? Limiting cruel and unusual punishments? Or, "hot spots" policing, which increases police patrols and the likelihood of arrest in high crime areas?

Crime Prevention in the Nineteenth-century Positivism Period

Beccaria and Bentham justified their views on deterrence and the call for reforms of the justice system on philosophical and moral grounds, not on the grounds that deterrence-based efforts were more effective than other approaches to prevention. While deterrence strategies continued to dominate crime prevention approaches during the nineteenth century, the introduction and application of the scientific method in biology, chemistry, and other physical and life sciences led to some dramatic new discoveries and a greater emphasis on scientific proof. The appeal of the scientific approach eventually extended to other disciplines, including the study of society, social behavior, and criminal behavior. For example, Auguste Comte (1798–1857), the founder of the discipline of sociology, believed that society, like the physical world, functions according to observable regularities or general "laws." These laws are the basis of all knowledge, and knowledge is established by the scientific method of observing regularities and testing or "verifying" hypothesized causal processes that account for these regularities. All knowledge can (and should) be verified using this process.

Positivism, which is the movement calling for the use of the scientific method to determine if hypothesized causes of crime could be demonstrated empirically (i.e., scientifically), dramatically changed thinking about criminology and crime prevention. Cesare Lombroso (1835–1909), a surgeon in the Italian army and later a professor and director of an insane asylum, was one of the first positivists to apply the scientific method to the study of crime. His first major study compared the cadavers of male criminals that had been executed to male inmates of insane asylums to determine if criminals were physically, biologically, and psychologically different from non-criminals. He made very detailed and precise measurements of body features to identify those shared by criminals. Based on interviews with living offenders, he also documented psychological traits common to criminals. These findings were summarized in *The Criminal Man* (1876/2006). The major conclusion of this book was that criminality can be linked to **atavism**, a less evolved form of humanity. That is, criminals represent a recurrence of an earlier form of the human species that is not fully evolved and are thus a subhuman or primitive form of our species. According to Lombroso, the offender is "a savage born into the modern world" (Elwood 1912: 721).

Drawing on the extensive data compiled from his studies, Lombroso identified **stigmata**, or physical signs of atavism. These physical markers included thin beards, physical weakness, small

> *[N]early all criminals have jug ears, thick hair, thin beards, pronounced sinuses, protruding chins and broad cheekbones ... Jug ears are found on 28% of criminals, but the proportion varies by region: 47% of Sicilian criminals have jug ears as do 33% from Piedmont, 11% from Naples, 33% from the Romagna, 9% from Sardinia and 36% from Lombardy. Nine percent of all criminals have very long ears, although that proportion rises to 10% in Lombardy and the Romagna and 18% in Sicily and Piedmont.*
>
> Lombroso, 1876/2006: 53

heads (which would indicate reduced brain capacity), receding foreheads, highly developed frontal sinuses (similar to animals who are more dependent on a sense of smell), exceptionally large jaws and cheekbones, thick hair, darker skin, jug-shaped ears, and low sensitivity to pain. He believed that these physical abnormalities were directly related to and could cause psychological deficits and/or personality traits such as being vain, vindictive or spiteful; laziness; being dominated by a thirst for blood; and having a preference for sexual behavior and orgies. He also characterized criminals as morally corrupt and degenerate.

In 1893, with the publication of *The Criminal Woman, the Prostitute, and the Normal Woman* (Lombroso and Ferrero, 1893/2004), Lombroso turned his attention to women. He found female criminals, like male criminals, to have physical stigmata and atavistic features including a narrow receding forehead, prominent cheekbones, short stature, excessive weight, left handedness, and prehensile feet, which can function like hands and have the ability to grip objects. Psychological stigmata included a lack of modesty, a bold and brazen attitude, an "irregular" lifestyle, laziness, vanity, and a fondness for amusement, orgies, and alcohol abuse. As reflected in the title of this book, Lombroso thought that the typical female offender was a prostitute and that the stigmata were specific to this type of criminal. Not surprisingly, he viewed females' criminal behavior as being rooted in their sexuality. He also noted that women had small brains, which indicated an intellectual inferiority, that women criminals were physically under-developed, and that female offenders could even be considered to be undeveloped males. Needless to say, Lombroso's views of female offenders were even less flattering than his views of male offenders.

Lombroso's early writings emphasized the fact that criminals were born criminals. In early editions of *The Criminal Man*, he claimed that as many as 70% of all criminals were atavistic and had criminal tendencies at birth. In his later writing, he allowed for social and environmental conditions to affect criminal behavior (a view that predated later theories, as we will discuss), and in his last book, *Crime: Its Causes and Remedies* (1912), he stated that only 33% of offenders were born criminals. In these writings, he distinguished between the **insane criminal** and the **criminaloid**. The insane criminal was not a born criminal; instead, offending was the result of an injury or brain impairment following birth which altered normal functioning. Kleptomaniacs and child molesters were primary examples of insane criminals. Criminaloids were also not born criminals but became involved in crime as a result of association with other criminals, excessive alcohol use/abuse, or exposure to stressful circumstances. He also argued that different types of criminals had different clusters of stigmata which make it easier to distinguish between them. For example, one could tell a robber from a murderer or burglar based on their pattern of stigmata.

Lombroso's theory of atavism and the idea that criminals could be identified by stigmata was attacked and discredited in the late nineteenth and early twentieth centuries. Several of his critics noted that many of their non-criminal friends had a number of these stigmata; indeed, these features were common in the general population and could be found among many non-criminals. While Lombroso is applauded as being one of the first to apply scientific methods to the study of crime, taking precise measurements and analyzing these data, his methods were also critiqued. Notably, his study sample and analysis involved *only* criminals and did not compare the physical and psychological characteristics of criminals and non-criminals. As we will discuss in Chapter 4, comparison groups allow for stronger conclusions regarding the causes of crime.

It was a study by Charles Goring (1870–1919), a medical officer in English prisons, which led most criminologists to reject Lombroso's atavism argument. Goring (1913/1972) also collected data on physical characteristics of prisoners, but he collected the same type of data on a sample of non-criminals and then compared the prevalence of these bodily attributes in the two samples. This analysis led Goring to reject the claim that criminals could be distinguished from non-criminals by the features Lombroso identified as stigmata. Goring's scientific methods were clearly superior to Lombroso's, and, as a result, the theory that criminals were atavistic and identifiable by certain stigmata was rejected. However, echoing some of Lombroso's writings, Goring believed criminality to be hereditary and also endorsed the idea that the interaction of biological and environmental factors led to crime.

Even though Goring's work discredited the idea of atavistic criminals, Lombroso's legacy for crime prevention continued well into the twentieth century. Two of his Italian students, Enrico Ferri (1856–1928) and Raphael Garofalo (1852–1934), continued to identify types of criminals based on physiological and psychological traits, and American criminologists also relied on this type of explanation for crime. Even more importantly, Lombroso was among the first to seek a scientific solution to the problem of crime and to collect and analyze data using observable events and experiences. He shifted the focus of criminology and crime prevention from thinking about the *crime* to concentrating on the *criminal*.

The clear prevention strategy from Lombroso's perspective was to punish and incarcerate offenders, but his view differed from the preceding deterrence perspective. In fact, some claim that Lombroso dealt a "death blow" to the rational choice and free will assumptions of the earlier deterrence theory (Elwood, 1912), although we disagree, given that deterrence theory lives on today. Lombroso claimed that most crime was biologically determined and beyond the control of the offender, but he also asserted that crime had multiple causes, including biological, psychological, and social/environmental factors. He argued that punishment should be proportionate to the dangerousness of the offender, not the specific offense committed. This was a new way of thinking about prevention; it addressed the (future) threat posed by the offender, not the seriousness of the (past) offense. Enrico Ferri extended Lombroso's logic to emphasize that there was no point in crime prevention or rehabilitation; given the biological and physiological basis of crime, criminals could not be reformed and should either be executed or locked up for life.

In the 1800s, as academics in the emerging disciplines of psychology and sociology began to study crime, they further extended ideas regarding the causes of offending and ways to prevent and control it. **Emile Durkheim** (1858–1917), a French sociologist born 20 years after Lombroso, adopted the positivism approach but proposed a new type of determinism to explain crime and other types of deviant behavior: a social determinism that viewed crime as socially rather than biologically determined. For Durkheim, crime was a fundamental condition of social life and a response to specific social structural and organizational conditions.

Durkheim first outlined his theory in *The Division of Labor in Society* (1893/1984) and further developed it in *The Rules of Sociological Method* (1895/1965) and *Suicide: A Study in Sociology* (1897/1951). Durkheim was interested in how traditional pre-industrial and modern societies function and change over time. He identified two types of social solidarity, or ways that members and groups in a society develop shared values and beliefs and work cooperatively toward common goals. For Durkheim, these processes were critical in establishing a stable social order and, by extension, promoting conformity.

The first type, **mechanical solidarity,** was used in pre-literate and pre-industrial societies. It involved self-sufficient families or larger groups that functioned independently of one another. These groups provided for all their own needs and did not need to rely on other groups; there was no need to divide work across multiple groups or to cooperate to ensure that everyone was taken care of. Ties to others were based primarily on family relationships and established tradition. Groups were homogeneous, meaning members were similar to one another, which produced high levels of group cohesion and cooperation.

In contrast, Durkheim wrote that larger and more complex post-industrial societies are character-ized by **organic solidarity**. In these societies, families are no longer self-sufficient. Instead, there is a high division of labor and individuals have specialized roles and tasks. This arrangement creates mutual dependency between groups and members, which in turn produces societal cohesion, solidarity, and a stable social order. As populations grow and become more dense and diverse, they evolve from a mechanical to an organic form of solidarity.

Durkheim also identified social conditions that lead to a breakdown of solidarity and produce social disintegration rather than integration. The most important condition he discussed, and the one most related to crime prevention, was **anomie**. Anomie is derived from the Greek term *nomus*, meaning "without norms." Durkheim stated that during the transition from mechanical to organic sources of solidarity, the old norms, values and shared understandings that regulate behavior are weakened and break down. For example, during the Industrial Revolution, when masses of people moved from farms and rural communities into cities and metropolitan areas to find work, old sources of solidarity were no longer effective and new sources were not yet established. Durkheim called the resulting condition anomie: a temporary social structural condition in which norms and laws are ineffective in regulating behavior. In such conditions, society's social control mechanisms cannot maintain control over the population's behavior and compliance with norms and laws is weakened.

Anomie can result from any rapid change in the structure and organization of the society. For example, a severe and sustained economic crisis, war, famine, societal disasters, and technological revolutions can all produce anomie. Durkheim believed that during periods of anomie, personal goals become too ambitious, to the point where there are no realistic opportunities for achieving them. The gap between one's aspirations and the ability to fulfill them puts great pressure on con-ventional and socially approved ways of achieving goals, resulting in the adoption of new, creative, unconventional, and even deviant and criminal alternatives for realizing them.

Durkheim was heavily influence by the ideology of the French Revolution and believed that opportunities were equal for all social classes, rich and poor alike. The problem of anomie was thus more related to increasing societal aspirations than to limited opportunities. He also thought that the middle and upper social classes were more likely than the lower class to develop very high and unattainable aspirations because poverty placed a natural restraint on aspirations while the wealthy could always desire more wealth. In today's society, for example, we talk about the 1% class as being the small group of the very rich, a group that many wealthy individuals aspire to be part of. According to Durkheim, anomic conditions could produce crime as well as suicide, especially among the higher income classes.

Durkheim argued that some level of crime is normal and functional for every society. While not a positive experience at the individual level, at the societal level crime can serve as a prelude to social change and reform and thus contributes to the stability of the social order. Society's collective response to crime can help reinforce the existing norms and values embodied in the law as well as challenge their legitimacy. The first response can draw a society together and help build public support for the law. The second response can also bring people together; however, in this case, they will work together to challenge conventional values and beliefs, change moral boundaries and/or produce moral and legal reforms. A recent example of the latter situation would be the acts of civil disobedience and public protests of discriminatory law enforcement practices. Durkheim would view these situations as illustrating the functionality of crime in a society. Crime can also provide a way to release tensions and frustrations associated with anomie. The looting of stores and riots that occurred in New Orleans following Hurricane Katrina and again after the shooting of unarmed Michael Brown in Ferguson, MO are examples of this type of functionality.

Durkheim's contributions to contemporary theories of crime are profound. His work marked a radical break from the older deterrence paradigm which emphasized individual free will and rational choice. He established a new paradigm for studying crime and its prevention which attributed the causes of crime to the social organization and structures in which individuals live. Anomie is primarily a **macro theory**, an explanation of variation in the rates of crime in societies or communities, rather than a **micro theory** explaining variation among individuals' participation in crime. However, Durkheim did offer some suggestions about how anomie might function at the individual level to produce the aggregate rates found at the societal, contextual level. Other theorists drew upon these ideas when developing many of the micro contemporary theories we will discuss in the next section.

To summarize, Durkheim's new paradigm facilitated the development of both macro and micro theories of criminal behavior which locate the causes of crime in social interactions and in various features of the social context. While differing significantly from prior work, Durkheim's paradigm is still based in the major principles of positivism, including the assumptions that: (i) there are invariable laws of social relationships; (ii) these laws can be discovered with scientific methods; and (iii) the data of scientific inquiry are quantitative rather than qualitative. Durkheim's positivism was more strongly committed to the scientific method than Lombroso's work and relied heavily on the use of hypothesis testing to verify theoretical propositions. These differences are shown in Table 2.1.

Table 2.1 Notable historical figures in the eighteenth and nineteenth centuries.

Person	Major contribution
18th century	
Beccaria	• Laws should have specific punishments that are known to the public, their severity should be proportionate to the offense committed and they should be applied swiftly and with certainty after a law is broken
Bentham	• Punishments that are too severe are immoral and unfair
19th century	
Lombroso	• Crime is the result of atavism and criminals are less evolved humans who can be recognized by their abnormal physical characteristics
Durkheim	• Crime is determined by the social structure and anomie, a social condition in which norms and laws fail to regulate citizens' behavior. Crime can be functional for a society

Crime Prevention in the Twentieth Century

In the USA, crime prevention in the twentieth century was strongly influenced by the theories and prevention practices developed in Europe during the nineteenth century described earlier. Deterrence, with some important elaborations, continued to be the dominant theoretical model for prevention strategies utilized in the USA and Europe. Biological explanations for crime also continued to be proposed well into the twentieth century, with relatively minor modifications from Lombroso. It was not until the middle of the twentieth century that social structural theories began to appear and prevention strategies derived from this paradigm began to be implemented and evaluated, primarily in the USA, but also in the UK. In the following sections, we describe the development of each of these theoretical traditions and their applied crime prevention strategies.

Deterrence-based prevention

Crime prevention strategies in twentieth-century USA continued to rely on deterrence theory with little theoretical development beyond the work of Beccaria and Bentham until the late 1970s. Prevention was left to law enforcement and criminal justice agencies and relied primarily on the use of punishment in various forms, but especially the use of monetary fines and incarceration. There was little evaluation of the effectiveness of these strategies before the 1960s. Instead, "studies" involved philosophical debates over what constituted fair and morally acceptable punishments for specific crimes – with capital punishment the main focus of these conversations – and the physical and sanitary conditions of jails and prisons (Gibbs, 1975; Toby, 1964).

During most of the twentieth century, the basic deterrent strategy remained unchanged, except for one important event which had a significant, but temporary, impact on views regarding crime prevention and treatment. In 1825, the Society for the Prevention of Juvenile Delinquency began calling for the removal of juvenile offenders from the criminal justice system and the creation of a separate justice system for juveniles. At that time, children as young as seven could stand trial in a criminal court. In 1899, the Illinois legislature passed the *Juvenile Court Act* and the first juvenile court was established in Cook County, IL.

The juvenile court was founded on the British doctrine of **parens patriae**, which means "the state as parent." The philosophy was that the court should be able to intervene in the lives of juvenile offenders to protect and provide for their basic needs when their natural parents were not doing so. This view is clearly intended as a non-punitive strategy, focuses on the offender rather than the offense, and emphasizes treatment to address the basic individual and environmental causes of criminal behavior. While some punitive options were still available to the juvenile court, its creation and philosophy signified a radical departure from the sole reliance on punishment to deter subsequent offending. By 1925, all but two states in the USA had established juvenile courts and a juvenile justice system (Office of Juvenile Justice and Delinquency Prevention, 1999). At the national level, the Office of Juvenile Justice and Delinquency Prevention was established in 1974.

In the early years of their existence, juvenile court hearings were informal and dispositions (i.e., "sentences") included warnings only, supervision by a probation officer, mandated treatment by some welfare agency and, the most serious option, commitment to a state training school. Over time, it became clear that the treatment options for juvenile offenders were limited and/or ineffective and the promise that the juvenile justice system could successfully reform delinquent youth was rarely realized. In actuality, the system began relying more and more on punitive sanctions and less on rehabilitation. By the 1950s, the number of juveniles locked up in correctional institutions for extended periods in the name of "treatment" was alarming. In the 1960s, the US Supreme Court required that many of the protections offered adults in criminal courts be offered to juveniles, the juvenile court process became more formal and adversarial, like the adult system, and the **parens patriae** philosophy was essentially abandoned. Deterrence was again the basic prevention strategy, and prevention was still the responsibility of law enforcement and the justice system. Today, there have been some reforms to the juvenile justice system and some treatments have been demonstrated to reduce recidivism (see Chapter 9), although more progress is needed.

Challenges of deterrence theory

In the mid-1960s, the prevention programs and practices implemented in the justice system began to be seriously challenged. Crime prevention efforts became a political issue in the USA, as politicians of both parties began to question the effectiveness of crime prevention efforts used by the justice system. In 1965, President Lyndon Johnson created the first Presidential Commission to evaluate crime prevention efforts in the USA and to make recommendations for improving their effectiveness. This report, *The Challenge of Crime in a Free Society* (1967), highlighted the failure of the criminal justice system to effectively deter or prevent crime and recommended the creation of new types of prevention strategies, including efforts that would take place outside the criminal justice system. In fact, the report asserted that crime could not be controlled without "… the interest and participation of schools, businesses, social agencies, private groups and individual citizens" (President's Commission on Law Enforcement and the Administration of Justice, 1967: 38). This call for community involvement in prevention efforts was followed in June 1968, a few days after the assassination of Senator Robert Kennedy and two months after the assassination of the Reverend Martin Luther King, with the establishment of a second Presidential Commission, *The National Commission on the Causes and Prevention of Violence*. Again, the Commission recommended new prevention approaches involving agencies outside the justice system, taking the position that these would be more effective in addressing the underlying social conditions that were at the root of crime.

The response to these challenges and recommendations was underwhelming. In fact, the recommendations were ignored by politicians and policy-makers. Prevention strategies did not change and the responsibility for prevention remained almost exclusively with law enforcement and criminal justice systems.

It was also in 1968 that the first somewhat rigorous tests of the deterrence strategy were reported (Gibbs, 1968). These studies found support for some parts of the theory but not others. The most consistent findings were that the *certainty* of punishment was associated with reductions in criminal behavior and that the *severity* of sanctions had a deterrent effect only when certainty was high (Chiricos and Waldo, 1970; Gibbs, 1968; Tittle, 1969). There was almost no research testing the effect of **celerity**, or the speed at which punishment follows from the commission of an offense (for an exception, see Nagin and Pogarsky, 2001), although policies have been based on this part of the theory; for example, the Speedy Trial Act. The early finding that certainty is the critical deterrent variable has been consistently supported by additional tests of deterrence theory (National Institute of Justice, 2014). But, again, this information had little effect on deterrence-based crime prevention programs, practices, or policies, which continued to prioritize the seriousness of punishments until the late twentieth century; for example, imposing mandatory and lengthy prison sentences for serious offenses.

Modifications and extensions of deterrence theory

Around 1980, several new criminological theories in the deterrence tradition were proposed. A variation that considers both individual and societal opportunities for crime prevention is **routine activities theory** (Cohen and Felson, 1979). This perspective considers both the environmental context and individual decision-making as primary causes of crime. It states that a person's general lifestyle determines the likelihood of his/her involvement in crime and that the more exposed you are to crime and criminal opportunities in your everyday activities, the greater your chances of becoming both a perpetrator of crime and a victim. For example, an elderly person who spends most of the day and evening at home is unlikely to encounter criminals or opportunities to break the law, which lessens the likelihood of both crime victimization and perpetration.

According to routine activities theory, a crime event is most likely to occur when one's everyday routines allow three factors to come together at the same time and place: (i) a motivated offender, (ii) a suitable target, and (iii) an absence of capable guardians (Clarke, 1995). Regarding the first factor, like deterrence, routine activities theory considers individuals to be rational thinkers who will be motivated to commit crime if the benefits are considered greater than the costs. Suitable targets for crime include individuals, objects, or places that are deemed attractive based on their actions, appearance, or perceived vulnerability and ease of attainment or access. The third factor recognizes the importance of having human or non-human surveillance systems in place to deter individuals from committing a crime. Individuals will be less able to break the law and more deterred from doing so if they believe they will be caught and punished for their actions by these guardians.

Crime prevention efforts based on routine activities theory do not try to change individuals. This perspective emphasizes that there will always be motivated offenders and even if a particular person is deterred from crime, there will be others to take his/her place (Clarke, 1995). Prevention efforts instead target the last two components of the theory and seek to reduce opportunities for offending and to make particular crimes more difficult to commit. These efforts often rely on practices used every day by ordinary citizens. For example, home-owners try to prevent burglary by reducing the attractiveness of the home as a target (e.g., by hiding expensive items from plain view and installing bright lights over the doorways) and by increasing guardians (e.g., getting a dog and installing an alarm system). Similarly, if one wants to avoid being the victim of an assault, it is best to refrain from wearing expensive jewelry and clothes, pay attention to one's surroundings, and avoid going to risky places (e.g., bars and nightclubs) that have many motivated offenders and few guardians who will try to control deviant behavior.

Situational crime theory originated in Great Britain's and the British Home Office's efforts to reduce crime in the 1970s (Clarke, 1983). Similar to routine activities theory, the focus of this theory is on the immediate social and physical settings of crime events as well as the broader social context in which they occur, rather than on the offender. The recommended prevention strategy is to reduce the opportunities for crime by changing the characteristics of the situation or environment that may facilitate crime, including the physical design or layout of a building or neighborhood and its social management. These activities are often referred to as **place-based prevention**. They can include "target hardening" practices such as installing fences, metal detectors, and locks so that items or objects are more difficult to vandalize, damage, or steal. Crime prevention also includes efforts to increase guardianship and surveillance of properties; for example, hiring security guards and installing surveillance cameras. Cornish and Clarke (2003) identified 25 specific techniques for changing crime-prone places and situations to prevent illegal activities.

Rational choice theory (Cornish and Clark, 1986) provides another variation of deterrence theory. It became a popular explanation of criminal behavior in the UK and USA in the 1980s. Based on the "expected utility" philosophy applied to criminal behavior by Beccaria and Bentham and to economic theory in eighteenth-century Europe, rational choice theory proposes that people will make rational decisions in an effort to maximize their profits or rewards and minimize their losses or costs. According to this theory, people act according to their own self-interests and we are all motivated to maximize pleasure and minimize pain (Clarke and Cornish, 1985).

Rational choice theorists recognize that law-breaking can result in many benefits for offenders: stealing can provide extra income and material goods that they might not otherwise be able to obtain, assaulting an enemy helps to seek revenge or right a wrong, and breaking into a building can provide thrills and alleviate boredom. While human beings prefer engaging in behaviors that will bring them pleasure, they also try to avoid pain and minimize costs or losses. So, if illegal behavior carries a certain punishment and we believe we will face this punishment if we break the law, we will refrain from offending – unless the reward for doing so outweighs the cost.

Compared to deterrence theory, prevention activities based on rational choice theories focus less on societal actions that can be used to deter crime (e.g., passing new laws with more severe punishments for certain crimes) and more on efforts to influence the individual and his/her decision-making processes related to criminal behavior. More specifically, these efforts will try to reduce an individual's perceived benefits of crime and increase the costs or pain thought to follow from illegal behavior. Examples of popular prevention efforts based on rational choice theory include "scare tactics" such as having criminals or drug addicts talk to youth about the dangers of illegal behaviors and, in the case of the **Scared Straight** program (see Chapter 9), describe their terrible jail or prison experiences. They also include "three strikes and you're out" legislation which increases the severity of sanctions for repeated, serious offenders, and media campaigns showing the long-term effects of drug use on one's health. All these strategies emphasize the costs of crime.

All the variations of deterrence theory shown in Table 2.2 retain the perspective's basic assumption that humans are rational decision-makers who weigh the costs and benefits of criminal activity and in that respect they are all rational choice theories. They differ in how much emphasis is placed on individual (micro) and societal (macro) level interventions, but they all call for increasing the cost of crime as the basic approach to prevention. By expanding upon the early versions of deterrence theory, they have also increased the variety of possible prevention strategies that could be used to deter individuals from offending. For example, rather than solely focusing on imposing severe punishments for offending, routine activities and situational theories also recommend increasing offenders' perceived difficulty of committing a criminal act and their anticipated certainty of apprehension for offending.

Table 2.2   Deterrence theories and crime prevention.

Theory	Summary of the theory	Crime prevention strategies suggested by the theory
Deterrence	The threat of punishment will deter individuals from committing crime, especially when punishments are known, certain, similar in severity to the offense committed, and swiftly applied	Fines, incarceration, boot camps
Routine activities	Crime is more likely when there are motivated offenders, suitable targets/victims, and few guardians	Hiring of security guards, installing burglar alarms
Rational choice	Crime is more likely when individuals view its benefits as greater than its costs	"Scare tactics" such as having criminals talk to youth about prison life (e.g., Scared Straight programs) and drug addicts talking about the dangers of drug use
Situational crime prevention	Crime is most likely to occur in certain places based on their physical and social conditions	Removal of graffiti and abandoned buildings, increased street lighting

We will review many of the prevention strategies recommended by these more modern variations of deterrence theory in Chapter 6. In general, empirical tests of the newer deterrence-based theories have found some, but not consistent support that the variables hypothesized to affect crime (e.g., the certainty severity, and swiftness of punishments) actually have such effect; and when effects are found, they are relatively weak (for reviews, see: Akers and Sellers, 2013; Birkbeck and LaFree, 1993; Massey, Krohn, and Bonati, 1989; Weisburd, 1997).

Well-conducted scientific evaluations (see Chapter 4) of specific prevention programs, practices and policies based on these theories have been relatively rare, even at the end of the twentieth century. Reviewing evaluations of situational crime prevention strategies, Weisburd (1997: 11) concludes: "The enthusiasm surrounding situational prevention must be tempered by the weakness of the methods used in most existing evaluation studies." This conclusion applies equally well to nearly all evaluations of deterrence-based prevention strategies (Akers and Sellers, 2013), with some exception regarding certain law enforcement interventions (e.g., hot spots policing).

Biological, physiological, and psychogenic prevention strategies

The prediction that Lombroso's theory attributing criminal behavior to atavism was dead was greatly exaggerated. In 1939, Earnest A. Hooton (1887–1954), a cultural anthropologist from Harvard University, published *The American Criminal: An Anthropological Study*. Hooton studied 17,000 persons (14,000 who were prisoners), taking body measurements similar to those used by Lombroso in order to test his idea that criminals are "organically inferior" and that inferiority was genetically inherited. Like Lombroso in his later work, Hooton believed the environment also contributed to crime but the primary cause was a biological inferiority. He stated that crime occurred when low-grade human organisms were exposed to negative social environments (Hooton, 1939/1969).

Ten years later, the psychologist William Sheldon (1898–1977) published his theory of delinquency, **constitutional psychology**, in *Varieties of Delinquent Youth* (1949). In this work, Sheldon matched particular body types, which he called **somatotypes**, to particular temperaments and to involvement in delinquent behavior. He studied nude photos of 200 young men living in a rehabilitation center in Boston between 1939 and 1946 and measured various physiological characteristics of their bodies. He identified three somatotypes: (i) Endomorphs were overweight, with soft tissue, round bodies, slow reactions, and temperaments that were relaxed and jolly. They loved eating, good company and emotional support from others. (ii) Mesomorphs were rectangular in shape, had rugged, strong and muscular bodies, and were assertive, courageous, physically active, and risk takers. (iii) Ectomorphs had thin, fragile bodies and were flat-chested, tense, anxious, restrained, and shy. Sheldon asserted that delinquents were most likely to be mesomorphs because this body type and temperament naturally led them into risky and dangerous activities.

Sheldon's theory was tested in a landmark study by Harvard Law School professors Sheldon and Eleanor Glueck. The Gluecks studied 500 delinquent and 500 non-delinquent boys, obtaining measures of 402 factors from each boy relating to their family background, body types, health, intelligence, and temperament/character. Their findings, published in *Unraveling Juvenile Delinquency* (1950), described the characteristics that were more likely to be found among the delinquents compared to the non-delinquents: delinquents typically had mesomorph constitutions and came from unstable homes with unloving parents who were essentially unfit to serve as models for their children.

The Gluecks' study provided the basis for some, albeit short-lived, delinquency prevention strategies. In 1952, the Boston School Committee approved a plan to train teachers to identify delinquents and those with delinquent tendencies among elementary school children using methods outlined in *Unraveling Juvenile Delinquency*. At about the same time, the New York City School Board and the New York City Youth Board expressed interest in using these methods to identify potential delinquents (Lucas, 1952), but exactly what intervention was planned for those children, and for youth identified as delinquents, was unclear as the plan was never realized.

Most criminologists responded to the Gluecks' research and conclusions with skepticism and were critical of this largely biological approach to crime (for example, see Hartung, 1958). Edwin Sutherland was particularly opposed to Hooton's, Sheldon's, and the Gluecks' work (Cohen, Lindesmith, and Schuessler, 1956), as seen in the following quote:

> The futility of this study (*Varieties of Delinquent Youth*) in constitutional psychology should have been obvious in advance from the previous failures of analogous studies. Sheldon adds himself to the list of Lombroso, Kretschmer, Hooton and others who have attempted to demonstrate a physical difference between criminals and non-criminals. Unfortunately, the administrators of research funds can be seduced into wasting many hundreds of thousands of dollars on such projects [a possible reference to a $200K Ford Foundation grant to the Gluecks] even after the results of previous studies have been repeatedly shown not to be worth a nickel. (Sutherland, 1951: 288; parens added)

The prevention implications of these theories are very limited given the contention that biological inferiority and biological constitutions are inherited. If criminals are born with a propensity to offend, the logical prevention strategy would be, as Lombroso proposed, to identify those persons and lock them up in prisons or mental institutions, or, as the Gluecks recommended, to remove young offenders from their biological families. There is some acknowledgment in all of these theories that the environment contributes to crime, which would suggest that improvements to the social and physical environment would help prevent crime, but these theorists offer few specific recommendations for how to change environmental influences on crime.

More modern twenty-first-century biological and biosocial theories are much more sophisticated. Technological advances have made it possible to examine the impact on crime of biological characteristics that could not have been studied just a few decades ago, such as genetic make-up and brain functioning and development. Biosocial research increasingly emphasizes that these factors alone cannot fully explain criminal involvement. Rather, it is the interaction of biological and social factors that is most important in leading to crime, and that individuals with particular traits may be much more sensitive to environmental risk and protective factors. For example, some studies have shown that the relationship between child maltreatment and violent offending varies by the genetic make-up of the individual (Caspi *et al.*, 2002).

The crime prevention implications of biosocial research have not yet been clearly established. Findings indicating that individuals with certain genotypes are more at risk for offending, at least under certain conditions, might suggest a preventive approach that requires genetic testing followed by efforts to provide "at-risk" individuals with prevention or treatment service (Boardman *et al.*, 2014; Dobbs, 2009). However, serious ethical issues must be addressed regarding how to collect and store such information and how to use it without stigmatizing those with "deficient" genes. Nonetheless, some emphasize that even without genetic testing, universal prevention services can be delivered to the general population with the expectation that they will be beneficial for those with and without genetic risk factors (Brody *et al.*, 2013; Rocque, Welsh, and Raine, 2012). As this debate plays out, the search for biological influences on crime, and their interaction with social conditions, continues.

Anomie-based prevention strategies

Social disorganization theories

All of the early explanations for criminal behavior hinted that the physical and social environment might play a causal role in leading to offending, but these possibilities were not made explicit until Durkheim's anomie theory was proposed. This concept was revisited in the twentieth century in **social disorganization** theory, which emphasized the role of neighborhoods in producing crime. By studying maps indicating the residential locations of Chicago youth referred to the juvenile court, Park *et al.* (1928) and Shaw and McKay (1942) found that illegal activities were concentrated in certain areas or zones of the city. They noted that youth offenders disproportionately resided in lower class neighborhoods located closest to the center of the inner city. Fewer juvenile court youth lived in areas more distant from the inner city. Moreover, they discovered that this systematic variation in rates of delinquency, with crime less likely to occur the more removed from the inner city youth lived, was relatively constant over time. Even when there was a complete turnover of persons living in these neighborhoods, the neighborhood delinquency and adult crime rates remained relatively the same.

Shaw and McKay (1942) interpreted these data as indicating that *crime was not a function of the characteristics of persons living in a neighborhood, but was linked directly to the characteristics of the neighborhood itself.* They argued that delinquency and crime become a way of life and a cultural tradition in these neighborhoods, and that these lifestyles and beliefs are passed on from one generation to another and influence all those who might come to live in these high-crime neighborhoods. They termed this process and their theory as "social disorganization," though some criminologists refer to it as a social ecological theory to highlight the environmental focus.

Shaw and McKay proposed that the causal process that linked geographic neighborhoods to crime and other problems was the social and cultural features of these neighborhoods. They observed that high-crime-rate neighborhoods in Chicago tended to have high rates of poverty, population turnover, single-parent and divorced families, and racial diversity. They reasoned that these characteristics led to a broken, unstable social order, weak institutions and limited informal controls on behavior. In these areas, residents lacked the financial resources to address problems, the high resident turnover made stable relationships and ongoing sources of social support more difficult, and the racial/ethnic diversity created competing value systems and differences in expectations of behavior. Together, these conditions produced social disorganization, which made crime more likely to occur.

While not derived directly from Durkheim's anomie theory, social disorganization and anomie share the view that stable relationships, shared values and norms, and social cohesion among residents produces a stable, orderly social order and conformity to conventional forms of interaction and behavior. In contrast, brief and unstable relationships, a lack of consensus on values and norms and low levels of cohesion lead to disrupted interactions and unconventional behavior, including deviant and illegal behavior (Bursik Jr. and Grasmick, 1993). Shaw and McKay (1942) called neighborhoods with the latter characteristics *disorganized* neighborhoods while Durkheim would have called them *anomic* neighborhoods. Like Durkheim's theory, social disorganization provides a macro-level explanation for criminal behavior.

The crime patterns first noted by Park *et al.* (1928) and Shaw and McKay (1942) in Chicago have been replicated across many other American cities, and there are clear differences in official crime rates across regions of a county, state, and whole society (Sampson, 2012; Scheurman and Kobrin, 1986; Taylor and Covington, 1988). Although such data support social disorganization theory, specific tests of this theory are challenging to conduct (Leventhal and Brooks-Gunn, 2000). It can be difficult to define the precise boundaries of a "neighborhood" which is needed in order to compare crime rates across neighborhoods. Many early tests of the theory relied on census tract boundaries created by the US Census data to define neighborhoods, but the extent to which these census tract areas actually correspond to "true" neighborhoods is questionable. It is also difficult to obtain direct measures of the processes identified by Shaw and McKay as indicators of social disorganization. Although some measures, like turnover of residents and poverty, can be found in the US Census data, data reflecting social and cultural processes are more challenging to collect. Finally, many of the early tests of social disorganization theory relied on official arrest data, rather than self-reported crime data, and studies based on self-reported data have indicated relatively weak support for the theory (Akers and Sellers, 2004; Elliott *et al.*, 2006; Gottfredson, McNeil, and Gottfredson, 1991). However, there have been some important extensions and refinements to social disorganization theory in recent years, as well as more sophisticated tests of the theory (Bursik Jr. and Grasmick, 1993; Sampson, 2012; Sampson and Groves, 1989).

From a crime prevention perspective, social disorganization shifted the focus of prevention efforts from punishment and other deterrence-based practices to interventions designed to change the social environments that generate and sustain criminal behavior. Correspondingly, rather than view prevention as the sole responsibility of law enforcement agencies, it also places responsibility with agencies outside the justice system, such as social welfare and community agencies.

The first well-documented community-based delinquency prevention initiative based on social disorganization theory was the Chicago Area Project (CAP) created by Shaw in the 1930s (Welsh and Pfeffer, 2013). He began the CAP in three of the highest crime areas in Chicago with the goal of improving the quality of life in these areas, eliminating aspects of the community that attracted youth into delinquent gangs, providing youth with increased opportunities for conventional activities, and encouraging law-abiding families to take leadership roles in the community. Initially, over 20 specific youth programs were created, including recreational teams, counseling services, summer camps, boys clubs, hobby groups, school-related activities, and "detached street worker" programs to intervene directly with gang members. Efforts were also made to improve sanitation services and restore dilapidated and rundown properties. Shaw established parent–teacher groups to rally parents to work together to improve the community and community committees with delinquent and paroled youth as members to help plan and oversee prevention activities. By the 1940s, the project had expanded to seven other low-income areas in Chicago. In addition, CAP was asked to help the Boy Scouts of America with their goal of increasing integration and participation of African American youth.

An initial evaluation of CAP by Shaw in 1944 indicated significant reductions in youth arrests in two of the three CAP neighborhoods. However, later evaluations failed to demonstrate significant differences in crime between CAP and similar non-CAP neighborhoods (Finestone, 1976; Kobrin, 1959), and even Shaw eventually noted that a strong claim of effectiveness for the CAP could not be made (Schlossman and Sedlak, 1983). More recent prevention strategies that can be viewed as based on social disorganization theory involve cleaning up and patrolling neighborhood parks, tearing down damaged and abandoned buildings and reducing visible signs of criminal activity (e.g., empty syringes, graffiti). In addition, Neighborhood Watch and community mobilization programs are aligned with this theory as they encourage residents to get to know each other, discuss local problems and agree to work together to implement crime prevention strategies.

Strain theories

Durkheim's theory of anomie was more directly extended by Robert Merton (1938) and by Richard Cloward and Lloyd Ohlin (1960) in their **strain theory** perspectives. Merton's version of strain theory, outlined in *Social Structure and Anomie* (1938), provided a macro-level explanation that accounted for the observed concentration of crime in lower social class and minority groups in the USA. He argued that crime rates were higher among these groups due to a disconnect between the strong American cultural emphasis on achieving success and the "American Dream" of wealth, power, and status, and the realistic opportunities of actually achieving this goal. According to Merton, although all youth are socialized in their families, at school and by the media to try to achieve these goals, those from the lower classes and especially those from lower class minority groups do not have access to the educational and economic resources and personal connections necessary for achieving these goals. When unable to attain wealth and status, they must accept their failure and revise their goals or find alternative, unconventional ways to achieve them. Crime is one of these alternative strategies. For Merton, like Durkheim, crime represents a particular response to a socially produced condition. The behavior is caused by the disjunction between socially desired goals and opportunities to achieve these goals, and is experienced primarily by the poor, disadvantaged, and minorities in our society.

Merton (1938) also proposed a micro-level explanation for crime. He identified five possible individual responses, or adaptations, to experiencing the anomic condition of being unable to achieve culturally valued goals: (i) *conformity*, which occurs when individuals simply accept their situation and do the best they can to achieve wealth/status using legitimate means; (ii) *innovation*, when individuals find alternative ways to achieve goals, even if doing so involves illegal activities; (iii) *rebellion*, or rejecting societal goals and opportunities and replacing them with a new system or subculture which identifies new goals and ways of achieving them; (iv) *retreatism*, or rejecting the goals and opportunities and withdrawing from society altogether; and (v) *ritualism*, which occurs when individuals give up on the goal of achieving success and hold on to what has been achieved while rigidly following conventional norms. Merton (1938) saw criminals as primarily innovators. For example, people will use the "innovative" strategy of stealing in order to achieve material goods and money.

Cloward and Ohlin built on Merton's individual theory of adaptations to anomie in their book *Delinquency and Opportunity* (1960). Here, they argued that delinquency is a result of differential access to criminal as well as conventional opportunities. They also drew upon the works of Shaw and McKay (1942), Cohen (1955), and Sutherland (1947) in viewing criminal behavior as a way of life in certain neighborhoods which can be passed on from generation to generation through normal socialization processes occurring in small groups, or subcultures.

For Cloward and Ohlin (1960), not everyone experiencing anomie has access to illegitimate opportunities. To be successful as a criminal, one must also have access to a criminal opportunity structure, just as success for non-criminals requires access to conventional opportunity structures. Also like a legitimate career, success in crime requires one to acquire specific skills, training, and knowledge, such as learning how and where to sell (i.e., fence) stolen goods and how to best avoid detection and arrest. Learning how to be a successful criminal and social support for this way of life occurs in subcultures such as gangs and organized crime networks. Some socially disorganized areas have such subcultures and can provide illegitimate opportunity structures, while others do not. They also stated that the specific types of illegal opportunities that are available also vary across neighborhoods. For example, some areas will have opportunities mostly for illicit drug sales, while others may provide access to subcultures focused on theft or violence.

Also building on Merton's work, Cloward and Ohlin (1960) noted that when individuals do not have access to criminal subcultures, they will be forced to choose other types of adaptations such as those identified by Merton. In areas without illegitimate subcultures, rates of crime will be relatively low, even if the neighborhood is disadvantaged or disorganized. If there are illegitimate opportunities, then the rates of crime will be high, and rates will be highest for the specific type of crimes supported by the subculture.

These versions of anomie theory are commonly referred to as **strain theories** since the basic motivation for involvement in crime is the strain or frustration experienced by those faced with limited opportunities to achieve conventional goals. There have been many tests of strain theory and overall, the results are mixed, with support for some of the concepts discussed and little support for others (for a review, see Akers and Sellers, 2013). For example, crime rates are greater among the lower class when using official measures of crime, but the relationship between class and crime is much less consistent when using self-reported measures. In addition, social class and race/ethnicity are consistently related to gang-related crime in both official and self-reported measures; school dropout is related to social class and race/ethnicity and is related to criminal behavior in some studies but not others; and the perceived gap between aspirations and opportunities and criminal behavior is supported only under specific conditions.

As we will discuss in Chapter 3, there are several modern versions of strain theory (Agnew, 1992; Messner and Rosenfeld, 1994) which expand upon the conditions that cause or are sources of strain, but even in these versions, the prevention implications remain essentially the same. Generally, prevention efforts will attempt to reduce strain and prevent criminal adaptations or reactions to it. Because there are both macro and micro versions of strain, prevention can take place at the community level or the individual level. At the macro or community level, similar to social disorganization theory, strategies could include changing the culture of disadvantaged neighborhoods and the functioning of social institutions serving these neighborhoods. At the individual level, strain theory would recommend: (i) providing more/better conventional opportunities for youth, especially those living in the disadvantaged, disorganized neighborhoods most likely to produce the stress of failed goal achievement; (ii) removing barriers and obstacles to accessing these opportunities; and (iii) removing or cutting off access to criminal opportunities. Specific interventions might include employment programs, housing subsidies for the poor, job training, educational subsidies, dropout programs, and eliminating neighborhood gangs and illicit drug distribution networks.

An early, large-scale, 50 million dollar prevention initiative based on strain theory, **Mobilization for Youth**, occurred in 1962 in neighborhoods on the Lower East Side of Manhattan, NY. Richard Cloward was the research director for the project at one time and President Johnson embraced the project as a vital part of his "War on Poverty" and "Great Society" initiatives. The major goal of the program was to increase opportunities for disadvantaged youth and to end the unfair distribution of resources in their neighborhoods. To achieve this goal, a large array of services were provided to youth living in the targeted areas including employment centers, job training programs, neighborhood service centers, a youth service corps, detached street workers, basic educational programs, and anti-discrimination activities (Short Jr., 1974). Unfortunately, there was no systematic evaluation of the effectiveness of the program on delinquency or crime. Nonetheless, it provided a model for similar, national crime prevention initiatives that followed, such as Job Corps and AmeriCorps.

Social control theory prevention strategies

Social control theories emerged in the 1950s and represent a very different approach to explaining crime and implementing crime prevention programs and practices. For all of the theories discussed earlier, the critical question to be addressed was: *Why do people engage in crime? What leads them to do* *that which is contrary to society's expectations and the behaviors they have been socialized to conform to?* For control theorists the main question is: *Why don't people engage in crime?* According to this perspective, and in contrast to most other theories, all persons have a natural, inherent propensity to achieve their wants and desires and they will use any means that is effective to do so (Hirschi, 1969). To keep these natural, criminal impulses in check and prevent crime, society must create strong internal controls in individuals and/or externally apply constraints on individual behavior.

Early control theorists saw crime as a result of: (i) a lack of internalized, normative controls; (ii) a breakdown in previously established controls; and/or (iii) conflict or inconsistency in rules or social controls (Nye, 1958; Reckless, 1961; Reiss, 1951). They focused primarily on the first and third conditions and left the second condition largely to strain theory to discuss. Control theorists also differentiated between (i) **internal** controls, which are personal, internalized restraints; (ii) **indirect** controls, which occur when individuals consider that involvement in crime will hurt or disappoint those closest to them (such as parents); and (iii) **direct** controls, which are applied externally by law enforcement, parents, friends, and others; these include the threat of or actual punishment for deviance and rewards for compliance to rules.

Travis Hirschi's control theory, published in *Causes of Delinquency* (1969), dominated American criminological theorizing in the latter part of the twentieth century. Although sometimes called **social bonding theory**, Hirschi's (1969) theory is clearly a version of social control theory in the tradition of Reiss (1951), Nye (1958), and Reckless (1961). His theory emphasizes the role of internal and indirect controls in fostering conformity and inhibiting crime. According to Hirschi, these controls are the result of early (and ongoing) socialization processes that result in the child's and adolescent's bonding to significant others and adopting their conventional norms and values.

Hirschi (1969) identified four elements of the social bond that are all important in inhibiting crime. Higher levels of all these components of the social bond are expected to be associated with lower levels of criminal behavior. *First*, emotional **attachments** or bonds to others provide effective restraints on our behavior. The premise is that we will not disobey or violate accepted rules and legal standards because we do not want to jeopardize our relationships or disappoint those who care about us and whose opinions we value. *Second*, **involvement** in conventional activities helps reduce crime, because the more time spent in positive behaviors, the less time one will have to break the law. *Third*, **beliefs**, or agreement with the norms and rules of society, help provide an internal, moral obligation to obey the law. *Fourth*, **commitment** to social institutions, like schools and jobs, helps promote abstinence from crime because those who have invested their time and devotion to such activities have "a stake in conformity" that they will not want to risk by engaging in illegal behaviors. For example, students who believe that education is important and who try to succeed in school will be less likely to cheat than those who have a lesser commitment to learning.

In a later control theory, Gottfredson and Hirschi (1990) argue that self-controls, or personal internalized controls, are sufficient to reduce crime; people with strong self-control should be able to stop themselves from acting on their impulses. In contrast, those with low self-control seek immediate gratification, have a preference for risky or exciting activities, and fail to consider the long-term consequences of their behaviors. These attributes make it more likely that individuals will give in to their natural inclination to commit crime and/or take advantage of opportunities to commit illegal behavior. External controls by law enforcement officers or informal actions by teachers, parents, employers, or spouses who set and enforce rules and expectations for behavior are also important, but these types of direct controls are less effective than self-control.

With some exceptions, early tests of control theory in both the USA and Europe supported its hypotheses (Hill *et al.*, 1999; Hirschi, 1969; Junger-Tas, 1992; Loeber and Stouthamer-Loeber, 1986). The major exception involved the consistent finding that delinquent youth often had strong bonds to their friends and that bonding to delinquent peers was the strongest predictor of initiating delinquent behavior (Elliott, Huizinga, and Ageton, 1985; Junger-Tas, 1992). Thus the effect of strong bonds was not always to inhibit delinquency; instead, it was dependent on the conventional or deviant orientation of the person or group to which one was bonded. The evidence also suggested that the effect of bonds on delinquency was largely limited to involvement in minor forms of delinquency and was weaker when more serious types of offending were considered (Agnew, 1991; Krohn and Massey, 1980).

The basic prevention strategy recommended by control theory is to increase internal and external controls and strengthen attachments to conventional others. This could involve teaching youth or adults how to regulate and control their emotions and impulses, or helping parents to set clear expectations for their children's behavior and to enforce these standards using fair and consistent discipline practices. Still other crime prevention efforts based on social control might involve mentoring programs to foster attachments to prosocial role models and tutoring programs to help children with academic challenges do better in school and become more committed to finishing their education.

Social learning theory prevention strategies

Social learning theories contend that children learn positive and negative behaviors, including crime, by interacting with others. The first iteration of this perspective in the twentieth century was Sutherland's (1947) **differential association theory**. According to this theory, the more one is exposed to criminal role models, the more likely one will be to commit crime. Interestingly, Lombroso also made this argument when discussing the criminoloid type of criminal, but Sutherland's discussion is much more involved. He stated that crime is especially likely when criminal role models exist in primary and intimate groups (e.g., such as the family) and when **associations** (i.e., relationships) with these role models occur early in life, are frequently occurring, and last for a long time (Akers and Sellers, 2013).

How does learning occur? Associations with criminals allow an individual to learn both the techniques necessary to engage in an illegal behavior (since you are not born knowing how to pick a lock or smoke marijuana) and the attitudes that can promote and help to rationalize such behaviors. These attitudes, which Sutherland called **definitions**, are the most important part of the learning process. When you are exposed to a greater number of criminal attitudes than noncriminal attitudes, criminal behavior is most likely to occur. For example, the more your friends or family members hold the view that fighting, cheating, or stealing are okay, then the more likely you are to endorse similar definitions. In turn, the more likely you will be to engage in crime. Cloward and Ohlin drew from Sutherland's theory in their work detailing the criminal opportunity structure.

Akers' (1985, 2009; Burgess and Akers, 1966) **social learning theory** describes the learning process in more detail. In addition to agreeing with Sutherland that associations and definitions are important, this theory adds the concepts of **imitation** and **differential reinforcement**, which are based on the work of behavioral psychologists, especially Bandura and Walters (1963). According to Akers, the onset of crime is best explained by imitation: an individual observes someone else commit an illegal behavior and mimics it. This is not hard to believe if you have a younger brother or sister; children often learn by imitation and crime is no exception. Once participation in crime has occurred, its persistence is best explained by the extent to which it is reinforced – either encouraged, which leads to more offending, or discouraged, which should promote desistence. That is, the likelihood that crime will be committed or repeated is directly related to how often one receives rewards and favorable responses to it and does not receive unpleasant reactions or punishments (Akers, 2009).

Empirical tests of social learning theory generally show support for it, although there is some mixed evidence when specific propositions are considered (for a detailed review of this evidence, see Akers and Sellers, 2013). This theory also serves as the foundation for many crime prevention programs, especially those which focus on minimizing exposure to criminal peer or family role models. Many drug prevention curricula, for example, try to adjust children's perceptions about the numbers of people who drink or use drugs, so that substance use is not considered to be common and acceptable behavior. These programs also have adolescents consider the negative consequences of using drugs (e.g., smoking makes you smell bad and cigarettes cost a lot of money) and practice declining a peer's offer to use drugs. Programs for parents emphasize the importance of monitoring their children's friends and discouraging association with troublemakers, displaying positive behaviors and promoting non-criminal attitudes (e.g., telling children that "fighting is not how we solve problems in this family"), as well as consistently rewarding children for pro-social behavior and punishing aggressive or criminal behaviors.

Integrated theories and prevention strategies

Cloward and Ohlin's (1960) differential opportunity theory was an early example of an integrated theory, as it combined ideas from many different theories, including Merton's (1938) anomie theory, Shaw and McKay's (1942) social disorganization theory, and Sutherland's (1947) differential association theory. However, it did not formally integrate these theories. That is, it made no attempt to reconcile the basic assumptions of each theory or to create a single consistent set of propositions.

A more intentional integrated theory, which did attempt to formally integrate several theories into a single coherent theory, was Elliott and colleagues' (1979) integration of strain, social learning, and social control theories. In doing so, they identified two major pathways that can lead to crime: (i) youth who experience few social controls and weak bonds will be more likely to associate with delinquent peers, which will increase their risk for crime; and (ii) youth who have strong social controls/bonds initially but then experience strains will face a weakening of controls, which places them at risk for being exposed to delinquent peers and for becoming delinquent.

In outlining these pathways, Elliott *et al.* (1985) describe a chain of events that unfolds early in life and over subsequent stages of a person's life in which significant events, like encountering strain, can influence criminal behavior. In addition, the theory recognizes that different people can follow different routes into crime and be influenced by different factors. These concepts are well supported by the **life-course developmental paradigm**, which describes how causal factors and involvement in crime can vary across one's life; we will explain this perspective much more in Chapter 3.

From a crime prevention standpoint, strengthening social controls and attachments should reduce crimes committed by those following the first pathway outlined by Elliott and colleagues (1985). The second group, however, may or may not benefit from this strategy, depending on when they receive such an intervention. If it is implemented *prior* to their experiencing strain, it will likely not affect their involvement in crime since their bonds to society were already strong. If it occurs *after* the strains have been faced, then delinquency is more likely to be reduced. As this example shows, the timing of an intervention, the particular risk factors it seeks to address and the population for whom it is intended are all critical to its success. We will also elaborate on these basic tenets of crime prevention in Chapter 3.

Thornberry's (1987; Thornberry *et al.*, 1991) **interactional theory** is also an integrated theory. It relies on concepts from social control and social learning theories to explain criminal behavior from childhood to adulthood. Like Elliott and colleagues' (1985) theory, interactional theory considers social bonds to be important because they affect the degree to which one will associate with deviant peers. In addition, the theory states that bonding to family is the most important causal factor during childhood. During adolescence, as children seek independence from parents and spend less time at home, their relationships with teachers and peers take precedence. During adulthood, one's attachments to work and family are most important.

A unique feature of this theory is its recognition of reciprocity in social interactions.[1] Whereas social learning and social control theory typically describe one-way processes in which delinquent peers or parenting practices affect an individual's likelihood of crime, interactional theory also credits individuals with influencing their peers' and parents' behaviors. For example, the types of rules set by parents, how they enforce these rules, and the degree to which they are warm and loving can be affected by the child's behavior. "Difficult" children who act out and break rules may elicit harsher reactions from parents than compliant children. Adolescents who are frequently delinquent may, over time, cause their parents to reduce their efforts at social control, giving up in the face of constant failure (Jang and Smith, 1997). This component of the theory suggests that interventions intended to improve child management skills, such as parent training programs, include both adults and children in the intervention and have these individuals practice effective communication and interaction.

The **Social Development Model (SDM)** integrates social control theory, particularly Hirschi's (1969) version of the theory, and social learning theory (Catalano and Hawkins, 1996). The theory describes what is necessary to create strong relationships and social bonds, recommending that adults: (i) provide youth with opportunities to positively contribute to their families, schools and communities; (ii) actively teach youth the skills they need to make such contributions; (iii) recognize them when they have succeeded in doing so; and (iv) offer specific suggestions for how to improve poor performances. What does this look like? Teachers might choose a child to be their helper in the classroom, show the student how to erase the chalkboard or prepare materials for a lesson and reward him or her for a job well done. While these kinds of actions should create closer attachments to teachers, to most effectively reduce crime, teachers must also communicate to children that they are opposed to law-breaking activities and that youth should refrain from delinquency (Catalano and Hawkins, 1996). Likewise, parents, police officers, and other adults can use these techniques to promote youth bonds to positive adults and reduce crime.

Similar to the discussions by Elliott and colleagues' (1985) and Thornberry (1987), the SDM states that bonding can occur with deviant persons as well as conventional persons. If children are bonded to prosocial adults, their own criminality will be suppressed; if they are bonded to individuals who are deviant, they are likely to commit crime. The SDM thus considers how both crime and conformity can be influenced by social bonds and social learning processes.

Prevention strategies based on integrated theories include all those guided by the specific theories included in the more comprehensive theory. Thus, any of the prevention efforts recommended by strain, social control and social learning theories could be recommended by the integrated theories described in this section. Generally, integrated theories support the idea of implementing multiple prevention strategies that can address the many causes of crime and the multiple pathways leading to criminal behavior. Table 2.3 summarizes all of the non-deterrence-based theories and provides examples of how they would prevent crime.

Table 2.3   Non deterrence-based theories of crime and crime prevention.

Theoretical perspective	Summary of the theory	Crime prevention strategies suggested by the theory
Biological and physiological Anomie	Crime is related to inferior biological and physical characteristics of individuals	Imprisonment, placement in mental institutions
Social disorganization	Crime is related to geographical residence, with low-income and socially unstable areas having higher rates of crime	Neighborhood watch Community mobilization
Strain	Crime occurs when there is a disjunction between socially desired goals such as wealth and status and opportunities to achieve those goals	Job training programs Housing subsidies School dropout programs
Social control	Crime occurs when internal and external controls are weak	Parent training to improve child monitoring and discipline skills Therapeutic interventions to teach impulse control and anger management Mentoring programs to promote bonding to conventional others
Social learning Differential association	Crime occurs when individuals are exposed to criminal role models	Drug prevention curricula to help youth resist peer influences to use drugs Gang prevention
Social learning	Crime occurs when individuals are exposed to criminal role models and when they receive rewards for engaging in crime	Parent training to improve child monitoring and discipline skills
Integrated	There are many causal influences on crime, as identified in multiple theories of criminology	Multi-component programs which seek to change multiple causes of crime

Crime Prevention in the Era of "Nothing Works"

As we have emphasized throughout the previous sections, in the period leading up to the mid to late twentieth century, crime prevention efforts were (i) largely based on deterrence theories, and (ii) rarely evaluated for their effectiveness in rigorous scientific studies. Neither situation seemed to be of concern to policy-makers or the public; presumably, so long as offenders were being punished for their crimes, justice was being served. However, between 1970 and 1980, a series of publications drew considerable attention to crime and crime prevention in the USA. At this time, several reviews were conducted to evaluate evidence of the effectiveness of existing programs, practices, and policies intended to prevent crime, mostly treatment strategies designed to reduce recidivism among offenders, as implemented in either the justice system or in the community[2] (Lipton, Martinson, and Wilks, 1975; Martinson, 1976a; Romig, 1978).

The findings from this research, summarized in Table 2.4, were not encouraging. Summarizing the results of his review of 231 correctional evaluations studies in the USA and abroad, Martinson (1976a: 10), concluded: "With few and isolated exceptions, the rehabilitative (treatment) efforts that have been reported so far have had no appreciable effect on recidivism." Rather quickly, these findings led to a widely shared view among politicians, researchers, and the general public that "nothing works" to reduce crime.

Not only was there little or no evidence for the effectiveness of these crime prevention strategies, some were also shown to have negative effects. In these cases, those receiving the intervention were *more likely* to recidivate compared to those not receiving the "treatment." While most of the

Table 2.4 Evidence for specific prevention/treatment programs.★

Program	Evidence
Casework	No consistent evidence of effectiveness
Teaching academic skills	Not effective
Behavior modification	Limited success but should not be used with juvenile offenders
Work and vocational training	Not effective
Educational programs	Not effective
Training adult inmates	No consistent evidence of effectiveness
Group counseling	Not effective
Individual psychotherapy	Not effective
Therapeutic camping	Not effective
Diversion	Not effective
Milieu therapy	Not effective
Medical treatment	Not effective
Less restrictive custody	No consistent evidence of effectiveness
Early release and short sentences	No consistent evidence of effectiveness
Intensive supervision	Effective with limited studies
Probation	No consistent evidence of effectiveness

★Information taken from Martinson (1976a) and Romig (1978).

ineffective interventions were deterrence-based programs delivered to offenders in correctional settings, the results also applied to deterrence- and non-deterrence-based strategies being implemented in the community. Similarly pessimistic findings were found almost 20 years later in a review conducted by the National Academy of Sciences Panel on the Understanding and Control of Violent Behavior (Reiss and Roth, 1993).

Despite the very negative publicity generated by the Martinson studies, the conclusion that "nothing works" was actually a bit overstated (see also Andrews *et al.*, 1990). A correct interpretation of this evidence is that *evaluations of these treatment strategies failed to find any consistent, reliable, and compelling evidence of their effectiveness.* This is an important distinction, since all of these reports acknowledged that both the number and quality of the available evaluations was very low. It is thus logically possible that some of these programs were in fact effective, but due to limitations of their evaluations, this could not be demonstrated. The failure to find positive effects was probably a reflection on the quality of the evaluations as much as the quality of the programs being evaluated.

Within a short time, the conclusion that nothing worked was challenged and new evaluations of interventions provided more positive findings, at least for a few specific interventions (Cullen, 2005). Nonetheless, the practical effect of these reports remains essentially the same: *prior to the end of the twentieth century, there was little credible scientific evidence that any crime prevention programs were effective and little scientifically grounded confidence that placing youth or adults in these programs would have any positive effects on their behavior.* The view that nothing worked led to calls for major reforms of the justice system and to an intellectual debate about scientific methods and evaluation. Martinson (1976b: 93) noted that the crisis "... *reflects a number of conflicting tendencies: fear of public accountability, a flight from the findings of good research, a yearning for business-as-usual, substitution of methodological sophistry for substantive issues and a scapegoat to be blamed for all this.*"

The good news is that the findings did, in fact, spark interest in evaluation and resulted in new and improved research designs and methods, as well as more funding for evaluations. We will discuss these methods, and what constitutes "good evaluation," in more detail in Chapter 4. The debates also led to more innovative prevention approaches, expanding the deterrence-based efforts enacted largely by law enforcement and justice officials to community-based interventions which focused on families, neighborhoods, and schools. Finally, the discussions led to a new focus on public accountability for the dollars invested in crime prevention programs, practices, and policies (Welsh and Pfeffer, 2013), a conversation that is ongoing, as we will discuss in Chapter 11.

Contemporary Crime Prevention

Considering the numbers of persons subject to crime prevention efforts and the amount of money invested in these efforts, contemporary prevention strategies are still primarily deterrence-based strategies implemented by the justice system, at least in the USA. The most commonly used methods to prevent crime are fines, confiscation of property, jail, prison, probation, parole, boot camps, detention centers, and state training schools.

Yet, these views are changing. Growing public concerns about crime rates and questions about the effectiveness of justice system prevention strategies have resulted in a wider range of prevention programs and more shared responsibility for crime prevention. For example, police departments have begun to work with neighborhood groups and concerned citizens to jointly plan and sometimes carry out crime prevention strategies. Other community organizations have also become involved in prevention activities. Today, crime prevention efforts occur in schools, churches, recreation centers, and doctor's offices. They are carried out by teachers, parents, health care providers, community volunteers and other adults as well as youth. In Chapters 6 to 9, we will consider the evaluation evidence for all of the crime interventions currently being implemented, in communities and correctional settings, and identify those with good evidence of their effectiveness and those for which the evidence indicates they are ineffective.

Summary

From the earliest thinking about the causes of crime, deterrence has been the dominant approach to prevention in all societies. This theoretical model with its focus on punishment remains the philosophical foundation for modern Western criminal law, criminal justice systems and crime prevention programs, practices, and policies. Stopping people from breaking the law, locking up offenders and keeping the public safe have been seen as the responsibility of the police, jails and prisons. Early explanations also included biological and demonic theories and punitive prevention strategies that persisted into the twentieth century. The arguments for rejecting these prevention strategies were based more on philosophical and moral grounds than evidence of their ineffectiveness. Biological explanations have taken different forms, have gone through periods of rejection and recasting, and the latest versions of biological determinism were largely discredited in the early twentieth century.

Not until the twentieth century were alternative theoretical explanations, emphasizing the role of social and environmental factors in leading to crime, introduced and new strategies involving other agencies in the community proposed as crime prevention efforts. While the research testing the validity of these new theoretical explanations was encouraging, their implied prevention approaches were just beginning to be implemented, were not widely adopted, and few were evaluated. Reviews of the prevailing law enforcement treatment interventions found little evidence these prevention strategies were effective. In spite of these findings, deterrence strategies implemented by law enforcement agencies continued to dominate crime prevention activities in the United States and other Western societies.

Critical Thinking Questions and Practice Activities

1. What is the distinction between general and specific deterrence? How is this related to the distinction between crime prevention and crime control?
2. Trace the idea that the causes of crime are found in the social and physical environment from the earliest explanations for crime to the latest explanations.

3. Which of the theories discussed in this chapter suggest both micro and macro level prevention strategies? Explain.

4. Think about a crime that interests you. Then, choose two theories discussed in this chapter and compare how each would explain this crime and how each would try to prevent it. Which theory provides the better explanation and the most effective crime prevention strategy? Explain and justify your answer.

5. What do you consider the greatest contribution to crime prevention made during the Positivism period of criminology? What is its legacy for contemporary thinking about crime prevention?

6. What are the advantages and disadvantages of integrated theories compared to individual theories for guiding the development of prevention strategies?

Endnotes

1. The claim that the relationships between these theoretical variables and delinquent behavior were likely reciprocal relationships was made earlier by Elliott *et al.* (1979: 11), but this theoretical proposition was not fully developed until Thornberry (1987).

2. Martinson (1976a) does not consider treatment interventions to be prevention interventions. Instead, he views treatment as a type of crime control. As we discussed earlier in the chapter, we take the position in this book that treatment and other control interventions are types of prevention interventions.

Helpful Websites (last accessed July 19, 2016)

- http://www.iep.utm.edu/home/about/
  The Encyclopedia of Philosophy provides detailed, scholarly information on important philosophers of history, including Beccaria, Bentham, Durkheim, and others referenced in this chapter.
- http://durkheim.uchicago.edu/
  The Durkheim Pages provides summaries of Durkheim's four major books and electronic copies of some of this literature.
- http://www.chicagoareaproject.org/historical-look-chicago-area-project
  This website provides information on the history and current implementation of the Chicago Area Project (CAP).

Further Reading

- Akers, R. L., and Sellers, C. S. 2013. *Criminological Theories: Introduction, Evaluation and Application*, 6th ed. New York, NY: Oxford University Press.
  Textbook describing the major criminological theories and their suggestions for crime prevention.
- Welsh, B. C., and Pfeffer, R. D. 2013. Reclaiming crime prevention in an age of punishment: An American history. *Punishment and Society*, 15:534–553.
  Article summarizing the history of crime prevention in the United States during the twentieth century.

References

Agnew, R. 1991. A longitudinal test of social control theory and delinquency. *Journal of Research in Crime and Delinquency*, 28:126–156.

Agnew, R. 1992. Foundation for a general strain theory of crime and delinquency. *Criminology*, 30:47–88.

Akers, R. L. 1985. *Deviant Behavior: A Social Learning Approach*, 3rd ed. Belmont, CA: Wadsworth.

Akers, R. L. 2009. *Social Learning and Social Structure: A General Theory of Crime and Deviance*. New Brunswick, NJ: Transaction Publishers.

Akers, R. L., and Sellers, C. S. 2004. *Criminological Theories: Introduction, Evaluation and Application*, 4th ed. Los Angeles, CA: Roxbury Publishing Company.

Akers, R. L., and Sellers, C. S. 2013. *Criminological Theories: Introduction, Evaluation and Application*, 6th ed. New York, NY: Oxford University Press.

Andrews, D. A., Zinger, I., Hoge, R. D., *et al.* 1990. Does correctional treatment work? A clinically relevant and psychologically informed meta-analysis. *Criminology*, 28:369–404. doi: 10.1111/j.1745-9125.1990.tb01330.x

Bandura, A., and Walters, R. H. 1963. *Social Learning and Personality Development*. New York, NY: Holt, Rinehart and Winston.

Beccaria, C. 1764/1983. *On Crimes and Punishments*. Indianapolis, IN: Bobbs-Merrill.

Bentham, J. 1789/1970. An introduction to the principles of morals and legislation. In: J. H. Burns and H. L. A. Hart (eds), *The Collected Works of Jeremy Bentham*. London, England: The Athlone Press.

Birkbeck, C., and LaFree, G. 1993. The situational analysis of crime and deviance. *Annual Review of Sociology*, 19:113–137.

Boardman, J. D., Menard, S., Roettger, M. E., *et al.* 2014. Genes in the dopaminergic system and delinquent behaviors across the life course: The role of social controls and risks. *Criminal Justice and Behavior*, 41:713–731.

Brody, G. H., Beach, S. R. H., Hill, K. G., *et al.* 2013. Using genetically informed, randomized prevention trials to test etiological hypotheses about child and adolescent drug use and psychopathology. *American Journal of Public Health*, S1:S19–S24.

Burgess, R., and Akers, R. L. 1966. A differential association reinforcement theory of criminal behavior. *Social Problems*, 14:128–147.

Bursik Jr., R. J., and Grasmick, H. G. 1993. *Neighborhoods and Crime: The Dimensions of Effective Community Control*. New York, NY: Lexington Books.

Caspi, A., McClay, J., Moffitt, T. E., *et al.* 2002. Role of genotype in the cycle of violence in maltreated children. *Science*, 297:851–859.

Catalano, R. F., and Hawkins, J. D. 1996. The Social Development Model: A theory of antisocial behavior. In: J. D. Hawkins (ed.), *Delinquency and Crime: Current Theories*, pp. 149–197. New York, NY: Cambridge University Press.

Chiricos, T. G., and Waldo, G. P. 1970. Punishment and crime: An examination of some empirical evidence. *Social Problems*, 18:200–217.

Clarke, R. V. 1983. Situational crime prevention: Its theoretical basis and practical scope. In: M. Tonry and N. Morris (eds), *The Annual Review of Criminal Justice Research*, pp. 225–256. Chicago, IL: Chicago University Press.

Clarke, R. V. 1995. Situational crime prevention. In: M. Tonry and D. P. Farrington (eds), *Crime and Justice, Building a Safer Society: Strategic Approaches to Crime Prevention*, pp. 91–150. Chicago, IL: The University of Chicago Press.

Clarke, R. V., and Cornish, D. B. 1985. Modeling offenders decisions: A framework for research and policy. In: M. Tonry and N. Morris (eds), *Crime and Justice*, pp. 147–185. Chicago, IL: The University of Chicago Press.

Cloward, R., and Ohlin, L. 1960. *Delinquency and Opportunity*. Glencoe, IL: Free Press.

Cohen, A. K. 1955. *Delinquent Boys: The Culture of the Gang*. Glencoe, IL: Free Press.

Cohen, A. K., Lindesmith, A., and Schuessler, K. 1956. *The Sutherland Papers*. Bloomington, IN: Indiana University Press.

Cohen, L. E., and Felson, M. 1979. Social change and crime rate trends: A routine activity approach. *American Sociological Review*, 44:588–608.

Cornish, D. B., and Clark, R. V. 1986. *The Reasoning Criminal: Rational Choice Perspectives on Offending*. New York, NY: Springer Verlag.

Cornish, D. B., and Clark, R. V. 2003. Opportunities, precipitators and criminal decisions: A reply to Wartley's critique of situational crime prevention. *Crime Prevention Studies*, 16:41–96.

Cullen, F. T. 2005. The twelve people who saved rehabilitation: How the science of criminology made a difference. *Criminology*, 43:1–42.

Dobbs, D. 2009. The science of success. *The Atlantic*.

Durkheim, E. 1893/1984. *The Division of Labor in Society*. New York, NY: Free Press.

Durkheim, E. 1895/1965. *The Rules of Sociological Method*. New York, NY: Free Press.

Durkheim, E. 1897/1951. *Suicide: A Study in Sociology*. New York, NY: Free Press.

Elliott, D. S., Ageton, S. S., and Canter, R. J. 1979. An integrated theoretical perspective on delinquent behavior. *Journal of Research in Crime and Delinquency*, 16:1–27.

Elliott, D. S., Huizinga, D., and Ageton, S. S. 1985. *Explaining Delinquency and Drug Use*. Beverly Hills, CA: Sage.

Elliott, D. S., Menard, S., Rankin, B., *et al.* 2006. *Good Kids from Bad Neighborhoods: Successful Development in Social Context*. New York, NY: Cambridge University Press.

Elwood, C. 1912. Lombroso's theory of crime. *Journal of Criminal Law and Criminology*, 2:716–723.

Finestone, H. 1976. *Victims of Change*. Westport, CT: Greenwood Press.

Gibbs, J. 1968. Crime, punishment and deterrence. *Social Science Quarterly*, 48:515–530.

Gibbs, J. 1975. *Crime, Punishment and Deterrence*. New York, NY: Elsevier.

Glueck, S., and Glueck, E. 1950. *Unraveling Juvenile Delinquency*. Cambridge, MA: Harvard University Press.

Goring, C. 1913/1972. *The English Convict: A Statistical Study*. Montclair, NJ: Patterson Smith.

Gottfredson, D. C., McNeil, R. J., and Gottfredson, G. D. 1991. Social area influences on delinquency: A multilevel analysis. *Journal of Research in Crime and Delinquency*, 28:197–226.

Gottfredson, M. R., and Hirschi, T. 1990. *A General Theory of Crime*. Stanford, CA: Stanford University Press.

Hartung, F. E. 1958. A critique of the sociological approach to crime and correction. *Law and Contemporary Problems*, 23:703–734.

Hill, K. G., Howell, J. C., Hawkins, J. D., and Battin-Pearson, S. R. 1999. Childhood risk factors for adolescent gang membership: Results from the Seattle Social Development Project. *Journal of Research in Crime and Delinquency*, 36:300–322.

Hirschi, T. 1969. *Causes of Delinquency*. Berkeley, CA: University of California Press.

Hooton, E. A. 1939/1969. *The American Criminal: An Anthropological Study*. Westport, CT: Greenwood Press.

Jang, S. J., and Smith, C. 1997. A test of reciprocal causal relationships among parental supervision, affective ties, and delinquency. *Journal of Research in Crime and Delinquency*, 34:307–337.

Junger-Tas, J. 1992. An empirical test of social control theory. *Journal of Quantitative Criminology*, 8:9–28.

Kobrin, S. 1959. The Chicago Area Project: A 25-year assessment. *Annals of the American Academy of Political and Social Science*, 322:19–29.

Krohn, M. D., and Massey, J. L. 1980. Social control and delinquent behavior: An examination of the elements of the social bond. *The Sociological Quarterly*, 21:529–543.

Lejins, P. P. 1967. The field of prevention. In: W. E. Amos and C. F. Wellford (eds), *Delinquency Prevention: Theory and Practice*, pp. 1–21. Englewood Cliffs, NJ: Prentice Hall.

Leventhal, T., and Brooks-Gunn, J. 2000. The neighborhoods they live in: The effects of neighborhood residence on child and adolescent outcomes. *Psychological Bulletin*, 126:309–337.

Lipton, D., Martinson, R., and Wilks, J. 1975. *The Effectiveness of Correctional Treatment: A Survey of Evaluation Studies*. New York, NY: Praeger Publishers.

Livy, T. 2002. *The Early History of Rome: Books I–V of the History of Rome from its Foundation*. London, England: Penguin Books.

Loeber, R., and Stouthamer-Loeber, M. 1986. Family factors as correlates and predictors of juvenile conduct problems and delinquency. In: M. Tonry and N. Morris (eds), *Crime and Justice: An Annual Review of Research*, pp. 29–149. Chicago, IL: University of Chicago Press.

Lombroso, C. 1876/2006. *The Criminal Man*. Durham, NC: Duke University Press.

Lombroso, C. 1912. *Crime: Its Causes and Remedies*. Montclair, NJ: Patterson Smith.

Lombroso, C., and Ferrero, G. 1893/2004. *The Criminal Woman, the Prostitute, and the Normal Woman*. Translated by N. Hann Rafter and M. Gibson. Durham, NC: Duke University Press.

Lucas, A. J. 1952. Gluecks' study of 500 delinquents to determine root causes of criminal behavior. *The Harvard Crimson*, April 11, 1952.

Martinson, R. 1976a. What works? Questions and answers about prison reform. In: M. Matlin (ed.), *Rehabilitation, Recidivism, and Research*, pp. 7–40. Hackensack, NJ: National Council on Crime and Delinquency.

Martinson, R. 1976b. Evaluation in crisis – A postscript. In: M. Matlin (ed.), *Rehabilitation, Recidivism, and Research*, pp. 93–96. Hackensack, NJ: National Council on Crime and Delinquency.

Massey, J. L., Krohn, M. D., and Bonati, L. 1989. Property crime and the routine activity of individuals. *Journal of Research in Crime and Delinquency*, 26:378–400.

Merton, R. K. 1938. Social structure and anomie. *American Sociological Review*, 3:672–682.

Messner, S. F., and Rosenfeld, R. 1994. *Crime and the American Dream*. Belmont, CA: Wadsworth.

Nagin, D. S., and Pogarsky, G. 2001. Integrating celerity, impulsivity and extralegal sanction threats into a model of general deterrence: Theory and evidence. *Criminology*, 39:865–892.

National Institute of Justice. 2014. Five things about deterrence. Washington, DC: Office of Justice Programs.

Nye, F. I. 1958. *Family Relationships and Delinquent Behavior*. New York, NY: John Wiley & Sons, Inc.

Office of Juvenile Justice and Delinquency Prevention. 1999. Juvenile justice: A century of change. In: *Juvenile Justice Bulletin*. Washington, DC: Office of Justice Programs.

Park, R. E., Burgess, E. W., and McKenzie, R. D. 1928. *The City*. Chicago, IL: University of Chicago Press.

President's Commission on Law Enforcement and the Administration of Justice. 1967. The challenge of crime in a free society. Washington, DC: US Government Printing Office.

Reckless, W. 1961. A new theory of delinquency and crime. *Federal Probation*, 25:42–46.

Reiss, A. J. 1951. Delinquency as the failure of personal and social controls. *American Sociological Review*, 16:196–207.

Reiss, A. J., and Roth, J. A. 1993. *Understanding and Preventing Violence*. Washington, DC: National Academy Press.

Rocque, M., Welsh, B. C., and Raine, A. 2012. Biosocial criminology and modern crime prevention. *Journal of Criminal Justice*, 40:306–312.

Romig, D. A. 1978. *Justice for our Children: An Examination of Juvenile Delinquent Rehabilitation Programs*. Lexington, MA: Lexington Books.

Sampson, R. J. 2012. *Great American City: Chicago and the Enduring Neighborhood Effect*. Chicago, IL: University of Chicago Press.

Sampson, R. J., and Byron Groves, W. B. 1989. Community structure and crime: Testing social-disorganization theory. *American Journal of Sociology*, 94:774–802.

Scheurman, L., and Kobrin, S. 1986. Community careers in crime. In: M. Tonry (ed.), *Crime and Justice: Communities and Crime*, pp. 67–100. Chicago, IL: University of Chicago Press.

Schlossman, S., and Sedlak, M. 1983. The Chicago Area Project revisited. *Crime and Delinquency*, 26:398–462.

Shaw, C. R., and McKay, H. D. 1942. *Juvenile Delinquency and Urban Areas*. Chicago, IL: University of Chicago Press.

Sheldon, W. H. 1949. *Varieties of Delinquent Youth*. New York, NY: Harper.

Short Jr., J. F. 1974. The natural history of an applied theory: Differential opportunity and "mobilization for youth." In: N. J. Demerath, O. Larsen, and K. F. Schuessler (eds), *Social Policy and Sociology*, pp. 193–210. New York, NY: Academic Press.

Sutherland, E. H. 1947. *Principles of Criminology*. Philadelphia, PA: J. B. Lippincott.

Sutherland, E. H. 1951. Varieties of delinquent youth. In: A. K. Cohen, A. Lindesmith, and K. Schuessler (eds), *The Sutherland Papers*, pp. 279–290. Bloomington, IN: Indiana University Press.

Taylor, R. B., and Covington, J. 1988. Neighborhood changes in ecology and violence. *Criminology*, 26:553–589.

Thornberry, T. P. 1987. Toward an interactional theory of delinquency. *Criminology*, 25:863–891.

Thornberry, T. P., Lizotte, A. J., Krohn, M. D., Farnworth, M., and Jang, S. J. 1991. Testing interactional theory: An examination of reciprocal causal relationships among family, school, and delinquency. *Journal of Criminal Law and Criminology*, 82:3–35.

Tittle, C. R. 1969. Crime rates and legal sanctions. *Social Problems*, 16:409–422.

Toby, J. 1964. Is punishment necessary? *Journal of Criminal Law and Criminology*, 55:332–337.

Weber, E. 1971. *A Modern History of Europe*. New York, NY: Norton.

Weis, J. G., and Hawkins, J. D. 1981. Preventing delinquency. Washington, DC: Office of Juvenile Justice and Delinquency Prevention, US Department of Justice.

Weisburd, D. 1997. Reorienting crime prevention research and policy: From the causes of criminality to the context of crime. Washington, DC: National Institute of Justice, US Department of Justice, Office of Justice Programs.

Welsh, B. C., and Pfeffer, R. D. 2013. Reclaiming crime prevention in an age of punishment: An American history. *Punishment and Society*, 15:534–553.

Section II

The Foundations of Crime Prevention

3

How Theory and Research Inform the Science and Practice of Crime Prevention

Learning Objectives

Upon finishing this chapter, students should be able to:

- Understand the different criminological theories which inform crime prevention
- Identify the nine elements of the criminal career framework
- Summarize the public health and prevention science approaches to crime prevention
- Identify specific risk and protective factors related to involvement in crime
- Explain the differences between universal, selective, and indicated crime prevention
- Explain the differences between situational, contextual, and individually focused crime prevention approaches.

Introduction

The goal of this textbook is to describe the range of activities that can be considered "crime prevention" and to identify the effectiveness of these strategies in reducing rates of crime. In the last chapter, we reviewed the different ways societies have attempted to explain and prevent crime throughout time. History reveals that crime prevention efforts up through the twentieth century were most often based on deterrence theory and were rarely tested for their effectiveness. When evaluations were conducted, relatively few programs and practices were found to be effective. In fact, reviews of correctional and law enforcement program evaluations near the end of the twentieth century suggested that "nothing works."

The Prevention of Crime, First Edition. Delbert Elliott and Abigail Fagan.
© 2017 John Wiley & Sons, Inc. Published 2017 by John Wiley & Sons, Inc.
Companion website: www.wiley.com/go/elliott/prevention_of_crime

We noted in Chapter 2 that, in our opinion, the conclusion that nothing worked to prevent crime was overly pessimistic. Nonetheless, at the time of those reviews, credible, scientific evidence of effective crime prevention strategies was very limited. The good news is that, in recent years, theories about what leads to crime have become more sophisticated and there have been many more, and better conducted, scientific tests of these theories and of evaluations of crime prevention strategies guided by these theories. As a result, today we can identify a greater number of prevention programs, practices, and policies that have credible evidence of effectiveness. We also know a lot more now about how to create prevention strategies so that they have the strongest likelihood of achieving reductions in crime.

To summarize what we have learned over the years, *first*, we know that the most effective crime prevention efforts are based on criminological theories and that they try to change the specific factors described in those theories and shown in research studies to actually affect criminal behavior. For example, if studies testing strain theory show that poverty makes crime more likely, then prevention efforts should focus on helping individuals get better paying jobs. In contrast, if there is no evidence that crime is caused by poverty, then attempts to reduce poverty will not be effective in preventing crime. As became clear in Chapter 2, different theories identify different factors as important in causing crime, which means that crime prevention can take many different forms. Because theories are tied so directly to the creation and effectiveness of crime prevention efforts, we begin this chapter by reviewing and updating information from Chapter 2 about the theories that are most widely endorsed in criminology and most often used to guide crime prevention.

Second, we know that crime prevention strategies can differ depending on the specific form or type of illegal behavior that a community is trying to reduce. For example, some programs are designed to prevent persons from committing their very first criminal act; that is, from making the transition from being a non-offender to being an offender. Other strategies are designed to help offenders give up their involvement in criminal behavior. In this chapter, we will introduce the **criminal careers** framework, which has strongly influenced the ways modern criminologists define and conceptualize criminal behavior, and, correspondingly, the types of crime we might want to prevent and the individuals who should be targeted by prevention efforts.

> *Nothing is so practical as good theory.*
>
> Kurt Lewin, psychologist (1951: 169)

Third, it is now generally accepted that strategies designed to change individual involvement in crime should take into account the age of the person and the characteristics or experiences, which are called **risk and protective factors**, most likely to affect crime at each stage of life. This view, and its corresponding implications for crime prevention, is emphasized in the **life course development paradigm**, as well as in the **public health approach** to prevention and the emerging discipline of **prevention science**. Each of these frameworks will be described in this chapter and their impact on contemporary crime prevention strategies noted. The chapter will conclude by identifying a typology of prevention strategies that will guide this textbook and previewing the discussion of how preventive interventions are developed using **logic models**.

Theoretical Foundations of Crime Prevention

The development of any prevention program or strategy begins with two questions: (i) What causes individuals or groups to engage in criminal behavior? And, (ii) given some understanding of these causes, how can we intervene to eliminate or block them? The first question is a theoretical question. A crime theory proposes an explanation about the motive for committing a crime as well as the set of circumstances or conditions that connect this intention with actual criminal behavior. The logic of crime prevention is that if we know why an individual or group engages in criminal behavior, we can try to avoid, counteract, or eliminate these causes. Doing so will prevent crime. *Theoretical explanations about the causes of crime underlie all prevention efforts.* Even if the theory guiding the approach is not explicitly stated, which is frequently the case, it can be determined by reading the descriptions of the interventions and thinking about which causes of crime they seek to change.

As reported in Chapter 2, research that tests criminal theories demonstrates better support for some theories than others and for some specific causal claims (hypotheses) within theories than others. For example, there is little support for Lombroso's (1911) theory that **atavism** or primitive physical features of an individual (e.g., overly long arms, misshapen noses, or large jawbones) are associated with crime. But, there is good support for Sutherland's (1947) claim of **differential association**, that associating with criminals is causally related to criminal behavior. The stronger the research evidence supporting a causal claim hypothesized by a theory, the greater confidence can be placed in the expectation that eliminating or blocking that cause or set of causes will prevent criminal behavior. In other words, theories with stronger evidence should be those upon which crime prevention strategies are based.

It should be noted, however, that research evidence rarely meets the very high scientific standards required to demonstrate a true causal relationship described in a criminological theory. The evidence often shows that a *natural* change in the characteristic or condition hypothesized to be a cause predicts a subsequent change in criminal behavior. For example, studies have found that individuals who start spending time with friends who engage in crime become more likely to break the law themselves (Elliott and Menard, 1996). This is pretty good evidence of a causal relationship between having criminal friends and associates and being involved in crime. This research also supports Sutherland's differential association theory. But, since the change in friendship was natural, meaning it was unplanned or accidental, and was not the result of an *intentional* or experimental manipulation, a causal claim about the effect of delinquent peers on delinquency cannot be made with certainty. As we will explain later in this chapter, given this uncertainty, we refer to the causal characteristics, conditions and processes derived from criminological theories and addressed by prevention programs as **risk and protective factors**. There is good but not conclusive evidence for their causal effects on crime.

The second question that guides crime prevention is a more practical one: having identified a risk factor(s) that increases the likelihood of crime, can we realistically expect to eliminate or change it, and, if so, what strategies and resources are needed to do so? Some risk factors will be easier to change or eliminate than others. For example, unemployment, poverty, child abuse, academic failure, and involvement with a gang are all risk factors for criminal behaviors. Yet, they are not equally amenable to change. The cost, resources, and time required to reduce or eliminate these conditions will vary considerably. In addition, the power of these risk factors to influence crime also varies considerably. Improving academic performance will have a much smaller effect on crime than breaking up a gang. The design of a prevention program or strategy involves the selection of a risk factor(s) to be reduced and/or a protective factor(s) to be increased and the design of a set of activities, policies, processes, and procedures to make these changes happen.

With this background in mind, what do theories say about the causal conditions that are most likely to lead to criminal behavior? And, how can this information help us develop effective crime prevention strategies? To answer these questions, we now review the theories most often discussed in criminology and used to create prevention strategies.

Deterrence theories guiding crime prevention by law enforcement agencies

Historically, **deterrence and rational choice theories** have been the main theoretical perspectives guiding crime prevention, particularly as undertaken by law enforcement agents. As described in Chapter 2, these theories assume that individuals are rational thinkers who consider the risks and rewards of their actions before making a decision to commit an illegal act. When the potential benefits of committing a crime are viewed as outweighing the potential risks, then individuals will be more likely to break the law. Where these theories differ is in the degree to which they focus on societal versus individual considerations of the benefits and risks of crime and the emphasis on the seriousness or certainty of punitive sanctions. Nonetheless, because they both assume that individuals are rational thinkers who will be deterred from offending when costs and punishments are high, they advocate similar types of crime prevention strategies. **Routine activities theory** also takes the perspective that offenders are rational thinkers and will consider the costs and benefits of crime prior to breaking the law, particularly the amount of effort needed to commit an illegal act and the likelihood of getting caught.

Of the three theories, **deterrence theory** takes the most macro or societal level view of crime and of crime prevention. This perspective emphasizes that societies must have punishments in place to deter would-be offenders from breaking the law. Indeed, deterrence theory provides the foundation for virtually all law, law enforcement, and correctional systems. According to deterrence theory, public awareness of the fact that certain actions are illegal and that violation of these laws can result in specific punishments should be enough to prevent crime. If the rate of a specific crime in a society is going up, the prevention strategy would be to increase the seriousness and/or certainty of punitive sanctions for that crime. Prevention activities based on deterrence theory involve societal-level strategies, especially the creation of laws that focus on the certainty, speed, and particularly the severity of punishment following the commission of a crime. Longer sentences for crimes involving the use of a firearm and "three strikes" laws that require a life sentence for a third felony offense are based on deterrence theory.

The concepts of **general deterrence** and **specific deterrence** refer to the types of individuals who will be prevented from breaking the law. Simply having laws and punishments in place creates a risk of punishment for offending that should be enough to deter the general public from committing crime; this is the concept of general deterrence. Once an individual breaks the law, is apprehended and punished, this experience will function as a deterrent for that person committing additional criminal acts; this is the concept of specific deterrence (Akers, 1997). There are different implied intervention targets and strategies for these two types of deterrence. General deterrence interventions will focus on general populations, persons who have not yet committed a crime. They can also include public awareness strategies which make the public aware of the law and potential punishment for violating it. For example, if you read in the paper that the local police will be conducting **sobriety checkpoints** and stopping drivers to assess if they are driving under the influence of alcohol, you can assume that law enforcement is using a general deterrence practice. Specific deterrence practices will focus on offenders, punishing them for breaking the law with the expectation that negative experiences in the criminal justice system will deter them from future offending.

Rational choice theory focuses more on individuals and individual decision-making. It hypothesizes that if illegal behavior carries a certain punishment, and individuals believe they will face this punishment if they break the law, they will refrain from offending unless the reward for doing so outweighs the cost. Given this orientation, crime prevention based on rational choice theory will try to influence one's decision-making processes in order to reduce the perceived benefits of crime and increase the costs or pain thought to follow from illegal behavior. Examples include media campaigns showing the long-term effects of drug use on one's health or individual treatment programs which emphasize the consequences of offending or drug use on one's scholastic and vocational achievements.

Routine activities theory considers both individual and societal opportunities for offending and prevention. It states that crime is most likely to occur when three factors are present at the same time and place: (i) a motivated offender, (ii) a suitable target, and (iii) an absence of capable guardians (Clarke, 1995). Although all three are considered important, crime prevention efforts do not focus on trying to change individuals, but rather try to reduce opportunities for offending, the attractiveness of a target and the lack of guardianship of a place or object. For example, installing time-lock safes and bullet proof windows in banks should reduce robberies.

Have you ever spent time in a risky, high-crime urban neighborhood such as those found in the south side of Chicago or upper east-side of Detroit? How would you try to reduce crime in these neighborhoods? Another theory related to the deterrence perspective, and especially routine activities theory, is **situational crime prevention**. This theory focuses on how physical environments and geographical locations, rather than individual characteristics, influence crime. These theories might suggest that law enforcement agencies examine crime maps that show the geographical locations of every crime that has occurred in their district. After identifying the **hot spots** (Sherman and Weisburd, 1995) where rates of crime are highest, they will increase patrol and surveillance of these areas to deter would-be offenders. **Place-based** prevention activities might also be undertaken by law enforcement agents, business owners, or private citizens. These efforts focus on very small geographical units, such as individual buildings or streets that are known to be hot spots of crime (Eck and Guerette, 2012). The goal is to make these areas less attractive and more difficult targets for criminals; for example, by installing alarm systems in homes or buildings that have been repeatedly vandalized or broken into, increasing street lighting and using closed circuit televisions to increase surveillance of a particular block or building.

Developmental theories guiding community-based crime prevention strategies

In the last few decades, crime prevention efforts have moved somewhat away from deterrence-based theories and become more informed by **developmental** theories of offending. These perspectives recognize that crime is a complex behavior influenced by many factors, that there are multiple causal paths to crime, that individuals' involvement in crime can develop and change over time, and that factors influencing offending can differ depending on characteristics of the individual, the physical and social environment and the type of crime being considered. Moreover, these theories locate prevention efforts primarily in families, schools, and the community rather than in the criminal justice system.

> *The theory that can absorb the greatest number of facts, and persist in doing so, generation after generation, through all changes of opinion and detail, is the one that must rule all observation.*
>
> Adam Smith

Yes, this makes for a complicated picture of crime. But, it is also true that crime is a complex social problem requiring comprehensive explanations. If criminal behavior was easy to figure out, we would have already solved the problem and eliminated crime altogether! Criminologists are increasingly acknowledging this complexity and adjusting their theoretical views on crime accordingly. Before describing the developmental theories guiding more contemporary and community-based crime prevention, it is essential to understand the **criminal career** framework, which describes the kinds of behavior and dimensions of crime targeted by these prevention strategies.

The criminal career framework

In Chapter 2, we discussed the controversy over the terms "crime prevention" and "crime control." The focus of this debate is whether crime prevention should be concerned only with the *first* crime a person ever commits (i.e., the transition from being a non-offender to being an offender) or with preventing *any* criminal act, no matter how many the individual has previously committed. We have chosen to refer to **crime prevention** as interventions that seek to stop any criminal event, regardless of when it occurs in the series of crimes. But we acknowledge that the distinction between the first criminal behavior and repeated offending is important and that the prevention of an initial offense may require something different than that needed to prevent ongoing criminal behavior. But where a criminal act falls along a sequence of criminal activities is not the only type of distinction we might consider when describing criminal behavior and designing prevention programs, practices, or policies. What other dimensions of crime and criminal behavior do you think are important? Is the distinction between preventing aggravated assaults and vandalism an important one? What are the dimensions of crime that prevention programs should address?

Blumstein and his colleagues (Blumstein, Cohen, and Farrington, 1988; Blumstein *et al.*, 1986) proposed the **criminal career** framework to identify and organize a set of concepts that distinguish between different types and levels of involvement in crime. Their framework was one of the first to view criminal behavior as having a definite progression, beginning with the initiation or first act of crime, continuing for a defined period, then ending. This view has expanded both theories about and research on crime. For example, it has led to new and more comprehensive measures of

Table 3.1 Dimensions of the criminal career.

Dimension	Definition
Onset (initiation)	The beginning of the career; the point at which one's first offense is committed
Participation	Percentage of the population who engages in crime during some time period
Frequency	Number of crimes per year committed by those who are actively participating in crime
Seriousness	The degree to which one commits predatory offenses, such as burglary, assault, or robbery
Specialization	Primarily engaging in only offense or one group of related offenses
Escalation	Increases in the number and/or seriousness of offending over time
De-escalation or desistance	Decreases in the number and/or seriousness of offending over time
Length (duration)	The amount of time between an offender's first and last crime
Termination	The end of the career; the point at which an offender's last crime is committed

Source: Based upon Blumstein *et al.*, 1986.

offending which move beyond the simple crime rates provided by the UCR and other official sources of crime data discussed in Chapter 1. It also has many implications for crime prevention programs, practices, and policies, as we will describe.

The main elements of the criminal career described by Blumstein and colleagues include **onset, participation, frequency, seriousness, specialization, escalation, desistance, length,** and **termination** (see Table 3.1 for brief descriptions of each). The criminal career begins with *onset*, the very first offense in a criminal career. The onset rate reflects the proportion of persons in a population (e.g., all youth in the United States or all adults in a particular city or state) whose initial offense occurs in a given year. *Participation* refers to the proportion of all people in a population who have committed at least one offense in a given time period (usually defined as one year). A lifetime participation rate would reflect the proportion of persons in a population that were involved in at least one crime during their lifetime. In any given year, the participation rate includes both those whose onset occurred in that year and those who initiated their offending earlier and also are active offenders in that period. All other dimensions describe the criminal involvement of individuals after onset: the *frequency* of their offending, the *seriousness* of their offenses, changes in that frequency or seriousness over time (*escalation/de-escalation*), the number of years from the first to the last offense (*length* or *duration*), and the ending (*termination*) of all offending.

In developing this framework, Blumstein and colleagues (Blumstein, Cohen, and Farrington, 1988; Blumstein *et al.*, 1986) were among the first to recognize what is now seen as an indisputable fact: that youth are much more likely to participate in crime than are adults. The strong relationship between age and offending, often referred to and visually displayed as an **age/crime curve** (see Figure 3.1), has been confirmed using official data and self-reports of offending. Research has shown that the onset or initiation of offending usually occurs in early to middle adolescence, participation in crime increases from late adolescence to early adulthood and desistence begins after that. Although there can be some variation in these patterns across time periods, types of offenses (e.g., violent vs

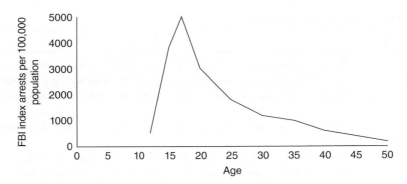

Figure 3.1   The age/crime curve. Source: Blumstein *et al.*, 1988.

non-violent crimes) and characteristics of offenders (e.g., males vs females), the age/crime curve typically tells the same story over and over again: adolescents are much more likely than adults to participate in offending.

It is important to remember, however, that there are more adults than youth in every society; in the USA, only about 15% of the population is aged 14–24 (National Center for Educational Statistics; http://nces.ed.gov/pubs2012/2012026.pdf). As a result, the total number of adult offenders will always be higher than the total number of youth offenders. But, the proportion of *all* adults who engage in crime will be lower than the proportion of *all* youth who engage in crime.

Additional research investigating the criminal career has indicated that for most offenders, participation in crime begins with the least serious types of offenses, such as minor forms of drug use and perpetration of minor assaults or thefts. Some offenders will escalate to more frequent and serious forms of drug use, non-violent crimes and/or violence over time, but people are very unlikely to begin their criminal career by committing a very serious offense such as an aggravated assault, robbery, or murder (Blumstein *et al.*, 1986; Elliott, 1994; Farrington, 2003). In addition, most serious offenders do not specialize in particular types of crime but are generalists, showing variation in the types of crimes they commit. For example, gang members may engage in drive-by shootings but will also be likely to use illegal drugs, get into fist-fights and/or commit vandalism.

Finally, evidence has shown that the earlier one's age of onset, the more likely s/he is to engage in persistent, serious offending that continues into adulthood. For example, findings from a national self-report survey showed that 45% of those whose first act of violence occurred before age 11 also committed violence during their 20s. However, only about 25% of those who initiated violence at ages 11–12 were violent during adulthood, and even fewer of those whose age of onset was later than 13 years continued to be violent as adults (Elliott, 1994). Table 3.2 shows similar statistics linking the age of onset among males in Denver to their later involvement in serious and chronic (i.e., of a long duration) offending.

What does information about the criminal career mean for crime prevention? First, if the age of onset is important in predicting serious and frequent offending and most individuals experience the onset of offending when they are adolescents, then prevention efforts that seek to delay onset and reduce participation in crime should probably be focused on children and those in the early years

Table 3.2 The relationship between age of onset and later offending.

Age of initiation	Percent who became serious offenders	Percent who became chronic violent offenders
Before age 9	67%	62%
Ages 12–14	53%	48%
Ages 15–17	27%	20%

Source: Adapted from Huizinga *et al.*, 2003 (Tables 2 and 3); information is based on self-reported information from males participating in the Denver Youth Survey.

of adolescence. Since these interventions are targeting people *before* they become involved in crime, they will not be implemented by the criminal justice system. Instead, they will likely occur in a community setting with the general population. If the goal is to reduce frequent and serious crime among active offenders, then crime prevention efforts should focus on older adolescents and/or adults – those who are already participating in crime (Blumstein *et al.*, 1986). These actions are likely to be initiated and overseen by the criminal justice system.

Second, Blumstein and colleagues (1988) speculated that different dimensions of the criminal career are influenced by different causal factors and so require different types of prevention strategies. For example, the factors that lead to the onset of crime (among youth) are likely to differ from the factors that influence the frequency of offending among serious (and older) offenders. Efforts to prevent or delay the initiation of crime might, then, try to minimize the influence of having delinquent peers or improve children's success in school, while efforts intended to prevent recidivism may require more intensive and multicomponent prevention strategies.

To summarize, research on criminal careers suggests the following for crime prevention:

1. The onset, frequency, escalation/de-escalation, and termination of crime may each have a unique set of causes requiring different prevention strategies.
2. Services to prevent criminal onset should focus primarily on youth.
3. Crime prevention efforts intended to bring about termination should focus on all active offenders.
4. Given the developmental progression of crime, prevention at early stages of the career should reduce the frequency and seriousness of crime and the length of one's criminal career.

The life course developmental paradigm

Do you know what a "paradigm shift" is? In science, it refers to a very large change in how we view a particular event or set of events. What does this have to do with criminology and crime prevention? Our view, and that of some other criminologists (e.g., Cullen, 2011), is that criminology has recently experienced such a shift with the introduction of the life course development paradigm. The application of this view of human behavior to crime has had a strong impact on our understanding of the factors that lead to crime and the types of strategies that should be used to prevent illegal behaviors.

Backing up a bit, we should mention that a **paradigm** is a worldview or a research tradition within a scientific discipline (Laudan, 1977). It is a descriptive framework that identifies what types of things need to be observed or measured, what kinds of questions need to be answered, and what types of conclusions we should draw from research findings and integrate into any one discipline (Kuhn, 1996). The **life course developmental paradigm** is one such paradigm. It has its roots in several academic disciplines, including psychology, sociology, and biology, and is now gaining popularity in criminology. In a nutshell, this perspective considers personal growth and development to be a complex process that evolves and changes over time, particularly in response to the changing social environments we experience as we age (Elder Jr., 1995; Elder Jr. and Caspi, 1990). *We repeat: this paradigm presents a very complex view of human development and behavior,* so bear with us as we explain some of its key concepts. Do not worry: we will also describe exactly how this paradigm relates to crime prevention.

Concept #1: Person-in-context interactions. The life course paradigm sees human behavior as the result of many different individual characteristics (biological, psychological, and social) and experiences interacting with many different environments that are also changing over the life course. We move from the family environment in early childhood to family, school, and peer groups in adolescence, and to college, work, and marriage in adulthood. Individuals have **agency**, or freedom, to choose some environments but not others. For example, we actively seek out our friends – and we may choose delinquent friends or very conventional friends – but we have very little control over who makes up our family. All the environments that surround us affect our opportunities to engage in particular behaviors, the social roles we play (e.g., "girlfriend" or "parent") and our understanding of social norms – what society considers to be acceptable and unacceptable, or approved of or not approved of, behaviors. Even though everyone experiences the same general contexts (e.g., school or work), individuals are different. Each individual brings particular skills, attitudes, beliefs, and experiences into each context, and the particular behavior that emerges is the result of our personal characteristics and choices *and* the social roles, norms, and opportunities found in our social environments.

Concept # 2: Developmental stages. As we age, we move through distinct phases of the life course that are defined, in part, by our age; for example, infancy, childhood, early adolescence, late adolescence, early adulthood, and late adulthood. Movement from one stage to the next occurs when we experience changes in psycho-biological processes (e.g., puberty, which indicates a movement from childhood to adolescence) and in social roles and statuses (e.g., becoming a legal driver or gaining more independence from parents). Development, then, is a continuous process of maturation and change. Changes in social contexts, social roles, norms, and demands or responsibilities all contribute to our development as human beings—and can affect involvement in crime. Problems arise for those who are not well equipped to meet the demands of or successfully complete important developmental tasks present in each stage of the life course (e.g., failing to graduate from high school on time). Those who do not progress normally, or on the expected timeline, can experience much personal stress. They may become marginalized or separated from their peers or others, they may experience a delay or failure to successfully complete important tasks in future stages, and they may be less able to attain conventional social roles and statuses.

Concept #3: Transitions and trajectories. Transitions are abrupt events or experiences that typically mark movement from one developmental stage to the next. Often, they represent changes in social status and/or roles (e.g., graduation from elementary to middle school, getting married, or getting arrested). Adolescence is the stage of maximum change. More changes in social contexts and more transitions occur in this stage compared to any other, making it a critical period of development. A **trajectory** is a long-term sequence showing the pattern of transitions and changes that occur during one's life. It is a history recording how individuals adapt to changes in social contexts and how well they navigate significant transitions and turning points.

Concept #4: Timing. If significant events, tasks, and transitions that should occur during a particular developmental stage do not occur – if they are "off time" or out of sequence – problems can arise not only during that particular period but also in future stages. For example, the timing of both puberty and employment are important for ensuring healthy development and one's potential for crime. Girls who experience an early onset of puberty are at greater risk of delinquency than those with a normal or late onset (Zahn *et al.*, 2008). Likewise, being employed prior to high school graduation is a risk factor for crime but not after graduation (Mihalic and Elliott, 1997).

Concept #5: Stability and change. The concepts of stability and change are central to the life course paradigm and refer to continuity or discontinuity in behavior across different developmental stages. According to this perspective, one's behavior is *not* a stable personality trait or inherent propensity. Individuals are not born criminals; they do not have an inherent propensity to commit crimes. Instead, behavior can be stable *or* changing, depending on how one responds or adapts to each stage of life. If an individual shows stability in positive or negative behaviors, this stability cannot be attributed simply or solely to one's genetics or biological tendencies. Instead, it may be that an individual responded in a certain way in one environment and decides to repeat the performance in another context, probably because s/he had similar opportunities to behave in that manner and/or was rewarded for doing so in both contexts (Elliott and Williams, 1995).

Now that we have explained the life course paradigm in some detail, it's completely apparent how this perspective relates to criminal behavior and crime prevention, right? Not yet? Well, let's think about it some more …

In the life course paradigm, crime is viewed as an adaptation made because one has not achieved the goals or successfully completed the demands faced at a particular stage. Or, crime occurs because one has not experienced important transitions or turning points at the right time. Remember that, in this paradigm, both individual characteristics and social environments affect behavior and development, which means that both personal and contextual factors, as well as their interactions, affect one's likelihood of overcoming or failing to overcome challenges faced during the life course. A major goal of crime prevention programs is to provide individuals with the skills they need to successfully complete tasks, adapt to new circumstances and take on new responsibilities so that they do not resort to criminal adaptations. Recall that adolescence is the stage where most of these demands occur and crime is most likely to be initiated, which also makes it an important period for crime prevention. The specific individual and contextual risk and protective factors that affect adaptations and which can be targeted by prevention efforts are described in various developmental theories, which we will review in the next section.

Similar to the criminal career framework, the life course perspective considers and seeks to answer questions about how offending behavior can change over the life course but also investigates how these patterns may vary across individuals and contexts. Some of the questions that life course theories seek to answer include: How big a failure or departure from the normal course of

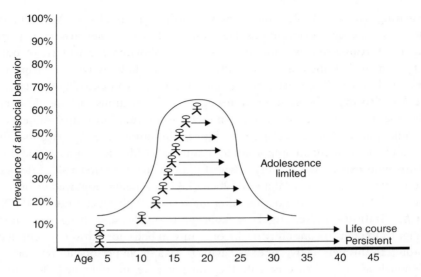

Figure 3.2 Two groups of individuals with different levels of participation in offending over the life course. Source: Moffitt, 1993. Reproduced with permission of the American Psychological Association.

development is required before crime becomes a likely adaptation? Why would an individual choose a criminal adaptation rather than some other non-criminal adaptation (e.g., why react to a failure to meet goals with crime versus depression or just by lowering your goals or aspirations)? What personal traits, conditions, experiences, or interactions explain the specific form of crime one chooses to commit (e.g., violence compared to theft or drug use)? Why is involvement in crime temporary for some individuals but more stable or persistent for others? Is stability in offending likely to be the result of an accumulation of failures experienced across multiple stages of development, or is a critical failure experienced very early in life enough to create an ongoing pattern or trajectory of offending?

   Also like the criminal career paradigm, the life course paradigm recognizes the definite relationship between age and crime, but also points out that the age/crime curve shown in Figure 3.1 reflects an aggregate or overall pattern, meaning that it is based on averaging crime rates across all individuals in a population. Presenting information in this way can hide differences in crime rates for particular individuals or groups of individuals. For example, Moffitt's (1993) examination of offending rates has shown that although most offenders do limit their participation in crime to the adolescent period of life (and are, as a result, **adolescent-limited offenders**), this is not true of all individuals. A small proportion of the population (5–10%) are **life-course persistent offenders** (Moffitt, 1993; Sampson and Laub, 1993). As depicted in Figure 3.2, these individuals usually commit their first deviant or illegal behavior during childhood and are persistent offenders, continuing to offend through adulthood.

   To further complicate matters, additional patterns of offending are also possible. For example, some studies have shown that there are distinct groups of individuals who: (i) initiate offending during adolescence and persist into adulthood, and (ii) have a delayed onset of crime, offending for the first time after age 20 (Jennings and Reingle, 2012; Nagin, Farrington, and Moffitt, 1995; US Department of Health and Human Services, 2001). Moreover, even for life course persisters, involvement in crime can be unstable, increasing or decreasing depending on life circumstances.

This variation in offending means that there are many opportunities to prevent involvement in crime. We must provide services early in life before the age of onset has occurred as well as later in the life course to guard against a late onset of crime and to reduce recidivism among those who have already initiated. Crime prevention efforts must also consider the different developmental stages that individuals are experiencing and recognize that the factors influencing criminal adaptations will be different at different stages. That is, risk factors that are most important in childhood are likely to be different from those that are most important in adolescence and from those that are most salient during adulthood. This means that prevention services have to address the *right* factors at the *right* time. Similarly, because the circumstances that predict onset and persistence or which influence adolescent-limited offending and life course persistent offending may differ, prevention programs will need to focus on different factors depending on the outcome one wishes to prevent and/or the types of individuals targeted for services.

As we have been emphasizing, different theories offer different explanations for criminal involvement. From a life course perspective, it is important to consider the degree to which theories take into account the age of the individual, the turning points and transitions affecting their involvement in crime and the degree to which they allow for different pathways to crime for different individuals. With these thoughts in mind, let's review some of the theories we discussed in Chapter 2 and reflect again on their implications for crime prevention.

Theories within the life course development paradigm

Strain theories predate the emergence of the life course paradigm but nonetheless reflect some of its main principles. Strain theories assume that humans are basically law-abiding and will engage in crime only when pushed to do so. The central proposition in strain theory is that crime is a response to the pain and emotions produced by stress, which can act as a turning point in the life course, especially if it results in the inability to successfully achieve important tasks and goals.

The primary theories in this tradition that guide current prevention efforts are Cloward and Ohlin's (1960) version of strain theory, sometimes called **Opportunity Theory** and Agnew's (1991, 2006) **General Strain Theory (GST)**. According to both these theories, an important motivation for involvement in crime is having limited access to conventional opportunities, which leads to an anticipated failure to achieve goals that are universally valued in society (e.g., a high-quality education, a good job, accumulated wealth and social status, and a happy marriage). Agnew's GST identified two other important types of stressors: (i) the loss of positive influences and relationships like close friends, a favorite teacher, or a beloved coach; and (ii) a dramatic negative event like the death of a loved one or exposure to violence and victimization. All of these experiences can evoke strong emotions (e.g., anger, anxiety, or depression), which, in turn, prompt a search for ways to deal with this condition.

Strain theory views crime as one possible solution or adaptation to stressful situations. But according to Cloward and Ohlin (1960), choosing a criminal adaptation depends on access to criminal opportunities, those learning environments and subcultures where the required skills and knowledge to be successful in crime can be acquired. The specific form of criminal behavior is determined, at least in part, by the specific criminal subculture available. In addition, Agnew (1991, 2006) states that social support is very important in determining which adaptation is chosen: individuals with high levels of social support are less likely to respond to strain with crime compared to those with less social support.

What crime prevention strategies are suggested by strain theories? An obvious recommendation they would make is to reduce the occurrence of problematic strains in individuals' lives. For example, we could provide housing subsidies for the poor, increase welfare programs, provide educational or job training programs, and seek to reduce or eliminate racial and ethnic discrimination. This theory would also advocate for programs that help individuals more positively cope with life stress. We might, for example, teach people how to recognize and respond to the physiological signs of stress (e.g., increased heartbeat, difficulty breathing) or anger (e.g., clenched fists, reddening of the face) in non-violent and healthy ways.

Social learning theories assume that human nature is determined by socialization processes and that individuals are not inherently predisposed to either conventional or antisocial behavior. The central proposition is that children learn positive and negative behaviors, including crime, when interacting with others in social situations. Sutherland's (1947) **differential association theory** and Akers' (1985, 2009) **social learning theory** are the primary criminological theories in this tradition. These theories both assert that the more one is exposed to criminal role models and to the attitudes and values they convey, the more likely one will be to engage in crime. Associations with criminals allow an individual to learn both the techniques necessary to engage in an illegal behavior (since you are not born knowing how to pick a lock or hack into someone's bank account) and the attitudes that can promote and help to rationalize such behaviors. Learning processes also include imitation and reinforcement. In the first case, an individual who observes someone else commit an illegal behavior will be at risk for mimicking the behavior. Once participation in crime has occurred, its persistence is best explained by the extent to which it is reinforced – either encouraged, which leads to more offending, or discouraged, which should promote desistence.

Social learning theory serves as the foundation for many crime prevention programs, especially those that focus on minimizing exposure to risky family and peer influences – those social groups encountered relatively early in life and which are especially important to the individual. Programs for parents will emphasize the importance of modeling positive behaviors and refraining from committing illegal acts or sharing deviant attitudes with youth. They can also help parents be more aware of their children's behaviors, more effectively discipline children and discourage children's association with deviant peers. Schools can offer drug prevention curricula in order to adjust students' perceptions about the numbers of people who drink or use drugs, so that it is not considered to be common and acceptable behavior. Likewise, these programs may have adolescents consider the negative consequences of using drugs (e.g., smoking makes you smell bad and cigarettes cost a lot of money) and practice declining a peer's offer to use drugs.

Social control theories assume that humans are basically hedonistic and driven by the need to satisfy their own needs and desires, which creates a natural tendency to engage in crime. The central theories in this tradition are Hirschi's (1969) **social control/bonding theory** and Gottfredson and Hirschi's (1990) **general theory of crime**. The first focuses on the importance of having strong emotional attachments or bonds to others, which act as informal and indirect social controls. We are more likely to conform to the rules and expectations set by those we respect and care about even when they are not actively trying to control our behavior because we do not want to jeopardize our relationships or disappoint those who care about us. The second theory prioritizes the role of internal self-control; people with strong self-control should be able to stop themselves from acting on their desires and impulses and from committing crime when faced with opportunities to do so.

These theories have clear and logical applications for crime prevention: to prevent crime and/keep criminal impulses in check, we must externally apply controls, strengthen bonds, and/or create strong internal controls in individuals. Attempts to increase external controls may include formal actions by law enforcement officers or informal actions by teachers or parents who set and enforce rules for behavior. To increase bonds, we could increase individuals' involvement in conventional activities and strengthen their beliefs in the norms and rules of society. To increase self-control, we could help individuals better regulate their impulses and emotions and help them evaluate the consequences of their actions.

We discussed several examples of **integrated theories** in Chapter 2, including those proposed by Elliott and colleagues (Elliott, 1985; Elliott, Ageton, and Canter, 1979), **Interactional Theory** (Thornberry, 1987; Thornberry *et al.*, 1991), and the **Social Development Model** (Catalano and Hawkins, 1996). The last two theories include an integration of social control and social learning theories, and Elliott and colleagues also include strain theory. It is easy to see how these theories are related to the life course developmental paradigm. They all describe a chain of events that unfolds over the early stages of the life course, in which significant experiences in specific social contexts constitute turning points that influence the development of crime. In addition, they recognize that different people can follow different life course trajectories and that they may be influenced by different causal factors that lead them into crime. These theories have been used to explain not only the initiation into crime, but also continuity and desistance from crime, as well as particular life course trajectories followed by individuals (Catalano *et al.*, 2008; Elliott, Huizinga, and Menard, 1989; Thornberry and Krohn, 2008).

Prevention strategies based on integrated theories tend to be multifaceted and have the goal of implementing strategies recommended by all the theories included in the integrated model. In addition, they emphasize that these strategies take into account the developmental life stage/age of the individual and target the influences that are most likely to be affecting the particular population intended to receive services. (See Table 3.3 for a summary of all the theories that fall within the life course paradigm.)

A Public Health Approach to Crime Prevention

Although illegal behavior has always been the focus of law enforcement and other criminal justice agencies, crime is increasingly being considered a matter of public concern. This means that crime is now more likely to be viewed as having consequences for everyone. Clearly, crime is harmful to those who are victims of or commit illegal acts. Indeed, violence is responsible for 9% of all deaths worldwide among males aged 10–24 (Patton *et al.*, 2009) and is the second leading cause of death of all those aged 10–24 in the USA (Centers for Disease Control and Prevention, 2015). In addition,

Table 3.3   Theories within the life course developmental paradigm.

Theory	Definition	Crime prevention strategies suggested by the theory
Strain	Crime is produced by strains and stressors that create pressures that must be alleviated	• School curricula to improve social-emotional learning • Job training programs
Social learning	Crime is learned through interactions with others	• Drug or violence prevention curricula helping children resist peer or media influences to use drugs or be aggressive
Social control	Crime is more likely to occur when internal, external, and indirect controls are weak	• Parent training programs that improve child management and discipline skills • Mentoring programs
Integrated	Many factors influence crime and their effects may differ across individuals and stages of development	• Multiple component programs targeting multiple causes of crime • Developmentally sensitive interventions that address causal factors when they are most influential

offenders are more likely to self-report the use and/or abuse of illegal drugs compared to non-offenders and to have mental and physical health problems. Those involved in the criminal justice system must also contend with the social stigma that follows from having a criminal record and from the subsequent lack of access to important services and/or social processes (e.g., being unable to vote, having more difficulty finding employment, etc.).

We also know that people do not have to directly experience crime, as perpetrators or victims, to be harmed by it. Given that significant tax dollars are spent to prevent crime and punish criminals, we all suffer when crime rates are elevated. There is also evidence that **vicarious victimization** (Agnew, 2006) – hearing about or witnessing crimes perpetrated against others – can cause stress, emotional trauma, and fear of crime, particularly when loved ones are victimized. For all of these reasons, crime can be seen as threatening the health and well-being of the general public, similar to other serious problems such as poverty, obesity, and cancer.

Viewing crime as a public health problem has increased public support for crime prevention and generated demand for broader-based actions to reduce crime that extend beyond law enforcement. Such efforts are modeled after the medical and public health approaches to reducing disease and other health problems. These perspectives emphasize the importance of *early* and *proactive activities*

> An ounce of prevention is worth a pound of cure.
> Ben Franklin

that will alter the factors that lead to disease or increase the risk of disease. This orientation is in contrast to *reactive* efforts that are implemented after problems have emerged. That is, instead of waiting until an individual becomes sick, then trying to treat the disease, public health approaches try to reduce the chance that illness will occur.

As an example, consider how we might prevent heart disease using a public health approach. First, we would identify the factors that scientific studies have shown to influence, either positively or negatively, the potential that an individual will develop this sickness. These factors include stress and poor diets, which increase the risk for heart disease, and regular exercise, which reduces its chances of occurring. Secondly, we would create and test a strategy designed to reduce the factors that make heart disease more likely and to increase the factors that make it less likely to develop. To prevent heart disease, then, we might teach individuals strategies to effectively manage stress (e.g., practice yoga, reduce caffeine intake, etc.) and encourage them to eat healthier meals and engage in regular exercise.

Extending this logic to the prevention of crime, rather than wait until crimes are committed and responding with punishments, we want to reduce the probability that individuals will break the law. Doing so requires that we first identify the factors that increase or decrease the likelihood of illegal behavior and then create and test strategies to change these factors. In the next section, we will describe more fully the progress that has been made in identifying the causes of offending. For now, consider what preventive actions might be put in place if there was evidence that academic failure during elementary school increased the likelihood of adolescent delinquency. What might we do based on this knowledge? One strategy would be to encourage parents and schools to enroll children with low grades in tutoring programs. What action could be taken if it was clear that steady employment reduced the probability of offending? This information would suggest increasing access to educational and job training.

Risk and Protective Factors Related to Crime

We have already mentioned several times and will continue to emphasize in this text that crime prevention strategies should try to change the factors that have been identified in theories and shown in scientific studies to affect criminal behavior. These influences are called **risk factors** and **protective factors**. They are the circumstances or experiences encountered during life that predict the onset and/or persistence of crime. **Risk factors** increase the likelihood that one will engage in an illegal act; for example, academic failure as described in the earlier example. **Protective factors** reduce, counteract, or buffer the impact of risk factors; that is, risks have weaker influence on criminal behavior when protective factors are present (Rutter, 1985; US Department of Health and Human Services, 2001).[1] Risk and protective factors can be encountered in all stages of the life course. As shown in Table 3.4, they include characteristics and experiences associated with individuals and with the social contexts of families, peer groups, schools, and neighborhoods.

How do we know which risk and protective factors actually affect crime? As we have discussed, the first place to start looking is criminological theory, since its goal is to explain criminal behavior. To be sure that factors discussed in theories do, in fact, lead to offending, we must also consult findings from scientific research. Longitudinal studies, which follow individuals over time to investigate how their encounters with risk and protective factors subsequently affect their criminal behavior, provide strong evidence that these factors increase and/or decrease offending (US Department of Health and Human Services, 2001). Keep in mind, however, that the strongest evidence of causality comes from criminological experiments which intentionally change a risk or protective factor then measure its effect on crime.

Longitudinal studies typically rely on self-report surveys rather than official data to assess the impact of risk and protective factors on offending. Although official data can provide information on

Table 3.4 Risk and protective factors associated with adolescent delinquency.

Type of influence	Risk factor	Protective factor
Individual	• Childhood behavioral problems (e.g., conduct disorder, hyperactivity) • Temperament/disposition (e.g., low self-control, impulsivity, having a preference for risk taking) • Antisocial attitudes (e.g., holding a belief that violence or law-breaking is acceptable) • Exposure to violence	• High intelligence • Religiosity • Positive social orientation • Strong moral beliefs opposed to deviance
Family	• Poverty • Child neglect and abuse • Parental conflict • Poor child management (low or inconsistent levels of monitoring, discipline, and supervision) • Parental substance abuse or criminality	• Warm and supportive relationships with parents or other adults • Parent involvement in school and support for child's education
Peer group	• Delinquent peers • Gang membership • Social rejection by peers	• Friends who engage in conventional behavior
School	• Academic failure	• Commitment to school • Involvement in conventional activities
Community	• High rates of crime • Concentration of poor residents • Concentration of single-parent families	• Collective efficacy • Close ties between neighbors

Source: Hawkins *et al.*, 1998; Lipsey and Derzon, 1998; Losel and Farrington, 2012; US Department of Health and Human Services, 2001. See also http://www.cdc.gov/violenceprevention/youthviolence/riskprotectivefactors.html.

offenders' demographic characteristics (e.g., sex, race/ethnicity, age, and possibly socioeconomic status), these are generally stable qualities that cannot be changed using crime prevention strategies. Self-report surveys are a better source for information on experiences that can potentially be modified using crime prevention strategies. These surveys ask individuals to report whether or not or how often they have encountered risk and protective factors of various types, and they also gather information on illegal behaviors, which allows the researcher to assess the degree to which the former impact the latter.

> The **Communities That Care Youth Survey** developed by the Social Development Research Group http://www.sdrg.org/ctcresource/CTC_Youth_Survey_2006.pdf and the **School Climate Surveys** from the Center for the Study and Prevention of Violence http://www.colorado.edu/cspv/safeschools/surveys.html are both self-report surveys which measure risk and protective factors and involvement in crime. We encourage you to read through these surveys to see for yourselves how they ask about a variety of experiences that can affect crime.

When this information is gathered multiple times during a person's life, as in longitudinal studies, the ability to detect whether or not risk and protective factors lead to crime is facilitated.

According to information from longitudinal self-report studies, many different risk and protective factors affect illicit substance use and other types of crime. Table 3.4 lists factors shown in multiple studies conducted with children and adolescents to be related to illegal behaviors among youth. Although there is much support for the risk and protective factors listed here, scientists disagree as to which risk and protective factors are most influential. There is no agreed-upon list of risk and protective factors and some sources will have different lists than others, primarily as a result of requiring different levels of evidence to establish that such factors actually predict crime. It is also true that we currently know more about individual and family risk factors compared to risk factors in the peer, school, and neighborhood contexts. In addition, there has been less investigation of protective factors compared to risk factors (US Department of Health and Human Services, 2001), and fewer self-report studies have attempted to measure risk and protective factors that influence the offending of adults compared to youths.

There is also some disagreement as to how to measure risk and protective factors (Losel and Farrington, 2012). In some research, a particular variable may be identified as both a risk and a protective factor; for example, low intelligence is sometimes considered a risk factor for offending, while high intelligence is considered to be a protective factor. In general, we prefer not to measure risk and protective factors in this way. If risk factors are just the opposite of protective factors, distinguishing between the two is not very useful (Hall, Simon, Mercy, *et al.*, 2012; US Department of Health and Human Services, 2001). To be most meaningful, risk and protective factors should assess separate constructs, not the same factor at opposite ends of the spectrum. For example, holding beliefs favorable to violence can be viewed as a risk factor that is separate from and not simply the absence of having strong moral beliefs, which is a protective factor. Similarly, religiosity is commonly viewed as a protective factor, but failing to attend religious services is not seen as a risk factor.

To what degree do risk and protective factors predict crime?

Longitudinal studies provide information about the risk and protective factors that affect involvement in crime, but it is important to understand that these relationships are *predictive*, on average, for the whole set of persons reporting exposure to particular risk and protective factors. They do not necessarily apply to each individual person who is studied; they are not *proscriptive*. In other words, an individual who encounters a risk factor has a greater probability of offending compared to someone who does not experience the same risk factor, but criminal behavior does not automatically follow from risk exposure (US Department of Health and Human Services, 2001). For example, doing poorly in school is a risk factor for violence, meaning that, among all students doing poorly in school, a higher proportion will be violent compared to the proportion of all students doing well in school who are violent.

> *One of the things I learned is that you've got to deal with the underlying social problems if you want to have an impact on crime – that it's not a coincidence that you see the greatest amount of violent crime where you see the greatest amount of social dysfunction.*
>
> Eric Holder, former US Attorney General

But not all individual youth with low grades will engage in violence. The prediction applies to the group of students with low grades, not to specific individuals. Knowing the degree to which one faces risk and protection can help us predict who may become involved in crime, but we cannot know with certainty that offending will occur for any one individual based on his/her exposure to risk and protective factors.

We also know that humans are vastly different from one another. Just consider your siblings, close friends, or romantic partners: although you may have similar interests and sometimes act in similar ways, you are likely to be affected in different ways by the same experience. In addition, what is most important in shaping your behavior may be different from that affecting your significant other(s). Moreover, individuals vary in their levels of exposure to risk. For example, members of minority racial/ethnic groups are much more likely than Caucasians to live in risky, high poverty, high-crime neighborhoods (Sampson, 2012; Wilson, 1987), and males are more likely than females to experience victimization committed by strangers or acquaintances (Finkelhor *et al.*, 2009; Lauritsen and Heimer, 2008). Research has also shown that risk factors have different effects on individuals depending on their genetic make-up (Belsky and Pluess, 2009; Simons *et al.*, 2011).

As we have already mentioned, research in the life course development paradigm has shown that different risk and protective factors affect involvement in crime at different stages of the life course (Catalano and Hawkins, 1996; Moffitt, 1993; Sampson and Laub, 1993). During early childhood, individuals spend the most time with parents and other family members, making family risk and protective factors such as child maltreatment, parental monitoring and supervision of children and close, positive relationships with parents most important (Thornberry, 1987). During middle childhood and adolescence, school and peer experiences become more influential (Cleveland *et al.*, 2008; Elliott, Huizinga, and Ageton, 1985). For adults, community factors gain influence, as do employment and romantic relationships (Sampson and Laub, 1993). Even more complicated, some experiences may act as a risk factor at one stage of life and a protective factor at another time. For example, romantic relationships have been shown to increase the likelihood of delinquency among girls (Haynie, 2003) but to decrease crime among women (Petras, Nieuwbeerta, and Piquero, 2010). Working more than 20 hours per week before graduation from high school increases the risk of crime and drug use for teens, but employment acts as a protective factor after graduation (Mihalic and Elliott, 1997). It is also true that some risk and protective factors have stable effects throughout life. For example, having a preference for risk-taking and being unable to control one's impulses can affect criminal involvement at all ages (US Department of Health and Human Services, 2001).

Variation in the impact of risk and protective factors means that efforts to prevent crime may have differing levels of success for different groups, depending on their age, demographic characteristics, and other attributes. It also means that, to have maximum impact, the content of a program should try to change the risk and protective factors that are most likely to occur and to be influential for the group targeted to receive the intervention. To do so, those who create prevention strategies must be familiar with both theories of crime and empirical studies that test these theories, especially longitudinal research that indicates how influences may change over one's lifetime. Our descriptions of effective interventions in Section III will describe the risk and protective factors targeted by each program, the age(s) of the population targeted by the program and, when the information is available, the degree to which the intervention has shown variation in effectiveness for different individuals.

How does experiencing many risk and protective factors affect criminal involvement?

Have you heard the expression: "*What doesn't kill you makes you stronger*"? The idea behind this quote is that human beings are resilient: we can bounce back from hardships, although there are limits in how successful we will be in doing so. In criminology, studies show that individuals who encounter just a few risk factors are no more likely to engage in crime than those experiencing no risk factors. However, the more risk factors one is exposed to, the greater the likelihood of engaging in crime (Bry, McKeon, and Pandina, 1982; Coie *et al.*, 1993). For example, a longitudinal study showed that Seattle youth reporting more than five risk factors when aged 10 were 10 times more likely to engage in violence at age 18 compared to those who experienced zero or one risk factor (Herrenkohl *et al.*, 2000). Some call this a **dose–response** relationship (Losel and Farrington, 2012) meaning that, as the number or dose of risk factors increases, the odds of substance use, delinquency, and violence also increases (Newcomb, Maddahian, and Bentler, 1986; Stoddard, Zimmerman, and Bauermeister, 2012; Wikstrom and Loeber, 2000).

Although somewhat less frequently examined, protective factors appear to operate in the same way: the more protection experienced, the less likely one is to offend (Ostaszewski and Zimmerman, 2006; Stoddard *et al*, 2012). In a longitudinal study of teenage boys in Pittsburgh, Stouthamer-Loeber and colleagues (2002) found that 22% to 37% of the study participants engaged in persistent and serious offending during mid- to late-adolescence. For those reporting no protective factors, 41% to 66% became serious offenders, but among those who reported five or six protective factors, none (0%) became persistent, serious offenders.

These findings indicate that it is the accumulation of risk and protection that has the strongest potential to predict criminal behavior. However, such relationships are not completely straightforward. There are four reasons to be cautious when trying to determine the collective impact of risk and protective factors. *First*, research has not yet examined the extent to which the effects of different risk factors are independent from one another. Likewise, individual protective factors may or may not be independent predictors of less crime. As a result, we do not know whether the effect of one factor is totally separate from another or if their effects on crime overlap. There is good reason to believe that there is some overlap and that they may be measuring, to some degree, the same type of causal influence. For example, the impact of parent divorce and family conflict are likely to be related; the effect of one will largely capture the same effect on crime as the other.

Second, the predictive strength of individual risk and protective factors varies. Some have a greater impact on crime than others. For example, having delinquent peers is a much stronger predictor of subsequent offending than frequently watching violent movies (US Department of Health and Human Services, 2001).

Third, there is some evidence people differ in the number of risk and protective factors they have to experience before their involvement in crime is affected (Stoddard *et al.*, 2012). Some people have a very low threshold, or tolerance, for risk, while others have very high thresholds. For example, in the television show *Breaking Bad*, the main character, Walter White, begins producing and selling crystal meth after he has been diagnosed with cancer. However, his son Walt Jr., who has significant physical disabilities caused by cerebral palsy, a father diagnosed with cancer, a mother who is pregnant (no doubt embarrassing for a teenager) and who is in the risky developmental stage of adolescence is able to refrain from crime.

Fourth, we cannot simply add up the number of factors reported and calculate exactly how likely crime will be for any one person (Losel and Farrington, 2012). It is not necessarily true that those experiencing four risk factors will be twice as likely to engage in crime than those experiencing two risk factors, or that those with nine protective factors will be three times less likely to engage in crime than those experiencing three protective factors.

How can this information be used in crime prevention efforts? The most obvious implication is that, to have the best chance of reducing crime, an intervention should try to change the most influential and greatest number of risk and protective factors possible (Coie *et al.*, 1993). As we will discuss in Section III, **boot camps** try to increase discipline and self-control among offenders, and although they have been frequently used to try to reduce recidivism, there is no evidence that they are effective (MacKenzie, 2000). This may be because they only focus on changing one or two individual risk factors. They make no attempt to change family, school, peer, or community relationships that also impact youth offending. In contrast, **Multisystemic Therapy**, which tries to improve parent–child relationships, reduce the negative influence of delinquent peers and improve teenagers' commitment to school has been shown in multiple studies to reduce recidivism among youth offenders (Henggeler, 2011).

The impact of risk and protection on multiple problem behaviors

Although this textbook is focused on crime prevention, it is well known that negative behaviors cluster together and co-occur (Huizinga *et al.*, 2000; Jessor and Jessor, 1977; Tolan and Gorman-Smith, 1998). That is, those who engage in crime are also more likely to be unemployed or employed in low-paying jobs, suffer from substance abuse and addiction, engage in other risky behaviors such as drunk driving, have failed marriages, and have poor physical and/or mental health (Gottfredson and Hirschi, 1990). Given this pattern, it should not be surprising to learn that a particular risk factor can make crime more likely *and* increase the potential for other related problem behaviors (Coie *et al.*, 1993). For example, living in a high poverty, high crime neighborhood can increase the likelihood of aggression and violence, as well as victimization, school drop-out, unemployment, and mental health problems (McLoyd, 1998; Sampson, 2012).

These findings have encouraging implications for crime prevention. By targeting risk and protective factors in order to reduce crime, we can also reduce other public health problems. Prevention efforts can thus have a large pay-off. For example, the **Multisystemic Therapy** program just mentioned has been shown to lower rates of youth offending; to reduce mental health problems, school drop-out and substance abuse; and to improve social skills among youth who receive treatment (Henggeler, 2011). Implementing effective prevention programs can also result in significant financial benefits. As we will discuss in Section IV, when we prevent crimes from occurring, we also reduce the costs associated with law enforcement and the operation of the criminal justice system. When these services also improve educational outcomes and mental health and lower the likelihood of substance use and abuse, additional financial benefits are seen. We save money by not having to provide as many individuals with drug and psychiatric treatment services, and we have a better educated and more productive workforce (Washington State Institute for Public Policy, 2014).

Prevention Science

The multiple benefits of effective prevention are emphasized in the developing field of **prevention science**. Similar to the **public health** approach we described earlier, the goal of prevention science is to prevent major social problems and dysfunctions (Coie *et al.*, 1993: 1013) such as crime, physical illness, mental health problems, substance abuse, obesity, and HIV/AIDS. According to this perspective, the best way to prevent these problems is to reduce the risk factors and strengthen the protective factors associated with these outcomes. Prevention science is also concerned with ensuring healthy outcomes and positive development among children and adults, which can also be achieved by lowering risk and increasing protection (Botvin and Griffin, 2005).

The field of prevention science has rapidly progressed over the last few decades. A professional organization (the Society for Prevention Research; http://www.preventionresearch.org/) has been formed to help academics, practitioners, and policymakers from diverse disciplines share their work with one another. These include criminologists as well as professionals working in education, medicine, psychology, public health, social work, and sociology. What unites all of these individuals is the use of a scientific approach to conducting research intended to prevent problems and improve well-being.

The scientific approach to prevention means starting with theory. Prevention scientists draw from multiple theories to develop interventions that will attack the causes of crime and interrupt the processes that make offending more likely. That is, they create interventions that attempt to minimize risk factors and enhance protective factors identified as important in theory. The next step in the scientific process is to test the ability of these interventions to reduce crime and related problem behaviors in rigorous, well-conducted experiments. As we will explain in Chapter 4, methods for testing interventions can vary significantly in their quality. Prevention scientists use the most appropriate and strongest possible research designs to test programs' effectiveness in order to increase public confidence in their results. They also use appropriate statistical procedures to identify whether or not and how much crime is actually reduced for those involved in the prevention program. Ideally, interventions are re-tested under different conditions and with different populations to ensure their findings can apply in many different situations and for as many people as possible. The last steps in the prevention science approach are to compile the results of experimental studies, share information about what works with governmental and public agencies and use the findings to guide future research (Botvin and Griffin, 2005).

Types of Crime Prevention

Universal, selective, and indicated crime prevention strategies

Prevention strategies that are based on criminological theories and tested using scientific methods can take many different forms. One way of classifying interventions is according to the types of individuals or groups for whom they are intended. Following the public health and prevention science perspectives, we will classify interventions as **universal**, **selective**, and **indicated**, as defined in Table 3.5 (Mrazek and Haggerty, 1994; National Research Council and Institute of Medicine,

Table 3.5 Universal, selective, and indicated crime prevention strategies.

Type	Intended population	Examples of crime prevention strategies
Universal	All individuals in a general setting (e.g., a community, school, or demographic group)	• School-wide anti-bullying program • Neighborhood watch program
Selective	Individuals, groups, or settings known to have experienced one or more risk factors	• Head Start educational services for low-income families • Mentoring for youth from single-parent families
Indicated	Individuals who have already begun to engage in crime	• Drug courts • Boot camps

2009). **Universal** preventive interventions are intended for the general public or for all the individuals in a particular setting, regardless of whether or not they have begun to engage in crime or have experienced any risk or protective factors. For example, if a prevention program were offered to all students in a middle school, it would be considered to be universal. Similarly, universal prevention programs could be implemented with all students entering college or with all residents of a particular neighborhood. **Selective** preventive efforts are intended for individuals or groups considered to be at risk for engaging in crime because they are known to have already experienced one or more risk factors and/or to have low levels of protection. For example, students who are not doing well at school might be offered a selective tutoring program, and families living in high-poverty and violent neighborhoods might be the focus of selective family-focused or community-based interventions. **Indicated** preventive strategies are offered to individuals who are already engaging in crime, but who are doing so at relatively low levels. For example, youth or adults who have had their first contact with the correctional system could participate in an indicated prevention program to increase the likelihood they will not continue or escalate their offending.

Prior to 1994, the fields of medicine and public health used a different classification of programs. They identified interventions as being **primary**, **secondary**, and **tertiary** (Mrazek and Haggerty, 1994). In this classification, only **primary** programs were considered true prevention programs – interventions that tried to decrease the onset of crime and other physical and mental health problems. **Secondary** programs were considered "interventions" to be used with those already engaging in crime and/or displaying problems. **Tertiary** programs were "treatment" programs for those who had a definite disorder requiring intervention. The new classification system was developed to better clarify the differences in risk for engaging in crime across individuals, to better reflect the differences in service needs for different individuals and to expand the types of activities included in the prevention phase (Mrazek and Haggerty, 1994). Thus, under the new system, universal, selective, and indicated interventions are all considered prevention options. The distinction between prevention and treatment has also been clarified, with treatment programs reserved for persons who have a formal diagnosis of a disorder; for example, those with an antisocial personality disorder, those with a substance abuse disorder, or those with a psychopath disorder.

Although the categories of primary, secondary, and tertiary prevention have historically been used by criminologists to classify crime prevention programs (Lab, 2014; US Department of Health and

Human Services, 2001), we will use the new classification system differentiating universal, selective, and indicated interventions given its greater clarity, expanded recognition of prevention approaches and widespread usage in public health and prevention science. In Section III, we will identify effective prevention programs as being universal, selective, or indicated.

In Section IV, we will describe some of the challenges faced by communities when deciding whether it is best to implement universal, selective, or indicated strategies. There is debate about whether services should be directed at the general population, those at greater risk for becoming involved in crime, or those who are already engaging in serious, frequent offending. Those in favor of implementing universal interventions point out two main advantages: (i) Even if the majority of the population will not offend or will engage only in minor offenses, universal services can reach more individuals. In contrast, the higher risk individuals targeted by selective and indicated programs make up a relatively small percentage of the population (Rose, 1985). (ii) Universal interventions can affect the larger environments in which individuals reside without having to target and change particular individuals. For example, a school-based bullying prevention program might be able to change the policies and climate of an entire school, reinforcing the message for all students that bullying will not be tolerated.

Those in favor of selective and indicated approaches also make two arguments: (i) Providing services to individuals who may never break the law is a waste of resources. In contrast, higher risk groups will likely see greater benefits from participation in a crime prevention strategy (Andrews et al., 1990; Lipsey, 2009), making this approach more cost effective (Aos et al., 2004). (ii) Society is obligated to provide services to at-risk groups (e.g., members of racial/ethnic minority groups or those from low socioeconomic backgrounds), because doing so can help reduce social disparities and inequalities in those who are most likely to end up in prison (Frohlich and Potvin, 2008).

These controversies are difficult to resolve and each set of arguments has merit. In fact, the strategy we recommend is to offer a range of services that reaches all population groups, from those who may never participate in crime to those who are most likely to do so. In doing so, however, we must remember that it will be very difficult to identify with certainty who will become involved in crime, given that exposure to risk and protective factors does not automatically lead to offending (i.e., these factors are predictive but not proscriptive). Moreover, identifying and seeking out high-risk groups for services can backfire. There is evidence that labeling individuals as potential or actual offenders can increase their future involvement of crime by negatively affecting their self-concept and their interactions with others (Becker, 1963). Prevention efforts that focus on higher risk individuals must be careful to avoid stigmatizing these populations.

Situational/environmental, social context, and individual crime prevention strategies

A second way of categorizing crime prevention strategies, and how we will organize Section III of this text, is according to the setting or level at which they seek to make changes. Interventions can try to change: (i) the situations, physical environments or places in which crimes are likely to occur; (ii) the social contexts and/or social interactions that give rise to crime; and (iii) characteristics of individuals which affect their criminal behavior (see Table 3.6). The first group includes **situational and environmental** crime prevention practices and policies, such as **place-based** interventions

Table 3.6 Situational/environmental, social context, and individual crime prevention strategies.

Type	Intended target(s)	Examples of crime prevention strategies
Situational/ environmental	Changes in *places* (neighborhoods, streets, and buildings) to reduce opportunities for crime and in *law enforcement practices* to increase the likelihood that offenders will be caught and punished	• Installing locks and improving security procedures in campus dormitories • Installing ignition locks and Breathalyzers in cars • Hot spots policing • Increasing the minimum drinking age from 18 to 21
Social context	Changes in the organization, structure and/or relationships occurring in *peer, family, school, and neighborhood groups*	• Parent training programs • School climate change efforts • Gang prevention programs
Individual	Changes in risk and protective factors that affect *individuals*	• School curricula to improve child social skills or drug resistance skills • Afterschool programming

and **Crime Prevention Through Environmental Design (CPTED)**. These interventions try to change the physical features of places (neighborhoods, streets, or buildings) in which crimes are likely to occur. They may also focus on reducing opportunities that can give rise to crimes, making crimes more difficult to commit and increasing the likelihood of arrest. For example, efforts may be taken to make homes or commercial buildings more difficult to burglarize (by installing better locks or brighter lighting), bar fights less likely to occur (by increasing staff or educating servers about how to recognize intoxicated patrons), and neighborhoods less attractive to criminals (e.g., by tearing down abandoned buildings). Law enforcement practices and criminal justice policies which increase the probability that crimes will be detected and offenders punished can also fit under this heading.

The second category includes interventions designed to change aspects of the **family, school, peer group, and community context** which can affect crime. These strategies may focus on altering the organization of these groups or improving the social relationships and interactions that take place in these environments. For example, some family-based programs teach parents and children to more effectively communicate; school-wide interventions may try to change school rules, policies, or interactions between administrators, staff, and students; gang prevention programs try to weaken the gang's structure and hierarchy and prevent youth from joining gangs; and neighborhood efforts may try to reduce social disorganization and improve residents' trust and collaboration.

Finally, **individually focused** interventions seek to change individual risk and protective factors, improve how individuals respond to life events, and provide skills in how to effectively communicate and interact with others. For example, early childhood education programs provide children in nursery school with high-quality educational services so they can be better prepared for later school experiences. Other individually focused programs help children, teenagers, or adults improve their ability to regulate emotions, respond to stress more effectively, make better decisions without acting impulsively and/or resist social influences to engage in offending.

These three types of crime prevention have some overlap, making these distinctions somewhat arbitrary. We will do our best to classify interventions into one category or another but will also indicate when interventions fit into multiple types of programming.

Programs, policies, and practices

One last way of classifying prevention efforts is to differentiate programs from practices and policies (see Table 3.7). These terms are often used interchangeably but they do refer to different approaches. A **prevention program** is based on one or more theories of crime and tries to change risk and protective factors and mechanisms shown to affect crimes among particular populations. Programs have specific delivery requirements that are clearly outlined for the program implementer to follow, including not only content or activities to be covered, but also protocols and procedures that should be followed during implementation (e.g., requirements regarding the credentials of program implementers, number of program lessons, number of participants per implementer, how often discussions or role plays must be incorporated into the intervention, etc.). Furthermore, programs should include a package of services that includes implementation manuals detailing program protocols, opportunities for implementers to be trained and to receive consultation from program developers or trainers during delivery, and tools that will allow them to monitor their performance, identify challenges if they arise and implement solutions to these problems (Elliott, 2013).

Prevention practices are more general strategies, approaches, or procedures that utilize similar, but not necessarily the same activities to reduce crime or other problems (http://www.crimesolutions.gov/about_whyprogs_pracs.aspx). Tutoring, mentoring, and community policing can all be considered crime prevention practices. These practices may be incorporated into many different interventions in many different ways. For example, tutoring provides additional instructional assistance to students who are not doing well in school but specific tutoring interventions can differ in the number or duration of sessions being offered, characteristics of participants, credentials of implementers, and specific goals or outcomes targeted for change. Practices are considered effective when evidence from multiple evaluations of studies that involved implementation of the general practice indicates that the strategy was shown, on average, to reduce crime (Elliott, 2013).

Table 3.7 Prevention programs, practices, and policies.

Type	Definition	Examples of crime prevention strategies
Programs	Set of specific activities with defined protocols, manuals, and methods of delivery	• Drug Abuse Resistance Education (D.A.R.E.) • Functional Family Therapy • Perry Preschool program
Practices	General type of approach which can be used as part of many specific programs	• Mentoring • Drug counseling • Prison-based vocational training
Policies	Regulations or laws intended to reduce crime across large populations	• Increasing the minimum drinking age from 18 to 21 • Three Strikes laws

Prevention policies seek broad reductions in crime across a large population. They are not directed towards individuals but try to affect much larger groups, such as all youth attending a school, all residents of a neighborhood, or all citizens of a country (http://www.thecommunityguide.org/uses/policy_development.html). Policies are usually enacted by local, state, or federal decision-makers, such as heads of agencies (e.g., schools or philanthropic institutions) or law-makers (Dickerson, Haggerty, and Catalano, 2011). They usually take the form of regulations and/or laws that govern the behavior of a particular population. For example, school rules against bullying, restrictions on alcohol sales and laws restricting gun carrying can all be considered prevention policies.

Although prevention programs, practices, and policies will all be reviewed in this book, more research has investigated the effectiveness of programs compared to practices and policies. As a result, more examples of the former than the latter will be identified. In Section III, when describing scientific studies testing the effectiveness of programs, practices, and policies, we will take care to use the term that best describes the type of strategy being reviewed. To avoid being too wordy or overly complicated, in the other chapters of this book, we will refer to preventive *interventions*, *strategies*, *efforts*, and *actions*. These are general terms that can indicate any type of prevention.

Crime Prevention Logic Models

In the next chapter, we will discuss in more detail how prevention strategies are created and tested. To preview this information, we want to introduce the concept of **logic models**. Logic models provide the foundation for all interventions and include a theoretical model and a change model. As you now know, to have the best chance of reducing crime, prevention efforts must be based on a theory that identifies the causal factors and processes that lead to criminal behaviors. So, when developing an intervention, one first decides on the theoretical model that will provide the foundation for the content of the program. The next step is to design an intervention that reduces the risk factors and/or enhances the protective factors identified in this theory. The specific factors to be changed, the processes that will be used to change them, and the participants or settings to be changed, should all be incorporated in this change model. The program designer defines these elements in advance and makes specific hypotheses regarding the particular attitudes and/or behaviors to be changed in the short term and long term. These hypotheses are then tested using strong scientific research methods.

It is useful for program developers to diagram their logic models in order to show visually both the content and targets of an intervention and its expected changes. Increasingly, funding agencies require that the logic model for a program be submitted with requests for a grant to implement or test it. Figure 3.3 provides an example of a crime prevention logic model for **the Project Towards No Drug Abuse (TND)** program. The content of the 12-lesson program is summarized on the left-hand side of the model, along with a description of the length and delivery format of the sessions. The hypothesized changes in attitudes/motivations and skills are outlined in the middle of the logic model, representing the most immediate outcomes to be produced by the program. The longer term impact on risk and protective factors, as well as behavioral changes in substance use and crime, are shown on the right-hand side of the logic model. Creating logic models such as this one allows the program

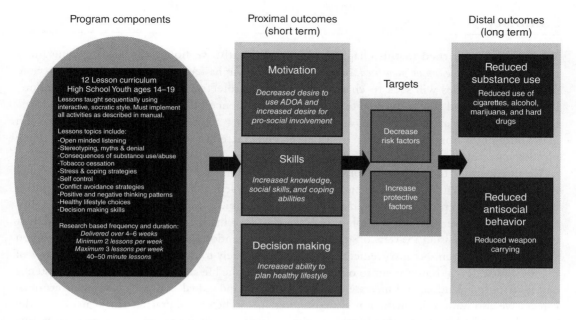

Figure 3.3 Example of the Project Towards No Drug Abuse (TND) logic model. Source: The Penn State Evidence-based Prevention and Intervention Support Center (EPISCenter); http://www.episcenter.psu.edu/sites/default/files/EPISCenter%27s%20Project%20TND%20Logic%20Model_4-4-12LAC.pdf

developer to carefully consider how the components of the intervention will produce anticipated changes in behavior. Sharing the logic model with potential participants and implementers is also helpful, as it can quickly communicate the nature of the program and its expected benefits.

When designing their programs and logic models, it is important for developers to consider the **malleability** of risk and protective factors associated with crime: that is, the degree to which these factors can actually be changed. As discussed earlier, certain demographic characteristics (e.g., age and gender) and genetic predispositions have been linked to offending, but we cannot alter these individual characteristics. Certain societal, structural, or cultural processes shown to affect crime may also prove very difficult to change, such as beliefs that individuals have the right to carry guns or the percentage of the population living in poverty. Even if these influences are identified as important causes of crime, it may not be feasible to design and test prevention programs that target these factors.

It is also important for the evaluation to assess whether or not the targeted risk and protective factors changed for those who received the intervention compared to those who did not, as well as whether or not crime was reduced. In our review, the final determination of whether or not prevention strategies are effective will be based on evidence indicating that they have been shown to reduce crime in high-quality, well-conducted scientific studies. If an intervention has affected only a risk or protective factor, but has not been shown to reduce offending, then it will not be considered effective and the validity of the underlying theory should be questioned.

Summary

What have you learned in this chapter? Most importantly, we hope you have become more convinced that *crime can be prevented*. In this chapter, we emphasized that the most effective crime prevention strategies will seek to change the risk and protective factors identified in criminological theories and shown in scientific research to influence offending. Many different criminological theories exist, many risk and protective factors are described in these theories and many different crime prevention strategies have been created to reduce risk factors and increase protective factors.

We also discussed the fact that historically, crime prevention has been considered the responsibility of law enforcement, but today, crime is seen as a social problem affecting everyone. Taking a public health approach to crime prevention means involving multiple agencies and individuals in the delivery of prevention services. Prevention efforts can thus take many forms and target many different types of individuals using a variety of strategies. Crime prevention should certainly focus on children and adolescents, given that involvement in crime is most likely to begin during these early stages of the life course. It is also important to offer services later in the life course, to help reduce persistence and severity in offending and increase the likelihood that individuals will terminate their criminal careers. We also want to implement prevention programs, policies, and practices that can change the physical and social environments in which crime occurs, as well as the risk and protective factors that shape individual behavior.

Finally, it is important to remember that all crime prevention efforts must be well evaluated, using the strongest and most appropriate research methods possible. Only those that show reductions in crime using high-quality scientific evaluations provide convincing evidence of success. The next chapter will provide a crash course in research methods so that you become very familiar with what it takes to show success. Get ready!

Critical Thinking Questions and Practice Activities

1. Select two of the theories discussed in this chapter you find most interesting. Identify the factors each theory considers most important in affecting crime, then describe how these factors could be changed by a prevention program, practice, or policy.
2. Thinking back over your adolescent years, consider those times when you may have broken the law or been tempted to do so. Looking at the risk factors listed in Table 3.4, which had the strongest influence on your potential delinquency? Then, consider a time when you considered breaking the law but did not. Looking at the list of protective factors in Table 3.4, were any important in helping you refrain from delinquency? How so?
3. Go to the website for the EPISCenter at Pennsylvania State University: http://www.episcenter. psu.edu/. Select one of the evidence-based programs (EBPs) listed on the site and find its logic model. Based on the information shown in the logic model, what criminological theory do you think the program is based on? Why?

4. Now, select a different program from the EPISCenter list. Based on the program description and logic model, would you classify it as a universal, selective, or indicated program? Why?

5. Consider the differences between environmental/situational, social context, and individual crime prevention strategies summarized in Table 3.6. If you were advising your home town on which type of strategy to invest money in, which of the three would you recommend? Which do you think has the greatest potential to reduce crime? Why? Which of the three types do you think would be the most challenging to implement? Why?

6. Select a particular crime that interests you. Identify the risk and protective factors that you think influence it. Then, consider how this crime might be prevented. Would it be best to use a strategy that targets individual factors, social interactions/relationships, or environmental/situational factors? Why?

Endnote

1. **Promotive factors** (Sameroff, 2006; Stouthamer-Loeber *et al.*, 2002) and **direct protective factors** (Hall, Simon, Lee, *et al.*, 2012) have also been identified as circumstances or experiences which directly reduce the probability of delinquency and/or increase the likelihood of positive, non-criminal behaviors. Because these types of factors are not widely used in current prevention science, they will not be used in this text.

Helpful Websites (last accessed July 23, 2016)

- Society for Prevention Research: www.preventionresearch.org
  Describes the mission and activities of members of this academic society devoted to prevention science.
- EPISCenter, Pennsylvania State University: www.episcenter.psu.edu
  Provides logic models of many effective crime prevention programs.

Further Reading

- Coie, J. D., Watt, N. F., West, S. G., *et al.* 1993. The science of prevention: A conceptual framework and some directions for a national research program. *American Psychologist,* 48(10):1013–1022.
  Short, easy-to-understand summary of the principles of prevention science.
- US Department of Health and Human Services. 2001. Youth Violence: A Report of the Surgeon General. Rockville, MD: US Department of Health and Human Services.
  Chapter 4 defines and summarizes research on risk and protective factors related to crime.
- http://www.ca-sdfsc.org/docs/resources/SDFSC_IOM_Policy.pdf.
  Detailed discussion of the program classifications used by the Institute of Medicine.

References

Agnew, R. 1991. A longitudinal test of social control theory and delinquency. *Journal of Research in Crime and Delinquency,* 28:126–156.

Agnew, R. 2006. *Pressured Into Crime: An Overview of General Strain Theory.* Cary, NC: Roxbury Publishing Company.

Akers, R. L. 1985. *Deviant Behavior: A Social Learning Approach*, 3rd ed. Belmont, CA: Wadsworth.

Akers, R. L. 1997. *Criminological Theories*. Los Angeles, CA: Roxbury Publishing Company.

Akers, R. L. 2009. *Social Learning and Social Structure: A General Theory of Crime and Deviance*. New Brunswick, NJ: Transaction Publishers.

Andrews, D. A., Zinger, I., Hoge, R. D., *et al.* 1990. Does correctional treatment work? A clinically relevant and psychologically informed meta-analysis. *Criminology*, 28:369–404. doi: 10.1111/j.1745-9125.1990.tb01330.x

Aos, S., Lieb, R., Mayfield, J., Miller, M., and Pennucci, A. 2004. *Benefits and Costs of Prevention and Early Intervention Programs for Youth*. Olympia, WA: Washington State Institute for Public Policy.

Becker, H. S. 1963. *Outsiders: Studies in the Sociology of Deviance*. New York, NY: Macmillan.

Belsky, J., and Pluess, M. 2009. The nature (and nurture?) of plasticity in early human development. *Perspectives on Psychological Science*, 4:345–351.

Blumstein, A., Cohen, J., and Farrington, D. P. 1988. Criminal career research: Its value for criminology. *Criminology*, 26:1–35.

Blumstein, A., Cohen, J., Roth, J. A., and Visher, C. A. 1986. *Criminal Careers and "Career Criminals," Vol.* I. Report of the Panel on Research on Criminal Careers, National Research Council. Washington, DC: National Academies Press.

Botvin, G. J., and Griffin, K. W. 2005. Prevention science, drug abuse prevention, and Life Skills Training: Comments on the state of the science. *Journal of Experimental Criminology*, 1:63–78.

Bry, B. H., McKeon, P., and Pandina, R. J. 1982. Extent of drug use as a function of number of risk factors. *Journal of Abnormal Psychology*, 91:273–279.

Catalano, R. F., and Hawkins, J. D. 1996. The Social Development Model: A theory of antisocial behavior. In: J. D. Hawkins (ed.), *Delinquency and Crime: Current Theories*, pp. 149–197. New York, NY: Cambridge University Press.

Catalano, R. F., Park, J., Harachi, T. W., *et al.* 2008. Mediating the effects of poverty, gender, individual characteristics, and external constraints on antisocial behavior: A test of the Social Development Model and implications for developmental life-course theory. In: D. P. Farrington (ed.), *Integrated Developmental and Life-Course Theories of Offending*, pp. 93–123. New Brunswick, NJ: Transaction Publishers.

Centers for Disease Control and Prevention. 2015. Understanding youth violence: Fact sheet. Atlanta, GA: Centers for Disease Control, National Center for Injury Prevention and Control.

Clarke, R. V. 1995. Situational crime prevention. In: M. Tonry and D. P. Farrington (eds), *Crime and Justice, Building a Safer Society: Strategic Approaches to Crime Prevention*, pp. 91–150. Chicago, IL: The University of Chicago Press.

Cleveland, M. J., Feinberg, M. E., Bontempo, D. E., and Greenberg, M. T. 2008. The role of risk and protective factors in substance use across adolescence. *Journal of Adolescent Health*, 43:157–164.

Cloward, R., and Ohlin, L. 1960. *Delinquency and Opportunity*. Glencoe, IL: Free Press.

Coie, J. D., Watt, N. F., West, S. G., *et al.* 1993. The science of prevention: A conceptual framework and some directions for a national research program. *American Psychologist*, 48:1013–1022.

Cullen, F. T. 2011. Beyond adolescence-limited criminology: Choosing our future – the American Society of Criminology 2010 Sutherland address. *Criminology*, 49:287–330.

Dickerson, M. L., Haggerty, K. P., and Catalano, R. F. 2011. *The Use of Evidence-Based Policy for State and Local Decision Makers*. Seattle, WA: Social Development Research Group, School of Social Work, University of Washington.

Eck, J. E., and Guerette, R. T. 2012. Place-based crime prevention: Theory, evidence, and policy. In: B. C. Welsh and D. P. Farrington (eds), *The Oxford Handbook of Crime Prevention*, pp. 354–383. New York, NY: Oxford University Press.

Elder Jr., G. H. 1995. The life course paradigm: Social change and individual development. In: P. Moen, G. H. Elder Jr., and K. Luscher (eds), *Examining Lives in Context: Perspectives on the Ecology of Human Development*, pp. 101–139. Washington, DC: APA Press.

Elder Jr., G. H., and Caspi, A. 1990. Studying lives in a changing society: Sociological and personological explorations. In: A. I. Rabin, R. A. Zucker, R. A. Emmons, and S. Frank (eds), *Studying Persons and Lives*, pp. 201–247. New York, NY: Springer.

Elliott, D. S. 1985. The assumption that theories can be combined with increased explanatory power: Theoretical integration. In: R. F. Meier (ed.), *Theoretical Methods in Criminology*, pp. 123–149. Beverly Hills, CA: Sage.

Elliott, D. S. 1994. Serious violent offenders: Onset, developmental course, and termination – The American Society of Criminology 1993 Presidential Address. *Criminology*, 32:1–21. doi: 10.1111/j.1745-9125.1994. tb01144.x

Elliott, D. S. 2013. Crime prevention and intervention over the life course: Emerging trends and directions for future research. In: C. L. Gibson and M. D. Krohn (eds), *Handbook of Life-Course Criminology*, pp. 297–316. New York, NY: Springer.

Elliott, D. S., and Menard, S. 1996. Delinquent friends and delinquent behavior: Temporal and developmental patterns. In: J. D. Hawkins (ed.), *Delinquency and Crime: Current Theories*, pp. 28–67. Cambridge, England: Cambridge University Press.

Elliott, D. S., and Williams, K. R. 1995. *A Life Course Developmental Perspective*. Boulder, CO: Center for the Study and Prevention of Violence.

Elliott, D. S., Ageton, S. S., and Canter, R. J. 1979. An integrated theoretical perspective on delinquent behavior. *Journal of Research in Crime and Delinquency*, 16:1–27.

Elliott, D. S., Huizinga, D., and Ageton, S. S. 1985. *Explaining Delinquency and Drug Use*. Beverly Hills, CA: Sage.

Elliott, D. S., Huizinga, D., and Menard, S. 1989. *Multiple Problem Youth: Delinquency, Substance Use, and Mental Health Problems*. New York, NY: Springer-Verlag.

Farrington, D. P. 2003. Developmental and life-course criminology: Key theoretical and empirical issues – the 2002 Sutherland Award address. *Criminology*, 41:221–255.

Finkelhor, D., Turner, H. A., Ormrod, R. K., and Hamby, S. 2009. Violence, abuse, and crime exposure in a national sample of children and youth. *Pediatrics*, 124:1411–1423.

Frohlich, K. L., and Potvin, L. 2008. The inequality paradox: The population approach and vulnerable populations. *American Journal of Public Health*, 98:216–221.

Gottfredson, M. R., and Hirschi, T. 1990. *A General Theory of Crime*. Stanford, CA: Stanford University Press.

Hall, J. E., Simon, T. R., Lee, R. D., and Mercy, J. A. 2012. Implications of direct protective factors for public health research and prevention strategies to reduce youth violence. *American Journal of Preventive Medicine*, 43:S76–S83.

Hall, J. E., Simon, T. R., Mercy, J. A., *et al.* 2012. Centers for Disease Control and Prevention's expert panel on protective factors for youth violence perpetration: Background and overview. *American Journal of Preventive Medicine*, 43:S1–S7.

Hawkins, J. D., Herrenkohl, T. I., Farrington, D. P., *et al.* 1998. A review of predictors of youth violence. In: R. Loeber and D. P. Farrington (eds), *Serious and Violent Juvenile Offenders*, pp. 106–146. Thousand Oaks, CA: Sage.

Haynie, D. 2003. Contexts of risk? Explaining the link between girls' pubertal development and their delinquency involvement. *Social Forces*, 82:355–397.

Henggeler, S. W. 2011. Efficacy studies to large-scale transport: The development and validation of multisystemic therapy programs. *Annual Review of Clinical Psychology*, 7:351–381.

Herrenkohl, T. I., Maguin, E., Hill, K. G., *et al.* 2000. Developmental risk factors for youth violence. *Journal of Adolescent Health*, 26:176–186. doi: 10.1016/S1054-139X(99)00065-8

Hirschi, T. 1969. *Causes of Delinquency*. Berkeley, CA: University of California Press.

Huizinga, D., Loeber, R., Thornberry, T. P., and Cothern, L. 2000. Co-occurrence of delinquency and other problem behaviors. Washington, DC: US Department of Justice, Office of Juvenile Justice and Delinquency Prevention.

Jennings, W. G., and Reingle, J. M. 2012. On the number and shape of developmental/life-course violence, aggression, and delinquency trajectories: A state-of-the-art review. *Journal of Criminal Justice*, 40:472–489.

Jessor, R., and Jessor, S. L. 1977. *Problem Behavior and Psychosocial Development: A Longitudinal Study of Youth*. San Diego, CA: Academic Press.

Kuhn, T. S. 1996. *The Structure of Scientific Revolutions*, 3rd ed. Chicago, IL: University of Chicago Press.

Lab, S. P. 2014. *Crime Prevention: Approaches, Practices and Evaluations*, 8th ed. New Providence, NJ: Anderson Publishing.

Laudan, L. 1977. *Progress and Its Problems: Toward a Theory of Scientific Growth*. Berkeley, CA: University of California Press.

Lauritsen, J. L., and Heimer, K. 2008. The gender gap in violent victimization, 1973–2004. *Journal of Quantitative Criminology*, 24:125–147.

Lewin, K. 1951. Problems of research in social psychology. In: D. Cartwright (ed.), *Field Theory in Social Science: Selected Theoretical Papers*, pp. 155–169. New York, NY: Harper and Row.

Lipsey, M. W. 2009. The primary factors that characterize effective interventions with juvenile offenders: A meta-analytic overview. *Victims and Offenders*, 4:124–147.

Lipsey, M. W., and Derzon, J. H. 1998. Predictors of violent or serious delinquency in adolescence and early adulthood: A synthesis of longitudinal research. In: R. Loeber and D. P. Farrington (eds), *Serious and Violent Juvenile Offenders: Risk Factors and Successful Interventions*, pp. 86–105. Thousand Oaks, CA: Sage.

Lombroso, C. 1911. *Criminal Man: According to the Classification of Cesare Lombroso*. New York, NY: Putnam.

Losel, F., and Farrington, D. P. 2012. Direct protective and buffering protective factors in the development of youth violence. *American Journal of Preventive Medicine*, 43:S8–23.

MacKenzie, D. 2000. Evidence-based corrections: Identifying what works. *Crime and Delinquency*, 46:457–471.

McLoyd, V. C. 1998. Socioeconomic disadvantage and child development. *American Psychologist*, 53:185–204.

Mihalic, S., and Elliott, D. S. 1997. Short and long-term consequences of adolescent work. *Youth and Society*, 28:464–498.

Moffitt, T. E. 1993. Adolescence-limited and life-course persistent anti-social behavior: A developmental taxonomy. *Psychological Review*, 100:674–701.

Mrazek, P. J., and Haggerty, R. J. 1994. *Reducing Risks for Mental Disorders: Frontiers for Preventive Intervention Research*. Washington, DC: The National Academies Press.

Nagin, D. S., Farrington, D. P., and Moffitt, T. E. 1995. Life-course trajectories of different types of offenders. *Criminology*, 33:111–139.

National Research Council and Institute of Medicine. 2009. Preventing mental, emotional, and behavioral disorders among young people: Progress and possibilities. Washington, DC: The National Academies Press.

Newcomb, M. D., Maddahian, E., and Bentler, P. M. 1986. Risk factors for drug use among adolescents: Concurrent and longitudinal analyses. *American Journal of Public Health*, 76:525–531.

Ostaszewski, K., and Zimmerman, M. A. 2006. The effects of cumulative risks and promotive factors on urban adolescent alcohol and other drug use: A longitudinal study of resiliency. *American Journal of Community Psychology*, 38:237–249.

Patton, G. C., Coffey, C., Sawyer, S. M., *et al.* 2009. Global patterns of mortality in young people: A systematic analysis of population health data. *Lancet*, 374:881–892.

Petras, H., Nieuwbeerta, P., and Piquero, A. R. 2010. Participation and frequency during criminal careers across the life span. *Criminology*, 48:607–637.

Rose, G. 1985. Sick individuals and sick populations. *International Journal of Epidemiology*, 14:32–38.

Rutter, M. 1985. Resilience in the face of adversity: Protective factors and resistance to psychiatric disorder. *British Journal of Psychiatry*, 147:598–611.

Sameroff, A. 2006. Identifying risk and protective factors for health child development. In: A. Clarke-Stewart and J. Dunn (eds), *Families Count: Effects on Child and Adolescent Development*, pp. 53–76. Cambridge, England: Cambridge University Press.

Sampson, R. J. 2012. *Great American City: Chicago and the Enduring Neighborhood Effect*. Chicago, IL: University of Chicago Press.

Sampson, R. J., and Laub, J. H. 1993. *Crime in the Making: Pathways and Turning Points Through Life*. Cambridge, MA: Harvard University Press.

Sherman, L. W., and Weisburd, D. 1995. General deterrent effects of police patrol in crime "hot spots": A randomized, controlled trial. *Justice Quarterly*, 12:625–648.

Simons, R. L., Lei, M. K., Beach, S. R. H., *et al.* 2011. Social environment, genes, and aggression: Evidence supporting the differential susceptibility hypothesis. *American Sociological Review*, 76:883–912.

Stoddard, S. A., Zimmerman, M. A., and Bauermeister, J. A. 2012. A longitudinal analysis of cumulative risks, cumulative promotive factors, and adolescent violent behavior. *Journal of Research on Adolescence*, 22:542–555.

Stouthamer-Loeber, M., Loeber, R., Wei, E., Farrington, D. P., and Wikstrom, P.-O. H. 2002. Risk and promotive effects in the explanation of persistent serious delinquency in boys. *Journal of Consulting and Clinical Psychology*, 79:111–123.

Sutherland, E. H. 1947. *Principles of Criminology*. Philadelphia, PA: J. B. Lippincott.

Thornberry, T. P. 1987. Toward an interactional theory of delinquency. *Criminology*, 25:863–891.

Thornberry, T. P., and Krohn, M. D. 2008. Applying interactional theory to the explanation of continuity and change in antisocial behavior. In: D. P. Farrington (ed.), *Integrated Developmental and Life-course Theories of Offending*, pp. 183–209. New Brunswick, NJ: Transaction Publishers.

Thornberry, T. P., Lizotte, A. J., Krohn, M. D., Farnworth, M., and Jang, S. J. 1991. Testing interactional theory: An examination of reciprocal causal relationships among family, school, and delinquency. *Journal of Criminal Law and Criminology*, 82:3–35.

Tolan, P. H., and Gorman-Smith, D. 1998. Development of serious and violent offending careers. In: R. Loeber and D. P. Farrington (eds), *Serious and Violent Juvenile Offenders*, pp. 68–85. Thousand Oaks, CA: Sage.

US Department of Health and Human Services. 2001. Youth violence: A report of the Surgeon General. Rockville, MD: US Department of Health and Human Services, Centers for Disease Control and Prevention, National Center for Injury Prevention and Control; Substance Abuse and Mental Health Services Administration, Center for Mental Health Services; National Institutes of Health, National Institute of Mental Health.

Washington State Institute for Public Policy. 2014. Benefit-cost results. Olympia, WA: Washington State Institute for Public Policy.

Wikstrom, P.-O. H., and Loeber, R. 2000. Do disadvantaged neighborhoods cause well-adjusted children to become adolescent delinquents? A study of male juvenile serious offending, individual risk and protective factors, and neighborhood context. *Criminology*, 38:1109–1142.

Wilson, W. J. 1987. *The Truly Disadvantaged: The Inner City, the Underclass, and Public Policy*. Chicago, IL: University of Chicago Press.

Zahn, M. A., Hawkins, S. R., Chiancone, J., and Whitworth, A. 2008. The Girls Study Group – Charting the way to delinquency prevention for girls. Washington, DC: Office of Juvenile Justice and Delinquency Prevention.

4

Evaluation Science

Introduction

Now that you understand the historical and theoretical foundations of crime prevention, it is time for a brief review of how rigorous scientific evaluations are conducted. Briefly stated, an evaluation is a study to test whether an intervention works the way it was designed to work, whether it is effective in achieving what it intended to do. Good evaluations provide evidence of an intervention's effectiveness by assessing the amount of change in criminal behavior that can be uniquely attributed to the program, practice, or policy being investigated. Since there is no theory-free program design, evaluations are also tests of the validity of criminological theories (Shadish, Cook, and Leviton, 1991).

Although this chapter will provide a more detailed and sometimes technical description of different evaluation designs and methodologies, we will cover most issues fairly briefly. If you have already taken a Research Methods course, much of this information should be familiar. If you are intrigued by the material and want to learn about evaluation designs in more depth, we encourage you to

The Prevention of Crime, First Edition. Delbert Elliott and Abigail Fagan.
© 2017 John Wiley & Sons, Inc. Published 2017 by John Wiley & Sons, Inc.
Companion website: www.wiley.com/go/elliott/prevention_of_crime

consult the suggested readings listed at the end of this chapter. Our goal is to help you understand the most important issues related to evaluation so that you can judge for yourselves if claims about an intervention's effectiveness are to be believed. This knowledge will be important not only in interpreting the information on effective interventions described in Section III of this text, but also more generally in your future careers in criminology, criminal justice, public health, social work, and other professions.

There are three basic purposes of such evaluations. *First*, evaluations are undertaken to provide feedback to a program developer about the particular intervention features and/or content which are working well and contributing to positive outcomes and the aspects that are not working well. This information guides the developer in making specific changes to the program to increase its ability to reduce crime. The *second* purpose is to test the validity of the **causal mechanisms** underlying the intervention. Recall from Chapter 3 that effective prevention programs, practices, and policies are based on theories of crime and attempt to change the underlying causes and processes that the theory states are related to criminal behavior. Evaluations play a critical role in validating theories of crime and extending our understanding about the causal mechanisms that increase or decrease the likelihood of offending. They can evaluate the claim that if a specific treatment, based on a particular criminological theory, is delivered to participants, it will cause them to be less involved in criminal behavior. If crime is reduced, support for the theory is demonstrated. The theory is further supported if the particular mechanisms identified by the theory as leading to crime are also changed. For example, if the intervention shows that participants' relationships with others are strengthened and their criminal behavior is reduced, then **social control theory** is supported. *Third*, evaluations provide valuable information to decision-makers who are responsible for taking action to reduce social problems like criminal behavior. By reviewing the results of evaluation studies, policy-makers can decide whether or not they will encourage or even mandate the use or discontinuation of particular crime prevention strategies. All three reasons for conducting evaluation research are important, but our focus in this book will be on the latter two purposes: on how evaluations can identify effective interventions based on sound causal mechanisms and how this information can lead to informed choices about which programs, practices, and policies to implement in order to reduce rates of crime.

The processes used to evaluate the effectiveness of crime prevention strategies are similar to those used in medical research to determine the effectiveness of prescription drugs or medical procedures and protocols, like how to provide lifesaving CPR. In the USA, the Federal Drug Administration (FDA) is charged with reviewing evidence from evaluations to determine if a specific drug has the desired effect on the targeted disease or medical condition, identifying important negative side effects and judging if its benefits outweigh its potential harms. Only drugs shown to be effective and to have minimal side effects are certified or approved by the FDA and allowed to be sold to consumers. As we will describe further in Chapter 5, although determinations of the effectiveness of crime prevention programs, practices, and policies are modeled after the procedures used in medical research, no federal agency regulates these processes or certifies crime prevention programs as effective and ready to be marketed and implemented. Several governmental agencies and universities have compiled lists of interventions they consider to be effective in reducing crime, but the criteria and processes for making this determination vary considerably across institutions. As a result, the available lists of effective crime interventions differ substantially in what they consider to be effective, as you will see in Chapter 5. In this chapter, we describe how scientific evaluations should be conducted and which types of evaluations are likely to produce the most persuasive evidence about an intervention's effectiveness.

The Stages of Evaluation

Evaluation is a process with distinct and sequenced stages. Each stage is designed to answer specific questions about the intervention being evaluated, as shown in Table 4.1. Evidence of effectiveness can be obtained from each stage, and conclusions about whether or not a program is effective should be based on the overall, cumulative evidence produced across all stages. The evaluation design differs according to the questions being asked, and methods typically become more complex as the evaluation sequence progresses.

Process evaluation

The evaluation sequence typically begins with a **process evaluation**. This type of evaluation is designed to answer the first three questions in Table 4.1. It examines the nature of the intervention and its chances of being successfully implemented. Until the foundations of the intervention are well understood, there is no reason to move to the next stage of evaluation, which examines the outcomes produced by an intervention.

Process evaluations rely on a review of the intervention's **theoretical model** and descriptions of the theory(ies) underlying the program, the specific risk and/or protective factors the

Table 4.1 Questions addressed during the three stages of the evaluation process.

Evaluation stage	Question
1. Process evaluation	1. Is the intervention based on theory, practical to implement, and logical?
	2. How difficult is the intervention to implement?
	3. Can the intervention be integrated into existing agencies and social systems without significantly changing its content or methods of delivery?
2. Pre-post outcome evaluation	*Provides tentative answers to the questions:*
	4. Does the intervention have the desired effect on the targeted risk factors, protective factors, and outcomes?
	5. How strong are the effects?
	6. Does the intervention have high social, economic, and political importance?
3. Experimental outcome evaluation	*Provides more definite answers to the questions:*
	7. Does the intervention have the desired effect on the targeted risk factors, protective factors, and outcomes?
	8. How strong are the effects?
	9. Does the intervention have high social, economic, and political importance?

intervention will target for change based on this theory, and evidence from other empirical studies that show support for the theory and its stated causal mechanisms. As noted in Chapter 3, risk and protective factors differ in: (i) their impact on crime, with some showing a more powerful influence on offending, which means that they are also likely to have a stronger prevention effect in reducing crime; (ii) their malleability or ability to be changed by an intervention (e.g., it is harder to change poverty than academic performance); and (iii) the prevalence of these factors or conditions in the population or environment targeted to receive the intervention. For example, parent/child conflict is likely to be highest in adolescence compared to other stages of the life course. The theoretical model guides the development of the intervention by indicating which risk and protective factors should be targeted for change based on their impact on crime, their malleability, and their prevalence in the targeted population. The theory should also suggest the most appropriate developmental timing for the intervention. For example, social learning theory and tests of this perspective indicate that peer interactions will be most important in affecting criminal involvement during adolescence.

The process evaluation also requires a review of the **program change model**, which specifies the attitudes and behaviors to be changed by the intervention and the research evidence that these factors will change the prevalence of the targeted risk and protective factors. For example, research has shown that child abuse (a risk factor) can be reduced by teaching parents how to be more effective in disciplining and monitoring their children and that academic performance and high school graduation rates (protective factors) can be improved by creating close mentoring relationships between youth and adults. The program change model should also identify the participants who will be recruited or enrolled in the intervention; the setting or context in which the intervention will be delivered; the number and length of lessons, sessions, or treatments to be provided; the specific types of instruction to be used (e.g., lectures, discussions, or one-on-one therapy); and the credentials and experience required of implementers. As we discussed in Chapter 3, the theoretical rationale and the program change model together are referred to as the intervention **logic model** and provide a detailed description of why and how the intervention is expected to work.

In addition to considering the nature of the intervention, or what it looks like *on paper*, the process evaluation also examines how the intervention is delivered *in practice*. That is, it addresses the second question listed in Table 4.1: how difficult is it to implement the intervention? Can it be implemented as planned, particularly as specified in the change model, without too many problems? A process evaluation may, for example, investigate the degree to which an intervention has successfully recruited the types of individuals, groups, or communities targeted to receive it; provided the correct number of treatment sessions, contacts, or classes using the methods outlined in the change model; and ensured that implementers have the required skills and backgrounds needed to deliver the intervention.

The answers to these process evaluation questions require the careful collection and review of data describing all aspects of the implementation process. For example, a process evaluation of an individually focused crime prevention program should record each person's eligibility for the intervention, their attendance and completion of program sessions, and the content actually delivered to them during each session. It may also collect information on participants' levels of risk and protective factors and criminal involvement at the start of the intervention and after it has ended. To assess prevention practices and policies, data should be recorded to document the date they begin, the number of persons trained to deliver the practice or implement the policy, the length and content of any training required of implementers, how the policy was enforced, and crime rates before and after the practice or policy was delivered or enacted. All of these records are used to establish that the program is being implemented with **fidelity**, as closely as possible to the model described by the program designer, a concept we will describe much more fully in Chapter 10.

A process evaluation can also begin to evaluate the third question listed in Table 4.1: how well the intervention is integrated into the agencies and systems charged with delivering or supporting it. Such issues may be assessed by surveying agency administrators or systems leaders (e.g., school superintendents, the head of the state juvenile justice agency, etc.) about their use of and support for the intervention. These issues become very important when effective prevention programs are taken to scale and widely used across a state or country. We will continue the discussion of how to evaluate implementation fidelity in large-scale replications in Section IV.

What does a typical process evaluation look like? To provide a real-life example, consider the **Life Skills Training Program (LST)**, a school-based drug prevention program which has been subject to several process evaluations. One such evaluation, performed as part of the Blueprints for Healthy Youth Development initiative (Fagan and Mihalic, 2003), examined the theoretical and program change model during replications taking place in middle schools in the USA. The results supported that developer's descriptions of the program (see: www.lifeskillstraining.com/ and www.blueprint sprograms.com/LST), as follows:

- **Theoretical rationale**. LST is based on social learning theory.[1] As we described in Chapters 2 and 3, this theory states that individuals learn behaviors during social interactions by observing, imitating, and modeling behaviors of others. Especially during adolescence, behaviors like substance use and violence are likely to be learned during interactions with peers. Such behaviors help individuals achieve goals they believe they are unable to achieve in more conventional, law-abiding ways.
- **Risk factors** identified as important in social learning theory and targeted for change in LST include: favorable attitudes toward drug use, interactions with delinquent and/or substance-using peers, and neighborhood laws and norms favorable to drug use or crime. Protective factors include: having clear standards for behavior, believing that drug use is risky, having strong problem-solving skills, and being able to refuse offers of drugs.
- **Program Change Model**. LST is designed to improve the general social and personal skills needed to successfully navigate developmental challenges faced when moving from childhood to adolescence. It also teaches young people ways to resist pro-drug influences, refuse drug offers from peers, and identify and resist pro-drug messages shown in movies, TV, and other media. The program is a universal, classroom-based intervention for middle school or junior high school students. It involves 37 sessions taught by teachers over three years who use a variety of instructional techniques, including lecture, demonstration, feedback, reinforcement, and practice.

During the Blueprints process evaluation, data describing program implementation processes were collected in over 400 schools across the country (Fagan and Mihalic, 2003; Mihalic, Fagan, and

Argamaso, 2008). A review of these data indicated that LST could be delivered as planned. All schools were successful in recruiting and training teachers to deliver the intervention to the targeted, eligible population of students in middle schools and junior high schools. Most teachers taught all of the lessons over a three-year period and delivered all of the required material in each session. However, the process evaluation indicated that implementation procedures were not perfectly followed in all cases. A few teachers did not cover specific lessons, not every student attended all sessions in all three years and some students did not fully participate in every lesson. As we will discuss in Chapter 10, programs are not always implemented exactly as they were designed, but when deviations from the program logic model are relatively minor, the replication should still be able to produce its anticipated effects on crime.

Programs that show positive results from process evaluations, like LST, are then ready for the next stage of evaluation. If a program fails to demonstrate that it is grounded in theory, fails to alter relevant risk and protective factors, has no clear change strategy or cannot be implemented as planned (with fidelity), the program is not ready to move to the next stage of evaluation. Instead, the program should be re-designed and re-evaluated or completely abandoned.

Pre–post outcome evaluation

The next stages of the evaluation process involve **outcome** or **impact evaluations**, which seek to answer Evaluation Questions #4–6 (see Table 4.1) relating to the effects of the intervention on criminal behavior. Outcome evaluations vary in their level of rigor and sophistication. More basic designs, like a **non–experimental pre–post design** associated with Stage 2 of the evaluation process, provide tentative or preliminary answers to the evaluation questions. Pre–post evaluations involve the collection of data from individuals who receive a particular treatment at the start of the study and again when they complete the intervention or when they drop out of the study prior to its completion. As shown in Figure 4.1, all individuals participating in the study are expected to receive the intervention and the degree to which their criminal behaviors change is assessed using data collected at two time points: pre-test and post-test. If participation in the intervention has some effect on crime, the level of initiation or involvement in offending should be lower at post-test compared to pre-test. If no change is seen, there is reason to question the effectiveness of the intervention. If the average level of crime actually *increases* from pre-test to post-test, the intervention is potentially **iatrogenic** or harmful. The impact on crime is referred to as the **main effect** of the intervention and is the outcome of greatest interest to practitioners, funders, and policy-makers.

The pre–post evaluation can also compare participants' levels of targeted risk and protective factors before and after the intervention. As with the main effect on crime, if the intervention is effective, then changes in these **secondary effects** should also be seen. That is, levels of risk should decline from pre-test to post-test and the levels of protection should increase. If this does not occur, the program's effectiveness is less certain. It is also possible to test the degree to which a reduction in crime is directly related to a reduction in a risk factor and/or an increase in a protective factor. This type of analysis, shown in Figure 4.2, is called a **mediating analysis**, because the change in the risk or protective factor is thought to *mediate* or be responsible for the change in outcomes produced by the intervention.

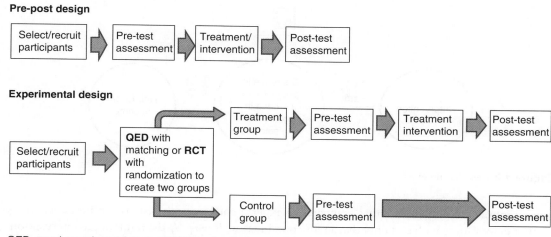

QED, quasi-experimental design; RCT, randomized control trial.

Figure 4.1 Outcome evaluation designs.

Mediating effects are often not examined, especially if no main effect on crime is produced, but they are important in helping to understand a program's main effects and evaluate its logic model. For example, if the main effect indicates a reduction in crime (Path C in Figure 4.2), the intervention shows secondary effects on risk and protective factors (Path A), and the risk and protective factors are shown to reduce crime (Path B), we have more confidence in the theoretical rationale of the intervention, the claim that these particular risk and protective factors are causally linked to crime and that the intervention change strategy was effective. If the main effect shows reductions in crime (Path C) but there is no evidence that the risk and protective factors were changed by the intervention (Path A), this may lead us to question whether or not crime was actually reduced. The outcome could have been produced simply by chance (it happens!); or, if it was truly reduced, the intervention change strategy is likely to be faulty since the outcome was not due to changes in the targeted risk or protective factors.

The pre–post impact evaluation provides an initial test of an intervention's effectiveness. If an intervention appears to be ineffective or does not work the way it was expected to work, this design can help pinpoint whether or not the problem is with the theoretical rationale or the program change model. However, keep in mind that a failure to show a main effect may also be due to poor implementation of the program. If a process evaluation indicates that the intervention was not fully implemented or that major deviations from the program change model were made, then the expected outcomes are less likely to be seen. Thus, it is helpful to conduct a process evaluation along with the pre–post evaluation, even if a process evaluation was conducted in the past.

Although pre–post impact evaluations can provide *preliminary* evidence of program effectiveness, they have several limitations which, together, reduce their ability to show with confidence that an outcome like crime has been reduced. We review some of these problems below and will continue this discussion when describing more rigorous **experimental outcome evaluations**. What is

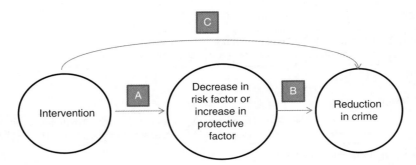

Figure 4.2 Mediating effects.

most important to remember is that, compared to experimental research designs, pre-post evaluations cannot demonstrate with certainty that a reduction in crime is *uniquely* the result of the intervention. They cannot rule out other alternative explanations for how a reduction in crime might or might not have occurred.

Consider, for example, an indicated intervention designed to reduce the frequency of offending among 17–20 year olds who have a history of frequent and serious offending. These offenders attend a "wilderness survival camp" lasting two weeks, followed by five hour-long employment counseling sessions. A pre-post evaluation finds that the average frequency of offending in the year following participation in this program is 20% less than it had been the year before entering the program, indicating a substantial pre-post reduction in crime. *Can we conclude that program participation caused this decrease in the rate of offending?* Not necessarily. As noted in the discussion of the life-course developmental paradigm in Chapter 3, studies consistently show that involvement in crime increases in early adolescence, peaks between ages 17 and 18 and then declines. This drop-off in offending is called the **maturation effect**. For the majority of the population, criminal behavior lessens as one gets older, develops more mature ways of thinking and enters new social roles like work and marriage. This "natural" decrease in offending means that individuals are likely to reduce their involvement in crime during this age period whether they participated in the program or not. Maturation, or aging, cannot be ruled out as a possible explanation for the observed decline in offending, and any claim that the program caused this reduction is debatable.

History effects may also affect individual offending during the implementation period. A history effect is when an event that is not part of the intervention occurs during the same time period the intervention is being delivered – an event that might have some effect of its own on criminal behavior. Suppose a bullying prevention program is introduced into a school that was known to have high rates of bullying. A pre-post assessment based on students' self-reported bullying perpetration revealed less bullying in the 3 months following the intervention compared to the 3 months prior to it. But a month after the program started, three senior boys known to be bullies were arrested by the police for breaking into cars and stealing CD players and were then expelled from school. Assuming the school had a relatively small student population, can we conclude the bullying prevention program caused the decline in bullying? Can we rule out the removal from school of three frequent bullies as an alternative explanation? Probably not.

Next, consider a community that implemented a drug prevention program in all three of its high schools. The pre-post assessment of drug use, based on student self-reports, indicated that while the levels of alcohol use declined slightly after the intervention, the rate of marijuana use actually increased substantially in all schools. This finding would point to an iatrogenic program effect. However, while the intervention was going on, the city district attorney announced that she would no longer prosecute anyone for the possession or use of marijuana. Can we conclude the program actually increased marijuana use? Can we rule out the possible history effect caused by the DA's announcement?

As these examples show, what at first appears to be an intervention success based on a pre-post evaluation may actually be due to some other explanation. Similarly, concluding that an intervention has failed based on the results of a pre-post design may be premature; other possible explanations could explain why crime increased rather than decreased following the intervention. Given the inability to completely rule out alternative explanations of program success/failure, the findings of pre-post evaluations must be considered tentative and taken with much caution. Why, then, do evaluators rely on this design? Why not just move to the next stage of the evaluation process and use a more rigorous methodology which can provide more definitive evidence of an intervention's effectiveness?

There are three main reasons why pre-post evaluations are conducted. *First*, such evaluations are not very expensive or difficult. They do not necessarily require experts in research methodology and so can be undertaken by local program developers or staff. *Second*, it is very difficult to obtain enough funding or professional expertise to conduct a more rigorous outcome evaluation, like an experimental research design, without preliminary evidence of intervention effectiveness such as that provided by a pre-post evaluation. Policy-makers and evaluators want to know in advance that more complex evaluations will be worth their time and money. *Third*, the pre-post evaluation results can be helpful in making changes to an intervention to improve its effectiveness. If the primary goal, at least at this stage of program development, is to refine the intervention and maximize its ability to reduce crime, then pre-post evaluations can serve a critical role.

Before describing experimental outcome evaluations, we must mention a few technical points relating to the evaluation of program outcomes. Evaluations that claim to find a pre-post difference in the onset, prevalence or frequency of criminal behavior are usually referring to a change in crime from pre-test to post-test that is **statistically significant**. This means that the difference was unlikely to occur accidently or by chance. Usually, if the difference could occur more than 5 times out of every 100 comparisons, it is considered a non-significant difference and no claim of intervention effectiveness is made. If the effect could occur 5 or fewer times per 100 comparisons, the difference is considered a significant or "real" difference. In this case, the risk of claiming program effectiveness when, in fact, the difference in outcomes occurred by chance is very low; the difference can be attributed to the intervention with much confidence. This "5% rule" for determining statistically significant differences in program outcomes is used in nearly all quantitative evaluations.

Does this rule mean that you have to conduct 100 evaluations to determine if your outcome is the result of chance? Thankfully, the answer is "no." Using appropriate statistical procedures to evaluate pre-post differences, you can assess program effectiveness using a single study. Although we could explain in more detail the mathematical calculations needed to identify the statistical probability of finding observed differences, we will leave that issue for you to investigate on your own (one good source to consult is Weisburd and Britt, 2014). What is important to remember is that when we state that an evaluation shows an effect on crime or a statistically significant difference in criminal behavior, we mean that this outcome has been found using the 5% rule.

A related statistical measure that is used to measure the size of a difference in outcomes is the **effect size (ES)**. Although effect sizes are described in more detail later in this chapter, we mention the concept now to make the point that, while it is generally true that the bigger the observed difference, the more likely it is to be statistically significant, it is possible to find a statistically significant difference that is actually not very meaningful. That is, the difference could be relatively small, even if it is statistically significant, and have no practical value if our goal is to substantially reduce rates of crime. Statistical significance is directly related to the sample size of an evaluation, meaning that studies involving more participants have a greater likelihood of achieving statistical significance compared to studies with fewer participants even if the actual difference in criminal behavior is the same in both evaluations. For example, an evaluation of a probation program might indicate that it reduced the recidivism rate by 1%. If the number of participants in the evaluation study is small, this difference will not be statistically significant. If the number of participants is large, this 1% change may be statistically significant. Regardless, the size of the difference is small and does not reflect a very important reduction in crime. Furthermore, if the program is expensive, costing $20,000 per participant, then the change may be viewed as having very little practical value.

The goal in evaluation studies is to find differences that are both statistically significant and substantively important. The ES helps to evaluate the second issue since it identifies the size of an intervention effect without being overly influenced by sample size. The larger the ES, the greater the reduction of crime and the larger the potential social value of the intervention. Although not all program evaluations calculate effect sizes or include them in their published findings, we will note the ES of interventions described in Section III when they are available. We will also report on the **return–on–investment (ROI)**, or financial return on investment of programs, a measure that takes into account both the effect size and the cost of the program as we will discuss at the end of this chapter. By examining these issues, evaluations can help address the fifth and sixth evaluation question listed in Table 4.1.

Experimental outcome evaluation

The third stage of evaluation involves an **experimental research design**, which can take several forms, including a **causal comparative design**, a **quasi-experimental design**, or a **true experimental design**. Unlike pre-post evaluations, these all involve a comparison or control group that does not receive the intervention, as well as a group that is provided the program or treatment. As such, these designs are better able to rule out alternative explanations for observed pre-post intervention differences and provide more convincing evidence that the intervention caused a reduction in criminal behavior or some other outcome. They provide a more definitive answer to Evaluation Questions #4–6 in Table 4.1. We describe **quasi-experimental** and **true experimental** evaluations in the next two sections of this chapter. **Causal comparative** evaluations, also called **ex-post-facto** studies, are rarely used in contemporary crime prevention evaluations and are not discussed here.

Quasi-experimental design (QED) outcome evaluations

As shown in Figure 4.1, in a QED, a group of individuals (the study participants) is divided into a treatment group that receives the intervention to be evaluated and a "matched" comparison group that does not receive the intervention. Levels of risk and protection and targeted crime outcomes are assessed for both groups prior to the start of the intervention using the same measures and procedures. These results are examined in order to "match" the two groups, or make them as similar as possible before the study starts, particularly on their levels of risk and protection and involvement in crime. In practice, it is often not possible to achieve two groups that are completely matched in these outcomes. Sometimes, it is only possible to match the two groups in their demographic characteristics; for example, on the age or gender distribution of individuals in the two groups. However, if there is a close match on all of the intervention's targeted risk and protective factors and outcomes at pre-test, the evaluation is better able to rule out alternative explanations for program effects and make causal claims. After matching, the treatment group receives the intervention while the comparison group does not. At the end of the intervention, both groups are again assessed on the same measures of risk, protection, and criminal behaviors. Although Figure 4.1 shows only one post-intervention assessment, multiple assessments can be made following the end of the intervention in order to determine longer term effects. As we will describe in Section III, some studies have conducted follow-up assessments 10 to 20 years following the intervention!

True experimental outcome evaluations

True experiments also involve two groups of individuals and pre-test and post-test assessments of outcomes, but they require an additional and important feature: **random assignment** to the treatment and control groups. This type of experimental evaluation, also shown in Figure 4.1, is typically referred to as a **randomized control trial (RCT)**.[2] Whereas QEDs attempt to create two similar groups using a matching process, random assignment is much better able to produce treatment and control groups that are equivalent in key outcomes. Using this method, any participant or group (e.g., a family, classroom, or geographical area) in the study has the same chance of being placed in the treatment or control group. Who is assigned to each group is completely random. To ensure that group assignment is random, an evaluator may actually flip a coin and assign all participants who receive a "heads" to the treatment group and all those receiving a "tails" to the control group. Random assignment helps ensure that any differences between the two groups that may exist at the start of the study are due completely to chance, which will minimize bias when interpreting the results of the evaluation. *To repeat, using randomization to create treatment and control groups is much better than the matching procedure employed in QEDs because it insures that the participants in the two groups are essentially the same, except for chance.* It controls for *all* possible differences between those in the treatment and control groups, not just those characteristics that an evaluator thinks of ahead of time and includes in a matching process.

Random assignment allows us to rule out the possibility that the observed difference between those receiving or not receiving the intervention was due to some pre-intervention difference. In fact, in a RCT, a pre-test assessment is not required if the evaluator can be sure that the assignment to treatment and control groups was truly random. In practice, however, a pre-test assessment is usually conducted and it can be helpful, particularly when the size of the treatment and control groups is relatively small. When less than 100 participants are involved in the study, the randomization process is less likely to produce equivalent groups and pre-tests will be more necessary. Even with large sample sizes, pre-tests can verify that the assignment was truly random and the two groups are equivalent. Having this information also increases the ability to rule out alternative explanations and calculate group differences more precisely.

Judging the Merit of Evaluation Designs

How can we judge the merits of these different types of evaluation strategies and determine which is best able to identify effective crime prevention programs, practices, and policies? Doing so relies on an assessment of each one's **validity**, or its accuracy in determining that a change in criminal behavior is actually the result of participation in an intervention. When an evaluation has strong validity, we can place more confidence in its findings. Three types of validity must be considered.

First, evaluations should be judged according to their **construct validity**, or the degree to which their measures of targeted risk and protective factors, crime outcomes and any other processes or conditions related to the intervention accurately assess the constructs they are intended to measure. "Constructs" can be abstract ideas about some quality or trait of persons or contexts that cannot be seen, felt or heard by an outside observer; for example, an individual's intelligence or self-control, or the amount of bonding between a child and a parent. Since these types of constructs are abstract, they present a challenge to a scientific researcher who wants to accurately assess their presence or absence. Other constructs can be directly observed and counted and thus present a less significant measurement challenge. Such constructs, like "criminal behavior," are typically measured using a direct count of the number of acts observed, recorded, or reported.

For crime prevention programs, we are usually interested in assessing the construct validity of criminal behavior. Recall from Chapter 1 that criminal acts can be defined and measured (i.e., counted) in different ways and that not all measures are equally "good." In fact, this means that different types of measures have different levels of construct validity. We noted that arrests are less able to measure actual levels of criminal behavior because most criminal acts are undetected or are reported or observed but do not lead to an arrest. Using the number of arrests to evaluate the effectiveness of a youth employment program in reducing adolescent offending would therefore have weak construct validity. However, an arrest measure would have good construct validity if evaluating the effectiveness of a law enforcement policy designed to increase the use of arrests for domestic violence.

Compared to crime outcomes, it is more difficult to achieve high construct validity of measures of risk and protective factors because constructs like attitudes regarding violence or bonding to family or school represent abstract ideas or qualities which cannot be easily observed or counted. Knowing this, researchers have spent much time developing and testing measures of such factors. These usually rely on self-reported surveys or observations to do so. They also tend to use multiple items or **indicators** to create **scales** which are better able to measure these more complex and abstract events or conditions. For example, a well-known scale used to measure the individual risk factor of "low self-control" relies on a set of 24 indicators or items assessing various aspects of this construct (Grasmick *et al.*, 1993). Individuals are asked to rate their level of agreement with 24 statements including: "*I don't devote much thought and effort to preparing for the future;*" "*When things get complicated, I tend to quit or withdraw;*" and "*I lose my temper pretty easily.*" Parental warmth, a protective factor, has been measured using home observations in which trained researchers count the number of times caregivers display different behaviors thought to indicate their love for and affection towards the child (Caldwell and Bradley, 1984). For example, observers rate whether or not or how often the parent *praises*; *caresses, kisses, or hugs*; or *voices positive feelings to the child*. Many established measures, already evaluated and shown to have good construct validity, are available for use in evaluation research. When there is no existing measure, the evaluator must pay careful attention to construct validity and create a new measure which accurately reflects the attitude, behavior, or condition of interest.

The *second* way to judge an evaluation is by its **internal validity**, the extent to which the evaluation has eliminated alternative explanations of an intervention's effectiveness. We mentioned earlier that pre-post evaluation studies have relatively weak internal validity, given that they cannot rule out alternative explanations like **maturation** and **history effects**. Other threats to the internal validity of an evaluation include **testing effects**, **instrumentation effects**, **non-equivalence**, **regression to the mean**, and **attrition** (Shadish, Cook, and Campbell, 2002).

A **testing effect** refers to the situation whereby participants in an evaluation learn something from taking the pre-test which artificially affects their responses to the post-test. The more "practice" they have in completing assessments, especially when multiple post-tests are given in a short period of time, the more problematic testing effects can be. Participants may become too familiar with the items used to measure particular outcomes, since the same items are supposed to be used during every assessment. Prior to the next assessment, participants may have thought about the questions to be asked and decided to answer them differently based on what they think the researcher is trying to study. Or, they may simply become "better" at test-taking because they know what to expect and/or are less anxious about the testing process. Testing effects can result in higher or lower post-test scores even if the intervention has had no real effect. If testing effects are known to have occurred, the evaluation will be less valid. One solution to this problem is to increase the length of the interval between pre-test and post-test. There is also a very sophisticated type of experimental design which actually controls for this possible effect called the **Solomon Four Group Design** (for more information on this type of design, see: Shadish, Cook, and Campbell, 2002).

An **instrumentation effect** indicates a change in the way a risk factor, protective factor, or crime outcome has been measured from pre-test to post-test. Any observed changes in the outcome may then be due to the change in the survey item(s) or in its meaning, rather than changes in the participants. To understand how this might occur, consider a multi-year evaluation of a program implemented during the transition from adolescence to young adulthood. This period coincides with changes in the legal definition of what constitutes crime: some behavior that is illegal for adolescents is not illegal for adults, like purchasing alcohol, carrying a concealed weapon, or failing to attend school (i.e., truancy). If this difference is not taken into account, a simple count of the number of self-reported crimes could show a pre-post reduction that is not the result of the intervention, but rather a change in what is defined as a crime. This situation then introduces a potential alternative explanation for any observed pre-post changes.

Another type of instrumentation effect is related to the possible bias introduced when a person delivering or involved with the intervention is the one completing the pre- and post-test. For example, teachers delivering a violence prevention program may be asked to evaluate student participants' levels of aggression in the classroom, or correctional officers delivering a vocational training program may be asked to assess inmates' job skills. Knowing that a person is receiving an intervention can influence the rater's perception of whether or not this person has changed, particularly if the rater believes the intervention is effective. In such cases, any improvement between pre-test and post-test may be due to rater bias, rather than a true change in risk, protection, or criminal behavior.

Regression effects can result when individuals assigned to a treatment group were selected or recruited because they were serious or frequent offenders at the peak of their criminal involvement. Given the age/crime curve described in Chapter 3, it can be assumed that without any intervention, rates of criminal behavior will decline as adolescents move into early adulthood. What may be interpreted as a decline in crime produced by an intervention is actually the result of the aging process. More generally, **regression to the mean** occurs as individuals with very high or very low levels of any outcome or measure move towards an average level of the outcome over time without any intervention. This "natural" change from an extreme to more typical level can skew evaluation findings and make it appear as if an intervention has either been successful or failed when, in fact, this is not the case.

We previously mentioned the problem of **non-equivalence**, which occurs when participants in the treatment and control groups differ significantly in the outcomes of interest at the start of the study. One group might have higher levels of criminal behavior than the other or may be at greater risk of offending because they live in more disadvantaged neighborhoods or are exposed to more violence at home. Any control-treatment group difference at pre-test on a main outcome can provide an alternative explanation for an observed difference at post-test. Matching participants in the control group to those in the treatment group to achieve groups that are similar in their outcomes is one way to try to achieve equivalence, but this can be difficult to do. Groups need to have similar levels not only of crime, but also of all risk and protective factors that could be related to crime. Unless *all* differences are removed, non-equivalence remains an alternative explanation for differences at post-test. As noted earlier, random assignment is a much stronger method than matching for achieving group equivalence at pre-test.

Even the best evaluation study typically has participants drop out before the intervention is over. This loss is called **attrition** and poses another threat to the internal validity of an evaluation. If participants leaving the study have different characteristics than those remaining, especially different rates of criminal behavior, attrition could be alternative explanation for any observed differences at post-test. For example, if males are more likely to drop out of a treatment group than a control group, greater reductions in crime for the treatment than the control group at post-test could be due to this loss, given that males are more likely to commit crimes than females. Attrition is related to the problem of **non-equivalence**, because treatment and control groups that were equal at pre-test can become unequal at post-test due to attrition. In the prior example, if both groups had equal numbers of males and females at pre-test, at post-test the control group will have more males than the treatment group. Even if the actual rate of attrition is relatively low, when attrition affects group equivalence, it can provide an alternative explanation for any observed post-test differences.

The *third* aspect of an evaluation to consider is **external validity**. External validity is the degree to which the intervention is **generalizable** and can be transported to other settings and replicated with other participants with the same level of effectiveness. The greater the external validity or generalizability of an intervention, the broader its impact on crime is expected to be. Programs that have very strong external validity and are expected to work for diverse populations could potentially be replicated across a country or internationally and produce widespread reductions in crime.

There are three major types of external validity to consider: **population**, **ecological** and **operations external validity**. **Population external validity** evaluates whether or not the results of an evaluation shown for specific types of participants can be generalized to all persons with these same characteristics and to other types of persons. An intervention shown to be effective for Caucasians but not Asians, for example, would have low population external validity.

Ecological external validity is concerned with how the social or physical setting of the study influences outcomes and if effects can be replicated in other types of settings. For example, a program shown to reduce crime in urban, high-poverty neighborhoods, wealthy neighborhoods, and rural communities would have high ecological external validity. Or consider an evaluation of a family-based program seeking to increase parent/child bonding, reduce family conflict and prevent the initiation of delinquency. If children are asked to rate the quality of their interactions with parents and their illegal behaviors on surveys conducted in their homes, they may be reluctant to answer honestly for fear that their parents may see the results of their survey. If a second evaluation of the intervention relied on assessments conducted in a more neutral setting such as the child's school, the youth's responses may differ. The two evaluations may then produce different results due to poor ecological external validity, even if the change in behaviors was the same.

There are two ways to assess an evaluation's population or ecological external validity. First, and ideally, the evaluation team would randomly select a sample of participants from the population of all persons who are eligible to receive the intervention. Specific study settings would also be randomly selected from the broad set of all possible contexts where the intervention was designed to take place. If these procedures are followed, the findings can be generalized from the smaller groups and settings to the larger population of all eligible persons and all possible study locations using statistical probability arguments. In practice, however, these procedures are rarely followed, at least in studies of crime prevention.[3] A random process is almost never used to select participants or settings. As a result, there are few crime prevention programs that can claim to have very strong population or ecological external validity.

A second and more common strategy involves making a logical argument that the participants actually selected are typical of some larger group of intended and eligible persons and settings. To make this argument, the evaluation should describe in detail the characteristics of the participant sample, including their age, sex, socioeconomic status, race/ethnicity, level of education, and involvement in or general risk for criminal behavior. The intervention setting should also be described, including the types of families, schools, neighborhoods, or correctional facilities involved in the study. To the extent that these sample characteristic are similar to those intended to be targeted by the intervention, an informed judgment can be made regarding the external validity of the evaluation. Keep in mind, however, that this practice will provide much weaker evidence for external validity than the randomization strategy.

The third type, **operational external validity**, examines the degree to which findings from one evaluation are **replicated** in a second evaluation conducted by different investigators.[4] This concern arises from the considerable evidence that evaluations completed by the developer of an intervention are more likely to find positive findings and stronger effects than when they are undertaken by other investigators (Eisner, 2009; Gandhi *et al.*, 2007; Petrosino and Soydan, 2005). Typically, the developer of an intervention leads the first evaluation of the program and often has a personal interest, and sometimes a financial one, in its success. As a result, s/he may ensure that the intervention and the evaluation are implemented with a very high level of rigor and care that is difficult to duplicate in later tests by investigators who have no connection to the developer or intervention.

In general, the greater the number of **replications**, that is, of evaluations showing similar effects, the stronger the claim of external validity. Although some programs and policies have been subject to multiple replications, many have been tested only once. In these cases, investigators often avoid discussing the intervention's external validity and simply note that the evaluation findings are limited to those individuals, groups, or settings actually participating in the evaluation. In our reviews of effective crime prevention programs, we will take care to describe the number of replications that have been conducted and to evaluate the logical claims that can be made for external validity.

Considering all three types of validity shown in Table 4.2, evaluations are most commonly judged by their construct and **internal validity** and less often for their external validity given the costs and complexity involved in doing so.[5] Internal validity is actually of greatest concern and is very difficult to fully establish. Of the different designs we have discussed, RCTs are considered the "gold standard" and best method of achieving internal validity and producing the strongest claims of intervention effectiveness (National Science Foundation, 2013; Shadish, Cook, and Campbell, 2002). This design

Table 4.2   The three types of validity to be assessed when judging evaluation designs.

Type	Definition	Example
Construct validity	The degree to which a measure adequately captures or represents the construct it is intended to measure	*Higher construct validity*: using self-reports of offending to measure criminal behavior *Lower construct validity*: using self-reports of fear of crime to measure criminal victimization
Internal validity	The degree to which an evaluation can rule out other explanations of an intervention's effectiveness	*Higher internal validity*: experimental evaluations, especially randomized control trials (RCTs) *Lower internal validity*: pre-post evaluations
External validity	The degree to which an intervention's effectiveness applies to a broad population of individuals, groups and/or contexts	*Higher external validity*: the Multisystemic Therapy (MST) program lowers recidivism for males and females, youth of different racial/ethnic groups and those with different levels and types of offending at pre-test *Lower external validity*: the Project Northland program reduces alcohol use among Caucasian students from rural Minnesota but not among racially diverse students in urban Chicago

has the greatest potential for addressing the threats to internal validity and of eliminating the potential alternative explanations for an observed difference between control and treatment groups. The RCT design evaluation can, at least in theory, successfully deal with maturation, history, regression, and non-equivalence threats.

Well-conducted QEDs can also address many of the threats to internal validity but are particularly vulnerable to the threat of **non-equivalence** given that they rely on matching rather than randomization when trying to establish comparable treatment and comparison groups. Because the randomization requirement of RCTs is often difficult to achieve, and QEDs are often used, a fair amount of research has been conducted to compare results obtained using QEDs and RCTs. For example, studies have compared outcomes obtained using randomly assigned intervention and control groups and those obtained using the same intervention participants and a comparison group selected through methods other than randomization. Cook, Shadish, and Wong's (2008) review of 12 such studies suggested that when comparison groups are obtained without very close matching, estimates of an intervention's effects are likely to be inaccurate. This is true even when statistical techniques are used to adjust for observed differences between the two groups at pre-test. Often QED studies match groups only on demographic variables, not on the outcomes of greatest interest to the evaluator, and these studies consistently fail to reproduce the results of RCTs. QED designs are more likely to produce valid results when there is very careful matching of the treatment and comparison groups at pre-test, especially on measures of the outcome, risk/protective factors, and geographic location of the study.

RCTs and QEDs are more or less equally subject to testing, instrumentation and attrition threats. Since these evaluation designs cannot fully address these issues, evaluators must turn to statistical procedures to do so. We review some of these techniques and provide additional description of analysis strategies used to estimate the size and duration of program effects in the next section.

Evaluation Analyses

The main goal of a crime prevention evaluation is to establish a causal relationship between participation in a program or between the introduction of a new practice or policy and a reduction in criminal behavior. Evaluations involve a **causal analysis**, an analysis in which a cause(s) of crime is manipulated or controlled by a researcher via an intervention that is purposely delivered to some persons or in some contexts and not others. The demonstration of a causal relationship requires three conditions: (i) finding a statistically significant relationship between the cause and the effect, (ii) ensuring that the cause occurred prior to the effect, and (iii) ruling out possible alternative causes of the effect. It is relatively easy to satisfy the second condition, as the program, practice, or policy (the cause) always precedes the measure of change and the analysis of the effect (criminal behavior). As we have discussed, evaluations can also address the third condition by ruling out some of the threats to internal validity. To satisfy the first condition, statistical analyses must be used. In addition to identifying whether or not a cause produces an effect, these statistical procedures can also rule out some of the potential alternative explanations of changes in crime, like **testing effects**, **instrumentation effects**, and **attrition effects**.

The most basic analysis involves an assessment of the amount of change in the measures of risk, protection, and crime outcomes between pre-test and post-test. If the intervention is effective, the targeted risk and protective factors and crime measures will all have changed in a positive direction, demonstrating a statistically significant relationship between participation in the program (the cause), a reduction in risk and criminal behavior, and an increase in protection (the effects). When the evaluation includes both a treatment and a control group, the assessment of pre- to post-intervention change is made for both groups, and the amount of change between groups is compared. If the program is effective, the amount of change will be in the expected direction and significantly greater for the treatment group than the control group. As noted earlier, the measured change in criminal behavior is the **main effect**. It is the primary goal of the intervention and often the only effect that is actually measured and reported. While the evaluation may assess secondary effects on risk or protective factors, or mediating effects examining whether or not changes in the risk and protective factors led to changes in outcomes, such analyses are not routinely performed at this time in the study of crime prevention.

Marginal and absolute effects

It is easy when reading results from **experimental outcome** studies to focus on changes that have occurred for the treatment group, but it is important to remember that in this type of evaluation, unlike the **pre–post design**, outcomes are based on a comparison of the treatment group with a control group. It is also important to realize that there are two types of control groups: those who receive no treatment at all during the study period and those who receive an alternative intervention. The second group is often referred to as a "treatment as usual" control group. Providing control group participants with some type of service or treatment is common in crime prevention studies because it allows researchers to avoid the ethical dilemma faced when withholding services from those who may seem in need of assistance. In addition, a goal of many evaluations is to estimate whether a new intervention is more effective than what is usually offered. For example, probation is a standard type of intervention used by virtually all criminal and juvenile courts. If researchers or court officials sense that probation is not working very well to reduce crime – for example, they see that a growing number of offenders are violating the terms of their probation and being sent back to court – then a new intervention may be offered to some offenders (who would be in the intervention group) and its effectiveness compared to those who receive probation (the control group).

When the control group receives no intervention, the main effect is considered an **absolute effect**. It compares the effect of participating in the intervention to getting no services. When the control group participates in an alternative intervention, the **marginal effect** will indicate how much better or worse the new intervention is compared to the alternative intervention. The interpretation of main effects is quite different for these two types of evaluations. In the first scenario, if no differences in crime are found, the intervention would be considered ineffective. In the second case, finding no differences would indicate that the new treatment is no better than the alternative intervention or the treatment as usual. A decision-maker could still decide to use the new treatment, especially if it was cheaper or considered easier to implement than existing services.

Attrition analyses

No matter what types of services a control group receives, main effects can be misleading if there is a high degree of participant attrition, a different attrition rate for treatment and control groups, or a loss of different types of participants in the two groups. As a first step in trying to minimize the threat of attrition, it is important to document how many and what types of participants drop out of the evaluation before it is over. This analysis can involve a simple count of the number of participants who complete the pre-test and the post-test and a calculation of the attrition rate. So, if 100 participants were enrolled at the start of the study and 90 completed the post-test, the attrition rate is 10% (100-90 divided by 100). If this rate is low, ideally less than 5% (Shultz and Grimes, 2002), or if the rate is about the same for the treatment and control groups, attrition is unlikely to threaten the internal validity of the study or to bias the estimate of the main effect.

A more problematic but somewhat common scenario is **differential attrition**, which indicates a difference between the treatment and control groups in the amount of attrition or in the type of participant that drops out. Even if the rates of attrition are the same in both groups, differential attrition can occur. For example, an evaluation may indicate a loss of 10% of participants in the treatment group and 10% in the control group. But, what if the majority of drop-outs in the first group were high-rate offenders, while most of those lost in the control group were low-rate offenders? How might this situation affect the analysis of main effects? The evaluation may find that the treatment group showed greater reductions in offending compared to the control group. Differential attrition is problematic because it can introduce the threat of **non–equivalence**, even in an RCT, if groups that were comparable at the start of a study are no longer equal at the end of the study and the difference is related to dropping out, not to the intervention itself.

Attrition makes it more difficult to conduct an **intent-to-treat (ITT)** analysis. In an ideal evaluation, all participants assigned to the treatment or control groups complete the pre-test, are followed over time and complete the post-test. This allows for an ITT analysis in which data from all participants is included in the analysis of main effects. When attrition occurs and data are missing from some participants, it is still possible to use an ITT approach. Because participant drop-out is so common, several statistical methods have been developed to minimize the threat of attrition (Graham, 2012; Shafer, 1999). However, many evaluations with attrition problems have not used such statistical techniques to compensate for participant loss or have used them incorrectly.

Some evaluators choose to abandon an ITT analysis and purposefully exclude information from those who failed to complete the treatment or who had no post-test assessment. Those who endorse this practice claim that individuals who received none or only part of a treatment would have no reason to change their behaviors and thus should not be included in estimates of the intervention effect (Gupta, 2011). Although this rationale makes sense, the general consensus among prevention scientists (e.g., Moher, Schultz, and Altman, 2001) and our view

> *What I advocate is treatment effectiveness research done well enough to produce both results we can trust and sufficient explanatory detail to understand why we got those results. Unfortunately, much contemporary treatment effectiveness research not only falls well short of this mark, but is, frankly, horrid.*
>
> Lipsey, 1988: 6

is that failure to use an ITT approach can bias the estimate of the program's effectiveness for several reasons. *First*, in any real world implementation some participants will drop out of the treatment condition. Subjects may move out of the intervention area; experience unexpected, negative side effects; feel threatened by the intervention or stigmatized by participation; or can no longer afford the cost of the intervention. Individuals may also switch from the control group into the treatment group or vice versa. Any of these changes can threaten the equivalence of the treatment and control groups and bias evaluation results. *Second*, when data are analyzed from a subset of individuals who had been randomly assigned to the treatment group at the start of the study, the results will be less generalizable to the program's intended population of persons. In this case, the external validity of the evaluation is threatened. *Third*, the sample size of the subsample of individuals who complete the treatment will be smaller than the original group, which will reduce the evaluation's ability to detect differences that are statistically significant. Given all of these potential problems, it is critical that evaluators make every effort to obtain post-test assessments for all participants initially assigned to treatment and control groups. They should also become familiar with the statistical techniques than can help minimize attrition and missing data problems.

Mediation and moderation analyses

Although most evaluations focus on assessing main effects, additional analyses like **mediation** and **moderation analyses** can significantly add to the understanding of the intervention's main effects and external validity. A **mediation analysis**, illustrated in Figure 4.2, helps explain exactly how the treatment produced a change in criminal behavior and tests the program's logic model. The mediation analysis determines if the treatment changed the targeted risk and/or protective factors (Path A in the Figure) and if the change in risk/protection led to the change in criminal behavior (Path B in the Figure) as hypothesized in the theoretical rationale. If this type of analysis shows that the targeted risk/protective factors were changed by the treatment as expected, and this change led to the reduction in criminal behavior, a strong claim can be made for the effectiveness of the intervention and for the validity of the theoretical model underlying the intervention.

In some cases, however, a mediation analysis could show a significant main effect (Path C) and a significant change in the risk and protective factors (Path A), but fail to show that the change in the risk and protective factors was related to the main effect (Path B). This finding would weaken any conclusions about the effectiveness of the intervention and challenge the program's theoretical rationale. The intervention would appear to work, but it would not be clear why or how it worked. If there were no main effect (Path C), but the treatment was effective in changing risk/protection (Path A), this also would challenge the intervention's theoretical rationale. Finally, if the intervention failed to change the targeted risk/protective factors (Path A) but produced a significant main effect (Path C), this would challenge the program change model, since the change did not occur using the intended mechanisms. Even though these types of findings weaken causal claims about the intervention, they can still be useful in helping developers refine their theoretical and program change models in order to improve intervention effectiveness.

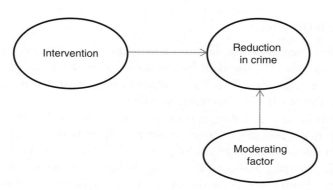

Figure 4.3 Moderating effects.

An analysis of **moderator effects** determines whether or not a third factor, usually related to participant characteristics like sex, race/ethnicity, or neighborhood poverty influence the direction or strength of the intervention's effect. This type of effect is shown in Figure 4.3. Many evaluations have tested for and found evidence that a moderator variable influences an intervention's main effect. For example, several of the evaluations of the **Good Behavior Game** (see Chapter 8) have shown that it is effective *only* with high-risk participants (i.e., students who show aggressive behavior in kindergarten) and with males (Kellam *et al.*, 2008). The intervention does not appear to reduce crime among lower risk students or females. For this program, both the "risk status" and sex of the participants would be considered moderating variables.

In some cases, interventions may have a significant and positive main effect but show harmful outcomes for a sub-set of participants.[6] Moderating analyses can help identify these types of **differential effects** and assess the generalizability of an intervention: whether it appears to work equally well for all participants, is more effective for some groups than others, or has harmful effects on a specific subgroup. Like mediating analyses, moderating analyses can provide important feedback to program developers about how and for whom their program works, as well as inform potential users of a program of these differences. For example, developers may make changes to their program change model to make the intervention more effective with low-risk participants. Or, they could ensure that the program is used only with the population for whom it has been shown to be effective. Knowing that certain conditions are necessary for program success can also help decision-makers determine if an intervention is appropriate for the specific population they serve.

Given the value of the information provided by mediating and moderating analyses, it is surprising that such statistical procedures are not routinely included in crime prevention evaluations. A moderator analysis is more frequently performed than a mediator analysis, but typically, only a small number of potential moderating factors are considered, most often the sex or race/ethnicity of participants. Our descriptions of specific crime prevention programs and practices will identify, when the analyses have been conducted, the types of populations for whom the intervention has been shown to be effective.

Short- and long-term effects

To this point we have referred to analyses that measure the effect of an intervention from pre-test to post-test, from before the intervention started to immediately after it ended. This type of analysis assesses the short-term effect of an intervention. While important, such analyses do not provide the most complete or accurate test of an intervention's effectiveness.

Consider an evaluation of a work program in a state correctional facility. Inmates interested in this program are randomly assigned to participate or not participate in the program. Pre-test and post-test assessments are made and official reports of prison infractions are used as the outcome measure. The measure of effectiveness is based on the change in rates of infraction during the six months before entering the program compared to the rate at the end of the intervention, a short-term effect. Why is this time frame inadequate to assess the effectiveness of the program? For one reason, participants have been in custody throughout the entire intervention, including during the pre-test assessment, have been closely supervised and have had limited opportunities to engage in criminal behavior. Secondly, the goal of the program was to provide work experience that would help inmates secure jobs after leaving prison. The theoretical rationale was that employment is a protective factor that would have its beneficial effect *after* the offenders had left the institution; it would keep them from re-offending once they were released back to their communities. However, the short-term analysis did not extend past the time of release, and given the restrictions imposed while participants were in custody, is this a fair test of the program's effectiveness? It is likely that such an evaluation would find no effect on prison infractions, but does this mean that the program should be stopped on the grounds that it did not work?

A better evaluation would investigate the longer term effects of the program, using multiple post-tests extending over a greater duration, at least until there is time for the intervention to have its intended effect. The specific amount of time needed between the pre-test and final post-test should be guided by the intervention's logic model, as well as research relating to the developmental timing of particular behaviors. For example, an intervention providing academic enrichment services to preschool children in order to reduce delinquency should follow participants at least until the teenage years, since this is when crime is likely to occur. However, there will be pressure to have results from the study, and secondary effects on risk and protective factors like children's reading skills and their attachment to teachers could still be examined in the short term, prior to adolescence.

In the case of the prison work program, a second post-test one year after release from the correctional facility and a third post-test two years after leaving would likely be adequate to capture the program's main effects. A comparison of recidivism rates from the initial post-test at the end of the program to the third post-test is called a **time-to-failure** analysis. This analysis compares the treatment and control groups' tendency to re-offend right away or to delay offending for a longer period of time. If the treatment group remains crime free for a longer period of time (on average) than the control group, even if the actual rate of recidivism at the last post-test is the same, this would be considered a positive outcome. In the shorter term, the evaluation could also measure secondary effects such as the acquisition of specific work skills, good work habits, and changes in attitudes toward work. Changes in these effects could then be incorporated into a mediating analysis to see if they led to reductions in recidivism.

All types of evaluations can incorporate multiple follow-up periods and post-tests, but these additional assessments will require more resources and effort compared to the administration of a single post-test. Nonetheless, they are important to help determine the **sustainability** or durability of intervention effects.

> *Science is always worth the wait.*
> The New York Times, 2011

Outcomes could be brief or could last for many years, indicating that they are sustained over time. For example, a program operating in a correctional facility may demonstrate positive effects while prisoners are in custody, are closely guarded and receive reinforcements for good behavior. However, these effects could be quickly lost once prisoners are released into the same neighborhoods, homes, schools, or peer groups that helped shape their criminal behaviors and led to their incarceration. Longer term effects may be more difficult to achieve, but they are possible and we will provide many examples in Section III of interventions that have been shown to reduce criminal behavior many years following the end of an intervention. Although sustainable effects are optimal, an intervention that can delay the onset of criminal behavior, even if it does not ultimately prevent it, is still effective, particularly in light of the evidence discussed in Chapter 3 showing that early onset of crime is linked to more frequent and serious criminal behavior over the life course.

Effect size

Effect sizes were discussed earlier in the chapter, but a few additional comments are relevant here. The effect size is a measure of the relative strength and substantive significance of the intervention main effect. It is intended to indicate how big a reduction in criminal behavior can be expected from participation in the intervention.

The effect size may be an unstandardized measure or a standardized measure. When the outcome is measured in units that have some intrinsic meaning, like criminal acts, arrests, or victimizations, an unstandardized effect size is typically used. For example, an evaluation may report that the effect size represents an average reduction of four crimes per person for those receiving the intervention. If the outcome is measured in units that have no intrinsic meaning, like 3 points on a 10-point scale intended to assess the seriousness of an offense, a standardized measure is typically used. In this case, the effect size will vary from 0 to 1, with *small* effect sizes ranging from 0 to 0.20, *moderate* effects ranging from 0.21 to 0.40, and values greater than 0.40 representing *large* effects (Cohen, 1988), as shown in Figure 4.4. An added advantage of the standardized effect size measure is that the effects of different interventions can be compared even when the measure of the outcome is different.

Another advantage of the effect size is that it is not influenced by the sample size of an evaluation, as is the test for statistical significance. Both small and large samples can be problematic when trying to identify the substantive or practical value of an intervention if you have to rely solely on tests of statistical significance. Small samples are said to have **low statistical power**. The smaller the sample, the greater the treatment-control difference must be to pass the 5% rule and achieve the accepted level of statistical significance.[7] But a calculation of the effect size can be performed in these cases in order to identify meaningful changes in crime. Conversely, in a large study (e.g., involving 1000 or more participants), it is much easier to find a statistically significant main effect even if the intervention has virtually no meaningful effect on criminal

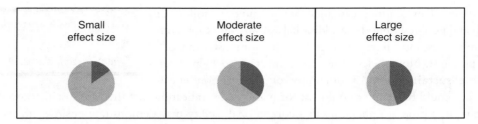

Figure 4.4   Effect sizes indicating the amount of criminal behavior reduced by an intervention.

behavior, as would be indicated by a very small effect size. It is useful, then, to consider both the statistical significance and effect size of an intervention. If the main effect is not statistically significant, the effect size has little practical significance; if it is statistically significant, the effect size provides an estimate of how powerful the intervention is for reducing criminal behavior.

Meta-analysis and systematic reviews

Meta-analysis is also a useful strategy in studies with small samples sizes and low statistical power. A meta-analysis provides an "analysis of analyses" and allows the results from multiple evaluation studies to be combined and analyzed together. This process eliminates the small sample size problem because results from participants involved in *all* studies are analyzed together. Meta-analyses are useful when multiple evaluations of an intervention have shown conflicting evidence of effectiveness, such as differences in the strength of the main effect or both positive and negative outcomes. Meta-analyses provide an estimate of the *average* effect size across all the studies included in the analysis and help make sense of contradictory evidence. This estimate is also considered more reliable than those from a single study as multiple evaluations contribute to the estimate.

In Section III, we will refer to findings from two types of meta-analysis. A meta-analysis of a prevention *program* will analyze the overall effects on crime of a single program, such as **Scared Straight** or **Functional Family Therapy**, which has been tested in multiple studies. A meta-analysis of a prevention *practice* will be based on multiple evaluations of different interventions that use a common change strategy or target a common outcome, such as the law enforcement practice of increasing surveillance in **hot spots**, or areas in a police beat known to have high levels of crime. Most meta-analyses in crime prevention are of the second type. Meta-analyses of single programs and policies are relatively rare, primarily because most of these types of interventions have been evaluated only one or two times, which is not enough to justify a meta-analysis.

A related approach to summarizing the evidence from multiple evaluations involves a **systematic review**. These reviews are based on having a set of procedures, specified in advance, which will guide the search, selection, evaluation, and synthesis of evaluation findings from multiple studies. The procedures should be clearly described so that other researchers could replicate the review. As we will describe more fully in Chapter 5, the Campbell Collaboration was one of the first organizations dedicated to conducting systematic reviews of interventions in crime and justice. As described on their website (www.campbellcollaboration.org/what_is_a_systematic-review), a systematic review must have: clear criteria regarding the types of evaluations that will be included and excluded from the analysis, which should include published and unpublished reports, as well as international studies; a description of exactly how the search for evaluations will proceed; a detailed plan describing how evaluation findings will be reviewed and coded; and use of meta-analysis where possible to estimate the average impact of a program, practice, or policy. In addition, they require that all procedures and findings be reviewed by other scientists prior to publication. This is a very rigorous review process that provides reliable estimates of effect sizes for individual programs, practices, and policies when there are multiple evaluations. As we will also describe in Chapter 5, the Office of Justice Programs' CrimeSolutions.gov website (http://www.crimesolutions.gov/Programs.aspx#programs) uses findings published by the Campbell Collaboration to identify effective and ineffective crime prevention practices.

Return on investment (ROI)

Last, but certainly not least, we want to mention a statistical analysis strategy that allows estimation of the economic value, or **return on investment (ROI)**, of a prevention intervention. This type of calculation is intended to help decision-makers evaluate taxpayers' and society's financial benefits and determine the worthiness of investing in particular programs, practices, or policies. It places a monetary value on the intervention outcomes, based on the effect sizes for all analyzed outcomes, and compares these benefits to the costs of the intervention. Although we will not get into the technical details of how the ROI is estimated, recall from Chapter 1 that crime has significant costs to society, including expenses related to law enforcement, corrections and drug treatment services. Such figures are all considered in the ROI.

The ROI is helpful not only for evaluating the economic importance of a single intervention (recall this question from Table 4.1) but also in comparing different interventions. For example, according to the Washington State Institute for Public Policy (2015), providing vocational training while adult offenders are in prison has an ROI of $13.22. That is, this practice returns $13.22 in savings to taxpayers for every $1.00 invested in it. In comparison, the provision of vocational education and job assistance to offenders after they are released from prison is $47.79. Such information can provide useful guidance to correctional officials when evaluating potential treatment services, though it should not be the *only* consideration. When describing crime prevention strategies in Section III, we will provide the ROI where it has been calculated. As you will see, some interventions have a negative ROI, meaning that their costs exceed their benefits. For example, the Scared Straight intervention has an ROI of -$201; it *costs* taxpayers about $201 for every dollar put into it (Washington State Institute for Public Policy, 2015). As you will read in Chapter 9, this is because Scared Straight has no demonstrated impact on criminal behavior.

A Critical View of Current Evaluation Research

Although we have already pointed out some of the limitations of evaluation research, we summarize some of the most serious concerns here given their importance for conducting evaluations and informing decision-makers' views about which interventions to replicate. A first concern is over

developer bias, a type of bias resulting from the involvement of program developers in evaluations of their own interventions that can distort estimates of the intervention's effectiveness. To date, most high-quality evaluations of crime prevention programs have been undertaken by the program developer (Gorman and Conde, 2007), and such evaluations have been shown to provide higher estimates of a program's effect size compared to studies led by independent investigators (Gandhi *et al.*, 2007; Petrosino and Soydan, 2005). This situation means that claims of program effectiveness may be exaggerated, and that if replicated on a wide-scale, many interventions will not produce the same impact on crime as we would expect based on their developer-based evaluation evidence.

Publication bias can also contribute to inflated estimates of a program's effect size. It is commonly accepted among scientists that academic journals accept articles that report positive evaluation findings at a higher rate than articles reporting no significant findings or iatrogenic effects (Hunter and Schmidt, 1990; McCord, 2003; Wilson, 2009). Unpublished studies receive far less attention and are often not included in systematic reviews of the evaluation literature (although the Campbell Collaboration is an exception). As a result, their findings will not be able to balance out the more positive effects documented in published studies, thus contributing to biases in the estimate of an intervention's average effect size. Although it is difficult to determine exactly how serious this problem is, it is likely that when agency decision-makers evaluate different options for addressing crime, they will not have all relevant information.

Next, there is the problem of evaluations failing to assess the long-term effectiveness of prevention programs, practices, and policies. Historically, the majority of evaluations have focused only on short-term effects, largely because it is more costly and difficult to conduct multiple follow-up assessments. Just consider the challenge in getting participants to complete two surveys, then think about how much more difficult it is to secure their agreement to participate in repeated assessments and in tracking them down year after year to do so. While easier to conduct, short-term evaluations could produce misleading results of an intervention's effectiveness if the treatment initially shows positive effects, but weaker or iatrogenic effects emerge in the long term. This has been known to occur (e.g., McCord, 2003; St. Pierre *et al.*, 2005). Conversely, interventions may have "sleeper effects" which are not present early on but become evident over time (e.g., Hawkins *et al.*, 1999). Such programs may be dismissed as ineffective if outcomes are evaluated only in the short term.

Findings can also be misinterpreted and interventions falsely perceived to be ineffective when evaluating **marginal effects**. The failure to find a statistically significant main effect when a new intervention is compared to "treatment as usual" should not be interpreted as evidence that the intervention was ineffective. This assessment may be correct if it is known that the treatment provided to the control group had no impact on crime. Otherwise, this finding means that the new intervention is no more effective than that the control group received. Stated differently, if the control group treatment reduced crime, and the new intervention's effects were no different than those of the control group program, it also produced positive changes in offending.

An issue that we have not yet considered is the potential for evaluations to overlook problematic **side effects** caused by participation in the intervention. Although the developer's review of research relating to the theoretical and change model should provide some guidance about possible negative effects, due to practical reasons such as having limited time to conduct surveys or the evaluator's specialization in a particular field of study, evaluations often limit their analysis of effects to only one or two outcomes. In doing so, they may fail to identify unanticipated negative effects on unassessed outcomes. For example, the National Women's Health Initiative Study examined the effects of a medical intervention intended to reduce heart disease in women. During the evaluation, the treatment provided to study participants was shown to increase women's risk for stroke and breast cancer, outcomes which were not expected but which happened to be measured by the evaluators (Manson *et al.*, 2013). These iatrogenic effects eventually led to the suspension of the intervention. In crime prevention, a long-term follow-up of the Milwaukee Domestic Violence Experiment revealed that domestic violence perpetrators who were randomly assigned to be arrested for their offenses were three times more likely to die of a homicide than those assigned to receive only a warning but not an arrest (Sherman and Harris, 2014). A somewhat higher death rate was also found for victims whose perpetrators had been arrested. Such outcomes were unanticipated and could have easily been overlooked if deaths had not been examined.

> *There is a moral imperative for … randomized experiments in crime and justice. That imperative develops from our professional obligation to provide valid answers to questions about the effectiveness of treatments, practices and programs.*
>
> David Weisburd, 2003: 339

A frequently cited ethical issue related to experimental evaluations, particularly RCTs, is that they recruit individuals who could all benefit from an intervention, but half are denied treatment: those assigned to the control group (Weisburd, 2003). In our view, this concern lacks validity because it assumes that the intervention is effective. But, the main goal of evaluation research is to answer the question: does this intervention work? If the treatment was known to reduce crime, it would be delivered to all participants. The ethical question could easily be turned around to ask: how can the justice system mandate individuals into interventions that have not been evaluated and which have no evidence of effectiveness? Such practices seem unethical given that some interventions, even those intended or expected to reduce crime, have been shown to be harmful, as you will see in Section III.

Another critique of RCTs is that they cost too much and that their high costs make them impractical to conduct. This concern has merit. For example, even a RCT considered "modest" in scope and complexity, such as an evaluation of a school-based prevention program involving 20 schools and 2 post-tests, can cost several million dollars and take 5 years to complete. Larger studies cost even more. The National Women's Health Initiative mentioned earlier, which involved over 160,000 American women, cost 625 million dollars (Parker-Pope, 2011). Costs can easily reach $10 to $15 million if an intervention is subject to an initial RCT and one or two replications to increase its external validity. Costs place a heavy burden on federal governments, as most experimental evaluations of crime prevention efforts are funded by national agencies like the Department of Justice and the National Institute on Drug Abuse in the USA. Local agencies are unlikely to be able to secure large grants from federal agencies or to have the required resources to conduct their own high-quality RCT or even QED, leading to a shortage of information about the effectiveness of interventions commonly implemented in communities. Nonetheless, it is possible for local programs to move through the early stages of the evaluation process and conduct process and pre-post evaluations. These studies can provide local providers with valuable information about their interventions and increase their chances of eventually obtaining funding for an experimental evaluation.

For all of these reasons, there has been some resistance to claims that experimental evaluations and especially RCTs are the "gold standard" in evaluation research and that only programs evaluated using these designs should be promoted as effective (Lab, 2014; Laycock, 2002). Critics also raise concerns about the limited external validity of RCTs, claiming they are too artificial and cannot adequately capture processes occurring in the real world. The heavy reliance on measuring outcomes using quantitative data based on official or self-reported data has been critiqued and arguments made for the use of **qualitative** data. Such studies might, for example, rely more heavily on in-depth interviews and/or observations of program participants, implementers and implementing agencies to understand the complex processes that affect criminal behavior. Pawson and Tilley (1997) have proposed the use of "realistic" or "realist" evaluation strategies which rely on a combination of qualitative and quantitative data to assess outcomes and change mechanisms of an intervention operating in different contexts.

In our view, qualitative studies have made significant contributions to the development of criminological theory, hypotheses about the causes of crime and identification of potential strategies to prevent or control it. However, this type of research is not equipped to validate these hypotheses or test the validity of proposed causal mechanisms. It is concerned with observing natural conditions, not manipulating causal variables. The latter is the specific purpose of an experimental study and the foundation for making a strong argument for a causal argument and/or intervention's effectiveness. We will return to this debate in the next chapter, when we describe variation in standards across agencies in determining what works to reduce crime. As you might realize, we will be making the case that such claims require the use of well-conducted RCTs and strong statistical analyses such as those described in this chapter.

The *Blueprints for Healthy Youth Development* Experience Reviewing Evaluations

As a final commentary on judging the quality of evaluation research, we conclude this chapter by sharing some of the first author's experiences leading the *Blueprints For Healthy Youth Development* project (www.blueprintsprograms.com/). Since 1996, Blueprints staff and members of its scientific advisory board have systematically compiled and reviewed findings from over 1300 prevention interventions, many of them aimed at reducing crime, delinquency, violence, and drug use (Mihalic and Elliott, 2015). The goal of the project is to identify interventions that have been demonstrated as effective in high-quality research designs. The merit of each research evaluation is judged according to the criteria described in this chapter. (See Chapter 5 for more detail about the Blueprints project and criteria.)

To date, about 80% of the interventions reviewed by Blueprints have not been subject to a credible scientific evaluation. These findings suggest that most crime prevention programs currently in use in the USA and internationally have never been assessed using the evaluation process described earlier. Of those that have been evaluated using experimental designs, most of the experiments were judged to have low merit because most failed to adequately address threats to internal validity. By far the most frequent problem encountered has been the threat of **non-equivalence** caused by contamination of the random assignment to treatment and control groups in RCTs, significant pre-test differences in QEDs, failure to perform an intent-to-treat analysis, and differential attrition that is not addressed in the analysis (Mihalic and Elliott, 2015). When high-quality evaluations have been performed, they have often indicated no significant effects on outcomes and a few studies have reported negative and harmful effects. These problems have resulted in a relatively short list of interventions identified as effective by Blueprints.

On the positive side, Blueprints has identified some interventions that have been evaluated using very high-quality research designs and which have demonstrated positive effects and good ROI rates. Moreover, over time, the quality of crime prevention evaluations has improved. RCTs are now more frequently employed and new methods for addressing some of the threats to internal validity have been developed and utilized by evaluators (for further commentary on progress made in evaluation research, see: Farrington and Welsh, 2005; Flay and Collins, 2005).

Summary

This chapter has provided a complete but fairly general overview of the purpose, process, and nature of evaluation research. Evaluation has three purposes: (i) to provide feedback to developers to help them improve their interventions, (ii) to test the validity of the causal processes underlying the intervention, and (iii) to provide critical information to funders, policy-makers and other decision-makers so that they can make informed choices about what interventions to implement to reduce crime.

Evaluation is a process with stages that involve a progression from the use of more basic to more sophisticated research designs. This sequence begins with a process evaluation, followed by a pre-post impact evaluation and then an experimental outcome evaluation. Each stage provides useful answers to particular research questions and information from all parts of the process should be considered when judging the overall effectiveness of an intervention. The merits of different types of evaluation are judged by their construct validity, internal validity, and external validity. In practice, few evaluations have provided good information on external validity and they are judged primarily on how well they address the threats to internal validity. Based on these criteria, RCTs are considered to be the "gold standard" when trying to determine the effectiveness of crime prevention programs, practices, and policies. When they are well conducted, RCTs do the best job of addressing the threats to internal validity and ruling out alternative explanations for the study findings.

We also reviewed different types of statistical analyses that can be used to help rule out alternative explanations of observed changes in criminal behaviors. Analytic procedures can also be used to confirm the underlying logic model and causal processes of the intervention, test for conditions that moderate the effects of the intervention and provide valuable feedback about the strengths and weaknesses of the intervention.

This chapter has identified the optimal practices to use when evaluating crime prevention interventions. Some of these methods have been critiqued and many are not followed in practice. Many experimental evaluations of crime interventions have weak levels of external or internal validity, have limited their design and analysis to short-term rather than long-term effects, may overstate their effect size, and are very expensive to undertake. For all of these reasons, Section III of this text, which describes interventions shown to be effective in reducing crime when evaluated in high-quality research projects, may be shorter than you expect and may not include interventions that you may have heard about or seen used. In fact, many commonly used crime prevention strategies have not been evaluated using rigorous research methods and some have failed to show positive effects on offending. However, this situation is slowly changing and evaluations are increasingly relying on better methods and statistical procedures.

Critical Thinking Questions and Practice Activities

1. Imagine you have been asked to speak to correctional staff at a nearby prison about how to evaluate a new program designed to reduce inmate recidivism. Although the program has only been operating for 8 months, the staff are interested in seeking funding to conduct a RCT to evaluate its effectiveness. Explain to them why doing so may not be the best way to begin the evaluation process and propose an alternative evaluation method.
2. Using Figures 4.2 and 4.3 as a guide, state the difference between **mediation** and **moderation** analyses. Be sure to contrast the types of information that each method provides about an intervention's effectiveness.
3. Consider the logic model of the Towards No Drug Abuse program shown in Chapter 3 (Figure 3.3). If you were conducting a **process evaluation** of this program, what kinds of data would you collect to determine if the program components were well implemented? If you conducted a **pre-post outcome evaluation** and it indicated significant reductions in substance use and weapons carrying, would you conclude with certainty that the program was effective? Why or why not? Describe an alternative explanation for these findings. If you conducted an **experimental outcome evaluation** of this program and it showed reductions in substance use but not in the risk and protective factors targeted by the program, what would you conclude about the program's theoretical and program change models?
4. Review the criticisms of evaluation designs, especially RCTs, described in this chapter. In your opinion, what is the most serious critique? Defend your position by explaining why the criticism you select has merit in questioning the ability of evaluations to adequately and ethically assess the effectiveness of crime prevention interventions.
5. Describe what is meant by **external validity**. How would you judge the external validity of a program designed to reduce violence between prison inmates that is tested only one time, with female offenders incarcerated in all women's prisons in New Zealand?

Endnotes

1. The LST program description lists two theories, social learning theory and problem behavior theory, but problem behavior theory is a specific version of social learning theory.
2. There are other types of experimental outcome designs, but we only describe those that are most often used in crime prevention evaluations. For a full description of other types of designs, see Shadish *et al.* (2002).

3. For an example of a RCT that did use randomly selected samples of participants and settings, and thus has high population and ecological external validity, see the National Head Start Impact Study (US Department of Health and Human Services, 2010). It assessed changes in children's academic performance using a random sample of all Head Start programs and children in these programs in the United States.

4. Other operations effects, like **task effects** and **Hawthorne effects**, are not discussed here but are reviewed in detail in Smith and Glass (1987).

5. For an interesting discussion of challenges involved with program replications and assessment of external validity, see Valentine and colleagues (2011), as well as reactions to this article (Aos *et al.*, 2011; Hansen, 2011).

6. Iatrogenic effects were found in an evaluation of the Family Foundations program (Feinberg *et al.*, 2010) conducted by the Blueprints for Healthy Youth Development Advisory Board based on detailed results provided by the first author of the evaluation.

7. Technically, statistical significance is a function of both the size of the difference and the standard error of the difference.

Helpful Websites (last accessed July 24, 2016)

- www.campbellcollaboration.org/what_is_a_systematic-review
  The Campbell Collaboration website includes a description of rigorous guidelines for conducting a systematic review, as well as completed systematic reviews for many crime prevention programs, practices, and policies.

- http://www.eblcprograms.org/docs/pdfs/NREPP_Non-researchers_guide_to_eval.pdf
  This online document from the National Registry of Evidence-based Programs and Practices (NREPP) provides a very basic overview of the purposes of research evaluation, types of evaluation design, and steps in the evaluation process.

- www.wsipp.wa.gov
  The Washington State Institute of Public Policy (WSIPP) website provides definitions of return on investment (ROI), details about how this measure is calculated, and ROI estimates for many crime prevention programs and practices.

Further Reading

- Fairchild, A. J., and MacKinnon, D. P. 2014. Using mediation and moderation analyses to enhance prevention research. In: Z. Sloboda and H. Petras (eds), *Defining Prevention Science*, pp. 537–556. New York, NY: Springer-Verlag.
  This book chapter provides a discussion of the use of mediation and moderation analysis and how these analyses can confirm the underlying theoretical rationale of an intervention and inform the development of future interventions.

- National Research Council. 2005. Improving Evaluation of Anticrime Programs. Committee on Improving Evaluation of Anti-Crime Programs, Committee on Law and Justice, Division of Behavioral and Social Sciences and Education. Washington, DC: The National Academies Press.
  This report provides recommendations for improving evaluations of crime prevention interventions.

- Shadish, W. R., Cook, T. D., and Campbell, D. T. 2002. *Experimental and Quasi-Experimental Designs for Generalized Causal Inference*. Boston, MA: Houghton-Mifflin.
  This classic text on experimental design provides an in-depth review of experimental and quasi-experimental evaluation designs, their strengths and weaknesses and threats to internal and external validity.

- Wilson, S. J., and Tanner-Smith, E. 2014. Meta-analysis in prevention research. In: Z. Sloboda and H. Petras (eds), *Defining Prevention Science*. New York, NY: Springer-Verlag.
  This book chapter provides a good introduction to the basic elements of a meta-analysis and its use in prevention science.

References

Aos, S., Cook, T. D., Elliott, D. S., *et al.* 2011. Commentary on Valentine, Jeffrey, *et al. Prevention Science*, 12:121–122.

Caldwell, B., and Bradley, R. 1984. *Home Observation for Measurement of the Environment (HOME)*, Revised edition. Little Rock, AR: University of Arkansas.

Cohen, J. 1988. *Statistical Power Analysis for the Behavioral Sciences*, 2nd ed. Hillsdale, NJ: Lawrence Erlbaum Associates.

Cook, T. D., Shadish, W. R., and Wong, V. C. 2008. Three conditions under which observational studies produce the same results as experiments. *Journal of Policy Analysis and Management*, 274:724–750.

Eisner, M. P. 2009. No effects in independent prevention trials: Can we reject the cynical view? *Journal of Experimental Criminology*, 5:163–183. doi: 10.1007/s11292-009-9071-y

Fagan, A. A., and Mihalic, S. 2003. Strategies for enhancing the adoption of school-based prevention programs: Lessons learned from the Blueprints for Violence Prevention replications of the Life Skills Training Program. *Journal of Community Psychology*, 31:235–254.

Farrington, D. P., and Welsh, B. C. 2005. Randomized experiments in criminology: What have we learned in the last two decades? *Journal of Experimental Criminology*, 1:9–38. doi: 10.1007/s11292-004-6460-0

Feinberg, M. E., Jones, D. E., Goslin, M. C., and Kan, M. L. 2010. Effects of Family Foundations on parents and children: 3.5 years after baseline. *Journal of Family Psychology*, 24:532–542.

Flay, B. R., and Collins, L. M. 2005. Historical review of school-based randomized trials for evaluating problem behavior prevention programs. *The Annals of the American Academy of Political and Social Science*, 599:115–145.

Gandhi, A. G., Murphy-Graham, E., Petrosino, A., *et al.* 2007. The devil is in the details: Examining the evidence for "proven" school-based drug abuse prevention programs. *Evaluation and Program Planning*, 30:422–429.

Gorman, D. M., and Conde, E. 2007. Conflict of interest in the evaluation and dissemination of "model" school-based drug and violence prevention programs. *Evaluation and Program Planning*, 30:422–429. doi: 10.1016/j.evalprogplan.2007.06.004

Graham, J. W. 2012. *Missing Data: Analysis and Design*. New York, NY: Springer.

Grasmick, H. G., Tittle, C. R., Bursik, R. J., and Arneklev, B. J. 1993. Testing the core empirical implications of Gottfredson and Hirschi's general theory of crime. *Journal of Research in Crime and Delinquency*, 30:5–29.

Gupta, S. K. 2011. Intention-to-treat concept: A review. *Perspectives in Clinical Research*, 2:109–112. doi: 10.4103/2229-3485.83221

Hansen, W. B. 2011. Was Herodotus correct? *Prevention Science*, 12:118–120.

Hawkins, J. D., Catalano, R. F., Kosterman, R., *et al.* 1999. Preventing adolescent health-risk behaviors by strengthening protection during childhood. *Archives of Pediatric and Adolescent Medicine*, 153:226–234.

Hunter, J. E., and Schmidt, F. I. 1990. *Methods of Meta-analysis: Correcting Error and Bias in Research Findings*. Newbury Park, CA: Sage.

Kellam, S. G., Hendricks Brown, C., Poduska, J. M., *et al.* 2008. Effects of a universal classroom behavior management program in first and second grades on young adult behavioral, psychiatric, and social outcomes. *Drug and Alcohol Dependence*, 95S:S5–S28. doi: 10.1016/j.drugalcdep.2008.01.004

Lab, S. P. 2014. *Crime Prevention: Approaches, Practices and Evaluations*, 8th edn. New Providence, NJ: Anderson Publishing.

Laycock, G. 2002. Methodological issues in working with policy advisors and practitioners. In: N. Tilley (ed.), *Analysis for Crime Prevention*, pp. 205–237. Monsey, NY: Criminal Justice Press.

Lipsey, M. 1988. Practice and malpractice in evaluation research. *Evaluation Practice*, 9:5–24.

Manson, J. E., Chlebowski, R. T., Stefanick, M. L., *et al.* 2013. Menopausal hormone therapy and health outcomes during the intervention and extended poststopping phases of the Women's Health Initiative randomized trials. *Journal of the American Medical Association*, 310:1353–1368.

McCord, J. 2003. Cures that harm: Unanticipated outcomes of crime prevention programs. *The Annals of the American Academy of Political and Social Science*, 587:16–30.

Mihalic, S., and Elliott, D. S. 2015. Evidence-based programs registry: Blueprints for Healthy Youth Development. *Evaluation and Program Planning*, 48:124–131.

Mihalic, S., Fagan, A. A., and Argamaso, S. 2008. Implementing the LifeSkills Training drug prevention program: Factors related to implementation fidelity. *Implementation Science*, 3:5.

Moher, D., Schultz, K. F., and Altman, D. 2001. The CONSORT statement: Revised recommendations for improving the quality of reports of parellel-group randomized trials. *Journal of the American Medical Association*, 285:1987–1991.

National Science Foundation. 2013. Common Guidelines for Education Research and Development. Washington, DC: Institute of Education Sciences, US Department of Education and the National Science Foundation.

Parker-Pope, T. 2011. The women's health initiative and the body politic. *The New York Times, Week in Review*, April 9, 2011.

Pawson, R., and Tilley, N. 1997. *Realistic Evaluation*. London, England: Sage.

Petrosino, A., and Soydan, H. 2005. The impact of program developers as evaluators on criminal recidivism: Results from meta-analyses of experimental and quasi-experimental research. *Journal of Experimental Criminology*, 1:435–450.

Shadish, W. R., Cook, T. D., and Campbell, D. T. 2002. *Experimental and Quasi-Experimental Designs for Generalized Causal Inference*. Boston, MA: Houghton-Mifflin.

Shadish, W. R., Cook, T. D., and Leviton, L. C. 1991. *Foundations of Program Evaluation: Theories of Practice*. Newbury Park, CA: Sage.

Shafer, J. L. 1999. Multiple imputation: A primer. *Statistical Methods in Medical Research*, 8:3–15.

Sherman, L. W., and Harris, H. M. 2014. Increased homicide victimization of suspects arrested for domestic assault: A 23-year follow-up of the Milwaukee Domestic Violence Experiment (MilDVE). *Journal of Experimental Criminology*. doi: 10.1007/s11292-013-9193-0

Shultz, K. F., and Grimes, D. A. 2002. Sample size slippages in randomized controlled trials: Exclusions, lost and wayward. *Lancet*, 359:781–785.

Smith, M. L., and Glass, G. V. 1987. *Research and Evaluation in Education and the Social Sciences*. Englewood Cliffs, NJ: Prentice-Hall.

St. Pierre, T. L., Osgood, D. W., Mincemoyer, C. C., *et al.* 2005. Results of an independent evaluation of Project ALERT delivered in schools by cooperative extension. *Prevention Science*, 6:305–317.

US Department of Health and Human Services. 2010. Head Start impact study: Final report. Washington, DC: US Government Printing Office.

Valentine, J. C., Biglan, A., Boruch, R. F., *et al.* 2011. Replication in prevention science. *Prevention Science*, 12:103–117.

Washington State Institute for Public Policy. 2015. Benefit-cost results. Olympia, WA: Washington State Institute for Public Policy.

Weisburd, D. 2003. Ethical practice and evaluations of interventions in crime and justice: The moral imperative for randomized trials. *Evaluation Review*, 27:336–354.

Weisburd, D., and Britt, C. 2014. *Statistics in Criminal Justice*. New York, NY: Springer.

Wilson, D. B. 2009. Missing a critical piece of the pie: Simple document search strategies inadequate for systematic reviews. *Journal of Experimental Criminology*, 5:429–440. doi: 10.1007/s11292-009-9085-5

5

Establishing a Standard for Judging Intervention Effectiveness

Learning Objectives

Upon finishing this chapter, students should be able to:
- Understand why it is important to have standards, and consensus on these standards, for determining the effectiveness of crime prevention programs, practices, and policies
- Summarize the challenges in establishing rigorous, agreed-upon standards for identifying effective crime prevention programs, practices, and policies
- Identify multiple web-based databases that list effective crime prevention programs, policies, and practices
- Summarize the differences in standards and review processes used to determine program effectiveness across these databases
- Recommend a set of rigorous standards that should be used in future determinations of "what works" to prevent crime.

Introduction

Have you ever received an inoculation, vaccine, or other preventive medicine (e.g., a flu shot) in order to prevent an illness? How confident were you that this treatment would prevent you from getting sick? How worried were you that the medicine would make you feel worse?

When was the last time you were prescribed or bought over-the-counter medicine to cure a cold or other illness? How confident were you that this medicine would work to alleviate your symptoms? Were you worried

The Prevention of Crime, First Edition. Delbert Elliott and Abigail Fagan.
© 2017 John Wiley & Sons, Inc. Published 2017 by John Wiley & Sons, Inc.
Companion website: www.wiley.com/go/elliott/prevention_of_crime

about potential side effects, particularly whether or not taking the medicine would make you feel worse rather than better?

Although there are some exceptions, most people tend to place a lot of confidence in the medical profession, in doctors and in the medications offered to us when we are sick. When prescribed a medicine, we usually assume it will work and that harmful side effects will be minimal. Most of the time, we do not even give the topic much thought: we have faith that there are regulations governing the testing and approval of medications and that some capable group or organization is watching to make sure these policies are followed. Don't we?

Can we have this same confidence in the work of prevention scientists? Are there any standards governing the creation, testing, and distribution of crime prevention programs, practices, and policies? Are there any regulations for how this work is done or any agencies or organizations charged with ensuring that such regulations are upheld and that harmful interventions are not implemented?

This chapter will consider these issues. We will describe the degree to which there are standards governing the work of prevention scientists and the challenges faced when trying to create, reach consensus on and apply these standards in crime prevention. We will identify the varied sets of standards currently used by different groups when identifying and recommending effective crime prevention strategies, and the resulting disparity in the interventions promoted on web-based databases as "evidence-based," "best practices," "model," or "promising." The chapter will conclude with our recommendations for a set of standards we would like to see used more consistently across agencies seeking to identify "what works" in crime prevention.

The Need for Standards about "What Works" to Prevent Crime

Today, many federal agencies emphasize the importance of using "what works" to improve public health and prevent or reduce crime, meaning that these problems should be addressed using evidence-based or effective programs, practices, and policies. Yet, there are many different views about "what works", what constitutes "evidence" and how to determine if a particular intervention is "effective" in achieving a particular outcome. These views vary across agencies, federal policy-makers, scientists, and potential implementers of an intervention.

Although the increased focus on using evidence-based interventions is encouraging, without clear definitions and agreed-upon standards describing what this means, success is unlikely to be realized. Without such guidelines, practitioners have to decide for themselves what is effective or evidence-based and what is not, and these decisions are very complicated. As we will describe, many organizations now promote evidence-based prevention programs, but the number, type, and quality of interventions recommended vary widely across these agencies, resulting in a confusing array of options for practitioners. Some agencies judge the merits of interventions using strict and scientifically rigorous criteria, such as that described in Chapter 4, when trying to identify what works, which usually results in a smaller list of recommended programs. Other agencies have lower standards, which generally increases the number of options but may also result in programs being nominated that have a weaker evidence base. There is a greater chance, then, that these interventions will be ineffective in reducing crime and a greater likelihood that taxpayers' money will be wasted if such programs are replicated in communities.

By failing to provide practitioners with consistent, easy-to-access and valid information about what works, we risk their becoming frustrated with and skeptical about prevention science and scientists. They may ask themselves, for example: *how can I trust a bunch of people who can't even agree among themselves about what works?* In the absence of good information, agencies and communities may also implement ineffective strategies, and when positive results are not achieved, they will become even more doubtful about the scientific process and prevention scientists.

How can we prevent this skepticism and ensure that effective crime prevention efforts are implemented and ineffective strategies avoided? The answer is straightforward, at least in theory: we must reach agreement on a set of standards or guidelines for what constitutes evidence that a program works and then ensure that these guidelines are consistently and widely used to identify effective interventions. If this is not accomplished, there is a real danger of promoting programs of questionable value and losing public confidence in prevention science.

How Politics, Science, and Practice Influence Decisions about What Works

If we want to have any chance of success in achieving consensus on guidelines for determining what works, we must first understand why such differences exist. Why is there such disparity across agencies and individuals in the standards used to identify effective crime prevention programs? What stands in the way of a "master list" of recommended programs and an agreed-upon set of standards for identifying programs that all parties can agree to? In criminology, as in most disciplines, determinations about the level of evidence needed to determine program effectiveness, and which programs should be promoted based on this evidence, are influenced by politics, scientific ideals, ethical concerns, and practical considerations.

First, political ideologies strongly influence evaluation standards and the identification of effective and ineffective programs. One of the major differences across different lists of what works is whether or not a particular intervention must be evaluated using a **randomized control trial (RCT)**. Although the RCT is widely promoted as the "gold standard" in evaluation research, meaning it is the best methodology for determining effectiveness (Cook and Campbell, 1979; Sherman, 2003; Weisburd, 2010), criminal justice agencies have not generally advocated for the use of RCTs. For example, the agencies responsible for funding most criminal justice research in the USA, the National Institute of Justice (NIJ) and the Office of Juvenile Justice and Delinquency Prevention (OJJDP), have historically not required that evaluations rely on RCTs. Instead, most of their funded research has supported non-randomized trials. There have been some exceptions, usually coinciding with the arrival of a leader who is personally supportive of RCTs, but generally, these agencies have not widely encouraged the use of RCTs (Farrington, 2003; Weisburd, 2003). These views strongly influence scientific practices: when the political climate does not fund or support RCTs, scientists will be less likely to use and endorse RCTs.

There was a similar reluctance to support RCTs in the field of medicine. Until the early 1960s, the RCT was often viewed as too difficult, costly, and unethical to implement. But, in

1962, a law passed by President Kennedy dramatically changed this point of view in the USA. At that time, a sedative used to treat morning sickness in pregnant women, thalidomide, was shown to result in birth defects in children born in Europe, Canada, and other countries. The public demanded that the government do something to prevent such catastrophes in America, and the result was federal legislation, in the form of

> *Failure to discover whether a program is effective is unethical.*
> Boruch, 1975: 135

the US Kefauver-Harris Drug Amendments Acts. These laws called for stricter guidelines and more safeguards to ensure that drugs sold in the USA went through rigorous testing prior to being released. They required that drug manufacturers prove scientifically, using RCTs, that medications were not only effective but also safe. In time, the National Institutes of Health, which provides billions of dollars to fund health-related research each year, adopted similar standards and strongly emphasized the use of RCTs in their funded studies. In the fields of medicine and public health, thanks to political and public support, RCTs are now widely considered as *the* way to determine effectiveness.

Politics do matter when it comes to emphasizing particular standards for determining effectiveness. It is also true, of course, that political forces can be difficult to overcome, and there is often political pressure to support particular programs even if scientific evidence indicates they are not effective. Federal and state agencies may be reluctant to identify as ineffective strategies which have been supported by public funds and endorsed by political allies. For example, mandating that some juvenile offenders be tried in the adult criminal justice system, **Scared Straight** interventions that involve visits to prisons for youth considered at high risk for engaging in crime, and the **Drug Abuse and Resistance Education (D.A.R.E.)** program taught in schools by police officers have received a lot of federal funding and have much political and popular support. This backing, and the considerable amount of personnel, materials, and training invested in these strategies, is difficult to counteract. Even though multiple studies have shown that each strategy is ineffective (see Section III for the facts), they are hard to remove from society. How can political and public pressures to use ineffective strategies be overturned? We will explore that question more fully in Section IV of this text, but the solution, we believe, lies in increasing support for prevention science, publicizing more broadly interventions that *do* work, requiring that criminal justice agencies be accountable for the outcomes they achieve with public funds, showing that effective prevention is cost effective and helping communities implement effective strategies.

Scientists, like politicians, play a key role in determining the standards to be used in judging program effectiveness. Unfortunately, they can be just as stubborn in their convictions about what works and what does not and in their views about what is needed to determine effectiveness. Returning to the example of the RCT, some criminologists support RCTs as the gold standard of evaluation research while others doubt their necessity, question their feasibility and emphasize their costs and difficulty in comparison to other methodologies (Hough, 2010; Sampson, 2010). Some argue that the methodological rigor of the RCT should not be the sole basis on which intervention effectiveness is determined, in large part because experiments are too artificial and have low **external validity** (Sampson, Winship, and Knight, 2013; Weisburd, 2003). That is, some critics contend that the experimental conditions manipulated by scientists to fit the demands of

RCTs have little resemblance to everyday experiences and practices (Pawson and Tilley, 1994). As a result, an intervention deemed effective for participants in a research trial may not actually work in practice.

Sampson and colleagues (2013) contend that although RCTs can tell us *what works*, they are less able to tell us what *will work* in naturalistic conditions. They recommend that much more evidence must be accumulated prior to making recommendations for the use of particular interventions. Specifically, they would like to wait until programs document in detail the populations for whom they are most effective, exactly how and why outcomes are achieved and the larger contexts in which positive effects are most likely to be evidenced. Others assert that quantitative methodologies cannot capture all of the processes, outcomes and experiences potentially related to program effectiveness and that qualitative methods are better able to capture why and how behaviors change (Pawson and Tilley, 1994). Finally, some point out that local programs are usually not subject to randomized studies, because knowledge of how to conduct RCTs and sufficient funding to implement this methodology are often lacking in communities. This means that lists of what works often exclude local programs, even though these may be most appealing to local practitioners.

As discussed in Chapter 4, ethical concerns about experiments and RCTs have also been raised. Randomizing some individuals to a potentially effective treatment and withholding such services from other individuals is troubling to many. There may be concerns that decisions about who receives treatment and who does not will be biased and that, regardless, all individuals should be provided potentially beneficial treatments (Weisburd, 2003). Others point to the difficulty in convincing judges, parole officers, schools, families, or communities to agree to randomization. If participants are unlikely to agree to such a methodology, then more feasible approaches should be adopted. Finally, some suggest that randomized experiments cost more than other types of evaluations.

All of these concerns result in resistance to standards that limit the determination of what works to interventions that have been evaluated using RCTs. Most critics of the RCT advocate for more flexible standards that will allow for a variety of research evaluation methods and types of evidence. The advantage of loosening criteria is that doing so will likely increase the number of recommended programs that communities can adopt. Having more options can, in turn, increase the number of interventions in use. However, there is a corresponding increase in the risk of program failure, in that less rigorous standards generally correspond to more uncertainty that programs actually work. Then, as we have discussed, if programs are widely replicated and fail to produce results, confidence in science is undermined. Higher standards carry a lower risk of program failure, but also fewer choices for communities. When few options are available, practitioners may feel forced to implement a strategy that they do not agree with or which is difficult given their resources or capacity. Aware of this dilemma, public agencies may feel pressured to loosen standards of effectiveness.

This quickly begins to resemble a "chicken and egg" dilemma and leaves us with the question: how can we balance scientific standards with practical considerations in a way that will best ensure reductions in crime? We try to answer this question in the conclusion of this chapter. Before doing so, however, let's review in more detail the standards that are currently used to determine program effectiveness and how these standards have come to be.

Historical Development of "What Works" Databases

The emphasis on identifying evidence-based crime prevention strategies using high-quality research evaluations emerged in the mid-1990s in the USA. During this period, Martinson's (1974) and others' claims that "nothing works" (see Chapter 2) were still widely accepted. It was also recognized that many crime prevention efforts had not been evaluated for effectiveness and if they were, evaluations were generally of poor quality (Farrington, 2003). This was also a period in which crime rates, especially for youth-perpetrated offenses, were surging, drawing public attention to the crime problem and increasing demands to do something to reverse these trends. What followed was the publication of various guides describing effective crime prevention strategies, though there was little description of the standards used to produce the lists of effective programs contained in these guides. Early guides to "what works" included the following:

- **1995: *Guide for Implementing the Comprehensive Strategy for Serious, Violent, and Chronic Juvenile Offenders*, Office of Juvenile Justice and Delinquency Prevention (OJJDP).** The goal of this publication was to identify "Effective" and "Promising" programs evaluated in the USA. Given its sponsorship by OJJPD, all interventions in the *Guide* were aimed at preventing juvenile delinquency. The *Guide* also emphasized comprehensive approaches to prevention and included an array of universal, selected, and indicated programs – from interventions implemented early in life for non-offenders to juvenile justice programs for incarcerated offenders. The *Guide* did not include information about criteria used to determine program effectiveness. It simply stated that Promising programs "did not have sufficiently strong research designs" compared to Effective programs (Office of Juvenile Justice and Delinquency Prevention, 1995: xi).
- **1996: *Communities That Care Prevention Strategies Guide.*** This book was published as a resource for communities implementing the Communities That Care (CTC) prevention system (see Chapter 7 to learn more about CTC). It listed interventions considered to be "Effective" in reducing juvenile substance use and delinquency. Determinations about effectiveness were based on evidence showing that programs tried to reduce risk factors and increase protective factors and "showed positive effects in high-quality" evaluations (*Communities That Care: Prevention Strategies Guide to What Works*, 1996: xvi).
- **1997: *Preventing Drug Use Among Children and Adolescents: A Research-Based Guide*, National Institute on Drug Abuse (NIDA).** This was the first attempt by NIDA to compile information on effective substance use prevention programs appropriate for children and adolescents. The *Redbook* (so named because of its red cover) reviewed information on risk and protective factors related to substance use and how interventions could target these factors to reduce substance use. Examples of "research-tested" prevention programs were also given but criteria used to determine inclusion in the book were not provided.
- **1996–1997: *Blueprints for Violence Prevention*.** In 1996, the Center for the Study and Prevention of Violence at the University of Colorado began the Blueprints Initiative. Its goal was to identify effective youth violence and substance use prevention programs based on systematic reviews of evaluation studies and rigorous, clearly identified criteria to judge effectiveness (see later for more details on these criteria). By 1997, 10 "Model" programs with strong evidence of effectiveness

had been identified, were listed on the Blueprints website and were described in a series of short books (i.e., "blueprints") designed for practitioners and agencies (Elliott, 1997).

- **1996–1997:** *Preventing Crime, What Works, What Doesn't, What's Promising*. In 1996, Congress required that the US Attorney General provide a comprehensive evaluation of the effectiveness of crime prevention programs funded by the Department of Justice. The review, conducted by criminologists at the University of Maryland, included juvenile- and adult-focused prevention programs as well as strategies that could be implemented by communities, law enforcement agencies, and correctional institutions (Sherman *et al.*, 1997). In addition to listing effective and ineffective strategies, the review was important in creating a rating system known as the "Maryland Scale of Scientific Methods" (Sherman *et al.*, 1998). It outlined specific criteria for differentiating between "Effective," "Promising," and "Ineffective" programs based on the methodological rigor of their evaluations.

- **2001:** *Youth Violence: A Report of the Surgeon General*. This report was created by the US Department of Health and Human Services at the request of the US Surgeon General at that time, David Satcher, largely in response to concerns about increases in youth violence in the 1990s and the 1999 shootings at Columbine High School in Littleton, CO. This review of prevention programs was guided by life course developmental theories and focused on universal, selective, and indicated strategies aimed at youth. It did not review interventions for law enforcement or correctional agencies. The *Report* classified interventions as "Model," "Promising," and "Ineffective," based on criteria including the Maryland Scale of Scientific Methods, the Blueprints ratings, and effect sizes produced by the interventions. Coincidently, its Senior Scientific Editor, Dr Del Elliott, is also the developer of the Blueprints Initiative and co-author of this textbook.

Current Crime Prevention Lists and Criteria

As noted above, early efforts to identify effective crime prevention strategies did not clearly identify the criteria used to determine program effectiveness, likely used less rigorous criteria and published their findings in reports that may or may not have been widely read. In this section, we will review current efforts to identify effective crime prevention programs, practices, and policies. These lists tend to have stricter and more clearly defined standards for determining what works and a greater emphasis on communicating results to policy-makers, agency administrators, and practitioners. Instead of relying solely on published reports, agencies are increasingly releasing their findings directly to practitioners via online databases, many of which have user-friendly search engines and practical information about recommended programs.

> *Basing policy on evidence requires somebody, or some body, to ordain and proclaim the 'best evidence'. An authorized group has to select that evidence which is worth attending to and give it visibility and standing.*
>
> Weiss *et al.*, 2008: 43

We summarize here some of the best known and widely used lists, sometimes referred to as "what works" databases. Note that *we restrict our discussion to online databases which are regularly updated*. Given these parameters, we will not be reviewing other lists that you may or may not have heard about, such as the **California Evidence-based Clearinghouse for Child Welfare** (www. cebc4cw.org/), which focuses on effective programs for children and families in the child welfare system; the **Centers for Disease Control (CDC) Community Guide** (http://www. thecommunityguide.org/index.html),[1] which includes violence and substance use prevention strategies; the **Child Trends' What Works/LINKS** database (http://www.childtrends.org/ what-works/), a comprehensive list of programs to promote children's healthy development; and **Investing in Children** (www.investinginchildrten.eu), a list of interventions for children created using standards similar to Blueprints standards and including cost–benefit information developed and maintained by the Dartington Social Research Unit in the UK. While these websites have useful information, they are not regularly updated, which is problematic given the numerous evaluations conducted each year.

As will quickly become apparent, the six databases we will describe in detail use different criteria to determine program effectiveness. Because we draw heavily upon the Blueprints list and criteria when identifying effective crime prevention programs in this textbook, we begin by describing its criteria. When describing the other lists, we note similarities and differences in their standards compared to Blueprints.

Blueprints for Healthy Youth Development (www.blueprintsprograms.com)

Blueprints has very rigorous criteria for determining the effectiveness of crime prevention programs. The database is restricted, however, to interventions which show an impact on youth behavior. That is, interventions focused solely on adult outcomes are not reviewed by Blueprints. However, programs with adult participants may be included if they have been shown to affect youth behaviors. Blueprints is also limited to reviewing programs, not practices or policies.

Blueprints was begun in 1996 and underwent an expansion and revision in 2013, including changes to the criteria used to determine program effectiveness. As of Spring 2014, programs are reviewed based on four criteria: (i) **intervention specificity**, (ii) **evaluation quality**, (iii) **intervention impact**, and (iv) **system readiness**.[2] The first criterion is not typically used by other lists of evidence-based programs, but it is considered important by Blueprints because it takes into account the theoretical basis for the program and its logic model, both key features of interventions as described in Chapters 3 and 4. In order to meet this criterion, programs have to clearly identify the theory(ies) guiding the intervention, the risk and protective factors targeted for change, the populations to be served and the specific services to be offered. The second and third criteria focus more on the research methods used in the evaluation; every other database takes these features into account in some way. For Blueprints, Evaluation Quality is assessed according to the number of well-conducted experimental and quasi-experimental evaluations conducted, and the Intervention Impact relates to the number and size of positive and negative effects on youth outcomes. For the fourth criterion, System Readiness, even if a program has been well evaluated and shown to reduce crime, if the developer does not have the desire or ability to help communities replicate it – or to authorize other parties to provide such assistance – it will not be promoted as effective by Blueprints.

Table 5.1   Blueprints criteria.

Designation	Intervention specificity	Evaluation quality	Intervention impact	System readiness
Model	√	2 RCTs *or* 1 RCT and 1 QED	Sustained for ≥1 year	√
Promising	√	1 RCT *or* 2 QEDs	Post-test	√

Programs meet this criterion if developers can provide training, tools, manuals, and ongoing support to those who wish to implement the intervention.

Programs that meet all four criteria are rated as "Model" or "Promising" and those that do not are not listed on the website. This means that the Blueprints website does not contain information about ineffective or harmful programs. As shown in Table 5.1, designation as a **Model** program requires: (i) well-described and logical intervention specificity; (ii) at least two well-conducted RCTs or one RCT and one QED; (iii) positive effects on crime, no harmful or iatrogenic effects and sustainability of effects for at least one year after the intervention has ended; and (iv) readiness for replication. As the name implies, designation of "Model" is reserved for the best programs; that is, interventions that have the strongest chance, based on scientific evidence, of producing significant and lasting effects. Thus, programs must have been replicated at least once and show some evidence of long-term effectiveness in high-quality evaluations.

What does a "high-quality" evaluation mean for Blueprints? Reviewers judge the quality of RCTs and QEDs based on the study design features and analysis strategies we reviewed in Chapter 4. For example, they take into account the validity and reliability of the measures, equivalence of participants at the start of the study, attrition and missing data and the quality of the statistical analyses performed. When three or more high-quality evaluations of a program have been conducted, a meta-analysis is performed to determine the average effect size across the studies.

Promising programs must meet the same criteria as Model programs, except that replication and evidence of sustained effects are not required. That is, a program can be certified as Promising if only one well-conducted RCT or two QEDs have been conducted and positive effects shown only in the short term. Programs meeting this designation are effective but are designated "Promising" because widespread use across a state or nation may not be warranted until further evaluations are conducted.

In addition to understanding the criteria used to determine effectiveness, it is important to understand the processes by which these criteria are applied. Blueprints uses a **systematic review** approach, which in this case means that staff: (i) conduct an exhaustive search for all evaluation reports related to the intervention, (ii) document findings from each of these studies using the same set of standards, and (iii) evaluate the overall effectiveness of the program based on the quality, strength, and consistency of findings across all studies. A panel of scientific experts in evaluation methodology, intervention design and testing, and the content areas of interest to Blueprints (e.g., crime/delinquency, substance use, mental health, and education) meet to discuss the evidence. They make the final determination of program effectiveness according to the Blueprints criteria and periodically update these ratings as new evaluations are conducted.

Coalition for Evidence-based Policy (www.coalition4evidence.org)

The Coalition is a non-profit organization that seeks to identify effective programs influencing broad social outcomes including education, health, housing, employment, welfare, mental health, and emotional well-being, as well as substance use and crime. Its primary goal is to influence government funding of "the most promising social interventions," which it considers to be those evaluated using well-conducted RCTs. Unlike the Blueprints systematic review approach, the Coalition limits its reviews to programs likely to be effective based on their inclusion in other databases. Together, these restrictions have resulted in a short list of recommended programs. As of August 1, 2015, only eight interventions on the Coalition website were considered to have reduced any of the criminal behaviors reviewed in this textbook.

Similar to Blueprints, Coalition reviews are conducted by a panel of scientific experts who meet twice per year to review evaluation evidence. Their criteria, however, are focused entirely on the scientific quality of the evaluation and do not take intervention specificity or dissemination readiness into account, although there is a preference for evaluations conducted in what they determine to be "typical community settings." Designation as a **Top Tier** program requires: (i) two well-conducted RCTs or one RCT taking place in multiple sites, and (ii) statistically significant, sizeable and sustained positive effects and no evidence of contradictory findings from well-conducted RCTs. In determining whether or not an evaluation is "well conducted," the Coalition rates elements of the research design using similar criteria as Blueprints, assessing features like the validity of the measures, baseline equivalence, participant attrition, and statistical techniques. Unlike Blueprints, "sustained" effects do not mean that findings have to be demonstrated at a particular time point following the end of the intervention. Instead, this criterion could be met, for example, if positive effects are shown in Years 2 and 3 of a three-year program.

To achieve **Near Top Tier** status, a program must be evaluated in one well-conducted RCT and have sizeable positive effects. There is no requirement of replication or sustained effects. The Coalition does not specify the size of the effect needed to qualify for Top Tier or Near Top Tier status. However, the website notes that they will take into account the program's cost and ease of implementation when deciding if the size of the effect is worth the investment in the program. The Coalition criteria are summarized in Table 5.2 using the four Blueprints categories.

The Coalition also designates programs as **Promising**. These programs are listed on the website and have some positive effects but do not fully meet the criteria for Near Top Tier status and are not considered good candidates for widespread replication. They may have mixed evidence of

Table 5.2 Coalition criteria.

Designation	Intervention specificity	Evaluation quality	Intervention impact	System readiness
Top Tier	Not considered	2 RCTs *or* 1 RCT with multiple sites	Sustained*	Not considered
Near Top Tier	Not considered	1 RCT	Post-test	Not considered

*Sustained effects do not mean that outcomes must be shown following the end of the intervention; they could be demonstrated during a multi-year intervention.

effectiveness (e.g., some outcomes are affected but others are not), somewhat flawed measures, or very short follow-up assessments. They may also lack evaluations conducted in "typically community settings"; that is, evidence of effectiveness may be restricted to studies in which all programming was delivered by research staff under the direction of the program developer or evaluator.

> *We all have tight budgets today. CrimeSolutions.gov helps us take a 'smart on crime' approach that relies on data-driven, evidence-based analysis to identify and replicate justice-related programs that have shown real results in preventing and reducing crime and serving crime victims.*
>   Laurie O. Robinson, Assistant Attorney General, 2011 (see http://www.justice.gov/opa/pr/department-justice-launches-crimesolutionsgov-website)

The Office of Juvenile Justice and Delinquency Prevention's (OJJDP) *Model Programs Guide* (MPG) and the Office of Justice Programs' *CrimeSolutions.gov*

The OJJPD Model Programs Guide (www.ojjdp.gov/mpg) was developed in 2000 to identify effective youth delinquency prevention programs and was later expanded to include treatment and re-entry programs for youth involved with the juvenile justice system. In 2011, CrimeSolutions.gov (www.crimesolutions.gov) was developed. It used more rigorous criteria to rate programs than did the MPG and reviewed a more comprehensive set of services, including adult crime prevention programs and practices as well as programs and practices used by law enforcement and correctional agencies. Since 2011, the two sites have been using the same guidelines and reviewers and share a database listing juvenile-focused programs. For this reason, we describe the standards of these two sites together.[3]

Although the lists are maintained by federal agencies, program reviews are conducted by academic scientists who are experts in the fields of criminology and criminal justice and in research methodology and evaluation. A Lead Reviewer is designated for every intervention, and his/her first responsibility is to search for all evaluations of the program and select up to three studies considered to have the most rigorous research design. The quality of these studies and the program overall are evaluated by two reviewers using detailed scoring instruments.

Programs are designated as **Effective**, **Promising**, or having **No Effects**. Both **Effective** and **Promising** programs must show positive effects but there is no requirement that they be sustained or of a particular size. Neither designation is dependent on using an RCT; QEDs are acceptable as long as they include a comparison group. However, Effective programs are more likely to have been evaluated using RCTs and will have fewer research design problems, whereas Promising programs may be of somewhat lower quality (e.g., smaller sample sizes, more threats to internal validity, shorter follow-up periods, etc.). To be Effective, a program must not have shown harmful effects or no effects when evaluated in a well-conducted study. Promising programs may include an evaluation that showed no effects on crime as long as at least one evaluation demonstrated positive effects.

Table 5.3 Model programs guide and crime solutions criteria.

Designation	Intervention specificity	Evaluation quality	Intervention impact	System readiness
Effective	√	1 well-conducted study (RCT or QED) with a comparison group	Significant, positive effects and no evidence of harmful or null effects	Not considered
Promising	√	1 well-conducted study (RCT or QED) with a comparison group	Post-test	Not considered
No Effects	√	1 well-conducted study (RCT or QED) with a comparison group	Harmful or null effects	Not considered

For both categories, replication of effects is not required, but if positive outcomes have been shown in multiple studies, the website indicates that replication has occurred using a particular icon.

As shown in Table 5.3, MPG/CrimeSolutions.gov reviewers rate Intervention Specificity based on similar information as Blueprints. Specifically, they score each program on a scale that ranges from "0" to "3" based on its theoretical basis, logic model, duration/frequency, targeted population, and targeted outcomes. Unlike Blueprints, this rating is not a stand-alone criterion but is averaged with ratings assessing the quality of each evaluation and its intervention impact. This score also includes a rating of implementation quality denoting how well the program was delivered in accordance to its requirements. There is no requirement related to system readiness; programs may be recommended even if the materials, training, and technical assistance are not available to replicate them or if the program is no longer available for dissemination.

These criteria for determining evaluation quality are less rigorous than those used by Blueprints and the Coalition. A program can be designated as **Effective** by MPG/CrimeSolutions.gov even if it was evaluated one time, in a quasi-experimental study and with no evidence of sustained effects. Such findings would not warrant inclusion in either the Blueprints or Coalition databases. The standards that need to be met to be designated as Promising in CrimeSolutions.gov are even less rigorous and we do not consider Promising interventions to have credible evidence of effectiveness.

A strength of the MPG and CrimeSolutions.gov, however, is that they are the only websites to identify ineffective interventions. Programs designated as having **No Effects** have been evaluated in at least one well-conducted study and shown to produce no effects or harmful effects on crime, and no well-conducted studies have demonstrated positive effects. This designation does not differentiate between iatrogenic and ineffective programs but the actual findings are described on the website. Program reviews are updated periodically.

In Fall 2013, CrimeSolutions.gov began evaluating the effectiveness of crime prevention practices. Practices are also designated as **Effective**, **Promising**, and having **No Effects** but the criteria and process differ somewhat from those used to evaluate programs. For practices, reviewers consider evidence reported in one or more meta-analyses conducted by other researchers. They rate the quality of the meta-analysis using structured instruments that take into account how the individual studies were selected for the meta-analysis (at least two must be included), the rigor and research design of the individual studies, the statistical techniques used in the meta-analysis and the effect sizes produced. **Effective** practices show the most consistent evidence of positive effects in well-conducted meta-analyses; **Promising** practices have demonstrated reductions in crime in somewhat less rigorous studies; and practices with **No Effects** are those which high-quality meta-analyses have shown do not affect crime or actually increase illegal behaviors.

The Substance Abuse and Mental Health Services Administration's (SAMHSA) National Registry of Evidence-based Programs and Practices (NREPP) (http://www.nrepp.samhsa.gov/Index.aspx)

The NREPP database was created to review programs and practices affecting youth and adult substance use and abuse and mental health. Unlike the other databases, interventions listed on NREPP are typically reviewed at the request of the program developer, who works with NREPP staff to identify studies to be included in the review. Two pairs of volunteer reviewers then rate each evaluation, with one pair (usually academics with a PhD) assessing the evaluation quality and the other pair (usually practitioners) rating the program's readiness for dissemination. Raters work independently using standardized protocols and criteria. They submit their assessments to the NREPP lead reviewer who makes the final determination of the program ratings.

When begun in 1997, NREPP categorized interventions as Model, Effective, and Promising, but these designations were discontinued in 2004. Under the current rating system, programs receive a score of 0 to 4 on their **quality of research** and **readiness for dissemination**, with higher scores indicating better programs.[4] The quality of research score is an average of six indicators relating to the reliability and validity of the measures, evidence of implementation fidelity, assessment of missing data and attrition and use of appropriate statistical procedures. Readiness for dissemination is the average of three ratings assessing the availability of materials (e.g., program manuals), training and support services and quality assurance procedures. To be eligible for review, an evaluation must be conducted using an RCT or QED with a comparison group and have at least pre- and post-test measures of outcomes. At least one positive effect on substance use must be demonstrated, but whether or not a negative effect is allowable is unclear. There are no stipulations regarding program replication or sustained effects.

The NREPP standards, summarized in Table 5.4, are the weakest of all the databases we review and have been critiqued as such (Gruner Gandhi *et al.*, 2007; Wright, Zhang, and Farabee, 2012). The ratings also have questionable validity given the developer's involvement in nominating programs and supplying the evaluations to be reviewed. Program scores can be updated every five

Table 5.4 NREPP criteria.

	Intervention specificity	Evaluation quality	Intervention impact	System readiness
Inclusion in the database	Not considered	1 RCT or QED with a comparison group and pre-test/post-test assessments	At least one significant, positive effect	√

years, but this is usually done only at the developer's request, meaning that replications showing negative effects may not come to NREPP's attention. Also problematic is the fact that programs are not rated as effective or ineffective. The quality of research and readiness for dissemination scores are listed on the website but no guidance is provided to help users determine how high scores should be in order to merit replication. Although the NREPP website includes some user-friendly information about programs and (to a lesser extent) practices, the fact that the site does not identify particular programs as effective or ineffective limits its utility to practitioners.

Campbell Collaboration (C2)

The Campbell Collaboration (C2) was begun in 2000 to review programs, practices, and policies seeking to affect crime and justice and other social and behavioral outcomes. It was modeled after and is part of the international Cochrane Collaboration, an independent and non-profit organization which conducts systematic reviews of health-related interventions (http://www.cochrane.org/about-us). Like the larger organization, C2 relies on an international group of researchers to voluntarily conduct systematic reviews. Results of these reviews are provided on their website (http://www.campbellcollaboration.org/background/index.php) and updated every two to three years.

The C2 systematic review process involves a careful and comprehensive systematic review of published and unpublished evaluations of crime prevention programs conducted by at least two independent researchers. There are no specific standards governing the collection, review and analysis of evaluations. The criteria used by authors to assess evaluations can vary across reports, but such practices must be clearly described and are reviewed by the C2 Editorial Board to ensure they are clear and rigorous.

Given this variety, some C2 reviews are limited to evaluations based on RCTs while others may include RCTs and/or QEDs. Most reviews focus on identifying crime prevention practices; for example, mentoring, school-based bullying programs or "hot spots" policing in which law enforcement efforts are directed towards high-crime areas (see Chapter 6 for more information about this practice). However, some analyze the impact of individual programs which have been evaluated in multiple studies.

Meta-analytic techniques are generally used to report an average effect size based on all evaluations reviewed. If relatively few evaluations have been conducted or if the specific interventions subjected to evaluation are too varied in their content or methodology to be meaningfully combined, then C2 reviewers will use a "count" method for reporting the proportion of evaluations that have reported statistically significant results across all the studies reviewed. In some cases, the review may report both types of figures. For example, a meta-analysis of the "pulling levers" law enforcement strategy, in which prosecutors, police, and community members all communicate to active offenders that violent crimes will be not be tolerated, reported an overall effect size of 0.60 – indicating a medium to large reduction in crime – and noted that 9 of 10 evaluations showed statistically significant reductions (Braga and Weisburd, 2012).

Similar to NREPP, C2 does not have specific criteria or designations to differentiate effective and ineffective programs and practices. Instead, reviewers and readers have to use their own judgment when interpreting the results. For example, in the pulling levers meta-analysis, Braga and Weisburd (2012: 6) concluded that such strategies "seem to be effective in reducing crime." However, they also urged "caution in interpreting these results because of the lack of … rigorous randomized controlled trials in the existing body of scientific evidence on this approach." None of the 10 evaluations they reviewed was an RCT, which resulted in their recommendation for the reader to use caution when considering the evidence (see Chapter 6 for more information about the effectiveness of this practice).

Given that criteria can differ across C2 studies, it is difficult to compare the C2 standards to those of the other databases reviewed. Most C2 reviews do not seem to take intervention specificity or system readiness into account. However, most appear to use a systematic and rigorous approach to collect and review evaluations, and meta-analysis is a valid and useful statistical method for quantifying the size of a program's impact. This is also the only rigorous and updated database we know of (other than its parent organization, the Cochrane Collaboration) that is explicitly international (Boruch, Snyder, and DeMoya, 2000). The organization relies on reviewers from multiple countries and emphasizes the inclusion of international evaluations. Given all of these strengths and its attention to crime prevention practices, we draw upon findings from C2 when describing effective interventions in Section III.

Similarities and differences across lists

It should now be clear that databases of crime prevention programs differ in significant ways. Their only similarity is an interest in making available information about crime prevention strategies, but different databases focus on different types of crime, different populations to be served (e.g., youth versus adults) and different types of intervention strategies (e.g., programs versus practices). They also vary in whether or not they designate interventions as effective or ineffective and in the processes and standards used to make these determinations. Finally, the degree to which standards take into account evaluation quality as well as the underlying theoretical frameworks and program mechanisms (i.e., intervention specificity) and practical issues related to program replication (i.e., system readiness) also differ across lists. In Table 5.5, we compare databases across all of these dimensions in order to better illustrate the variety of approaches.

To demonstrate how these differences can affect the identification and/or recommendation of evidence-based interventions, Table 5.6 compares the six databases on their designation of five crime prevention programs and practices. In only one case does an intervention (**Nurse–Family Partnership, NFP**) achieve the same and highest designation among the three databases that provide such classifications. NFP is a Blueprints Model program, a Top Tier Coalition program, and an Effective program according to MPG/CrimeSolutions.gov. The program received a 3.5 rather than the highest possible rating (a 4.0) on Evaluation Quality by NREPP. C2 did not evaluate NFP as a stand-alone program but it was included in a meta-analysis assessing the impact of family-based programs on child behavior problems (Piquero *et al.*, 2008). The overall effect size of this type of practice was 0.35, which the authors characterized as small to moderate in size (Piquero *et al.*, 2008: 85).

Ratings of the **Big Brothers/Big Sisters (BBBS)** program were even more varied across lists. This program received the second-best rating by Blueprints (Promising), the third-best rating by the Coalition (Promising), the best rating by MPG/CS (Effective), and an Evaluation Quality score of

Table 5.5 Key dimensions of crime prevention databases.

Database	Intervention types included	Targeted participants	Review process	Designations	Study design needed for top rating	Sustained effects	Replication needed for top rating	Harmful or ineffective interventions	Rates system readiness
Blueprints	Programs	Youth	Staff driven/comprehensive	Model Promising	RCT	Yes – 1 year	Yes	Not listed	Yes
Coalition	Programs	Youth	Staff driven/limited	Top Tier Near Top Tier (Promising)	RCT	Yes*	No	Not listed	No
MPG/CS	Programs Practices	MPG: Youth CS: Youth and Adults	Staff and developer driven/limited	Effective Promising No Effects	RCT or QED	No	No	Listed	No
NREPP	Programs Practices	Youth	Developer driven/limited	None	n/a, but RCT or QED to be listed	No	No	May be listed	Yes
C2	Programs Practices	Youth and Adults	Staff driven/limited	None	n/a	No	n/a	Listed	No

* Sustained effects do not mean that outcomes must be shown following the end of the intervention; they could be demonstrated during a multi-year intervention.

Table 5.6 Program ratings across databases.

Database	Nurse-Family Partnership	Big Brothers/Big Sisters	Project Alert	Functional Family Therapy	Hot Spots Policing
Blueprints	Model	Promising	Not listed	Model	Not reviewed
Coalition	Top Tier	Promising	Not listed	Not listed	Not reviewed
MPG/CS	Effective	Effective	No Effects	Effective	Effective
NREPP	Eval Quality: 3.2–3.5 Readiness: 3.7	Eval Quality: 3.0–3.1 Readiness: 3.7	Eval Quality: 3.2–3.4 Readiness: 2.9	Eval Quality: 4.0 Readiness: 3.8	Not reviewed
C2	Included in meta-analysis of "Family Programs" which produced a small to moderate effect size of 0.35	Included in meta-analysis of "Mentoring" which produced a small effect size of 0.21	Not reviewed	Not reviewed	Included in meta-analyses of "Pulling Levers" and "Hot Spots" which produced effect sizes of 0.60 and 0.18, respectively

3.0–3.2 by NREPP. It is difficult to determine exactly why these different ratings are given, as websites do not provide detailed explanations of why programs meet or do not meet particular designations. However, in this case, both the Coalition and NREPP critique the BBBS study for relying solely on self-reported information of delinquency and failing to have objective or official measures of crime. The Blueprints review does not note these measurement issues as problematic but indicates a concern that positive effects were strongest in the original RCT evaluation compared to subsequent replications. The other databases only considered the original RCT of the program in their review, which underscores the value of basing ratings on all available information. C2 included BBBS as one of the programs evaluated in a meta-analysis of mentoring of at-risk youth, which found a small to moderate effect size of 0.21 (Tolan *et al.*, 2013).

The third program, **Project Alert**, received the highest possible rating of Evaluation Quality (a 4.0) by NREPP but is not listed by Blueprints or the Coalition and is rated as having **No Effects** by MPG/CS. Project Alert had been listed as a Promising program on Blueprints until additional evaluations indicating null effects were published and taken into account. These evaluations were not part of the NREPP review, which indicates the problem with relying solely on program developers to provide and/or update evaluation findings.

Functional Family Therapy (FFT) received the highest possible ratings by Blueprints and MPG/CS. The Coalition website indicates that the program was reviewed but did not meet criteria, but no explanation for its exclusion is given. A version of the program targeting substance use has been rated as 3.2–3.4 by NREPP, depending on the substance use outcome evaluated, and C2 has not reviewed FFT.

Finally, the law enforcement practice of **Hot Spots Policing** was not reviewed by three of the five databases (Blueprints, the Coalition, and NREPP) because this type of intervention does not meet their inclusion criteria; none of these sites reviews law enforcement practices. The strategy is considered Effective by MPG/CS, and this rating was given based largely on the meta-analyses conducted by the C2 organization which indicated effect sizes of 0.18 to 0.60 depending on the studies included in the review (Braga, Papachristos, and Hureau, 2012; Braga and Weisburd, 2012).

> *List review processes are generally not transparent, and concerns have been raised about differences in criteria and methods, conflict of interest, and poorly defined or operationalized criteria. Perhaps the greatest problem is that for most lists "evidence" about program effectiveness comes from a single small efficacy trial by program developers.*
>
> Hallfors *et al.*, 2007: 79

Recommendations for Achieving Consensus on Standards of Evidence

As all this information makes clear, at present, there is limited consensus regarding the standards of scientific evidence that should be used to designate or certify an individual program as effective or evidence-based. The current lists use different selection processes and scientific standards to review and classify interventions. Not all use systematic search processes that take into account all relevant studies. Furthermore, they are not all regularly updated as new findings emerge. These limitations are problematic given recent increases in the number of program evaluations being conducted (Fagan and Eisenberg, 2012; Farrington and Welsh, 2005), and because findings from program replications are not always consistent with results from earlier studies (Valentine *et al.*, 2011). Databases also vary in how well they describe their criteria for determining intervention effectiveness and in the level of rigor they apply when making these decisions. The result, as illustrated in Table 5.6, is that the same intervention can be considered very effective, somewhat effective, or not at all effective depending on the database one consults. This is confusing for the public, for policymakers, for funding agencies, for practitioners, and for scientists as well. The conflicting recommendations also threaten to undermine everyone's confidence in the power of prevention science.

What can we do to improve what is currently a very messy process? How can we move towards a system – such as that used in medicine to regulate drug sales – that will certify programs as effective or ineffective, using consistent and transparent guidelines that will appeal to all stakeholders? Our recommendations are threefold. First, we call for *more consistent use of the systematic review process to identify effective crime prevention programs, practices, and policies.* Secondly, *where there is enough evidence* (e.g., at least three evaluations of the same or very similar programs), *we recommend the use of meta-analyses to calculate standardized effect sizes of programs and practices.* Thirdly, where evidence has not accumulated sufficiently to allow for a meta-analysis of the overall impact of an intervention, we put forth a *set of rigorous but increasingly achievable criteria for determining program effectiveness.*

As we have discussed, the systematic review process involves having a clearly described set of explicit procedures to find and evaluate the effectiveness of particular interventions. A comprehensive search of all studies that have evaluated a particular program, practice, or policy should be conducted and all such evaluations, not a subset of them, should be considered in the review (Wilson, 2009).

In addition, the review should be as up-to-date as possible, with new findings incorporated as they emerge. When a sufficient number of evaluations are identified using a comprehensive search process, a meta-analysis should be conducted to synthesize the findings and estimate an average effect size across all studies. This methodology allows for a more precise and reliable judgment of the degree to which a program, practice, or policy is likely to affect crime rates, as it takes all relevant research into account. Effect sizes are also fairly easy for practitioners and policy-makers to understand, as a value of "zero" clearly indicates no effect on crime and scores between "zero" and "one" indicating a linear progression from having little effect to having a large impact on crime.

Unfortunately, relatively few programs currently have a sufficient number of high-quality evaluations to allow for a reliable meta-analysis of their impact. In these cases, we still need a standardized and rigorous method for identifying what works. Our recommendation is for databases to utilize the criteria developed by the Federal Collaboration on What Works (2005). In 2005, this group of federal agencies[5] was directed by the White House Task Force on Disadvantaged Youth to set standards to be used across all federal agencies to identify effective prevention programs. After some no doubt very heated debate, the group agreed that determinations of program effectiveness should be based on ratings of: (i) the quality of the evaluation design, (ii) replication of the intervention, (iii) independence of the program developer and the program evaluator, and (iv) sustainability of effects after the intervention had ended (Working Group of the Federal Collaboration on What Works, 2005). Criterion #1, #2, and #4 should sound familiar, as they are already used by many groups and have been discussed in this chapter. Criterion #3, however, has not yet been discussed. This standard is based on the desire to keep science objective and uncontaminated from the potential bias that exists for program developers to show positive effects of their interventions (Gorman, 2005; Petrosino and Soydan, 2005). To guard against this bias, there is a preference that evaluations be conducted by researchers who are independent from program developers.

Under the guidelines of the Federal Collaboration on What Works, to be considered **Effective**,[6] a program would need to have statistically significant, positive effects in a well-conducted RCT, have at least one external or independent RCT replication, demonstrate evidence of sustained effects at least one year post-intervention from at least one study and have no iatrogenic or harmful effects. The standard to be considered **Promising** required statistically significant positive effects from at least one well-conducted RCT or QED (i.e., no replication required), sustained effects at least one year post-intervention and no evidence of iatrogenic effects. The guidelines also allowed for identification of **Ineffective, Inconclusive,** and **Harmful** programs. Each designation had to meet all the requirements to be Promising, but instead of showing positive effects, **Ineffective** programs would demonstrate no statistically significant effects, **Inconclusive** programs would have mixed effects, and **Harmful** programs would show negative effects.

Although the goal of this group was to create uniform standards to be used by all federal agencies, including criminal justice agencies like NIJ and OJJDP, the criteria were never adopted by any organizations. We suspect there was reluctance to do so because the standards are very high and enforcement of these criteria would limit the number of interventions that could be recommended. As is evident in Table 5.7, none of the databases we reviewed in this chapter has fully adopted these standards. However, the criteria for consideration as a Blueprints Model program approach this level of rigor and, in Spring 2015, Blueprints decided to create a new classification: **Model+** programs.

Table 5.7   Comparison of current databases with the federal collaboration on what works (2005) criteria.

Database	Study design for top rating	Replication	Independent replication	Sustained effects ≥1 year post-intervention
Blueprints (Model)	RCT	Yes	Yes, for Model Plus programs	Yes
Coalition (Top Tier)	RCT	Yes	No	No
MPG/CS (Effective)	RCT or QED	No	No	No
NREPP	n/a, but requires a RCT or QED to be reviewed	No	No	No
C2	n/a	Yes	No	No

These interventions have to meet all the criteria to be certified as Model, as well as the independent evaluation criterion.

Despite the legitimate concern of limiting the number of programs recommended for use, we strongly advocate that the What Works standards be adopted and applied across agencies and databases. In our opinion, the government has a responsibility to spend public monies responsibly, to prevent public health problems, and to avoid harming individuals. As such, programs advocated by the government, which will result in considerable financial and human investment, should meet a high standard of effectiveness.

With this view in mind, we have some additional recommendations to ensure that standards have practical and scientific merit. First, given the importance of ensuring that interventions are based on credible theories and knowledge of the risk and protective factors associated with crime, *we recommend that the Federal Collaboration on What Works criteria be expanded to include a rating of Intervention Specificity similar to that used in Blueprints.* This would mean that, to be considered effective, interventions would have to clearly identify and describe their theoretical and empirical foundations, logic model, and the types of individuals or areas targeted for intervention. Even though we suspect that programs that fail to meet this criterion would be unlikely to achieve positive outcomes, having the standard draws program developers' and users' attention to the importance of these issues. Secondly, *we advocate for the addition of the Blueprints Dissemination Readiness standard.* Designating a program as effective and desirable for replication makes no sense if the program is not available for use. In addition, as we will discuss in Chapters 10 and 11, prevention programs can be challenging to implement, and if program developers lack the capacity to train and provide ongoing support to implementers, then successful replication is much less likely to occur.

We hesitate to add more criteria to our set of recommended standards at this point, for fear of limiting the number of options available to communities. However, as replications and evaluations continue to emerge, it may be possible to add two more standards: an analysis of mediating factors that produce behavioral changes and a cost–benefits analysis. As we discussed in Chapter 4, mediation analyses allow evaluation of the degree to which the risk and protective factors targeted for change are actually altered by the intervention and lead to anticipated reductions in crime. Demonstration of mediating pathways allows for a better understanding of why a program works and strengthens claims of its effectiveness. Documentation of the financial costs and benefits of an intervention has important practical implications. Potential users have limited funds and will want to know which program provides a "bigger bang for the buck." Savvy consumers will want to compare the relative costs and effect sizes of different programs. It is also true that many practitioners and policy-makers will be reluctant to spend funds on a new intervention even if it has scientific evidence of success. Being able to show that the program will generate financial returns as well as improve crime rates can help encourage adoption and widespread dissemination, a subject we will return to in Section IV. Although evaluations are increasingly incorporating analysis of mediating effects and costs versus benefits, this information is still not readily available for most programs and, as such, we will not yet recommend they be added to a list of required standards.

Summary

This chapter has reviewed the processes by which programs, practices, and policies are determined to be effective in preventing crime and the many challenges associated with making such recommendations. We have discussed the importance of setting high standards to differentiate effective and ineffective interventions, identified the range of standards that currently exist, and made recommendations for a set of rigorous standards we would like to see adopted by agencies in the future. We compared six web-based databases that are currently in use and periodically updated in terms of the criteria and methods used to review intervention effectiveness and demonstrated how these differences result in different determinations across lists about what works.

   As emphasized throughout this chapter, some lists have more rigorous criteria than others, which affects both the number of interventions that are designated as effective and our level of confidence that, if replicated, recommended programs will be likely to reduce crime. These two outcomes are inversely related: higher standards result in fewer nominated programs but a greater level of certainty in program effectiveness. In order to balance these two demands, our textbook will rely on multiple databases when describing interventions in Section III. The Blueprints and Coalition databases have the most rigorous standards for assessing the quality of prevention programs, and we will prioritize their recommendations. We rely more heavily on Blueprints, given that it is more comprehensive approach and has crime as a priority outcome of interest. Because Blueprints and the Coalition focus on programs intended to change *youth* outcomes, and because they do not review prevention *practices*, we will rely on the MPG/CrimeSolutions.gov and the C2 databases to identify adult-focused interventions as well as law enforcement and situational crime prevention programs and practices. Since these databases often rely on less rigorous criteria, we will note their recommendations with some caution. We will not include ratings by NREPP given their reliance on less rigorous criteria.

Critical Thinking Questions and Practice Activities

1. Choose two delinquency prevention programs from the CrimeSolutions.gov website (http://www.crimesolutions.gov/TopicDetails.aspx?ID=62). Create a table similar to Table 5.6 and identify how these programs are rated on CrimeSolutions.gov and the other databases described in this chapter. If there are differences in ratings across lists, summarize why these differences exist.

2. Find a program that is listed on the Blueprints, CrimeSolutions.gov, and NREPP websites. If you were a practitioner interested in replicating this program, which site do you think provides the best explanation of the program and its effectiveness? Be sure to justify your choice and compare the extent to which each site is "user friendly."

3. Using any of the databases reviewed in this chapter, select an effective crime prevention program or practice that interests you. Summarize the intervention in one or two sentences using your own words. Based on the information you find on the website, (i) identify two strengths of the program. You can focus on the program's effectiveness in reducing crime, its content or approach, or how the population targeted by the program seems like the right group to focus on when trying to prevent crime. Then, (ii) identify two challenges you think would be faced by practitioners who try to implement this program. Comparing these strengths and weaknesses, would you recommend that the program be replicated in your home town?

4. Consider the four criteria used by Blueprints to rate program effectiveness: Intervention Specificity, Evaluation Quality, Intervention Impact, and System Readiness. Which criterion do you think is most important for determining program effectiveness and which is least important?

5. Imagine that a teacher, social worker, or correctional officer asks you for advice about how to reduce crime in his/her community. S/he has heard about a few different programs that may be effective but is not sure how to decide which one to implement. What advice would you give this person?

Endnotes

1. We will, however, draw upon recommendations from the CDC Guide when reviewing policies intended to reduce under-age drinking and Driving While Intoxicated (DWI) in Chapter 6.

2. These standards are described in detail on the Blueprints website; see: http://www.blueprintsprograms.com/resources/Blueprints_Standards_full.pdf

3. These standards are described in detail on the CrimeSolutions.gov website; see: http://www.crimesolutions.gov/about_starttofinish.aspx

4. In July, 2015, NREPP announced that it would be updating its criteria and review processes (https://www.federalregister.gov/articles/2015/07/07/2015-16573/national-registry-of-evidence-based-programs-and-practices#h-8); in particular, it would no longer be scoring interventions according to their Readiness for Dissemination. Because the changes had yet to take effect at the time this textbook was being prepared for publication, the description of the NREPP standards in this chapter reflects the pre-existing standards and procedures.

5. The Working Group of the Federal Collaboration on What Works included members from the Center for Substance Abuse Prevention, SAMHSA; the National Institute of Drug Abuse; the National Center for Education Evaluation, Institute of Education Sciences; the Office of Justice Programs, the National Institute of Justice; and the Office of Juvenile Justice and Delinquency Prevention.

6. Programs were further differentiated as **Effective** and **Effective With Reservation**, with the main distinction that the former relied on a replication study conducted by an independent evaluator and the latter did not.

Helpful Websites (last accessed August 2, 2016)

- Drilling Down: An Analytical Look at Evidence-Based Practice Resources
  https://www.nttac.org/index.cfm?event=trainingCenter.traininginfo&eventID=472&from=training&dtab=0
  Webinar comparing different website lists of evidence-based practices.
- The Office of Justice Programs CrimeSolutions.gov
  https://www.youtube.com/watch?v=lr8PS_f-xx0&feature=youtu.be
  Webinar explaining the CrimeSolutions.gov website.
- http://www.criminaljusticeprograms.com/
  Interview with Dr Phelan Wyrick explaining the CrimeSolutions.gov database.

Further Reading

- Flay, B. R., Biglan, A., Boruch, R. F., *et al.* 2005. Standards of evidence: Criteria for efficacy, effectiveness, and dissemination. *Prevention Science*, 6:151–176.
  This article outlines a set of scientific standards for determining program effectiveness advocated by the Society for Prevention Research.
- The following three articles provide critical reviews of various "what works" databases, including differences in the standards used to rate the effectiveness of interventions:
  1. Gruner Gandhi, A., Murphy-Graham, E., Petrosino, A., Schwartz Chrismer, S., and Weiss, C. H. 2007. The devil is in the details: Examining the evidence for "proven" school-based drug abuse prevention programs. *Evaluation Review*, 31:43–74.
  2. Hallfors, D., Pankratz, M., and Hartman, S. 2007. Does federal policy support the use of scientific evidence in school-based prevention programs? *Prevention Science*, 8(1):75–81.
  3. Wright, B. J., Zhang, S. X., and Farabee, D. 2012. A squandered opportunity? A review of SAMHSA'S National Registry of Evidence-Based Programs and Practices for offenders. *Crime and Delinquency*, 58(6):954–972.

References

Boruch, R. F. 1975. On common contentions about randomized field experiments. In: R. F. Boruch and H. W. Reicken (eds), *Experimental Testing of Public Policy: The Proceedings of the 1974 Social Sciences Research Council Conference on Social Experimentation*, pp. 107–142. Boulder, CO: Westview Press.

Boruch, R. F., Snyder, B., and DeMoya, D. 2000. The importance of randomized field trials. *Crime and Delinquency*, 46:156–180.

Braga, A. A., Papachristos, A. V., and Hureau, D. 2012. Hot spots policing effects on crime. *Campbell Systematic Reviews*, 2012:8. doi: 10.4073/csr.2012.8

Braga, A. A., and Weisburd, D. L. 2012. The effects of "pulling levers" focused deterrence strategies on crime. *Campbell Systematic Reviews*, 2012:8(6).

Communities That Care: Prevention Strategies Guide to What Works. 1996. Seattle, WA: Developmental Research and Programs, Inc.

Cook, T. D., and Campbell, D. T. 1979. *Quasi-Experimentation: Design and Analysis Issues for Field Settings*. Boston, MA: Houghton Mifflin.

Elliott, D. S. 1997. *Blueprints for Violence Prevention*. Boulder, CO: University of Colorado, Institute of Behavioral Science, Center for the Study and Prevention of Violence.

Fagan, A. A., and Eisenberg, N. 2012. Latest developments in the prevention of crime and anti-social behaviour: An American perspective. *Journal of Children's Services*, 7:64–72.

Farrington, D. P. 2003. A short history of randomized experiments in criminology: A meager feast. *Evaluation Review*, 27:218–227.

Farrington, D. P., and Welsh, B. C. 2005. Randomized experiments in criminology: What have we learned in the last two decades? *Journal of Experimental Criminology*, 1:9–38. doi: 10.1007/s11292-004-6460-0

Gorman, D. 2005. Drug and violence prevention: Rediscovering the critical rational dimension of evaluation research. *Journal of Experimental Criminology*, 1:39–62.

Gruner Gandhi, A., Murphy-Graham, E., Petrosino, A., Schwartz Chrismer, S., and Weiss, C. H. 2007. The devil is in the details: Examining the evidence for "proven" school-based drug abuse prevention programs. *Evaluation Review*, 31:43–74.

Hallfors, D., Pankratz, M., and Hartman, S. 2007. Does federal policy support the use of scientific evidence in school-based prevention programs? *Prevention Science*, 8:75–81. doi: 10.1007/s11121-006-0058-x

Hough, M. 2010. Gold standard or fool's gold? The pursuit of certainty in experimental criminology. *Criminology and Criminal Justice*, 10:11–22.

Martinson, R. 1974. What works? Questions and answers about prison reform. *The Public Interest*, 35:22–54.

Office of Juvenile Justice and Delinquency Prevention. 1995. Guide for implementing the Comprehensive Strategy for Serious, Violent, and Chronic Juvenile Offenders, edited by James C. Howell. Washington, DC: Office of Juvenile Justice and Delinquency Prevention.

Pawson, R., and Tilley, N. 1994. What works in evaluation research. *British Journal of Criminology*, 34:291–306.

Petrosino, A., and Soydan, H. 2005. The impact of program developers as evaluators on criminal recidivism: Results from meta-analyses of experimental and quasi-experimental research. *Journal of Experimental Criminology*, 1:435–450.

Piquero, A. R., Farrington, D. P., Welsh, B. C., Tremblay, R., and Jennings, W. G. 2008. Effects of early family/parent training programs on antisocial behavior and delinquency. *Campbell Systematic Reviews*, 2008:11.

Sampson, R. J. 2010. Gold standard myths: Observations on the experimental turn in quantitative criminology. *Journal of Quantitative Criminology*, 26:489–500.

Sampson, R. J., Winship, C., and Knight, C. 2013. Translating causal claims: Principles and strategies for policy-relevant criminology. *Criminology and Public Policy*, 12:587–616.

Sherman, L. W. 2003. Misleading evidence and evidence-led policy: Making social science more experimental. *The Annals of the American Academy of Political and Social Science*, 589:6–19.

Sherman, L. W., Gottfredson, D. C., MacKenzie, D., et al. 1997. Preventing crime: What works, what doesn't, what's promising: A report to the United States Congress. Washington, DC: US Department of Justice, Office of Justice Programs.

Sherman, L. W., Gottfredson, D. C., MacKenzie, D. L., et al. 1998. Preventing crime: What works, what doesn't, what's promising. Washington, DC: National Institute of Justice.

Tolan, P., Henry, D., Schoeny, M., et al. 2013. Mentoring interventions to affect juvenile delinquency and associated problems: A systematic review. *Campbell Systematic Reviews*, 2013:9(10).

Valentine, J. C., Biglan, A., Boruch, R. F., et al. 2011. Replication in prevention science. *Prevention Science*, 12:103–117.

Weisburd, D. 2003. Ethical practice and evaluations of interventions in crime and justice: The moral imperative for randomized trials. *Evaluation Review*, 27:336–354.

Weisburd, D. 2010. Justifying the use of non-experimental methods and disqualifying the use of randomized controlled trials: Challenging folklore in evaluation research in crime and justice. *Journal of Experimental Criminology*, 6:209–227. doi: 10.1007/s11292-010-9096-2

Weiss, C. H., Murphy-Graham, E., Petrosino, A., and Gandhi, A. G. 2008. The fairy godmother and her warts: Making the dream of evidence-based policy come true. *American Journal of Evaluation*, 29:29–47.

Wilson, D. B. 2009. Missing a critical piece of the pie: Simple document search strategies inadequate for systematic reviews. *Journal of Experimental Criminology*, 5:429–440. doi: 10.1007/s11292-009-9085-5

Working Group of the Federal Collaboration on What Works. 2005. The OJP what works repository. Rockville, MD: Office of Justice Programs.

Wright, B. J., Zhang, S. X., and Farabee, D. 2012. A squandered opportunity? A review of SAMHSA'S National Registry of Evidence-Based Programs and Practices for offenders. *Crime and Delinquency*, 58:954–972. doi: 10.1177/0011128710376302

Section III

What Works to Prevent Crime?

6

Situational and Legal Crime Prevention Practices, Programs, and Policies

Learning Objectives

Upon finishing this chapter, students should be able to:

- Identify effective and ineffective situational crime prevention programs, practices, and policies and those which have inconclusive evidence of effectiveness
- Identify effective and ineffective law enforcement and legal crime prevention programs, practices, and policies and those which have inconclusive evidence of effectiveness
- Summarize the extent to which effective situational and legal programs, practices, and policies are being implemented to prevent crime
- State the most important research tasks that must be accomplished in order to increase the number of effective situational and legal programs, practices, and policies available and in use.

Introduction

Prior to taking this course, you probably had some ideas about how to best prevent crime. We are willing to bet that, like most citizens, you naturally thought about **law enforcement practices** and **legal sanctions** that result in the arrest and incarceration of offenders. These punitive activities are hypothesized by **deterrence theory** to prevent crime among the general public, as individuals will be less likely to break the law if they think that doing so will result in punishment. They are also expected to prevent recidivism among active offenders who, following contact with the criminal justice system, will want to avoid such sanctions in the future.

The Prevention of Crime, First Edition. Delbert Elliott and Abigail Fagan.
© 2017 John Wiley & Sons, Inc. Published 2017 by John Wiley & Sons, Inc.
Companion website: www.wiley.com/go/elliott/prevention_of_crime

We are also willing to bet that you did *not* consider strategies that take place "behind the scenes" to prevent crime, actions often taken by private citizens with no involvement from law enforcement. For example, when business owners install security cameras or hire security guards, they are engaging in **situational crime prevention**. You probably use some of these strategies too, to protect yourself or your property from harm. In fact, every time you set your car alarm and leave your porch lights on when you go out for the evening, you are taking steps to prevent crime. There are many other types of situational crime prevention. What they have in common is the goal of making crimes more difficult to commit and easier to detect.

This chapter will review the effectiveness of **situational** and **legal** crime prevention programs, practices, and policies in reducing crime. Recall from Chapters 3 and 4 that prevention **programs** have specific delivery requirements and protocols that will be clearly identified in a manual and which must be carefully followed. Programs are typically evaluated using an experiment that compares individuals or groups who receive the program to those who do not (i.e., those in the control condition), with randomized controlled experiments considered the strongest research design. Prevention **practices** are more general approaches that do not need to be implemented the exact same way every time but rely on similar procedures to prevent crime. These are typically classified as effective following a systematic review or meta-analysis of multiple evaluations of the approach which indicate that the practice, on average, reduces crime. Finally, prevention **policies** are legal regulations or formal standards that seek to affect the behavior of a large population. Their effectiveness can be evaluated using experiments or meta-analyses. We will consider evidence of the effectiveness of all of these types of interventions in this chapter and the other chapters in this section of the textbook.

To be considered effective in reducing crime in this book, programs, practices, and policies have to show a significant impact on rates of crime in rigorous, scientific evaluations which include valid and reliable measures of criminal behavior. When identifying effective crime prevention programs, we will primarily rely upon the recommendations listed on the Blueprints and Coalition websites mentioned in Chapter 5. These sites do not include many practices or policies, especially those related to situational and law enforcement strategies. For this information, we will rely on systematic reviews conducted by the Campbell Collaboration (C2) and CrimeSolutions.gov, as well as reviews conducted for the Centers for Disease Control's (CDC) *Community Guide*.

In our view, programs, practices, and policies rated as "Effective with Multiple Studies" by CrimeSolutions.gov have an acceptable level of evidence, comparable to the level required by Blueprints and the Coalition. We will, in most cases, also consider those rated as "Effective" by CrimeSolutions.gov to be effective, since the evidence for practices and some policies is almost always based on meta-analysis and consideration of multiple studies. However, in our view, programs, practices, and policies rated as "Promising" on the CrimeSolutions.gov website do not meet a high enough standard to be considered effective. We will characterize these types of interventions as having "inconclusive" evidence of effectiveness, meaning that more research is required to demonstrate whether or not they can reduce crime. Policies and practices reviewed by other sources that have had no or few high-quality evaluations will also be considered as having inconclusive evidence, as will interventions for which the effects on crime are so mixed (with some evaluations showing reductions in crime and others showing no effects) that conclusions about effectiveness cannot be made with certainty. We suspect that the majority of crime prevention efforts that occur every day in communities have inconclusive evidence of effectiveness. Given space limitations, we restrict our identification of inconclusive crime prevention strategies to those that are most commonly used and/or discussed in the crime prevention literature.

While it is important to understand what works to reduce crime, it is just as important to understand what does *not* work, and ineffective interventions will also be reviewed in this chapter and book. We will classify interventions as ineffective if they have been *well evaluated*, using the same standards as effective programs, practices, and policies, *and shown* not *to reduce crime*. In some cases, ineffective strategies may produce **iatrogenic** effects, meaning that the program, practice, or policy actually led to an *increase* in offending. We will identify these types of outcomes when they exist.

In the sections that follow, information about crime prevention strategies is organized according to the type of intervention that has been evaluated. For each type, we begin with a brief description of the approach and its theoretical basis, followed by information on the specific practices, programs, and policies shown to reduce crime using this approach. We will also identify the types of crimes that have been affected, the size of the reduction(s) in crime produced by the intervention and the degree to which the practice, program, or policy is currently being used in communities.

We will identify the amount of change produced by interventions in three ways. First, we may identify the **effect size** produced by the intervention. Recall from Chapter 4 that effect sizes provide a standardized metric indicating the degree to which an outcome has been changed. In non-technical terms, effect sizes represent the average change produced by the intervention among the population/area which received it compared to the group/area which did not. Values range from 0 to 1, with larger values indicating larger effects. These figures can be compared across different evaluations since they are on the same scale which is helpful when trying to assess the relative benefits of multiple interventions. In criminology, as in other social sciences, it is rare to see effects anywhere close to 1.0; there are just too many influences that affect criminal behavior. It is common to see *small* effect sizes, those that are less than 0.20. Effects between 0.21 to 0.40 are considered to be *moderate* in size, while values greater than 0.40 are considered *large* (Cohen, 1988).

Second, we will identify changes in crime using **odds-ratios** when the outcome is measured with a binary variable that has only two categories of responses, such as whether or not an individual was arrested following the intervention. Odds-ratios are measured on a scale that includes only positive values. An odds-ratio that is greater than 1.0 indicates that an increase in the outcome occurred, an odds-ratio of exactly 1.0 indicates that no change occurred, and an odds-ratio of less than 1.0 indicates that a decrease in the outcome occurred. Whether or not increases or decreases are desirable depends on how the outcome is coded and how the groups are compared, but we will be sure to let you know if interventions have shown a reduction or increase in crime for those in the intervention compared to the control group. The important thing to remember is that the more the value of the odds-ratio differs from 1.0, the larger the change in crime.

Third, we may describe the percentage reduction in crime produced by the intervention. This method can be used when outcomes are measured using binary variables or continuous variables, such as when comparing the average number of days that participants spent incarcerated following the intervention. This figure is usually calculated by dividing the outcome achieved in the intervention group by the outcome achieved in the control group, then subtracting that amount from 100.

For example, an evaluation of the **Behavioral Monitoring and Reinforcement Program** (see Chapter 8) found that three of the students who received the intervention had a criminal record, compared to nine of the students in the control group, which is equivalent to a 66% reduction in crime.

Situational Crime Prevention

The goal of **situational crime prevention strategies** is to make crimes more difficult to commit and more risky for offenders (Clarke, 1995; Eck and Guerette, 2012). These methods do not try to change the offender or the social risk or protective factors associated with individuals' involvement in crime. Instead, they try to alter the environments in which crimes occur and the immediate, situational factors that provide opportunities for crime. Situational crime prevention began in the UK in the early 1970s when individually focused attempts to rehabilitate offenders seemed to be unsuccessful and difficult to implement. Based on the work of Ronald Clarke and others, the British government began investing in strategies they considered to be more practical and less focused on social influences on crime (Clarke, 1995). Some other European countries and the USA began implementing situational crime prevention in the 1980s.

Situational crime prevention is based, in part, on **deterrence theory**, which states that offenders will be less likely to break the law if they believe with more certainty that they will be caught doing so. It is also based on **rational choice** and **routine activities theories** (Smith and Clarke, 2012). Rational choice theory states that potential offenders consider the risks and benefits of engaging in crime, as well as the amount of effort needed to complete the act and the likelihood of getting caught. They will break the law if the rewards for doing so are greater than the risks and the chances of being detected are seen as small (Clarke and Felson, 1993). For example, installing bullet-proof barriers between bank tellers and customers and using time-release safes would be suggested by rational choice theory as an ideal way to prevent bank robberies because those actions would increase the difficulty of the crime, make it seem more risky and reduce its perceived benefits. Routine activities theory states that crime is most likely when there are motivated offenders, few guardians and appealing targets, such as victims who could be physically overpowered or goods which are valuable and easy to steal (Clarke and Felson, 1993). Of these three factors, only the second two are subject to situational crime prevention efforts. Individual factors that may motivate criminal behavior, as well as social risk and protective factors, are assumed to be too difficult to change and too widespread in society. In contrast, increasing guardianship and reducing the attractiveness of targets are considered to be relatively easy and very feasible, and situational crime prevention offers many suggestions for how to make these types of changes in order to reduce opportunities for crime.

These practices can take many different forms and various typologies have been created to organize these different types of actions (e.g., see Smith and Clarke, 2012). Situational crime prevention does not usually involve actions taken by law enforcement, but rather relies on other government officials or private citizens to prevent crime. Involving the general public in crime prevention is seen as a major advantage of situational crime prevention, as doing so can potentially increase the reach of crime prevention in communities and transfer some of the costs otherwise paid for by the general public (through taxes) to individual citizens (Eck, 2003; Eck and Guerette, 2012). Although most situational crime prevention activities are aimed at reducing property offenses, they can prevent personal crimes to the extent that they help protect victims and reduce their encounters with offenders (Lab, 2014).

One over-arching type of situational crime prevention is **place-based** crime prevention (Eck, 2003; Eck and Guerette, 2012). As its name suggests, place-based prevention occurs in very small geographical areas, such as homes, public buildings, or retail stores. Place-based prevention can also be used in public transportation facilities such as bus or metro stations or recreational areas like parks and playgrounds. Places are targeted for crime prevention based on information regarding their history of criminal activity. As we will also discuss later in the chapter when reviewing **hot spots policing**, crime statistics indicate that crimes are not uniformly distributed across geographical areas, but rather tend to occur in the same places at very high rates year after year. Focusing crime prevention activities in these areas can potentially have a large pay-off.

Place-based crime prevention includes efforts to **increase the guardianship** and surveillance of these areas and **target hardening** practices which make places more difficult to vandalize or burglarize. Common prevention activities intended to increase guardianship are the installation of **closed circuit televisions (CCTV)**, **increasing street lighting**, and **hiring security guards** or **place managers**. As will be true of all situational crime prevention practices discussed in this chapter, all of these strategies are routinely used to prevent crime, but there have been very few rigorous evaluations of their impact on illegal activity. *As a result, we currently have inconclusive evidence that increasing guardianship of places reduces crime.* Again, this means that such practices may decrease crime or they may not; we just do not have enough information to make such a determination.

Of all the types of situational crime prevention we reviewed, **CCTV** and **street lighting** have undergone the most testing and show promise in reducing crime, but the evidence is still inconclusive. **CCTV** is classified as a Promising practice by CrimeSolutions.gov based on studies showing that its use can reduce property offenses but not violent crimes. Welsh and Farrington (2008a) conducted a meta-analysis of 41 CCTV evaluations occurring mainly in the UK, with a few studies in the USA, Canada, Sweden, and Norway. Based on all the evaluations, public places that had installed CCTVs experienced small but statistically significant reductions in crime. The average odds-ratio across studies was 1.19, corresponding to a 16% reduction in criminal behavior in intervention versus comparison areas. However, about half the studies showed no effects on crime and there was no significant decrease in violent crime when consid-

ering the 23 studies that evaluated this type of illegal behavior. Furthermore, most of the studies did not involve a rigorous research design. A more recent randomized evaluation of the impact of CCTV conducted in Philadelphia in the USA had somewhat stronger results. This study showed a 16% reduction in disorder crimes like vandalism and drug sales in areas in which cameras had been installed and a 13% reduction in crime when disorder and violent crimes were combined (Ratcliffe, Taniguchi, and Taylor, 2009). However, there was no impact on violent crime specifically and not all areas with cameras had lower rates of disorder crimes. Given this variation, as well as the mixed results of other studies, Ratcliffe and colleagues (2009) conclude that it is still too soon to advocate for widespread use of CCTVs. There is still too much that is not known about how, where, and why they may work, and more rigorous evaluation of this strategy is needed to answer these questions. We agree with their assessment. Nonetheless, use of CCTV is widespread, particularly in Great Britain. Welsh and Farrington (2008a: 2) note that 170 million pounds were spent by the British federal government on CCTVs in 1999–2001, making it the "single most heavily funded non-criminal justice [crime prevention] program" in that country. In addition, *The Telegraph* newspaper in the UK reported in 2013 that there were between 4.9 and 5.9 million CCTVs in that country, or one camera per 11–14 people (Barrett, 2013).

Welsh and Farrington (2008b) have also conducted a meta-analysis on the impact of **street lighting** on crime in public areas. Their review was based on 13 studies, none of which were randomized trials. About half the studies conducted in the USA showed that improved lighting was related to fewer crimes, while four of the five studies in the UK showed positive results. Across all studies, crime was reduced by 21% following enhancements to street lighting. Although the authors conclude that street lighting has a significant impact on crime, we consider the methodological rigor of these evaluations as too poor to consider this an effective practice.

Security guards and **place managers** provide human surveillance of public buildings and other areas. Place managers are those who function as guardians by virtue of their particular position but who are not hired specifically to provide security or surveillance (Welsh, Mudge, and Farrington, 2010). For example, bus drivers may observe and/or prevent passengers' crimes and parking lot attendants keep watch over the cars residing in public lots. While most public places have guardianship in place, there has been little rigorous evaluation of this practice. We could find only one systematic review that analyzed effects on crime from five studies evaluating the use of security guards and two evaluations of place managers (Welsh *et al.*, 2010). The review found very mixed evidence of effectiveness across studies, with some indicating reductions in crime and some demonstrating no effects. Furthermore, few evaluations involved rigorous methodologies. The lack of research emphasizes the need for more high-quality studies to determine the effectiveness of this practice (Hollis-Peel *et al.*, 2011).

There are also few rigorous evaluations of the effectiveness of **target hardening practices** which make items more difficult to steal or buildings more difficult to break into and/or vandalize. Common target hardening practices include installing locks and engine immobilizers in cars; alarm systems in buildings; metal detectors in airports, schools, and other public buildings; and stronger materials in the construction of payphones, parking meters, doors and windows. Target hardening can also rely on product design and technology to guard against theft or damage (Ekblom, 2012). For example, electronic tags can be used to prevent the theft of clothes, books, and other products. Beer bottles can be designed so that they do not shatter into sharp pieces of glass which could then be used as weapons in a bar fight. And, laptops and phones can be fitted with anti-virus programs, data encryption programs, and tracking devices that will help protect their data and recover the items if they are stolen. These practices are especially important for objects considered highly susceptible to theft, sometimes referred to as **CRAVED** products: those that are easily Concealable, Removable, Available, Valuable, Enjoyable, and Disposable (Clarke, 1999).

Comprehensive reviews of this type of situational crime prevention have indicated that many target hardening practices reduce crime (Eck, 2003; Eck and Guerette, 2012; Ekblom, 2012). However, none have strong evidence of effectiveness because, to date, most have not been rigorously evaluated. Almost no randomized evaluations of these practices have been conducted. As Ekblom (2012: 398) states, while there is circumstantial and anecdotal evidence that target hardening works, "the effort to find hard evidence must continue" before we can say that this practice is effective.

One exception to this conclusion may be the use of **ignition interlocks** in automobiles driven by individuals convicted of driving under the influence (DUI). These devices disable use of a vehicle until the driver provides a breath sample. If the individual's blood alcohol concentration is lower than a preset level, then the driver is allowed to start the car. Breath samples are collected periodically while the car is in use and the information is logged into a recorder which can be reviewed by those monitoring the offender (Willis, Lybrand, and Bellamy, 2004). Systematic reviews of the effectiveness of this type of target hardening have been conducted for C2 (Willis *et al.*, 2004) and the CDC Community Guide (Elder *et al.*, 2011). Both reviews noted that, compared to those who were not assigned to receive ignition interlocks, drivers whose cars were fitted with ignition interlocks had decreased rates of DUI recidivism during the time that the locks were in the car, with relative reductions ranging from 0.25 to 0.36. However, longer term studies showed that after the locks were removed, there were no significant differences in DUI re-arrest rates for those who received the locks compared to those who did not. Based on this evidence, both the World Health Organization (2010) and the CDC consider this practice to be effective in reducing DUI offenses *while immobilizers are installed in offenders' cars* (Elder *et al.*, 2011).

Two randomized trials conducted in Maryland show longer-term effects of ignition interlocks. The first study (Beck *et al.*, 1999) involved random assignment to intervention and control groups of mostly White, single males in their early 30s who had committed two or more alcohol-related traffic offenses in the five years prior to the study. Those in the intervention group were mandated to have locks installed on their cars for one year while those in the control group had their licenses suspended. Consistent with the findings from the meta-analysis, use of the interlocks was associated with significant differences in re-arrests at the end of the first year for the intervention versus control group, but no differences were seen one year after the locks were removed. However, there was a significant impact on alcohol traffic violations which favored the intervention group when outcomes were considered across the entire two-year evaluation period. In the second study (Rauch *et al.*, 2011), significant effects on alcohol-related traffic violations were shown after two years of mandatory locks, as well as two years later. Across the four-year study period, alcohol convictions were significantly reduced, by 32%, for the intervention versus control group. Based on these studies, CrimeSolutions.gov rates the use of ignition interlocks as Effective.

Taken as a whole, we consider ignition interlocks to be effective in reducing alcohol-related traffic offenses in the short term, while the locks are installed in vehicles. However, their ability to produce long-term changes in offenders' behavior is still uncertain. Rauch and colleagues (2011) recommend that ignition interlocks be mandated for at least a two-year period in order to have a sustained effect on drinking and driving. Elder and colleagues (2011) recommend that to have a widespread impact on DUI and alcohol-related offenses, the use of interlocks must be significantly increased. Although 47 states in the USA have interlock programs, these programs are optional for offenders; they can choose to have ignition locks installed in their vehicles or to have their licenses suspended. Only about 10% of eligible offenders select the interlock option, which means that only a small proportion of the targeted population can hope to benefit from this type of intervention (Elder *et al.*, 2011). Similar barriers to dissemination have been noted in other countries (Willis *et al.*, 2004).

A last type of situational crime prevention used to reduce illegal behavior is **Crime Prevention Through Environmental Design** (**CPTED**). This practice was developed in the early 1970s in the USA by criminologist C. Ray Jeffrey and architect Oscar Newman. Although they were not collaborators, they each saw ways to reduce opportunities for criminal behavior by changing the **built environment**; that is, the physical designs and structures of buildings and neighborhoods. Like other types of situational crime prevention, CPTED aims to increase guardianship and reduce the attractiveness of targets and does not directly intervene with offenders. In CPTED, changes are made to the design of residential or commercial buildings and their surrounding areas in order to increase surveillance and detection of offenders. CPTED would recommend, for example, that home owners remove or trim trees and bushes in order to ensure easy lines of sight in and out of their windows. Likewise, to reduce shoplifting and burglary, stores should be designed with few entries and exits and should clearly mark areas that are off-limits to customers. CPTED can also be used in city and street planning. For example, dead-end streets, cul-de-sacs and locked gates that bar access to alleyways facing the backs of homes can be used to limit outsiders' ability to enter neighborhoods. Similarly, street closures and traffic barriers can block entrances to important landmarks in order to prevent vandalism, theft, or terrorist acts. Sometimes these practices are referred to as creating **defensible space**, meaning that public areas are fortified and strengthened to guard against crime (Newman, 1972).

Defensible space is also considered important in increasing the safety of residential areas (Newman, 1972). For example, fences and gates can be built around individual homes to mark property lines and convey to strangers that the area is private and off-limits. In addition, housing complexes can be designed such that residents can see each other's properties, which can increase "natural" surveillance and communicate to would-be offenders that there is a good chance they will be seen if they commit a crime in the area. Such designs, as well as those used to create common areas where residents can socialize, can also foster **territoriality** among residents. Territoriality creates a sense of pride and collective ownership among all those living in the housing complex, with the goal of ensuring that all residents will help to control crime in all areas of the property (Mair and Mair, 2003). This concept is similar to that of **collective efficacy** (Sampson, Raudenbush, and Earls, 1997) from **social disorganization theory**, which emphasizes the importance of having residents know one another, be aware of strangers who may enter their neighborhoods with the intent to commit crimes and feel a sense of collective ownership of this area so that they work together to prevent crime.

CPTED strategies may also include efforts to remove signs of **physical and social disorder** from private and/or public property. Such actions are guided by **broken windows theory** (Wilson and Kelling, 1982), which emphasizes the importance of environmental influences on crime.

According to this theory, neighborhoods with an excess of rundown buildings, graffiti, and trash (i.e., physical disorder), as well as homeless persons, prostitution, and open drug-dealing (i.e., social disorder) are appealing targets for crime. These signs of disorder convey to potential offenders that no one in the area cares if crimes are committed and that if laws are broken, they are unlikely to be apprehended. Conversely, tearing down old buildings and fixing broken windows will help prevent crime and could generate more territoriality, or collective pride and ownership, among residents (Lab, 2014).

Although CPTED is now decades old, rigorous evaluations of CPTED practices, including the creation of defensible space and territoriality, are rare. One review (Casteel and Peek-Asa, 2000) evaluated whether or not CPTED strategies such as installing CCTVs, hiring security guards, ensuring limited access in and out of buildings and keeping stores well-lit reduced robberies of public stores. The results indicated that when just one of these types of strategies was used, robberies were not affected. However, when multiple CPTED activities were implemented simultaneously, which was often the case, robberies were reduced from 30% to 85% across studies. Although such effects are fairly large, of the 26 studies considered, most were not published in peer review journals, all but one involved quasi-experimental research designs, there were few comparisons groups, and most were based on pre/post comparisons with no long-term analysis of impact (Casteel and Peek-Asa, 2000).

A separate review of five evaluations of CPTED that involved changes in street design showed some positive effects (Welsh *et al.*, 2010). However, the evaluations were too few in number and of too poor quality to allow conclusions about the effectiveness of this practice. Likewise, strong evidence that reducing physical and social disorder prevents crime is currently lacking, primarily because too few rigorous evaluations of this approach have been conducted (Braga and Bond, 2008). *Taken together, these findings indicate that there is currently inconclusive evidence of the effectiveness of CPTED practices.* More rigorous research is needed before these types of situational crime prevention can be considered effective in reducing crime.

Considering all that has been discussed, can situational crime prevention practices as a whole be considered effective in reducing crime? Common sense dictates that a home that is well lit, easy to see from the street and protected by a guard dog should be less appealing to burglars compared to a home without these features. Likewise, placing security guards in public places, metal detectors in airports and traffic barriers in front of important landmarks makes sense. But, as we will emphasize throughout this book, basing crime prevention activities on what we *think* might work is risky. Instead, we want to carefully evaluate whether or not there is strong, scientific evidence that taking an action *will* reduce crime. *Based on this standard, we currently do not have enough evidence to conclude that situational crime prevention practices result in lower rates of crime.* As summarized in Table 6.1, the only practice with some evidence of effectiveness is the use of ignition interlocks in vehicles owned or operated by individuals with multiple convictions for alcohol-related traffic crimes. Even with this practice, however, the evidence suggests that locks are effective in preventing drinking and driving only while installed in vehicles; they do not necessarily produce a sustained change in offenders' behaviors. All of the other situational crime prevention practices we reviewed have inconclusive evidence of effectiveness. We cannot say with certainty that they reduce, increase or have no impact on crime.

Table 6.1 Effectiveness of situational crime prevention practices.

Practice	Effective?	Rating by CrimeSolutions.gov
Closed circuit TV (CCTV)	Inconclusive	Promising
Increased street lighting	Inconclusive	Not reviewed
Target hardening	Inconclusive	Not reviewed
Ignition interlock programs	Effective	Effective
Crime Prevention Through Environmental Design (CPTED)	Inconclusive	Not reviewed

Several critiques of situational crime prevention have been raised that may explain the uncertainty of their effectiveness. *First*, although there are some advantages to focusing on the immediate and situational factors that can foster crime, situational crime prevention makes no attempt to change the underlying causes of offending. That is, individual and social risk and protective factors that lead to crime are not addressed by these methods. As such, they may be less able to produce long-term changes in offending because individuals who may be deterred in the short term from committing a particular offense will likely find an alternative outlet for their illegal activities.

A related *second* critique is that situational crime prevention does not truly prevent crime, but rather **displaces** it to another time or location. That is, an offender who encounters guardians and well-protected targets in one location can simply choose a new target or move to a different location to commit the crime. Clarke (1995) counters this critique by stating that many criminal acts are spontaneous and undertaken after a quick assessment of perceived rewards and risks. If risks are considered to be too large, an individual simply chooses not to commit the act. Most criminals are not so driven to break the law that they will spend a lot of time and effort to commit an offense.

Third, some situational crime prevention practices are considered overly restrictive and intrusive. For example, widespread use of CCTVs in public spaces can infringe upon citizens' privacy and may provide law enforcement and government too much power (Norris and McCahill, 2006). In addition, building "fortress-like" homes and housing complexes can lead to isolation of residents and increase fear of crime rather than creating increased ownership, territoriality and security (Lab, 2014).

It is difficult to evaluate the merit of these critiques. Regarding displacement, many studies have not investigated the potential that crime simply "moves around the corner" when situational crime prevention efforts are enacted in particular places (Guerette and Bowers, 2009). The studies that have examined the issue have tended to find little support for displacement. Although displacement of crime to nearby areas sometimes occurs, so does a **diffusion** of benefits. That is, when crime is decreased by situational crime prevention, surrounding areas that were not directly targeted for prevention often see reductions of crime as well (Guerette and Bowers, 2009; Johnson, Guerette, and Bowers, 2012). While this is promising news, reviews of this literature emphasize that most evaluations of situational crime prevention do not rely on strong research designs, and so their ability to draw conclusions about displacement and diffusion is limited.

It is clear that additional research is needed to evaluate the effectiveness of situational crime prevention strategies. More rigorous evaluation is needed to determine if these efforts work, what types of crimes they are most likely to affect and if changes can be sustained in the long term and with no negative consequences for the public. Given that many situational crime prevention practices are used in combination, more complex research designs will also be required to identify the specific actions or combinations of actions that are most likely to produce reductions in crime.

Law Enforcement Practices

> *The police do not prevent crime. This is one of the best-kept secrets of modern life. Experts know it, the police know it, but the public does not know it. Yet the police pretend that they are society's best defense against crime … This is a myth. First, repeated analysis has consistently failed to find any connection between the number of police officers and crime rates. Secondly, the primary strategies adopted by modern police have been shown to have little or no effect on crime.*
>
> Bayley, 1994: 3

Law enforcement practices with evidence of effectiveness

Although crime prevention can be undertaken by anyone, just about every society relies heavily on the police to prevent crime. Law enforcement's ability to stop law-breakers is predicted by **deterrence theory**, which states that the general public and criminals will refrain from illegal behavior when they perceive or actually receive punishments for doing so. Indeed, their mere presence in a neighborhood can stop potential offenders from breaking the law, as predicted by **general deterrence**, and police do spend considerable time apprehending offenders, which should reduce crime according to **specific deterrence**.

What does the research say about the ability of law enforcement to prevent crime? As illustrated in the quote by David Bayley, a retired American professor who studied police practices, some criminologists are very skeptical about the potential for law enforcement to effectively reduce and prevent crime. In the 1970s, the prevailing view that "nothing works" in crime prevention applied to most standard law enforcement practices (Telep and Weisburd, 2012; Weisburd and Eck, 2004). For example, there was little evidence that increasing the number of officers on the streets, using random patrols across all parts of a community and ensuring rapid responses to calls for service affected crime rates. We should point out, however, that evaluations of these practices were usually based on poor research designs which made it difficult to draw any firm conclusions about their effectiveness.

In response to this critique, police were forced to become more innovative and consider new methods of law enforcement. They are now more likely to use proactive and preventive approaches, including partnering with local community members to address crime problems (Lab, 2014). They are also more strategic and focused; for example, routine policing practices now involve targeting locally specific causes of crime and more frequently patrolling parts of a city known to have

Table 6.2   Effective law enforcement practices.

Practice	Rating by CrimeSolutions.gov
Hot spots policing	Effective

particularly high rates of crime rather than spending equal amounts of time in all areas of the police beat. Are these new strategies any better than the old ones at preventing crime? Are evaluations of these approaches based on more sophisticated research designs than before?

According to reviews of the literature, evaluations of most law enforcement practices still suffer from low methodological rigor and many show mixed evidence of effectiveness. As a result, many commonly used police practices currently have inconclusive evidence of reducing crime, and we are still far from being able to clearly identify "evidence-based policing strategies" (Sherman, 2011; Weisburd and Eck, 2004). The most promising law enforcement practices are those that (i) are more proactive than reactive, and (ii) focus attention on high crime areas or high-risk times of day/night rather than using random patrols (Lum, Koper, and Telep, 2011; Sherman and Eck, 2006). Across these different strategies, however, *the only policing practice which, in our view, has relatively strong evidence of effectiveness is **hot spots policing***. (See Table 6.2.)

Hot spots policing is based on both **social disorganization** and **deterrence** theories. Social disorganization theory recognizes that crime is not uniformly distributed across cities but rather clusters in certain geographical areas, typically neighborhoods closest to the city center where rates of poverty are high and social relationships are weak. **Hot spots** are even smaller geographical areas, usually streets or intersections, in which crime rates are very high and consistently elevated over time. Moreover, these areas account for the majority of crimes in the larger area (Braga, Papachristos, and Hureau, 2012; Lab, 2014). For example, a study of gun crimes in Boston showed that 74% of all shootings taking place from 1980 to 2008 occurred on 5% of street corners; these were Boston's crime hot spots (Braga, Papachristos, and Hureau, 2010).

In **hot spots policing**, the first step is for police to identify the high crime areas in their beats, often using crime mapping computer software. They then focus law enforcement activities in these areas, rather than spending equal amounts of time across the entire beat. The specific actions taken in hot spots areas can vary but usually include increased patrol and surveillance, regular "crack-downs" resulting in numerous arrests, and efforts to reduce physical and social disorder. Based on deterrence theory, the greater visibility of police in these places and increased likelihood of arrest will deter potential offenders from breaking the law.

A meta-analysis of 19 evaluations of hot spots policing showed an average effect size of 0.18, indicating a small but significant reduction in officially recorded crimes (Braga, Papachristos, and Hureau, 2012, 2014). When restricted to the 10 studies that were evaluated using RCTs, the effect size was smaller (0.12) but still statistically significant. Based on this review, CrimeSolutions.gov rates this **practice** as Effective. It also rates as Effective several studies which evaluated the use of hot spots policing in specific cities (e.g., in Lowell, MA; see: Braga and Bond, 2008; and in Minneapolis, MN; see: Sherman and Weisburd, 1995). Given these reviews, we also consider hot spots policing to be an effective practice.

In a 2008 survey of 176 law enforcement agencies in the USA, 63% said they used hot spots policing to reduce violent crime (Telep and Weisburd, 2012). However, Lum and colleagues (2011) caution that what many police agencies claim to be hot spots policing has more in common with traditional law enforcement strategies such as using random patrols across police beats. As we will discuss in Chapter 11, changing organizational practices to make greater use of evidence-based prevention strategies is difficult, and law enforcement agencies are no exception.

Law enforcement practices with inconclusive evidence of effectiveness

One challenge with hot spots policing is that, as a general **practice**, the particular actions that should be taken by police are not specified and may vary across agencies. This diversity makes evaluation difficult and can lead to variation in effects across studies. An even more general law enforcement practice that is specifically intended to take different forms in different agencies is **problem-oriented policing (POP)**. The goal of POP is to help law enforcement agencies use more strategic, proactive, and locally specific approaches which better address the underlying causes of crime (Lab, 2014; Weisburd and Eck, 2004). In this approach, police are to identify crime problems occurring in their jurisdiction and focus their efforts on these problems and their causes rather than simply reacting to all crimes after they have occurred. In the **SARA** model, Eck and Spelman (1987) identify four important actions that should occur when departments use POP: (i) **S**canning local crime data to identify and prioritize particular problems; (ii) **A**nalyzing the data in order to develop appropriate responses to prioritized problems; (iii) **R**esponding by implementing these responses; and (iv) **A**ssessing the impact of the responses on the targeted problems. This model guides police to use different tactics to address different crimes in different areas under their jurisdiction.

A meta-analysis of 10 evaluations of POP reported a significant but small average effect on crime of 0.13 (Weisburd et al., 2008, 2010). When considering the four RCTs, the average effect size was similar in size (0.15) and also statistically significant. However, the authors caution that the findings are based on a relatively small number of studies and that the specific law enforcement activities varied across sites, which makes it difficult to determine if some particular responses work better than others. They also noted that some sites reported significant implementation challenges. The assessment phase of the SARA model seems to be particularly challenging for police agencies to complete (Telep and Weisburd, 2012).

The **pulling levers** police practice combines the problem identification element of POP with a **focused deterrence** approach that emphasizes certain and severe sanctions for criminal behaviors. As we also describe in Chapter 7, the pulling levers practice is modeled after the **Boston Ceasefire** project, which showed some positive effects in reducing youth homicides, gun crimes (Braga et al., 2001) and gang-related shootings (Braga, Hureau, and Papachristos, 2014). In that project, following POP principles, Boston law enforcement officials and their community partners analyzed Boston crime data to determine the types of violent crime which were accounting for the majority of homicides, especially youth homicides, in the city. These data indicated that most homicides were committed by a small number of gang-involved youth. Based on deterrence theory, the Boston officials decided they needed to send a message to gang members that their future violent crimes would not be tolerated and would be subject to an increased likelihood of arrest, prosecution, and long sentences. This message was communicated in face-to-face meetings between law enforcement agents and known gang members, often with participation by local community members (Braga and Weisburd, 2012; Lab, 2014).

Hoping to replicate the findings in Boston, other cities implemented what came to be known as the pulling levers approach. A meta-analysis of outcomes from 10 of these studies, including the Boston project, indicated an overall effect size of 0.60, reflecting a large impact on crime (Braga and Weisburd, 2012). However, all of the studies were evaluated using QEDs rather than more rigorous designs and not all showed significant crime reductions. Based on this evidence, CrimeSolutions.gov rates pulling levers as a Promising practice. Given the quasi-experimental nature of the evaluations, we agree with Braga and Weisburd (2014: 574) that "these strategies need to be subjected to more rigorous tests that generate more robust evidence on program impacts." Until that time, we consider the pulling levers practice to have inconclusive evidence of effectiveness.

Despite the uncertain level of effectiveness, both POP and pulling levers are widely used. Weisburd et al. (2008) report that POP is popular in the UK, and about two-thirds of large police agencies in the USA reported on a 2007 survey that they "actively encourage problem-solving" (Telep and Weisburd, 2012). The US Department of Justice has made a significant investment in these practices. It enacted the **Strategic Approaches to Community Safety Initiative (SACSI)** in the late 1990s, which involved collaboration between US Attorneys and local communities to analyze crime data and create strategic crime prevention plans which could entail pulling levers meetings and cracking down on repeat offenders via increased arrests and prosecution (Lab, 2014; Roehl et al., 2008). A quasi-experimental evaluation of SACSI based on implementation in 10 cities from 1998 to 2000 showed mixed results across sites in reducing levels of homicide (Roehl et al., 2008; Rosenbaum and Schuck, 2012). Nonetheless, the initiative was expanded to more cities in 2001 in the **Project Safe Neighborhoods (PSN)** initiative (Lab, 2014). A QED evaluation of PSN in Chicago showed that 24 police beats in Chicago's West Side which used PSN had significant reductions in homicide, gun homicides, and aggravated assaults compared to 30 beats in the South Side which did not (Papachristos, Meares, and Fagan, 2007). Although this initiative is rated as Promising by CrimeSolutions.gov, a larger QED which compared 82 PSN sites to 170 cities across the country failed to show an overall impact of PSN on crime (McGarrell et al., 2009).

Another policing practice intended to reduce gun crimes is the use of **directed patrols**. Similar to hot spots policing, but usually focused on larger geographical areas, in this practice, officers increase their patrols of areas known for having elevated levels of gun-related crime. They may stop more vehicles, make more arrests and confiscate more guns compared to standard policing. Unlike the pulling levers practice, directed patrols are carried out only by law enforcement officers; they do not include collaborations with community members to send general deterrence messages or prosecutors to increase specific deterrence. Of the police practices reviewed here, directed patrols have been evaluated least often. We could find only one review of their effectiveness, which was based on four studies, three conducted in the USA and one in Colombia. Across the four evaluations, 10% to 71% reductions in gun-related violent crimes and homicides were found in areas using directed patrols (Koper and Mayo-Wilson, 2012). While suggesting that this practice may work, none of the studies relied on RCTs and strong evidence of effectiveness is not yet available.

The last policing practice we consider to have inconclusive evidence of effectiveness is **community-oriented policing (COP)**. This practice is similar to POP in emphasizing the use of proactive and preventive measures to address the root causes of crime, rather than reacting to crimes after they occur, and in carefully identifying and prioritizing local crime problems. The main emphasis in COP is the creation of partnerships between law enforcement agents and community residents. To foster communication and collaboration, law enforcement agencies host community meetings to talk to residents about crime issues and collaboratively prioritize the most serious issues to be addressed. In addition, small "storefront" law enforcement stations are placed in neighborhoods where they will be accessible to citizens, and the same officers are assigned to regularly patrol neighborhoods, often on foot, so that residents and officers get to know one another (Lab, 2014). Another key element of COP is the decentralization of police bureaucracy and decision-making, so that individual officers are more empowered to work with community members (Gill et al., 2014).

A meta-analysis of studies that defined COP very broadly, as any type of collaboration between police and citizens, found inconclusive evidence of effectiveness for this practice. Based on 25 evaluations, use of COP was associated with odds-ratios of 1.05 to 1.10, indicating 5% to 10% reductions in crime depending on the specific crimes included in the analysis (Gill et al., 2014). The authors caution that only one study utilized a RCT and that effects were small and inconsistent across studies. Other reviews have failed to show effects of COP in reducing crime and have noted a lack of methodological rigor in most COP evaluations (Lab, 2014; Telep and Weisburd, 2012). In addition, COP is challenging to fully implement; research indicates that many agencies do not implement all parts of this practice, especially decentralization of agencies' hierarchical structures (Gill et al., 2014; McDonald, 2002).

It should be noted that the review by Gill et al. (2014) did find a significant impact of COP on citizen satisfaction with police officers. This finding is important given highly publicized displays of citizen outrage and displeasure with law enforcement, such as the riots in Ferguson, MO following the shooting of a young African American male by a white police officer. Furthermore, there is some evidence that whether or not people obey the law depends on their perceptions of the legitimacy, fairness, and satisfaction with laws and law enforcement (Tyler, 2004). It is possible then, that COP could have an indirect effect on crime by increasing favorable attitudes towards law enforcement, but this hypothesis has not yet been tested (Gill et al., 2014).

Taking into account the practices reviewed in this section and in the previous section, we conclude that the quote by Bayley is overly pessimistic. We do not have strong evidence that police fail to prevent crime or that the main strategies used by police have little or no impact on offending. Instead, most of the evidence regarding the effectiveness of law enforcement practices is inconclusive, as shown in Table 6.3; we do not yet know with certainty if these actions reduce, increase, or have no effect on crime. As with situational crime prevention, more rigorous evaluation of policing practices is needed to determine if these efforts work and to identify the specific law enforcement activities that are best able to prevent crime.

Table 6.3 Law enforcement practices and policies with inconclusive evidence of effectiveness.

Practice	Rating by CrimeSolutions.gov
Problem-oriented policing (POP)	Promising
Pulling levers	Promising
Directed patrols	Not reviewed
Community-oriented policing (COP)	Not reviewed

Alcohol-Related Policies Intended to Prevent Crime

Because drinking alcohol is an illegal behavior for youth and alcohol use by adults has been linked to increased drinking and driving and other criminal behaviors (Anderson, Chisholm, and Fuhr, 2009; Boyum, Caulkins, and Kleiman, 2011), various policies have been enacted to reduce alcohol use and related problems. **Alcohol-related policies** include local, state or national ordinances and laws which restrict the supply of or demand for alcohol. They also include the passage and enforcement of laws making driving while intoxicated (DWI) illegal. Such laws are based on **general deterrence theory**, as they are enacted with the expectation that increasing the certainty and severity of punishments will deter the general population from driving while intoxicated.

DWI studies can examine changes in rates of drinking and driving based on official data, usually police records indicating drivers' blood alcohol concentration (BAC) levels, or self-reported data. In addition, they often rely on official records of motor vehicle crashes and/or fatalities, some of which provide information on BAC levels but some of which are "proxy" measures in which the drivers' BAC is unknown but presumed to be elevated. For example, single-car accidents occurring at night have been demonstrated as more likely than daytime accidents to be alcohol-related, so some studies evaluate changes in rates of nighttime, single-car accidents before and after the passage of a new alcohol-related law or enforcement strategy (Shults *et al.*, 2001). In order to restrict our review to studies with the most rigorous research methods, we have tried to avoid citing evidence from studies in which actual levels of alcohol use are unknown.

Probably the most well-known alcohol-related law, especially among college students, is that establishing a **minimum legal drinking age (MLDA)**. The impact of MLDA laws on both under-age drinking and drinking and driving has been examined. A meta-analysis found that about one-third of 132 MLDA evaluations showed that increasing the minimum drinking age to 21 years in the USA produced statistically significant lower rates of alcohol use by those aged 18 to 20 (Wagenaar and Toomey, 2002). However, about half the studies showed a non-significant impact of this policy and a few evaluations showed increased rates of drinking. This study and other reviews (Anderson *et al.*, 2009; Gruenewald, 2011; Wagenaar, Lenk, and Toomey, 2005) identify MLDA as an effective policy for reducing under-age drinking. However, *based on the mixed evidence, our interpretation is that there is currently inconclusive evidence of effectiveness for the impact of these laws on under-age drinking.*

There is stronger evidence that MLDA laws produce reductions in under-age DWI and car crashes. A review of 33 studies conducted by the CDC found that increasing the MLDA reduced alcohol-related crashes by 18–20-year-old drivers by 10% to 16% (Shults *et al.*, 2001). The CDC Community Guide indicates that these results provide "strong evidence" that MLDA laws are effective in preventing alcohol-related motor vehicle crashes among young adults (Shults *et al.*, 2001: 75), and we agree that there is evidence of effectiveness.

In the USA, all states have set the legal drinking age at 21 years, but some groups, including presidents of some American liberal arts colleges, have lobbied the government to reduce the drinking age (see the Amethyst Initiative website, http://www.theamethystinitiative.org/statement/). In fact, in many other countries the legal drinking age is 18, and New Zealand lowered its age from 20 to 18 years in 1999 (Gruenewald, 2011). Based on the evidence, however, reducing the MLDA is not recommended. The public, at least in the USA, seems to agree. A Gallup poll conducted in 2014 indicated that 74% of respondents aged 18 and older opposed lowering the drinking age to 18 (http://www.gallup.com/poll/174077/lowering-drinking-age.aspx).

Local, state, or federal statutes that **raise prices or taxes on alcohol** are intended to reduce the demand for alcohol by making it more expensive. The effect of this type of policy on under-age drinking has been evaluated in a systematic review of nine studies conducted mostly in the USA (Elder *et al.*, 2010). In four of the studies, increasing the price of alcohol was significantly associated with less drinking by adolescents and young adults; in the other five studies, a similar pattern was found but not all relationships were statistically significant. In another review, increased pricing was associated with lower rates of youth drinking in 10 of the 13 studies considered, and this association was found in four of the seven high-quality studies included in the analysis (Wagenaar *et al.*, 2005).

Alcohol pricing has also been shown to affect DWI. Elder and colleagues (2010) found that in two of three studies reviewed, increases in alcohol pricing or taxation were significantly associated with fewer alcohol-related car crashes and/or fatalities, while five of eight studies relying on proxy measures like nighttime crashes found significant reductions. In addition, two of three other studies showed a relationship between increases in pricing and taxation and lower self-reported alcohol-impaired driving. A meta-analysis of 14 studies examining the impact of alcohol pricing on other types of crime showed that higher pricing was significantly associated with child abuse, violent assaults, and other types of criminal behavior (Wagenaar, Tobler, and Komro, 2010). However, effect sizes were very small for these outcomes (0.02 for child abuse/violence and 0.01 for other crimes).

Based on this research, we conclude that policies which increase the price of alcohol are effective in reducing youth drinking and DWI, but the evidence indicating an impact on other types of crime is inconclusive. Although the USA and most nations impose some taxes on alcohol, the consensus is that taxation tends to be relatively low and has not kept up with inflation (Anderson *et al.*, 2009; Wagenaar *et al.*, 2005). For example, Xu and Chaloupa (2011) report that more than 20 states in the USA have not raised their taxes on beer in the last 20 years and only 10 states have raised beer taxes in the last decade.

Laws can also be passed to prohibit DWI. When first established, such laws did not require evidence that drivers had a certain **blood alcohol concentration (BAC)** level, but now "**per se**" **laws** make it illegal to operate a car when the driver is at or above a certain BAC level (Shults *et al.*, 2001). Different states and nations specify different BAC levels and 19 countries have established lower BACs for young or inexperienced drivers. A CDC evaluation of eight studies assessing the impact of lowering BAC levels from 0.10 to 0.08, which occurred in 21 states in the USA between 1983 and 2001, indicated a median reduction in alcohol-related motor vehicle fatalities of 7% following this change in law (Shults *et al.*, 2001). The same report analyzed data from six studies, four in the USA and two in Australia, examining the effects of lowering BAC levels to even less than 0.08 for drivers younger than 21 years old (in the USA) or newly licensed drivers (in Australia). All six studies showed reductions in fatal and non-fatal crashes following the more restrictive laws, ranging from 4% to 24%, results which the CDC considers to be "sufficient evidence" of effectiveness (Shults *et al.*, 2001: 72).

Taken as a whole, these studies demonstrate that legal statutes setting BAC levels are effective in reducing DWI and alcohol-related car accidents. As of 1995, the federal government in the USA has required states to enact a BAC limit of 0.02 or lower for youth drivers and all have done so (Wagenaar, O'Malley, and LaFond, 2001). Voas and Fell (2011) recommend that the USA lower BAC levels for adult drivers from 0.08 to 0.05, the minimum standard used in Australia, New Zealand, the European Union, and various other countries (for more information on BAC levels internationally, see: www.icap.org). In addition, Wagenaar *et al.* (2001) recommend that public awareness campaigns be implemented to increase knowledge of BAC laws, given that most youth and adult drivers are unaware of BAC limits.

There is evidence that proactive enforcement of DWI and BAC laws can help reduce alcohol-impaired driving and related accidents. Although these activities are the responsibility of law enforcement officers, we cover these practices in this section rather than earlier in the chapter given their relationship to alcohol policies. Two different practices have been used to prevent DWI: **random breath testing (RBT)** and **selective breath testing (SBT)**. When RBT is used, police can regularly stop drivers at random, regardless of whether or not they have been observed to be driving erratically, and require that they submit to a BAC test (Fell, Lacey, and Voas, 2004). This practice is used in Australia and some other European countries but, in the USA, RBT is considered a violation of the Fourth Amendment which prohibits unreasonable searches and seizures. However, a Supreme Court ruling in the *Michigan Department of State Police v. Sitz* case allowed police to use SBTs to check for alcohol-impaired drivers. In this practice, police create "sobriety checkpoints" in which they stop all vehicles at a particular location, ask drivers questions, observe their responses and detain those who show signs of alcohol use and impairment (Fell *et al.*, 2004; Shults *et al.*, 2001).

Based on their systemic review of the literature, the CDC has concluded that both RBT and SBT have "strong evidence" of effectiveness in reducing alcohol-related crashes (Shults *et al.*, 2001: 78). Their analysis of 12 RBT studies indicated median reductions in fatal and non-fatal crashes of 20% to 24%, while the 11 SBT studies reviewed demonstrated median reductions of 16% to 22%. Other reviews have also identified these practices as effective (Anderson *et al.*, 2009; Voas and Fell, 2011). Because deterrence theory emphasizes that offenders are more likely to be deterred when they are aware of laws and believe that they will be enforced, RBTs and SBTs should be well publicized and frequently conducted. A CDC review of 10 highly publicized SBT programs in the USA showed a median reduction in alcohol-related crash fatalities of 8.9% (Bergen *et al.*, 2012).

To summarize, there is evidence that a variety of alcohol-related practices are effective in reducing DWI and alcohol-related crashes, though impact on under-age drinking and other crimes is less conclusive, as shown in Table 6.4. Based on this research as a whole, the 2010 World Health Organization's

Table 6.4 Effectiveness of alcohol-related policies.

Policy	Effective?	Rating by CrimeSolutions.gov
Increasing the minimum legal drinking age	Inconclusive in reducing under-age drinking	Not reviewed
	Effective in reducing DWI	Not reviewed
Raising taxes on alcohol	Effective in reducing under-age drinking	Not reviewed
	Effective in reducing DWI	Not reviewed
	Inconclusive in reducing adult crime	Not reviewed
"Per se" laws regulating drivers' blood alcohol content (BAC) levels	Effective in reducing DWI	Not reviewed
Random breath testing (RBT) and Selective breath testing (SBT) by law enforcement	Effective in reducing DWI	Not reviewed

DWI, driving while intoxicated.

Global Strategy to Reduce the Harmful Use of Alcohol emphasizes the need for all countries to enact stricter alcohol policies in order to reduce alcohol consumption and problems caused by drinking, such as vehicle crashes and the perpetration of violent crimes (World Health Organization, 2010).[1] This report recognizes that most of the evidence for the impact of alcohol-related policies has been based on studies conducted in English-speaking and high-income countries, and that these nations tend to have many alcohol policies already in place. Nonetheless, the report calls for all nations, and especially lower income countries, to take additional steps to reduce the availability and consumption of alcohol and to set and enforce DWI policies. We would add that in the USA, 12 states currently ban SBTs, considering them to violate the Fourth Amendment, and most states have been shown to use sobriety checkpoints less than once per month (Voas and Fell, 2011).

Effectiveness of Other Legal and Criminal Justice Policies Intended to Prevent Crime

In this final section of the chapter, we consider the effectiveness of other legal and criminal justice policies that are enacted locally, in states, or nationally with the intention of preventing crime. Some of these policies are aimed at deterring the general population from committing crime and are based on **general deterrence theory**. Others are designed to reduce recidivism among those already engaged in crime, with the expectation that legal punishments will reduce future crime by these individuals, as hypothesized by **specific deterrence theory**. In Chapter 9, we also review the effectiveness of practices and some policies intended to reduce recidivism, but that chapter focuses on interventions implemented in correctional facilities. In this chapter, our discussion focuses on legal statutes making certain behaviors illegal or mandating particular punishments for particular offenses.

Policies with inconclusive evidence of effectiveness

As was true with many of the practices reviewed in this chapter, we lack conclusive evidence regarding the effectiveness of many policies enacted by the criminal justice system to punish offenders, even those that are widely used, as shown in Table 6.5. The uncertainty is largely related to a lack of high-quality evaluations of these policies. As we will repeat throughout this book, policies of any type are particularly difficult to evaluate using high-quality research designs. They are often passed by federal or state governments with the expectation that all jurisdictions will comply, such that randomization to intervention and control groups is not possible and suitable comparison groups are difficult to find. Policies can be evaluated using some high-quality quasi-experimental research designs, such as **time series designs**, in which outcomes are assessed before and after a policy has been enacted (Cook and Campbell, 1979; Rossi, Lipsey, and Freeman, 2004). Even with this design, however, it can be difficult to rule out other potential explanations for demonstrated effects (Biglan, Ary, and Wagenaar, 2000).

The first criminal justice policy that has been subject to numerous evaluations but shown to have inconclusive evidence of effectiveness in reducing crime is **capital punishment**. A report assessing the deterrent effect of capital punishment on homicides, based on studies conducted in the USA, concluded that evaluations of this policy have not been strong enough to provide valid evidence of effectiveness (Nagin and Pepper, 2012). As the authors state: "research to date on the effect of capital punishment on homicides is not informative about whether capital punishment decreases, increases or has no effect on homicide rates" (Nagin and Pepper, 2012: 2). Until additional high-quality studies are conducted, we cannot say with any certainty whether or not the death penalty reduces homicides.

Three strikes laws also provide harsh punishments for offenders with the goal of reducing their involvement in crime. Three strikes laws mandate increased sentences, sometimes life in prison

Table 6.5   Legal and criminal justice policies with inconclusive evidence of effectiveness or shown to be ineffective.

Practice	Evidence?	Rating by CrimeSolutions.gov*
Capital punishment	Inconclusive	Not reviewed
Three strikes laws	Inconclusive	Not reviewed
Longer sentences for gun crimes	Inconclusive	Not reviewed
Weapons bans	Inconclusive	Not reviewed
Mandatory background checks and waiting periods to purchase guns	Inconclusive	Not reviewed
Concealed weapons laws	Inconclusive	Not reviewed
Gun buyback programs	Inconclusive	Not reviewed
Youth curfew laws	Inconclusive	Not reviewed
Transfer of juvenile offenders to the adult criminal justice system	Ineffective	Not reviewed
Arresting perpetrators of misdemeanor domestic violence offenses	Ineffective	Not reviewed

* CrimeSolutions.gov identifies as "Promising" policies intended to reduce gun violence, based on a review of various types of gun-related practices by Makarios and Pratt (2012).

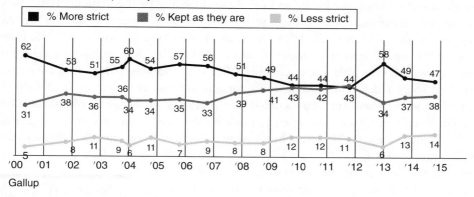

Laws covering the sale of firearms – Americans' preferences since 2000

In general, do you feel that the laws covering the sale of firearms should be made more strict, less strict, or kept as they are now?

Figure 6.1 The views of American citizens on gun purchase restrictions.

without parole, for offenders convicted of their third crime, usually a serious felony. These laws were passed in the early 1990s in the USA, when crime rates were increasing and policy-makers were intent on "getting tough on crime."

To date, evaluations have not provided a clear indication that three strikes laws reduce crime (Chalfin and McCrary, 2014). In regards to **general deterrence**, some states have not seen any changes in crime rates following the passage of three strikes policies, while some have seen reductions and other have seen increases (Kovandzic, Sloan, and Vieraitis, 2004). Iatrogenic effects, particularly increases in homicide seen in three strikes states, have been explained as a reaction of criminals to the threat of harsh sanctions that is in opposition to that predicted by deterrence theory. Instead of refraining from committing a third offense, some offenders try to reduce their chances of getting caught for their third strikeable offense by killing witnesses (Kovandzic *et al.*, 2004). On the other hand, some studies have shown that criminals who have already been convicted of two felony crimes and are at risk for three strikes sentencing are less likely to commit a third strikeable offense compared to those whose second crime did not result in a felony conviction (Chalfin and McCrary, 2014). This evidence is more supportive of deterrence theory.

Various **gun control policies** have also been created based on general and specific deterrence theories. These laws assume that having strict punishments for gun-related crimes will both deter the general public from committing these offenses and reduce recidivism among criminals who have used weapons during their offenses. Although the general public seems to favor firearms sentencing laws which mandate increased sentence length for gun-related crimes (Marvell and Moody, 1995), policies intended to reduce the supply of guns are more controversial. For example, proponents of the Second Amendment, which allows American citizens to keep guns in their homes for self-defense, often oppose policies which restrict the sales of weapons and ammunition, require extensive background checks, or impose waiting times before guns can be purchased. As shown in Figure 6.1, a 2015 Gallup Poll indicated that 47% of Americans favored stricter laws for the sale and purchase of firearms (Swift, 2014). However, this same poll indicated that 73% of citizens did not want handguns to be banned in the USA.

Pro-gun attitudes among the public and significant lobbying by the National Rifle Association (NRA) and gun manufacturers has led to a very limited body of research evaluating the effects on crime of gun control policies in the USA (American Psychological Association, 2013; Institute of Medicine (IOM) and National Research Council (NRC), 2013). Until very recently, the US Government invested very little funding in gun policy evaluation research and has barred scientific agencies from using federal funds to advocate for gun control. However, in 2013 following the Sandy Hook shooting, President Obama called for stricter gun policies, better implementation and enforcement of current policies and more research on the causes and prevention of gun violence (see the President's *Now is the Time* plan, http://www.whitehouse.gov/sites/default/files/docs/wh_now_is_the_time_full.pdf).

Given the limited high-quality research to date, it is difficult to determine the effectiveness of most gun-related policies. A meta-analysis of the impact on crime of various gun laws, nearly all of which were enacted in the USA, showed a significant but small overall effect size of 0.09 (Makarios and Pratt, 2012). Based on this review, CrimeSolutions.gov identifies gun policies as a Promising practice. However, a systematic review of firearms policies conducted by the CDC (Hahn *et al.*, 2005) concluded there is currently insufficient evidence to determine the effectiveness of any particular firearms law, given that high-quality evaluations of gun policies are rare and findings are mixed across studies. Although the CDC review was not restricted to studies conducted in the USA, nearly all were based on American laws. The World Health Organization emphasizes that information about violent crimes is very difficult to obtain globally and that 60% of countries do not have reliable data even on homicides. This lack of data severely restricts the ability to evaluate the impact on crime of any type of prevention policy including gun laws.

> *What we don't know about gun control can hurt us.*
> Zimring, 1991: 48

When considering specific gun policies, Makarios and Pratt's (2012) review of studies showed significant effects on crime for both the use of **longer prison terms for gun-related crimes** and **banning ownership of particular weapons** (e.g., high-capacity assault rifles). However, other comprehensive reviews have indicated that these policies are either ineffective or that there is insufficient evidence to draw conclusions about their effectiveness (Hahn *et al.*, 2005; IOM and NRC, 2013). Research has also shown little evidence of effectiveness for **mandatory background checks** and **waiting periods** prior to gun purchase (Hahn *et al.*, 2005; IOM and NRC, 2013; Makarios and Pratt, 2012). These types of policies are unlikely to be effective because many criminals do not purchase guns through legal markets, but rather steal them, buy them on the black market, or receive them from friends or family members.

The CDC has evaluated the impact on crime of **shall issue concealed weapons carry laws**, which require authorities to issue permits to carry concealed weapons to all applicants who meet background checks (Hahn *et al.*, 2005). Their review found only four evaluations that met their standards, and the results were mixed across studies, leading them to classify these laws as having insufficient evidence of effectiveness.

Evaluations of **gun buyback programs** in the USA have not been linked to reductions in crime (Braga and Wintemute, 2013; IOM and NRC, 2013; Makarios and Pratt, 2012). There are several explanations for this failure to reduce crime, including that: (i) firearms are widely available in the USA, (ii) most buyback programs collect a very small number of weapons and do not significantly reduce the supply of weapons, (iii) the weapons returned are typically not the types used in crimes, and (iv) participants are usually law-abiding citizens, not criminals (Braga and Wintemute, 2013). Despite the lack of results in the USA, there is some evidence of effectiveness for gun buyback programs implemented in Australia (Braga and Wintemute, 2013; IOM and NRC, 2013). Following a mass shooting in Tasmania in 1996, the Australian Government banned certain firearms and instituted a national buyback program which resulted in the collection and destruction of about one-fifth of the total supply of firearms. An analysis of this policy indicated significant reductions in firearm homicides by 2006, which the authors attribute to the greatly reduced access to firearms across the country (Leigh and Neill, 2010).

Specific to youth crime, evaluations of **youth curfew laws** have shown mixed evidence of success, with participation in crime sometimes increasing, sometimes decreasing and often not changing at all following the adoption of a curfew law (Adams, 2003). As with many policies, however, most evaluations of the impact of curfew laws have not been rigorously conducted. Despite inconclusive evidence of their effectiveness, youth curfews are widely used in communities across the USA. Although the specific restrictions vary across communities, most ban youth under a certain age (typically 16 or 17) from being in public places during specified hours (Adams, 2007).

Ineffective policies

Some policies based on deterrence theory's hypothesis that harsh sanctions will reduce crime have been demonstrated as ineffective. Evaluations of the impact of **transfers** or **waivers of juvenile offenders to the adult criminal justice system** have shown that these policies do not reduce juvenile recidivism. Transfer laws allow offenders under age 18 who have committed particular offenses, usually violent felonies, to be tried in the adult criminal justice system where they are likely to receive harsher sentences. Evaluations indicate that youth who are waived to the adult court are *more* likely to recidivate than youth who remain in the juvenile justice system. A meta-analysis of four studies showed a median effect size of 0.34, indicating a medium-sized increase in arrests for violent and general offenses for youth who received waivers compared to similar offenders who did not (McGowan *et al.*, 2007). These findings have led the CDC to state that policies facilitating the transfer of juveniles to the adult system are not recommended because they are "counterproductive for the purposes of reducing juvenile violence and enhancing public safety" (McGowan *et al.*, 2007: S20). Similarly, a review of six evaluations by OJJPD concluded that transferring juveniles to adult courts "substantially increases recidivism" (Redding, 2010). In response to this evidence, states in the USA are decreasing their use of waivers and sending fewer juvenile offenders to the adult criminal justice system (Brown, 2012).

In terms of adult offenders, there is evidence that **arresting individuals for misdemeanor domestic violence offenses** does not reduce future domestic violence. An evaluation of this policy conducted in Minneapolis in the 1980s showed evidence of effectiveness, as those who were arrested for domestic violence had lower recidivism rates than offenders who were not arrested

(Sherman and Berk, 1984). Consequently, many police departments changed their policies and enacted mandatory arrest policies to be used for domestic violence misdemeanors. However, replications of this project did not produce similarly positive effects (Dunford, Huizinga, and Elliott, 1990; Farrington and Welsh, 2005; Maxwell, Garner, and Fagan, 2002) and the original study failed to show a long-term impact on recidivism (Sherman and Harris, 2014). Today, the general consensus is that mandatory arrests are not effective in reducing crime (Telep and Weisburd, 2012).[2] This example indicates the dangers of making widespread policy changes prior to a careful review of scientific evidence, ideally collected in studies with relatively long follow-up periods, a subject we will return to in Part IV of this text.

Need for Further Research

The information in this chapter highlights both the breadth of prevention practices and policies that are implemented every day to reduce crime and the lack of strong evidence of effectiveness for many of these interventions. As we will emphasize in this book, many of the most common strategies used to prevent crime have never been well evaluated. As a result, we cannot know with certainty if they reduce, increase, or have no effect on crime. *The fact that some preventive interventions actually do increase crime further emphasizes the importance of evaluation.* If we want to avoid harming the individuals and public we are trying to protect, then we must rigorously evaluate our crime prevention efforts. As discussed in Chapters 4 and 5, there is skepticism regarding the usefulness and feasibility of using randomized controlled trials to evaluate criminal justice practices. In fact, some of the most vocal critics of RCTs are advocates of situational crime prevention (e.g., Pawson and Tilley, 1994). Yet, there are many others, including authors of studies reviewed in this chapter, who recognize that use of less rigorous approaches limits our ability to make valid recommendations to policymakers and practitioners about how to prevent crime (e.g., Ekblom, 2012). Indeed, there appears to be growing consensus that additional, more rigorous evaluations are needed to determine the effectiveness of situational, law enforcement, and legal crime prevention practices and policies.

Clearly, it will be challenging to conduct these evaluations. Many of the strategies reviewed in this chapter are general practices which can take many different forms. In addition, sometimes multiple strategies are used simultaneously, which makes it difficult to determine if a particular practice is responsible for changes in crime or if it was the combination of actions that produced outcomes. Although situational crime prevention is considered to be relatively easy to implement, many of the law enforcement practices are more difficult to enact, particularly those that involve changes to agency structure and decision-making processes. All of these issues mean that evaluations must pay close attention to exactly what has been implemented and take this information into account when investigating outcomes.

> *The quest for a miracle cure for crime and violence sometimes leads to an early or excessive embrace of an unproven technology.*
>
> Cook, 2011: 162

While existing practices warrant further evaluation, new strategies are being implemented all the time and their outcomes will also need to be investigated. For example, rapid growth in technology is leading to the creation of many new "hot products" fitting the CRAVED criteria (Clarke, 1999), and new target hardening practices will need to be created and tested to determine if they reduce theft and damage of these products. In terms of policing strategies, recent years have seen many anti-law enforcement demonstrations and some erosion in the public's confidence in the police. Given research linking negative views of police to increased law-breaking, we need to know more about practices which can enhance citizen satisfaction with police, such as community-policing efforts, and the degree to which better citizen–police relationships lead to reductions in crime.

There is also a need for more evaluation of current and new alcohol-related and criminal justice policies. The World Health Organization (2010) has called for more evaluation of alcohol policies in low- and middle-income countries as well as greater examination of the impact of such policies on minority and marginalized groups. In the USA, President Obama has called for the implementation and evaluation of stricter gun policies, and it remains to be seen if such legislation will be passed and if new laws will impact gun crime. New policies related to medical and recreational marijuana use also require careful evaluation. We will want to know if these laws impact both juvenile and adult illegal substance use and what impact, if any, they have on other types of crime.

More information about the effectiveness of these approaches will help us come closer to our goal of achieving widespread reductions in crime. Although the practices discussed in this chapter do not try to change the risk and protective factors shown to be related to offending, they can be used in combination with individually focused prevention efforts to ensure that both the immediate and underlying causes of crime are addressed.

Summary

This chapter has reviewed many situational crime prevention practices and legal practices and policies which try to change, respectively, the environmental characteristics that provide opportunities for crime and the ways in which law enforcement and criminal justice agencies interact with potential and/or active offenders. Although commonly used, most of the activities we discussed have inconclusive evidence of effectiveness, largely due to a lack of high-quality evaluations that can adequately assess their impact on crime. Nearly every study reviewed concluded with a recommendation that the strategy(ies) assessed required more rigorous evaluation.

For example, while there is some indication that increasing guardianship, reducing the attractiveness of targets and changing the physical design of buildings and neighborhoods sometimes reduce crime, none of these situational crime prevention practices has strong enough evidence to suggest that, if widely used in communities, it will have a significant impact on rates of crime. Of the policing practices we considered, hot spots policing was the only method with credible evidence of effectiveness in reducing crime. Practices such as pulling levers, problem-oriented policing, and community policing have weaker evidence of effectiveness and appear to be challenging for agencies to fully implement.

Legal sanctions can also be used to reduce crime, although not all are successful in meeting this goal. Laws that restrict the availability of alcohol and make it illegal to drive while intoxicated have been shown to reduce rates of DWI, though their impact on under-age drinking and other types of crime is less certain. Many laws intended to limit the supply and use of guns have inconclusive evidence of effectiveness in reducing crime and require more evaluation. Of the criminal justice policies reviewed, harsh punishments like capital punishment and three strikes laws may or may not reduce adult offending. For juveniles, curfew laws have inconclusive evidence of effectiveness and waiver laws, which transfer juvenile offenders to adult courts, have been shown to increase recidivism.

Critical Thinking Questions and Practice Activities

1. Discuss with your classmate(s) the degree to which you regularly use situational crime prevention practices to protect yourself, your family, and your property from crime. Which do you use? Are there any new practices you plan to use more regularly after reading this chapter?
2. Conduct a careful observation of your home or apartment complex and the few blocks surrounding the area in which you live. Do you think these buildings and streets have been designed with CPTED practices in mind? What features do you see that should reduce opportunities for crime? What could be changed to increase the defensible space of the area? Who would be responsible for making these changes?
3. Although hot spots policing has evidence of effectiveness in reducing crime, concerns have been raised that this practice can cause residents to feel unfairly targeted by police. Do you think this concern has merit? To what degree might hot spots policing influence citizens' perceptions of police legitimacy? How can hot spots policing be implemented to minimize concerns about police misconduct and discrimination?
4. Consider the impact on crime that may result from laws that de-criminalize the possession and use of marijuana in the USA. Do you expect that these laws will increase marijuana use among youth? Among adults? Will other types of substance use be affected? Why or why not? Do you think that other forms of crime will increase, decrease, or be unaffected by these laws?
5. Imagine that your town has passed a new curfew law aimed at reducing youth crime and that you have been asked to help evaluate its effectiveness. Describe the type of evaluation you would conduct. In doing so, consider: (i) whether or not you would have a comparison or control group and what it would be; (ii) the data you would collect and/or analyze to measure changes in crime; and (iii) how you would investigate the degree to which the curfew law was being implemented and enforced as intended.

Endnotes

1. The World Health Organization (2010) and some other reviews (Anderson *et al.*, 2009; Martineau *et al.*, 2013) consider local or state zoning laws that control **alcohol outlet density** by restricting the number of places that can legally sell alcohol in a particular geographical region, and attempts to regulate the **days and times during which alcohol can be sold** as effective in reducing alcohol consumption and related harmful behaviors. While there is some evidence that areas with a greater number of places to purchase liquor have higher crime levels (Campbell *et al.*, 2009) and that restricting or loosening the days or times during which alcohol can be sold affects alcohol-related driving crashes (Hahn *et al.*, 2010; Middleton *et al.*, 2010), most of the research on these factors comes from cross-sectional research studies rather than experimental studies which examine changes in outcomes following changes in policies (Martineau *et al.*,

2013). In fact, it is relatively uncommon for communities or states to make significant changes in these types of laws, which limits the ability to analyze their impact (Campbell *et al.*, 2009). In addition, when changes are made, they often co-occur with other actions, making it difficult to assess the effectiveness of any one policy (Gruenewald, 2011). Until more high-quality evaluations are conducted, the effectiveness of alcohol outlet density and sales restrictions remains inconclusive.

2. A review by Sherman and Eck (2006) concludes that there is mixed evidence of the effectiveness of arresting those who commit domestic violence misdemeanors. This conclusion is based on findings from several studies indicating that arrests of unemployed offenders are associated with increases in recidivism, while arrests of employed offenders are associated with decreases in recidivism. However, these results are based on post hoc analyses conducted after studies have been completed, rather than evaluations that have randomly assigned employed and non-employed offenders to separate conditions. Until more rigorous tests are conducted, we base our conclusion that arrests of domestic violence perpetrators are ineffective in preventing recidivism on the main findings of the relevant research.

Helpful Websites (last accessed August 4, 2016)

- http://www.securedbydesign.com/index.aspx
  The Secured by Design website is maintained by the UK Police and provides advice to architects, housing developers, home owners, and police on CPTED methods that can be used to reduce crime.
- http://www.popcenter.org/
  The Center for Problem-Oriented Policing website provides very detailed information on many types of situational crime prevention practices and on POP. It includes recommendations for police agencies and others who may be interested in implementing these strategies.
- http://cebcp.org/evidence-based-policing/
  The Center for Evidence-Based Crime Policy at George Mason University maintains this website describing the evidence of effectiveness of law enforcement practices.
- http://www.cops.usdoj.gov/
  This US Department of Justice website describes the practice of community policing and its use in the USA.
- http://www.jhsph.edu/research/centers-and-institutes/johns-hopkins-center-for-gun-policy-and-research/
  The Center for Gun Policy and Research, maintained by Johns Hopkins University, describes effective and ineffective policies intended to reduce gun-related crime.
- http://alcoholpolicy.niaaa.nih.gov/and http://www.icap.org/
  The Alcohol Policy Information System (APIS) and International Center for Alcohol Policies provide detailed information on alcohol-related policies adopted in the USA and internationally.
- http://www.thecommunityguide.org/mvoi/AID/index.html
  The Centers for Disease Control Community Guide provides recommendations and links to research on alcohol policies intended to reduce under-age drinking, alcohol-related traffic crashes, and other problems.

Further Reading

- Gruenewald, P. J. 2011. Regulating availability: How access to alcohol affects drinking and problems in youth and adults. *Alcohol Research and Health*, 34:249–256.
  Reviews the purpose and effectiveness of various policies intended to affect alcohol use and related crime.

- Telep, C. W., and Weisburd, D. 2012. What is known about the effectiveness of police practices in reducing crime and disorder? *Police Quarterly*, 15:331–357.
  Describes the effectiveness of different law enforcement practices.
- World Health Organization. 2010. *Global Strategy to Reduce the Harmful Use of Alcohol*. Geneva, Switzerland: World Health Organization.
  Reviews information on the harmful effects of alcohol use on public health and crime and provides policy recommendations to reduce alcohol use globally.

References

Adams, K. 2003. The effectiveness of juvenile curfews at crime prevention. *The Annals of the American Academy of Political and Social Science*, 587:136–159.

Adams, K. 2007. Abolish juvenile curfews. Criminology and Public Policy, 6:663–670.

American Psychological Association. 2013. *Gun violence: Prediction, prevention, and policy*; http://www.apa.org/pubs/info/reports/gun-violence-prevention.aspx (accessed August 2, 2016). Washington, DC: American Psychological Association.

Anderson, P., Chisholm, D., and Fuhr, D. 2009. Effectiveness and cost-effectiveness of policies and programmes to reduce the harm caused by alcohol. *The Lancet*, 373:2234–2246.

Barrett, D. 2013. One surveillance camera for every 11 people in Britain, says CCTV survey, *The Telegraph*. Retrieved from http://www.telegraph.co.uk/technology/10172298/One-surveillance-camera-for-every-11-people-in-Britain-says-CCTV-survey.html (accessed August 4, 2016).

Bayley, D. H. 1994. *Police for the Future*. Oxford, England: Oxford University Press.

Beck, K. H., Rauch, W. J., Baker, E. A., and Williams, A. F. 1999. Effects of ignition interlock license restrictions on drivers with multiple alcohol offenses: A randomized trial in Maryland. *American Journal of Public Health*, 89:1695–1700.

Bergen, G., Pitan, A., Qu, S., *et al.*; Community Preventive Services Task Force. 2012. Publicized sobriety checkpoint programs: A Community Guide systematic review. *American Journal of Preventive Medicine*, 46:529–539.

Biglan, A., Ary, D. V., and Wagenaar, A. C. 2000. The value of interrupted time-series experiments for community intervention research. *Prevention Science*, 1:31–49.

Boyum, D. A., Caulkins, J. P., and Kleiman, M. A. R. 2011. Drugs, crime and public policy. In: J. Q. Wilson and J. Petersilia (eds), *Crime and Public Policy*, pp. 368–410. New York, NY: Oxford University Press.

Braga, A. A., and Bond, B. J. 2008. Policing crime and disorder hot spots: A randomized controlled trial. *Criminology*, 46:577–607.

Braga, A. A., and Weisburd, D. L. 2012. The effects of "pulling levers" focused deterrence strategies on crime. *Campbell Systematic Reviews*, 2012:8(6).

Braga, A. A., and Weisburd, D. L. 2014. Must we settle for less rigorous evaluations in large area-based crime prevention programs? Lessons from a Campbell review of focused deterrence. *Journal of Experimental Criminology*, 10:573–597. doi: 10.1007/s11292-014-9205-8

Braga, A. A., and Wintemute, G. J. 2013. Improving the potential effectiveness of gun buyback programs. *American Journal of Preventive Medicine*, 45:668–671.

Braga, A. A., Hureau, D. M., and Papachristos, A. V. 2014. Deterring gang-involved gun violence: Measuring the impact of Boston's Ceasefire on street gang behavior. *Journal of Quantitative Criminology*, 30:113–139.

Braga, A. A., Papachristos, A. V., and Hureau, D. M. 2010. The concentration and stability of gun violence at micro places in Boston, 1980–2008. *Journal of Quantitative Criminology*, 26:33–53.

Braga, A., Papachristos, A., and Hureau, D. 2012. Hot spots policing effects on crime. *Campbell Systematic Reviews*, 2012:8. doi: 10.4073/csr.2012.8

Braga, A. A., Papachristos, A. V., and Hureau, D. M. 2014. The effects of hot spots policing on crime: An updated systematic review and meta-analysis. *Justice Quarterly*, 31:633–663.

Braga, A. A., Kennedy, D. M., Waring, E. J., and Piehl, A. M. 2001. Problem-oriented policing, deterrence, and youth violence: An evaluation of Boston's Operation Ceasefire. *Journal of Research in Crime and Delinquency*, 38:195–225.

Brown, S. A. 2012. Trends in juvenile justice state legislation: 2001–2011. Washington, DC: National Conference of State Legislatures.

Campbell, C. A., Hahn, R. A., Elder, R. W., *et al.*; Task Force on Community Prevention Services. 2009. The effectiveness of limiting alcohol outlet density as a means of reducing excessive alcohol consumption and alcohol-related harms. *American Journal of Preventive Medicine*, 37:556–569.

Casteel, C., and Peek-Asa, C. 2000. Effectiveness of crime prevention through environmental design (CPTED) in reducing robberies. *American Journal of Preventive Medicine*, 18:99–115.

Chalfin, A., and McCrary, J. 2014. Criminal deterrence: A review of the literature. University of California. Working paper.

Clarke, R. V. 1995. Situational crime prevention. In: M. Tonry and D. P. Farrington (eds), *Crime and Justice, Building a Safer Society: Strategic Approaches to Crime Prevention*, vol. 19, pp. 91–150. Chicago, IL: University of Chicago Press.

Clarke, R. V. 1999. Hot products: Understanding, anticipating and reducing demand for stolen goods. *Police Research Series, Paper 112*. London, England: Home Office.

Clarke, R. V., and Felson, M. 1993. *Routine Activity and Rational Choice*. New Brunswick, NJ: Transaction Publishers.

Cohen, J. 1988. *Statistical Power Analysis for the Behavioral Sciences*, 2nd ed. Hillsdale, NJ: Lawrence Erlbaum Associates.

Cook, P. J. 2011. The impact of drug market pulling levers policing on neighborhood violence: An evaluation of the High Point Drug Market Intervention. *Criminology and Public Policy*, 11:161–164.

Cook, T. D., and Campbell, D. T. 1979. *Quasi-Experimentation: Design and Analysis Issues for Field Settings*. Boston, MA: Houghton Mifflin.

Dunford, F., Huizinga, D., and Elliott, D. S. 1990. The role of arrest in domestic assault: The Omaha experiment. *Criminology*, 28:183–206.

Eck, J. E. 2003. Preventing crime at places. In: L. W. Sherman, D. P. Farrington, B. C. Welsh, and D. L. MacKenzie (eds), *Evidence-Based Crime Prevention*, pp. 241–294. New York, NY: Routledge.

Eck, J. E., and Guerette, R. T. 2012. Place-based crime prevention: Theory, evidence, and policy. In: B. C. Welsh and D. P. Farrington (eds), *The Oxford Handbook of Crime Prevention*, pp. 354–383. New York, NY: Oxford University Press.

Eck, J. E., and Spelman, W. 1987. Problem solving: Problem-oriented policing in Newport News. Washington, DC: Police Executive Research Forum.

Ekblom, P. 2012. The private sector and designing products against crime. In: B. C. Welsh and D. P. Farrington (eds), *The Oxford Handbook of Crime Prevention*, pp. 384–403. New York, NY: Oxford University Press.

Elder, R. W., Lawrence, B., Ferguson, A., *et al.*; The Task Force on Community Preventive Services. 2010. The effectiveness of tax policy interventions for reducing excessive alcohol consumption and related harms. *American Journal of Preventive Medicine*, 38:217–229.

Elder, R. W., Voas, R. B., Beirness, D. J., *et al.*; Task Force on Community Prevention Services. 2011. Effectiveness of ignition interlocks for preventing alcohol-impaired driving and alcohol-related crashes: A Community Guide systematic review. *American Journal of Preventive Medicine*, 40:362–376.

Farrington, D. P., and Welsh, B. C. 2005. Randomized experiments in criminology: What have we learned in the last two decades? *Journal of Experimental Criminology*, 1:9–38. doi: 10.1007/s11292-004-6460-0

Fell, J. C., Lacey, J. H., and Voas, R. B. 2004. Sobriety checkpoints: Evidence of effectiveness is strong, but use is limited. *Traffic Injury Prevention*, 5:220–227. doi: 10.1080/15389580490465247

Gill, C., Weisburd, D., Telep, C. W., Vitter, Z., and Bennett, T. 2014. Community-oriented policing to reduce crime, disorder and fear and increase satisfaction and legitimacy among citizens: A systematic review. *Journal of Experimental Criminology*, 10:399–428.

Gruenewald, P. J. 2011. Regulating availability: How access to alcohol affects drinking and problems in youth and adults. *Alcohol Research and Health*, 34:249–256.

Guerette, R. T., and Bowers, K. J. 2009. Assessing the extent of crime displacement and diffusion of benefits: A review of situational crime prevention evaluations. *Criminology*, 47:1331–1368.

Hahn, R. A., Bilukha, O., Crosby, A., *et al.* 2005. Firearms laws and the reduction of violence: A systematic review. *American Journal of Preventive Medicine*, 28:40–71.

Hahn, R. A., Kuzara, J. L., Elder, R. W., *et al.*; Task Force on Community Prevention Services. 2010. Effectiveness of policies restricting hours of alcohol sales in preventing excessive alcohol consumption and related harms. *American Journal of Preventive Medicine*, 39:590–604.

Hollis-Peel, M. E., Reynald, D. M., van Bavel, M., Elffers, H., and Welsh, B. C. 2011. Guardianship for crime prevention: A critical review of the literature. *Crime, Law and Social Change*, 56:53–70.

Institute of Medicine (IOM) and National Research Council (NRC). 2013. Priorities for research to reduce the threat of firearm-related violence. Washington, DC: The National Academies Press.

Johnson, S. D., Guerette, R. T., and Bowers, K. J. 2012. Crime displacement and diffusion of benefits. In: B. C. Welsh and D. P. Farrington (eds), *The Oxford Handbook of Crime Prevention*, pp. 337–353. New York, NY: Oxford University Press.

Koper, C. S., and Mayo-Wilson, E. 2012. Police strategies to reduce illegal possession and carrying of firearms: Effects on gun crime. *Campbell Systematic Reviews*, 2012:11. doi: 10.4073/csr.2012.11

Kovandzic, T. V., Sloan, J. J., and Vieraitis, L. M. 2004. "Striking out" as crime reduction policy: The impact of "three strikes" laws on crime rates in U.S. cities. *Justice Quarterly*, 21:207–239.

Lab, S. P. 2014. *Crime Prevention: Approaches, Practices and Evaluations*, 7th ed. Waltham, MA: Anderson Publishing.

Leigh, A., and Neill, C. 2010. Do gun buybacks save lives? Evidence from panel data. *American Law and Economics Review*, 12:509–557. doi: 10.1093/aler/ahq013

Lum, C. M., Koper, C. S., and Telep, C. W. 2011. The evidence-based policing matrix. *Journal of Experimental Criminology*, 7:3–26.

Mair, J. S., and Mair, M. 2003. Violence prevention and control through environmental modifications. *Annual Review of Public Health*, 24:209–225.

Makarios, M. D., and Pratt, T. C. 2012. The effectiveness of policies and programs that attempt to reduce firearm violence: A meta-analysis. *Crime and Delinquency*, 58:222–244.

Martineau, F., Tyner, E., Lorenc, T., Petticrew, M., and Lock, K. 2013. Population-level interventions to reduce alcohol-related harm: An overview of systematic reviews. *Preventive Medicine*, 57:278–296.

Marvell, T. B., and Moody, C. E. 1995. The impact of enhanced prison terms for felonies commited with guns. *Criminology*, 33:247–281.

Maxwell, C. D., Garner, J. H., and Fagan, J. A. 2002. The preventive effects of arrest on intimate partner violence: Research, policy and theory. *Criminology and Public Policy*, 2:51–80.

McDonald, J. M. 2002. The effectiveness of community policing in reducing urban violence. *Crime and Delinquency*, 48:592–618.

McGarrell, E. F., Hipple, N., Corsaro, N., *et al.* 2009. Project Safe Neighborhoods – A national program to reduce gun crime: Final project report. Washington, DC: National Institute of Justice.

McGowan, A., Hahn, R., Liberman, A., *et al.*; Task Force on Community Prevention Services. 2007. Effects on violence of laws and policies facilitating the transfer of juveniles from the juvenile justice system to the adult justice system: A systematic review. *American Journal of Preventive Medicine*, 32:S7–S28.

Middleton, J. C., Hahn, R., Kuzara, J. L., *et al.*; Task Force on Community Prevention Services. 2010. Effectiveness of policies maintaining or restricting days of alcohol sales on excessive alcohol consumption and related harms. *American Journal of Preventive Medicine*, 39:575–589. doi: 10.1016/j.amepre.2010.09.015

Nagin, D. S., and Pepper, J. V. (eds). 2012. *Deterrence and the Death Penalty*. Washington, DC: National Research Council, Committee on Law and Justice, Division of Behavioral and Social Sciences and Education.

Newman, O. 1972. *Defensible Space: Crime Prevention Through Urban Design*. New York, NY: Macmillan.

Norris, C., and McCahill, M. 2006. CCTV: Beyond penal modernism? *British Journal of Criminology*, 46:97–118.

Papachristos, A. V., Meares, T. L., and Fagan, J. A. 2007. Attention felons: Evaluating Project Safe Neighborhoods in Chicago. *Journal of Empirical Legal Studies*, 4:223–272.

Pawson, R., and Tilley, N. 1994. What works in evaluation research. *British Journal of Criminology*, 34:291–306.

Ratcliffe, J. H., Taniguchi, T., and Taylor, R. B. 2009. The crime reduction effects of public CCTV camera: A multi-method spatial approach. *Justice Quarterly*, 26:746–770. doi: 10.1080/07418820902873852

Rauch, W. J., Ahlin, E. M., Zador, P. L., Howard, J. M., and Duncan, G. D. 2011. Effects of administrative ignition interlock license restrictions on drivers with multiple alcohol offenses. *Journal of Experimental Criminology*, 7:127–148.

Redding, R. E. 2010. Juvenile transfer laws: An effective deterrent to delinquency? Washington, DC: Office of Juvenile Justice and Delinquency Prevention.

Roehl, J., Rosenbaum, D. P., Costello, S. K., *et al.* 2008. Paving the way for Project Safe Neighborhoods: SACSI in 10 U.S. cities. Washington, DC: US Department of Justice, Office of Justice Programs.

Rosenbaum, D. P., and Schuck, A. M. 2012. Comprehensive community partnerships for preventing crime. In: B. C. Welsh and D. P. Farrington (eds), *The Oxford Handbook of Crime Prevention*, pp. 226–246. New York, NY: Oxford University Press.

Rossi, P. H., Lipsey, M. W., and Freeman, H. E. 2004. *Evaluation: A Systematic Approach*. Thousand Oaks, CA: Sage.

Sampson, R. J., Raudenbush, S. W., and Earls, F. 1997. Neighborhoods and violent crime: A multilevel study of collective efficacy. *Science*, 277:918–924.

Sherman, L. W. 2011. Democratic policing on the evidence. In: J. Q. Wilson and J. Petersilia (eds), *Crime and Public Policy*, pp. 589–618. New York, NY: Oxford University Press.

Sherman, L. W., and Berk, R. A. 1984. The specific deterrent effects of arrest for domestic assault. *American Sociological Review*, 49:261–272.

Sherman, L. W., and Eck, J. E. 2006. Policing for crime prevention. In: L. W. Sherman, D. P. Farrington, B. C. Welsh, and D. L. MacKenzie (eds), *Evidence-Based Crime Prevention*. New York, NY: Routledge.

Sherman, L. W., and Harris, H. M. 2014. Increased homicide victimization of suspects arrested for domestic assault: A 23-year follow-up of the Milwaukee Domestic Violence Experiment (MilDVE). *Journal of Experimental Criminology*. doi: 10.1007/s11292-013-9193-0

Sherman, L. W., and Weisburd, D. 1995. General deterrent effects of police patrol in crime "hot spots": A randomized, controlled trial. *Justice Quarterly*, 12:625–648.

Shults, R. A., Elder, R. W., Sleet, D. A., *et al.*; Task Force on Community Prevention Services. 2001. Reviews of evidence regarding interventions to reduce alcohol-impaired driving. *American Journal of Preventive Medicine*, 21:66–88.

Smith, M. J., and Clarke, R. V. 2012. Situational crime prevention: Classifying techniques using "good enough" theory. In: B. C. Welsh and D. F. Farrington (eds), *The Oxford Handbook of Crime Prevention*, pp. 291–315. New York, NY: Oxford University Press.

Swift, A. 2014. Less than half of Americans support stricter gun laws. Retrieved from http://www.gallup.com/poll/179045/less-half-americans-support-stricter-gun-laws.aspx (accessed July 21, 2016).

Telep, C. W., and Weisburd, D. 2012. What is known about the effectiveness of police practices in reducing crime and disorder. *Police Quarterly*, 15:331–357.

Tyler, T. 2004. Enhancing police legitimacy. *Annals of the American Academy of Political and Social Science*, 593:84–99.

Voas, R. B., and Fell, J. C. 2011. Preventing impaired driving: Opportunities and problems. *Alcohol Research and Health*, 34:225–235.

Wagenaar, A. C., and Toomey, T. L. 2002. Effects of minimum drinking age laws: Review and analyses of the literature from 1960 to 2000. *Journal of Studies on Alcohol*, 14S:206–225.

Wagenaar, A. C., Lenk, K. M., and Toomey, T. L. 2005. Policies to reduce underage drinking: A review of the recent literature. In: M. Galanter, C. Lowman, G. M. Boyd, *et al.* (eds), *Recent Developments in Alcoholism: Alcohol Problems in Adolescents and Young People*, pp. 275–297. New York, NY: Springer.

Wagenaar, A. C., O'Malley, P. M., and LaFond, C. 2001. Lowered legal blood alcohol limits for young drivers: Effects on drinking, driving, and driving-after-drinking behaviors in 30 states. *American Journal of Public Health*, 91:801–804.

Wagenaar, A. C., Tobler, A. L., and Komro, K. 2010. Effects of alcohol tax and price policies on morbidity and mortality: A systematic review. *American Journal of Public Health*, 100:2270–2278.

Weisburd, D., and Eck, J. E. 2004. What can police do to reduce crime, disorder, and fear? *The Annals of the American Academy of Political and Social Science*, 593:42–65.

Weisburd, D., Telep, C. W., Hinkle, J. C., and Eck, J. E. 2008. The effects of problem-oriented policing on crime and disorder. *Campbell Systematic Reviews*, 2008:14.

Weisburd, D., Telep, C. W., Hinkle, J. C., and Eck, J. E. 2010. Is problem-oriented policing effective in reducing crime and disorder? Findings from a Campbell systematic review. *Criminology and Public Policy*, 9:139–172.

Welsh, B. C., and Farrington, D. P. 2008a. Effects of closed circuit television surveillance on crime. *Campbell Systematic Reviews*, 2008:17.

Welsh, B. C., and Farrington, D. P. 2008b. Effects of improved street lighting on crime. *Campbell Systematic Reviews*, 2008:13.

Welsh, B. C., Mudge, M. E., and Farrington, D. P. 2010. Reconceptualizing public area surveillance and crime prevention: Security guards, place managers and defensible space. *Security Journal*, 23:299–319. doi: 10.1057/sj.2008.22

Willis, C., Lybrand, S., and Bellamy, N. 2004. Alcohol ignition interlock programmes for reducing drink driving recidivism. *Cochrane Database of Systematic Reviews*, (3):CD004168. doi: 10.1002/14651858. CD004168.pub2

Wilson, J. Q., and Kelling, G. L. 1982. Broken windows. *The Atlantic Monthly*, 249:29–38.

World Health Organization. 2010. Global strategy to reduce the harmful use of alcohol. Geneva, Switzerland: World Health Organization.

Xu, X., and Chaloupka, F. J. 2011. The effects of prices on alcohol use and its consequences. *Alcohol Research and Health*, 34:236–245.

Zimring, F. E. 1991. Firearms, violence and public policy. *Scientific American*, 265:48.

7

Contextual Interventions

Learning Objectives

Upon finishing this chapter, students should be able to:
- Identify effective family-, school-, peer- and community-focused prevention programs, practices, and policies
- Identify family-, school-, peer-, and community-focused programs, practices, and policies which are not effective and those that have inconclusive evidence of effectiveness
- Summarize the extent to which contextual prevention programs, practices, and policies are being implemented
- State the most important research tasks that must be accomplished in order to increase the number of effective contextual programs, practices, and policies available and in use.

Introduction

During your teenage years, was there ever a time when you considered drinking alcohol, smoking marijuana, shoplifting, or hitting someone because you were angry at them? If you thought about committing these delinquent acts, but decided not to, what influenced your decision to refrain from offending? Did you consider how your parents might react to your behavior? Were you too worried about getting caught by a school official or neighbor? Did you fear that your friends would find out and think less of you, or were they the ones encouraging you to be delinquent?

If you answered "yes" to any of these questions, then you know firsthand that social interactions and social contexts can affect criminal behavior. And, you might suspect that if you want to reduce

The Prevention of Crime, First Edition. Delbert Elliott and Abigail Fagan.
© 2017 John Wiley & Sons, Inc. Published 2017 by John Wiley & Sons, Inc.
Companion website: www.wiley.com/go/elliott/prevention_of_crime

crime, a good strategy would be to change the groups and environments we encounter every day so that they are more likely to
encourage positive behavior and discourage negative behavior.
We might also provide individuals with better skills so that they
can more successfully interact with individuals, groups, and agencies in these environments. The goal of this chapter is to review
such strategies.

In Chapter 6, we also described efforts to reduce crime by
changing environments. However, that chapter described interventions guided largely by **deterrence** and **routine activities**
theories which promote the idea of changing physical environments or using legal tactics to reduce opportunities for crime.
The strategies described in this chapter are guided primarily by
the **life course developmental** paradigm and theories related to it. Life course theories support
the use of contextual interventions because they recognize that development is affected by each of
the environments we live in: families, schools, peer groups, and communities. Each of these contexts
has particular risk and protective factors that can influence crime and which should be addressed by
interventions. In addition, since development is affected by the interaction of individual and social
influences, the broader context has the potential to support or undermine the effectiveness of crime
prevention strategies that target individual risk and protective factors. It is important to bolster social
contexts so that they can support and reinforce individually focused crime prevention efforts.
We will review those types of interventions in Chapters 8 and 9.

Because the life course paradigm emphasizes the importance of early experiences in leading to
criminal involvement, most of the successful interventions we will describe in this chapter are
intended for children and adolescents. They try to ensure that children are raised in supportive
families, have positive school experiences and have prosocial rather than delinquent peers. This
chapter also discusses strategies intended to change neighborhoods and communities so that they
more effectively support and encourage prosocial development for all youth living in these places.
These interventions typically help community residents to work together to provide positive opportunities and resources for children, endorse conventional norms and values and create organized
opposition to criminal activity. Most of these strategies rely on the collective action of residents to
prevent crime rather than law enforcement officials to patrol neighborhoods and make arrests.

As we did in Chapter 6, in the sections which follow, information about effective practices,
programs, and policies will be organized according to the type of crime prevention strategy that has
been evaluated. We will begin by describing the criminological theory(ies) and empirical evidence
supporting the use of crime prevention strategies in each social context and will discuss the risk and
protective factors typically targeted by these interventions. We will then review evidence of effectiveness regarding specific practices, programs, and policies implemented in each context and the
degree to which effective interventions are currently used in communities.

In this chapter and in Chapters 8 and 9, we will also include information on cost effectiveness
when it is available from the Washington State Institute of Public Policy (WSIPP) (http://www.
wsipp.wa.gov/BenefitCost). We did not include this information in Chapter 6 because WSIPP has

> *Prevention programs
> cannot hope to have
> lasting effects unless the
> broader social environment ...
> is also changed to be more
> supportive and reinforcing of
> newly changed attitudes,
> normative beliefs, and
> social skills.*
>
> Flay, 2000: 861

not analyzed the cost effectiveness of most of the situational and legal interventions reviewed in that chapter. In order to calculate monetary benefits, WSIPP begins by estimating the average effect size on crime produced across all evaluations of a program, practice, or policy. These are the **unadjusted effect sizes**. WSIPP may also adjust this effect size if the evaluation was not well conducted, if there were problems with the validity or reliability of the measures, if the person who developed the program was also the one to evaluate it, or if the intervention was tested under very artificial conditions like a scientific laboratory. WSIPP assumes that all of these issues can artificially affect the size of the program effect on crime, often inflating it, and they try to counteract this problem using various statistical procedures to adjust the effect size by particular amounts, depending on the problems identified in the evaluation. Because it is difficult to know whether or how much to reduce effect sizes if there are problems with the design of a study, and because we are already limiting our review to high-quality evaluation studies, we will report mostly the unadjusted effect sizes calculated by WSIPP. But, we will report **adjusted effect sizes** if they are less than half the unadjusted effect sizes, so that you can consider the potential bias in intervention evaluations.

Family-focused Practices and Programs with Evidence of Success in Preventing Crime

The environmental context that individuals encounter first in life is the family. The family setting contains both risk and protective factors related to crime, as specified in many of the life course developmental theories discussed in Chapter 3. For example, **differential association** and **social learning** theories indicate that exposure to criminal role models is a risk factor for crime. They further specify that children are at particular risk for crime when they observe those closest to them (e.g., parents and siblings) engaging in crime, when their family members communicate deviant attitudes and when parents fail to appropriately punish children's delinquent behaviors. Prevention programs based on these theories would thus try to minimize family members' deviant behavior and attitudes. **Social control** theories emphasize that the best way to deter crime is by setting and enforcing rules for behavior. Since parental controls are considered to be very important, interventions based on these theories will try to improve parents' ability to communicate to children which behaviors are acceptable and which are unacceptable, monitor compliance with these rules and provide appropriate reinforcements for positive and negative behaviors. These theories also identify emotional attachment as an important protective factor which can inhibit crime and would recommend interventions that promote close, warm relationships between parents and children.

As you will learn, a variety of family-focused interventions have been created and shown to reduce crime. We will discuss three types of family-focused interventions in this chapter: **home visitation**, **parent training**, and **family therapy**. These differ in terms of the specific family risk and protective factors they seek to change, their content, duration, implementers and other implementation requirements. In addition, some require involvement from parents or care-givers only, while others involve parents and children. What they have in common is the desire to improve parents' ability to set rules or guidelines for children's behavior, monitor children's behaviors, provide appropriate consequences for positive and negative behaviors and improve parent/child bonding and attachment.

Many effective family-focused programs are implemented with parents of young children, given that early family experiences are very important in affecting later criminal involvement. Some evaluations of these interventions have followed child participants into adolescence and adulthood and can report long-term effects on their criminal behavior. In other cases, however, evaluations are limited to assessing shorter term effects on child behavior problems, such as conduct disorder or oppositional defiant disorder. Actual illegal behaviors may not be assessed because child participants are too young to engage in crime during the period of evaluation. We still consider these types of outcomes to be important for crime prevention, given that early antisocial behaviors have been shown to strongly predict delinquency and crime during adolescence and/or adulthood (Broidy et al., 2003; Loeber and Farrington, 2000; Yoshikawa, 1994).

Home visitation

Home visitation programs are based on the idea that it is never too early to prevent crime. These interventions try to improve the home environment even before children are born, by providing services to pregnant women before they give birth. They also continue programming after children are born to improve family risk and protective factors during the first few years of life. Such programs may be recommended by **social control theories** which prioritize the role of parent/child attachment and effective child discipline practices in helping prevent children's subsequent involvement in crime. Parenting skills are promoted through regular home visits by health care professionals who provide information and training to parents in how to care for their newborn and very young children (Bilukha et al., 2005). A major goal is to create a strong and supportive relationship between caregivers and home visitors that parents can draw upon to help them personally and when caring for children. These attachments also provide a model of a trusting, caring, and supportive relationship that parents can emulate when interacting with their child (Gomby, Culross, and Berhman, 1999). In this way, home visitation programs also recognize the importance of social bonds for adults and hypothesize that parents' own involvement in crime will be lessened through contact with the visitors, especially their abuse and/or neglect of children.

While program content and participant characteristics differ a bit across programs, there is enough similarity to allow home visitation to be evaluated as a general prevention **practice**. A meta-analysis of four home visitation programs (Farrington and Welsh, 2003) showed an average effect size on youth misbehavior and delinquency of 0.24, indicating small to moderate effects. A second meta-analysis, based on eight studies, showed similar results and an overall effect size of 0.30 (Piquero et al., 2009). However, the Centers for Disease Control (CDC) (Bilukha et al., 2005) reported mixed evidence that home visitation programs reduce youth-perpetrated violence. Only two of the four programs included in their review reported such effects, leading the CDC to conclude that there is "insufficient evidence" that home visitation reduces youth violence (http://www.thecommunityguide. org/violence/home/index.html). *Taken as a whole, these results suggest that home visitation can produce moderate reductions in children's delinquency, but perhaps not violence.*

As shown in Table 7.1, our review identified two home visitation programs shown to reduce crime: **Nurse-Family Partnership (NFP)** and **Child and Family Interagency, Resource, Support, and Training (Child FIRST)**. **NFP** is a selective intervention in which trained registered nurses

Table 7.1 Effective home visitation prevention practices and programs.

Effective practice?	Yes		
Effective programs	Rating by Blueprints	Rating by the Coalition	Rating by CrimeSolutions.gov
Nurse-Family Partnership (NFP)	Model	Top Tier	Effective
Child FIRST	Not rated	Near Top Tier	Not rated

(RNs) visit first-time, mostly low-income and unmarried mothers every two weeks during pregnancy and for two years post-birth. Nurses share information on how mothers can reduce their use of tobacco, alcohol, and other drugs during pregnancy; improve their prenatal health and diet; sensitively and responsibly care for their infants; achieve their own educational and occupational goals; avoid unwanted future pregnancies; and access community services (Olds, 2002). Three randomized controlled trials of NFP have been conducted with Caucasian, Hispanic, and African American families in rural (New York State) and urban (Memphis, TN and Denver, CO) areas of the USA. All three have shown evidence of effectiveness in reducing mothers' or children's involvement in crime. In the NY study, some outcomes were significant only when comparing women in intervention and control groups who were "high risk"; that is, mothers who were unmarried and had a very low income.

Both the Denver and NY studies showed significant effects on mother's involvement in crime. In Denver, NFP mothers reported significantly less victimization by a domestic partner. When children were aged 4, 7% of NFP women reported experiencing any domestic violence in the six months prior to the survey compared to 14% of those in the control group (Olds et al., 2004). In the NY study, the high-risk mothers who received NFP reported fewer arrests and convictions compared to the high-risk females in the control group, and they had fewer officially recorded arrests and convictions by the time children were aged 15. For example, intervention women reported an average of 0.18 arrests, compared to 0.58 for the control group women, and they had an average of 0.16 officially recorded arrests compared to 0.90 for the control group (Olds et al., 1997). This study also showed a reduction in child abuse and neglect perpetrated by the high-risk mothers. Only 4% of those receiving NFP had an officially verified case of maltreatment when children were aged 2 compared to 19% of the control group, an 80% reduction (Olds et al., 1986). When children were aged 15, the high-risk mothers in the NFP group had 0.11 officially verified incidents of maltreatment compared to 0.53 for the control group (Olds et al., 1997). This outcome was also significant when assessing the full sample, as NFP mothers had an average of 0.29 incidents compared to 0.54 for those in the control group.

Effects on child substance use were seen in the Memphis study, which involved mostly African American families. When children were aged 12, those whose mothers received NFP were less likely to report any use of cigarettes, alcohol, or marijuana, with use reported by 1.7% of the NFP group and 5.1% of the control group (Kitzman et al., 2010). The NY study showed reductions in children's delinquency. At age 15, 17% of the NFP children had been arrested, compared to 36% of the control group, a 52% reduction. Convictions were 69% lower, with 10% of the intervention children having official convictions versus 27% of the control group. Finally, among children of the high-risk mothers, those in the intervention condition reported fewer days of using alcohol than those in the control group (Olds, Henderson, and Cole, 1998). Children also had lower rates of offi-cially recorded crime at age 19, but these effects were significant only for girls (Eckenrode *et al.*, 2010). Girls whose mothers received NFP had a delayed onset of their first criminal arrest. They were also 67% less likely to have ever been arrested compared to those in the control group, with arrest rates of 10% and 30%, respectively, and 80% less likely to have ever been convicted of a crime (4% vs 20%).

Based on the findings from all three study sites, WSIPP (2015) reports overall adjusted effect sizes of 0.25 for mothers' crime, 0.32 for child maltreatment, and 0.04 for children's crime (which is not significant). Unadjusted effect sizes are much larger (0.70, 0.88, and 0.27, respectively). WSIPP identifies NFP as cost beneficial, returning $2.89 for every dollar spent.

The **Child FIRST** home visitation program is also a **selective** intervention for low-income mothers with children aged 6 months to 3 years old (Lowell *et al.*, 2011). Families are referred to the program if children have social-emotional and behavioral problems and/or parents are known to have individual risk factors such as depression or substance abuse. Families receive 12 visits over 22 weeks by health clinicians who teach effective child management techniques, encourage positive parenting behaviors like reading and playing with children and encourage parents to utilize needed community-based services such as housing programs or drug treatment programs. This program has been evaluated in one RCT in CT, involving 127 Latino and African American families, most of whom received welfare. The evaluation showed a reduction in maternal and/or official reports of child maltreatment by caregivers. Three years following the intervention, 28% of the intervention group had at least one contact with the state's Child Protective Services, compared to 42% of the control group (Lowell *et al.*, 2011).

Home visitation programs have been in existence for many decades, giving them ample time to be disseminated. A 2009 report estimated that home visitation programs operate in every state in the USA and that 400,000 to 500,000 families receive programs each year, representing about 3% of all families with children under age 6 (Stoltzfus and Lynch, 2009). However, the use of *effective* services is likely to be less common. According to the **NFP** website (http://www.nursefamilypartnership.org/assets/PDF/Fact-sheets/NFP_Snapshot), about 190,000 families have received this program since it began in 1996. The program is currently being offered in 43 states in the USA.

The number of families receiving home visitation services is likely to grow substantially in the USA given the Maternal, Infant, and Early Childhood Home Visiting (MIECHV) initiative begun in 2011. This program provides funding to states to implement home visitation programs (http://mchb.hrsa.gov/programs/homevisiting/index.html), including NFP and Child FIRST, with 400 million dollars allocated in 2014. While this investment in home visitation is exciting, the list of programs eligible for funding includes several that have inconclusive evidence of effectiveness in reducing crime by mothers or youth. Many have not actually evaluated their impact on crime or have done so using low quality evaluations.

Parent training

Parent training services contain a more diverse group of programs compared to home visitation programs. They can be implemented with universal or selective families and with children of all ages. They also tend to utilize community volunteers rather than professional staff to deliver services.

Given this diversity, the specific content and approach varies across parent training programs, but most try to improve parents' monitoring and discipline of youth, communication between children and parents and parent–child bonding.

Several meta-analyses have evaluated whether or not parent training is an effective crime prevention **practice**. In a meta-analysis of 47 programs intended for parents of children younger than 5 years old, Piquero and colleagues (2009) reported a moderate effect on children's delinquency and/or behavior problems, with an average effect size of 0.36. A meta-analysis of 10 parent training programs for youth aged 2–8 years old also indicated a moderate impact on children's behavioral problems, with an overall effect size of 0.40 (Farrington and Welsh, 2003). When considering the impact on behavior problems of 63 parent training programs targeting children and adolescents, Lundahl and colleagues (2006) reported a mean effect size of 0.42. A review of universal parent training programs by the Cochrane Collaboration found that 9 of the 12 reduced adolescent alcohol use, but an effect size was not calculated given the diversity of interventions assessed (Foxcroft and Tsertsvadze, 2011). Finally, based on a review of 12 programs, the CDC (Burrus *et al.*, 2012) reported that parent training programs reduced adolescent problem behaviors and violence by about 30%, but effects on substance use were much smaller (13%) and non-significant. *Taken as a whole, these studies indicate that parent training is an effective practice and produces, on average, a moderate reduction in child behavior problems and/or delinquency.*

Our review identified 12 specific parent training program which are effective in reducing child behavior problems, adolescent substance use and/or other types of crime, as summarized in Table 7.2. Proceeding according to the age of the targeted child, the first effective program is **Family Foundations**.

Table 7.2 Effective parent training practices and programs.

Effective practice?	*Yes*		
Effective programs	*Rating by Blueprints*	*Rating by the Coalition*	*Rating by CrimeSolutions.gov*
Family Foundations	Promising	Not rated	Promising
Incredible Years	Promising	Reviewed but not rated	Effective
Parent–Child Interaction Therapy (PCIT)	Promising	Not rated	Effective
New Beginnings	Model	Not rated	Not rated
Guiding Good Choices	Promising	Reviewed but not rated	Effective
Strengthening Families Program 10–14	Promising	Not rated	Effective
Strong African American Families (SAAF)	Promising	Not rated	Effective
Familias Unidas	Promising	Not rated	Promising
Effekt	Promising	Not rated	Not rated
Positive Family Support/Family Check-Up	Promising	Not rated	Effective
Parent Management Training/The Oregon Model (PMTO)	Model	Near Top Tier	Not rated
Triple P	Promising	Near Top Tier	Effective

This is a universal program delivered to two-parent couples expecting their first child. Mixed-sex, two-person teams of facilitators meet with small groups (6 to 10) of parents in four sessions prior to the birth of the child and four sessions after the birth to promote "co-parenting" among care-givers. Facilitators discuss ways to enhance communication between parents, avoid conflicts about how to raise children and work together as parents (Feinberg, Jones, Goslin, et al., 2010). In a randomized trial involving mostly White parents in Pennsylvania, children of intervention parents had fewer behavioral problems and less aggression when aged 3 (Feinberg, Jones, Goslin, et al., 2010). These effects were also seen when children were aged 6 but outcomes were significant only for boys, not girls.

The **Incredible Years (IY)** is a set of interventions designed to reduce children's conduct problems. The **BASIC parent training program** has been the most extensively evaluated of all the Incredible Years programs and is usually implemented as an indicated intervention for parents of children aged 2–10 who are showing conduct problems. It can be offered alone or in combination with youth- and teacher-focused programs. BASIC involves 12–14 weekly sessions, each 2–2.5 hours long, delivered to small groups of parents by pairs of facilitators. During interactive sessions that involve watching and discussing videos of parents responding to youth behavior problems, participants learn to set up routines for children, create rules, respond to misbehavior with proactive discipline and promote positive behaviors using praise and incentives (Webster-Stratton and Taylor, 2001).

The program has been evaluated numerous times in the USA, the UK, Norway, the Netherlands, and Ireland, in randomized trials conducted by both the program developer and independent scientists. Together, these studies have shown significant reductions in child conduct problems for males and females and children of various racial/ethnic and income groups (Webster-Stratton and Taylor, 2001). A meta-analysis of 50 evaluations of the program reported an overall effect size of 0.27, indicating modest reductions in disruptive, problem behaviors among children whose parents received BASIC compared to those in control groups (Menting, de Castro, and Matthys, 2013).[1] Analyses conducted by WSIPP (2015) reported adjusted effect sizes on disruptive behavior of 0.12 to 0.22, with larger unadjusted effect sizes (0.44 to 0.60 depending on the specific problem). WSIPP (2015) considers the BASIC program to be cost beneficial, with $1.26 in benefits for every dollar spent on the program. Although all of these results indicate that BASIC is effective at reducing child conduct problems, it is important to note that most evaluations have not involved a long-term follow-up period, so it is somewhat uncertain if BASIC reduces adolescent delinquency and adult crime.

Parent–Child Interaction Therapy (PCIT) is a parent training program intended to improve positive parenting behaviors and create better parent–child interactions. The intervention is intended for families with children aged 2–12 years who display conduct disorder and other behavior problems. During 12 weekly, half-hour sessions, therapists observe parents interacting with children. They provide real-time, individual feedback to assist parents in positively communicating with children and taking turns leading and letting children lead play activities. In a randomized trial involving Australian parents of 4-year-old, mostly male children, the intervention reduced conduct problems among those in the treatment compared to the control group (Nixon et al., 2004). Small, quasi-experimental studies in Puerto Rico (Matos, Bauermeister, and Bernal, 2009) and Hong Kong (Leung et al., 2009) have also shown reductions in conduct problems.

There is also an indicated version intended to reduce future episodes of child abuse and neglect among parents involved with the child welfare system. In addition to the regular, 12-week curriculum, trained therapists provide one-on-one coaching over six sessions to increase parents' motivation and ability to use non-violent discipline strategies. In a RCT of this version of the program involving 110 White and African American families with children aged 4–12, families receiving PCIT had lower rates of reported child physical abuse (19% of the sample) compared to those in the control group (49% of the sample) 4 years following the intervention (Chaffin et al., 2004). A second RCT involving 153 families also showed reductions in physical abuse of children, with a recidivism rate of 29% for the intervention group and 41% for the control group (Chaffin et al., 2011).

According to a review by WSIPP (2015), PCIT's has modest effects on children's disruptive behaviors, with adjusted effect sizes ranging from 0.26 to 0.38. This version of the program is not cost beneficial, as the costs and benefits are about the same. However, WSIPP (2015) reports that PCIT is cost effective when implemented with families involved in the child welfare system due to maltreatment, with financial returns of $24.28 for every dollar spent on services.

The rest of the effective parent training interventions described in this section are for parents of adolescents and all have evaluated effects on children's illegal behaviors. **New Beginnings** is a selective intervention for recently divorced women with children aged 9–12. It involves 11 sessions delivered to small groups of mothers or to mothers and children, as well as two home visits. The program seeks to provide mothers with information about and opportunities to practice effective discipline of children and the creation of positive and supportive relationships with youth. It also helps mothers consider how to reduce children's exposure to conflict with the divorced spouse. In a randomized trial involving 240 mostly White families in Arizona, children whose mothers received the program had fewer externalizing (i.e., acting out and aggressive) behaviors six months following the intervention compared to the control group (Wolchik et al., 2000). Six years later, when children were aged 15–19, externalizing problems were reduced among children who participated in sessions along with their mothers (Wolchik et al., 2002). Effects on children's substance use were not affected by program participation at the 6-year follow-up, but at the 15-year follow-up, males (but not females) whose families received the program had less illegal drug use compared to those in the control group (Wolchik et al., 2013).

Guiding Good Choices (GGC) is a universal parent training program intended to prevent adolescent alcohol and drug use. It is taught to small groups of parents in five weekly, two-hour sessions; one of these sessions involves children aged 10–14 years. Based on a randomized trial involving mostly White 6th grade students and their families in Iowa, those who participated in GGC were less likely to initiate tobacco, alcohol, or marijuana use and more likely to remain drug-free at Grades 8 (Spoth, Lopez Reyes, et al., 1999) and 10 (Spoth, Redmond, and Shin, 2001). Among those who had used drugs prior to the intervention, program participation resulted in a lower frequency of drinking at Grade 10, with an effect size of 0.28 (Spoth et al., 2001). The program also decreased the rate of growth in substance use and in general delinquency from Grades 6 to 10 (Mason et al., 2003). A long-term follow-up study showed that earlier reductions in substance use were related to less drug use when participants were aged 21. WSIPP's (2015) review of GGC indicated small reductions in alcohol use, with an adjusted effect size of 0.12, and non-significant effects on other outcomes. Their cost–benefit analysis shows a return of $2.48 for every dollar invested in GGC.

The **Strengthening Families Program for Parents and Youth 10–14 (SFP 10–14)** uses a similar parent training approach to reducing adolescent substance use, but involves both parents and children in sessions. Families attend seven weekly two-hour sessions. For the first hour, parents and youth meet separately with facilitators to discuss and practice skills related to effective parental monitoring and discipline (for parents) and recognizing and refusing social pressures to use drugs (for youth). In the second hour, parents and children meet together to work on communication skills and enhance family bonding (Spoth and Redmond, 1996).

A randomized trial of mostly White families in Iowa showed that participation resulted in less initiation and lower rates of substance use. Specifically, participants who received the program in 6th grade had a lower likelihood of initiating alcohol use at Grades 7 and 8 (Spoth, Redmond, *et al.*, 1999) and in initiating alcohol and marijuana use at Grade 10 (Spoth *et al.*, 2001). At age 21, SFP participants reported a lower frequency of substance use (Spoth *et al.*, 2009). The program has also reduced delinquency. According to self-reports, SFP youth reported fewer aggressive behaviors (e.g., beating someone up) and property offenses at Grade 10 compared to those in the control group, with an effect size of 0.35 (Spoth, Redmond, and Shin, 2000). A meta-analysis by WSIPP (2015) indicated adjusted effect sizes of 0.29 for marijuana use, 0.13 for alcohol use, and 0.11 for other illegal drug use. Their cost–benefit analysis shows a return of $3.59 for every dollar invested in SFP 10–14.

Although SFP 10–14 was originally designed for and tested with White families, changes were made to the program content to be more culturally relevant for African American families living in the rural South. This version, known as the **Strong African American Families (SAAF)** program, involves the same number, frequency, and format of program sessions as SFP 10–14, but content has been added to help parents and youth discuss and deal with racial discrimination. Children also learn how to maintain positive future expectations, self-esteem and academic success even when faced with discrimination (Brody *et al.*, 2004). When evaluated with African American families in rural Georgia, those who received the program in Grade 6 were less likely than those in the control group to initiate alcohol use at Grade 8 and to increase alcohol use from Grade 6 to Grade 8 (Brody *et al.*, 2006) and Grade 11 (Brody *et al.*, 2010). At Grade 8, participants had 54% fewer conduct problems (measured by a combination of having delinquent peers, low self-control and engaging in five delinquent acts) compared to the control group (Brody *et al.*, 2008).

Another culturally specific parent training program designed to reduce adolescent substance use is **Familias Unidas**. The 3-to-5 month-long intervention involves small group sessions and home visits to allow discussion of and practice in parent–child involvement, bonding, and communication. The content integrates Hispanic cultural norms, expectations, and values, such as the belief that family is most important and that parents are the family's leaders and decision-makers (Prado *et al.*, 2007). Two evaluations of the program involving low-income Hispanic families from Miami showed reductions in children's substance use. In the first study (Prado *et al.*, 2007), the intervention significantly reduced teenager's growth in self-reported smoking and hard drug use (but not alcohol use) from ages 13–16. In the second trial (Pantin *et al.*, 2009), substance use during adolescence increased less for youth who participated in the program compared to those in the control group, from ages 14–16, about 2.5 years (30 months) after receiving the intervention, as shown in Figure 7.1.

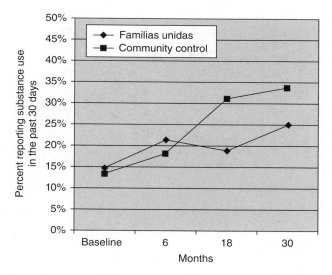

Figure 7.1 Effects of the Familias Unidas program in reducing substance use, from baseline to the 30-month post-test. Source: Pantin *et al.*, 2009. Reproduced with permission of the American Psychological Association.

The **EFFEKT** program, also known as the Orebro Prevention Program, was developed to reduce teenage alcohol use. The main goal of the universal intervention is to provide parents with information about the harmfulness of adolescent substance use and the importance of setting strict rules regarding children's drinking. These messages are shared during short parent–teacher meetings at the beginning of the school year and in brief letters mailed home during the year (Koutakis, Stattin, and Kerr, 2008). When tested in Sweden, students whose parents received the program had less increase in drunkenness and delinquency from Grades 7–9 compared to control group youth (Koutakis *et al.*, 2008), as shown in Figure 7.2. Effect sizes for these two outcomes were 0.35 and 0.38, respectively. A replication in the Netherlands also indicated reductions in adolescent drinking 2 years following implementation of an expanded version of the program, which added a short classroom-based curriculum to the parent training condition (Koning *et al.*, 2009).

The **Positive Family Support** middle school intervention includes multiple components intended to reduce substance use and delinquency. The first is a universal intervention which involves the creation of a family resource center in schools to provide parents with access to information and consultation about how to manage their children's behavior. Secondly, students receive a six-week classroom curriculum based on the **Life Skills Training** drug prevention program (see Chapter 8 for more information on this program) designed to improve school success, increase contact with positive peers, and provide problem-solving and emotional competency skills. The third component is a selective intervention for parents of students who have begun to engage in disruptive behaviors at school or home. Teachers are trained to communicate more regularly with parents of these children and to work collaboratively to monitor children's behaviors. Parents may also receive the Family Check-Up, which is a series of three face-to-face meetings with therapists who rely on **Motivational Interviewing (MI)** techniques (see Chapter 9 for more information on this

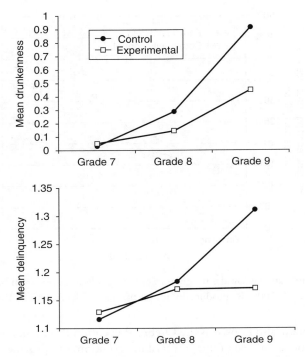

Figure 7.2   Reductions in drunkenness and delinquency for EFFEKT and control group participants from Grades 7 to 9. Source: Koutakis *et al.*, 2008. Reproduced with permission of John Wiley & Sons.

approach) to help parents assess family problems and better supervise and interact with children. If these efforts fail to be effective, therapists provide families with referrals to more intensive, indicated community-based programs designed to reduce students' behavioral or substance use/abuse problems (Dishion and Kavanagh, 2000).

The first randomized evaluation of Positive Family Support, involving Caucasian and African American families in the northwestern USA, showed that youth who participated in the program were less likely than those in the control group to initiate smoking and drinking by Grade 9 and had smaller increases in these behaviors from Grades 6–9 (Connell, Dishion, and Deater-Deckard, 2006). Program participation also reduced the likelihood of arrest by Grade 11 (Connell, Klosterman, and Dishion, 2011) and delinquency by age 19 (Van Ryzin and Dishion, 2012). Despite these positive effects, a review of the intervention by WSIPP (2015) indicated very small and mostly non-significant effects on substance use and crime, with the exception of smoking, which had an adjusted effect size of 0.24. They report that the program was not cost effective, as costs ($328 per person) exceeded benefits ($77 per person).

The **Parent Management Training/Oregon Model (PMTO)** is a parent training program designed to improve parents' effective discipline and monitoring of youth, increase their positive involvement with children and reduce parent/child conflict. The program can be used with small groups of universal or selective families, such as low-income, recently divorced mothers. In a randomized trial of divorced mothers and young boys in Oregon, intervention males had less delinquency than control group boys according to teacher ratings 3.5 years after the intervention ended (DeGarmo and Forgatch, 2005). At the nine-year follow-up, teacher reports indicated smaller increases in delinquency for intervention compared to control group boys. Intervention youth also had a lower rate of arrests at age 17, with an average of 0.76 arrests for PMTO boys and 1.34 for those in the control group (Forgatch *et al.*, 2009). According to official arrest records, there was a 32% reduction in the number of arrests for mothers who participated in PMTO compared to those in the control group (Patterson, Forgatch, and DeGarmo, 2010). The universal, small group program has also been tested and shown to reduce children's conduct problems with families in Norway (Bjorknes *et al.*, 2012; Kjobli, Hukkelberg, and Ogden, 2013). WSIPP's (2015) review of the program indicated an unadjusted effect size of 0.18 for children's crime, which was not statistically significant, and a financial return of $7.18 for every dollar invested, indicating that it is cost-beneficial.

The last intervention, the **Triple P Positive Parenting Program**, is a comprehensive intervention designed for families with children aged 1–12 years. Recognizing the variation in family needs and children's behavioral difficulties, Triple P offers a range of programmatic options that vary in content and intensity from short, universal approaches that focus on providing parents with information about effective parenting strategies to more intensive services that allow parents to learn and practice skills related to child monitoring and discipline (Sanders, Turner, and Markie-Dadds, 2002). Although the program was developed and tested many times in Australia, the only study meeting the Blueprint quality standard and responsible for inclusion on the Blueprints website was conducted in South Carolina in the USA. In this large, randomized trial, counties that implemented Triple P with families with children 0–8 years old showed a smaller increase in officially substantiated cases of child abuse and neglect from pre-test to post-test compared to counties that did not implement these services (Printz *et al.*, 2009). The intervention counties also had a 33% reduction in the number of children being removed from the home and placed in foster care and a 35% reduction in hospitalizations or emergency room visits due to child maltreatment injuries compared to the control group counties. WSIPP (2015) estimated that this version of the program had an adjusted effect size of 0.05 for child maltreatment cases and that it returned $9.58 for every dollar spent.

While our review has identified numerous parent training interventions with evidence of reducing child behavior problems, substance use, and delinquency, are they being used by communities? This question is somewhat difficult to answer. Starting from an optimistic point-of-view, several parent training programs shown in Table 7.2 are reaching large numbers of families in the USA. For example, the **Incredible Years** program has trained over 12,000 facilitators in the USA (http:// incredibleyears.com/programs/implementation/implementation-examples/) and has reached over 35,000 children from low-income families in Colorado since 2002 (Institute of Medicine (IOM) and National Research Council (NRC), 2014a). **SFP 10–14** and **Guiding Good Choices** have also been implemented across the USA.

Of all the program types reviewed in this book, effective parent training interventions may have the largest international presence. Two of the interventions were developed abroad: **EFFEKT** in Sweden and **Triple P** in Australia. Triple P has reached over 4 million families and trained over 55,000 facilitators in Australia and 24 other countries (http://www.triplep.net/glo-en/triple-p-at-a-glance/). **Incredible Years** has been implemented in Canada and many European countries (e.g., in the UK, Norway, Denmark, Sweden, the Netherlands, and Finland), as well as in diverse nations such as Russia, China, Singapore, Portugal, Chile, Australia, and New Zealand. In Norway, the government funds local communities across the country to implement **PMTO**. As of 2011, almost 400 therapists had been trained to deliver the program (Ogden *et al.*, 2012).

Despite these positive signs, there is a long way to go to ensure that all families who *could* benefit actually receive such services. Given that many are universal programs, meaning they could target *all* parents, it is likely that only a small proportion of the intended population has ever participated in an effective parent training program (Printz and Sanders, 2007). In addition, despite signs of international dissemination, Knerr *et al.* (2013) point out that very few parent training programs, especially those for parents of teenagers, have been tested in low and middle income countries (also see Catalano *et al.*, 2012).

There are many challenges to recruiting families to participate in effective interventions, including the fact that many parents may not perceive their need for services, especially if their children are not currently engaging in delinquency. They may also avoid programs for fear of being labeled a "bad parent" or may lack the time or financial means to attend sessions (Printz and Sanders, 2007; Spoth and Redmond, 2002). Finally, parents of teenagers may view strained relationships as inevitable, and they may view participation in a prevention program as counter to their goal of helping adolescents seek independence (Dishion, Nelson, and Bullock, 2004). These challenges are widely acknowledged and strategies for overcoming some of these problems are currently being tested (IOM and NRC, 2014a), as we will discuss in Section IV.

Family therapy

Family therapy programs represent a more intensive and comprehensive approach to changing the family environment compared to **parent training** interventions. The effective family therapy programs described in this chapter are **indicated** interventions designed for families of youth who have already broken the law. They involve the entire family in treatment, not just the youth or just the parents. Therapy is typically provided by trained clinicians (e.g., social workers or psychologists) who have relatively small caseloads so that they can be available to work with families as much as needed during the treatment period, which usually lasts 4–6 months. Families receive one-on-one services that take place either in their own homes or in community-based clinics at least once per week. Thus, although these programs are designed for offenders, they are delivered in the community setting with the expectation that treating families in their natural environment will improve the relevance and effectiveness of program content.

Family therapy programs are based on criminological theories that emphasize the influence of the family environment in shaping children's likelihood of offending, such as **social control theories**. Many seek to improve parenting practices like child management and discipline skills and to promote parent–child emotional attachments and communication. They also recognize that **social learning** contributes to offending. To reduce such influences, family therapy interventions try to help parents reduce their own involvement in crime and drug use/abuse, and they teach both children and parents the importance of minimizing youth contact with delinquent peers. In most cases, therapy begins with the clinician working with family members to identify the particular needs of the family then providing individualized services to help achieve these goals.

Table 7.3 Effective family therapy programs.

Effective practice?		Inconclusive	
Effective programs	Rating by Blueprints	Rating by the Coalition	Rating by CrimeSolutions.gov
Multisystemic Therapy (MST)	Model	Promising	Effective
Functional Family Therapy (FFT)	Model	Not rated	Effective
Treatment Foster Care Oregon (TFCO)	Model	Top Tier (when implemented with girls)	Effective

Three community-based family therapy programs have evidence of effectiveness in reducing youth crime, as shown in Table 7.3. Although meta-analyses of some of these individual programs have been performed, we are not aware of meta-analyses that have investigated the effectiveness of the general practice of providing community-based family therapy to families of known juvenile offenders. *As a result, at this point, we cannot identify family therapy as an effective crime prevention practice.*

Multisystemic Therapy (MST) views juvenile delinquency as the result of multiple risk and protective factors in the family environment as well as in the neighborhood and peer group. Therapists undergo intensive training in the MST model, are assigned small caseloads of 4–6 families, and are closely supervised by a supervisor. They provide individualized services to families in their own homes over 3–5 months. Sessions focus on (i) improving parenting skills such as monitoring, supervision and discipline of children; (ii) promoting bonding and communication between family members; and (iii) encouraging youth to refrain from friendships with deviant peers and develop closer friendships with prosocial individuals. School achievement is also emphasized in order to ensure that youth are successful in all major contexts of their lives.

MST has probably been subject to more RCTs than any other intervention reviewed in this book, with 22 such studies published as of 2014. Given this amount of research, several meta-analyses have been conducted using MST evaluations. Based on evidence from six RCTs, Farrington and Welsh (2003) reported that MST had an overall effect size of 0.41, indicating a moderate reduction in youth delinquency.[2] WSIPP (2015) reported a similar unadjusted effect size of 0.43 based on 11 evaluations, but their adjusted effect size of 0.14 was much smaller. WSIPP (2015) also reported an unadjusted effect size on crime of 0.36 when MST is implemented with substance-abusing juvenile offenders and of 0.71 when implemented with juvenile sex offenders, although these calculations are based on only a few studies each and are reduced when adjusted for evaluation design issues.

Results from individual studies have shown that youth whose families receive MST have lower rates of recidivism according to both official arrest records and self-reported offending. For example, in a study of 84 families in South Carolina, MST youth had about half as many arrests as those in the control group (0.87 vs 1.52) at post-test and 58% had no re-arrests, compared to 38% of those receiving usual services from the juvenile justice system (Henggeler, Melton, and Smith, 1992). Long-term reductions in recidivism were also found for those receiving MST in Columbia, MO. Four years after receiving treatment, 26% of MST youth had been re-arrested versus 71% of those in the control group (Borduin *et al.*, 1995). Recidivism rates were 50% and 81%, respectively, at the 14-year follow-up, when participants were aged 29 years, and rates for violent offending were 14% for MST youth versus 30% for those in the control group (Schaeffer and Borduin, 2005). When implemented with 118 drug-abusing adolescents aged 12–17 years, MST reduced convictions for violent crimes by 75%, decreased self-reported aggressive offenses and increased marijuana use abstinence, with 55% of MST youth compared to 28% of control group youth having no marijuana use four years after receiving treatment (Henggeler *et al.*, 2002).

Positive results have been found for male and female and African American as well as White youth participants. The program has also shown positive results when implemented in countries other than the USA, specifically Norway and Great Britain. However, a study of 409 youth offenders in Canada (Leschied and Cunningham, 2002) did not show significant effects in reducing recidivism for those who received MST. This failure is likely why MST is designated as only a Promising program by the Coalition for Evidence-based Policy, as shown in Table 7.3. However, the overall impact of MST is clearly positive and with this much replication across different sites and with different types of participants, a logical claim can be made that MST has **external validity** and is effective for many different youth populations.

Analyses by WSIPP (2015) have indicated that MST is cost effective, with a return of $3.03 for every dollar invested in the program and $3.99 when used with substance abusers. Its cost effectiveness, as well as its ability to reduce youth involvement in the juvenile justice system, may help explain the relatively high rates of use of the MST program. According to the MST website (http://www.mstservices.com/), the program is being used in 34 states in the USA and in 15 other countries and provides services to more than 23,000 youth and families annually.

Functional Family Therapy is also a short but intensive therapy program for juvenile offenders and their families. Trained therapists provide about 30 hours of one-on-one counseling in 12–14 sessions held over 3–5 months. Sessions can be delivered in the family's home or in clinics. The program content focuses on improving family communication, parent–child emotional attachment and parents' monitoring and discipline of youth. A meta-analysis of eight FFT evaluations by WISPP (2015) indicated moderate to large reductions in criminal behaviors, with an average unadjusted effect size of 0.59.

FFT has had positive effects when implemented in several US states and in Sweden. For example, the first RCT involving 46 families in Utah showed that 26% of FFT youth were re-arrested compared to 50% of the control group 1.5 years after receiving services (Alexander and Parsons, 1973). Moreover, fewer siblings of the FFT youth had court records, suggesting that the program has preventive effects for youth not already involved in the juvenile justice system (Klein, Alexander, and Parsons, 1977). When implemented in Sweden, the rate of recidivism two years after the program ended was 41% for FFT youth compared to 82% for those in the control group (Hansson, Cederblad, and Hook, 2000). The program has also been shown to reduce substance use. When tested with 120 adolescents in Albuquerque, NM, those receiving FFT had lower rates of marijuana use and heavy marijuana use compared to the control group (Waldron *et al.*, 2001).

FFT is cost effective, whether implemented for youth in correctional institutions or those on probation, returning $11.19 and $8.92, respectively, for every dollar invested (WSIPP, 2015). FFT is currently being implemented in 45 states and 11 countries (http://www.fftllc.com/). About 1,600 therapists have been trained in FFT and nearly 50,000 families have received services. Like MST, this program has good logical evidence of its external validity.

Treatment Foster Care Oregon (TFCO, formerly known as **Multidimensional Treatment Foster Care**, or **MTFC)** seeks to reduce recidivism by placing adolescent offenders in foster families. Unlike typical foster care placement, only one child at a time is placed with foster parents, and therapists ensure that foster parents provide a very structured environment for youth which emphasizes positive reinforcement for appropriate behavior (Hahn *et al.*, 2005), which is consistent with both **social control** and **social learning theories**. Youth are encouraged to minimize contact with delinquent peers and to become involved in community-based recreational and social skills programs. Services usually last about 6 months and may involve some therapy after children are reunited with their biological families.

The program has been tested primarily in Oregon with White youth and with male and female participants. When tested with 79 boys aged 12–17, those receiving TFCO had fewer arrests one year after participation and less self-reported delinquency, including index offenses and felony assaults, compared to the control group (Chamberlain and Reid, 1998). Participants also self-reported less tobacco, marijuana, and other drug use at the 18-month follow-up (Smith, Chamberlain, and Eddy, 2010). At the two-year follow-up, the program youth had lower rates of arrest for violent offenses (21% vs 38%) and less self-reported violence than those in the control group (Eddy, Bridges Whaley, and Chamberlain, 2004). A study of 81 female offenders indicated that TFCO resulted in fewer criminal referrals, with 1.38 for TFCO girls versus 3.04 for control group girls, and fewer days in correctional facilities (47 vs 149 days) at the two-year follow-up (Chamberlain, Leve, and DeGarmo, 2007).

A meta-analysis by WSIPP (2015) based on three evaluations of TFCO indicated an average unadjusted effect size of 0.54 and an adjusted effect of 0.11, indicating small to moderate reductions in recidivism. A review of three TFCO evaluations by the CDC (Hahn *et al.*, 2005) concluded that the program was effective in reducing youth violence and produced a median reduction of 72%. According to WSIPP (2015), for every dollar spent on TFCO, there is a benefit of $2.11. The program is currently implemented in eight states in the USA and has been replicated in five other European countries (the UK, Denmark, the Netherlands, Norway, and Sweden) (http://www.tfcoregon.com/).

As the program descriptions have indicated, the dissemination of MST, FFT, and TFCO in communities is occurring. An evaluation designed to identify rates of use of these programs in seven US states concluded that we have "come a long way" in disseminating these programs but that, even still, only about 5% of youth offenders receive effective programs (Greenwood and Welsh, 2012).

School Context Practices, Programs, and Policies with Evidence of Success in Preventing Crime

In Chapter 8, we identify many effective school-based programs that have been shown to reduce youth delinquency and/or substance use. Most of those interventions are taught by teachers to all students in certain classes and/or grades. Their goal is to change individual and/or peer risk and protective factors known to be associated with crime. In this chapter, we describe interventions that are implemented more broadly in the school setting and which seek to change the social, cultural, or structural aspects of the school environment that can affect delinquency and crime.

School-wide prevention efforts are guided by the recognition that students spend a substantial amount of time in school and, as a result, are very likely to be influenced by school-level risk and protective factors (Langford *et al.*, 2014). Because they are intended to affect *all* students attending the school, a major advantage of these interventions is their potential to impact a large number of students, many more than would be reached by an individually focused program or a program taught to all students in a single classroom. In addition, the more students who are positively affected by a school-wide intervention, the more potential for a positive **peer contagion** effect (Dishion and Dodge, 2005). That is, the more likely it will be for adolescents to spread and reinforce the prosocial norms and values promoted in the intervention to each other.

Several criminological theories support the use of school-wide interventions. **Social control theory** emphasizes that monitoring and supervision of youth will help reduce their delinquency. The physical structure and organization of a school can affect the ability of school staff to monitor and regulate students' behavior, as can teachers' classroom management skills. Likewise, school officials can create clear policies outlining acceptable and unacceptable behaviors and consistently enforce these rules (Gottfredson, Cook, and Na, 2012). According to **social bonding theory**, children's attachment to prosocial role models such as teachers, as well as their commitment to education, can also reduce their involvement in delinquency. This theory may thus suggest programs that try to improve the school climate or atmosphere or which encourage teachers to use more engaging and interactive instructional techniques. These changes should make students feel more supported, safe, and respected at school; improve teacher–student relationships; and increase students' attachment to school. Although schools are usually viewed as a protective context, they can increase exposure to delinquent peers (Gottfredson *et al.*, 2012; Jacob and Lefgren, 2003), and according to **social learning theory**, exposure to delinquent peer role models will increase the likelihood of offending. Effective monitoring and supervision by staff are needed to help counteract these deviant influences. Finally, **strain theory** views the competition at school for academic success, sports and peer popularity as potential sources of strain. Students who are not successful in these areas will experience the highest levels of stress and be at greatest risk for engaging in violence and delinquency. Changing the structure of the school, reducing the emphasis on competition and success and providing a wider range of opportunities for success can reduce school-related stressors and risks for offending.

The last reason why school-based crime prevention interventions are needed is because much crime occurs in school buildings and on school grounds. Data from the National Crime Victimization Survey (NCVS) in the USA indicate that students are somewhat more likely to be victims of theft and violence at school compared to away from school, although serious crimes, like aggravated assaults and homicides, rarely occur at school (Robers, Kemp, and Truman, 2013). Other national studies have found that about 18% of students report gang activity at their schools, 28% experience bullying at school and more students report being fearful at school than away from school (Robers *et al.*, 2013).

Although criminological theories and empirical evidence suggest the need for school-wide crime prevention efforts, and the majority of schools do implement school-wide change efforts with the hope of reducing problem behaviors, relatively few of these practices have been tested using high-quality, rigorous research designs (Flay, 2000; Langford *et al.*, 2014). In addition, many of these

Table 7.4 Effective school-wide practices and programs.

Practice	School-bullying prevention programs (Effective, CrimeSolutions.gov)		
Program	Rating by Blueprints	Rating by the Coalition	Rating by CrimeSolutions.gov
Steps to Respect	Promising	Not rated	Effective
Olweus Bullying Prevention Program	Promising	Not rated	Reviewed but not rated
Good Behavior Game	Promising	Near Top Tier	Effective
Raising Healthy Children	Promising	Not rated	Promising
Incredible Years: teacher training version	Promising	Reviewed but not rated	Not reviewed

interventions have not investigated their impact on criminal behaviors, but rather evaluate changes in students' academic performance, disruptive behaviors or violations of school policies (Cook, Gottfredson, and Na, 2010). As a result of these limitations in the research, *our review of interventions intended to affect the school environment identified very few well-evaluated practices or programs with strong evidence of reducing crime and no effective crime prevention policies*. The only practice identified as effective is **bullying prevention**, and a few effective programs exist, as shown in Table 7.4.

Bullying prevention

Bullying is defined by the Centers for Disease Control as "*any unwanted aggressive behavior(s) by another youth or group of youths who are not siblings or current dating partners that involves an observed or perceived power imbalance and is repeated multiple times or is highly likely to be repeated*" (Gladden et al., 2014: 7). According to this definition, bullying can include verbal or physical behavior which may or may not be illegal. We include bullying prevention programs in this book because some programs have demonstrated reductions in delinquency as well as bullying behaviors, some bullying is technically a crime (e.g., an assault) and bullying perpetration and victimization have both been linked to later criminal involvement (Ttofi, Farrington, and Losel, 2012). We classify bullying prevention as a school context intervention because most bullying programs involve prevention actions that affect the entire school, such as efforts to create a school climate that is not conducive to bullying perpetration, the development and consistent enforcement of policies that specify consequences for bullying and regular monitoring of student behavior by all school staff.

There is evidence that school **bullying prevention** is an effective crime prevention **practice**. According to a meta-analysis of 44 school anti-bullying programs, these interventions significantly reduced bullying perpetration and victimization by about 20% each (Farrington and Ttofi, 2009). When limited to the 14 randomized studies included in the review, significant but small effects on bullying victimization were found but bullying perpetration was not significantly reduced. A meta-analysis of six anti-bullying interventions evaluated using RCTs showed similar results (Langford *et al.*, 2014). On average, these programs significantly reduced bullying victimization by about 17% but did not decrease bullying perpetration. Another review of 26 programs indicated that bullying prevention programs which involve school-wide interventions were more effective than those which only included classroom-based skills training (Vreeman and Carroll, 2007). However, both that review and another study emphasized that rigorous evaluations of bullying prevention programs are rare, and that, as a result, it is difficult to draw firm conclusions about the overall effectiveness of anti-bullying initiatives (Ryan and Smith, 2009). *Nonetheless, CrimeSolutions.gov considers school-based bullying prevention to be an Effective practice, and we agree.* Effects appear to be stronger for reductions in bullying victimization than perpetration.

Two individual bullying prevention programs have been tested in high-quality research trials and shown to reduce bullying and/or adolescent delinquency. The **Steps to Respect (STR)** elementary school program provides training for all school staff in how to identify and appropriately respond to bullying, and all students in Grades 3–6 receive a 10-session classroom-based curriculum to help foster positive peer relationships, increase students' emotion management and encourage students to report bullying behaviors (Brown *et al.*, 2011). STR has been evaluated in two randomized trials in the USA. The first, conducted in six elementary schools, indicated reductions in observed bullying perpetration on the playground, but no differences in student- or teacher-reported bullying (Frey *et al.*, 2005; Frey *et al.*, 2009). When tested in 33 elementary schools in CA, teacher reports indicated a reduction in physical bullying in intervention compared to control schools, but no differences in bullying were found according to student reports (Brown *et al.*, 2011). Neither study evaluated changes in illegal behaviors by students.

The **Olweus Bullying Prevention Program** is a year-long intervention with school-wide, classroom-based and individually focused components. These activities include: administering a survey to all students and teachers to identify the extent and nature of bullying in the school, creating school rules against bullying, training for all school staff on how to identify and intervene in bullying incidents, providing regular classroom sessions to help students learn about the negative effects of bulling and having teachers facilitate meetings with students involved in bullying and their parents. The program was created and originally tested in Norway in a QED involving 42 middle schools. That evaluation indicated significant reductions in bullying perpetration and victimization, as well as delinquent behaviors such as theft and vandalism (Olweus and Alsaker, 1991). Similar findings were found in a quasi-experimental study in South Carolina middle schools, with reductions in bullying and delinquency shown one year after the program ended (Melton *et al.*, 1998).

The prevalence and harms associated with bullying have been increasingly recognized, and there is growing pressure on schools to address this issue. For example, a study of 19 European countries found that six had national legislation requiring that schools address bullying and three others mandated school-based interventions to address student violence and/or bullying (Ananiadou and Smith, 2002). In the USA, 49 states and the District of Columbia have mandated that schools enact anti-bullying policies which should clearly define for students the types of behaviors that are considered to be bullying and identify the consequences for engaging in such acts. While this is an important step in trying to reduce bullying, to date, there is no evidence that such policies, when enacted in isolation from other efforts, are effective in preventing bullying perpetration or victimization.

Most states do not mandate that schools implement comprehensive prevention programs such as **STR** and **Olweus**. As a result, the use of effective school-based bullying prevention programs is relatively uncommon. A study of 4,726 public schools conducted by the US Department of Education (2011) found that only 1.1% of schools implemented the Olweus Prevention Program in 2004–2005. As one government official in the USA has noted regarding the lack of dissemination of effective programs: "when it comes to bullying prevention, we know we can still do a lot better" (IOM and NRC, 2014b: 3).

Classroom management techniques and/or instructional practices

As mentioned earlier in this chapter, improving **teachers' classroom management skills and instructional practices**, such as increasing the use of interactive teaching methods, is expected to prevent students' problem behaviors and increase their bonding to school. Wilson and colleagues' (2001) meta-analysis of 15 interventions intended to improve teachers' classroom management and/ or instructional practices identified small but significant effect sizes on delinquency (0.13) and alcohol/drug use (0.10) for these types of practices. However, because very few evaluations in this review had strong research designs, we do not consider this practice to have evidence of effectiveness in reducing crime.

However, we have identified three specific programs that have shown effects in reducing crime by improving teachers' classroom management techniques and/or instructional practices, as shown in Table 7.4. Two of these programs, the **Good Behavior Game** and **Raising Healthy Children**, are discussed in more detail in Chapter 8. Briefly, the **Good Behavior Game** trains teachers to effectively manage student behavior by creating explicit rules about acceptable and unacceptable classroom behaviors and consistently enforcing those standards with students' help. **Raising Healthy Children** is a multi-component program which includes training for teachers in the use of cooperative learning techniques meant to improve students' engagement in lessons and commitment to school.

The third program, the **Incredible Years Teacher Classroom Management Program** is intended to help teachers prevent student misbehavior and build positive relationships with students. It involves training for preschool and early elementary school teachers delivered 1 day a month for 5–6 months. Instructors are taught to increase their use of praise and encouragement, give clear and specific directions to students, stay calm when interacting with difficult children, regularly communicate with parents, and monitor student relationships to reduce peer aggression. The program has been evaluated when used alone and in combination with the Incredible Years BASIC parent training program described earlier in this chapter. In a randomized trial of the teacher program conducted in Wales, students in the Incredible Years classrooms were less likely to show off-task and non-compliant behavior (Hutchings et al., 2013). When used in conjunction with the BASIC parent program, child conduct problems were reduced for those in the intervention compared to control groups (Webster-Stratton, Reid, and Hammond, 2004).

School-based practices and policies with inconclusive evidence of effectiveness

Just as we lack conclusive evidence regarding the **effectiveness of teachers' classroom management skills and instructional practices**, other school practices and policies also have uncertain evidence of effectiveness, as shown in Table 7.5. Our inability to draw strong conclusions about these practices is mainly due to a lack of rigorous evaluations, especially randomized studies. In truth, it is challenging to evaluate the effectiveness of school practices using *any* type of research design. It is difficult to specify the particular components or actions comprising some of these practices and to differentiate their impact from other related activities occurring in the school. Until these evaluation limitations can be overcome, we will not be able to specify the effects on crime of many commonly implemented school-wide practices and policies.

For example, most schools have **discipline policies** which identify the school's expectations for positive and negative student behaviors, describe how such behaviors will be monitored and identify the punishments for rule violations. A meta-analysis of discipline policies indicated that they produce small to moderate reductions in crime and substance use, with average effect sizes of 0.27 and 0.24, respectively (Gottfredson, Wilson, and Najaka, 2002). However, most of the evaluations were not rigorously conducted, leading to a lack of confidence in their findings.

Disciplinary policies that are more punitive in nature appear to be less effective in reducing crime. Most notably, **zero-tolerance policies** are likely to be ineffective in reducing delinquency (Cook *et al.*, 2010). Such policies are aligned with **deterrence theories** and began to emerge in the USA during the late 1980s as part of the "get tough on crime" movement. They identify particular behaviors that will not be tolerated at school, such as having weapons or illegal drugs of any sort, and they mandate certain punishments for rule violation by any student. In many cases, students found to be in violation of the policy will be given out-of-school suspension or expulsion, even for a first offense and regardless of the circumstances surrounding the behavior (Kang-Brown *et al.*, 2013).

As with other school-wide policies, high-quality evaluations of zero-tolerance policies are rare and conclusions about their effectiveness must be taken with caution. Nonetheless, the available evidence suggests that these policies are unlikely to improve school safety or reduce student crime, and that they can have several unanticipated negative effects (Gottfredson *et al.*, 2012; Komro *et al.*, 2013). *First*, while removing problem students from school is supposed to improve the school climate and deter future misbehavior, research suggests that schools that apply such harsh sanctions have less positive climates, and that school suspension can increase student misbehavior and school

Table 7.5 School-wide practices and policies with inconclusive evidence of effectiveness.

Practices and policies	Evidence of effectiveness
Improving teachers' classroom management skills and instructional practices	Inconclusive
School discipline policies	Inconclusive
Zero-tolerance policies	Inconclusive
Placing police officers in schools	Inconclusive

dropout in the long term (American Psychological Association (APA) Zero Tolerance Task Force, 2008). *Second*, although such policies are meant to increase the consistency and fairness of punishment, research has indicated that youth of minority racial/ethnic backgrounds and special education students are disproportionately likely to be punished under zero-tolerance policies (APA Zero Tolerance Task Force, 2008; Kang-Brown *et al.*, 2013). *Third*, while they are meant to reduce crime, zero-tolerance policies tend to increase referrals to the juvenile justice system, often for behaviors that are relatively minor and which would have been informally handled by administrators in the past.

> *Like many social programs that are motivated by a sense of urgency to do something about a perceived crisis situation, [placing police officers in schools] has grown dramatically without the benefit of scientific evaluation. No rigorous study to date has demonstrated that placing police in schools promotes school safety.*
>
> Na and Gottfredson, 2011: 26

Coupled with evidence indicating that academic failure, suspensions, and dropout can increase the likelihood of crime (Cook *et al.*, 2010), critics note that zero-tolerance policies create a **school-to-prison pipeline** that will likely result in more youth, especially minority students, being processed through the juvenile justice system and subject to the negative effects of having a formal police record (APA Zero Tolerance Task Force, 2008; Lab, 2014). Based on the potential for zero-tolerance policies to do more harm than good, as well as recommendations from the US Departments of Justice and Education, many states are reforming their policies to allow more discretion by school authorities to decide appropriate punishments, reduce the use of suspension and expulsion, apply more positive reinforcements and limit the use zero-tolerance policies to the most serious misbehaviors (Kang-Brown *et al.*, 2013).

Another common practice in schools is to **place armed guards and/or police officers in school buildings**. According to data from the 2011 National Crime Victimization Survey, 70% of students aged 12–18 reported that their school had security guards or police officers, an increase from 1999 when 54% of students reported such security measures (Robers *et al.*, 2013). The increase in police presence in schools is likely due to media coverage of school shootings and violent incidents as well as the public's belief that law enforcement officials will deter students' crime. This practice is also facilitated by significant federal funding in the USA. Notably, the Department of Justice has provided schools with approximately 750 million dollars in funding for police officers since 1995 through its Community-Oriented Policing Services (COPS) program (Cook *et al.*, 2010). An additional 45 million dollars was set aside to hire school resource officers in 2013 following the shooting at Sandy Hook Elementary School in Newtown, CT (http://www.cops.usdoj.gov/).

Despite the vast resources spent on such initiatives, there has been very little high-quality research evaluating the effectiveness of this practice (Gottfredson *et al.*, 2012). Moreover, some evidence suggests that schools with officers report *more* crime to criminal justice officials (e.g., Na and Gottfredson, 2011) which can also contribute to the school-to-prison pipeline. As the quote from Na and Gottfredson (2011) suggests, the wisdom of continuing to invest in school police officers is questionable, given that we do not, as yet, know if police presence in schools reduces or increases student crime.

Peer- and Gang-focused Practices and Programs

Peer influences are widely considered one of the most important risk factors for crime. Meta-analyses examining the impact of exposure to delinquent peers on delinquency have reported moderate effect sizes ranging from 0.27 (Pratt *et al.*, 2010) to 0.37 (Lipsey and Derzon, 1998). **Differential association** (Sutherland, 1947) and **social learning** (Akers, 1985) theories both emphasize the importance of peer influences on crime. They state that criminal behavior is learned during interactions with important social groups, and that the peer group is the most influential social group for adolescents. One's peers may model delinquent behaviors and/or communicate norms and attitudes that are supportive of delinquency and substance use. **Social control** theory (Hirschi, 1969) suggests that strong and supportive relationships with prosocial peers can help protect against crime. Guided by these theories, peer-focused prevention programs typically try to reduce deviant peer influences, change peer interactions and improve positive peer relationships. They include **universal** programs for youth who have not yet begun to engage in crime and substance use, as well as **indicated** programs designed to reduce recidivism among known offenders (Dodge, Dishion, and Lansford, 2006; Gottfredson, 1987; Weiss *et al.*, 2005).

Despite the potential to reduce crime by altering peer influences, *our review of the literature identified no peer group-focused practices, programs, or policies shown to reduce offending in high-quality research trials.* There is some evidence that substance abuse prevention programs have stronger effects when they rely on peer facilitators to help model and reinforce positive behaviors (Botvin, 1990; Tobler and Stratton, 1997). In addition, as we will discuss in Chapter 8, several classroom-based curricula which provide youth with information and training in how to resist deviant peer influences and to correct their (mis)perceptions that their peers are using drugs have been shown in high-quality evaluations to reduce drug use and delinquency. However, those programs target individual risk and protective factors. Interventions that focus more directly on changing peer relationships and interactions have been less successful. Moreover, as described at the end of this chapter, some prevention programs that group together high-risk youth and isolate them from their mainstream peers have produced **iatrogenic** effects, increasing substance use and offending, likely because they provide youth with more opportunities to interact with and establish closer relationships with delinquent peers (Dishion, McCord, and Poulin, 1999).

Gangs provide even greater opportunities for exposure to delinquent peers and for involvement in crime. In fact, research shows that delinquency tends to increase after youth join gangs and decrease after members leave gangs, and that gang members engage in more crime than non-gang members (Howell, 2010; Maxson, 2011; Thornberry *et al.*, 2003). **Gang prevention programs** may seek to prevent youth from joining gangs, in which case they are truly preventive interventions, or they may try to break up the gang and/or reduce gang members' involvement in crime, typically using crackdowns by law enforcement. The latter are referred to as **gang suppression** strategies (Howell, 2010).

Our review indicated only one gang prevention program that has been evaluated in a high-quality research study and shown to reduce gang membership. The **Montreal Longitudinal and Experimental Study**, listed in Table 7.6 and also described in Chapter 8, is a **selective** intervention for boys showing behavioral problems in kindergarten. The program provides boys with social skills training in school and their care-givers with parent training programming. In a randomized study in Montreal, boys who received treatment were less likely to report being in a gang compared to those who did not receive treatment (Tremblay *et al.*, 1996). Significant differences in gang members were seen two, four, and six years after the intervention ended.

Gang prevention practices and programs with inconclusive evidence of effectiveness

The **Boston Ceasefire** gang suppression project, which was mentioned in Chapter 6, involves joint efforts by local and federal prosecutors, law enforcement officers, and community members to reduce youth homicides and gun crimes, especially those perpetrated by gang members. Law enforcement officers meet with gang members newly released from prison and communicate the message that future gun violence will not be tolerated and will result in arrest and full prosecution (Lab, 2014). Local social workers may also provide gang members with referrals to community-based services to assist with educational, vocational, or other needs. A quasi-experimental evaluation of the Boston Ceasefire program indicated a 63% reduction in youth homicides in Boston one year after the intervention, a larger decline compared to comparable cities in the USA during this period (Braga *et al.*, 2001). A decade later, after the project had been stopped and re-initiated, a quasi-experimental evaluation indicated greater reductions in gang-involved shootings for Boston compared to other cities (Braga, Hureau, and Papachristos, 2014). Although the Boston Ceasefire project is rated as Effective by CrimeSolutions.gov, *given that it has not been subject to a randomized trial, we consider it to have inconclusive evidence of effectiveness.*

A few other gang prevention and suppression programs are considered **Promising** by CrimeSolutions. gov, but we consider these interventions to currently have insufficient evidence of effectiveness, as shown in Table 7.6. In most cases, these interventions have been evaluated using QEDs and in a single

Table 7.6   Gang prevention practices, programs, and policies.

Program	Rating by Blueprints	Rating by the Coalition	Rating by CrimeSolutions.gov
Montreal Longitudinal and Experimental Study	Promising[a]	Promising	Promising
Boston Ceasefire	Not rated	Not rated	Effective
Cease-Fire Chicago/Cure Violence	Not rated	Not rated	Promising
Practice			
Pulling levers	Inconclusive (Promising, CrimeSolutions.gov)		
OJJDP's Comprehensive Gang Model	Inconclusive		
OJJDP's Gang Reduction Program (GRP)	Inconclusive		
OJJDP's Comprehensive Anti-Gang Initiative (CAGI)	Inconclusive (Promising, CrimeSolutions.gov)		

[a]This program does not seem to be available for replication or dissemination. For this reason it is not listed on the Blueprints website. However, the evaluation evidence meets the Blueprint standard to be a Promising intervention.

study with no replications. Or, they have been tested in multiple sites with mixed evidence across communities. For example, **Cease–Fire Chicago**[3] (also called **Cure Violence**) has been evaluated in three QEDs, but not all sites demonstrated reductions in crime (Picard-Fritsche and Cerniglia, 2010; Skogan *et al.*, 2009; Webster *et al.*, 2012) and an adaptation of the program evaluated in a QED failed to show positive effects on crime (Wilson and Chermak, 2011).

A few **practices** intended to reduce gang crimes also have mixed and/or inconclusive evidence of effectiveness. For example, following the claims of success of the **Boston Ceasefire** project, similar programs were implemented and evaluated in other US cities. These are referred to as **pulling levers** interventions (see Chapter 6) due to the emphasis on communicating to gang members that "every lever will be pressed" to combat gang violence (Braga *et al.*, 2001). A meta-analysis of 10 such programs indicated an overall effect size on crime of 0.60 (Braga *et al.*, 2001). However, there was much variation in findings across studies, with some of the initiatives showing significant reductions in violence and/or gang-related crimes (Corsaro and McGarrell, 2009; McGarrell *et al.*, 2006), and others failing to demonstrate significant effects (Wilson and Chermak, 2011). Moreover, all of the evaluations were based on QEDs, leading the study authors to "urge caution in interpreting these results because of the lack of more rigorous randomized controlled trials" (Braga and Weisburd, 2012: 6). CrimeSolutions.gov rates the **pulling levers** practice as **Promising**.

The Office of Juvenile Justice and Delinquency Prevention has developed a series of guidelines to govern communities' efforts to reduce gang activities (Howell, 2010). The **Comprehensive Gang Model** (National Gang Center, 2010) emphasizes that the best way to combat gangs is to implement both universal prevention services to stop youth from joining gangs and criminal justice interventions to suppress gang activities. Specifically, this model advocates that local communities offer five coordinated strategies: (i) community mobilization of citizens and agencies to work together to reduce gang activities; (ii) delivery of social interventions to youth at risk for joining gangs or those already involved in gangs, including universal programs to increase social skills, reduce bullying and violence and improve academic performance; (iii) provision of community-based educational and vocational opportunities to gang-involved youth; (iv) suppression of gang activities by law enforcement and other criminal justice agencies, including increased surveillance of gang "hot spots" and monitoring of gang member activities; and (v) organizational change to ensure collaboration across community agencies and effective use of resources.

Although this type of comprehensive approach may seem reasonable, it does not provide specific guidance on particular actions to be taken and it does not mandate that activities should have strong evidence of effectiveness. Evaluations of the model have shown mixed effects in its ability to reduce crime or gang activities (Lab, 2014; Maxson, 2011; Spergel *et al.*, 2003). The approach has been revised over time, but more recent versions also have inconclusive evidence of effectiveness. For example, when tested in quasi-experimental studies, both the **Gang Reduction Program (GRP)** (Cahill and Hayeslip, 2010) and the **Comprehensive Anti-Gang Initiative (CAGI)** (McGarrell *et al.*, 2012; McGarrell *et al.*, 2013) have shown mixed results across sites, as well as implementation problems in ensuring participation and collaboration by community agencies (Lab, 2014; Maxson, 2011; McGarrell *et al.*, 2012; Rosenbaum and Schuck, 2012).

Given concerns about gang violence, most communities in the USA are currently implementing some type of gang prevention strategy. The Bureau of Justice Assistance (BJA) provides funding to communities via its **Project Safe Neighborhoods** initiative (https://www.bja.gov/programdetails. aspx?program_id=74) to target gangs, and OJJDP provides training for its Comprehensive model to communities across the country. The **Cure Violence** website indicates that this program is currently implemented in 22 US cities and in 7 other countries, with many more potential additions (http:// cureviolence.org/). Given that none of these approaches has strong evidence of effectiveness, it is difficult to believe they will result in widespread reductions in gang activities.

Community-focused Interventions

Community-focused interventions with evidence of effectiveness in preventing crime

In Chapter 6, we discussed **situational crime prevention** strategies, guided by **deterrence** and **routine activities** theories, which try to reduce opportunities for crime in neighborhoods. The community-based strategies described in this chapter also try to alter neighborhoods conditions, but they do so by addressing the social and cultural characteristics identified as important in **social disorganization** theories (Sampson, Raudenbush, and Earls, 1997; Shaw and McKay, 1942). These theories suggest that crime rates are highest in communities with structural problems such as poverty, physical deterioration, and residential turnover (Shaw and McKay, 1942) as well as social problems including a lack of cohesion and trust between neighbors and a reluctance of residents to informally control crime (Sampson *et al.*, 1997). Recognizing the significant challenges faced when trying to increase employment rates and income levels, most neighborhood prevention strategies based upon social disorganization theory try to counteract the negative effects of poverty by changing cultural norms and strengthening social interactions between residents (Sampson, 2011). For example, they may try to increase the number of residents who condemn violence and decrease tolerance of crime, foster communication and trust between neighbors and encourage residents to take action if they see the potential for crime (Sampson *et al.*, 1997).

Similar to school-context programs, the benefits of community-based programs include the potential to reach large numbers of individuals – ideally, all members of the community – and to support prevention messages taught in other contexts (Gates *et al.*, 2006; Specter, 2008; Wagenaar and Perry, 1994). Because they are aimed at entire communities, most try to involve as many individuals as possible in prevention activities. For example, many rely on broad-based coalitions of individuals from key organizations in the community such as schools, police agencies, churches, businesses, and public health agencies. These community members discuss local crime problems and collectively determine how to reduce them. In contrast to many of the interventions discussed in this book, which are delivered by a single agency to a particular group of individuals, community-based prevention efforts often involve the coordinated delivery of multiple interventions by multiple agencies (Wandersman and Florin, 2003).

> *Never doubt that a small group of thoughtful, committed citizens can change the world; indeed, it's the only thing that ever has.*
>
> Margaret Mead

Table 7.7 Effective community-focused programs.

Program	Rating by Blueprints	Rating by the Coalition	Rating by CrimeSolutions.gov
PROSPER	Promising	Near Top Tier	Not rated
Communities That Care	Promising	Reviewed but not rated	Promising

Two effective programs which take a collective and coordinated approach to crime prevention are **PROmoting School–community–university Partnerships to Enhance Resilience (PROSPER)** and **Communities That Care (CTC)** (see Table 7.7). The **PROSPER** program (Spoth *et al.*, 2004) involves the delivery of universal classroom curricula (such as those described in Chapter 8) and parent training interventions such as those described earlier to prevent the onset of substance use. These interventions are overseen by a community coalition, whose members include university staff from Cooperative Extension Systems, public school teachers and administrators, youth, parents, and other community members interested in reducing youth crime. This group ensures that programs delivered in the community have strong evidence of effectiveness and that they are delivered to as many people as possible in a coordinated fashion, over at least a two-year period.

A randomized study of PROSPER in 28 rural and suburban communities in Iowa and Pennsylvania demonstrated positive reductions in youth substance use based on data from about 8,000 mostly White youth who were in Grade 6 when their towns began to implement PROSPER. By the end of Grade 7, significantly fewer students in the PROSPER communities had initiated use of marijuana, inhalants, methamphetamine and ecstasy compared to those in the control communities. In addition, a smaller proportion of PROSPER youth reported use of marijuana and inhalants in the past year, with effect sizes of 0.53 and 0.49, respectively (Spoth *et al.*, 2007). From Grades 6 to 10, there was less growth in tobacco, alcohol, and marijuana use for intervention versus control group youth (Spoth *et al.*, 2011). By the end of Grade 12, those in PROSPER communities compared to control communities were less likely to have used any drugs in their lifetime, to report current use of substances and to increase their use of drugs over adolescence. Reductions in use for intervention compared to comparison youth ranged from 3% to 14% across outcomes (Spoth *et al.*, 2013).

The **Communities That Care (CTC)** prevention system also relies on community coalitions to learn about and implement effective delinquency prevention programs, practices, and policies. Compared to PROSPER, CTC promotes a wider range of evidence-based interventions in recommending use of any of the interventions listed as Model or Promising on the Blueprints website. The particular programs to be implemented are to be community-specific and selected because they address the risk and protective factors of concern to the community (Hawkins, Catalano, and Arthur, 2002). Community coalitions oversee the administration of community-wide surveys of youth conducted in middle and high schools. They then select interventions that will lower the risk factors identified by students as being elevated and increase the protective factors identified as depressed.

Two evaluations have demonstrated that use of the CTC system can lead to community-wide reductions in youth substance use, delinquency, and violence. In a quasi-experimental evaluation in Pennsylvania, greater reductions in self-reported rates of past-month smoking, drinking, binge drinking, and drug use were found for middle and high school students in cities implementing the CTC system compared to those in communities not using CTC (Feinberg *et al.*, 2007). Reductions

Table 7.8 Effects of CTC on increasing abstinence of substance use and delinquency from Grade 5 to Grade 12.

Outcome	CTC	Control
Any drug use	24.5%	17.6%★
Gateway drugs (tobacco, alcohol, or marijuana)	29.4%	21.0%★
Alcohol	32.2%	23.3%★
Cigarettes	49.9%	42.8%★
Marijuana	52.6%	48.2%
Binge drinking	50.4%	43.9%
Delinquency	41.7%	33.0%★

Source: Adapted from Hawkins *et al.*, 2014.

★ denotes a statistically significant effect ($p < 0.05$) between CTC and control conditions in the percentage of youth reporting abstinence of behaviors.

in property and violent delinquency were also found, with relatively small effects sizes (0.19) favoring students in CTC communities (Feinberg, Jones, Greenberg, *et al.*, 2010).

A randomized trial conducted in 24 communities across the USA also showed positive effects (Hawkins, Catalano, *et al.*, 2008). Based on annual surveys of about 4,000 youth started in Grade 5, when CTC began in the intervention communities, those in CTC communities were less likely than those in control communities to have ever engaged in delinquent behavior by Grades 7, 8, 10, and 12 (Hawkins, Brown, *et al.*, 2008; Hawkins *et al.*, 2009; Hawkins *et al.*, 2012; Hawkins *et al.*, 2014). At Grade 10, intervention youth reported fewer delinquent and violent behaviors (Hawkins *et al.*, 2012), but these differences were not significant at Grade 12 (Hawkins *et al.*, 2014). CTC youth also had lower rates of initiation of alcohol and tobacco use by Grades 8, 10, and 12 (Hawkins *et al.*, 2009; Hawkins *et al.*, 2012; Hawkins *et al.*, 2014). A summary of the intervention effects in delaying substance use and delinquency is shown in Table 7.8. The percentages represent the proportion of youth in CTC and control communities who abstained from, or never engaged in, the behavior by the end of high school.

According to WSIPP (2015), CTC produces small effects on crime (0.14), drinking (0.15), and smoking (0.09), with even smaller adjusted effect sizes. The system is cost beneficial, returning $3.04 for every dollar spent.

Community-focused prevention practices with inconclusive evidence of effectiveness

The evidence from evaluations of **PROSPER** and **Communities That Care** suggest that the general practice of **community mobilization**, or encouraging community members to work together to prevent crime, may be effective. However, this claim cannot yet be made with certainty given that other efforts to encourage local residents to work together to reduce problems such as drug use and crime have not been successful. The ability of community partnerships to reduce crime is thought to be related to the community's commitment to use evidence-based, effective interventions, and when untested or ineffective strategies dominate coalition activities as is often the case, crime rates are less likely to be affected (Fagan and Hawkins, 2012; Rosenbaum and Schuck, 2012).

The ability of **neighborhood watch groups** to reduce crime is also unclear. Like coalitions, these groups provide the opportunity to build cohesion, trust, and collective action among neighborhood residents. The particular activities of watch groups vary across neighborhoods, but they commonly include meetings of community residents to discuss local crime problems, share crime prevention tips and plan citizen patrols, such as having neighborhood volunteers walk the streets to watch for suspicious activities and report potential crimes to police (Lab, 2014; Rosenbaum, 1987). They may also establish crime hotlines, conduct security surveys of residents and/or coordinate activities with **community policing** efforts (see Chapter 6) (Bennett, Holloway, and Farrington, 2008; Lab, 2014). Neighborhood watch activities might be recommended by **routine activities** theory as a way of increasing guardianship and by **social disorganization** theory as a mechanism for increasing collective efficacy.

CrimeSolutions.gov identifies **neighborhood watch** as a Promising practice, based on a meta-analysis of 24 such programs. This review indicated that 19 of the 24 interventions had positive results and when averaged together, reduced crime by 16% to 26% in intervention areas versus comparison neighborhoods (Bennett *et al.*, 2008). However, most evaluations were QEDs and there was significant variation in effects across studies, with some showing increases in crime and some showing decreases. The findings also showed that programs conducted in the USA and Canada had stronger effects than those in the UK. Reasons for the disparity in outcomes are not certain, but Lab (2014) suggests it may be related to implementation challenges, notably variation in participation by community members. Although the effectiveness of this practice is still somewhat tentative, neighborhood watch programs are widely used, particularly in the USA, Asia, and Western Europe (Lab, 2014). According to studies cited in Bennett *et al.* (2008), 41% of US communities have neighborhood watch initiatives and 27% of adults in the UK have reported involvement in such programs.

Ineffective Social Context Practices and Programs

A few contextual practices and programs have been evaluated in high-quality research trials and been shown to have harmful or no effects on crime. A family-focused intervention, the **Adolescent Transitions Program (ATP)** was shown to *increase* adolescent delinquency and tobacco use in a randomized study of 119 White families with children aged 11–14 years (Dishion *et al.*, 1999). In this evaluation, families reporting high levels of family or child risk factors were assigned to receive: (a) parent training only, (b) teen/peer training only, (c) a combined parent and teen/peer group, or (d) no services (i.e., the control group). Parents and teens met in small groups for 12 weeks to learn, respectively, positive parenting skills and the development of prosocial goals and self-regulation. Although children of those attending the parent group showed some benefits, at the one-year follow-up, those who participated in the teen/peer-only group and those in the combined group had greater increases in smoking and teacher reports of delinquency compared to those in the control group (Dishion and Andrews, 1995). As shown in Figure 7.3, these iatrogenic effects were also found at the three-year follow-up, with those in the teen/peer-only and combined groups

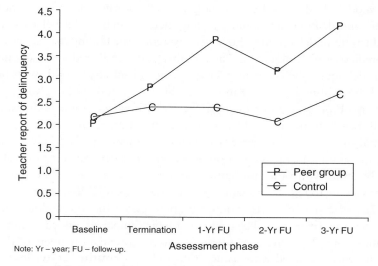

Teacher report of delinquency as a function of the teen focus intervention

Note: Yr – year; FU – follow-up.

Figure 7.3 Increases in delinquency for teens participating in the teen (peer) group intervention of the Adolescent Transitions Program compared to those in the control condition. Source: Dishion *et al.*, 1999. Reproduced with permission of the American Psychological Association.

continuing to have higher levels of delinquency and tobacco use compared to the control group (Poulin, Dishion, and Burraston, 2001).

Subsequent analysis and observation of participants suggested that negative outcomes were the result of **deviancy training**, which refers to the negative peer influences especially likely to occur when groups of delinquent adolescents are brought together (Dishion *et al.*, 1999). Especially if youth activities and conversations are not well monitored by adults, deviant adolescents may model and reinforce others' delinquency through verbal communication as well as non-verbal gestures (e.g., smiling and laughing) (Dishion *et al.*, 1999; Gottfredson, 2010).

One universal gang prevention program, **Gang Resistance Education and Training (G.R.E.A.T.)**, has been evaluated and shown to produce no significant changes in adolescent delinquency. G.R.E.A.T. is a 13-lesson, classroom-based curricula taught by police officers in elementary and middle schools. The program attempts to reduce gang membership by improving students' communication, peer refusal, and anger management skills; increase their ability to resolve conflicts; and change positive beliefs about gangs and gang membership. Early tests of the intervention failed to show a significant effect on gang membership (Esbensen *et al.*, 2011; Lab, 2014). In a recent randomized trial in 31 US elementary schools, students who received the intervention in Grades 6 or 7 were less likely to report gang membership, at both one and four years following the program (Esbensen *et al.*, 2012; Esbensen *et al.*, 2013). However, the size of this effect was small and, at the four-year follow-up, there were no differences between the G.R.E.A.T. and control group participants on any of the five peer-related variables (e.g., having delinquent peers or prosocial peers) or any of the four measures of delinquent behavior (Esbensen *et al.*, 2013).

This combination of findings is problematic as it fails to support the intervention's theoretical basis and causal model. As discussed earlier, gang research clearly indicates a relationship between gang membership and delinquency: joining a gang increases delinquent behavior and leaving the gang leads to reductions in delinquency. Equally consistent is the finding that association with delinquent peers is predictive of delinquency. The fact that G.R.E.A.T. reduced gang membership but had no effect on delinquent behavior or peer associations is clearly at odds with both theoretical expectations and the existing body of empirical research on gangs. Although CrimeSolutions.gov rates G.R.E.A.T. as a Promising program, given the inconsistency of these findings, Blueprints does not consider G.R.E.A.T. to be an effective crime prevention program.

Media campaigns can be considered a community-focused practice given that most try to change social norms among a large proportion of residents in a defined geographical area. They can be used in combination with other prevention activities or as a stand-alone intervention. Many media campaigns seeking to reduce substance use are based on **social learning** theory (Akers, 1985; Sutherland, 1947), as they try to correct youth (mis)perceptions that most adolescents or adults use drugs and emphasize the harms caused by drug use. Media campaigns guided by **deterrence** theory often try to reduce crime by increasing awareness among potential offenders of the certainty and severity of punishments associated with crimes. Or, guided by **routine activities** theory, they may encourage the public to report suspicious behaviors to police or take individual preventive actions to reduce their own chances of victimization (Lab, 2014). No matter what content they emphasize, media campaigns involve the spread of information via print (e.g., newspapers or magazines), television, or online media.

There is no doubt that media campaigns can be successful in spreading their messages. How many of you have seen pictures of methamphetamine addicts who have lost their teeth, smokers who need voice boxes to speak or, for slightly older readers, McGruff the crime dog "taking a bit out of crime" (www.ncpc.org)? But, how effective are these campaigns in reducing actual levels of substance use and crime? A meta-analysis of five American mass media campaigns found no impact on adolescent or young adult substance use; the overall effect size was 0.02 (Ferri *et al.*, 2013). Similarly, four evaluations of the Meth Project showed inconsistent effects on substance use. Combining data from all four evaluations, 12- to 17-year olds who had greater exposure to the campaign reported significantly lower rates of methamphetamine use in the past year compared to those with less exposure, with an overall effect size of 0.59. However, there were no significant differences in past month meth use or use by young adults aged 18–24.

Based on the Meth Project evaluation, CrimeSolutions.gov classifies media campaigns as having **No Effects** on adolescent illicit drug use, and we agree that media campaigns are ineffective in reducing youth drug use. We also consider the practice to have inconclusive evidence of effectiveness in reducing other forms of crime, given the lack of high-quality research evaluations examining their impact. Individuals are increasingly exposed to media of all types, which could potentially reduce the impact of media campaigns, as they will have to compete with many other sources of influence. On the other hand, the ability to reach large numbers via electronic and social media could enhance the potential for mass media campaigns to influence potential offenders. At this point, however, the effectiveness of this approach in reducing most types of crime is unknown.

Need for Further Research

Our review of the literature had indicated much disparity in the number of effective crime prevention strategies across the primary social contexts in which individuals reside. While a relatively large number of family-focused programs have been shown to reduce crime, there are far fewer models of effective school-, peer-/gang- and community-focused interventions. This gap in the research is very troubling given the potential for school- and community-wide interventions to reach large numbers of youth and adults. In addition, given that peer influences are considered by most criminologists to be the most important risk factor for adolescent delinquency, it is very disappointing that we cannot identify any successful interventions that alter the peer context. Likewise, research indicates that a large proportion of crime, particularly violent offenses, are committed by gang members, yet relatively few gang prevention programs have been tested in high-quality research trials and only a couple have evidence of effectiveness (Lab, 2014; Maxson, 2011). The limited number of effective gang prevention programs constitutes a serious gap in our crime prevention efforts.

Clearly, a priority for future research is to create and evaluate more contextual interventions using rigorous research methods. This goal will be challenging to meet, however. Compared to interventions focused on individuals, contextual programs are more difficult to evaluate and may be less likely to show positive effects. *First*, they require that groups, not individuals, be recruited. In practice, this means that consent to participate in the study must be obtained from the group leader(s), such as a school principal or city leader, and from the individuals in the group, and securing participation from all necessary parties will likely be difficult. *Second*, enough groups must be recruited to ensure that appropriate statistical analyses can be conducted; comparing one school with a program to a second one without the program will not allow for a multilevel statistical analysis which is the best means of testing group-level interventions.[4] *Third*, manipulating group processes may be more difficult than changing an individual's attitudes or behaviors. For example, improving family interactions means altering the ways that mothers, fathers, children, and siblings all relate to one another, and any one individual has the potential to deviate from the program's protocols and/or undermine the program's effectiveness.

In terms of school-based interventions, we have noted that many schools have now adopted certain practices that could potentially affect crime, such as anti-bullying and zero-tolerance policies and having police officers in the building. When new policies are adopted widely, in all schools in a district or region, it is very difficult to evaluate their effectiveness because there is no valid comparison group that has not adopted the intervention (Cook *et al.*, 2010; Evans-Whipp *et al.*, 2004). Nonetheless, it may be even more imperative to evaluate these strategies, given their potential to affect very large numbers of students.

Community-based initiatives also pose unique and significant evaluation challenges. Unlike families and schools, which have clear boundaries, it can be difficult to determine the precise area that defines the "neighborhood" or "community" to be changed. In addition, many community-based initiatives involve the simultaneous implementation of multiple prevention strategies, which can also vary from community to community, making for a very complicated analysis (Fagan and Hawkins, 2012; Lab, 2014).

In addition to recommending more general evaluation of contextual interventions, we also note the need for these evaluations to assess crime as an outcome. Many of the family-focused interventions reviewed in this chapter evaluated changes in children's conduct problems or externalizing behaviors, but not illegal activities. In part, this was due to having limited follow-up periods, and more long-term evaluations are needed to assess effects on adolescent delinquency and adult crime. Many school-based initiatives have evaluated changes in academic performance, school climate, or school disciplinary infractions, but not crime. Given the relationship between school risk and protective factors and crime (Cook *et al.*, 2010), it seems very plausible that an intervention that is effective in changing school-related outcomes will have an impact on crime, but to be sure, that outcome must be measured. Relatedly, quite a few of the interventions reviewed in this chapter examined substance use but not other forms of crime, and it would be useful for interventions that can plausibly affect both of these related forms of behavior to measure both of them.

Summary

This chapter has reviewed interventions that try to create more supportive social contexts for individuals. We identified many effective family-based programs, including home visitation, parent training, and family therapy interventions which improve parenting practices such as monitoring and discipline of youth and create stronger parent–child relationships. Fewer school-, peer-, gang-, and neighborhood-focused interventions were identified as effective in reducing crime. These gaps represent a significant limitation in our current ability to address crime problems.

Although it is difficult to determine how many effective social context programs, practices, and policies are currently being implemented in the USA and abroad, we suspect that the number is limited. Furthermore, many commonly used practices, programs, and policies, especially those in schools and to address gangs, have either little evidence of effectiveness or have never been well evaluated to determine if they affect crime. Priorities for future research are the creation, testing and increased dissemination of effective social context interventions. Given their potential to positively affect very large numbers of individuals, if used more widely, contextual interventions could make a substantial impact on crime.

Critical Thinking Questions and Practice Activities

1. Of all the contexts discussed in this chapter, which do you think is most important for influencing crime? Why? Does it depend on the age of the individual? Explain.
2. In your opinion, which type of contextual program would be most difficult to evaluate: those that try to change families, schools, peers, gangs, or communities? Why? Identify some of the main challenges a researcher would face when evaluating the effectiveness of the social context program you have chosen. Consider issues related to program participants, program implementation, and measurement and analysis of outcomes.

3. Police officers are increasingly being placed in schools even though there is little evidence that doing so will reduce crime. What do you think about this practice? Should we be advocating for more police officers in our schools? What are some of the benefits and consequences of doing so?

4. Imagine that you have been charged with creating a mass media campaign to reduce crime. Identify the specific crime(s) you want to prevent and the population(s) you will target with your intervention. Then, describe your intervention content and the types of media you will use to spread your prevention messages. Be sure to base your idea on criminological theories.

Endnotes

1. A meta-analysis of 13 evaluations of group-based parent training interventions for parents of children with conduct problems reported effect sizes of 0.44 based on observer reports and 0.53 based on parent reports (Furlong et al., 2012). Nine of these studies evaluated the BASIC parent training program, providing additional evidence of its effectiveness.

2. A meta-analysis by Littell and colleagues (2005) based on eight evaluations of MST concluded that the evidence of the program's effectiveness in reducing crime was inconclusive. However, the Blueprints Advisory Board identified several flaws in the meta-analysis's methodology which weaken the credibility of the study's conclusions.

3. The **Cease-Fire** program focuses on changing community and gang norms regarding violence to reduce gang crime. A key component is to have local community members (i.e., "violence interrupters"), who are typically former gang members with prior criminal records, spend time with gang members in order to find out about gang conflicts and prevent retaliatory strikes (Skogan et al., 2009). When they learn about a potential gang fight, they talk to gang members about the individual and community harms that are caused by gang violence. Although anti-violence norms are thought to be more salient when provided by credible messengers like the violence interrupters, as opposed to social workers, researchers or police officers, the effectiveness of this approach has been questioned. Critics note that using former gang members and criminals may not be effective, as they may not follow program guidelines, may have a difficult time believing the messages they are to communicate, can be difficult to manage and may increase rather than reduce gang cohesiveness (Klein, 2011).

4. When program participants are drawn from multiple groups, such as schools or neighborhoods, multilevel statistical analyses like hierarchical linear models (Raudenbush and Bryk, 2002) are recommended. These techniques take into account the potential that group members may share certain characteristics and that they will systematically differ from individuals in other groups in particular ways. Failing to account for these differences can introduce statistical biases and potentially result in unreliable estimates of a program's effects. For more information on multilevel analysis, see Diez-Roux (2000) or Johnson (2010).

Helpful Websites (last accessed August 3, 2016)

- http://www.wsipp.wa.gov/BenefitCost
  The Washington State Institute of Public Policy contains detailed information on how the organization calculates the costs and economic benefits of crime prevention programs, practices, and policies.
- http://www.stopbullying.gov/

This website is intended for schools and communities wanting to know more about the prevalence, consequences, and prevention of bullying, including the types of policies and rules that are recommended to reduce bullying.

- https://www.nationalgangcenter.gov/
  The National Gang Center website compiles information on gang activities from law enforcement officials across the United States and reviews gang prevention strategies.

Further Reading

- Dishion, T. J., McCord, J., and Poulin, F. 1999. When interventions do harm: Peer groups and problem behavior. *American Psychologist*, 54:755–764.
  This article reviews characteristics of peer-focused programs that have resulted in harmful effects to participants.
- Gomby, D. S., Culross, P. L., and Berhman, R. E. 1999. Home visiting: Recent program evaluations – analysis and recommendations. *The Future of Children*, 9: 4–26.
  Easy-to-read summary of the effectiveness of home visiting programs.
- Gottfredson, D. C., Cook, P. J., and Na, C. 2012. Schools and prevention. In: B. C. Welsh and D. P. Farrington (eds), *The Oxford Handbook of Crime Prevention*, pp. 269–287. New York, NY: Oxford University Press.
  This book chapter provides an overview of levels of school crime in the United States, school risk and protective factors, and various school- and classroom-based programs to reduce substance use and crime.
- Howell, J. C. 2010. Gang prevention: An overview of research and programs. Washington, DC: Office of Juvenile Justice and Delinquency Prevention.
  This OJJDP report summarizes official data related to gang-related crime and prevention and suppression approaches to reduce gang crime.
- Kumpfer, K., and Alvarado, R. 2003. Family-strengthening approaches for the prevention of youth problem behaviors. *American Psychologist*, 58:457–465.
  This article summarizes different family-focused interventions intended to reduce substance use and crime.
- Washington State Institute for Public Policy. 2014. *Benefit-Cost Results*. Olympia, WA: Washington State Institute for Public Policy.
  Up to-date estimates of the cost effectiveness of many evidence-based programs and practices reviewed in this chapter (and in other chapters of the textbook).

References

Akers, R. L. 1985. *Deviant Behavior: A Social Learning Approach*, 3rd ed. Belmont, CA: Wadsworth.

Alexander, J. F., and Parsons, B. V. 1973. Short-term behavioral intervention with delinquent families: Impact on family process and recidivism. *Journal of Abnormal Psychology*, 81:219–225.

American Psychological Association Zero Tolerance Task Force. 2008. Are zero tolerance policies effective in the schools? An evidentiary review and recommendations. *American Psychologist*, 63:852–862.

Ananiadou, K., and Smith, P. K. 2002. Legal requirements and nationally circulated materials against school bullying in European countries. *Criminology and Criminal Justice*, 2:471–491.

Bennett, T., Holloway, K., and Farrington, D. P. 2008. The effectiveness of neighborhood watch. *Campbell Systematic Reviews*, 2008:18.

Bilukha, O., Hahn, R. A., Crosby, A., *et al.*; Task Force on Community Prevention Services. 2005. The effectiveness of early childhood home visitation in preventing violence: A systematic review. *American Journal of Preventive Medicine*, 28:11–39.

Bjorknes, R., Kjobli, J., Tanger, T., and Jakobsen, R. 2012. Parent training among ethnic minorities: Parenting practices as mediators of change in child conduct problems. *Family Relations*, 61:101–114.

Borduin, C. M., Mann, B. J., Cone, L. T., *et al.* 1995. Multisystemic treatment of serious juvenile offenders: Long-term prevention of criminality and violence. *Journal of Consulting and Clinical Psychology*, 63:569–578.

Botvin, G. J. 1990. Substance abuse prevention: Theory, practice, and effectiveness. In: M. Tonry and J. Q. Wilson (eds), *Crime and Justice, Vol. 13, Drugs and Crime*, pp. 461–519. Chicago, IL: University of Chicago Press.

Braga, A. A., and Weisburd, D. L. 2012. The effects of "pulling levers" focused deterrence strategies on crime. *Campbell Systematic Reviews*, 2012:8(6).

Braga, A. A., Hureau, D. M., and Papachristos, A. V. 2014. Deterring gang-involved gun violence: Measuring the impact of Boston's Operation Ceasefire on street gang behavior. *Journal of Quantitative Criminology*, 30:113–139.

Braga, A. A., Kennedy, D. M., Waring, E. J., and Piehl, A. M. 2001. Problem-oriented policing, deterrence, and youth violence: An evaluation of Boston's Operation Ceasefire. *Journal of Research in Crime and Delinquency*, 38:195–225.

Brody, G. H., Kogan, S. M., Yi-fu, C., and McBride Murry, V. 2008. Long-term effects of the Strong African American Families Program on youths' conduct problems. *Journal of Adolescent Health*, 43:474–481.

Brody, G. H., Yi-fu, C., Kogan, S. M., McBride Murry, V., and Brown, A. C. 2010. Long-term effects of the Strong African American Families Program on youths' alcohol use. *Journal of Consulting and Clinical Psychology*, 78:281–285.

Brody, G. H., McBride Murry, V., Gerrard, M., *et al.* 2004. The Strong African American Families Program: Translating research into prevention programming. *Child Development*, 75:900–917.

Brody, G. H., McBride Murry, V., Kogan, S. M., *et al.* 2006. The Strong African American Families Program: A cluster-randomized prevention trial of long-term effects and a mediation model. *Journal of Consulting and Clinical Psychology*, 74:356–366.

Broidy, L. M., Tremblay, R. E., Brame, R., *et al.* 2003. Developmental trajectories of childhood, disruptive behaviors and adolescent delinquency: A six-site, cross-national study. *Developmental Psychology*, 39:222–245.

Brown, E. C., Low, S., Smith, B. H., and Haggerty, K. P. 2011. Outcomes from a school-randomized controlled trial of Steps to Respect: A bullying prevention program. *School Psychology Review*, 40:423–443.

Burrus, B., Leeks, K. D. L., Sipe, T. A., *et al.*; Community Preventive Services Task Force. 2012. Person-to-person interventions targeted to parents and other caregivers to improve adolescent health: A Community Guide Systematic Review. *American Journal of Preventive Medicine*, 42:316–326.

Cahill, M., and Hayeslip, D. 2010. Findings from the evaluation of OJJDP's Gang Reduction Program. Washington, DC: Office of Juvenile Justice.

Catalano, R. F., Fagan, A. A., Gavin, L. E., *et al.* 2012. Worldwide application of prevention science in adolescent health. *The Lancet*, 379:1653–1664.

Chaffin, M., Funderburk, B., Bard, D., Valle, L. A., and Gurwitch, R. 2011. A combined motivation and parent–child interaction therapy package reduces child welfare recidivism in a randomized dismantling field trial. *Journal of Clinical Child and Adolescent Psychology*, 79:84–95.

Chaffin, M., Silovsky, J. F., Funderburk, B., *et al.* 2004. Parent–child interaction therapy with physically abusive parents: Efficacy for reducing future abuse reports. *Journal of Clinical Child and Adolescent Psychology*, 72:500–510.

Chamberlain, P., and Reid, J. B. 1998. Comparison of two community alternatives to incarceration for chronic juvenile offenders. *Journal of Consulting and Clinical Psychology*, 66:624–633.

Chamberlain, P., Leve, L. D., and DeGarmo, D. 2007. Multidimensional treatment foster care for girls in the juvenile justice system: 2-year follow-up of a randomized clinical trial. *Journal of Consulting and Clinical Psychology*, 75:187–193.

Connell, A. M., Dishion, T. J., and Deater-Deckard, K. 2006. Variable- and person-centered approaches to the analysis of early adolescent substance use: Linking peer, family, and intervention effects with developmental trajectories. *Merrill-Palmer Quarterly*, 52:421–448.

Connell, A. M., Klosterman, S., and Dishion, T. J. 2011. Family Check-Up effects on adolescent arrest trajectories: Variation by developmental subtype. *Journal of Research on Adolescence*, 22:367–380.

Cook, P. J., Gottfredson, D. C., and Na, C. 2010. School crime control and prevention. In: M. Tonry (ed.), *Crime and Justice*, vol. 39, pp. 313–440. Chicago, IL: University of Chicago Press.

Corsaro, N., and McGarrell, E. F. 2009. Testing a promising homicide reduction strategy: Re-assessing the impact of the Indianapolis "pulling levers" intervention. *Journal of Experimental Criminology*, 5:63–82.

DeGarmo, D., and Forgatch, M. S. 2005. Early development of delinquency within divorced families: Evaluating a randomized preventive intervention trial. *Developmental Science*, 8(3):229–239.

Diez-Roux, A. V. 2000. Multilevel analysis in public health research. *Annual Review of Public Health*, 21:171–192.

Dishion, T. J., and Andrews, D. W. 1995. Preventing escalation in problem behaviors with high-risk young adolescents: Immediate and 1-year outcomes. *Journal of Consulting and Clinical Psychology*, 63:538–548.

Dishion, T. J., and Dodge, K. A. 2005. Peer contagion in interventions for children and adolescents: Moving towards an understanding of the ecology and dynamics of change. *Journal of Abnormal Child Psychology*, 33:395–400.

Dishion, T. J., and Kavanagh, K. 2000. A multilevel approach to family-centered prevention in schools: Process and outcome. *Addictive Behaviors*, 25:899–911.

Dishion, T. J., McCord, J., and Poulin, F. 1999. When interventions do harm: Peer groups and problem behavior. *American Psychologist*, 54:755–764.

Dishion, T. J., Nelson, S. E., and Bullock, B. M. 2004. Premature adolescent autonomy: Parent disengagement and deviant peer process in the amplification of problem behaviour. *Journal of Adolescence*, 27:515–530.

Dodge, K. A., Dishion, T. J., and Lansford, J. E. 2006. Deviant peer influences in intervention and public policy for youth. *Social Policy Report*, 20: 3–19. Society for Research in Child Development.

Eckenrode, J., Campa, M., Luckey, D. W., *et al.* 2010. Long-term effects of prenatal and infancy nurse home visitation on the life course of youths: 19-year follow-up of a randomized trial. *Archives of Pediatric and Adolescent Medicine*, 164:9–15. doi: 10.1007/s11121-009-0126-0

Eddy, J. M., Bridges Whaley, R., and Chamberlain, P. 2004. The prevention of violent behavior by chronic and serious male juvenile offenders: A 2-year follow-up of a randomized clinical trial. *Journal of Emotional and Behavioral Disorders*, 12:2–8.

Esbensen, F. A., Matsuda, K. N., Taylor, T. J., and Peterson, D. 2011. Multimethod strategy for assessing program fidelity: The national evaluation of the revised G.R.E.A.T. program. *Evaluation Review*, 25:14–39.

Esbensen, F. A., Peterson, D., Taylor, T. J., and Osgood, D. W. 2012. Results of a multi-site evaluation of the G.R.E.A.T. program. *Justice Quarterly*, 29:125–151.

Esbensen, F. A., Osgood, D. W., Peterson, D., Taylor, T. J., and Carson, D. C. 2013. Short- and long-term outcome results from a multisite evluation of the G.R.E.A.T. program. *Criminology and Public Policy*, 12:375–411.

Evans-Whipp, T., Beyers, J. M., Lloyd, S., *et al.* 2004. A review of school drug policies and their impact on youth substance use. *Health Promotion International*, 19:227–234.

Fagan, A. A., and Hawkins, J. D. 2012. Community-based substance use prevention. In: B. C. Welsh and D. P. Farrington (eds), *The Oxford Handbook of Crime Prevention*, pp. 247–268. New York, NY: Oxford University Press.

Farrington, D. P., and Ttofi, M. M. 2009. School-based programs to reduce bullying and aggression. *Campbell Systematic Reviews*, 2009:6.

Farrington, D. P., and Welsh, B. C. 2003. Family-based prevention of offending: A meta-analysis. *Australian and New Zealand Journal of Criminology*, 36:127–151.

Feinberg, M. E., Jones, D. E., Goslin, M. C., and Kan, M. L. 2010. Effects of Family Foundations on parents and children: 3.5 years after baseline. *Journal of Family Psychology*, 24:532–542.

Feinberg, M. E., Greenberg, M. T., Osgood, D. W., Sartorius, J., and Bontempo, D. 2007. Effects of the Communities That Care model in Pennsylvania on youth risk and problem behaviors. *Prevention Science*, 8:261–270.

Feinberg, M. E., Jones, D., Greenberg, M. T., Osgood, D. W., and Bontempo, D. 2010. Effects of the Communities That Care model in Pennsylvania on change in adolescent risk and problem behaviors. *Prevention Science*, 11:163–171.

Ferri, M., Allara, E., Bo, A., Gasparrini, A., and Faggiano, F. 2013. Media campaigns for the prevention of illicit drug use in young people. *Cochrane Database of Systematic Reviews*, (6):CD009287.

Flay, B. R. 2000. Approaches to substance use prevention utilizing school curriculum plus social environment change. *Addictive Behaviors*, 25:861–885.

Forgatch, M. S., Patterson, G. R., DeGarmo, D. S., and Beldavs, Z. G. 2009. Testing the Oregon delinquency model with 9-year follow-up of the Oregon Divorce Study. *Development and Psychopathology*, 21:637–660.

Foxcroft, D. R., and Tsertsvadze, A. 2011. Universal family-based prevention programs for alcohol misuse in young people. *Cochrane Database of Systematic Reviews*, (9):CD009308.

Frey, K., Bobbitt Nolen, S., Van Schoiack Edstrom, L., and Hirschstein, M. K. 2005. Effects of a school-based social–emotional competence program: Linking children's goals, attributions, and behavior. *Applied Developmental Psychology*, 26:171–200.

Frey, K., Hirschstein, M. K., Edstrom, L. V., and Snell, J. L. 2009. Observed reductions in school bullying, nonbullying aggression, and destructive bystander behavior: A longitudinal evaluation. *Journal of Educational Psychology*, 101:466–481.

Furlong, M., McGilloway, S., Bywater, T., et al. 2012. Behavioural and cognitive-behavioural group-based parenting programmes for early-onset conduct problems in children aged 3 to 12 years. *Campbell Systematic Reviews*, 2012:12.

Gates, S., McCambridge, J., Smith, L. A., and Foxcroft, D. 2006. Interventions for prevention of drug use by young people delivered in non-school settings. *Cochrane Database of Systematic Reviews*, (1):CD005030.

Gladden, R. M., Vivolo-Kantor, A. M., Hamburger, M. E., and Lumpkin, C. D. 2014. Bullying surveillance among youths: Uniform definitions for public health and recommended data elements. Atlanta, GA: National Center for Injury Prevention and Control, Centers for Disease Control and Prevention and US Department of Education.

Gomby, D. S., Culross, P. L., and Berhman, R. E. 1999. Home visiting: Recent program evaluations – analysis and recommendations. *The Future of Children*, 9:4–26.

Gottfredson, D. C. 2010. Deviancy training: Understanding how preventive interventions harm: The Academy of Experimental Criminology 2009 Joan McCord Award Lecture. *Journal of Experimental Criminology*, 6:229–243.

Gottfredson, D. C., Cook, P. J., and Na, C. 2012. Schools and prevention. In: B. C. Welsh and D. P. Farrington (eds), *The Oxford Handbook of Crime Prevention*, pp. 269–287. New York, NY: Oxford University Press.

Gottfredson, D. C., Wilson, D. B., and Najaka, S. S. 2002. School-based crime prevention. In: L. W. Sherman, D. P. Farrington, B. C. Welsh, and D. MacKenzie (eds), *Evidence-Based Crime Prevention*, pp. 56–164. New York, NY: Routledge.

Gottfredson, G. D. 1987. Peer group intervention to reduce the risk of delinquent behavior: A selective review and a new evaluation. *Criminology*, 25:671–714.

Greenwood, P., and Welsh, B. C. 2012. Promoting evidence-based practice in delinquency prevention at the state level: Principles, progress, and policy directions. *Criminology and Public Policy*, 11:493–513.

Hahn, R., Bilukha, O., Lowy, J., et al.; Task Force on Community Prevention Services. 2005. The effectiveness of therapeutic foster care for the prevention of violence: A systematic review. *American Journal of Preventive Medicine*, 28.

Hansson, K., Cederblad, M., and Hook, B. 2000. Functional family therapy: A method for treating juvenile delinquents. *Socialvetenskaplig tidskrift*, 3:231–243.

Hawkins, J. D., Catalano, R. F., and Arthur, M. W. 2002. Promoting science-based prevention in communities. *Addictive Behaviors*, 27:951–976.

Hawkins, J. D., Oesterle, S., Brown, E. C., Abbott, R. D., and Catalano, R. F. 2014. Youth problem behaviors 8 years after implementing the Communities That Care prevention system: A community randomized trial. *JAMA Pediatrics*, 168:122–129.

Hawkins, J. D., Brown, E. C., Oesterle, S., et al. 2008. Early effects of Communities That Care on targeted risks and initiation of delinquent behavior and substance use. *Journal of Adolescent Health*, 43:15–22.

Hawkins, J. D., Catalano, R. F., Arthur, M. W., et al. 2008. Testing Communities That Care: Rationale and design of the Community Youth Development Study. *Prevention Science*, 9:178–190.

Hawkins, J. D., Oesterle, S., Brown, E. C., et al. 2009. Results of a type 2 translational research trial to prevent adolescent drug use and delinquency: A test of Communities That Care. *Archives of Pediatric Adolescent Medicine*, 163:789–798.

Hawkins, J. D., Oesterle, S., Brown, E. C., et al. 2012. Sustained decreases in risk exposure and youth problem behaviors after installation of the Communities That Care prevention system in a randomized trial. *Archives of Pediatrics and Adolescent Medicine*, 166:141–148.

Henggeler, S. W., Melton, G. B., and Smith, L. A. 1992. Family preservation using multisystemic therapy: An effective alternative to incarcerating serious juvenile offenders. *Journal of Consulting and Clinical Psychology*, 6:953–961.

Henggeler, S. W., Clingempeel, W. G., Brondino, M. J., and Pickrel, S. G. 2002. Four-year follow-up of Multisystemic Therapy with substance-abusing and substance-dependent juvenile offenders. *Journal of the American Academy of Child and Adolescent Psychiatry*, 41:868–874.

Hirschi, T. 1969. *Causes of Delinquency*. Berkeley, CA: University of California Press.

Howell, J. C. 2010. Gang prevention: An overview of research and programs. Washington, DC: Office of Juvenile Justice and Delinquency Prevention.

Hutchings, J., Martin-Forbes, P., Daley, D., and Williams, M. E. 2013. A randomized controlled trial of the impact of a teacher classroom management program on the classroom behavior of children with and without behavior problems. *Journal of School Psychology*, 51:571–585.

Institute of Medicine (IOM) and National Research Council (NRC). 2014a. Building capacity to reduce bullying: Workshop summary. Washington, DC: The National Academies Press.

Institute of Medicine (IOM) and National Research Council (NRC). 2014b. Strategies for scaling effective family-focused preventive interventions to promote children's cognitive, affective, and behavioral health: Workshop summary. Washington, DC: The National Academies Press.

Jacob, B. A., and Lefgren, L. 2003. Are idle hands the devil's workshop? Incapacitation, concentration and juvenile crime. Cambridge, MA: National Bureau of Economic Research.

Johnson, B. D. 2010. Multilevel analysis in the study of crime and justice. In: A. R. Piquero and D. Weisburd (eds), *Handbook of Quantitative Criminology*, pp. 615–649. New York, NY: Springer.

Kang-Brown, J., Trone, J., Fratello, J., and Daftary-Kapur, T. 2013. A generation later: What we've learned about zero tolerance in schools. New York, NY: Vera Institute of Justice, Center on Youth Justice.

Kitzman, H. J., Olds, D. L., Cole, R. E., *et al.* 2010. Enduring effects of prenatal and infancy home visiting by nurses on children: Follow-up of a randomized trial among children at age 12 years. *Archives of Pediatric and Adolescent Medicine*, 164:412–418.

Kjobli, J., Hukkelberg, S., and Ogden, T. 2013. A randomized trial of group parent training: Reducing child conduct problems in real-world settings. *Behaviour Research and Therapy*, 51:113–121.

Klein, M. W. 2011. Comprehensive gang and violence reduction programs: Reinventing the square wheel. *Criminology and Public Policy*, 10:1037–1044.

Klein, N. C., Alexander, J. F., and Parsons, B. V. 1977. Impact of family systems intervention on recidivism and sibling delinquency: A model of primary prevention and program evaluation. *Journal of Consulting and Clinical Psychology*, 45:469–474.

Knerr, W., Gardner, F., and Cluver, L. 2013. Improving positive parenting skills and reducing harsh and abusive parenting in low- and middle-income countries: A systematic review. *Prevention Science*, 14:352–363.

Komro, K. A., Tobler, A. L., Delisle, A. L., and O'Mara, R. J. 2013. Beyond the clinic: Improving child health through evidence-based community development. *BMC Pediatrics*, 13:172.

Koning, I. M., Vollebergh, W. A. M., Smit, F., *et al.* 2009. Preventing heavy alcohol use in adolescents (PAS): Cluster randomized trial of a parent and student intervention offered separately and simultaneously. *Addiction*, 104:1669–1678.

Koutakis, N., Stattin, H., and Kerr, M. 2008. Reducing youth alcohol drinking through a parent-targeted intervention: the Örebro Prevention Program. *Addiction*, 103:1629–1637. doi: 10.1111/j.1360-0443.2008.02326.x

Lab, S. P. 2014. *Crime Prevention: Approaches, Practices and Evaluations*, 7th ed. Waltham, MA: Anderson Publishing.

Langford, R., Bonell, C. P., Jones, H. E., *et al.* 2014. The WHO Health Promoting School framework for improving the health and well-being of students and their academic achievement. *Cochrane Database of Systematic Reviews*, (4):CD008958.

Leschied, A., and Cunningham, A. 2002. Seeking effective interventions for serious young offenders: Interim results of a four-year randomized study of Multisystemic Therapy in Ontario, Canada. London, ON: Centre for Children and Families in the Justice System.

Leung, C., Tsang, S., Heung, K., and Yiu, I. 2009. Effectiveness of Parent–Child Interaction Therapy (PCIT) among Chinese families. *Research on Social Work Practice*, 19:304–313.

Lipsey, M. W., and Derzon, J. H. 1998. Predictors of violent or serious delinquency in adolescence and early adulthood: A synthesis of longitudinal research. In: R. Loeber and D. P. Farrington (eds), *Serious and Violent Juvenile Offenders: Risk Factors and Successful Interventions*, pp. 86–105. Thousand Oaks, CA: Sage.

Littell, J. H., Campbell, M., Green, S., and Toews, B. 2005. Multisystemic Therapy for social, emotional, and behavioral problems in youth aged 10–17. *Cochrane Database of Systematic Reviews*, (4):CD004797.

Loeber, R., and Farrington, D. P. 2000. Young children who commit crime: Epidemiology, developmental origins, risk factors, early interventions, and policy implications. *Development and Psychopathology*, 12:737–762.

Lowell, D., Paulicin, B., Carter, A. S., Godoy, L., and Briggs-Gowan, M. J. 2011. A randomized controlled trial of Child FIRST: A comprehensive home-based intervention translating research into early childhood practice. *Child Development*, 82:193–208.

Lundahl, B., Risser, H. J., and Lovejoy, M. C. 2006. A meta-analysis of parent training: Moderators and follow-up effects. *Clinical Psychology Review*, 26:86–104. doi: 10.1016/j.cpr.2005.07.004

Mason, W. A., Kosterman, R., Hawkins, J. D., Haggerty, K. P., and Spoth, R. L. 2003. Reducing adolescents' growth in substance use and delinquency: Randomized trial effects of a preventive parent-training intervention. *Prevention Science*, 4:203–212.

Matos, M., Bauermeister, J. J., and Bernal, G. 2009. Parent–child interaction therapy for Puerto Rican preschool children with ADHD and behavior problems: A pilot efficacy study. *Family Process*, 48:232–252.

Maxson, C. 2011. Street gangs. In: J. Q. Wilson and J. Petersilia (eds), *Crime and Public Policy*, pp. 158–182. New York, NY: Oxford University Press.

McGarrell, E. F., Chermak, S., Wilson, J. M., and Corsaro, N. 2006. Reducing homicide through a "lever-pulling" strategy. *Justice Quarterly*, 23, 214–231.

McGarrell, E. F., Corsaro, N., Melde, C., *et al.* 2012. An assessment of the Comprehensive Anti-Gang Initiative: Final project report. Washington, DC: National Institute of Justice.

McGarrell, E. F., Corsaro, N., Melde, C., *et al.* 2013. Attempting to reduce firearms violence through a Comprehensive Anti-Gang Initiative (CAGI): An evaluation of process and impact. *Journal of Criminal Justice*, 41, 33–43.

Melton, G. B., Limber, S. P., Cunningham, P., *et al.* 1998. Violence among rural youth. Washington, DC: Office of Juvenile Justice and Delinquency Prevention.

Menting, A. T. A., de Castro, B. O., and Matthys, W. 2013. Effectiveness of the Incredible Years parent training to modify disruptive and prosocial child behavior: A meta-analytic review. *Clinical Psychology Review*, 33:901–913.

Na, C., and Gottfredson, D. C. 2011. Police officers in schools: Effects on school crime and the processing of offending behaviors. *Justice Quarterly*, 30:619–650.

National Gang Center. 2010. Best practices to address community gang problems: OJJDP's Comprehensive Gang Model. Washington, DC: Office of Juvenile Justice and Delinquency Prevention.

Nixon, R. D. V., Sweeney, L., Erickson, D. B., and Touyz, S. W. 2004. Parent–Child Interaction Therapy (PCIT): One- and two-year follow-up of standard and abbreviated treatments for oppositional preschoolers. *Journal of Abnormal Child Psychology*, 32:263–271.

Ogden, T., Bjørnebekk, G., Kjøbli, J., *et al.* 2012. Measurement of implementation components ten years after a nationwide introduction of empirically supported programs – a pilot study. *Implementation Science*, 7:49. doi: 10.1186/1748-5908-7-49

Olds, D. L. 2002. Prenatal and infancy home visiting by nurses: From randomized trials to community replication. *Prevention Science*, 3:153–172.

Olds, D. L., Henderson Jr., C. R., and Cole, R. 1998. Long-term effects of nurse home visitation on children's criminal and antisocial behavior: 15-year follow-up of a randomized controlled trial. *Journal of the American Medical Association*, 280:1238–1244.

Olds, D. L., Henderson Jr., C. R., Chamberlin, R., and Tatelbaum, R. 1986. Preventing child abuse and neglect: A randomized trial of Nurse Home Visitation. *Pediatrics*, 78:65–78.

Olds, D. L., Eckenrode, J., Henderson Jr., C. R., *et al.* 1997. Long-term effects of home visitation on maternal life course and child abuse and neglect: Fifteen-year follow-up of a randomized trial. *Journal of the American Medical Association*, 278:637–643. doi: 10.1001/jama.280.14.1238

Olds, D. L., Robinson, J., Pettitt, L. M., *et al.* 2004. Effects of home visits by paraprofessionals and by nurses: Age 4 follow-up results of a randomized trial. *Pediatrics*, 114:1560–1568.

Olweus, D., and Alsaker, F. 1991. Assessing change in a cohort-longitudinal study with hierarchical data. In: D. Magnusson, L. R. Bergman, and G. Rudinger (eds), *Problems and Methods in Longitudinal Research: Stability and Change*, pp. 107–132. Cambridge, England: Cambridge University Press.

Pantin, H., Prado, G., Lopez, B., *et al.* 2009. A randomized controlled trial of Familias Unidas for Hispanic adolescents with behavior problems. *Psychosomatic Medicine*, 71(9):987–995.

Patterson, G. R., Forgatch, M. S., and DeGarmo, D. 2010. Cascading effects following intervention. *Development and Psychopathology*, 22:949–970.

Picard-Fritsche, S., and Cerniglia, L. 2010. Testing a public health approach to gun violence: An evaluation of Crown Heights Save Our Streets, a replication of the CureViolence model. New York, NY: Center for Court Innovation.

Piquero, A. R., Farrington, D. P., Welsh, B. C., Tremblay, R., and Jennings, W. G. 2009. Effects of early family/parent training programs on antisocial behavior and delinquency. *Journal of Experimental Criminology*, 5:83–120.

Poulin, F., Dishion, T. J., and Burraston, B. 2001. 3-year iatrogenic effects associated with aggregating high-risk adolescents in cognitive-behavioral preventive interventions. *Applied Developmental Science*, 5:214–224.

Prado, G., Pantin, H., Briones, E., *et al.* 2007. A randomized controlled trial of a parent-centered intervention in preventing substance use and HIV risk behaviors in Hispanic adolescents. *Journal of Consulting and Clinical Psychology*, 75:914–926.

Pratt, T. C., Cullen, F. T., Sellers, C. S., *et al.* 2010. The empirical status of social learning theory: A meta analysis. *Justice Quarterly*, 27:765–802. doi: 10.1080/07418820903379610

Printz, R. J., and Sanders, M. R. 2007. Adopting a population-level approach to parenting and family support interventions. *Clinical Psychology Review*, 27:739–749.

Printz, R. J., Sanders, M. R., Shapiro, C. J., Whitaker, D. J., and Lutzker, J. R. 2009. Population-based prevention of child maltreatment: The US Triple P system population trial. *Prevention Science*, 10:1–12.

Raudenbush, S. W., and Bryk, A. S. 2002. *Hierarchical Linear Models: Applications and Data Analysis Methods*, 2nd ed. Newbury Park, CA: Sage.

Robers, S., Kemp, J., and Truman, J. L. 2013. Indicators of school crime and safety: 2012 (NCES 2013-036/NCJ 241446). Washington, DC: National Center for Education Statistics, US Department of Education, and Bureau of Justice Statistics, Office of Justice Programs, US Department of Justice.

Rosenbaum, D. P. 1987. The theory and research behind Neighborhood Watch: Is it a sound fear and crime reduction strategy? *Crime and Delinquency*, 33:103–134.

Rosenbaum, D. P., and Schuck, A. M. 2012. Comprehensive community partnerships for preventing crime. In: B. C. Welsh and D. P. Farrington (Eds.), *The Oxford Handbook of Crime Prevention*, pp. 226–246. New York, NY: Oxford University Press.

Ryan, W., and Smith, J. D. 2009. Antibullying programs in schools: How effective are evaluation practices? *Prevention Science*, 10:248–259.

Sampson, R. J. 2011. The community. In: J. Q. Wilson and J. Petersilia (eds), *Crime and Public Policy*, pp. 210–236. New York, NY: Oxford University Press.

Sampson, R. J., Raudenbush, S. W., and Earls, F. 1997. Neighborhoods and violent crime: A multilevel study of collective efficacy. *Science*, 277:918–924.

Sanders, M. R., Turner, K. M., and Markie-Dadds, C. 2002. The development and dissemination of the Triple P-Positive Parenting Program: A multilevel, evidence-based system of parenting and family support. *Prevention Science*, 3:173–189.

Schaeffer, C. M., and Borduin, C. M. 2005. Long-term follow-up to a randomized clinical trial of Multisystemic Therapy with serious and violent juvenile offenders. *Journal of Consulting and Clinical Psychology*, 73:445–453.

Shaw, C. R., and McKay, H. D. 1942. *Juvenile Delinquency and Urban Areas*. Chicago, IL: University of Chicago Press.

Skogan, W. G., Hartnett, S. M., Bump, N., and Dubois, J. 2009. Evaluation of CeaseFire-Chicago. Washington, DC: National Institute of Justice.

Smith, D. K., Chamberlain, P., and Eddy, J. M. 2010. Preliminary support for Multidimensional Treatment Foster Care in reducing substance use in delinquent boys. *Journal of Child and Adolescent Substance Abuse*, 19:343–358.

Specter, A. 2008. Making youth violence prevention a national priority. *American Journal of Preventive Medicine*, 34:S3–4.

Spergel, I. A., Wa, K. M., Grossman, S. F., *et al.* 2003. The Little Village gang reduction project in Chicago. Chicago, IL: Illinois Criminal Justice Information Authority.

Spoth, R., Redmond, C., and Lepper, H. 1999. Alcohol initiation outcomes of universal family-focused preventive interventions: One- and two-year follow-ups of a controlled study. *Journal of Studies on Alcohol*, Suppl 13:103–111.

Spoth, R., Lopez Reyes, M., Redmond, C., and Shin, C. 1999. Assessing a public health approach to delay onset and progression of adolescent substance use: Latent transition and log-linear analyses of longitudinal family preventive intervention outcomes. *Journal of Consulting and Clinical Psychology*, 67:619–630.

Spoth, R., Trudeau, L., Guyll, M., Shin, C., and Redmond, C. 2009. Universal intervention effects on substance use among young adults mediated by delayed adolescent substance initiation. *Journal of Consulting and Clinical Psychology*, 77:620–632.

Spoth, R., Redmond, C., Shin, C., *et al.* 2013. PROSPER Community-University Partnership delivery system effects on substance misuse through 6½ years past baseline from a cluster randomized controlled intervention trial. *Preventive Medicine*, 56:190–196. doi: 10.1016/j.ypmed.2012.12.013

Spoth, R. L., and Redmond, C. 1996. Illustrating a framework for rural prevention research: Project Family studies of rural family participation and outcomes. In: R. Peters and R. J. McMahon (eds), *Preventing Childhood Disorders, Substance Abuse, and Delinquency*. Thousand Oaks, CA: Sage.

Spoth, R. L., and Redmond, C. 2002. Project Family prevention trials based in community-university partnerships: Toward scaled-up preventive interventions. *Prevention Science*, 3:203–222.

Spoth, R. L., Redmond, C., and Shin, C. 2000. Reducing adolescents' aggressive and hostile behaviors. *Archives of Pediatric and Adolescent Medicine*, 154:1248–1257.

Spoth, R. L., Redmond, C., and Shin, C. 2001. Randomized trial of brief family interventions for general populations: Adolescent substance use outcomes 4 years following baseline. *Journal of Consulting and Clinical Psychology*, 69:627–642.

Spoth, R. L., Greenberg, M. T., Bierman, K. L., and Redmond, C. 2004. PROSPER Community-University partnership model for public education systems: Capacity-building for evidence-based, competence-building prevention. *Prevention Science*, 5:31–39.

Spoth, R. L., Redmond, C., Clair, S., *et al.* 2011. Preventing substance misuse through community–university partnerships randomized controlled trial outcomes 4½ years past baseline. *American Journal of Preventive Medicine*, 40:440–447.

Spoth, R. L., Redmond, C., Shin, C., *et al.* 2007. Substance use outcomes at eighteen months past baseline from the PROSPER community-university partnership trial. *American Journal of Preventive Medicine*, 32:395–402.

Stoltzfus, E., and Lynch, K. E. 2009. Home visitation for families with young children. Washington, DC: Congressional Research Service.

Sutherland, E. H. 1947. *Principles of Criminology*. Philadelphia, PA: J. B. Lippincott.

Thornberry, T. P., Krohn, M. D., Lizotte, A. J., Smith, C., and Tobin, K. 2003. *Gangs and Delinquency in Developmental Perspective*. Cambridge, England: Cambridge University Press.

Tobler, N. S., and Stratton, H. H. 1997. Effectiveness of school-based drug prevention programs: A meta-analysis of the research. *The Journal of Primary Prevention*, 18:71–128.

Tremblay, R., Masse, L. C., Pagani, L., and Vitaro, F. 1996. From childhood physical aggression to adolescent maladjustment: The Montreal Prevention Experiment. In: R. Peters and R. J. McMahon (eds), *Preventing Childhood Disorders, Substance Abuse, and Delinquency*, pp. 268–298. Thousand Oaks, CA: Sage.

Ttofi, M. M., Farrington, D. P., and Losel, F. 2012. School bullying as a predictor of violence later in life: A systematic review and meta-analysis of prospective longitudinal studies. *Aggression and Violent Behavior*, 17, 405–418.

US Department of Education. 2011. Prevalence and implementation fidelity of research-based prevention programs in public schools: Final report. Washington, DC: US Department of Education, Office of Planning, Evaluation and Policy Development, Policy and Program Studies Service.

Van Ryzin, M. J., and Dishion, T. J. 2012. The impact of a family-centered intervention on the ecology of adolescent antisocial behavior: Modeling developmental sequelae and trajectories during adolescence. *Development and Psychopathology*, 24:1139–1155. doi: 10.1017/S0954579412000582

Vreeman, R. C., and Carroll, A. E. 2007. A systematic review of school-based interventions to prevent bullying. *Archives of Pediatric and Adolescent Medicine*, 161:78–88.

Wagenaar, A. C., and Perry, C. L. 1994. Community strategies for the reduction of youth drinking: Theory and application. *Journal of Research on Adolescence*, 4:319–345.

Waldron, H. B., Slesnick, N., Brody, J. L., Turner, C. W., and Peterson, T. R. 2001. Treatment outcomes for adolescent substance abuse at 4- and 7-month assessments. *Journal of Consulting and Clinical Psychology*, 69:802–813.

Wandersman, A., and Florin, P. 2003. Community intervention and effective prevention. *American Psychologist*, 58:441–448.

Washington State Institute for Public Policy (WSIPP). 2015. *Benefit-Cost Results*. Olympia, WA: Washington State Institute for Public Policy.

Webster-Stratton, C., and Taylor, T. K. 2001. Nipping early risk factors in the bud: Preventing substance abuse, delinquency, and violence in adolescence through interventions targeted at young children (0–8 years). *Prevention Science*, 2:165–192.

Webster-Stratton, C., Reid, M. J., and Hammond, M. 2004. Treating children with early-onset conduct problems: Intervention outcomes for parent, child, and teacher training. *Journal of Clinical Child and Adolescent Psychology*, 33:105–124.

Webster, D. W., Whitehill, J. M., Vernick, J. S., and Parker, E. M. 2012. Evaluation of Baltimore's Safe Streets program: Effects on attitudes, participants' experiences, and gun violence. Baltimore, MD: Johns Hopkins Center for the Prevention of Youth Violence, Johns Hopkins Bloomberg School of Public Health.

Weiss, B., Caron, A., Ball, S., *et al.* 2005. Iatrogenic effects of group treatment for antisocial youth. *Journal of Consulting and Clinical Psychology*, 73:1036–1044.

Wilson, D. B., Gottfredson, D. C., and Najaka, S. S. 2001. School-based prevention of problem behaviors: A meta-analysis. *Journal of Quantitative Criminology*, 17:247–272.

Wilson, J. M., and Chermak, S. 2011. Community-driven violence reduction programs: Examining Pittsburgh's One Vision One Life. *Criminology and Public Policy*, 10:993–1027.

Wolchik, S. A., Sandler, I. N., Millsap, R. E., *et al.* 2002. Six-year follow-up of preventive interventions for children of divorce: A randomized controlled trial. *Journal of the American Medical Association*, 288:1874–1881.

Wolchik, S. A., Sandler, I. N., Tein, J.-Y., *et al.* 2013. Fifteen-year follow-up of a randomized trial of a preventive intervention for divorced families: Effects on mental health and substance use outcomes in young adulthood. *Journal of Consulting and Clinical Psychology*, 81:660–673.

Wolchik, S. A., West, S. G., Sandler, I. N., *et al.* 2000. An experimental evaluation of theory-based mother and mother-child programs for children of divorce. *Journal of Consulting and Clinical Psychology*, 68:843–856.

Yoshikawa, H. 1994. Prevention as cumulative protection: Effects of early family support and education on chronic delinquency and its risks. *Psychological Bulletin*, 115:28–54.

8

Individual-Level Crime Prevention
Preventing the Onset of Crime

Learning Objectives

Upon finishing this chapter, students should be able to:
- Identify effective programs, practices, and policies that prevent or delay the onset of crime
- Identify programs, practices and/or policies that are not effective in preventing the onset of crime and those which have inconclusive evidence of effectiveness
- Summarize the extent to which programs and practices that prevent the onset of crime are being implemented
- State the most important research tasks that must be accomplished in order to increase the number of effective programs, practices, and policies available and in use to prevent the onset of crime.

Introduction

When in elementary or middle school, do you recall your teacher ever warning you that drinking alcohol and using drugs could be dangerous? Did a police officer ever visit your classroom and tell you not to do drugs or show you a jar containing a blackened lung taken from the body of a deceased, long-time smoker? Or, did you ever spend time with a peer or adult tutor because you needed a little extra assistance with your schoolwork?

If any of these experiences sound familiar, it's because you probably participated in an **individually focused crime prevention program**, but not necessarily one that has evidence of effectiveness in reducing crime, as you will learn in this chapter. Whereas Chapter 7 described prevention strategies that try to improve the social contexts of the family, school, peer group, and community, this

The Prevention of Crime, First Edition. Delbert Elliott and Abigail Fagan.
© 2017 John Wiley & Sons, Inc. Published 2017 by John Wiley & Sons, Inc.
Companion website: www.wiley.com/go/elliott/prevention_of_crime

chapter focuses on crime prevention programs and practices designed to change *individuals*. These interventions seek to alter the personal attitudes, skills, experiences, and behaviors that influence offending.

As we have discussed throughout this book, to have the best chance of reducing crime, interventions should reduce the risk factors and enhance the protective factors identified in criminological theories and shown in scientific research to affect crime. In this chapter, you will learn about programs which use this approach to prevent the onset of offending. For example, some interventions help individuals better regulate their emotions, cope with stress and anxiety and refrain from impulsive and/or aggressive behaviors. These are the factors promoted as most important in **strain** and **social control** theories. Other programs focus on increasing children's academic achievement and school engagement, which are also identified as important in **strain** and **control** theories. Still other interventions seek to improve how individuals interact with others, such as by teaching them how to resist deviant peer influences or how to build strong relationships with positive peers and with parents. According to **social learning theory**, these interactions matter in either promoting or inhibiting criminal involvement. The interventions described in Chapter 7 also focus on improving environments and relationships, but they do so by changing these contexts directly, whereas the programs and practices reviewed in this chapter try to help individuals better respond to these contexts.

All of the interventions discussed in this chapter seek to reduce the **onset** or **initiation** of crime. That is, *their goal is to prevent individuals from committing their first illegal act*. In Chapter 9, we will also discuss programs, practices, and policies which focus on individual risk and protective factors, but they are **indicated** interventions which try to reduce **recidivism** and promote **desistence** among those who have already begun engaging in crime.

To show that an intervention prevents the **onset** of crime, its evaluation should first demonstrate that participants in both the intervention and control groups had never broken the law at baseline, prior to the start of the program or practice. This can be done by asking participants directly about their involvement in crime, using the self-report methodology described in Chapter 2, or by checking official records of their criminal histories. If anyone reported prior offending or had an official crime record, they should be removed from the analysis. If the evaluation then shows that, after the intervention has ended, crime participation is lower among those remaining in the intervention group, or that they were older when their first crime took place, compared to those remaining in the control group, the intervention can be considered effective in preventing the onset of crime.

In actuality, this type of analysis strategy is often not used. Evaluators may not collect information on criminal histories and they rarely remove from their samples those who had previously committed a crime. A more common approach is to compare rates of offending between intervention and control group participants at post-test, and, ideally, statistically controlling for offending reported at the pre-test. This second approach is still a valid method for determining if the program reduced crime, but it cannot guarantee that it reduced the *onset* of offending. In our summaries below, we will do our best to distinguish between evaluations that demonstrate reductions in onset using the first approach and those that show reductions in participation using the second approach.[1]

This chapter includes **universal** and **selective** interventions. As their name suggests, **universal** programs and practices are delivered universally, to a wide range of individuals. These interventions usually seek to prevent the onset of offending among a population considered to be at fairly low risk for offending. For example, interventions delivered in schools to all youth in a particular grade or afterschool programs open to all children in a neighborhood are considered to be universal. Because they involve many individuals with many different backgrounds, and because criminal behavior is not rare, some participants may have already engaged in some crime prior to receiving a universal prevention program. Universal programs do not try to screen out or exclude such individuals from participating in the intervention, but they generally assume that participants will be entering the program with no history of offending.

Selective programs are more restrictive in defining exactly who can receive the program (i.e., they are "selective"). These interventions are delivered to a specific set of individuals who are known to have already experienced a particular risk factor(s) for crime, but who have not yet had official contact with the juvenile or adult criminal justice systems. For example, tutoring programs are selective, in that they are intended for children who are not doing well in school.

Many of the interventions we will describe are designed for young people: children and adolescents. Why focus on youth when so many more adults engage in crime? Recall that, according to the **life course development paradigm** and research on the **criminal career**, while many adults do break the law, their first criminal act typically occurs in middle or late adolescence.

> *It is easier to prevent bad habits than to break them.*
> Ben Franklin

We also know that the earlier the age of onset, the more likely an individual is to become a frequent, violent and/or serious offender and to continue offending into adulthood. This information emphasizes the importance of preventing or delaying the onset of offending and suggests that, to do so, it is best to target youth rather than adults. That being said, some of the interventions described in this chapter will involve services for parents, teachers, or even community members, but most are designed to help these adults prevent or at least delay the onset of offending among children and adolescents.

Practices and Programs with Evidence of Success in Preventing the Onset of Crime

Early childhood education

In his 2013 State of the Union Address, President Obama urged Congress to expand the delivery of high quality preschool educational programs across the United States, stating, "*We know this works.*" Although he was referring to the impact of these programs on education and employment, how much evidence is there that this strategy can reduce crime? As we describe in this section, there is some evidence of effectiveness, but we have identified only one specific **early childhood education** program that has been well evaluated and shown to prevent illegal behavior, as shown in Table 8.1.

The main goal of early education programs is to increase school readiness and improve cognitive skills among very young children, aged 3–5 years old, especially those from lower income families. Because preschool education is not provided free of charge like elementary and secondary school

Table 8.1 Effective early childhood education prevention practices and programs.

Effective practice?	Yes		
Effective programs	Rating by Blueprints	Rating by the Coalition	Rating by CrimeSolutions.gov
Perry Preschool	Promising	Promising	Effective

education, poor families may not be able to afford to send their children to preschool. As a result, these children may fall behind other income groups in their educational attainment and social skills. According to **strain theories**, the failure to attain significant educational goals early in life can place youth at risk for involvement in crime later in life (Schindler and Yoshikawa, 2012). Early childhood education programs try to counteract these early disadvantages by providing free, high-quality preschool education services to young children. Classes are small so that teachers can spend time working individually with children and communicating with parents about what their children are learning in school. By increasing parents' involvement in their children's education and improving children's school experiences, these programs also try to strengthen youths' bonds to society (in particular, their attachments to parents and teachers) and their commitment to education, which are identified in **social control theories** as important protective factors that will reduce the likelihood of offending.

A meta-analysis by Farrington and Welsh (2003) examining the effectiveness of five preschool programs showed a significant but relatively small impact on children's delinquency, with an overall effect size of 0.26. A second meta-analysis (Washington State Institute for Public Policy (WSIPP), 2015) showed a similar impact on crime, with an average effect size of 0.25. Together, these studies indicate that the general **practice** of early childhood education reduces subsequent involvement in crime for youth enrolled in these services compared to those who do not receive such interventions. Research has also indicated that investing in early childhood education can be cost beneficial (Heckman and Masterov, 2007). WSIPP (2015) estimated that for every dollar invested in early childhood education services, $4.66 is saved. Reducing participants' involvement in crime saves money that would otherwise be spent processing offenders in the criminal justice system, and improving their educational attainment helps them to achieve better-paying jobs, leading to greater financial benefits for taxpayers.

Early childhood education can be considered an evidence-based and cost-effective practice, but what specific early childhood education programs have been demonstrated as effective? According to our review, only one program has the required level of evidence: the **HighScope Perry Preschool** program. The effectiveness of this program was tested with 123 low-income African American children and their families, 58 of whom were

Early childhood may provide an unusual window of opportunity for interventions because young children are uniquely receptive to enriching and supportive environments … As individuals age, they gain the independence and ability to shape their environments, rendering intervention efforts more complicated and costly.

Duncan and Magnuson, 2004: 102

randomly assigned to receive two years of preschool services when they were aged 3 and 4. Based on self-reported information at ages 15 and 19, which includes the age periods when individuals are likely to experience the onset of offending, those receiving the program were less likely to report crime than those in the control group (Parks, 2000; Schweinhart, 2005). Crime reductions were also shown using official records. For example, at age 19, 31% of the program youth had ever been arrested or detained by police compared to 51% of the control group (Schweinhart et al., 1985). The longest follow-up evaluation showed that program participants were less likely to have ever been arrested for a violent crime by age 40 compared to the control group participants, with arrest rates of 32% and 48%, respectively. Program participants were also less likely to be arrested for property crimes and for drug-related offenses (Schweinhart, 2005, 2013) and had fewer total arrests for any offense (Heckman et al., 2010). Given that the program was only offered to African American youth, it is unclear if the Perry Preschool program would be beneficial for other racial/ethnic groups. A cost-benefit analysis of this program shows that for every dollar invested, there is a saving of $12.90 (Belfield et al., 2006).

As suggested in the quote from President Obama, the US Government is very supportive of early childhood education programs. The government provides millions of dollars each year to states to implement the Head Start early childhood education program and estimates that one million children and families participate in Head Start each year (http://www.acf.hhs.gov/programs/ohs/about/head-start). Although Head Start uses some of the same instructional content and methods as the Perry Preschool program and also targets low income youth and families, its effectiveness in reducing crime has not been established (Schindler and Yoshikawa, 2012). Some speculate that when implemented widely and with fewer resources, many of the features that make the Perry Preschool program successful become "watered down," resulting in a less effective program (Yoshikawa et al., 2013). So, while early childhood education services reach large numbers of low-income children and families through the Head Start program, the degree to which national crime rates will be affected is questionable since the program has not (yet) been shown to reduce delinquency (Puma et al., 2012).

Afterschool programs

Afterschool programs (ASPs) encompass a range of activities which differ in their goals, content, and delivery formats. Some ASPs focus on improving youths' academic performance and rely on peers or adults to provide informal help with schoolwork or more structured tutoring in particular subjects. Others may offer recreational programs, sports and/or social events, such as can be found in Boys & Girls Clubs or YMCA facilities. Still other ASPs may seek to improve youths' social or emotional skills using more traditional teaching practices and structured classes offered on a regular basis. Finally, mentoring ASPs seek to create supportive relationships between youth from single-parent or low-income families and peer or adult role models.

ASPs are informed by different criminological theories, depending on their focus. Many are based on **routine activities theory's** premise that how individuals spend their time influences their opportunities for law-breaking activities. Afterschool programs try to fill children's time with positive activities so that they do not have time to engage in crime (Cross et al., 2009). This idea is also consistent with the **involvement** component of Hirschi's (1969) **social control theory**. As would also be recommended by Hirschi (1969), many ASPs try to create close and supportive relationships between participants and adult staff. Finally, they should ensure that all youth activities are closely supervised by facilitators, to provide **social control** and minimize the chances that children will engage in deviant or delinquent behaviors during programming time.

Because they can take so many different forms, it is difficult to evaluate the overall effectiveness of afterschool programming as a crime prevention practice, but some research has attempted to do so. A meta-analysis of 25 **mentoring** programs showed that use of this practice was related to reduced delinquency and substance use for youth under age 22 (Tolan *et al.*, 2013). The average effect sizes were 0.21 for delinquency and 0.16 for substance use. Both results indicate that youth who receive mentoring are significantly less involved in crime compared to those who do not participate, though the size of the impact is modest. Some of the mentoring interventions included in the review were **indicated** programs, implemented with youth involved in the juvenile justice system, while the rest were **selective**, targeting youth considered to be at risk for delinquency. Given these populations, it is difficult to determine if these programs actually delayed the **onset** of offending or if their effectiveness was restricted to reducing recidivism among those already participating in crime.

Other studies suggest that, as a general practice, ASPs do not reduce crime. We will describe such results in more detail later in this chapter, but some meta-analyses have concluded that ASPs do not reduce substance use or delinquency. Evaluations of ASPs focused on improving social and emotional skills (Durlak, Weissberg, and Pachan, 2010) as well as academic performance (James-Burdumy, Dynarski, and Deke, 2008; Zief, Lauver, and Maynard, 2006) have shown few effects on delinquency and some have shown harmful effects, sometimes *increasing* crime. This evidence suggests that we must be cautious about advocating for the dissemination of ASPs as a general practice if the goal is to reduce crime. *Based on credible scientific evidence, only mentoring approaches and the three specific programs shown in Table 8.2 and reviewed next can be used with confidence to prevent the onset of offending.*

The three ASPs we consider to have credible evidence of effectiveness are **Big Brothers, Big Sisters (BBBS)**, **Keep Safe**, and **Athletes Training and Learning to Avoid Steroids (ATLAS)**. These three programs use very different approaches. **BBBS** is a mentoring program for low-income youth from single-parent families or families in which a parent is incarcerated. Although a school-based version of the program has been developed, in which matches meet only during the school year and only on school grounds, only the community-based version of the program has shown evidence of

Table 8.2 Effective afterschool prevention practices and programs.

Effective practice?	Yes − mentoring only		
Effective programs	*Rating by Blueprints*	*Rating by the Coalition*	*Rating by CrimeSolutions.gov*
Big Brothers, Big Sisters	Promising	Promising	Effective
Keep Safe	Promising	Not rated	Promising
ATLAS	Promising	Not rated	Promising

reducing crime (Tierney, Grossman, and Resch, 1995). This program involves matching adult volunteers ("Bigs") with children ("Littles") based on their shared interests and commitment to forming a relationship that will last at least a year. Program staff screen and train mentors and supervise relationships to ensure that both parties and children's parents are satisfied with the match and that they are regularly meeting.

An evaluation based on data from eight BBBS programs across the USA showed that, after one year of mentoring, youth receiving BBBS were 32% less likely than those in the control group to report hitting someone in the past year. In addition, participants who had not used any illicit substances when the program started were 46% less likely than the control group to report any use by the time the study ended. However, reductions in the onset of substance use were significant only for males from minority racial/ethnic groups, not Caucasians or females (Tierney *et al.*, 1995). A review by WSIPP (Aos *et al.*, 2004) reported effect sizes on crime to be about zero. The initial effect size of 0.10 was adjusted to 0.00 because WSIPP considered "hitting someone" to be fairly minor delinquency and not highly predictive of future criminal involvement. Unadjusted effect sizes for the initiation of alcohol and illicit substance use were larger, at 0.19 and 0.17, respectively. WSIPP (Aos *et al.*, 2004) considers BBBS to be cost beneficial, with a return of $3.28 for every dollar invested in the program, based on its demonstrated reductions in substance use and improvements in children's academic success.

The **Keep Safe** program is designed for children living with foster care families. It involves six sessions for children offered the summer before they enter middle school. Program content focuses on improving peer relationships, setting goals, and fostering effective decision-making. Parents also receive six sessions to help them more effectively set and enforce rules for children. The program has been evaluated in Oregon with mostly non-Hispanic, Caucasian girls. In this study, girls who received Keep Safe, compared to those in the control group, reported less use of illegal substances (tobacco, alcohol, and marijuana) three years after the program ended. The effect size for the combined measure of illegal substance use was 0.47. When examined individually, only tobacco and marijuana use were significantly reduced; alcohol use was not changed. The study also showed a reduction in self-reported property and violent offenses for participants versus the control group. The effect size was 0.36 but only marginally significant, suggesting small reductions in delinquency (Kim and Leve, 2011).

The goal of the **ATLAS** program is to reduce illegal substance use and use of anabolic steroids among male athletes. The program is taught by sports coaches and integrated into team practice sessions. Sessions focus on sharing information about the negative impact of drug use on sports performance. They also try to promote health via good nutrition and strength training exercise rather than by using diet supplements or steroids. A randomized evaluation showed that, when delivered to mostly Caucasian, male high school football players, the program reduced substance use (alcohol, marijuana, amphetamines, and narcotics) more for participants than for those in the control group one year after the program had ended. Reductions in drinking and driving were also seen at the one-year follow-up (Goldberg *et al.*, 2000). Given that this program was delivered only to males and most were from middle-class families, it is unclear if this approach would benefit female athletes, members of minority racial/ethnic groups or those from lower income backgrounds.

To summarize, we can identify a few specific prevention programs delivered in the hours after school which reduce juvenile crime. However, few rigorous scientific evaluations or cost-benefit analyses of ASPs have been conducted, and the few programs we have identified have been tested with limited gender and racial/ethnic groups. As a result, it is difficult to determine their effectiveness for more diverse populations. It should also be noted that some afterschool programs (especially mentoring) are intended for selective rather than universal populations, such as at-risk youth who may need extra support and skills to avoid crime.

In terms of their dissemination, ASPs reach a large audience. It is likely that every reader of this chapter has participated in such an activity. According to Zief *et al.* (2006), two-thirds of school principals report afterschool programming in their schools and about 11% of all youth in the USA, or 6 million students, regularly participated in such programs in 2002–2003. Mentoring programs are also widespread, with over 5,000 organizations estimated to be delivering some type of mentoring program (Tolan *et al.*, 2014). According to their website (http://www.bbbs.org/site/c.9iILI3NGKhK6F/b.5960955/k.E56C/Starting_something_since_1904.htm), the BBBS program serves about 240,000 children and has offices in every state in the USA and in 11 other countries.

While it is encouraging to see widespread use of BBBS, we suspect that only a very small proportion of all afterschool programming offered to youth is evidence-based. In a national survey of high school administrators (Ringwalt *et al.*, 2008), only 1.2% reported the use of ATLAS with their students. In addition, 21st Century Community Learning Centers (CCLCs) deliver ASPs to large numbers of youth in the USA, with the government spending one *billion* dollars on these centers annually since 2004. Yet, evidence indicates that, on average, youth who participate in the CCLC programs have similar or even higher levels of delinquency compared to those who have not attended such services (James–Burdumy *et al.*, 2008). To summarize, we have a long way to go in order to increase the use of effective afterschool programs.

School-based curricula

School is not just for learning about reading, math, or science. It can also be an effective setting for preventing the onset of crime. In fact, schools are often used to deliver crime prevention programming. In part, this is due to the fact that youth are mandated to attend school, so we can reach lots of children with school-based prevention services. Programs can also be delivered cost effectively, as most are taught by teachers who are already paid to be in the classroom. Finally, the delivery of such programs can also benefit schools' primary mission of improving academics, as research indicates that behavioral problems can reduce students' academic success and interfere with the learning processes of other children (Durlak *et al.*, 2011).

In Chapter 7, we discussed school-based prevention practices and policies which try to alter the school context, such as the structure, climate, policies, or norms of the school. Effective interventions of this sort reduce student involvement in crime indirectly by changing aspects of the larger school environment that are likely to influence individual behavior. In this chapter, we

> *We cannot always build the future for our youth, but we can build our youth for the future.*
>
> Franklin D. Roosevelt

Table 8.3 Effective school-based prevention programs.

Effective practice?		Inconclusive	
Effective programs	Rating by Blueprints	Rating by the Coalition	Rating by CrimeSolutions.gov
Life Skills Training	Model	Top Tier	Effective
Project Towards No Drug Abuse	Model	Not rated	Promising
PATHS	Model	Not rated	Effective
Positive Action	Model	Not rated	Effective
Good Behavior Game	Promising	Near Top Tier	Effective
Achievement Mentoring	Promising	Not rated	Not rated
Sport	Promising	Not rated	Not rated
Safe Dates	Promising	Not rated	Effective

focus on programs intended to have a more direct impact on individuals. These interventions are targeted directly at students with the goal of teaching them strategies to avoid crime. Many of these programs are taught just like academic curricula: by teachers, during regular classroom periods and for multiple sessions spread over a few weeks, months, or even the entire school year. Unlike some academic subjects, which may be taught via lectures, school prevention programs often use classroom discussions and role-plays to better engage students and help them practice new skills.

Like afterschool programming, school-based crime prevention programs vary widely in their content and are based on different criminological theories. Many focus on individual risk and protective factors, such as enhancing students' ability to recognize and regulate their emotions, make good decisions, positively respond to stressful situations and resolve conflicts using assertive rather than aggressive behavior. These types of programs are based on **strain theory**, as they help students to avoid stressful situations and/or more effectively cope with strains. School programs that focus on peer risk factors and teach youth skills to resist peer pressures to engage in substance use and delinquency are modeled on **social learning theory**.

Given their diversity, it is difficult to determine if school-based curricula can be considered a general prevention **practice**. Several meta-analyses have investigated the effectiveness of different types of school-based prevention, including programs intended to teach social and emotional learning skills (Durlak et al., 2011), reduce violence (Hahn et al., 2007; Mytton et al., 2006), or prevent substance use (Faggiano et al., 2005; Foxcroft and Tsertsvadze, 2011b). Most of these studies have concluded that the programs being reviewed differ too much in their content, duration, and delivery methods to calculate an average effect size on crime. In other cases, the program evaluations vary too much in how crime is measured, with some combining illegal behaviors with less serious misconduct (e.g., being disruptive in the classroom), such that the overall impact on crime cannot be determined. *Based on these findings, we cannot state with certainty that the general practice of delivering a school-based prevention program will lead to reductions in crime.* We do, however, have many examples of specific, effective school-based programs, as shown in Table 8.3.

Life Skills Training (LST) is a classroom-based curriculum intended to reduce the onset and prevalence of substance use among middle school students. Teachers and/or trained students deliver 30 sessions over three years to improve youths': (i) decision-making and social skills, (ii) ability to resist peer and media pressures to use illegal substances, and (iii) recognition of the harmful consequences of substance use. LST has been tested in several studies with diverse groups of students and has been shown to reduce smoking, drinking, binge drinking, marijuana, and other drug use (Botvin, Griffin, and Nichols, 2006). According to a meta-analysis of the evaluations by WSIPP (2015), the average unadjusted effect sizes of these studies are small: approximately 0.08 to 0.13 for tobacco use, 0.03 to 0.08 for alcohol use, and 0.00 to 0.04 for marijuana use. They report a larger unadjusted effect size for binge drinking (0.25), which is reduced to 0.05 when taking study design issues into account.

LST has been shown to prevent the onset of substance use. In a study in Iowa, 4.3% of LST students reported first using marijuana during the one-year period following the program compared to 7.9% of those in the control group (Spoth et al., 2002). Long-term reductions in the onset and/or frequency of substance use have also been seen; for example, LST students have reported lower rates of drug use when seniors in high school, six years after receiving the program (Botvin et al., 1995). In one such study, New York students who received the curriculum in Grade 7 were less likely as 12th graders to report any smoking in the past month (reported by 26% of students receiving LST and 33% of those in the control group) and fewer instances of getting drunk (reported by 33% of LST youth and 40% of control group youth) (Botvin et al., 1995). For students in Iowa, those receiving LST were less likely to report any cigarette, alcohol, or marijuana use by Grade 12 compared to those in the control group (Spoth et al., 2008).

LST is also effective in reducing the continuity or frequency of substance use. One evaluation reported that, for those who had already used cigarettes, alcohol, or marijuana at the start of the study (in Grade 7), LST students reported less frequent use of all those substances at Grade 12 compared to the control group (Spoth et al., 2008). WSIPP (2015) rates LST as cost beneficial, returning $13.08 for every dollar spent.

Project Towards No Drug Abuse (TND) is 12-session, 3-week program taught by teachers in traditional or alternative high schools serving students with behavioral and/or academic problems. The program seeks to improve students' internal motivation not to use illegal substances and to increase their decision-making, self-control, and communication skills. Several evaluations, which included racially diverse students of both sexes, have shown that TND participation is related to less substance use (for a summary of these studies, see: http://tnd.usc.edu/). In a study conducted in 18 alternative high schools in California, the program was shown to reduce smoking by 27% and marijuana use by 22% (Sussman, Dent, and Stacy, 2002). The most consistent pattern of effects has been found for hard drug use (e.g., use of cocaine, hallucinogens, and stimulants), with intervention students reporting less use of these illicit substances compared to students in the control group, even five years after receiving the program (Sun et al., 2006). Alcohol use has also been reduced, but somewhat less so compared to other types of drugs (Sussman, et al., 2002).

The program appears to reduce the onset of marijuana and hard drug use, but not alcohol use. One study showed that marijuana use was reduced more for TND students versus those in the control group, but only among males who had never used marijuana prior to the start of the program

(Sussman *et al.*, 2003). In another study (Rohrbach, Sun, and Sussman, 2010), hard drug use was reduced only for those who had not yet used drugs at baseline. In terms of alcohol use, one evaluation indicated that TND did not reduce alcohol use for those who had never used alcohol at baseline, but there was a significant, 9% reduction in alcohol use for those who had reported drinking alcohol prior to the start of the study (Sussman *et al.*, 1998; Sussman, *et al.*, 2002). According to WSIPP (2015), TND has small effects on substance use, with unadjusted effect sizes for tobacco, alcohol, marijuana, and hard drug use of 0.04, 0.02, 0.03, and 0.10, respectively. The program is cost beneficial, returning $7.63 for every dollar spent.

The **Promoting Alternative Thinking Strategies (PATHS)** program is a comprehensive, multi-year program designed to reduce aggression and behavior problems by improving social and emotional competence in elementary school-age children. Developmentally appropriate lessons are taught 2–3 times per week by classroom teachers each year of elementary school to improve students' self-control, emotional understanding, self-esteem, healthy relationships, and interpersonal problem-solving skills. Homework assignments and information for parents are provided in order to increase parents' involvement (Crean and Johnson, 2013).

PATHS has been evaluated many times, in randomized trials conducted in the USA and in Europe. In one multi-site study, classrooms receiving the PATHS program in Grade 1 had lower rates of aggression compared to classrooms not receiving the program, with an effect size of 0.22 (Conduct Problems Prevention Research Group, 1999). Reductions in aggression were also seen in Grade 3, after three years of program implementation (Conduct Problems Prevention Research Group, 2010). Similar results were demonstrated in a replication taking place in Zurich, Switzerland, with intervention students showing greater decreases in aggression from Grades 2–4 compared to students in the control condition, with an effect size of 0.42 (Malti, Ribeaud, and Eisner, 2012). According to WSIPP (2015), PATHS is cost beneficial, returning $15.66 for every dollar spent. However, its impact on externalizing behaviors is small, as the unadjusted effect size across studies is 0.03 and not statistically significant.

Similar to PATHS, **Positive Action** is a comprehensive, multi-year program involving short classroom sessions taught two to four times a week throughout elementary and/or middle school. The program is designed to help students develop social and emotional skills, including their ability to make good decisions, regulate their emotions, communicate with others, set goals and follow through with commitments. Healthy physical behavior is also promoted by teaching students about the importance of nutrition, exercise, and adequate sleep. The school principal and all school staff help reinforce the messages students receive in the classroom.

Two evaluations involving relatively large numbers of students in Hawaii and Chicago have shown reductions in violence and substance use for students receiving the program compared to those in the control group. Neither evaluation specifically examined reductions in the onset of offending, but rather assessed the program's impact on participation in crime. In the Hawaii study, 5th graders receiving Positive Action had less self-reported violent behavior compared to those in the control group, with effect sizes ranging from 0.57 (for reports of carrying a gun) to 0.89 (for shooting someone). They were also less likely to report substance use, including smoking, drinking, and other drug use, with effect sizes ranging from 0.41 to 0.99 (Beets *et al.*, 2009). In Chicago, a 36% reduction in self-reported violence was found when comparing intervention and control group students at Grade 5 (Li *et al.*, 2011), and less violence (an effect size of 0.54) was also reported when students were in Grade 8 (Lewis *et al.*, 2013). This study also showed a 31% reduction in substance use at Grade 5 (Li *et al.*, 2011) and less drug use in Grade 8, with an effect size of 0.27. At Grade 8, 39% of students in Positive Action schools reported having ever used alcohol compared to 55% of those in the control group (Lewis *et al.*, 2012).

A meta-analysis of evaluations of Positive Action conducted by WSIPP (2015) indicated average adjusted effect sizes of 0.13 for smoking, 0.16 for alcohol use, 0.13 for marijuana use, and 0.29 for use of hard drugs, indicating small to moderate reductions in substance use among program participants. WSIPP reports that for every dollar spent on the program, there is a return of $20.57.

The **Good Behavior Game (GBG)** is designed to promote students' positive behavior by improving teachers' classroom management skills and encouraging positive peer influences. Because it seeks to change peer interactions and classroom dynamics, the GBG can also be considered a social context program, but we describe it in this chapter rather than Chapter 7 because evaluations have assessed changes in students' individual behaviors, not school-wide effects on crime. The program is typically implemented in first or second grade. The primary component involves the implementation of the "game." At the start of the school year, teachers and students jointly agree upon rules and standards for what constitutes proper classroom behavior. The class is then divided into teams of students balanced according to gender and student behavior. For the rest of the year, teachers periodically provide verbal praise and tangible rewards to the team whose members as a whole show the most positive behaviors. As the year progresses, the game becomes less predictable in terms of when teachers monitor and provide incentives. The goal is for students to learn to display good behavior frequently and with no certain expectation of rewards. The program also involves instruction to improve math and reading skills.

The GBG has been evaluated several times, with some of the longest follow-up periods of any program reviewed in this book. One of the first studies involved 1,084 1st grade students attending 19 inner-city Baltimore schools who were randomly assigned to participate in the GBG or to a control group. Program effects were shown only for a subset of students receiving GBG. Specifically, boys for whom teachers reported ongoing aggressive behavior from Grades 1–7 were less likely to have a diagnosis of antisocial personality disorder *and* officially recorded crime by young adulthood (ages 19–21) compared to boys in the control condition who were also rated as aggressive (Petras *et al.*, 2008). A second evaluation involving mostly low-income, African American students from Baltimore indicated that program participants were less likely to initiate smoking by Grade 7, with 26% reporting any use of tobacco compared to 33% of those in the control group (Storr *et al.*, 2002). They were also less likely to initiate tobacco use, with 34% of GBG compared to 47% of the control group reporting smoking at Grade 8, and to use hard drug use at this time (rates of 3% and 7%, respectively) (Furr-Holden *et al.*, 2004). When tested in the Netherlands, GBG students reported a moderate reduction in victimization by peers at age 10, compared to those in the control group, with an effect size of 0.35 (Van Lier, Vuijk, and Crijnen, 2005). This study also showed less tobacco and alcohol use from ages 10–13 for GBG compared to control group students (Van Lier, Huizink, and Crijnen, 2009).

According to WSIPP (2015), evaluations of GBG have shown average, unadjusted effect sizes of 0.11 for crime, 0.23 for the initiation of smoking, and 0.59 for regular smoking, but the adjusted effects are substantially reduced, at 0.04, 0.09, and 0.23, respectively. Nonetheless, these findings and additional positive effects on mental health problems and drug addiction result in GBG being very cost beneficial, returning $58.56 for every dollar spent.

The goal of the **Achievement Mentoring – Middle School** program (formerly known as **Behavioral Monitoring and Reinforcement**) is to improve middle and junior high school students' academic performance and reduce offending. The program provides increased and regular monitoring of adolescents' behavior, rewards for positive behavior and disincentives for poor behavior. By emphasizing increased controls on and reinforcements for behavior, the program is guided by **social control theory**. Over a two-year period, program staff: (i) create weekly "report cards" using information from school records and teachers regarding students' school behavior (attendance, discipline referrals, classroom behavior, and school performance); (ii) meet with students in small groups to discuss their report cards and recommend strategies to improve behaviors; and (iii) provide students with "points" for good behaviors that can be used to earn rewards at the end of the school year, such as a school trip to a destination of their choice.

A randomized trial in New Jersey showed that, one year after the program ended, students reported less hard drug use and less participation in delinquency. More specifically, 11 program students reported a total of 19 delinquent acts, compared to 45 offenses disclosed by 18 members of the control group. Five years after the program ended, there was a 66% reduction in officially recorded juvenile crimes, with three of the intervention and nine of the control group students having a criminal record (Bry, 1982). Note that these evaluations investigated changes in criminal participation, not reductions in the onset of offending, so it is unclear if this program delays onset. WSIPP (2015) reports that Achievement Mentoring has a relatively small effect on crime, with an adjusted effect size of 0.21 (the unadjusted effect size is 0.56). However, the intervention is cost beneficial, returning $4.29 for every dollar spent.

The **Sport** program attempts to promote healthy behaviors among high school students, especially increased physical activity and reduced substance use. During the school day, students are pulled out of class to complete a short questionnaire assessing their health and fitness practices. Then they meet one-on-one with a health care professional to discuss ways to improve health, are assigned a "prescription" with recommendations for improving their health and fitness, and are mailed a summary of this information as a reminder to keep working on their goals.

Based on a randomized trial involving students in Florida, the program was shown to delay the initiation and frequency of alcohol use at post-test and to reduce the initiation and frequency of smoking one year after the program ended (Werch et al., 2005). But, 18 months after the start of the study, the only participants who showed benefits were those who had smoked and used marijuana prior to the start of the study; that is, their onset of drug use had already occurred. These students showed lower frequencies of alcohol and marijuana use and less binge drinking compared to students in the control group who had already initiated substance use at baseline (Moore and Werch, 2009). These results suggest that the Sport program is less effective in delaying the onset of substance use and more effective in reducing levels of use among those who begin to use drugs relatively early in adolescence. According to WSIPP (2015), SPORT is cost beneficial, returning $34.57 for every dollar spent.

Unlike any of the programs reviewed so far, the goal of **Safe Dates** is to reduce violence in adolescent romantic relationships, a problem estimated to affect about 10% of all high school students involved in such relationships (Kann *et al.*, 2014). The program includes 10 lessons taught by teachers or health specialists to all 8th or 9th grade students. Participants learn and discuss how to maintain healthy relationships, communicate effectively with their dating partners, control anger, and manage conflicts. Based on a RCT in North Carolina, by the 12th grade, program participants reported between 56% and 92% less physical and sexual violence against a romantic partner than controls and lower rates of being victimized by a partner compared to those in the control group (Foshee *et al.*, 2005).

Given that a number of effective school-based programs exist, how likely are schools to implement such interventions? Although the evidence is somewhat mixed, our conclusion is that most schools are unlikely to be implementing effective crime prevention curricula. In a national survey of principals in US middle schools in 2008, 47% reported using at least one evidence-based substance use prevention program, which represented an increased use of effective programs since the prior decade (Ringwalt *et al.*, 2011). Of the specific programs mentioned in this chapter, 19.3% of school administrators reported the use of **LST** and 4.5% reported using **Positive Action**. Indeed, the **LST** program seems to be the most widely disseminated of all the evidence based-programs we reviewed. According to the LST website (http://www.lifeskillstraining.com/global-reach.php), the program has been taught by 50,000 teachers in 10,000 schools and reached 3 million students. It is used in all states in the USA and in 36 other countries.

Now for the bad news. According to a 2005 survey of high school administrators, only 10% reported that their school used an evidence-based substance abuse prevention program (Ringwalt *et al.*, 2008). Only 1.2% of administrators reported using **ATLAS**, 1.5% reported **Positive Action**, and 2.2% nominated **Project TND**. According to a different national survey, asking middle and high school administrators about their use of substance abuse prevention programs from 2001–2007, 55% reported using the **Drug Abuse and Resistance Education** (D.A.R.E.) program (Kumar *et al.*, 2013). This is very discouraging, given that, as you will learn shortly, D.A.R.E. is not effective in reducing illicit substance use. Lastly, national studies indicate that schools implement an average of 14 different delinquency prevention activities (Gottfredson and Gottfredson, 2002) and nine different substance abuse prevention programs (US Department of Education, 2011), but very few can be considered "evidence-based." As a whole, these results suggest that much improvement must be made to ensure that schools deliver effective prevention programming, especially if their goal is to reduce criminal behaviors other than substance use.

Multiple component programs

Programs that include multiple elements and/or deliver material in multiple settings, such as in the school and in the family, are based on the recognition in prevention science that risk and protective factors exist in all areas of children's lives (Catalano *et al.*, 2011; Coie *et al.*, 1993; Hawkins, Catalano, and Miller, 1992), that they may interact with one another to influence criminal behavior (Bronfenbrenner, 2005; Weissberg and Greenberg, 1998), and that the more risk factors and fewer protective factors encountered, the more likely one is to engage in crime (Herrenkohl *et al.*, 2000). Relatedly, if one context does not support the prevention messages or behaviors learned in another context, then their impact is likely to be weakened (Roth and Brooks-Gunn, 2003; Wagenaar and Perry, 1994). For example, if youth learn in a school-based program how to control their emotions

Table 8.4 Effective multi-component prevention practices and programs.

Effective practice?	Inconclusive		
Effective programs	Rating by Blueprints	Rating by the Coalition	Rating by CrimeSolutions.gov
Montreal Longitudinal and Experimental Study	Promising[a]	Promising	Promising
Coping Power	Promising	Not rated	Promising
Raising Healthy Children	Promising	Not rated	Promising
Midwestern Prevention Project	Promising[a]	Not rated	Effective
Project Northland	Promising	Not rated	Promising

[a]Neither of these programs appears to be ready for replication or dissemination using the Blueprints criteria. For these reasons, they are not listed on the Blueprints website. However, the evaluation evidence of each program meets the Blueprints standard to be a Promising program.

and respond to conflict assertively rather than aggressively, but they live in a neighborhood in which youth and adults frequently engage in violence, they may not benefit strongly from the school program. These findings suggest that to produce the greatest effect on crime, a prevention program should target for change multiple factors across multiple settings. This view is also supported by **integrated theories** of crime, which also emphasize that multiple factors affect delinquency.

Given that they are specifically intended to deliver a variety of strategies in a variety of settings, it is difficult to assess the effectiveness of multi-component approaches as a general prevention practice. We are aware of only one meta-analysis that attempted to do so (Foxcroft and Tsertsvadze, 2011a), and its authors concluded that the programs reviewed were too varied in content, participant characteristics and outcome measures to assess their overall impact on adolescent alcohol use (which was the focus of the meta-analysis). While we do not yet have enough information to recommend the delivery of multi-component programs as an effective crime prevention practice, we can say with confidence that the following five programs prevent criminal behavior; also see Table 8.4.

In Chapter 7, we introduced the **Montreal Longitudinal and Experimental Study (MLES)**, which is a two-year program designed to reduce aggression and crime among a selective population: boys aged 7–9 who are rated by kindergarten teachers as showing impulsive or disruptive behaviors in class. The intervention combines the delivery of a school-based curriculum to affect individual and peer risk and protective factors and training for parents to address family factors. The school program involves lessons for small groups of 5–7 students, including the targeted boys as well as peers who do not have behavioral problems. In these groups, boys learn and practice skills related to self-control, problem solving, and social interaction. For the family component, parents receive home visits to help them recognize children's behavioral problems, set clear rules for behavior and provide appropriate and consistent discipline.

A randomized trial conducted in Montreal assessed changes in crime participation, not onset, all the way to age 28, 19 years after the program ended. In this evaluation, MLES boys, compared to those in the control group, were less likely to report property and violent offenses at ages 11–13 (Vitaro *et al.*, 2013), had a lower frequency of alcohol use at age 13, and used fewer illicit drugs at ages

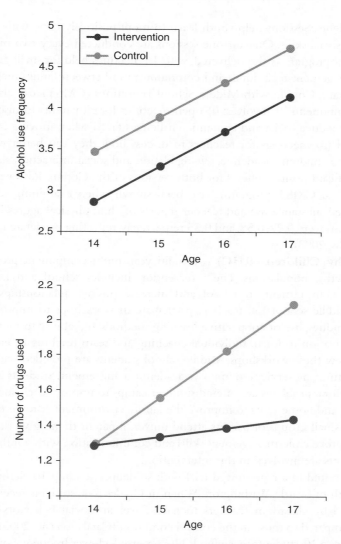

Figure 8.1 Effects on substance use for the MLES. Source: Adapted from Castellanos-Ryan *et al.*, 2013.

14–17 (Castellanos-Ryan *et al.*, 2013). Figure 8.1 shows the significant effects on substance use. At age 24, 22% of those in the intervention group had a criminal record, compared to 33% of the control group boys, a 33% reduction (Boisjoli *et al.*, 2007). In addition, those receiving MLES reported significantly fewer property offenses, but not violent offenses, from ages 17–28. The effect size for this outcome was 0.33, indicating a moderate reduction in property crime (Vitaro *et al.*, 2013).

The **Coping Power** program is also a two-year program designed for a selective population: students rated by their middle school teachers as verbally aggressive, physically aggressive and/or disruptive. It involves the delivery of 22 lessons in Grade 5 and 12 lessons in Grade 6, taught in small groups of 5–8 students. Sessions help youth learn to more positively cope with anger and anxiety and improve their social skills. One-on-one sessions are conducted every two months to reinforce these skills. A parent program is also delivered, with 16 meetings held for small groups of parents to improve child management techniques and communication between family members. A universal school-based program, Coping with Middle School Transitions (CMST), can also be added to the other program components. It involves: (i) open meetings for all parents to discuss ways they can help their children reduce social and academic challenges faced when moving from elementary to middle school, and (ii) meetings for teachers to discuss how they can better communicate with parents and enhance children's academic, self-regulation and social interaction skills (Lochman and Wells, 2002). Significant positive effects for both versions of the Coping Power program (with and without the universal CMST program) have been shown when examining self-reported delinquency, self-reported substance use and teacher reports of child physical aggression. Effect sizes for the standard program were 0.27, 0.58, and 0.35 respectively, reflecting moderate reductions in crime (Lochman and Wells, 2003).

Raising Healthy Children (RHC) is a multi-year, multi-component program delivered to universal and selective populations. The intervention includes school and family programs to improve students' commitment to school and increase positive relationships with parents. In elementary and middle schools, all teachers participate in workshops to improve their classroom management techniques, use of cooperative learning methods and ability to increase students' participation and motivation to learn. Individual coaching and team teaching to ensure that skills are used correctly follow these workshops. Middle school students are provided with opportunities to attend afterschool tutoring services to improve academic achievement. Students identified as having academic or behavioral problems are offered summer camps to improve their social skills and commitment to school and home visits to improve the family environment (Brown *et al.*, 2005). Also in the family setting, small groups of parents attend universal parent training workshops to learn and discuss ways to improve child management skills and communication with youth. Yes, indeed, many different components are involved in this intervention!

RHC has been tested in a randomized trial with students attending 10 elementary schools in a suburban area north of Seattle, Washington. When in Grades 3–4, students receiving the intervention were reported by classroom teachers to have fewer antisocial behaviors (fighting, stealing, vandalism, etc.) compared to those in the control condition (Catalano *et al.*, 2003). The program also showed that, by Grade 10, students receiving RHC reported a lower frequency of alcohol and marijuana use, with effect sizes of 0.40 and 0.57, respectively. As shown in Figure 8.2, although alcohol use became less frequent from Grades 8–10 for all students, those receiving the intervention had a significantly higher rate of decline than those in the control condition. The evaluation showed no differences in reducing the proportion of youth who indicated *any use* of alcohol or marijuana, suggesting that the program was not effective in promoting abstinence of drug use; its effects were limited to reducing the frequency of current users (Brown *et al.*, 2005).

The Midwestern Prevention Project/Project STAR is a five-year substance use prevention program for middle and high school students. It involves delivery of a school curriculum, parent education programming, media campaigns, and local policy changes. A two-year, 10-session social skills training curriculum is taught in Grades 6 and 7 to increase students' knowledge regarding the

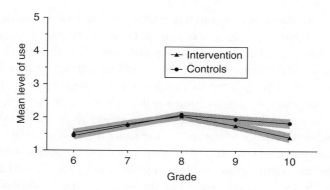

Figure 8.2 Effects on alcohol use for the Raising Healthy Children Program. Source: Brown *et al.*, 2005. Reproduced with permission of the American Psychological Association.

consequences of drug use, enhance their ability to identify and resist peer, adult and media influences to use drugs and encourage them to publically commit to abstaining from drug use. Homework is assigned to promote parent–child communication and parental support of children's commitment to abstain from drugs. Parents also help monitor the school grounds and surrounding neighborhoods to promote a drug-free environment. In the last three years of the intervention, community and local government leaders work together to enact policies that will reduce demand and supply of drugs, such as creating ordinances restricting smoking in public settings, increasing alcohol pricing, and creating drug-free zones. In all five years, television, radio and print media are used to reinforce anti-drug messages.

A quasi-experimental evaluation of MPP in 42 schools in Kansas City showed that it reduced students' substance use. After receiving one year of the school curriculum and media campaign, students in MPP versus comparison schools reported a 7% reduction in smoking, a 3% reduction in drinking, and a 3% reduction in marijuana use (Pentz *et al.*, 1989). Among 9th and 10th graders in eight of the schools, MPP students reported less past month tobacco and marijuana use, but not alcohol use, versus comparison students (Johnson *et al.*, 1990). In the MPP schools, 25% of students reported tobacco use and 12% marijuana use, compared to 31% and 20%, respectively, in the comparison schools. The program has also been shown to reduce the onset of smoking and marijuana use among MPP compared to control group students who had not initiated either substance prior to the start of the study. WSIPP (2015) reports small adjusted effect sizes for alcohol use (0.06), smoking (0.11), and marijuana use (0.12); unadjusted effects are about three times larger. MPP is somewhat cost beneficial, returning $1.56 for every dollar spent.

Project Northland is a 3–6-year program intended to reduce alcohol use among middle and high school students. It includes a school curriculum and extracurricular activities for students, information and meetings for parents, and opportunities for community members to reduce environmental risk factors for youth alcohol use. The three-year middle school curriculum helps youth: (i) communicate with their parents about alcohol use (through 4 lessons in Year 1), (ii) learn to resist peer and social pressures to use alcohol (in 8 sessions in Year 2), and (iii) increase attachments to positive role models in the community (in 8 sessions in Year 3). An evaluation of this program conducted with Caucasian youth in Minnesota showed less drinking for students receiving the program com-pared to those in the control group. At the end of Grade 8, 10.5% of those receiving Project Northland reported drinking in the past week compared to 14.8% of those in the control condition. Reductions in the onset of substance use have also been found (Perry *et al.*, 1996). For those who had not used alcohol or other drugs at the start of the study (in Grade 6), rates of smoking, drinking, and marijuana use were lower for intervention versus control group students, with effect sizes of 0.23, 0.15, and 0.15, respectively (Aos *et al.*, 2004). No effects were shown for students who had already initiated substance use prior to the start of the study (Perry *et al.*, 1996).

An evaluation conducted after students received an additional three years of programming in high school showed that program participants had less binge drinking up to Grade 12 compared to those in the control group. However, no effects were found for other types of alcohol use or for tobacco or marijuana use (Perry *et al.*, 2002). A separate evaluation conducted with African American youth attending schools in low-income neighborhoods in Chicago failed to demonstrate reductions in substance use or in self-reported violence (Komro *et al.*, 2008), indicating that the program might be effective only for Caucasian students from higher income families. Based on outcomes from the Minnesota and Chicago studies, as well as a replication in Croatia, WSIPP (2015) considers Project Northland to be cost beneficial, returning $3.80 for every dollar invested.

Very little information is available on the dissemination of multiple-component programs, but we suspect that use of these interventions is limited. Of the five programs we reviewed, **Project Northland** is the only one currently distributed by a publishing company (Hazelden; http://www.hazelden.org/web/go/projectnorthland). The other three are distributed on a case-by-case basis by the program developers, who are all university researchers. As we will discuss in Chapter 11, dissemi-nation is likely to be enhanced when there is an organization dedicated to publicizing the program, providing materials and helping agencies with implementation. University faculty will have more limited availability and resources to do so compared to a commercial organization, which will restrict program use. Even with a dedicated company marketing the program, dissemination can be challenging. For example, in the 2008 survey of middle school administrators (Ringwalt *et al.*, 2011), only 2.4% reported using Project Northland. These results suggest that there is room for improve-ment in increasing the use of multi-component prevention programs.

Ineffective Interventions

There is some evidence that **afterschool programs (ASPs)** are not an effective crime preven-tion practice. To evaluate the general practice of ASPs, specifically those intended to improve children's social and emotional skills such as problem-solving, conflict resolution, self-control, and decision-making, Durlak *et al.* (2010) conducted a meta-analysis of 69 such programs. The mean effect size on illegal substance use for youth 5–18 years old was small, 0.10, and not statistically significant. A meta-analysis of ASPs designed to enhance academic performance showed no impact on delinquency or substance use (Zief, Lauver, and Maynard, 2006). Although only five evaluations were included in the study, four involved the delivery of many ASPs to relatively large numbers of students. A third review of ASPs, this one analyzing the impact of academic-focused programs delivered to middle school students via 21st Century Community Learning Centers (CCLCs) (http://www2.ed.gov/programs/21stcclc/funding.html) showed no effects on self-reported rates of smoking, drinking, or using marijuana. Likewise, participation in the Centers did not reduce adolescents' self-reported violence, violent victimization, or likelihood of being arrested (Dynarski *et al.*, 2004). The only significant effects indicated *harmful* results for Center participants compared to the comparison group, as they reported more hard drug use (cocaine, ecstasy, or LSD) and a greater frequency of "breaking something on purpose" (James-Burdumy, Dynarski, and Deke, 2008).

Although **mentoring** programs as a general practice, and the BBBS program in particular, have been shown to reduce the onset of offending, the **Cambridge-Somerville Youth Study** has been demonstrated as ineffective. This mentoring program is likely the oldest of all we have reviewed, as it was implemented in the 1940s with 650 boys aged 5–13 from Massachusetts considered to be at risk for delinquency. Boys randomly assigned to the intervention received one-on-one counseling and tutoring from social workers, who also conducted home visits with parents. Recreational activities, including summer camps, were also offered to boys (Gottfredson, 2010; McCord, 2003). Thirty years later, according to official crime records, the intervention and control groups did not differ in terms of having ever been convicted of a crime, the number of serious crimes committed or the age of first offense (McCord, 1978). Additional analyses indicated that, as adults, intervention males who attended summer camps had at least twice had more contact with law enforcement compared to those in the control group (Dishion, McCord, and Poulin, 1999).

Although the specific reasons for the iatrogenic effects are unclear, McCord (2003) speculated that deviancy training, discussed in Chapter 7, was one possibility. In particular, the summer camps provided large amounts of unsupervised time in which boys could "brag about" their deviance and encourage one another to be more delinquent. Based on these types of findings, Dodge and colleagues (2006) recommend that interventions refrain from grouping together adolescents who are at risk for engaging in delinquency, minimize the amount of time adolescents spend in groups and reduce unstructured time spent by youth without intensive supervision and monitoring by adults.

Another program whose iatrogenic effects are hypothesized to be due to deviancy training is the school-based **Reconnecting Youth (RY)** intervention. The goal of RY is to improve academic performance, decrease the likelihood of school dropout and reduce substance use and delinquency among high-risk adolescents: those who have high rates of school truancy, low grades and involvement in illegal substance use. These students enroll in a semester-long class taught to small groups of 10–12 students. The program content focuses on increasing individual self-esteem, self-control, and decision-making skills. In addition, based on **social control** theory, teachers are trained to show concern for and provide social support to students to help "reconnect" them to the school (Sanchez *et al.*, 2007) and to model positive, empathetic behaviors in the hope that students will also learn to trust and care about one another. Although an initial evaluation showed the program to be effective in increasing contact with positive peers and decreasing substance use, a replication showed no significant effects on delinquency or substance use. Moreover, increasing students' contact and bonding with each other led to increased exposure to delinquent peers and less contact with prosocial peers (Cho, Hallfors, and Sanchez, 2005; Hallfors *et al.*, 2006). Based on this evidence, CrimeSolutions.gov has identified RY as having No Effects.

Two other school-based drug prevention programs have been demonstrated as ineffective. Likely the best-known example of this type is **Drug Abuse Resistance Education (D.A.R.E.)**.

Perhaps you have participated in this program, which is widely implemented in the USA and has even spread to 44 other countries (http://www.dare.org/d-a-r-e-international/)? For those of you who have not experienced it, the program relies on uniformed police officers to provide information to middle school students about illegal drugs and their harmful effects. It also teaches students skills to resist peer pressures to use substances (e.g., by just saying "no" to drugs). Despite its popularity, there is clear evidence that D.A.R.E. is not effective. Several evaluations of this program indicate that the program has very few, very small, and very short-lived effects on substance use (Rosenbaum, 2007).

> *DARE is a complete fraud on the American people, and has actually done a lot of harm by preventing the implementation of more effective programs.*
>
> Rodney Anderson, former mayor of Salt Lake City, 2000

One of the first studies to assess the long-term impact of the D.A.R.E. program showed no effects on self-reported delinquency or on substance use five years after intervention youth had received the curriculum. Worse, among participants living in suburban areas, D.A.R.E. students had *higher* rates of substance use compared to those in the control group (Rosenbaum and Hanson, 1998). Harmful effects were also demonstrated in the most recent evaluation of the program (Sloboda et al., 2009), even though the curriculum being studied had been revised (and re-named "Taking Charge of Your Life") to be more similar in content and delivery methods to some of the evidence-based programs discussed earlier. This evaluation indicated that, in 11th grade, two years after the program ended, students who had received D.A.R.E reported more smoking, drinking, and binge drinking compared to those in the control group. For example, 28% of those receiving D.A.R.E. reported binge drinking compared to 25% of those in the control group. Additional analyses showed that the program was especially harmful for those who did not use alcohol or cigarettes at the start of the study (when in Grade 7). In other words, the program *increased* the onset of smoking, drinking, binge drinking and getting drunk among students who were initially abstainers. These types of results led Rosenbaum (2007) to state that we should "Just say no to D.A.R.E." We concur that programs should definitely be discontinued when the evidence clearly indicates they are ineffective and harmful.

Project Alert is another example of school-based program with little evidence of effectiveness in reducing adolescent substance use and some evidence of iatrogenic effects. This two-year curriculum had been rated as Promising by Blueprints based on early evidence of effectiveness. Its first evaluation showed that, after receiving the program in 7th and 8th grades, Project Alert students reported less smoking and marijuana use among those who had not previously engaged in substance use at the start of the study compared to those in the control group, but these effects were no longer present by Grade 12 (Ellickson and Bell, 1990). The second study, involving 7th and 8th graders in South Dakota, showed more promise, reducing smoking and marijuana use by the end of Grade 8. However, the longer term impact was never assessed (Ellickson et al., 2003). Two subsequent studies showed weak evidence of effectiveness, with only one significant impact on substance use evidenced in each evaluation. In the first study, students receiving the program reported lower rates of drinking than those in the control group (Ringwalt et al., 2009), but the second study showed *higher* rates of marijuana use for those receiving the program (St. Pierre et al., 2005).

The overall pattern of weak results, and the presence of iatrogenic effects, resulted in the program being removed from the Blueprints website. As with D.A.R.E., however, schools continue to provide this curriculum to their students. According to its website (www.projectalert.com), Alert is used in all 50 states and reaches more than one million students each year. In a 2008 survey of middle school administrators (Ringwalt *et al.*, 2011), Alert was the second most nominated program, behind LST, with 19% of administrators reporting its use.

Need for Further Research

This review of programs, practices, and policies intended to reduce the onset of crime has both encouraging and discouraging implications for crime prevention. The most positive news is that there are multiple ways to ensure that young people refrain from offending. We identified many programs and some practices that reduce the onset of and participation in crime. Even though some of the reported effects were small in size, use of these programs can still produce substantial benefits for society. As just one example, reductions in cigarette smoking of 15% to 27% produced by the LST program can prevent 60,000–100,000 tobacco-related deaths (Botvin *et al.*, 1995). In addition, by preventing the onset of substance use and crime, we are likely to decrease the numbers of individuals who end up regularly using or abusing illegal substances and continuing to break the law into their adult years.

In some cases, these programs and practices are already known to and being used by practitioners, which we believe to be the ultimate goal of crime prevention. Moreover, by using such programs, we can save money. Reducing the onset of substance use and crime means that our society will, in the long run, spend less money on drug treatment services and the criminal justice system. In addition, by helping participants replace illegal behaviors with positive behaviors, like successfully graduating from school and getting jobs, we can realize financial benefits.

The bad news is that the list of well-evaluated and effective interventions is relatively short. Only a few early childhood education and afterschool programs have strong evidence that they reduce the onset of crime, few effective practices exist and we did not identify any effective policies in this area. We also have a lack of evidence regarding the **external validity** of some interventions. In some cases, programs and practices have been evaluated with, or are shown to be effective only for particular groups, so that we do not yet know if they will reduce the onset of offending if implemented with the general population. Clearly, there is a need for more interventions to be created and evaluated in high-quality, scientific studies.

More international prevention research is also needed. Almost every intervention described in this chapter was created and tested in the USA. Although rates of crime are higher in the USA than in many countries, other nations consider crime to be a social problem that must be addressed. It is important that programs deemed effective in the USA be replicated and tested for effectiveness in other countries and that other nations design and test locally developed interventions. Until more research of this type is conducted, we will have a limited understanding of what works to prevent crime in other countries.

Finally, the information reviewed in this chapter indicates that we have achieved only limited progress in disseminating effective programs. Not only is it uncommon for communities to use effective interventions, but "business as usual" usually means implementing untested or even ineffective prevention programs. Indeed, we know that nearly every community has a Head Start program, nearly every school implements some type of drug or crime prevention program and nearly every town offers afterschool activities. Yet, how many of these services has convincing evidence of effectiveness? We suspect very few. We also know that in the USA, implementation of D.A.R.E. is very common, despite the well-publicized fact that it does not reduce adolescent substance use and that participation may lead to *increased* drug use.

We will return to this subject in Chapter 11, when we discuss how to increase knowledge about and use of effective crime prevention programs, practices, and policies. Fortunately, some progress is being made. It is a very positive sign that, in the USA, the government is beginning to make funding contingent upon the use of effective and evidence-based services. Now, we have to make sure that "evidence-based" means that high-quality, rigorous, scientific studies have been conducted and shown to reduce involvement in crime.

Summary

This chapter provided information about prevention programs, practices, and policies that show strong evidence of preventing or delaying the onset of offending. Given that the onset of crime is likely to occur prior to adulthood, the interventions described in this chapter focused primarily on children and adolescents, although some also involved parents, teachers and/or community members. The interventions utilized various methods to prevent crime, but all were shown in rigorous scientific evaluations to reduce at least one type of criminal behavior. Such evidence is consistent with the fact that many theories of crime have been developed and, taken as a whole, indicate that many factors affect likelihood of crime. Thus, we have many options when it comes to preventing crime.

This chapter also provided information on ineffective crime prevention programs and practices, some of which are being used in communities every day, at least in the USA. Although such interventions were no doubt designed and tested with good intentions, the strong evidence that they fail to reduce crime, and that they may sometimes increase offending among participants, should lead to their being discontinued. Just as we want to see increased use of effective interventions, we must try to stop the use of ineffective programs. To do otherwise will undermine our attempts to significantly reduce rates of crime, and, more importantly, harm the very individuals we are trying to help.

Critical Thinking Questions and Practice Activities

1. There is often some reluctance among the public to implement universal prevention programs such as those described in this chapter. Youth crime, especially behaviors like smoking, drinking, fighting, and vandalism are often considered to be a normal part of growing up, and people may not feel it is necessary or worthwhile to spend money to prevent these behaviors. Imagine that you have to convince someone who holds such negative views that it is important to implement universal prevention programs. List the arguments you would make, drawing upon the life

course development paradigm and criminal career research reviewed in Chapter 3 and the positive results of the studies described in this chapter.

2. Even more specifically, there is often strong opposition to implementing the school-based prevention programs we describe in this chapter. Why do you think this resistance exists? Identify the specific reasons why school administrators, teachers, parents, and students may object to the implementation of these programs. Then, state the main argument or reason you would provide when trying to convince each group to support these programs.

3. Why do you think ineffective programs, practices, and policies are used so often?

4. Considering all the information you learned in this chapter, what were you most surprised to learn? Why? What was least surprising to you? That is, what information did you already know or suspect to be true?

5. Reflect on what you have learned about effective and ineffective interventions in this chapter. Identify three characteristics that appear to be common across many or most of the effective programs and practices described, taking into account their theoretical basis, content, methods of delivery, length, or other features. Then, identify three characteristics that appear to be shared by the ineffective interventions described in this chapter.

Endnote

1. Although we would prefer to limit this review to evaluations using the first and more rigorous approach, doing so would significantly reduce the number of effective interventions that we could discuss in this chapter. To avoid having too little to report, we will discuss programs evaluated using the second approach as well as the first. Because we focus on universal and selective interventions, most of which are implemented with young children, we have to make some assumptions that the intervention reduced the onset of crime. In cases when the evaluation clearly indicates that participants with criminal records were omitted from analyses, we do not have to make this assumption and will say with certainty that the program prevented the onset of offending.

Helpful Websites (last accessed August 7, 2016)

*   http://developingchild.harvard.edu/index.php/resources/multimedia/videos/inbrief_series/inbrief_science_of_ecd/
    The Center on the Developing Child website, sponsored by Harvard University, discusses the importance of early childhood and the need for effective interventions implemented during this stage of the life course.
*   http://www.episcenter.psu.edu/
    The EpisCenter website has useful information intended to help agencies and program providers implement prevention programs, including program logic models, frequently asked questions (and answers to them!), research summaries, tools for monitoring and evaluating programs and advice on how to receive training in the models.
*   http://www.drugabuse.gov/publications/preventing-drug-abuse-among-children-adolescents-in-brief/prevention-principles
    The National Institute on Drug Abuse discusses the need for school and community-based programs to prevent the onset of substance use.

Further Reading

- Gottfredson, D. C. 2007. Some thoughts about research on youth violence prevention. *American Journal of Preventive Medicine*, 33:S104–106.
  Short commentary on the strengths and challenges of school-based violence prevention programs.
- Gottfredson, D. C., Cross, A., and Soule, D. A. 2007. Distinguishing characteristics of effective and ineffective after-school programs to prevent delinquency and victimization. *Criminology and Public Policy*, 6:289–318.
  Discusses the strengths and weaknesses of afterschool programs based on an evaluation of services in Maryland.
- Ringwalt, C., Vincus, A. A., Hanley, S., et al. 2011. The prevalence of evidence-based drug use prevention curricula in US middle schools in 2008. *Prevention Science*, 12:63–69.
  Discusses the dissemination of school-based drug prevention programs in the United States based on a national survey of school administrators and staff.
- Yoshikawa, H. *et al.* 2013. *Investing in Our Future: The Evidence Base on Preschool Education.* New York, NY/Ann Arbor, MI: Foundation for Child Development/Society for Research in Child Development.
  Summarizes research related to the impact of early childhood education services on children's lives.

References

Aos, S., Lieb, R., Mayfield, J., Miller, M., and Pennucci, A. 2004. Benefits and costs of prevention and early intervention programs for youth. Olympia, WA: Washington State Institute for Public Policy.

Beets, M. W., Flay, B. R., Vuchinich, S., *et al.* 2009. Use of a social and character development program to prevent substance use, violent behaviors, and sexual activity among elementary-school students in Hawaii. *American Journal of Public Health*, 99:1438–1445. doi: 10.2105/AJPH.2008.142919

Belfield, C. R., Nores, M., Barnett, S., and Schweinhart, L. 2006. The High/Scope Perry Preschool Program: Cost-benefit analysis using data from the age-40 followup. *The Journal of Human Resources*, 41:162–190.

Boisjoli, R., Vitaro, F., Lacourse, E., Barker, E. D., and Tremblay, R. 2007. Impact and clinical significance of a preventive intervention for disruptive boys: 15-year follow-up. *The British Journal of Psychiatry*, 191:415–419.

Botvin, G. J., Griffin, K. W., and Diaz Nichols, T. 2006. Preventing youth violence and delinquency through a universal school-based prevention approach. *Prevention Science*, 7:403–408.

Botvin, G. J., Baker, E., Dusenbury, L., Botvin, E. M., and Diaz, T. 1995. Long-term follow-up results of a randomized drug abuse prevention trial in a white middle-class population. *Journal of the American Medical Association*, 273:1106–1112.

Bronfenbrenner, U. (ed.). 2005. *Making Human Beings Human: Bioecological Perspectives on Human Development.* Thousand Oaks, CA: Sage.

Brown, E. C., Catalano, R. F., Fleming, C. B., Haggerty, K. P., and Abbott, R. D. 2005. Adolescent substance use outcomes in the Raising Healthy Children project: A two-part latent growth curve analysis. *Journal of Consulting and Clinical Psychology*, 73:699–710.

Bry, B. H. 1982. Reducing the incidence of adolescent problems through preventive intervention: One- and five-year follow-up. *American Journal of Community Psychology*, 10:265–276.

Castellanos-Ryan, N., Seguin, J. R., Vitaro, F., Parent, S., and Tremblay, R. 2013. Impact of a 2-year multimodal intervention for disruptive 6-year-olds on substance use in adolescence: Randomised controlled trial. *The British Journal of Psychiatry*, 203:188–195.

Catalano, R. F., Haggerty, K. P., Hawkins, J. D., and Elgin, J. 2011. Prevention of substance use and substance use disorders: The role of risk and protective factors. In: Y. Kaminer and K. C. Winters (eds), *Clinical Manual of Adolescent Substance Abuse Treatment*, pp. 25–63. Washington, DC: American Psychiatric Publishing.

Catalano, R. F., Mazza, J. J., Harachi, T. W., *et al.* 2003. Raising healthy children through enhancing social development in elementary school: Results after 1.5 years. *Journal of School Psychology*, 41:143–164. doi: 10.1016/S0022-4405(03)00031-1

Cho, H., Hallfors, D. D., and Sanchez, V. 2005. Evaluation of a high school peer group intervention for at-risk youth. *Journal of Abnormal Child Psychology*, 33:363–374.

Coie, J. D., Watt, N. F., West, S. G., *et al.* 1993. The science of prevention: A conceptual framework and some directions for a national research program. *American Psychologist*, 48:1013–1022.

Conduct Problems Prevention Research Group. 1999. Initial impact of the Fast Track Prevention Trial for conduct problems: II. Classroom effects. *Journal of Consulting and Clinical Psychology*, 67:648–657.

Conduct Problems Prevention Research Group. 2010. The effects of a multiyear universal social–emotional learning program: The role of student and school characteristics. *Journal of Consulting and Clinical Psychology*, 78:156–168. doi: 10.1037/a0018607

Crean, H. F., and Johnson, D. B. 2013. Promoting Alternative Thinking Strategies (PATHS) and elementary school aged children's aggression: Results from a cluster randomized trial. *American Journal of Community Psychology*, 52:56–72.

Cross, A. B., Gottfredson, D. C., Wilson, D. M., Rorie, M., and Connell, N. 2009. The impact of after-school programs on the routine activities of middle-school students: Results from a randomized, controlled trial. *Criminology and Public Policy*, 8:391–412.

Dishion, T. J., McCord, J., and Poulin, F. 1999. When interventions do harm: Peer groups and problem behavior. *American Psychologist*, 54:755–764.

Dodge, K. A., Dishion, T. J., and Lansford, J. E. 2006. Deviant peer influences in intervention and public policy for youth. In: *Social Policy Report*: Society for Research in Child Development.

Duncan, G. J., and Magnuson, K. 2004. Individual and parent-based intervention strategies for promoting human capital and positive behavior. In: P. L. Chase-Lansdale, K. Kiernan, and R. J. Friedman (eds), *Human Development Across Lives and Generations: The Potential For Change*, pp. 93–135. New York, NY: Cambridge University Press.

Durlak, J., Weissberg, R. P., and Pachan, M. 2010. A meta-analysis of after-school programs that seek to promote personal and social skills in children and adolescents. *American Journal of Community Psychology*, 45:294–209.

Durlak, J. A., Dymnicki, A. B., Taylor, R. D., Weissberg, R. P., and Schellinger, K. B. 2011. The impact of enhancing students' social and emotional learning: A meta-analysis of school-based universal interventions. *Child Development*, 82:405–432.

Dynarski, M., James-Burdumy, S., Moore, M., *et al.* 2004. When schools stay open late: The national evaluation of the 21st Century Community Learning Centers Program: New findings. Washington, DC: US Department of Education, National Center for Education Evaluation and Regional Assistance.

Ellickson, P., and Bell, R. M. 1990. Drug prevention in junior high: A multi-site longitudinal test. *Science*, 247:1299–1305.

Ellickson, P. L., McCaffrey, D. F., Ghosh-Dastidar, B., and Longshore, D. L. 2003. New inroads in preventing adolescent drug use: Results from a large-scale trial of Project ALERT in middle schools. *American Journal of Public Health*, 93:1830–1836.

Faggiano, F., Vigna-Taglianti, F., Versino, E., *et al.* 2005. School-based prevention for illicit drugs use. *Cochrane Database of Systematic Reviews*, (2):CD003020.

Farrington, D. P., and Welsh, B. C. 2003. Family-based prevention of offending: A meta-analysis. *Australian and New Zealand Journal of Criminology*, 36:127–151.

Foshee, V. A., Bauman, K. E., Ennett, S. T., *et al.* 2005. Assessing the effects of the dating violence prevention program "Safe Dates" using random coefficient regression modeling. *Prevention Science*, 6:245–258. doi: 10.1007/s11121-005-0007-0

Foxcroft, D. R., and Tsertsvadze, A. 2011a. Universal multi-component prevention programs for alcohol misuse in young people. *Cochrane Database of Systematic Reviews*, (9):CD009307.

Foxcroft, D. R., and Tsertsvadze, A. 2011b. Universal school-based prevention programs for alcohol misuse in young people. *Cochrane Database of Systematic Reviews*, (5):CD009113.

Furr-Holden, C. D. M., Ialongo, N. S., Anthony, J. C., *et al.* 2004. Developmentally inspired drug prevention: Middle school outcomes in a school-based randomized prevention trial. *Drug and Alcohol Dependence*, 73:149–158. doi: 10.1016/j.drugalcdep.2003.10.002

Goldberg, L., MacKinnon, D. P., Elliot, D. L., *et al.* 2000. The Adolescents Training and Learning to Avoid Steroids program. *Archives of Pediatric and Adolescent Medicine*, 154:332–338.

Gottfredson, D. C. 2010. Deviancy training: Understanding how preventive interventions harm: The Academy of Experimental Criminology 2009 Joan McCord Award Lecture. *Journal of Experimental Criminology*, 6:229–243.

Gottfredson, D. C., and Gottfredson, G. D. 2002. Quality of school-based prevention programs: Results from a national survey. *Journal of Research in Crime and Delinquency*, 39:3–35.

Hahn, R., Fuqua-Whitley, D., Wethington, H., *et al.* 2007. Effectiveness of universal school-based programs to prevent violence and aggressive behavior: A systematic review. *American Journal of Preventive Medicine*, 33:S114–S129.

Hallfors, D. D., Cho, H., Sanchez, V., *et al.* 2006. Efficacy vs. effectiveness trial results of an indicated "model" substance abuse program: Implications for public health. *American Journal of Public Health*, 96:2254–2259.

Hawkins, J. D., Catalano, R. F., and Miller, J. Y. 1992. Risk and protective factors for alcohol and other drug problems in adolescence and early adulthood: Implications for substance abuse prevention. *Psychological Bulletin*, 112:64–105. doi: 10.1037/0033-2909.112.1.64

Heckman, J. J., and Masterov, D. V. 2007. The productivity argument for investing in young children. *Review of Agricultural Economics*, 29:446–493.

Heckman, J. J., Moon, S. H., Pinto, R., Savelyev, P. A., and Yavitz, A. 2010. Analyzing social experiments as implemented: A reexamination of the evidence from the HighScope Perry Preschool Program. *Quantitative Economics*, 1:1–46.

Herrenkohl, T. I., Maguin, E., Hill, K. G., *et al.* 2000. Developmental risk factors for youth violence. *Journal of Adolescent Health*, 26:176–186. doi: 10.1016/S1054-139X(99)00065-8

Hirschi, T. 1969. *Causes of Delinquency*. Berkeley, CA: University of California Press.

James-Burdumy, S., Dynarski, M., and Deke, J. 2008. After-school program effects on behavior: Results from the 21st Century Community Learning Centers Program national evaluation. *Economic Inquiry*, 46:13–18.

Johnson, C. A., Pentz, M., Weber, M. D., *et al.* 1990. Relative effectiveness of comprehensive community programming for drug abuse prevention with high-risk and low-risk adolescents. *Journal of Consulting and Clinical Psychology*, 58:447–456.

Kann, L., Kinchen, S., Shanklin, S., *et al.* 2014. Youth Risk Behavior Surveillance – United States, 2013. Surveillance Summaries, June 13, 2014. In: *Morbidity and Mortality Weekly Report 63*. Atlanta, GA: Centers for Disease Control and Prevention.

Kim, H. K., and Leve, L. D. 2011. Substance use and delinquency among middle school girls in foster care: A three-year follow-up of a randomized controlled trial. *Journal of Consulting and Clinical Psychology*, 79:740–750.

Komro, K., Perry, C. L., Veblen-Mortenson, S., *et al.* 2008. Outcomes from a randomized controlled trial of a multi-component alcohol use preventive intervention for urban youth: Project Northland Chicago. *Addiction*, 103:606–618.

Kumar, R., O'Malley, P. M., Johnston, L. D., and Laetz, V. B. 2013. Alcohol, tobacco, and other drug use prevention programs in U.S. schools: A descriptive summary. *Prevention Science*, 14:581–592.

Lewis, K. M., Bavarian, N., Snyder, F. J., *et al.* 2012. Direct and mediated effects of a social-emotional and character development program on adolescent substance use. *International Journal of Emotional Education*, 4:56–78.

Lewis, K. M., Schure, M. B., Bavarian, N., *et al.* 2013. Problem behavior an urban, low-income youth: A randomized controlled trial of Positive Action in Chicago. *American Journal of Preventive Medicine*, 44:622–630. doi: 10.1016/j.amepre.2013.01.030

Li, K.-K., Washburn, I. J., DuBois, D. L., *et al.* 2011. Effects of the Positive Action programme on problem behaviours in elementary school students: A matched-pair randomised control trial in Chicago. *Psychology and Health*, 26:187–204.

Lochman, J. E., and Wells, K. C. 2002. Contextual social-cognitive mediators and child outcome: A test of the theoretical model in the Coping Power Program. *Developmental Psychopathology*, 14:945–967.

Lochman, J. E., and Wells, K. C. 2003. Effectiveness of the Coping Power Program and of classroom intervention with aggressive children: Outcomes at a 1-year follow-up. *Behavior Therapy*, 34:493–515.

Malti, T., Ribeaud, D., and Eisner, M. P. 2012. Effectiveness of a universal school-based social competence program: The role of child characteristics and economic factors. *International Journal of Conflict and Violence*, 6:249–259.

McCord, J. 1978. A thirty-year follow-up of treatment effects. *American Psychologist*, 33:284–289.

McCord, J. 2003. Cures that harm: Unanticipated outcomes of crime prevention programs. *The Annals of the American Academy of Political and Social Science*, 587:16–30.

Moore, M. J., and Werch, C. 2009. Efficacy of a brief alcohol consumption reintervention for adolescents. *Substance Use and Misuse*, 44:1009–1020.

Mytton, J. A., DiGuiseppi, C., Gough, D., Taylor, R. S., and Logan, S. 2006. School-based secondary prevention programmes for preventing violence. *Cochrane Database of Systematic Reviews*. doi: 10.1002/14651858. CD004606.pub2

Parks, G. 2000. The High/Scope Perry Preschool Project. Washington, DC: Office of Juvenile Justice and Delinquency Prevention.

Pentz, M. A., Dwyer, J. H., MacKinnon, D. P., *et al.* 1989. A multicommunity trial for primary prevention of adolescent drug abuse. *Journal of the American Medical Association*, 261:3259–3266.

Perry, C. L., Williams, C. L., Veblen-Mortenson, S., *et al.* 1996. Project Northland: Outcomes of a community-wide alcohol use prevention program during early adolescence. *American Journal of Public Health*, 86:956–965. doi: 10.2105/AJPH.86.7.956

Perry, C. L., Williams, C. L., Komro, K. A., *et al.* 2002. Project Northland: long-term outcomes of community action to reduce adolescent alcohol use. *Health Education Research*, 17:117–132.

Petras, H., Kellam, S. G., Hendricks Brown, C., *et al.* 2008. Developmental epidemiological courses leading to antisocial personality disorder and violent and criminal behavior: Effects by young adulthood of a universal preventive intervention in first- and second-grade classrooms. *Drug and Alcohol Dependence*, 95:S45–S59.

Puma, M., Bell, S., Cook, R., *et al.* 2012. Third grade follow-up to the Head Start Impact Study final report, OPRE Report #2101-45. Washington, DC: Office of Planning, Research and Evaluation, Administration for Children and Families, US Department of Health and Human Services.

Ringwalt, C., Hanley, S., Vincus, A. A., *et al.* 2008. The prevalence of effective substance use prevention curricula in the Nation's high schools. *The Journal of Primary Prevention*, 29:479–488.

Ringwalt, C., Vincus, A. A., Hanley, S., *et al.* 2011. The prevalence of evidence-based drug use prevention curricula in U.S. middle schools in 2008. *Prevention Science*, 12:63–69.

Ringwalt, C. L., Clark, H. K., Hanley, S., Shamblen, S. R., and Flewelling, R. L. 2009. Project Alert: A cluster randomized trial. *Archives of Pediatric and Adolescent Medicine*, 163:625–632.

Rohrbach, L. A., Sun, P., and Sussman, S. 2010. One-year follow-up of evaluation of the Project Towards No Drug Abuse (TND) Dissemination Trial. *Preventive Medicine*, 51:313–319.

Rosenbaum, D. P. 2007. Just say no to D.A.R.E. *Criminology and Public Policy*, 6:815–824.

Rosenbaum, D. P., and Hanson, G. S. 1998. Assessing the effects of school-based drug education: A six-year multilevel analysis of Project D.A.R.E. *Journal of Research in Crime and Delinquency*, 35:381–412.

Roth, J. L., and Brooks-Gunn, J. 2003. Youth development programs: Risk, prevention and policy. *Journal of Adolescent Health*, 32:170–182.

Sanchez, V., Steckler A., Nitirat, P., *et al.* 2007. Fidelity of implementation in a treatment effectiveness trial of Reconnecting Youth. *Health Education Research*, 22:95–107.

Schindler, H. S., and Yoshikawa, H. 2012. Preventing crime through intervention in the preschool years. In: B. C. Welsh and D. P. Farrington (eds), *The Oxford Handbook of Crime Prevention*, pp. 70–88. New York, NY: Oxford University Press.

Schweinhart, L. 2005. *Lifetime Effects: The High/Scope Perry Preschool Study Through Age 40.* Ypsilanti, MI: High/Scope Press.

Schweinhart, L. J. 2013. Long-term follow-up of a preschool experiment. *Journal of Experimental Criminology*, 9:389–409. doi: 10.1007/s11292-013-9190-3

Schweinhart, L. J., Berrueta-Clement, J. R., Barnett, W. S., Epstein, A. S., and Weikart, D. P. 1985. Effects of the Perry Preschool Program on youths through age 19: A summary. *Topics in Early Childhood Special Education*, 5:26–35.

Sloboda, Z., Stephens, R. C., Stephens, P., *et al.* 2009. The Adolescent Substance Abuse Prevention Study: A randomized field trial of a universal substance abuse prevention program. *Drug and Alcohol Dependence*, 102:1–10. doi: 10.1016/j.drugalcdep.2009.01.015

Spoth, R. L., Redmond, C., Trudeau, L., and Shin, C. 2002. Longitudinal substance initiation outcomes for a universal preventive intervention combining family and school programs. *Psychology of Addictive Behaviors*, 16:129–134.

Spoth, R. L., Randall, G. K., Trudeau, L., Shin, C., and Redmond, C. 2008. Substance use outcomes 5 1/2 years past baseline for partnership-based, family-school preventive interventions. *Drug and Alcohol Dependence*, 96:57–68.

St. Pierre, T. L., Osgood, D. W., Mincemoyer, C. C., Kaltreider, D. L., and Kauh, T. J. 2005. Results of an independent evaluation of Project ALERT delivered in schools by cooperative extension. *Prevention Science*, 6:305–317.

Storr, C. L., Ialongo, N. S., Kellam, S. G., and Anthony, J. C. 2002. A randomized controlled trial of two primary school intervention strategies to prevent early onset tobacco smoking. *Drug and Alcohol Dependence*, 66:51–60.

Sun, W., Skara, S., Sun, P., Dent, C. W., and Sussman, S. 2006. Project Towards No Drug Abuse: Long-term substance use outcomes evaluation. *Preventive Medicine*, 42:188–192.

Sussman, S., Dent, C. W., and Stacy, A. W. 2002. Project Towards No Drug Abuse: A review of the findings and future directions. *American Journal of Health Behavior*, 26:354–365.

Sussman, S., Dent, C. W., Stacy, A. W., and Craig, S. 1998. One-year outcomes of Project Towards No Drug Abuse. *Preventive Medicine*, 27:632–642.

Sussman, S., Sun, P., McCuller, W. J., and Dent, C. W. 2003. Project Towards No Drug Abuse: Two-year outcomes of a trial that compares health educator delivery to self-instruction. *Preventive Medicine*, 37:155–162. doi: 10.1016/S0091-7435(03)00108-7

Tierney, J. P., Grossman, J. B., and Resch, N. L. 1995. Making a difference: An impact study of Big Brothers/Big Sisters. Philadelphia, PA: Public/Private Ventures.

Tolan, P. H., Henry, D. B., Schoeny, M., Lovegrove, P., and Nichols, E. 2014. Mentoring interventions to affect juvenile delinquency and associated outcomes of youth at risk: A comprehensive meta-analytic review. *Journal of Experimental Criminology*, 10:179–206. doi: 10.1007/s11292-013-9181-4

Tolan, P. H., Henry, D. B., Schoeny, M., *et al.* 2013. Mentoring interventions to affect juvenile delinquency and associated problems: A systematic review. *Campbell Systematic Reviews*, 9(10).

US Department of Education. 2011. Prevalence and implementation fidelity of research-based prevention programs in public schools: Final report. Washington, DC: US Department of Education, Office of Planning, Evaluation and Policy Development, Policy and Program Studies Service.

Van Lier, P. A. C., Huizink, A., and Crijnen, A. A. M. 2009. Impact of a preventive intervention targeting childhood disruptive behavior problems on tobacco and alcohol initiation from age 10 to 13 years. *Drug and Alcohol Dependence*, 100:228–233.

Van Lier, P. A. C., Vuijk, P., and Crijnen, A. A. M. 2005. Understanding mechanisms of change in the development of antisocial behavior: The impact of a universal intervention. *Journal of Abnormal Child Psychology*, 33:521–535.

Vitaro, F., Brendgen, M., Giguere, C.-E., and Tremblay, R. 2013. Early prevention of life-course personal and property violence: A 19-year follow-up of the Montreal Longitudinal-Experimental Study (MLES). *Journal of Experimental Criminology*, 9:411–427.

Wagenaar, A. C., and Perry, C. L. 1994. Community strategies for the reduction of youth drinking: Theory and application. *Journal of Research on Adolescence*, 4:319–345.

Washington State Institute for Public Policy (WSIPP). 2015. Benefit-cost results. Olympia, WA: Washington State Institute for Public Policy.

Weissberg, R. P., and Greenberg, M. T. 1998. School and community competence-enhancement and prevention programs. In: I. E. Siegel and K. A. Renninger (eds), *Handbook of Child Psychology*. Vol 4: *Child Psychology in Practice*, pp. 877–954. New York, NY: John Wiley & Sons, Inc.

Werch, C., Moore, M. J., DiClemente, C. C., Bledsoe, R., and Jobli, E. 2005. A multihealth behavior intervention integrating physical activity and substance use prevention for adolescents. *Prevention Science*, 6:213–226.

Yoshikawa, H., Weiland, C., Brooks-Gunn, J., *et al.* 2013. *Investing in Our Future: The Evidence Base on Preschool Education*. New York, NY/Ann Arbor, MI: Foundation for Child Development/Society for Research in Child Development.

Zief, S. G., Lauver, S., and Maynard, R. A. 2006. Impacts of after-school programs on student outcomes. *Campbell Systematic Reviews*, 2(3).

9

Individual-Level Crime Prevention
Reducing the Continuity of Offending

Learning Objectives

Upon finishing this chapter, students should be able to:
- Identify effective programs, policies, and practices that reduce recidivism among juvenile and adult offenders
- Identify programs, policies, and practices that are not effective in reducing recidivism among juvenile or adult offenders and those which have inconclusive evidence of effectiveness
- Summarize the extent to which effective recidivism programs and practices are being implemented in correctional institutions and community settings
- State the most important research tasks that must be accomplished in order to more effectively reduce recidivism.

Introduction

The previous chapter provided many examples of crime prevention programs and practices which have strong evidence of reducing the **onset** or **initiation** of crime. While it is exciting to have so many different and effective crime prevention strategies, we know that these interventions are not widely used and that even the best of them will not be 100% successful in preventing crime. Some individuals will break the law and some offenders will recidivate, perpetrating multiple offenses including criminal acts which have significant financial and emotional costs to society. These are the

The Prevention of Crime, First Edition. Delbert Elliott and Abigail Fagan.
© 2017 John Wiley & Sons, Inc. Published 2017 by John Wiley & Sons, Inc.
Companion website: www.wiley.com/go/elliott/prevention_of_crime

individuals the public would most like to see not only punished but also rehabilitated so that they do not commit any more crimes. But, what is the likelihood we can be successful in reaching this goal? Is there any hope of rehabilitating such individuals or is the situation still as Martinson (1974) described over 40 years ago, that nothing works to reform offenders? This chapter considers these questions and reviews what is currently known about attempts to reduce recidivism among those who have already begun engaging in crime.

There is clearly a need for effective rehabilitation programs. As shown in Figure 9.1, a study of offenders released from prisons in 30 states in the USA showed that 43% were re-arrested within one year and 77% were re-arrested within five years (Durose, Cooper, and Snyder, 2014). When using slightly different official measures of recidivism, this study also showed that 55% of prisoners were *convicted* for a new offense within five years of their release. In addition, 55% of those released *returned to prison* due to a new conviction or because they violated the terms of their original sentence or parole requirements, such as failing to remain drug-free or to refrain from associating with known criminals. Among those younger than age 24, recidivism rates were even higher, with 84% of such prisoners re-arrested within five years of their release.

These data suggest that our criminal justice system is failing to achieve its mission of reforming offenders. Instead of reducing crime, prisons seem to have a "revolving door" (Pew Center on the States, 2001) with only a short interval between one's release from prison and re-entry to the system. This failure runs counter to the predictions of **deterrence theory**, at least the idea of **specific deterrence** which posits that individuals who are punished for their offenses will be deterred from committing new crimes (Nagin, Cullen, and Jonson, 2009). The idea that prison time will reduce offending is also predicted by **rational choice theory**, which states that individuals weigh the pros and cons of potential behaviors and engage in crime when the benefits of doing so outweigh the drawbacks (Apel and Nagin, 2011; Clarke and Cornish, 1985). According to this theory, individuals who are caught committing a crime, and who serve time in jail or prison for doing so, will be less likely to offend again because they do not want to experience the negative consequences associated with incarceration.

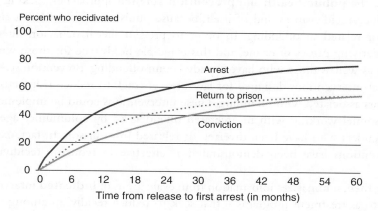

Figure 9.1   Recidivism rates in the United States for prisoners released in 30 states in 2005. Source: Durose *et al.*, 2014 (Bureau of Justice Statistics (2014), US Department of Justice).

While deterrence and rational choice theories provide the theoretical basis for arresting, convict-ing and imprisoning offenders, these perspectives have been critiqued on several grounds. **Labeling theorists** suggest that formal processing will be more likely to increase than decrease recidivism among those who break the law. Individuals may feel ashamed, stigmatized or angry by contact with law enforcement and correctional personnel, especially if they are ridiculed, treated with less respect or made to feel like outcasts by these officials or other members of society (Braithwaite, 1989; Sherman, 1993). They may also feel they have less to lose by offending because they are already treated like criminals. Labeling theories suggest that diverting offenders from the formal criminal justice system and offering alternative punishments and/or treatment services will be more likely to reduce recidivism. As we will describe later in this chapter, restorative justice is one example of an alternative sanction supported by labeling theory.

Social learning theory also predicts that time in prison will increase rather than decrease recidivism, as the following quote from Dodge and colleagues illustrates.

> *Deviant peer influences are among the most potent factors in the development of antisocial behavior ... Perversely, much of what we do as public policy is to segregate deviant youth from their mainstream peers and assign them to settings with other deviant youth.*
>
> Dodge *et al.*, 2006: 3

Incarceration by design increases contact among offenders. Spending time with other criminals allows reinforcement of the deviant attitudes and beliefs that can perpetuate offending (Akers, 1985; Sutherland, 1947). Incarceration also isolates offenders from prosocial role models and conventional beliefs, further increasing the chances of recidivism once offenders are released back to their communities.

According to the **public health** and **prevention science** approaches, locking up offenders is unlikely to reduce recidivism in and of itself, because punishment is neither a risk factor nor a protective factor related to offending. In order to prevent illegal behavior, interventions must address the underlying causes of crime, and this principle holds true for those who have not yet broken the law as well as those who have already begun offending. Prevention scientists therefore recommend that interventions designed for law-breakers seek to reduce risk factors and enhance protective factors associated with offending. These interventions could be implemented by crimi-nal justice personnel working with incarcerated offenders or by community agencies trying to rehabilitate offenders who have been diverted or released from prison. In fact, examples of both types of interventions have been demonstrated as effective in reducing recidivism, as we will describe.

This chapter, then, summarizes information from evaluations of **indicated** interventions – some-times referred to as treatment programs – that seek to reduce recidivism among those who have already begun engaging in crime. We will describe programs, practices, and policies tested in jails, prisons, and juvenile detention centers as well as those implemented in the community. Because these interventions target known offenders with the goal of reducing their subsequent contact with the criminal justice system, most evaluations of these strategies measure recidivism using official records of crime, but they often differ in the specific measure or measures chosen to represent recidivism. Like the research cited at the start of the chapter (Durose *et al.*, 2014), recidivism measures can include arrest, conviction and/or incarceration rates. Although all are valid indicators of contact with the criminal justice system, they represent different stages of this process and outcomes may vary depending on which indicator the evaluator selects.

It is also important to remember from Chapter 1 that official records under-estimate criminal offending, and recidivism by extension, since not all illegal behaviors will come to the attention of authorities. Arrest records also lack accuracy, given that not all those arrested will have necessarily committed a crime or be convicted of an offense. These measurement problems have often been noted by critics of recidivism research, who recommend assessing recidivism using self-reports of offending as well as additional measures of success, such as improvements in employment or socioeconomic status (Nagin *et al.*, 2009).

It is also important to note that while we will identify effective strategies that have been tested in rigorous scientific studies, the bulk of recidivism studies have relied on weak empirical methodologies and evaluation designs (Nagin *et al.*, 2009). In this way, Martinson's (1974) criticisms of correctional research still hold some merit. Relatively few RCTs have been conducted, due in part to challenges convincing criminal justice officials to agree to randomization of prisoners and because randomization is not possible when evaluating certain criminal justice policies. In addition, many of the RCTs and QEDs assessing recidivism outcomes have had relatively small sample sizes and high attrition rates and many of the interventions have suffered from poor implementation quality, all of which undermine the ability of these studies to produce valid and reliable results (Andrews and Dowden, 2005; Mears, 2007). Finally, many recidivism studies involve **marginal effects designs**, which occur when some type of service (e.g., incarceration or parole combined with restitution or community service) is delivered to the control group. This design complicates the interpretation of any observed effects on crime because there is no true comparison group which receives no services. All of these challenges have resulted in mixed and inconclusive evidence regarding the effectiveness of many recidivism programs and practices, and additional high-quality evaluations are needed to help us better understand what works and what does not work to reduce re-offending.

Interventions Intended to Reduce Youth Recidivism

We begin our review by identifying interventions intended to reduce recidivism among youth offenders. Later in the chapter, we will describe interventions for adult offenders. Although some of the same strategies are used for both age groups, the effectiveness of these interventions sometimes varies across the two populations. Such findings support the **life course developmental paradigm** which emphasizes that different factors may affect criminal behavior at different stages of life and that different intervention strategies may be needed for different age groups.

Effective community-based drug treatment programs

Rates of illegal substance use by adolescents are high in the USA and internationally (Hibell *et al.*, 2012; Johnston *et al.*, 2013), and 6% to 16% of adolescents worldwide are thought to have substance use disorders (National Research Council and Institute of Medicine, 2009). The negative effects of

Table 9.1 Effective drug treatment programs for youth.

Effective program	Rating by Blueprints	Rating by the Coalition	Rating by CrimeSolutions.gov
Adolescent Community Reinforcement Approach	Not rated	Not rated	Effective
BASICS	Model	Not rated	Effective

substance use on academic performance, social relationships and involvement in crime has led to the development and testing of programs designed to prevent the initiation of substance use, as described in Chapter 8, and to indicated interventions for those currently using and abusing drugs and alcohol. As shown in Table 9.1, *our review indicates that two programs have evidence of lowering rates of youth drug use and dependency among heavy users of alcohol and other drugs.*

The **Adolescent Community Reinforcement Approach** is a three-month-long program designed to reduce substance use among adolescents with diagnosed drug addiction and dependency. It focuses on improving individuals' problem-solving, coping, and communication skills. Families are also involved to support youths' attempts to refrain from drug use. This program content is consistent with **strain, social control** and **social learning theories**, as youth learn ways to cope with problems using positive rather than negative behaviors, build closer relationships with their parents and practice resisting peer influences to use substances (Godley *et al.*, 2006).

One randomized trial tested the effectiveness of the program with adolescents aged 12–17 recently released from a drug treatment center in IL. Most were Caucasian males and 82% had prior involvement with the juvenile justice system. The evaluation showed that nine months following treatment, more intervention youth reported abstaining from marijuana (41% abstained) than those in the control group (26% abstained). The effect size of 0.32 indicates a moderate reduction in marijuana use, but effects on alcohol use were smaller (0.10) and non-significant. A second evaluation conducted with 180 homeless 19 year olds in Albuquerque, NM found a moderate reduction in the frequency of alcohol and other drug use for program versus control group participants, with an effect size of 0.35 (Slesnick *et al.*, 2007).

The **Brief Alcohol Screening and Intervention for College Students (BASICS)** is intended to reduce alcohol use and related problems (e.g., poor school attendance and performance, risk for sexual assault, violence perpetration, etc.) among college students who are heavy drinkers. The intervention is guided in part by **social learning theory**, as it seeks to change individual expectations and attitudes regarding the positive and negative consequences of drinking, which may be influenced by peer substance use. It uses a therapeutic technique called **motivational interviewing (MI)**, reviewed in more detail later in this chapter, to help individuals recognize that their alcohol consumption may be problematic and interfere with their personal goals. Therapists work one-on-one with students to improve their motivation and ability to reduce their alcohol use by providing information regarding the harms associated with excessive drinking and the factors that may lead to alcohol use. Following MI principles, implementers are to be supportive, non-judgmental, and non-confrontational and allow participants to direct their own behavioral change efforts (Lundahl *et al.*, 2010; Marlatt *et al.*, 1998).

The first RCT of BASICS was conducted with incoming students at the University of Washington who had reported higher than average levels of alcohol use in their senior year of high school. For

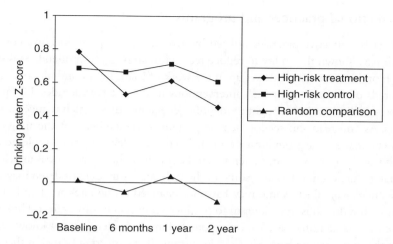

Figure 9.2 Effects of BASICS on college students' alcohol use. Source: Marlatt *et al.*, 1998. Reproduced with permission of the American Psychological Association.

example, on average, participants reported drinking twice a week and consuming 11 alcoholic drinks each week. The high-risk students selected to be in the intervention and control groups had much higher rates of drinking versus a "random comparison" group of other university students, as shown in Figure 9.2. Prior to their first meeting with therapists, students in the intervention group were asked to track their alcohol use and record problems that may have been caused by drinking over a two-week period. They were then provided with a personalized summary of their alcohol use and comparison to other students' use, reviewed this information with therapists in a face-to-face meeting and discussed possible changes to their behavior. Following the meeting, they were mailed information describing alcohol consequences and suggesting techniques for reducing use (Marlatt *et al.*, 1998).

As shown in Figure 9.2, six months after the study began, BASICS participants reported lower rates and frequency of drinking compared to the control group, though the effect size of 0.15 indicates a relatively small impact (Marlatt *et al.*, 1998). Similar reductions were evidenced at the two-year follow-up, with effect sizes ranging from 0.14 to 0.20 across the different types of alcohol use measured in the study. Effects of the intervention were maintained at the four-year follow-up, with students receiving BASICs still having lower rates of drinking than the control group (Baer *et al.*, 2001).

BASICS has also shown positive effects when replicated at other universities, including studies which targeted fraternity pledges (Larimer *et al.*, 2001) and athletes (Turrisi *et al.*, 2009). Based on 16 evaluations, the Washington State Institute of Public Policy (WSIPP) (2015) calculated an average effect size of 0.17 for BASICS' impact on alcohol abuse and dependence. WSIPP (2015) also report that BASICS is cost beneficial, returning $26.68 for every dollar spent. According to NREPP (http://legacy.nrep padmin.net/ViewIntervention.aspx?id=124), the program has been used in 1,100 sites and reached 20,000 students. This is good logical evidence of the program's generalizability or external validity.

Effective correctional practices and programs

This section describes effective practices utilized by juvenile justice personnel and community-based providers which have shown the ability to reduce recidivism among youth offenders, as summarized in Table 9.2. Much of this information draws upon the work of Mark Lipsey and his colleagues, who have reviewed hundreds of evaluations of such interventions in the last few decades. Using meta-analytic techniques, Lipsey and others have sought to identify general practices which reduce recidivism among youth offenders. As you read this section, it is important to remember that the individual programs evaluated in meta-analyses vary significantly in their content, delivery style, implementation fidelity, evaluation quality, and impact on crime. Even when the results of the meta-analysis indicate a statistically significant overall reduction in offending, some of the individual studies considered may have produced **iatrogenic** (i.e., negative) effects, some may have not changed crime rates at all and others may have shown large enough reductions in recidivism to produce an overall positive effect. Thus, even though a general practice may be identified as effective, a potential implementer may not know which particular intervention of that type will be best able to reduce crime. This uncertainty means that recommendations to replicate certain practices are made with caution, a subject we will return to in Section IV.

Lipsey's (2009) most recent meta-analysis was based on 548 evaluations of interventions designed to reduce recidivism among juvenile offenders aged 12–21. Most were conducted in the USA. Most youth (78%) received treatment from community providers, as they had been diverted out of the system (27%), were on probation or parole (33%), or were no longer under the supervision of the juvenile justice system at the time that services were provided. About one-fourth (22%) received programming while in a juvenile correctional institution. In our view, there are four notable findings emerging from this work:

1. The average effect size across these studies was 0.06, which was statistically significant but indicated a very small reduction in recidivism across programs. In most cases, the outcome was based on official data, specifically re-arrests of offenders occurring within one year after the treatment had ended.
2. There was large variation in effectiveness across the individual studies and some interventions increased rather than decreased recidivism.
3. Programs that were "control oriented" were much less effective than those that were "therapeutically oriented." The former interventions were primarily based on **deterrence theory** and involved supervising and controlling youth, restricting their opportunities to recidivate and using punishments to dissuade youth from future violations. As shown in Figure 9.3, interventions that emphasized discipline and deterrence tactics actually had harmful effects overall. That is, they increased recidivism among youth offenders, as indicated by the fact that the bars are on the left side of the x-axis, indicating smaller *reductions* in recidivism. We will describe some of these programs later in

Table 9.2 Interventions with evidence of effectiveness in reducing youth recidivism.

Practice/Program	Rating by CrimeSolutions.gov
Cognitive Behavioral Therapy (CBT)	Not reviewed
Aggression Replacement Therapy (ART)	Effective

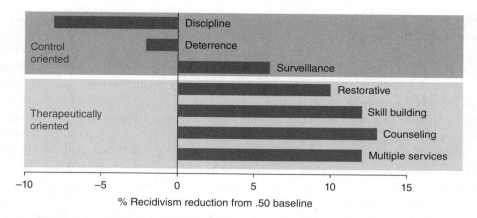

Figure 9.3   Effects on recidivism of control-oriented and therapeutically oriented interventions for juvenile offenders. Source: Howell and Lipsey, 2012. Reproduced with permission of Sage Publications.

the chapter. Therapeutic interventions, in contrast, provide offenders with skills, including educational and vocational training, fostering supportive relationships and providing counseling and other services to reduce risk factors and increase protective factors. As shown in Figure 9.3, these practices reduced recidivism rates by 10% to 13%, as indicated by the bars on the right side of the x-axis.

4. The therapeutic programs were generally more effective for youth offenders who had a larger number of prior offenses, who were considered to be at higher risk for recidivism.

Although not shown in Figure 9.3, one type of therapeutic practice identified as effective by Lipsey (2009) is **cognitive behavioral therapy (CBT)**. **CBT** considers behaviors of all types, not just illegal acts, to be strongly related to cognitive processes and decision-making. CBT involves helping individuals become more aware of their thoughts, beliefs and attitudes and to replace dysfunctional thought processes with healthier ones. CBT usually involves teaching skills related to decision-making and reasoning, anger management and emotional regulation and allowing participants to practice these skills in simulated interactions or situations.

In a meta-analysis of 14 CBT interventions delivered to juvenile offenders, Lipsey (2009) found an average effect size of 0.13, corresponding to a reduction in recidivism of 26% for youth receiving CBT compared to those in the control group. Armelius and Andreassen (2007) also report a small but significant effect of CBT on youth recidivism. Based on 12 studies (only 5 of which were RCTs) delivered to incarcerated youth aged 12–22, 8 in the USA, 2 in Canada, and 2 in the UK, they found that youth receiving CBT had a 10% lower rate of recidivism compared to those in the comparison groups one year after treatment had ended. However, this effect was not evident two years post-intervention. WSIPP (2015) reports a small unadjusted effect size of 0.12 for CBT programs for youth offenders, and the adjusted effect size is even smaller (0.04). Taken as a whole, these findings suggest that CBT is an effective practice but one that is likely to have a small impact on recidivism when used with youth offenders.

A specific program that relies on CBT to reduce recidivism among juvenile offenders is **Aggression Replacement Training (ART)**. ART targets youth in correctional or community settings who have a history of aggressive and violent behavior. Thirty one-hour sessions offered three times per week for 10 weeks are delivered to small groups of 8–12 offenders (WSIPP, 2004). Facilitators use CBT to teach youth how to control their impulses and manage anger. Discussion and role play allow youth to identify the types of situations that trigger their anger and to practice strategies to avoid aggressive responses to these difficult situations. Program content also focuses on helping youth develop stronger moral beliefs so they can respond to ethical dilemmas with prosocial behaviors.

An evaluation of ART conducted in WA with mostly male offenders indicated that the program significantly reduced recidivism when implemented by competent facilitators. When those conditions were met, ART youth experienced a 24% reduction in felony recidivism rates compared to those in the control group 18 months after treatment ended (WSIPP, 2004). ART has also been evaluated in other countries and shown positive effects in reducing problem behaviors and delinquency, though not all studies were of strong evaluation design. WSIPP (2015) reports an unadjusted effect size on crime of 0.51 across studies and an adjusted effect size of 0.12, indicating that ART is likely to have relatively small effects on recidivism. The program is rated as Effective by CrimeSolutions. gov and as cost beneficial by WSIPP (2015), returning $18.66 for every dollar spent when used with incarcerated youth and $10.25 when used with youth on probation.

Practices with inconclusive evidence of effectiveness in reducing youth recidivism

As discussed earlier in this chapter, different criminological theories predict that contact with the justice system can increase *or* decrease recidivism. Perhaps as a result, many evaluations of correctional practices have shown mixed results regarding their ability to impact youth recidivism. Coupled with the fact that many of these evaluations have relied on weak research designs, there are currently more interventions with *inconclusive* evidence of effectiveness than conclusive evidence, as shown in Table 9.3. In other words, we cannot say with much certainty whether or not many commonly used indicated interventions actually impact youth recidivism. More high-quality evaluations are needed before we can say with confidence that these practices work or do not work.

Our first example of an inconclusive practice is the use of **diversion** to limit youth offenders' contact with the juvenile justice system. Diversion is guided by **labeling theory**, which hypothesizes that contact with the juvenile justice will stigmatize young offenders and increase their chances of recidivism. The intent of diversion is to minimize this contact as much as possible, such as by dismissing offenders' cases as soon as possible or imposing conditions which, once met, will result in the dropping of charges and removal of all records of contact with the juvenile justice system. These sanctions could include, for example, having offenders pay fines, perform community service, or receive counseling and therapy.

A few meta-analyses have evaluated the effectiveness of diversion programs. Lipsey (2009) reported that recidivism rates did not differ between offenders who had been diverted from the system and those who received treatment in a juvenile correctional facility. Similarly, a study of 28 diversion programs indicated a small and non-significant impact on recidivism, with a recidivism rate of 31% for diverted youth and 36% for those in the control group (Schwalbe *et al.*, 2012).

Table 9.3   Interventions with inconclusive evidence of effectiveness in reducing youth recidivism.

Practice	Evidence of effectiveness?	Rating by CrimeSolutions.gov
Diversion	Inconclusive evidence	Not reviewed
Restorative justice	Inconclusive evidence	Not reviewed
Youth Courts	Inconclusive evidence	Not reviewed
Drug Courts	Inconclusive evidence	Promising (general recidivism)
		No effects (drug-related crimes)
Motivational interviewing	Inconclusive evidence	Not reviewed
Wilderness camps	Inconclusive evidence	Not reviewed

Wilson and Hoge (2013) report somewhat stronger effects for diversion programs. Their review of 45 studies indicated recidivism rates of 32% for diverted youth and 41% for the control group. However, when the evaluations were limited to the six studies with a rigorous methodological design, the impact of diversion became smaller and non-significant. A different meta-analysis of 29 studies suggested that formal processing increased juvenile recidivism compared to use of informal diversion programs (Petrosino, Turpin-Petrosino, and Guckenburg, 2010). However, this impact was only seen when youth were followed for at least a year, and the effect size of 0.15 was small. Finally, WSIPP (2006) reported that compared to formal processing, youth who receive diversion have less recidivism, with an average effect size of 0.06, but this is a very small effect and is reduced to 0.03 when adjusted for studies' methodological quality. WSIPP also reports that when diversion programs are compared to simply releasing youth into the community with no other contact, there is no effect on recidivism.

These findings suggest that diversion may be an effective strategy for reducing recidivism rates, at least when compared to the formal processing of offenders, but effects are very small. The reason we characterize diversion as having *inconclusive* evidence of effectiveness is that many of the evaluations described have had weak methodological designs. In addition, many studies have examined an array of different types of services, sometimes delivered to intervention and control groups, making it very difficult to determine what, specifically, has led to any observed changes in recidivism.

Although **restorative justice (RJ)** practices have become somewhat popular in the past few decades, there is mixed evidence of their effectiveness in reducing youth recidivism. This type of intervention is also based on labeling theory, particularly Braithwaite's (1989) **reintegrative shaming theory**. This theory states that when society responds to law-breaking by punishing and isolating offenders in prison, with no attempts to rehabilitate or maintain their connections to society, offenders will be stigmatized and more likely to recidivate. A more effective means of correcting offenders' behavior, particularly for those committing less serious crimes, is to maintain positive relationships between the offender and society. In particular, Braithwaite emphasizes that society must show offenders that their behaviors are wrong and at odds with the norms of their community, but to do so in a way that does not jeopardize their attachments to conventional society. As you might imagine, this theory is also related to Hirschi's (1969) **social control theory.**

RJ was developed simultaneously in the USA and in other countries including Australia, New Zealand, Canada, and the Netherlands in the 1970s and is currently used worldwide (Menkel-Meadow, 2007). It can take various forms, but most RJ practices involve providing offenders with a chance to hear from and respond to the victims of their crimes via a conference or meeting facilitated by a trained mediator or correctional staff person. Victims and offenders voluntarily participate, and offenders must admit their guilt prior to the meeting. Other attendees may include the offenders' or victims' friends, parents, or other family members, as well as representatives from the community. All parties have the opportunity to discuss how the crime affected their lives (Livingstone, Macdonald, and Carr, 2013). RJ may be used as a diversion practice or in combination with other sanctions, including incarceration.

Meta-analyses have provided mixed results of the potential of RJ to reduce youth recidivism. A review of four RCTs evaluating RJ conferences, two conducted in Australia and two in the USA, reported that none produced significant reductions in juvenile recidivism (Livingstone *et al.*, 2013). A review of six evaluations of victim–offender mediation by WSIPP (2015) indicated a non-significant effect size of 0.08. WSIPP's (2006) prior review of a larger and more diverse group of RJ studies showed a statistically significant effect size of 0.14, although the adjusted effect size was only 0.08. Both studies indicated that RJ was cost effective, saving $6.41 (WSIPP, 2015) to $9.03 (WSIPP, 2006) for every dollar spent. Strang and colleagues (2013) reviewed 10 RJ evaluations, not including victim–offender mediation programs, and found an overall mean effect size of 0.16, but a smaller effect (0.12) when restricted to programs for youth offenders only.

Another alternative sentencing option for youth offenders is the use of **youth (or teen) courts**. These target youth offenders who have committed relatively minor offenses and, based on **labeling theory**, are considered to be better served with informal processing (Lab, 2014). Teen courts are implemented in actual courtrooms, with youth volunteers acting as juries, attorneys, and sometimes judges. Adults supervise activities and sometimes act as judges. Similar to RJ, offenders must volunteer to participate and are provided an opportunity to discuss the reasons for and impact of their crime. Victim statements can also be included. Sanctions typically include community service, victim restitution and/or counseling, and once these conditions are met, offenders' records can be expunged (Stickle *et al.*, 2008). There is a definite need for more evaluation of youth courts. A review by WSIPP (2006) was based on only three studies and showed an overall effect size of 0.28. While this indicated significant reductions in recidivism, the adjusted effect size of 0.10 was much smaller. Teen courts were shown to be cost beneficial, returning $10.82 for every dollar spent (WSIPP, 2006). According to the National Association of Youth Courts (http://www.youthcourt.net/?page_id=24), as of 2010, teen courts were operating in all but one state in the USA.

Drug courts are another example of a specialized court system designed to treat offenders outside of the traditional juvenile justice system. Drug courts are based on the understanding that non-violent offenders with diagnosed substance abuse problems may be better served with drug treatment services than with incarceration. Rather than simply release offenders to the community, and based on **social control theory**, they provide regular, structured monitoring of substance-abusing offenders. More specifically, drug courts involve a series of graduated sanctions and rewards which involve frequent drug testing and court appearances to monitor whether or not offenders are complying with requirements to receive drug treatment services and fulfill other terms of their sentences, such as paying fines, making restitution and completing community service (Huddleston and Marlowe, 2011). Monitoring becoming less frequent over time until all conditions have been met, usually within 18 months of program entry (Lab, 2014; Mitchell *et al.*, 2012).

Evaluations of drug courts for youth offenders have shown mixed effects. According to a review of 34 evaluations (Mitchell *et al.*, 2012), juvenile drug court reduced offending in general, with an estimated recidivism rate of 42% for participants compared to 50% for those in the control group. However, there was no impact on drug-related crimes or on substance use. In addition, only three of these studies were RCTs, and when the results of these evaluations were assessed, significant reductions in recidivism were not produced. A review of seven studies by Latimer and colleagues (2006) also found a small and non-significant impact on juvenile recidivism. Finally, WSIPP's (2015) review of these evaluations found a small and non-significant effect on juvenile recidivism, with an effect size of 0.06, and some cost benefits, with a return of $2.34 for every dollar spent on the courts. CrimeSolutions.gov rates drug courts as Promising when considering youth recidivism in general and having No Effects when considering drug-related crimes and substance use. Despite the mixed evidence, the use of drug courts has been growing in the USA and they are now found in every state. Popularity is likely related to the ability of drug courts to help alleviate over-crowding of the correctional system (Lab, 2014).

Another practice used to reduce adolescent substance use and addiction, which can be utilized for youth offenders or those who have not had contact with the juvenile justice system, is **Motivational Interviewing (MI)**. MI is a general therapeutic practice which involves one-on-one therapy sessions to help increase individuals' intentions and ability to change problem behaviors (WSIPP, 2012). It uses a client-centered and supportive approach, such that therapists are non-judgmental and non-confrontational and allow participants to reflect on their own behaviors and decide on their future actions (Lundahl et al., 2010; Marlatt et al., 1998). Services are typically short in duration and often involve the implementation of surveys to document the occurrence of and reasons for participants' behaviors, followed by personalized feedback based on these results.

Evaluations of MI's ability to reduce substance use and dependency among adolescents and young adults have shown mixed evidence of effectiveness. In a review of 39 studies involving the use of MI for youth less than 19 years old, two of which took place in juvenile corrections facilities, two-thirds indicated significant reductions in tobacco, alcohol, marijuana and/or other illegal drug use for participants compared to those in the control group (Barnett et al., 2012). However, only about one-third of the evaluations used RCTs. A meta-analysis of RCTs which involved participants aged 15–26 indicated small but significant effects on the quantity (0.14) and frequency (0.11) of self-reported drinking, but no effects on binge drinking (Foxcroft et al., 2014). The authors of that review concluded that MI has "no meaningful benefits," given the small effects and mixed findings across outcomes. Given the varying conclusions about MI's effectiveness across studies, we cannot currently classify MI as an effective practice for reducing substance use among adolescents.

Wilderness camps or **challenge programs** are designed to rehabilitate youth by providing opportunities for physically challenging activities like rock climbing or backpacking in remote areas outside of correctional institutions (Wilson and Lipsey, 2000). The goal is to promote self-reliance and self-confidence. Loosely based on **social learning theory**, group-based problem-solving is also encouraged, with youth encouraged to work together to achieve certain tasks. A review by the University of Maryland (MacKenzie, 2000; Sherman et al., 1998) classified wilderness camps as ineffective in reducing recidivism. A more recent evaluation of 28 studies by Wilson and Lipsey (2000) reported a positive but modest effect of wilderness camps on youth recidivism, with an effect size of 0.18. However, they cautioned that some studies showed **iatrogenic** effects and increased recidivism among participants. WSIPP's (2006) meta-analysis of nine evaluations indicated positive outcomes, with an overall effect size of 0.25; however, the adjusted effect size was zero and non-significant. Furthermore, WSIPP (2006) concluded that wilderness camps were not cost beneficial; they cost $3,085 per offender and had no financial benefits. Overall, the evidence is too mixed to allow any conclusions regarding the ability of wilderness camps to reduce recidivism among youth offenders. Given this uncertainty, we would recommend against their widespread use at this time.

Programs and practices shown to be ineffective in reducing youth recidivism

If you have seen "Beyond Scared Straight" on the A&E channel, then you are already familiar with a popular, yet ineffective, program intended to reduce youth recidivism. **Scared Straight** programs are based on **rational choice** and **specific deterrence** theories' principle that exposing youth to the harsh conditions of the prison environment will scare them into good behavior. These programs involve arranging prison visits for at-risk youth or those who have already had contact with the juvenile justice system. Visits have included locking children in cells so they can experience prison first-hand and interactions with prisoners who may be confrontational, abusive and/or vulgar (Petrosino et al., 2013).

A meta-analysis of eight studies involving juvenile offenders or those at high risk for offending found those who participated in Scared Straight were *more likely* to engage in crime following the program, with the odds of offending being 1.68 for participants compared to non- participants (Petrosino et al., 2013). The authors conclude that Scared Straight is "more harmful than doing nothing" (Petrosino et al., 2013: 7). It costs more too. Based on a review of 10 programs, WSIPP (2015) calculated that participation in Scared Straight interventions increased juvenile crime, with an unadjusted effect size of 0.15, and cost taxpayers $201 for every dollar invested. CrimeSolutions. gov has classified Scared Straight as a practice with No Effects on recidivism (see Table 9.4).

Another punishment-oriented practice with no evidence of effectiveness in reducing recidivism is the use of **juvenile boot camps** for youth offenders. Boot camps vary in duration and content but have in common the goal of instilling discipline and obedience by requiring offenders to follow strict daily schedules, mandating that they engage in rigorous physical exercise and giving swift punishments for misbehavior (Wilson, MacKenzie, and Mitchell, 2008). According to a meta-analysis by Wilson and colleagues (2008), there is no evidence that boot camps reduce youth recidivism. Similarly, WSIPP's (2006) meta-analysis indicated an effect size of 0.03 for boot camps, and a cost of over $8,000 per participant with no financial returns. CrimeSolutions.gov rates this practice as having No Effects on youth crime, and Farrington and Welsh (2005) caution that boot camps sometimes increase recidivism for youth participants.

Table 9.4   Ineffective interventions intended to reduce youth recidivism.

Practice / Program	Evidence of effectiveness?	Rating by CrimeSolutions.gov
Scared Straight	Harmful	No Effects
Boot camps	Ineffective	No Effects

Interventions Intended to Reduce Adult Recidivism

Effective practices

Adults make up the majority of the prison population, and as discussed in Chapter 1, prison costs are enormous. As such, preventing recidivism among adult offenders should be a major goal of our society. What are our chances of achieving this goal? If the key to success is the implementation of evidence-based interventions, we are still a long way from success.

Our review of the evidence did not indicate any **programs** that were shown in high-quality evaluations to reduce recidivism among adult offenders. The only exception is **Parent–Child Interaction Therapy (PCIT)**, reviewed in Chapter 7, which reduced perpetration of child maltreatment among parents already involved with the child welfare system for their abuse and neglect of children. More promising is that a number of **practices** have been shown in meta-analyses to reduce adult re-offending (see Table 9.5). These practices may be implemented in correctional settings or in the community with adults on probation or parole following their release from prison.

Summarizing the results from multiple meta-analyses of correctional interventions, Lipsey and Cullen (2007) conclude that treatment practices shown to reduce adult recidivism do exist. However, they also acknowledge that there is great disparity in the size of effects produced by these interventions and some, especially punishment-oriented practices, have been shown to increase offending. What appears to be most effective, according to Lipsey and Cullen (2007), is when services follow the principles of **risk, need, and responsivity (RNR)**. These types of interventions: (a) are implemented with the highest-risk offenders – those expected to have the greatest chance of recidivism based on their past record of offending; (b) address criminogenic needs – the malleable or changeable risk factors known to be associated with crime; and (c) match the program content and approach to the demographic characteristics and risk factors of the offender. A meta-analysis of six evaluations of the RNR approach indicated a significant and moderate effect on recidivism when used with moderate- and high-risk adult offenders, with an average effect size of 0.27 (WSIPP, 2015). WSIPP (2015) also classifies this approach as cost beneficial, with economic returns of $3.78 for every dollar spent.

Another general practice with some evidence of effectiveness is the use of **cognitive behavioral therapy (CBT)**. WSIPP's (2015) review of CBT interventions targeting adults considered

Table 9.5 Effective correctional practices designed to reduce adult recidivism.

Practice or policy	Evidence of effectiveness?	Rating by CrimeSolutions.gov
Risk, Need and Responsivity (RNR)	Effective	Not reviewed
Cognitive Behavioral Therapy (CBT)	Effective	Not reviewed
Mental Health Courts	Effective	Not reviewed
Drug treatment programs	Effective	Not reviewed
Intensive supervision	Effective	Not reviewed
Electronic monitoring	Effective	Not reviewed

to be at moderate or high risk of recidivism indicates an overall effect size on recidivism of 0.15 and a financial return of $26.49 per dollar spent. Meta-analyses of 58 CBT studies by Lipsey (Landenberger and Lipsey, 2005; Lipsey, Landenberger, and Wilson, 2007) also show positive effects, with such programs reducing recidivism by 25% for those who received such services compared to those who do not. About half the programs reviewed were conducted in correctional settings and the other half in community settings in the USA (72% of all programs), Canada (17%), the UK (9%), and New Zealand (2%).

A specialized court system implemented for the many adult offenders who have mental health problems are **mental health courts**. They are managed by a combination of criminal justice personnel and mental health professionals who impose sanctions on offenders who have diagnosed mental health problems (Lab, 2014). Based on a review of six evaluations of American mental health courts, WSIPP (2015) found an average unadjusted effect size of 0.22, indicating small to moderate reductions in adult recidivism, and a return of $6.76 for every dollar spent.

For offenders known to be drug abusers or drug dependent, **drug treatment services** may be provided in correctional or community settings. These treatments can take a variety of forms, including less intensive services such as sharing information about the harmful consequences of drug use/abuse and group counseling as well as more intensive treatment, such as inpatient programs requiring participants to live apart from other inmates or family members (for those no longer incarcerated). According to a meta-analysis of eight studies, WSIPP (2015) reported that correctional drug treatment programs have an average effect size of 0.18 and that they return $10.47 to $17.35 for every dollar invested. However, services offered in the community have non-significant or only marginally significant effects (i.e., effect sizes of 0.03 to 0.08) and are less cost effective, returning $1.27 to $6.15 for every dollar spent.

A common practice to reduce recidivism based on **deterrence** and **social control** theories is to provide **intensive supervision** following incarceration. This monitoring technique involves more rigorous surveillance of offenders and more face-to-face meetings between offenders and parole officers (e.g., at least one per month) than is typically provided by probation and parole officers (WSIPP, 2015). Offenders may also be required to pay restitution, engage in community service, work or attend school, have curfews or undergo treatment services (Lab, 2014). WSIPP's (2015) meta-analysis of 11 evaluations of intensive supervision practices, conducted mostly in the USA, showed an average, unadjusted effect size of 0.21. The practice is somewhat cost beneficial, returning $1.58 for every dollar spent.

The last practice with some evidence of effectiveness in reducing recidivism by adult offenders is the use of **electronic monitoring (EM)** via phone, radio, or GPS systems. EM may be used instead of or following incarceration (e.g., during probation or parole) to restrict travel and minimize offenders' opportunities for criminal behavior. Offenders are usually mandated to stay at home, though allowances may be made for travel to school, work, or treatment services. According to a review of studies conducted in the USA, Canada, Sweden, and the UK, EM's effects on recidivism range from 0.15 to 0.35 (WSIPP, 2015). Lab (2014) notes that this strategy has become increasingly popular in the USA, particularly as prisons have become overcrowded and expensive, and more than 110,000 prisoners are tracked each day in the USA using EM. The technology is also being used in 17 other countries, primarily in Europe (the UK, Sweden, and Belgium), Asia, and Australia.

Correctional practices with inconclusive evidence of effectiveness in reducing adult recidivism

Although the practices mentioned earlier have been shown to reduce recidivism rates among adult offenders, with the exception of CBT, many of these practices have not been extensively evaluated. For other practices, the evidence is too mixed to draw conclusions regarding effectiveness or evaluations have been too few and/or of low quality (see Table 9.6). For example, studies assessing the impact of **restorative justice** programming have shown both positive and null effects on adult recidivism. Strang and colleagues' (2013) review of six RJ evaluations involving adult offenders showed a small but significant impact on recidivism, with an effect size of 0.15. However, a review by WSIPP (2006) of RJ interventions for low-risk adult offenders showed no changes in recidivism. The overall effect size of 0.09 was only marginally significant and the adjusted effect size was 0.00.

Drug courts have shown better success in reducing recidivism of adult offenders compared to juveniles, but the evidence is still mixed for this type of practice. WSIPP (2015) reports a significant and moderate impact on adult recidivism for drug courts, with an effect size of 0.27 based on a review of over 50 studies. A review of 92 adult drug courts operating mostly in the USA showed that adult participants had an overall recidivism rate of 38% compared to a rate of 50% for the comparison group (Mitchell et al., 2012). Significant reductions in arrests for drug-related crimes were also seen. While these results are promising, Mitchell and colleagues (2012) caution that of all the evaluations they reviewed, only three were rigorous RCTs and no significant effects on recidivism were seen in these studies. Based on this evaluation, CrimeSolutions.gov has classified drug courts as a Promising practice for adult offenders. Adult drug courts are widely used, operating in every state in the USA (Huddleston and Marlowe, 2011) and in other English-speaking countries such as Canada, the UK, South Africa, Bermuda, and Jamaica (Mitchell et al., 2012). WSIPP (2015) calculated a financial return of $3.00 for every dollar spent on drug courts.

Most inmates do not have a high school diploma and many have very poor reading and math skills, which will reduce their chances of future success and employment when released from prison (Cho and Tyler, 2010). For this reason, most correctional institutes offer voluntary or mandatory **educational services** for adults, often to help offenders achieve their General Educational Development (GED) certificate. A meta-analysis of educational programming by WSIPP (2015) showed significant reductions in recidivism, with an average effect size of 0.24. These services are also cost beneficial, with a return of $19.74 for every dollar spent. CrimeSolutions.gov rates educational services as a Promising practice, based on meta-analyses by several organizations.

Table 9.6 Correctional practices with inconclusive evidence of effectiveness in reducing adult recidivism.

Practice	Evidence of effectiveness?	Rating by CrimeSolutions.gov
Restorative justice	Inconclusive	Not reviewed
Drug courts	Inconclusive	Promising
Educational programming for inmates	Inconclusive	Promising
Job training for inmates	Inconclusive	Promising

Job training and **employment programs** are designed to provide offenders with vocational training and skills that will increase their chances of finding employment following their release. These may involve specific training for particular jobs or may focus on general employment skills like resumé-building and interviewing. These services appear to be more effective when delivered to incarcerated offenders versus those living in the community. According to a review of three evaluations, one of which included programs targeting youth, WSIPP (2015) reported an overall effect size of 0.26 for employment programs delivered in correctional settings and a smaller but still significant effect size of 0.08 for those delivered in the community. Both types were identified as cost effective, returning $13.22 and $47.79, respectively, for every dollar invested. CrimeSolutions.gov classifies vocational training as a Promising practice.

Correctional policies and practices shown to be ineffective in reducing adult recidivism

> *If any other institution in America were as unsuccessful in achieving their ostensible purpose as our prisons are, we would shut them down tomorrow … That is why it is vitally important how we treat [offenders] while they are incarcerated.*
>
> James Gilligan (2012), Professor, New York University

Two criminal justice interventions with relatively strong evidence that they fail to reduce adult recidivism are listed in Table 9.7. The first example may shock you, but a review of the evidence has indicated that **incarceration** does not decrease re-offending (Lipsey and Cullen, 2007; Nagin *et al.*, 2009; Villettaz, Killias, and Zoder, 2006). Nagin and colleagues (2009) emphasize the difficulties in conducting high-quality evaluation of the impact of incarceration on future offending, but nonetheless conclude that there is no evidence that locking up adult criminals reduces subsequent crime. Lipsey and Cullen (2007: 302) are more pessimistic, stating that imprisonment is iatrogenic: "*studies of incarceration compared with community supervision, or longer prison terms compared with shorter ones, all found that the average effect was increased recidivism.*"

Secondly, **boot camps** for adult offenders have not been demonstrated as effective in reducing recidivism. CrimeSolutions.gov identifies this type of practice as having No Effects, largely based on a meta-analysis by Wilson and colleagues (2008). That study of 26 evaluations of boot camps indicated a non-significant effect on adult recidivism. WSIPP (2006) also reported a non-significant and very small effect (0.03) of boot camps on adult recidivism, based on a review of 12 studies, only one of which was conducted outside the USA.

Table 9.7 Ineffective correctional practices and policies designed to reduce adult recidivism.

Practice or policy	Evidence of effectiveness?	Rating by CrimeSolutions.gov
Incarceration	Ineffective	Not reviewed
Boot camps	Ineffective	No effects

Need for Further Research

This review has identified a variety of programs and practices with evidence of reducing criminal recidivism among juvenile and adult offenders. It is encouraging to see that we have the ability to rehabilitate offenders, even those who may suffer from drug abuse or mental illness which may contribute to involvement in crime. These findings indicate that claims that "nothing works" (Martinson, 1974) are not absolutely true. Instead, treatment services provided within correctional settings, or in the community to individuals who have been diverted from formal processing or released from prison, do have the potential to reduce re-offending. Many of these interventions are cost beneficial according to the estimates of the Washington State Institute of Public Policy (www. wsipp.wa.gov). This is very good news considering the significant costs associated with processing offenders in the juvenile justice and criminal justice systems.

Nonetheless, some caution is required, for while we may have the *potential* to reduce re-offending rates, actually doing so will be very challenging. According to official data, recidivism rates are still very high in the USA (Durose *et al.*, 2014), suggesting that effective recidivism programs and practices are not being utilized nearly as much as they could or should be. Moreover, ineffective and harmful practices such as Scared Straight programs and applying harsh, punishment-oriented sanctions that do not change the underlying causes of offending (e.g., risk and protective factors) are being utilized at unacceptably high rates. Greenwood (2008) estimates that only about 5% of youth who could benefit from effective recidivism services actually receive them, and Taxman and colleagues' (2014) slightly more generous calculation estimates that only 10% of offenders receive evidence-based correctional treatment.

> *The juvenile justice and criminal justice systems trudge along, engaging in business as usual and all but ignoring the evidence-based practices that are staring them in the face – programs that cost less and keep communities safer.*
>
> Dr Robert K. Ross (2014: 18), President and CEO of the California Endowment

Lipsey and Cullen (2007: 314) similarly emphasize that "*the types of programs used in correctional practice are not the same mix represented in research literature.*" For example, giving offenders work experience by having them complete menial, physically demanding tasks (e.g., janitorial services) is far different than providing the types of vocational training shown in research studies to reduce recidivism. Recidivism rates are not likely to change until evidence-based, effective programs and practices become the norm and ineffective and harmful practices are discontinued. This shift in practices will likely need to be accompanied by a change in our philosophy of getting tough on crime (Lipsey and Cullen, 2007). While there is a clear need to punish offenders for illegal behaviors, if society wants to reduce and prevent crime, more will need to be done than simply ensuring that offenders are behind bars.

Much of the evidence cited in this chapter is drawn from meta-analyses based on multiple evaluations. While meta-analysis can be a useful technique for understanding what works, conclusions based on meta-analyses are only as good as the studies reviewed. Nearly all meta-analyses we cited in this chapter noted significant variation in the quality of the evaluations included in their calculations and in effect sizes produced by these studies. In many cases, only a minority of the evaluations were based on high-quality RCTs, many had problems with participant attrition and many were outdated. For example, in the review of the impact of formal processing of juvenile offenders (Petrosino *et al.*, 2010), two-thirds of the studies were conducted before 1990. While older research is not necessarily flawed, knowledge of risk and protective factors related to crime, research methodologies and statistical procedures have all become more sophisticated over the past few decades, and it is likely that interventions created and tested years ago will not have the greatest likelihood of demonstrating positive results.

The generalizability of these findings is also questionable. Many of the meta-analyses cautioned that their study samples were comprised largely of male offenders, which is not surprising given that males comprise the majority of those arrested and incarcerated. However, the lack of research on effective programs for female offenders is a limitation that should be addressed (Hipwell and Loeber, 2006; Zahn *et al.*, 2009). Our review also indicates a lack of evaluation research conducted outside the USA, particularly in non-English speaking countries. A meta-analysis of correctional programs for youth offenders implemented in European countries identified only 21 such studies, and two-thirds of the studies were conducted in the UK (Koehler *et al.*, 2013). Moreover, only four of the studies were RCTs, leading the authors to conclude that there is "a strong deficit of well-controlled program evaluations in most of the European countries" (Koehler *et al.*, 2013: 38). This limitation can likely be extended to most other areas of the world.

Despite these somewhat pessimistic observations, there is some room for optimism. In the USA, the emphasis on using effective treatments, the growing prison population and the rising costs of incarceration have led to some justice system reforms. Most notably, **justice reinvestment initiatives (JRI)** are occurring in about half the states in the USA (https://www.bja.gov/programs/justicereinvestment/what_is_jri.html). Begun in 2002 but bolstered in 2010 with funding from Congress, the goal of the JRI is to reduce prison populations and costs by increasing the use of strategies shown to reduce recidivism. Subsequent reductions in offending and correctional costs are expected to generate savings which can then be reinvested in community-based initiatives to improve public safety and strengthen neighborhoods, particularly severely disadvantaged areas with high rates of crime (Taxman *et al.*, 2014). Although there is much room for progress in meeting these goals, JRI is grounded in prevention science and fiscal accountability and could be successful if properly implemented (Austin *et al.*, 2013). The model has international appeal and has been embraced in European, South American and Asian countries as well as Australia (Homel, 2014).

Another encouraging sign in the USA is a recent review of the states' juvenile justice systems conducted by the National Research Council (2012). Informed by a panel of criminal justice experts, the report called for system reforms to better take into account life course developmental theories, as well as evidence from well-conducted experimental trials about what works to prevent offending. Recommendations included: (i) using incarceration of youth sparingly; (ii) increasing the use of clearly specified and developmentally informed interventions; and (iii) eliminating the use of interventions shown to be ineffective or harmful. The report concludes by stating that "*a harsh system of punishing troubled youth can make things worse, while a scientifically based juvenile justice system can make an enduring difference in the lives of many youth who most need the structure and services it can provide*" (National Research Council, 2012: viii). We agree wholeheartedly and hope to see these recommendations put into action in the future.

Summary

This chapter has described programs and practices with varying degrees of evidence of reducing recidivism among juvenile and adult offenders. All the interventions are designed to target individuals and/or their family members and may be offered at different points in the processing of offenders. Some are designed as diversion programs intended to minimize formal involvement in the system, while others are implemented by correctional staff with incarcerated offenders, and still others are designed for those who have been recently released from correctional facilities.

As in other chapters, we found that effective strategies include a variety of approaches and tend to be based on developmental theories of crime. There is some support for interventions guided by labeling theory, but strategies based solely on deterrence theory, which have an exclusive focus on punishing offenders without trying to change risk and protective factors, are unlikely to reduce recidivism and may even increase offending. Both effective and ineffective programs and policies are currently being used in the USA and worldwide. In order to significantly impact rates of offending, then, we must try to increase the use of effective strategies and eliminate the implementation of programs, policies, and practices that are ineffective or harmful.

Critical Thinking Questions and Practice Activities

1. Given the research on effective interventions in this chapter, which of the theories discussed in Chapters 2 and 3 has the best supporting evidence? Which theories have the weakest?
2. Imagine that you are in charge of rehabilitation services at a juvenile or adult correctional facility. Based on what you have read, and taking into account the effect sizes and quality of the studies reviewed, identify the intervention(s) you would implement for offenders.
3. Do you think it is possible to "get tough on crime" *and* implement effective interventions to reduce recidivism? Explain.
4. The interventions described in this chapter vary in their cost effectiveness. Do you think information on the costs versus benefits of interventions, especially those operating in correctional settings, should be considered when determining how to rehabilitate offenders? What are the benefits of doing so and what are the potential drawbacks?
5. Identify ONE ineffective or harmful program or practice discussed in this chapter. Read more about this intervention using the sources cited in the chapter. Based on the theories we have reviewed and evidence we have provided, why do you think this intervention does not lead to changes in recidivism? In your opinion, could the intervention be altered in any way to increase its likelihood of effectiveness? For example, might it be implemented with different types of offenders, in different settings, or with additional treatment components?

Helpful Websites (last accessed August 8, 2016)

- https://www.bja.gov/programs/justicereinvestment/index.html
  An Office of Justice Programs website detailing the Justice Reinvestment Initiative in the United States.
- http://nicic.gov/
  The National Institute of Corrections website, describing federal recommendations for the treatment of incarcerated offenders in the United States.

Further Reading

- Lipsey, M. W. 2014. Interventions for juvenile offenders: A serendipitous journey. *Criminology and Public Policy*, 13:1–14.
  First-person account of Lipsey's research on the effectiveness of rehabilitation programs, including changes in public perceptions of what works over the last few decades.
- Lipsey, M. W., and Cullen, F. T. 2007. The effectiveness of correctional rehabilitation: A review of systematic reviews. *Annual Review of Law and Social Science*, 3:297–320.
  Summarizes information from multiple meta-analyses of practices intended to reduce juvenile and adult recidivism.
- National Research Council. 2012. Reforming juvenile justice: A developmental approach. Washington, DC: The National Academies Press.
  Provides recommendations for reforms to the juvenile justice system, including the use of more effective prevention and treatment services.

References

Akers, R. L. 1985. *Deviant Behavior: A Social Learning Approach*, 3rd ed. Belmont, CA: Wadsworth.

Andrews, D. A., and Dowden, C. 2005. Managing correctional treatment for reduced recidivism: A meta-analytic review of programme integrity. *Legal and Criminological Psychology*, 10:173–187.

Apel, R., and Nagin, D. S. 2011. General deterrence: A review of recent evidence. In: J. Q. Wilson and J. Petersilia (eds), *Crime and Public Policy*, pp. 411–436. New York, NY: Oxford University Press.

Armelius, B., and Andreassen, T. H. 2007. Cognitive-behavioral treatment for antisocial behavior in youth in residential treatment: *Cochrane Database of Systematic Reviews*, (4):CD005650.

Austin, J., Cadora, E., Clear, T. R., *et al.* 2013. Ending mass incarceration: Charting a new justice reinvestment. Retrieved from http://sentencingproject.org/doc/publications/sen_Charting%20a%20New%20Justice%20 Reinvestment.pdf (accessed August 3, 2016).

Baer, J. S., Kivlahan, D. R., Blume, A. W., McKnight, P., and Marlatt, G. A. 2001. Brief intervention for heavy-drinking college students: 4-year follow-up and natural history. *American Journal of Public Health*, 91:1310–1316.

Barnett, E., Sussman, S., Smith, C., Rohrbach, L. A., and Spruijt-Metz, D. 2012. Motivational interviewing for adolescent substance use: A review of the literature. *Addictive Behaviors*, 37:1325–1334.

Braithwaite, J. 1989. *Crime, Shame and Reintegration*. New York, NY: Cambridge University Press.

Cho, R. M., and Tyler, J. H. 2010. Does prison-based adult basic education improve postrelease outcomes for male prisoners in Florida? *Crime and Delinquency*, 59:975–1005.

Clarke, R.V., and Cornish, D. B. 1985. Modeling offenders decisions: A framework for research and policy. In: M. Tonry and N. Morris (eds), *Crime and Justice*, vol. 6, pp. 147–185. Chicago, IL: The University of Chicago Press.

Dodge, K. A., Dishion, T. J., and Lansford, J. E. 2006. Deviant peer influences in intervention and public policy for youth. *Social Policy Report*, 20:3–19.

Durose, M. R., Cooper, A. D., and Snyder, H. N. 2014. Recidivism of prisoners released in 30 states in 2005: Patterns from 2005 to 2010. Washington, DC: Bureau of Justice Statistics, US Department of Justice.

Farrington, D. P., and Welsh, B. C. 2005. Randomized experiments in criminology: What have we learned in the last two decades? *Journal of Experimental Criminology*, 1:9–38. doi: 10.1007/s11292-004-6460-0

Foxcroft, D. R., Coombes, L., Wood, S., Allen, D., and Almeida Santimano, N. M. L. 2014. Motivational interviewing for alcohol misuse in young adults. *Cochrane Database of Systematic Reviews*, (8):CD007025.

Gilligan, J. 2012. Punishment fails. Rehabilitation works. Op. Ed, *The New York Times*, December 19, 2012.

Godley, M. D., Godley, S. H., Dennis, M. L., Funk, R. R., and Passetti, L. L. 2006. The effect of assertive continuing care on continuing care linkage, adherence and abstinence following residential treatment for adolescents with substance use disorders. *Addiction*, 102:81–93.

Greenwood, P. 2008. Prevention and intervention programs for juvenile offenders: The benefits of evidence-based practice. *The Future of Children*, 18:186–210.

Hibell, B., Guttormsson, U., Ahlström, S., *et al*. 2012. The 2011 ESPAD report: Substance use among students in 36 European countries. Stockholm, Sweden: The Swedish Council for Information on Alcohol and Other Drugs (CAN).

Hipwell, A. E., and Loeber, R. 2006. Do we know which interventions are effective for disruptive and delinquent girls? *Clinical Child and Family Psychology Review*, 9:221–255. doi: 10.1007/s10567-006-0012-2

Hirschi, T. 1969. *Causes of Delinquency*. Berkeley, CA: University of California Press.

Homel, R. 2014. Justice reinvestment as a global phenonomenon. *Victims and Offenders*, 9:6–12.

Howell, J. C., and Lipsey, M. W. 2012. Research-based guidelines for juvenile justice programs. *Justice Research and Policy*, 14:17–34.

Huddleston, W., and Marlowe, D. B. 2011. Painting the current picture: A national report on drug courts and other problem-solving court programs in the United States. Washington, DC: National Drug Court Institute.

Johnston, L. D., O'Malley, P. M., Bachman, J. G., and Schulenberg, J. E. 2013. Monitoring the Future national results on drug use: 2012 overview, key findings on adolescent drug use. Ann Arbor, MI: Institute for Social Research, University of Michigan.

Koehler, J. A., Losel, F., Akoensi, T. D., and Humphreys, D. K. 2013. A systematic review and meta-analysis on the effects of young offender treatment programs in Europe. *Journal of Experimental Criminology*, 9:19–43.

Lab, S. P. 2014. *Crime Prevention: Approaches, Practices and Evaluations*, 7th ed. Waltham, MA: Anderson Publishing.

Landenberger, N. A., and Lipsey, M. W. 2005. The positive effects of cognitive–behavioral programs for offenders: A meta-analysis of factors associated with effective treatment. *Journal of Experimental Criminology*, 1:451–476.

Larimer, M. E., Turner, A. P., Anderson, B. K., *et al*. 2001. Evaluating a brief alcohol intervention with fraternities. *Journal of Studies on Alcohol*, 62:370–380.

Latimer, J., Morton-Bourgon, K., and Chrétien, J.-A. 2006. A meta-analytic examination of drug treatment courts: Do they reduce recidivism? Department of Justice Canada, Research and Statistics Division.

Lipsey, M. W. 2009. The primary factors that characterize effective interventions with juvenile offenders: A meta-analytic overview. *Victims and Offenders*, 4:124–147.

Lipsey, M. W., and Cullen, F. T. 2007. The effectiveness of correctional rehabilitation: A review of systematic reviews. *Annual Review of Law and Social Science*, 3:297–320.

Lipsey, M. W., Landenberger, N. A., and Wilson, S. J. 2007. Effects of cognitive-behavioral programs for criminal offenders. *Campbell Systematic Reviews*, 3(6).

Livingstone, N., Macdonald, G., and Carr, N. 2013. Restorative justice conferencing for reducing recidivism in young offenders (aged 7 to 21): *Cochrane Database of Systematic Reviews*, (2):CD008898.

Lundahl, B. W., Kunz, C., Brownell, C., Tollefson, D., and Burke, B. L. 2010. A meta-analysis of motivational interviewing: Twenty-five years of empirical studies. *Research on Social Work Practice*, 20:137–160.

MacKenzie, D. 2000. Evidence-based corrections: Identifying what works. *Crime and Delinquency*, 46:457–471.

Marlatt, G. A., Baer, J. S., Kivlahan, D. R., et al. 1998. Screening and brief intervention for high-risk college student drinkers: Results from a 2-year follow-up assessment. *Journal of Consulting and Clinical Psychology*, 66:604–615.

Martinson, R. 1974. What works? Questions and answers about prison reform. *The Public Interest*, 22–54.

Mears, D. P. 2007. Towards rational and evidence-based crime policy. *Journal of Criminal Justice*, 35:667–682. doi: 10.1016/j.jcrimjus.2007.09.003

Menkel-Meadow, C. 2007. Restorative justice: What is it and does it work? *Annual Review of Law and Social Science*, 3:161–187. doi: 10.1146/annurev.lawsocsci.2.081805.110005

Mitchell, O., Wilson, D. B., Eggers, A., and MacKenzie, D. L. 2012. Drug courts' effects on criminal offending for juveniles and adults. *Campbell Systematic Reviews*, 4.

Nagin, D. S., Cullen, F. T., and Jonson, C. L. 2009. Imprisonment and reoffending. *Crime and Justice*, 38:115–200.

National Research Council. 2012. Reforming juvenile justice: A developmental approach. Washington, DC: The National Academies Press.

National Research Council and Institute of Medicine. 2009. *Preventing Mental, Emotional, and Behavioral Disorders Among Young People: Progress and Possibilities*. Washington, DC: The National Academies Press.

Petrosino, A., Turpin-Petrosino, C., and Guckenburg, S. 2010. Formal system processing of juveniles: Effects on delinquency. *Campbell Systematic Reviews*, 1.

Petrosino, A., Turpin-Petrosino, C., Hollis-Peel, M. E., and Lavenberg, J. G. 2013. Scared Straight and other juvenile awareness programs for preventing juvenile delinquency: A systematic review. *Campbell Systematic Reviews*, 5.

Pew Center on the States. 2001. State of recidivism: The revolving door of America's prisons. Washington, DC: The Pew Charitable Trusts.

Ross, R. K. 2014. We need more scale, not more innovation. *Stanford Social Innovation Review*, 12:18–20.

Schwalbe, C. S., Gearing, R. E., MacKenzie, M. J., Brewer, K. B., and Ibrahim, R. 2012. A meta-analysis of experimental studies of diversion programs for juvenile offenders. *Clinical Psychology Review*, 32:26–33.

Sherman, L. W. 1993. Defiance, deterrence, and irrelevance: A theory of the criminal sanction. *Journal of Research in Crime and Delinquency*, 30:445–473. doi: 10.1177/0022427893030004006

Sherman, L. W., Gottfredson, D. C., MacKenzie, D. L., et al. 1998. *Preventing Crime: What Works, What Doesn't, What's Promising*. Washington, DC: National Institute of Justice.

Slesnick, N., Prestopnik, J. L., Meyers, R. J., and Glassman, M. 2007. Treatment outcome for street-living, homeless youth. *Addictive Behaviors*, 32:1237–1251. doi: 10.1016/j.addbeh.2006.08.010

Stickle, W. P., Connell, N. M., Wilson, D. M., and Gottfredson, D. C. 2008. An experimental evaluation of teen courts. *Journal of Experimental Criminology*, 4:137–163.

Strang, H., Sherman, L. W., Mayo-Wilson, E., Woods, D., and Ariel, B. 2013. Restorative Justice Conferencing (RJC) using face-to-face meetings of offenders and victims: Effects on offender recidivism and victim satisfaction. A systematic review. *Campbell Systematic Reviews*, 10.

Sutherland, E. H. 1947. *Principles of Criminology*. Philadelphia, PA: J. B. Lippincott.

Taxman, F. S., Pattavina, A., and Caudy, M. 2014. Justice reinvestment in the United States: An empirical assessment of the potential impact of increased correctional programming on recidivism. *Victims and Offenders*, 9:50–75.

Turrisi, R., Larimer, M. E., Mallett, K. A., *et al.* 2009. A randomized clinical trial evaluating a combined alcohol intervention for high-risk college students. *Journal of Studies on Alcohol and Drugs*, 70:555–567.

Villettaz, P., Killias, M., and Zoder, I. 2006. The effects of custodial vs. non-custodial sentences on re-offending: A systematic review of the state of knowledge. *Campbell Systematic Reviews*, 13.

Washington State Institute for Public Policy (WSIPP). 2004. Outcome evaluation of Washington State's research-based programs for juvenile offenders. Olympia, WA: Washington State Institute for Public Policy.

Washington State Institute for Public Policy (WSIPP). 2006. Evidence-based public policy options to reduce future prison construction, criminal justice costs, and crime rates. Olympia, WA: Washington State Institute for Public Policy.

Washington State Institute for Public Policy (WSIPP). 2012. Return on investment: Evidence-based options to improve statewide outcomes. Olympia, WA: Washington State Institute for Public Policy.

Washington State Institute for Public Policy (WSIPP). 2015. Benefit-cost results. Olympia, WA: Washington State Institute for Public Policy.

Wilson, D. B., MacKenzie, D. L., and Mitchell, F. N. 2008. Effects of correctional boot camps on offending. *Campbell Systematic Reviews*, 1(6).

Wilson, H. A., and Hoge, R. D. 2013. The effect of youth diversion programs on recidivism: A meta-analytic review. *Criminal Justice and Behavior*, 40:497–518. doi: 10.1177/0093854812451089

Wilson, S. J., and Lipsey, M. W. 2000. Wilderness challenge programs for delinquent youth: A meta-analysis of outcome evaluations. *Evaluation and Program Planning*, 23:1–12. doi: 10.1016/S0149-7189(99)00040-3

Zahn, M. A., Day, J. C., Mihalic, S. F., and Tichavsky, L. 2009. Determining what works for girls in the juvenile justice system: A summary of evaluation evidence. *Crime and Delinquency*, 55:266–293. doi: 10.1177/0011128708330649

Section IV
Crime Prevention in Practice

10

Selecting and Implementing Effective Crime Prevention Practices, Programs, and Policies

---

Learning Objectives

Upon finishing this chapter, students should be able to:
- Describe the steps that communities should follow to select effective crime prevention interventions which best fit their needs and resources
- Define the four elements of implementation fidelity
- Understand how implementation quality affects the degree to which outcomes shown in research trials are achieved in community replications
- Describe the methods that can be used to ensure high-quality implementation of effective crime prevention interventions in communities.

Introduction

Have you ever had the opportunity to purchase a new or used vehicle or helped a friend or family member to do so? If so, you can probably appreciate the amount of time and consideration that goes into this decision. Cars are among the most expensive products we will ever buy and we want to be sure that the vehicle we choose is a worthy investment. Prior to making such a purchase, what factors must be considered? You will want to know about the vehicle's cost, reliability, safety features, and performance. To find this information, you'll have to do research, consulting sources like Consumer Reports, consumer ratings such as those found on Angie's List and asking friends and acquaintances about the cars they drive. You will also have to consider the type of vehicle that makes the most sense for your personal circumstances, such as where you live (do you need four-wheel drive capacity? Is a convertible a sensible option?), the number of human and canine passengers you will have to

The Prevention of Crime, First Edition. Delbert Elliott and Abigail Fagan.
© 2017 John Wiley & Sons, Inc. Published 2017 by John Wiley & Sons, Inc.
Companion website: www.wiley.com/go/elliott/prevention_of_crime

accommodate, whether or not you regularly transport large goods and the number of miles you typically drive per year (can you buy a gas guzzler or do you need a more fuel-efficient car?). After you create a "short list" of possible cars, you'll be ready to test drive them and get a hands-on feel for what it's like to drive the cars. Finally, after you select the make and model you want, you'll make a few final decisions that will help you customize the vehicle and truly make it your dream car.

All of this work takes place before you even take possession of the car and make your first payment! Is it worth it? Even if you aren't a car enthusiast, you'll probably agree that it's important to take the time to make sure you make the right choice. Similarly, most people wouldn't buy a car just because someone told them it was a great vehicle or because their local dealership was having a big sale.

If people are willing to spend this much effort to select a new car, why is it that communities often implement crime prevention programs without fully considering if the intervention(s) will actually solve their crime problems? Or because it's easier to continue implementing interventions already in place, even if they aren't working well? Is there a process that communities can follow to make better choices about prevention programming? How can they be sure they are selecting the right intervention and using it correctly?

This chapter addresses these issues and begins our discussion of how effective crime prevention can actually be achieved in communities, states, and nations. Although prevention science is a relatively new discipline, there is a growing body of research examining the process of **implementation**: the practice of selecting and using interventions shown to be effective in high-quality research evaluations. According to the National Implementation Resource Network (NIRN; see http://nirn.fpg.unc.edu/), simply providing agencies and organizations with a list of available effective interventions does not guarantee that they will actually select them, effectively implement them or achieve the outcomes that these interventions have produced in research trials. Rather, expected outcomes will only occur when effective interventions are well implemented and when the local context enables high-quality implementation (Fixsen *et al.*, 2009), as shown in the formula: **Effective innovations × Effective implementation × Enabling contexts = Socially significant outcomes** (Institute of Medicine and National Research Council, 2014a). To make all of this happen, organizations have to complete a series of tasks, beginning with an assessment of local levels of risk and protective factors, then comparing different interventions that can address these factors and investigating the community's ability to effectively implement each potential new intervention. This chapter describes these steps in detail. We also discuss methods for ensuring that the actual process of implementation is successful; that all aspects of the intervention are replicated with care and quality so that desired reductions in crime are achieved.

Conducting Needs Assessments and Establishing Local Priorities

To understand the first step of the implementation process, **needs assessments**, consider what happens when you are sick and require medicine to get better. Hundreds of medications are available in your local pharmacy, but you do not just pick one off the shelf and use it because it has been proven to work, right? To get well, you have to select the one that will treat your particular symptoms. In the same manner, a community that wants to reduce

> *If you don't know where you're going, you'll end up somewhere else.*
>
> Yogi Berra, US baseball player and manager

crime has to determine which prevention program, practice, or policy will address its particular crime problem and the factors contributing to it.

Much like a doctor performing a medical diagnosis, a local agency or community should begin with a scan of its symptoms, including: (i) what types of crime are occurring? and (ii) what risk and protective factors are contributing to these crimes? This work is important because there is often a misperception that a particular crime problem is larger or smaller than it really is and objective data can provide a more accurate picture of offending. For example, a gang shooting could lead to the belief that youth gangs are prevalent in a community when, in fact, they are not. Or, a series of drug overdoses among prominent community members could be covered up to avoid damaging the reputation of the group or the community. Using crime prevention dollars on the first issue but not the second would be misguided.

To assess its levels of crime, a community should collect both official and self-reported data. The goal is to identify the specific offenses occurring in the geographical region(s) in which prevention services will be implemented, as well as the types of crimes committed at the highest rates and the most consistently over time. Official data will be most informative when obtained from local law enforcement agencies. This information can be used to identify places where crime is elevated (i.e., **hot spots**) as well as rates of different offenses. It may or may not be able to provide details about individual offenders or groups of offenders who could be targeted for prevention services. Self-report surveys will be more helpful in that regard and can also identify crimes unlikely to come to the attention of law enforcement. Although these surveys can be costly and time-consuming to conduct, some surveys are regularly conducted in schools across the USA and it may be possible for a local agency to obtain regional data from those administrating the survey. For example, many public school students across the USA participate in the **Youth Risk Behavior Surveillance System (YRBSS**; http://www.cdc.gov/HealthyYouth/yrbs/index.htm) and **Monitoring the Future (MTF)** surveys (www.monitoringthefuture.org), both of which ask youth to report perpetration of particular crimes. Once the community has considered all its crime data, it should prioritize the offenses that are of most concern. These behaviors will be the focus of crime prevention efforts.

Because effective interventions are designed to reduce risk factors and increase protective factors, a community should also collect data on these experiences. Recall from Chapter 3 that multiple risk and protective factors are related to crime and can be experienced at different rates in different communities. Community members should collect information on a wide range of risk and protective factors, ideally using data collected over multiple years so that they can identify the risk and protective factors which are consistently elevated or depressed. Factors that are of greatest concern to the community should then be prioritized; these will be the focus of crime prevention programs, practices, and policies.

Official data provide limited information on risk and protective factors because such influences are usually related to individual characteristics or interpersonal situations, not objective behaviors easily captured by public records. However, data from the US Census can be used to measure community-level risk factors like poverty, high population turnover, and single-parent households. Schools also collect administrative data related to commitment to education (e.g., rates of absenteeism) and academic performance (e.g., grades and test scores). Information on individual, peer and family risk and protective factors will probably need to be collected directly from individuals using surveys or interviews. Again, it is possible that other agencies have collected such data, and local community groups should ask state-level offices related to education, juvenile justice, and child welfare if they have collected these types of data and are willing to share them. If such information is not available, the Blueprints (http://www.colorado.edu/cspv/safeschools/surveys.html) and Communities That Care (http://www.communitiesthatcare.net/getting-started/) websites provide detailed guidance for communities on how to implement community and/or school-based surveys to assess risk and protective factors.

Once an agency or community has identified the criminal behaviors it wishes to address and the risk and protective factors contributing to local crime, they should conduct a **resource assessment**. This work involves consulting local resource guides if they are available and interviewing or surveying staff at all agencies in the community likely to be offering crime prevention services. Questions should be asked regarding the types of programs or practices currently being implemented, including the risk and protective factors they address, whether or not services have been evaluated and demonstrated as effective in reducing crime and the population(s) targeted by the intervention. If no effective interventions are being used, there is good justification for adopting something new. If effective interventions do exist but do not seem to be reducing crime or changing risk and protective factors, it could be that they are not reaching enough people to make a difference in the community. The solution would then be to increase the reach of services by implementing the intervention more widely. It could also be that interventions are not being delivered with **fidelity**; that is, local implementers may be making considerable changes to the intervention's guidelines and protocols. For example, an agency may be delivering services to individuals who do not meet eligibility criteria, may be employing staff who do not have the training or credentials needed to effectively deliver the intervention or may be making substantial changes to the program content. In these cases, the solution is to improve implementation practices. We will provide specific examples of how to do so later in the chapter.

While they can be time-consuming, resource assessments serve three important functions. *First*, asking agencies to identify the degree to which they are using effective crime prevention services can increase awareness of the importance of both prevention and evidence-based prevention. *Second*, resource assessments can improve the quality of service delivery and ability of communities to reduce crime. They can identify services that should be abandoned because they have been tested and shown to have no effects or harmful effects on crime, as well as services whose effectiveness is questionable because they have never been evaluated. *Third*, such assessments can help avoid duplication of services and waste of resources. If one agency is already implementing an effective intervention targeting identified needs, it may not be necessary to start up a second program with similar aims. As we will discuss below, start-up costs for new programs can be significant and it may be better to invest money improving what is already in place than to launch an entirely new intervention.

Assessing Fit Between Local Needs and Effective Crime Prevention Interventions

Once the need for new crime prevention services has been identified, an agency must decide which new program, practice, or policy should be put in place. As reviewed in Section III, a number of effective interventions exist and there may be several interventions available to address a particular

Table 10.1 Questions to ask when conducting a fit assessment.

- How well do the new interventions address priority risk and protective factors?
- Are the new interventions aligned with the agency's/community's values and service priorities?
- Are the new interventions a good cultural fit for the community?
- Can implementation requirements be met?
- What are the relative costs and benefits of different interventions?

need. How, then, do practitioners choose between these options and make the choice that best fits their circumstances? Recall how confusing it can be when you first set out to buy a new car: how do you decide which one is the best investment and the best reflection of your personality?

The main task during this phase is to conduct a **fit assessment** and evaluate the degree to which potential interventions are a good fit for the agency or community in which they will be implemented (Meyers, Durlak, and Wandersman, 2012). Table 10.1 shows some important questions to ask during the fit assessment. First, one must consider if there is a good match between the new intervention and the risk and protective factors that have been prioritized as important by the community. Interventions should also be compared according to how well they align with the mission and service priorities of the agencies that will deliver them, as well as the norms and values of the larger community. For example, an agency dedicated to serving at-risk populations may be opposed to implementing a universal intervention, while a law enforcement agency with a rigid leadership structure would probably be reluctant to implement practices requiring extensive community involvement or officer discretion and decision-making power. Communities with diverse populations may prioritize interventions they consider to be most culturally relevant for their residents and which have been tested and shown to be effective for populations matching their demographic characteristics.

Implementation requirements must also be compared and interventions that cannot feasibly be delivered ruled out. For example, a community wishing to implement an early childhood education or parent training intervention has to consider whether there are local agencies suitable for delivering these services. It is also important to determine if there are enough eligible participants living in the community to make the delivery of services cost effective. For example, most home visitation programs target low-income, young, first-time mothers, and if there are relatively few women in the community meeting these eligibility requirements, then this type of service would not be a good fit. As another example, the **Multisystemic Therapy (MST)** program requires a five-day initial training for staff, low therapist:client ratios, strong supervisory oversight and active community referral mechanisms. If agencies do not believe they can accommodate all of these requirements, they should not adopt MST. Similarly, classroom curricula will require that a certain number of sessions be taught for a specified amount of time. If a school's schedule cannot allow for full delivery of the required lessons, a different program should be selected.

Cost will probably be the most important aspect of programming considered and interventions requiring the fewest resources may be viewed as most appealing. However, total costs should be considered along with the benefits of the program. As reviewed in Section III, different interventions produce different effect sizes, and a low-cost program with a small effect on crime may be less desirable than a more expensive program with a larger impact. In addition, some programs have been evaluated only a few times and may show inconsistent effects across studies, while others have been subject to much more investigation and show more stable and generalizable outcomes. Even if the latter cost more, they may be a better investment.

Obviously, some interventions may be too costly to implement and it is better to acknowledge this barrier as soon as possible so that other options can be considered. Human as well as financial resources should be taken into account during this discussion. For example, mentoring programs like **Big Brothers, Big Sisters** can only be successful if there are enough volunteers in the community willing to mentor young children. In addition, if this type of program is being implemented in a rural community, mentors and children will likely need access to public or private transportation in order to meet, and such services will not be available in some areas.

Assessing Readiness for Change

Fit assessments help communities identify interventions they perceive to be most cost effective, feasible, and appealing. Once fit is assessed, it will be tempting to immediately begin implementation of the intervention rated most highly on these dimensions. However, it is important to complete another set of activities before making the final decision on programming: conducting a **readiness assessment** (Edwards *et al.*, 2000; Meyers *et al.*, 2012). While there is some overlap in the issues considered during fit and readiness assessments, the former involves a comparison of multiple interventions while the latter typically focuses on one intervention, the one that rises to the top during the fit assessment. However, if multiple programs are all considered to be a good fit, all of those interventions may be compared during the readiness assessment.

As shown in Table 10.2, during the readiness assessment, the specific agency and/or system that will deliver the new program or practice should be identified. It may be an existing organization like a school or school district, health clinic, or justice system, or a newly created structure like a community coalition formed specifically to oversee the intervention (Durlak and DuPre, 2008). The readiness assessment focuses on the degree of support for the new intervention(s) within this organization and the capacity or ability of the agency to effectively deliver the new service(s). More specifically, Elliott and Mihalic (2004) identify six critical factors indicating readiness: (i) a champion who promotes and pushes for the program; (ii) strong administrative support from the agency or organization implementing the intervention;

Table 10.2 Critical steps in the readiness assessment.

- Identify the agency(ies) that will deliver the new intervention
- Identify the intervention champion(s)
- Assess levels of support and buy-in for the new intervention among all key personnel
- Identify and eliminate barriers which threaten support for the intervention
- Recruit implementers to be early adopters of the intervention
- Identify all intervention implementation requirements
- Assess the implementing agency's capacity to fully deliver the intervention
- Identify all financial and human resources needed to deliver the intervention

(iii) skilled and supportive staff; (iv) program credibility in the larger community; (v) consideration of the resources necessary for implementation; and (vi) the potential to successfully implement, sustain and obtain funding for all the required elements of the intervention.

One of the most important factors affecting the likelihood that a new intervention will be adopted and well implemented is the presence of a **champion** (Edwards *et al.*, 2000; Elliott and Mihalic, 2004). Program champions are individuals who enthusiastically endorse a particular intervention and who are fully committed to putting it into practice. They should also be well respected and have the necessary influence, connections and leadership in the community to bring together all partners necessary for the intervention, encourage their support and find the resources necessary for implementation. For example, the adoption of a new school-based program will be facilitated if the district superintendent or a principal is a champion, and the city mayor would be an excellent champion for a community-based intervention. In the Blueprints project, when replicating Model programs in sites across the USA, the degree to which there was a strong, supportive champion was strongly related to successful implementation (Fagan and Mihalic, 2003; Mihalic *et al.*, 2004).

Although the presence of a champion greatly increases the chances of success, new programs may not be adopted and probably will not be sustained over time without strong support from other key individuals. Thus, it is important to assess the readiness to endorse the new intervention of the agency and community as a whole. Support includes having a shared vision, recognizing the need for the intervention and believing the program can address that need (Kallestad and Olweus, 2003; Riley, Taylor, and Elliott, 2001).

The champion may take the lead in garnering support for the intervention, and a good first step is for the champion to arrange a meeting of all stakeholders whose buy-in will be needed to successfully implement the intervention. For example, during the readiness phase of **Communities That Care**, a Key Leader Orientation is held to bring together all individuals in the community whose influence and resources will be needed to form a broad-based coalition and to help find funding for new prevention programs. In this meeting, leaders discuss their willingness to implement a community-wide prevention system, the degree to which their community is able and willing to work together to implement effective prevention programs and the existence of any barriers or challenges which might prevent CTC from being a success (see: http://www.communitiesthatcare.net/getting-started/#prettyPhoto). For example, high levels of distrust between community members could signal a lack of readiness for CTC because this intervention requires active community involvement.

For school programs, champions might arrange a meeting of school administrators and staff to discuss potential interventions. Support from school principals will certainly be needed, as they will have to provide time and resources for implementation. For classroom-based interventions, teacher buy-in is also critical. Not only do teachers have to deliver the program content, they also have to do so with enthusiasm and excitement in order to increase the likelihood that students will practice and retain new skills (Fagan and Mihalic, 2003). Ideally, schools will ask for volunteers to be **early adopters** of the program – those who try it out for the first time in a trial run, sometimes referred to as a **pilot program**. These staff can later promote the program to other teachers in order to expand programming to other classrooms. Teachers who are not consulted in advance or who are pressured by administrators to implement a program are much less likely to support it and to implement it with enthusiasm (Berman and McLaughlin, 1976; Kam, Greenberg, and Walls, 2003).

If readiness assessments indicate that support for a new intervention is lacking, then it should either be abandoned and a new intervention selected, or time must be spent overcoming resistance. For example, communities vary in their tolerance of under-age drinking and their vigilance in enforcing policies intended to reduce alcohol use by teenagers. In communities where under-age drinking is seen as a "rite of passage" and not very harmful, champions may need to recruit influential community members to talk about the negative consequences of teen alcohol use and to participate in community events which highlight these problems. Or, if a school principal is reluctant to adopt a prevention program because s/he thinks it will take time away from academic instruction, a champion may need to find someone in the school who can help convince the principal that the intervention is necessary. No matter what the specific barrier is, it is essential that time be spent *prior* to program adoption to overcome resistance so that the lack of support does not lead to failure *after* resources have been invested.

Even if strong support for the new intervention exists, agencies must also have the **organizational capacity** needed to implement it. Capacity refers to the infrastructure, staffing, technology and resources that must be in place to fully implement the intervention (Elliott and Mihalic, 2004; Meyers *et al.*, 2012). To evaluate capacity, agency administrators and personnel must first become as familiar as possible with the intervention and its requirements. The Blueprints (www.blueprintsprograms.com) and CrimeSolutions.gov (www.crimesolutions.gov) websites provide useful summaries of intervention content and delivery protocols, costs, and contact information for developers. In addition to visiting these websites, it will be useful for agencies to discuss intervention requirements with program developers, obtain and read program materials and even talk to other agencies which have implemented the intervention and/or observe their programming in action.

> *What makes us human,*
> *I think, is an ability to*
> *ask questions.*
>
> Jane Goodall

Administrators must next consider staffing requirements: do they have enough staff in place with the necessary credentials to deliver the intervention, or will new staff need to be hired? For example, the **Nurse–Family Partnership** program must be delivered by registered nurses and **Functional Family Therapy** by therapists with master's degrees. If new staff will need to be hired, what is the likelihood that applicants will have the necessary qualifications? Many interventions require that staff receive ongoing supervision and feedback from supervisors who also must be familiar with and supportive of the program. If agencies do not routinely provide this type of coaching and feedback to staff, they will have to carefully consider if such a change in culture and practice can be made.

Agencies must also assess their capacity for monitoring and evaluating implementation practices. Some program developers require that local agencies collect data on program features such as the number of participants served, attendance and retention of participants, the number of sessions delivered, changes made to delivery requirements and outcomes demonstrated by the intervention. This information has to be regularly sent to developers or uploaded into their databases. In other cases, local agencies will have to create such systems themselves. For example, **hot spots policing** requires that law enforcement agencies regularly assess where in their jurisdictions crimes are being committed and if hot spots change over time. Police agencies will require software and technology to "geocode" crime data, as well as competent staff to manage these systems. Whether or not a particular police agency will have the capacity to complete this work must be assessed prior to adopting this type of intervention.

Development and maintenance of implementation monitoring systems will require financial investments, and agencies must assess their financial readiness to provide these and all other monetary and human resources needed for implementation. Costs associated with both start-up and maintenance must be considered. Start-up costs are usually one-time expenditures necessary to begin programming; for example, costs related to the initial training of staff; purchase of materials, equipment or technological services; and, in some cases, licensing fees. For example, there is a one-time $5,000 cost for opening a new **Big Brothers, Big Sisters** agency in a community. Ongoing costs of interventions usually include staff salary and benefits for implementers, supervisors and/or program managers; participant materials such as manuals or workbooks; fees to program developers for technical assistance and support during implementation; staff training; recruitment and advertising expenses; and facility costs for all sites where implementation will take place. Some interventions may also require money to be spent on participant incentives to ensure regular attendance, such as transportation, child care, and food/snacks.

Interventions will vary significantly in their costs and a full understanding of all resources required for implementation must be known prior to starting the new program. Otherwise, there is a danger of spending money on start-up costs only to have to discontinue the intervention because maintenance costs cannot be met. Although total program costs may be daunting, agencies should consider **unit costs**, or costs per person or per site, and keep in mind the potential for economies-of-scale. Costs for Blueprint programs range from a low of $50 to $100 per person for school drug prevention programs to a high of $3500 to $10,000 per person/family for community-based mental health programs. However, for many programs, the more people who receive services, the lower the costs per participant. For example, training costs are often based on the event rather than the number of people trained; therefore, an agency should train as many implementers as allowed by the developer, thereby expanding their delivery capacity and reducing their cost per trainee. Similarly, many parent training programs are delivered to groups of families, allowing a maximum of, for example, 10 families per session. If a parent training program costs $5000 to deliver, the cost per family would be $1250 if only four families attend but $500 per family if 10 families attend. Which scenario is more fiscally appealing?

Obviously, some interventions are quite expensive and limited financial resources may put a particular intervention out of reach for an agency. It is important to keep in mind, however, that most of the programs we describe in this book do show a return on investment over time. That is, while initial costs must be absorbed, there will be savings in the long term when crime is prevented. Thus, it is important to compare programs based on their costs *and* their costs/benefits.

The Process of Implementation

Implementation fidelity and intervention outcomes

After assessing needs, fit, readiness, and capacity, an agency is finally ready to put the new intervention into place. The goal in this stage is to implement the new program, practice, or policy with high **fidelity**: as closely as possible to the model that has been tested and shown to reduce crime (Durlak

Table 10.3   Four elements of implementation fidelity.

Element	Example of high-quality implementation
Adherence	Delivering all components of the intervention to the intended population using the recommended methods and materials
Dosage	Implementing the required number, length, and frequency of sessions and the right duration of programming
Quality of delivery	Implementer skill and enthusiasm in delivering program content and engaging participants
Participant responsiveness	Regular attendance, active participation and positive views of the intervention among those receiving services

and DuPre, 2008; Dusenbury *et al.*, 2003). Just as you are supposed to follow directions when taking a medicine that has been proven effective in treating your particular symptoms, interventions should also be implemented as directed. What happens if you do not take the entire dosage of medication prescribed by your doctor or if you do not take the medicine with food or avoid alcohol as recommended? You probably reduce your chances of feeling better and increase risks of harmful side effects. In the same way, deviating from intervention guidelines can undermine the likelihood of achieving the positive effects that were detailed in Section III.

Many studies have investigated the relationship between implementation and outcomes, and the findings from this research are conclusive: higher implementation fidelity is associated with better intervention outcomes (Durlak, 2013; Fixsen *et al.*, 2005; Lipsey, 2009). One of the first criminal justice studies to show this type of result, an evaluation of the Violent Juvenile Offender program, indicated that the two sites implementing the program with greater fidelity produced stronger effects on both the number and seriousness of arrests than the two sites with low implementation fidelity (Fagan, 1990). Many studies since then have documented similar relationships (Mihalic, 2004). A systematic review of this literature indicated that in two-thirds of the 59 studies considered, better implementation was related to improvements in at least half of the outcomes assessed (Durlak and DuPre, 2008). In meta-analyses of correctional programs intended to reduce recidivism, Lipsey (2009) found that when the quality of implementation was higher, stronger effects on recidivism were evidenced. In fact, adhering to implementation standards was estimated to reduce recidivism rates by 5 to 8 percentage points (Lipsey, 1999).

Attempts to document the relationship between fidelity and program outcomes typically focus on the four implementation characteristics shown in Table 10.3: **adherence**, **dosage**, **quality of delivery**, and **participant responsiveness** (Dusenbury *et al.*, 2003). All elements are important to achieve during implementation. **Adherence** is a comprehensive measure assessing the degree to which all essential elements of the intervention are delivered using the recommended methods and materials and to the intended population (Goncy *et al.*, 2015). For example, as discussed in Chapter 7, strong adherence to the **Strong African American Families (SAAF)** protocols means that: (i) youth and their parents receive separate as well as combined sessions, (ii) content related to targeted family risk and protective factors is shown in videos and discussed by participants, (iii) programming is delivered by three trained facilitators, and (iv) participants are limited to African American families with children aged 10–14.

As a prevention practice, **school-based bullying prevention** has fewer specified elements; nonetheless, implementation should include: (i) the creation of anti-bullying school policies, (ii) enforcement of these policies by all school personnel, (iii) a mechanism allowing schools officials and students to safely report bullying episodes, and (iv) classroom discussions of bullying and its negative consequences. One of the first studies to show a relationship between implementation adherence and program outcomes was an evaluation of the **Life Skills Training** drug prevention curriculum. In this trial, students whose teachers delivered at least 60% of the required information and activities had the greatest reductions in smoking, drinking, and marijuana use (Botvin *et al.*, 1995).

Dosage is the amount of programming that is delivered by implementers. It should mirror the number, length, frequency, and duration of programming specified by the intervention developer. For example, **Child First** requires that clinicians provide one or more home visits per week for 6–12 months. The total number of visits is not specified but is flexible and responsive to family needs. Although dosage requirements have not been clearly identified for **ignition interlocks**, a two-year installation period appears better able than a one-year dosage period to produce sustained reductions in drunk driving (Rauch *et al.*, 2011). Based on these types of findings, some prevention scientists maintain that interventions with longer dosage periods will be more likely to produce positive effects (Nation *et al.*, 2003). However, there is no rule of thumb regarding optimal dosage requirements and many programs and practices have shown effects even with relatively short intervention periods.

The **quality of delivery** refers to the competence, method, and style by which the intervention is delivered by program staff. Quality of delivery can be assessed by examining implementers' preparedness to teach, their support and enthusiasm for the program and mastery of delivery methods. For example, skilled implementers will be able to explain concepts clearly, without proceeding too quickly or too slowly and using relevant examples and stories. When programs call for interactive teaching methods, high-quality implementers will be able to facilitate participant discussion and practice without allowing disruptive behaviors or wasting of time. Staff who deliver therapeutic interventions like **Multisystemic Therapy (MST)** with quality will effectively build trust and rapport with clients, identify positive aspects of the family, avoid blaming family members for their problems and suggest specific actions they can take to achieve their goals (http://www.mstinstitute. org/qa_program/tam.html). An evaluation of **Functional Family Therapy (FFT)** indicated that quality of delivery strongly affected outcomes. As shown in Figure 10.1, in this study, youth whose families received services from therapists rated as "not competent" had *higher* rates of recidivism for felony offenses compared to both the control group and youth whose families received programming from more skilled therapists (Washington State Institute for Public Policy, 2002).

As its name suggests, **participant responsiveness** focuses on how well program participants are responding to services. When programs and practices are well implemented, participants will be more involved in sessions, react more positively to the content and activities and more regularly attend programming. In contrast, when responsiveness is low, participants will be visibly bored and distracted, will not complete practice assignments, will not regularly attend sessions and will have negative views regarding the intervention content. An analysis of the **Positive Family Support** program showed that participant responsiveness was significantly related to behavioral improvement (Stormshak *et al.*, 2005). As shown in Figure 10.2, adolescents whose families never utilized

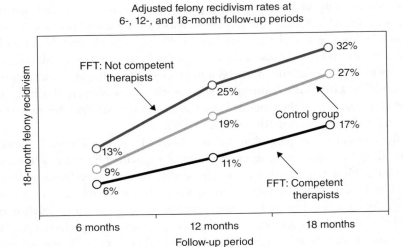

Figure 10.1 Relationship between therapist competence and felony recidivism rates in an evaluation of Functional Family Therapy. Source: Washington State Institute for Public Policy, 2002.

the Family Resource Centers offered in the intervention showed no changes in teacher reports of students' problem behaviors from Grades 6–8. However, those whose families had average levels of use (i.e., they accessed the FRC about eight times) showed decreases in problems from Grades 6–8, and those whose families were the top 5% (or 95th percentile) of users had the greatest reductions.

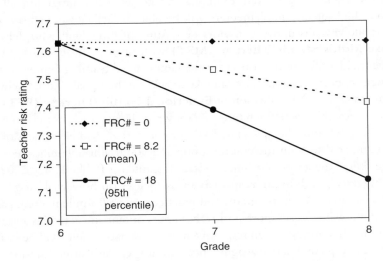

Figure 10.2 Relationship between the number of times families used the Family Resource Center (FRC) and teacher risk ratings of adolescent problem behaviors in the Positive Family Support program. Source: Stormshak *et al.*, 2005. Reproduced with permission of Springer.

Implementation and adaptation

Research on implementation processes not only indicates that higher quality implementation can improve participant outcomes, but also that interventions are often poorly replicated in communities and schools (Durlak, 2013; Gottfredson and Gottfredson, 2002). In research trials, program evaluators take many steps to ensure that implementation practices are followed, but when interventions are implemented in the "real world," fidelity is often lacking. Lipsey (2009) cautions that juvenile justice officials rarely implement programs with the same levels of care and quality as program developers and evaluators. In community settings, a review of family-focused programs estimated that only about one-fourth of practitioners implement such interventions according to their requirements (Kumpfer and Alvarado, 2003). The National Study of Delinquency Prevention in Schools (Gottfredson *et al.*, 2000) found that, on average, only half of school-based drug prevention programs met prescribed dosage levels, one-fourth of mentoring programs met dosage requirements and only 57% of all programs met a "quality of delivery" requirement. Similarly, a national assessment of school-based drug prevention programming (Hallfors and Godette, 2002) found that only 19% of districts implemented classroom curricula with fidelity, while the other districts delivered programs with untrained teachers, without the required materials or with misspecification of the population to be served (e.g., targeting high-risk students with universal programs). These findings suggest that perfect implementation rarely occurs during community replications of effective interventions (Bumbarger and Perkins, 2008).

There are many possible explanations for low fidelity and it is important to know that there is some debate in prevention science regarding the need for strict implementation fidelity (Elliott and Mihalic, 2004). Some scientists and many practitioners emphasize that complete fidelity may not be desirable and that local communities should make **adaptations** or changes to intervention protocols (Bumbarger and Perkins, 2008). These claims typically point out that most interventions are developed by academics, not practitioners, and tested in artificial conditions that do not match the settings or populations in which interventions will ultimately be used (Lau, 2006). As a result, it may not be possible for a community to adhere to implementation protocols. It could also be that the content and methods of delivery which produced results when tested with a particular group in a particular region will not be culturally relevant or effective when replicated in a new location or with participants from different backgrounds (Castro, Barrera, and Martinez, 2004). Thus, changes may be required to better respond to community composition, culture, or geographical setting (Morrison *et al.*, 2009). These types of adaptation are thought to increase both local support for the intervention and its intervention effectiveness, to the extent that they increase the relevance of the material and enhance participant engagement (Backer, 2001).

Advocates typically call for **planned adaptation**, whereby changes are made thoughtfully and carefully by local implementers and, ideally, in close consultation with program developers (Moore, Bumbarger, and Cooper, 2013). However, in practice, adaptations initiated by community practitioners tend to be *unplanned* and *reactive*. Changes tend to be made *during* implementation, not *before* programming starts. Many are made by implementers in response to a particular logistical problem(s), with no approval or input from program developers and often without their supervisors' knowledge. A survey of Pennsylvania practitioners replicating 10 of the effective programs discussed in this book found that 61% of those who reported making changes to the programs did so in a reactive fashion, while 33% did so proactively, altering the interventions prior to implementation (Moore *et al.*, 2013). When asked *why* they made changes, 80% reported that adaptations were due to having a lack of time to fully deliver the intervention and 72% were due to funding constraints. Although difficulty retaining (71%) and recruiting participants (62%) were also mentioned by a majority of respondents, only 22% of the changes described appeared to be efforts to make the program more culturally relevant.

A study of changes made by 41 practitioners implementing the **Strengthening Families Program (SFP) for Parents and Youth 10–14** in Washington State found similar types of and reasons for adaptations (Hill, Maucione, and Hood, 2006). A lack of time was the most frequent reason given for deleting or making changes to the program and cultural adaptations were not common. In both the PA and WA studies, changes were often made because program implementers disagreed with the program's content or philosophy (Hill *et al.*, 2006; Moore *et al.*, 2013). For example, school personnel implementing the LST program reported that a lesson focused on dating was inappropriate for the middle school population and was often not taught to students (Moore *et al.*, 2013).

These studies and other research suggest that adaptation rarely occurs in the careful, planned manner recommended by some prevention scientists. Instead, changes are made haphazardly and likely without a full consideration of whether the adaptation is consistent with the theoretical rationale or logic model of the intervention. These types of changes may threaten intervention effectiveness, although, in reality, it is difficult to know the degree to which adaptations may affect program outcomes. Nonetheless, there is some consensus that **surface adaptations**, or relatively minor alterations, will probably not be harmful. These changes may include, for example, providing participants with snacks or transportation to the program, updating any statistics or data included in program content, hiring staff who are ethnically matched to participants, translating materials to a new language or revising content and examples to be more relevant to the new population (Kumpfer *et al.*, 2002; Lau, 2006). These types of changes could also improve local support for the intervention and perhaps lead to better participant outcomes.

Deep structure adaptations, or more significant changes to program content, dosage or methods of delivery (Castro *et al.*, 2004), may be more risky. For example, an evaluation of the Adolescent Alcohol Prevention Trial, a drug prevention program with two core components, found that the intervention was effective in reducing alcohol use when both components were taught, but a shorter version of the program that included only one of the components was not effective (Donaldson, Graham, and Hansen, 1994). In deep structure adaptations, local practitioners may add, drop or change program content to make it easier to deliver, less costly to implement, or more culturally or geographically relevant. For example, in terms of dosage, they might offer one-on-one treatment rather than small group services or deliver an intervention over a weekend rather than once-per-week for seven weeks in order to accommodate participant transportation or scheduling conflicts. To the extent that these adaptations are inconsistent with a program's logical model or alter the parts of the intervention that produce positive outcomes, they will likely undermine program effectiveness. For these reasons, implementers should consult program developers prior to making adaptations to ensure they do not alter the program's causal mechanisms.

To summarize, adaptations often occur when local agencies replicate effective prevention programs and changes can impact program outcomes in a variety of ways. They may have no effect on a program's effectiveness, they could improve outcomes, they could reduce positive benefits and they may even lead to a total loss of effectiveness (Blase and Fixsen, 2013; Mihalic, 2004; Moore *et al.*, 2013). Given this level of uncertainty, and the amount of research indicating that lower rates of fidelity lead to less positive outcomes, our opinion is that there is a real danger in encouraging any type of adaptation by local implementers. Doing so sends the message that intervention protocols are optional and opens the door for a wide range of adaptations, some of which can undermine program effectiveness (Elliott and Mihalic, 2004).

Although not all prevention scientists share our perspective on adaptation, our views are informed by several bodies of research. *First*, evidence from systematic reviews (Elliott and Mihalic, 2004; Huey and Polo, 2008; Wilson, Lipsey, and Derzon, 2003; Wilson, Lipsey, and Soydan, 2003) and evaluations of specific programs (Allen and Philliber, 2001; Cook *et al.*, 1999; Cook, Murphy, and Hunt, 2000) indicate that program effects tend to be similar in size across participants of varying backgrounds. In a few cases, similar to the Adolescent Alcohol Prevention Trial described earlier, the effectiveness of the original and adapted versions of a program have been compared, along with an analysis of how results compare across different groups of participants. For example, the **Life Skills Training** program was originally shown to be effective in reducing substance use among a general population of students from multiple racial/ethnic groups. But given the hypothesis that a version tailored to students of minority racial/ethnic backgrounds might produce even stronger effects, an adaptation was developed to make the program more culturally relevant for African American and Hispanic youth. Changes included adding more pictures of minority youth to the student workbooks and using more culturally relevant language and role-play activities (Botvin *et al.*, 2001). The new version was then evaluated and the results compared to those found in the original study of the "generic" version. The findings showed that the effects of the original version and the culturally adapted version were similar for African American and Hispanic youth. That is, there was no increase in program effectiveness for African American and Hispanic students who received the adapted version compared to those who received the non-adapted version (Botvin, Mihalic, and Grotpeter, 1998).

Considering the research evidence as a whole, generic versions appear to have similar effects across racial, ethnic and gender groups (Elliott and Mihalic, 2004; Fagan and Lindsey, 2014; Huey and Polo, 2008; Wilson, Lipsey, and Soydan, 2003). There are a few cases where cultural adaptations improved effectiveness, but they are the exception rather than the rule. Still, the safest rule when evaluating programs is to test the degree to which effects are generalizable across groups (Flay *et al.*, 2005).

Secondly, as we have discussed, we know a lot about the challenges that can impede high-quality implementation and about the steps that communities can take to avoid these problems. If practitioners spend sufficient time planning for implementation, they can either avoid interventions they know cannot be successfully implemented or build their capacity to deliver programs with fidelity *prior* to implementation. Strong advocates of adaptation emphasize the need to change programs to fit the local environment, but it is also true that local conditions may need to change to successfully implement effective programs. As we described earlier, an agency's capacity-building efforts can result in a much more supportive environment for crime prevention. There are obvious practical limitations to an organization's ability and willingness to make changes, but it should not be assumed that adaption should take place solely at the program level with no changes to the local context.

A recipe for poor implementation

I didn't have potatoes, so I substituted rice.
I didn't have paprika, so I used another spice.
I didn't have tomato sauce, I used tomato paste—
A whole can, not a half a can — I do not like to waste.
A friend gave me the recipe, she said you couldn't beat it!
There must be something wrong with her
—I couldn't even eat it.

Anonymous

Methods for ensuring high-quality implementation

Once the new intervention has been selected, and before it is implemented, all of the steps shown in Table 10.4 should be taken to ensure that interventions are delivered with quality. To begin, an **implementation plan** should be created (Meyers *et al.*, 2012). This document is similar to the course syllabi your instructors develop before classes begin which provide information on the class schedule, material or concepts to be taught and desired student outcomes (i.e., learning objectives). In the same way, an implementation plan will include details on exactly when and where the intervention will be delivered, the number and characteristics of participants who will receive programming, the staff who will deliver it, how and when staff will be trained in the new intervention, the outcomes expected to be achieved at the end of the intervention and information on how implementation procedures and outcomes will be monitored. A detailed budget should also be part of the plan.

Implementation plans are important because all of the necessary steps, regulations and approvals needed, and the individuals who must be approached to complete these tasks may not be realized until documented. Likewise, the specific challenges that could affect implementation may not be recognized

Table 10.4 Methods for ensuring high-quality implementation.

- Create a detailed implementation plan
- Specify participant eligibility criteria, participation goals, and recruitment procedures
- Create implementation teams to oversee intervention delivery
- Hire all necessary staff, supervisors, and managers
- Ensure that all staff are trained and regularly supervised
- Seek regular technical assistance from intervention developers and purveyors
- Collect data on all aspects of implementation
- Regularly review implementation data and improve procedures as needed

until such details are written down. For example, until it sets goals regarding the number of participants to be served, an agency may not realize that it will have to hire additional staff to deliver an intervention at scale. Or, in the process of creating the implementation plan, school officials may recognize that in order to complete the 22-session **Coping Power** program during a trimester schedule, it

> *By failing to plan, you are planning to fail.*
> Ben Franklin

will be necessary to offer lessons twice a week instead of once per week as they had originally planned. Plans also serve as a useful communication tool when they are collaboratively developed and shared with all individuals and agencies who will be involved in implementation.

The section of the plan describing program participants should include eligibility criteria, the number to be reached with services and the steps that will be taken to recruit participants. In some cases, such as when implementing a school-based prevention program, participant information will be easy to document and recruitment and retention will not be very challenging. In other cases, ensuring adequate program reach may be the biggest problem faced. We know that the chances of achieving widespread reductions in crime are contingent upon implementing effective interventions, but it is equally true that to make a significant impact on crime, these services must be delivered to a significant proportion of the population (Fagan *et al.*, 2009). In practice, however, many agencies do not serve large numbers of individuals. They may lack staffing, resources or the desire to deliver interventions widely. Thus, it is important for agencies to consider in advance, and document in their plan, exactly how many individuals they will target for programming. They can then assess if this number will be high enough to achieve the goals they have set in terms of reducing risk factors and involvement in crime. If it is not, recruitment goals should be revised and all of the activities necessary to increase program reach detailed in the plan.

Plans should identify the agencies and individuals who will need to be contacted to assist with participant recruitment and the staff responsible for contacting them. For example, those delivering the **New Beginnings** program will want to ask local courts to identify recently divorced women who can receive services, while juvenile justice officials should be contacted to identify families for **MST** or **FFT** services. Asking individuals who have received services to help recruit new participants is also important. When participation is optional, as is the case with most of the interventions reviewed in Section III, word-of-mouth is one of the best ways to attract clients and communicate the message that the program or practice is worth their time (Sanders, Turner, and Markie-Dadds, 2002). Agencies must also be sure that individuals recruited for services match program requirements and that eligibility criteria are shared with community partners so they recommend the right clientele. For example, the **BASICS** intervention is intended for college students aged 18–24 years and has not been evaluated for effectiveness with older adults or young adults who do not attend college.

Implementation plans should identify any barriers that may impede participation and regular attendance and outline the steps that will be taken to avoid these challenges. For example, youth may not attend afterschool programs if transportation home is not provided, and parents may not be able to participate in parent training interventions unless there is childcare. In order to increase the attractiveness of prevention services, providers may also have to offer incentives or recognitions such as food and drinks, "graduation" certificates, or prizes for regular attendance, like gift certificates to local businesses. Asking community partners to donate such products can help to reduce costs and spread the word about the new intervention.

Implementation of any intervention is going to require collaboration among several parties, and creating **implementation teams** will help ensure cooperation and joint responsibility for the new initiative (Fixsen *et al.*, 2013; Meyers *et al.*, 2012). Beyond ensuring that certain tasks get accomplished, implementation teams also provide staff with ongoing support for the intervention. Exactly who and how many individuals should comprise an implementation team can vary across programs and will depend on the complexity of the intervention and the reach of services in a community. NIRN recommends that implementation teams include at least three individuals who know the intervention well and who are accountable for its delivery (http://nirn.fpg.unc.edu/learn-implementation/implementation-teams). Team members must include representatives from the primary agency(ies) charged with delivering the intervention, ideally an administrator whose support and resources are needed to carry out services, as well as an implementer with detailed knowledge of the intervention. Some interventions require a half- or full-time project director to oversee the intervention and these staff should also be on the implementation team. If the intervention involves regular communication with the program developer or trainer, that individual may also be part of the team. It is important to specify the roles and responsibilities of each team member in the implementation plan (Meyers *et al.*, 2012).

As mentioned earlier, one of the critical elements of implementation is ensuring high-quality delivery of services, which is contingent upon the skills and support of intervention staff. Organizations must be sure that all staff charged with delivering the intervention have the required credentials specified by intervention developers. These credentials should be specified in the implementation plan, along with the number of staff needed to deliver services. If an agency needs to hire new staff, timelines and procedures for doing so should be documented.

Staff must also receive training from program developers or **purveyors** – other individuals or agencies who have been certified by the developer to provide such services (Fixsen *et al.*, 2009). The importance of initial and ongoing training is emphasized in nearly all research on implementation (Fixsen *et al.*, 2005). As discussed, implementers often make adaptations to program content and delivery methods, and a major goal of training is to review exactly how and why an intervention works so that implementers do not alter the elements that make the program successful. Training also allows staff to practice teaching the new intervention, which is especially important if they have to master new methods of instruction, such as the ability to facilitate group discussions and role-play exercises. Finally, training helps build a sense of community and support among implementers, which they can draw upon in the future.

Staff turnover following training workshops is common, and implementing agencies must be sure that all new staff receive training from certified trainers. Some interventions also offer additional "booster" trainings to review and practice implementation delivery requirements and address any concerns that have arisen during implementation. Both the implementation plan and the budget should include details regarding initial and booster training sessions, including when they will be scheduled, who will need to attend them and what they will cost.

The implementation plan and budget should also include attention to **technical assistance (TA)**. TA includes advice and support from program developers or purveyors intended to ensure that staff are delivering interventions with fidelity (Chinman *et al.*, 2005). TA can be provided over the telephone or via on-site visits, and plans might list the types of TA that are desired and how often they will be requested. During these interactions, staff can discuss implementation challenges and receive coaching or guidance on how to overcome problems. TA providers might observe staff and provide detailed feedback on their performance, or they may teach or co-facilitate a lesson in order to demonstrate effective delivery methods. In the Blueprints initiative, TA was provided by program developers and research staff at the University of Colorado, and the active provision of TA was considered essential in ensuring high rates of implementation fidelity (Elliott and Mihalic, 2004; Mihalic and Irwin, 2003). Other research has also documented a relationship between TA and implementation quality (Durlak and DuPre, 2008; Fixsen *et al.*, 2005). Although TA will require additional funding, the investment will help ensure that interventions are well implemented and best able to achieve reductions in crime.

In addition to scheduling periodic consultation with program developers or purveyors, it is important that local agencies provide on-site coaching and feedback to program staff (Fixsen *et al.*, 2005). Methods for doing so should be outlined in the implementation plan and followed accordingly. Usually, coaching is the responsibility of the program manager or agency administrator directly overseeing implementation. These supervisors may periodically observe staff delivering interventions, rate their levels of implementation fidelity and discuss strategies to improve performance. For interventions without a specified manager, staff might meet regularly to discuss their implementation experiences and could observe one another and provide corrective feedback (Fagan and Mihalic, 2003).

Staff supervision is an essential element of **implementation monitoring** and **quality assurance**. Given the importance of implementation fidelity and the likelihood of unplanned adaptations, it is necessary to routinely track all implementation processes, including information on adherence, dosage, quality of delivery and participant responsiveness, as well as reach. Thus, information should be collected regarding: where and when services have been delivered; the number and credentials of implementers; the number, characteristics, and attendance of participants; deviations from intervention protocols and the factors contributing to these adaptations; and outcomes achieved by the intervention. Exactly how this information will be collected, the individual(s) responsible for monitoring implementation and the actions that will be taken based on these data should be specified in the implementation plan.

Program managers, if they exist, will be best able to track information on dosage and participant characteristics. Program attendance records and details regarding changes made to intervention requirements will probably have to be collected from implementers. Documentation of the quality of delivery and participant responsiveness will likely be more challenging because these aspects of implementation require subjective assessments of performance. However, this information could be obtained by asking participants to periodically rate implementers' knowledge of the material, enthusiasm, skill in addressing participant concerns and their poise and confidence. Implementers could be asked to gauge participants' enthusiasm, completion of activities and engagement in lessons. If agencies view surveys as too burdensome for staff or participants, they could have supervisors rate implementation procedures after observing live sessions or watching videotaped sessions.

Evaluation of program outcomes may also be difficult, as it will require administration of participant surveys or collection of official data such as arrest records or recidivism rates, which will then have to be analyzed to identify changes in outcomes from pre-test to post-test. Local agencies may not have staff with the statistical skills needed for this work, and they may need to partner with local researchers to conduct these analyses. Some program developers or purveyors may also provide this type of assistance as part of their TA services. For example, Hazelden publishing, the purveyor of the **Olweus Bullying Prevention Program**, will evaluate data on bullying incidents collected on the Olweus Bullying Questionnaire before and after program implementation (see: http://www. violencepreventionworks.org/public/olweus_preparation.page).

Exactly how all this information will be recorded and evaluated will have to be determined by agency administrators and/or program managers. Some interventions, including all those listed on the Blueprints website, will have tools that can be used to document implementation procedures, such as checklists completed by staff to document the delivery of required program content and activities. A few of the Blueprints programs require that local agencies input implementation details into a central database that the developer or purveyor maintains. If such systems do not exist, then local agencies may need to create their own databases.

Regardless of the system that is developed, it is critical that data about implementation can be easily accessed, periodically reviewed and routinely used to improve implementation quality, a process sometimes referred to as **continuous quality improvement (CQI)** (Wandersman *et al.*, 2000). Although the mere act of collecting data helps to remind staff that implementation procedures should be followed, using these data to identify implementation challenges and taking steps to overcome these problems will best ensure high-quality implementation. It is also true that implementation monitoring and CQI will be challenging and may require evaluation and/or technological skills not present in local agencies. For these reasons, it is critical that agencies be prepared to seek help from TA providers or other consultants during this stage.

What does CQI look like in practice? If records indicate that participation goals are not being met – either the targeted number of participants has not been met or attendance is irregular – then agencies will have to increase recruitment efforts and/or offer different incentives for attendance. If implementation data indicate that a classroom curriculum is not being taught in its entirety due to scheduling conflicts, then administrators may need to identify a different subject in which to teach the program. If implementers are rated as lacking enthusiasm and failing to effectively engage participants, supervisors should meet with the relevant staff and identify issues that need to be addressed. If problems cannot be solved, new implementers may need to be hired and trained.

The number and diversity of issues that may be uncovered through implementation monitoring is endless, as is the variety of steps that may need to be taken to solve these issues. What is important to remember, however, is that without monitoring, implementation problems are likely to grow and eventually undermine program success. Then, all the time and resources spent preparing for implementation and delivering services will be wasted. In turn, local support for evidence-based prevention will be weakened and public confidence shaken.

Future Directions

Although knowledge of effective implementation practices is accumulating, many issues require further consideration and investigation in order to ensure that effective interventions are successfully put into practice in communities. While many of the steps necessary for high-quality implementation have been identified, it is also clear that communities rarely follow these steps and that they require assistance to successfully complete this work. More information regarding the most commonly faced barriers to successful implementation and the best methods for helping communities overcome these challenges will help ensure effective local replication. Much of our understanding of implementation practices has been gathered during research trials conducted by scientists, rather than studies examining how practitioners actually implement effective interventions. Thus, more "real world" research is needed to understand both the general barriers that impair implementation as well as the specific challenges faced when particular programs and practices are used by practitioners (Spoth *et al.*, 2013).

Based on the available evidence, it appears that many communities require assistance to conduct needs assessments, especially gathering and analyzing local data on risk and protective factors. Selecting the right intervention depends on an analysis of the risk factors that are elevated and the protective factors that are depressed in a local area, and such information is typically not available in the public databases that can be accessed by community members. Rather than requiring every community to conduct its own needs assessment, it would be preferable to have state or federal agencies collect such information and make it readily accessible to the public (Catalano *et al.*, 2012).

Ensuring that prevention programs and practices reach sufficient numbers of individuals to impact crime rates is also difficult, particularly when implementing interventions outside of school settings and when participation is voluntary (Spoth *et al.*, 2013). Although barriers to participation have been identified across a range of intervention types, relatively few solutions to these challenges have been tested and demonstrated as effective. Some promising directions, which require further research and development, include the creation of web-based delivery systems which may be better able to reach more participants more cost effectively and reduce logistical barriers to participation (Institute of Medicine and National Research Council, 2014b; Kumpfer and Alvarado, 2003). Better marketing strategies are also needed to ensure that prevention programs and practices are promoted just like any other consumer product (Rotheram-Borus and Duan, 2003), but mass media strategies have yet to be developed for any one intervention. As we discussed in Chapter 5, it would also be useful for countries to have a national "seal of approval" and master list of effective crime prevention strategies, similar to how medicines are certified by the Food and Drug Administration (FDA) agency in the USA. This type of certification would help ensure that consumers know about, trust and are willing to participate in evidence-based prevention programs and practices (Rotheram-Borus and Duan, 2003).

Although we know that interventions are routinely altered when implemented in communities, surprisingly little research has examined in detail the types of adaptations actually made in practice, reasons for these adaptations or the types of changes that are likely to increase, lower or have no effect on participant outcomes. Thus, much more research is needed to document adaptations and their impact on program outcomes. It would also be useful to know if programs developed for one type of population are effective for another type of population, *prior* to and *after* adaptations are made.

Relatedly, more emphasis must be placed on the need for implementers to monitor and evaluate implementation practices. If implementers do not believe that implementation fidelity is important, they will be less likely to record implementation procedures. To counter this resistance, program developers should be sure to emphasize the need for implementation fidelity and monitoring during training and TA contacts. In doing so, they must also identify the **core components** of their interventions – those elements responsible for producing outcomes – and emphasize that these aspects of programming must be delivered as intended (Blase and Fixsen, 2013; Rhoades, Bumbarger, and Moore, 2012). In actuality, many developers have not clearly defined the core components of their interventions or tested whether or not particular elements lead to changes in outcomes (Blase and Fixsen, 2013). More research of this type will help ensure better local implementation and fewer potentially harmful adaptations.

Clearly, more research is needed to identify additional steps and processes that can facilitate the implementation of evidence-based crime prevention in communities. The next chapter continues to focus on these issues and takes a broader approach in considering how to more widely disseminate programs across communities, states, and nations.

Summary

This chapter has discussed methods for ensuring the successful adoption and implementation of effective prevention programs, practices, and policies in communities. Although we have made progress in the identification of effective crime prevention strategies, this success comes at a cost: it can be very challenging for communities to consider these options and select the intervention that is right for them. In addition, there is evidence that local implementers often make significant changes to implementation practices during replication and that adaptations can reduce intervention effectiveness.

As reviewed in this chapter, in order to ensure high-quality implementation, practitioners must spend sufficient time planning for implementation. Important steps that should be taken before selecting a particular intervention include conducting needs assessments, comparing the fit of and support for different interventions and assessing organizational capacity to implement interventions. Once an intervention has been selected, agencies should create detailed implementation plans specifying exactly when and where the intervention will be delivered, the number and characteristics of participants who will receive programming, the staff who will deliver it, how and when staff will be trained and supervised in the new intervention, the outcomes expected to be achieved and information on how implementation procedures and outcomes will be monitored. During implementation, interventions must be delivered with fidelity and with minimal adaptations. When challenges to implementation arise, solutions to these problems must be implemented so that interventions have the best possible chance of leading to reductions in crime.

Critical Thinking Questions and Practice Activities

1. Select one of the interventions reviewed in Section III of this book that has been rated as a "Model" or "Promising" program on the Blueprints website or as "Effective" on CrimeSolutions.gov. Using either or both of those websites, identify the implementation requirements and costs of

the program. Then, describe the implementation challenges you think would be most likely to be encountered if this program were to be replicated by an agency in your town. Consider challenges related to program length, delivery methods, staffing, recruitment, and cost.

2. Now select a second intervention that addresses at least one of the same risk and protective factors as the first intervention. Compare its implementation requirements, costs, and effectiveness to those of the other intervention. Which intervention do you think would be more appealing to a local agency in your home town? Why?

3. Imagine that you operate a youth agency interested in implementing an afterschool program to prevent crime. Consider one of the effective afterschool interventions described in Section III. Then, describe in detail your plans to recruit enough youth to this intervention to achieve a significant impact on youth delinquency, including how you plan to advertise the program and any partners you will need to assist you in recruitment activities. Also describe how you will ensure that youth regularly attend sessions. Identify any incentives you might provide to promote regular attendance, but keep in mind financial restrictions likely to be faced by a typical youth-serving agency.

4. Imagine that you are conducting a resource assessment of services in your community, during which you learn that an agency has been implementing the Strong African American Families (SAAF) program (described in Chapter 7). During your interview with the program coordinator for this program, you learn that many adaptations have been made to the program. These include:

   • Instead of relying on three African American staff to deliver sessions, the agency pairs a Caucasian and an African American facilitator to teach the separate youth and parent sessions, for a total of four facilitators

   • Instead of having participants watch videos about issues addressed by the intervention, facilitators describe the content shown in the video

   • Each session has been lengthened from 2 to 2.5 hours to allow time to serve a light dinner prior to the start of the intervention

   • When participants miss sessions, facilitators make home visits to review the program content that was missed

   • The agency has broadened the age range of youth participants from ages 10–14 to ages 8–14.

   Taking all of these factors into account, is the agency implementing the program with fidelity? Now, considering each adaption made, identify: (a) why you think the agency made the change; (b) whether or not the change is a surface adaptation or a deep structure adaptation; and (c) the degree to which the adaption is likely to increase or decrease program effectiveness.

5. Imagine you are the chief of a police agency that just began hot spots policing. Describe in detail the steps you would take to monitor and evaluate the quality of implementation of this practice. Consider how you would collect and record data on implementation fidelity and program effectiveness and how you would use these data to improve implementation services. Identify the staff and/or consultants you would require to assist you in these efforts.

Helpful Websites (last accessed August 8, 2016)

- http://www.episcenter.psu.edu/ebp
  The **EPISCenter** website provides communities with helpful information and resources on program implementation and evaluation.
- http://youth.gov/
  The **Find Youth Info** website provides a summary of effective prevention programs of various types as well as detailed information and guidance on how to effectively implement interventions (see the "Evidence and Innovation" tab).
- http://nirn.fpg.unc.edu/
  The **National Implementation Research Network (NIRN)** website provides comprehensive information about conducting fit and readiness assessments, as well as factors that affect the quality of implementation, how to prepare for implementation and how to monitor implementation.

Further Reading

- Durlak, J. 2013. The importance of quality implementation for research, practice, and policy. *ASPE Research Brief*. Washington, DC: Office of the Assistant Secretary for Planning and Evaluation, Office of Human Services Policy, US Department of Health and Human Services.
  This document provides a short, easy-to-understand review of implementation, including a list of 23 factors that can affect implementation and 14 steps necessary for achieving high-quality implementation.
- Fixsen, D. L., Blase, K. A., Naoom, S. F., and Wallace, F. 2009. Core implementation components. *Research on Social Work Practice*, 19:531–540.
  This article provides an overview of the different stages of implementation and factors affecting high-quality implementation, especially those related to staffing and monitoring implementation practices.
- Morrison D., Hoppe, M., Gilmore, M., *et al.* 2009. Replicating an intervention: The tension between fidelity and adaptation. *AIDS Education and Prevention*, 21:128–140.
  This article provides a good discussion of the issues surrounding the tension between fidelity and adaptation and ways to resolve this debate.

References

Allen, J. P., and Philliber, S. 2001. Who benefits most from a broadly targeted prevention program? Differential efficacy across populations in the Teen Outreach Program. *Journal of Community Psychology*, 29(6):637–655.

Backer, T. E. 2001. Finding the balance: Programme fidelity in substance abuse prevention: A state-of-the-art review. Rockville, MD: Substance Abuse and Mental Health Services Administration, Center for Substance Abuse Prevention.

Berman, P., and McLaughlin, M. W. 1976. Implementation of educational innovation. *The Educational Forum*, 40:345–370.

Blase, K. A., and Fixsen, D. L. 2013. Core intervention components: Identifying and operationalizing what makes programs work. Washington, DC: Office of the Assistant Secretary for Planning and Evaluation, US Department of Health and Human Services.

Botvin, G. J., Mihalic, S., and Grotpeter, J. K. 1998. Life Skills Training. In: D. S. Elliott (ed.), *Blueprints for Violence Prevention*, Book 5. Boulder, CO: Center for the Study and Prevention of Violence, Institute of Behavioral Science, University of Colorado.

Botvin, G. J., Griffin, K. W., Diaz, T., and Ifill-Williams, M. 2001. Drug abuse prevention among minority adolescents: Posttest and one-year follow-up of a school-based preventive intervention. *Prevention Science*, 2:1–13.

Botvin, G. J., Baker, E., Dusenbury, L., Botvin, E. M., and Diaz, T. 1995. Long-term follow-up results of a randomized drug abuse prevention trial in a white middle-class population. *Journal of the American Medical Association*, 273:1106–1112.

Bumbarger, B. K., and Perkins, D. F. 2008. After randomised trials: Issues related to dissemination of evidence-based interventions. *Journal of Children's Services*, 3:53–61.

Castro, F. G., Barrera Jr., M., and Martinez Jr., C. R. 2004. The cultural adaptation of prevention interventions: Resolving tensions between fidelity and fit. *Prevention Science*, 5:41–46.

Catalano, R. F., Fagan, A. A., Gavin, L. E., *et al.* 2012. Worldwide application of prevention science in adolescent health. *The Lancet*, 379:1653–1664.

Chinman, M., Hannah, G., Wandersman, A., *et al.* 2005. Developing a community science research agenda for building community capacity for effective preventive interventions. *American Journal of Community Psychology*, 35:143–157.

Cook, T. D., Murphy, R. F., and Hunt, H. D. 2000. Comer's School Development Program in Chicago: A theory-based evaluation. *American Educational Research Journal*, 37:535–597. doi:10.3102/00028312037002535

Cook, T. D., Habib, F.-N., Phillips, M., *et al.* 1999. Comer's school development program in Prince George's County, Maryland: A theory-based evaluation. *American Educational Research Association*, 36:543–597.

Donaldson, S. I., Graham, J. W., and Hansen, W. B. 1994. Testing the generalizability of intervening mechanism theories: Understanding the effects of adolescent drug use prevention interventions. *Journal of Behavioral Medicine* 17:195–216.

Durlak, J. A. 2013. The importance of quality implementation for research, practice, and policy *ASPE Research Brief*. Washington, DC: Office of the Assistant Secretary for Planning and Evaluation, Office of Human Services Policy, US Department of Health and Human Services.

Durlak, J. A., and DuPre, E. P. 2008. Implementation matters: A review of the research on the influence of implementation on program outcomes and the factors affecting implementation. *American Journal of Community Psychology*, 41:327–350.

Dusenbury, L., Brannigan, R., Falco, M., and Hansen, W. B. 2003. A review of research on fidelity of implementation: Implications for drug abuse prevention in school settings. *Health Education Research*, 18:237–256.

Edwards, R. W., Jumper-Thurman, P., Plested, B. A., Oetting, E. R., and Swanson, L. 2000. Community readiness: Research to practice. *Journal of Community Psychology*, 28:291–307.

Elliott, D. S., and Mihalic, S. 2004. Issues in disseminating and replicating effective prevention programs. *Prevention Science*, 5:47–53. doi: 10.1023/B:PREV.0000013981.28071.52

Fagan, A. A., and Lindsey, A. M. 2014. Gender differences in the effectiveness of delinquency prevention programs: What can be learned from experimental research? *Criminal Justice and Behavior*, 41:1057–1078. doi: 10.1177/0093854814539801

Fagan, A. A., and Mihalic, S. 2003. Strategies for enhancing the adoption of school-based prevention programs: Lessons learned from the Blueprints for Violence Prevention replications of the Life Skills Training Program. *Journal of Community Psychology*, 31:235–254.

Fagan, A. A., Hanson, K., Hawkins, J. D., and Arthur, M. W. 2009. Translational research in action: Implementation of the Communities That Care prevention system in 12 communities. *Journal of Community Psychology* 37:809–829.

Fagan, J. 1990. Treatment and reintegration of violent juvenile offenders: Experimental results. *Justice Quarterly*, 7:233–263.

Fixsen, D. L., Blase, K. A., Metz, A., and Van Dyke, M. 2013. Statewide implementation of evidence-based programs. *Exceptional Children*, 79:213–230.

Fixsen, D. L., Blase, K. A., Naoom, S. F., and Wallace, F. 2009. Core implementation components. *Research on Social Work Practice*, 19:531–540.

Fixsen, D. L., Naoom, S. F., Blase, K. A., Friedman, R. M., and Wallace, F. 2005. Implementation research: A synthesis of the literature. Tampa, FL: University of South Florida, Louis de la Parte Florida Mental Health Institute, The National Implementation Research Network (FMHI Publication #231).

Flay, B. R., Biglan, A., Boruch, R. F., *et al.* 2005. Standards of evidence: Criteria for efficacy, effectiveness, and dissemination. *Prevention Science*, 6:151–175. doi: 10.1007/s11121-005-5553-y

Goncy, E. A., Sutherland, K. S., Farrell, A. D., *et al.* 2015. Measuring teacher implementation in delivery of a bullying prevention program: The impact of instructional and procedural adherence and competence on student responsiveness. *Prevention Science*, 16:440–450. doi: 10.1007/s11121-014-0508-9

Gottfredson, D. C., and Gottfredson, G. D. 2002. Quality of school-based prevention programs: Results from a national survey. *Journal of Research in Crime and Delinquency*, 39:3–35.

Gottfredson, G. D., Gottfredson, D. C., Czeh, E. R., *et al.* 2000. Summary: National study of delinquency prevention in schools. Ellicott City, MD: Gottfredson Associates, Inc.

Hallfors, D., and Godette, D. 2002. Will the "Principles of Effectiveness" improve prevention practice? Early findings from a diffusion study. *Health Education Research*, 17:461–470.

Hill, L. G., Maucione, K., and Hood, B. K. 2006. A focused approach to assessing program fidelity. *Prevention Science*, 8:25–34.

Huey, S. J., and Polo, A. J. 2008. Evidence-based psychosocial treatments for ethnic minority youth. *Journal of Clinical Child and Adolescent Psychology*, 37:262–301.

Institute of Medicine and National Research Council. 2014a. *The Evidence for Violence Prevention Across the Lifespan and Around the World.* Workshop Summary. Washington, DC: The National Academies Press.

Institute of Medicine and National Research Council. 2014b. *Strategies for Scaling Effective Family-Focused Preventive Interventions to Promote Children's Cognitive, Affective, and Behavioral Health.* Workshop Summary. Washington, DC: The National Academies Press.

Kallestad, J. H., and Olweus, D. 2003. Predicting teachers' and schools' implementation of the Olweus Bullying Prevention Program: A multilevel study. *Prevention and Treatment*, 6(1), October.

Kam, C. M., Greenberg, M. T., and Walls, C. T. 2003. Examining the role of implementation quality in school-based prevention using the PATHS curriculum. *Prevention Science*, 4:55–63.

Kumpfer, K., and Alvarado, R. 2003. Family-strengthening approaches for the prevention of youth problem behaviors. *American Psychologist*, 58:457–465.

Kumpfer, K. L., Alvarado, R., Smith, P., and Bellamy, N. 2002. Cultural sensitivity and adaptation in family-based prevention interventions. *Prevention Science*, 3:241–246.

Lau, A. S. 2006. Making the case for selective and directed cultural adaptations of evidence-based treatments: Examples from parent training. *Clinical Psychology: Science and Practice*, 13:295–310.

Lipsey, M. W. 1999. Can intervention rehabilitate serious delinquents? *The Annals of the American Academy of Political and Social Science*, 564:142–166.

Lipsey, M. W. 2009. The primary factors that characterize effective interventions with juvenile offenders: A meta-analytic overview. *Victims and Offenders*, 4:124–147.

Meyers, D. C., Durlak, J. A., and Wanderman, A. 2012. The quality implementation framework: A synthesis of critical steps in the implementation process. *American Journal of Community Psychology*, 50:462–480.

Mihalic, S. 2004. The importance of implementation fidelity. *Emotional and Behavioral Disorders in Youth*, 4:83–105.

Mihalic, S., and Irwin, K. 2003. Blueprints for Violence Prevention: From research to real world settings – Factors influencing the successful replication of model programs. *Youth Violence and Juvenile Justice*, 1:307–329.

Mihalic, S., Irwin, K., Fagan, A. A., Ballard, D., and Elliott, D. S. 2004. Successful program implementation: Lessons from Blueprints. Washington, DC: Office of Juvenile Justice and Delinquency Prevention, US Department of Justice.

Moore, J. E., Bumbarger, B. K., and Cooper, B. R. 2013. Examining adaptations of evidence-based programs in natural contexts. *The Journal of Primary Prevention*, 34:147–161. doi: 10.1007/s10935-013-0303-6

Morrison, D. M., Hoppe, M., Gillmore, M. R., *et al.* 2009. Replicating an intervention: The tension between fidelity and adaptation. *AIDS Education and Prevention*, 21:128–140.

Nation, M., Crusto, C., Wandersman, A., *et al.* 2003. What works in prevention: Principles of effective prevention programs. *American Psychologist*, 58:449–456.

Rauch, W. J., Ahlin, E. M., Zador, P. L., Howard, J. M., and Duncan, G. D. 2011. Effects of administrative ignition interlock license restrictions on drivers with multiple alcohol offenses. *Journal of Experimental Criminology*, 7:127–148.

Rhoades, B. J., Bumbarger, B. K., and Moore, J. E. 2012. The role of a state-level prevention support system in promoting high-quality implementation and sustainability of evidence-based programs. *American Journal of Community Psychology*, 50:386–401.

Riley, B. L., Taylor, S. M., and Elliott, S. 2001. Determinants of implementing heart health promotion activities in Ontario public health units: A social ecological perspective. *Health Education Research*, 16:425–441.

Rotheram-Borus, M. J., and Duan, N. 2003. Next generation of preventive interventions. *American Academy of Child and Adolescent Psychiatry*, 42:518–526.

Sanders, M. R., Turner, K. M., and Markie-Dadds, C. 2002. The development and dissemination of the Triple P-Positive Parenting Program: A multilevel, evidence-based system of parenting and family support. *Prevention Science*, 3:173–189.

Spoth, R. L., Rohrbach, L. A., Greenberg, M. T., et al.; Society for Prevention Research Type 2 Translational Task Force. 2013. Addressing core challenges for the next generation of Type 2 translation research and systems: The translation science to population impact (TSci impact) framework. *Prevention Science*, 14:319–351.

Stormshak, E. A., Dishion, T. J., Light, J., and Yasui, M. 2005. Implementing family-centered interventions within the public middle school: Linking service delivery to change in student problem behavior. *Journal of Abnormal Child Psychology*, 33:723–733.

Wandersman, A., Imm, P., Chinman, M., and Kaftarian, S. J. 2000. Getting to outcomes: A results-based approach to accountability. *Evaluation and Program Planning*, 23:389–395.

Washington State Institute for Public Policy. 2002. Washington State's Implementation of Functional Family Therapy for Juvenile Offenders: Preliminary Findings. Olympia, WA: Washington State Institute for Public Policy.

Washington State Institute for Public Policy. 2004. Outcome Evaluation of Washington State's Research-Based Programs for Juvenile Offenders. Olympia, WA: Washington State Institute for Public Policy.

Wilson, S. J., Lipsey, M. W., and Derzon, J. H. 2003. The effects of school-based intervention programs on aggressive behavior: A meta-analysis. *Journal of Consulting and Clinical Psychology*, 71:136–149.

Wilson, S. J., Lipsey, M. W., and Soydan, H. 2003. Are mainstream programs for juvenile delinquency less effective with minority youth than majority youth? A meta-analysis of outcomes research. *Research on Social Work Practice*, 13:3–26.

11

Implementation Science
Taking Effective Crime Prevention Programs, Practices, and Policies to Scale

---

Learning Objectives

Upon finishing this chapter students should be able to:
- Identify the components of implementation science
- Understand the goals and objectives of dissemination research
- Identify the barriers to achieving sustainability of effective crime prevention programs, practices, and policies
- Identify several initiatives which have successfully taken crime prevention programs, practices, and policies to scale in communities and states
- Discuss strategies for building the national capacity for disseminating effective crime prevention programs, practices, and policies at scale.

Introduction

Thanks to the advances in prevention science discussed in this book, we now have some crime prevention programs, practices, and policies that really work. Given the availability of these interventions, we can easily get them implemented at the national and international levels needed to significantly reduce rates of crime in the USA and internationally, can't we? Given what we know, shouldn't we be able to cut crime rates by at least 20%, starting next year?

> *The world requires at least 10 years to understand a new idea, however important or simple it may be.*
>
> Sir Ronald Ross, English physician and Nobel Laureate

The Prevention of Crime, First Edition. Delbert Elliott and Abigail Fagan.
© 2017 John Wiley & Sons, Inc. Published 2017 by John Wiley & Sons, Inc.
Companion website: www.wiley.com/go/elliott/prevention_of_crime

If history really does repeat itself, as they say, we may not want to count on immediate success in drastically cutting crime rates. Consider that from 1881 to 1913, about 25,000 workers died during the construction of the Panama Canal. Malaria was one of the primary causes of their deaths. Also consider that in 1897, in the middle of the construction period, an English physician, Sir Ronald Ross, discovered through scientific research that malaria was a disease carried by mosquitos. *Yet, in 1904, the Canal Commission called the mosquito theory "balderdash" and refused to fund an initiative that would have tried to eliminate mosquitoes from the Canal Zone.* Fortunately, a fumigation effort was nonetheless undertaken in 1905. It was successful too. Whereas 85% of canal workers had been hospitalized at least once prior to the start of this project, by 1910, less than 1% of workers were hospitalized and deaths from yellow fever or malaria were rare (McCullough, 1977). Science eventually prevailed, but it took a while.

What can we learn from this lesson in regards to crime prevention? How close are we to a world in which effective crime prevention is the norm? How often are such programs, practices, and policies currently being used in the USA and internationally? What effects have the use of these interventions had on the rates of crime in our communities, states, and countries?

This chapter begins by summarizing current levels of **dissemination** of crime prevention strategies. In Section III, we provided information about levels of use of particular programs and practices. In this chapter, we take a more comprehensive approach to this subject. We review the progress made to date in increasing the use of effective interventions generally, in the USA and other countries, and we identify factors shown to facilitate and hinder widespread dissemination. In doing so, we also continue the discussion of **implementation** begun in Chapter 10. Whereas that chapter focused on ways that agencies and communities make decisions about which programs to use and how to implement them with fidelity, in this chapter, we take a larger scale approach and discuss ways to ensure that implementation proceeds smoothly when crime prevention is done at-scale, across communities, states, and nations. Throughout the chapter, we discuss findings from the newly emerging field of **implementation science** (Glasgow *et al.*, 2012), which seeks to understand the factors that promote the widespread use, high-quality implementation, and long-term sustainability of effective interventions.

Dissemination of Effective Crime Prevention Programs, Practices, and Policies

Concerned about worldwide rates of violence, in 2010 the World Health Organization (2014) surveyed 133 countries about their violence prevention initiatives. According to the survey, only one-third of the nations reported implementing one or more interventions on a "large scale"; for example, in many schools or with 30% or more of the targeted population (World Health Organization, 2014). The findings indicated that about one-third of the countries were implementing some type of home visitation practice, at least one parent training program and/or at least one school bullying program. Nearly 50% were implementing some form of social development or skill training program for youth. Although some of these statistics sound promising, the report cautioned that relatively few of the programs being used had been rigorously evaluated. As a result, it is likely that fewer than 10% of interventions could truly be considered "evidence-based" or effective. In addition, most interventions targeted individuals; few nations reported using community-level programs which have the potential to reach a large proportion of the population.

Several studies have been conducted in the USA to estimate the dissemination of effective drug and crime prevention programs. For example, a 2005 survey of school district administrators showed that 57% reported use of at least one substance use prevention program in their district's high school(s). However, only 10% reported use of an intervention listed on the Blueprints or NREPP websites and only 5.6% reported that, if they used such a program, it was used the most often out of all the drug prevention activities they implemented (Ringwalt *et al.*, 2008). *These results suggest that the most commonly used drug prevention programs are likely to be those with no credible evidence of effectiveness.*

Somewhat more promising news comes from a similar survey of middle school administrators. Based on reports collected in 2008 from almost 1,900 US middle schools, 47% were using a program considered effective on the Blueprints, NREPP, or US Department of Education lists (Ringwalt *et al.*, 2011).[1] However, only 26% of these programs were used "the most" out of all drug prevention activities, meaning that unevaluated and/or ineffective programs were used three-fourths of the time. These results indicate that, even in the USA, where the government has mandated the use of "evidence-based" drug prevention curricula, and where many effective programs are available, their use is not common.

It is somewhat more difficult to obtain information on the dissemination of non-school based programs. However, Greenwood and colleagues (2012) have been tracking use of three Blueprints Model programs – **Multisystemic Therapy (MST)**, **Functional Family Therapy (FFT)**, and **Treatment Foster Care (TFC) Oregon** (formerly Multidimensional Treatment Foster Care, or MTFC) – by state juvenile justice systems. The results of this study are shown in Figure 11.1. Despite evidence indicating that these programs are better able to reduce recidivism and are more cost effective than programs typically administered by state juvenile justice systems (see Chapter 7), 15 of the 50 US states did not appear to be using any of these programs. Another 20 states had fewer than 2 intervention "teams," or groups of therapists trained to provide services to juvenile offenders and their families, per million population. Only 5 states were using these interventions with 10 or more teams per million population, a level of implementation the authors considered to be reasonable given the number of youth in the justice system who would be eligible for this type of intervention.

Another Blueprints Model program, **Nurse–Family Partnership** (also see Chapter 7), has been estimated as reaching 2–3% of eligible pregnant women in the USA (Kristof and WuDunn, 2014). More generally, about 10% of child public service agencies are considered to be implementing effective programs and practices in the USA (Hoagwood and Olin, 2002), and in 2003, about 10% of family-serving agencies were thought to be using effective interventions (Kumpfer and Alvarado, 2003). Two former directors of the US Office of Management and Budget (OMB) estimate that less than 1% of government spending is actually used on evidence-based initiatives (Nussle and Orszag, 2014). Taken as a whole, this research suggests that in the USA, and probably in most countries worldwide, we actually invest relatively little in effective crime prevention programs and practices. This news is especially frustrating given cost-benefit studies suggesting that every dollar invested in

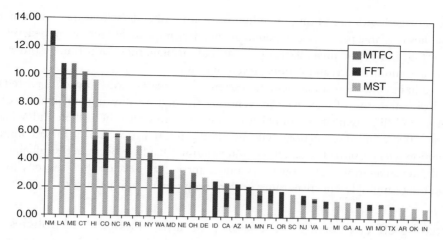

Figure 11.1 US States implementing three Family Therapy Programs rated as "Model" Programs by Blueprints, rank ordered according to the number of teams per million population. Source: Greenwood *et al.*, 2012.

effective and well-implemented programs would provide $7 to $10 in benefits to taxpayers, primarily in reduced spending for prison construction and operation (Drake, Aos, and Miller, 2009; Greenwood, 2006; Greenwood and Welsh, 2012).

Implementation Science

As the previous material has illustrated, and as we discussed in Chapter 10, the *availability* of effective interventions does not guarantee the *use* of these programs and practices. In medicine, it is now recognized that it can take at least 10 years before an effective medicine or disease prevention strategy becomes widely used (Institute of Medicine, 2001). Unfortunately, it appears to take even longer to ensure the successful, widespread implementation of effective mental health and crime prevention interventions, as long as 20 years by some estimates (Hoagwood, 2003). In fact, knowing how to prevent crime and actually utilizing this knowledge are two very different problems. Just as challenging, we know that some interventions are ineffective or even harmful, but they are often used in the criminal justice system and by other public and private systems.

How can we utilize the growing knowledge about what does and does not work to guide decision-making about crime prevention? What conditions and factors facilitate and impede our effective use of this knowledge? These are the issues addressed by **implementation science**, which is the study of how to replicate effective programs, practices, and policies at a level that can significantly impact communities, states, and nations (Glasgow *et al.*, 2012; Kelly and Perkins, 2014). Implementation science has been applied to many different public health problems and has great utility for crime prevention. Implementation science research can help us understand how to better disseminate information about effective crime prevention interventions, encourage their adoption by agencies charged with preventing offending or treating offenders, fund these interventions at a scale that addresses a large percentage of potential offenders, implement them with the level of fidelity required to realize their potential effects on crime and maintain them over time in order to significant impact community, state, and national levels of crime.

As implied in its definition, implementation science is concerned with processes related to the: (i) widespread dissemination of effective interventions, (ii) high-quality implementation of effective interventions, and (iii) sustainability of effective interventions over time (Elliott and Mihalic, 2004; Rabin *et al.*, 2008). The next sections will review the research on each of these components of implementation science, provide examples of interventions that have been successfully implemented at scale and offer suggestions as to how states and countries can develop their capacity for ensuring widespread use of multiple, effective crime prevention programs and practices.

Disseminating effective crime prevention programs, practices, and policies

Research on dissemination involves a systematic study of the processes and factors that lead to widespread adoption of effective interventions (Fixsen *et al.*, 2005; Rabin *et al.*, 2008). The goal is to identify methods that will best facilitate the adoption and use of these interventions by local agencies, communities, and state- or national-level systems, including those concerned with criminal justice as well as labor, health, and education. Such knowledge is important but under-developed because in prevention science, most research money is spent on creating and testing *new* interventions in order to establish "what works". Very little funding has been set aside to study how to disseminate and implement *existing* interventions. In large part this was because, until quite recently, there were no effective interventions to disseminate or implement. The situation is now improving as we have some very effective interventions, and some evidence that the return on investment for dissemination research far exceeds the return on money spent making new discoveries (Glasgow *et al.*, 2012). *These findings suggest that if effective interventions can be put into routine practice, we can greatly decrease rates of crime and gain a significant financial return on investment.*

Because funding has been historically lacking for this type of research, most of the studies that have investigated dissemination have been non-experimental. Many are longitudinal studies that report relationships between practices or strategies used to enhance dissemination and subsequent changes in the adoption of effective interventions. Although such predictive studies are useful, the level of evidence provided by these methods is not as good as that provided by experimental studies, as we discussed in Chapter 4.

Although not an experimental study, the Blueprints initiative involved a detailed investigation of the dissemination of effective violence and drug prevention interventions. Following the identification of 10 Model programs, in 1998 with funding from the Office of Juvenile Justice and Delinquency Prevention, Blueprints initiated a national dissemination project with the goal of replicating each of these interventions in 10 sites, for a total of 100 replications. Early in the project it was discovered that only 4 of the 10 programs were actually prepared to deliver their programs to 10 sites. Some were not prepared to deliver it to even one or two sites (Elliott and Mihalic, 2004).

These findings were somewhat surprising and very important because research on dissemination tends to assume that all the programs listed on the "what works" lists and websites have the ability to deliver their program to multiple sites simultaneously. In fact, this is often not the case. Many interventions rated as effective do not have the **organizational capacity** to do so;[2] that is, they lack the financial and human resources or the knowledge and skills needed to deliver their programs state-wide or to large urban school districts. While program developers may be well equipped to evaluate their interventions, dissemination requires a far different set of requirements. It entails, at a minimum, the creation and professional publication of manuals, protocols and other program materials; a qualified group of trainers and technical assistance providers who are available to travel long distances to work with implementers; tools and a data collection system that can be used to monitor implementation processes; and a well-developed advertising and marketing strategy.

Given these many requirements, program readiness for dissemination should not be assumed. Before any replication can occur, program developers have to establish some type of organization that will allow them to adequately prepare for dissemination. However, there is little published work describing how this should be done and what specific capabilities should be developed. Based on the early experiences encountered when trying to replicate the first set of Model programs, Blueprints now has explicit criteria that must be met for a program to be identified as effective; these are the **dissemination readiness** standards described in Chapter 5 and outlined in Table 11.1. Program developers at the early stages of dissemination can use these recommendations as a starting place to build their capacity to deliver programs at scale.

Once a program is ready for dissemination, what happens next? Several experimental studies have found that simply distributing information about an intervention or guidelines about a treatment protocol rarely leads to use of the intervention (Azocar et al., 2003; Fine et al., 2003; Schectman et al., 2003). As Fixsen et al. (2005: 20) summarize: "*Taken together, these experimental studies indicate that dissemination of information does not result in positive implementation outcomes (changes in practitioner behavior) or intervention outcomes (benefits to consumers).*" Adoption requires more than distributing information about a program to practitioners or potential users.

Harris et al. (2012) describe a practical framework for disseminating effective programs and practices based on their review of the dissemination literature and their own dissemination experiences. They identify two main elements necessary for dissemination: (i) a working partnership between the program developer and a dissemination organization that assumes the responsibility for the dissemination process, and (ii) the use of social marketing principles to reach potential users and/or their organizations. These are part of the Blueprints dissemination criteria shown in Table 11.1.

Table 11.1 Dissemination readiness criteria required to be rated as a Model or Promising program by Blueprints (see: http://www.blueprintsprograms.com/programCriteria.php).

- An organization dedicated to marketing the program and helping sites to implement the program
- Published program manuals, curricula, participant guides, or other explicit instructions regarding protocols and delivery methods
- A group of trainers who have adequate experience/certification in the program
- Ability to provide high-quality technical assistance (i.e., consultation) to sites
- A data management system and/or tools to allow sites to monitor and/or evaluate implementation of the program

A dissemination organization could be a for-profit company or a non-profit organization; it could specialize in marketing preventive interventions of various types (e.g., by distributing multiple interventions) or be created specifically to disseminate one intervention; and its administration may or may not include the program developer. In fact, some developers decide to sell their programs to such agencies and are not actively involved in their dissemination. Although many developers assume full responsibility for disseminating their programs, there are some advantages in hiring a professional dissemination agency to do so. Program developers tend to be academic scientists with relatively little skill or knowledge in marketing and dissemination, whereas professional organizations are devoted to these tasks and have the expertise and staffing to be successful in this area. Moreover, compared to the developer, they may better understand the culture and values of potential users. Blueprints-rated programs that have achieved the widest distribution all have dissemination organizations marketing and delivering their programs.

Implementing effective crime prevention programs, practices, and policies

Chapter 10 provided an in-depth discussion of all the factors that must be considered by individual agencies and organizations prior to implementation to be sure that the particular programs they choose to adopt can be successfully implemented. As described in that chapter, it is critical to ensure a good **fit** between the new program and the needs and resources of the agency, as well as high levels of support and **readiness** to fully implement the intervention (Fixsen *et al.*, 2005). In some cases, planning may reveal that there is *no* effective intervention that fits the particular needs, resources, and culture of a community. Although we have made progress in identifying effective interventions, there are still limited numbers of interventions with strong evidence of effectiveness. When effective programs are unavailable or considered to be a poor fit, agencies and communities should identify programs, practices, and policies currently being implemented that have at least some preliminary evidence of success and then work towards a more rigorous evaluation of their effectiveness. Evaluation of such interventions is essential because, in our view, *it is unethical to provide services that have no evidence of positive effects and make no attempt to determine their effects.* Chapter 4 provides some guidelines for how to conduct strong, scientific evaluations to determine program effectiveness.

Assuming that fit and readiness assessments are successful and particular programs have been selected for implementation, it is critical to ensure **training and technical assistance (TA)** for all staff involved in delivering the program. Although we reviewed some of the issues related to training and TA in Chapter 10, their importance calls for a more extended discussion here.

Some of the most important factors associated with successful training are listed in Table 11.2. One of the main goals of any program's training protocols is to provide local staff with the skills and self-confidence needed to implement the new intervention. In fact, staff participation in training and implementers' self-efficacy, or belief that they *could* deliver the program, have been linked to more successful implementation (Henderson, MacKay, and Peterson-Badali, 2006). Similarly, research on school-based programs has shown that trained teachers are more likely than untrained teachers to implement new interventions (McCormick, Steckler, and McLeroy, 1995). Ross *et al.* (1991)

Table 11.2 Recommendations for training implementers in effective crime prevention programs and practices.

- Hire all staff before training
- Review program requirements and local implementation plans with staff before training
- Arrange for substitute teachers/staff to allow implementers to attend all days of the training
- Ensure that administrators attend training sessions
- Communicate expectations for staff behavior during training
- Plan for staff turnover and multiple training sessions
- Be ready to implement the program soon after training

found that 50% of teachers who did not attend training either failed to deliver the intervention at all or implemented only part of it during the school year. Trained teachers have also been demonstrated as better prepared for implementation, better able to implement school curricula with fidelity and more likely to positively affect student outcomes compared to partially trained or untrained teachers (Connell, Turner, and Mason, 1985; Fors and Doster, 1985; Parcel *et al.*, 1991). Ensuring attendance at training by implementers of any type of crime prevention program is thus very important, and staff absenteeism as well as staff turnover following training are both significant threats to intervention success (Bjorklund *et al.*, 2009; Joyce and Showers, 2002; Mihalic *et al.*, 2004). Communities must be aware of these challenges and plan in advance for substitute teachers and alternative staff to allow program implementers to attend training. They must also be ready to recruit new staff and arrange additional training sessions when turnover occurs.

The specific length, content, and methods used to train staff vary widely across programs. However, as mentioned earlier, programs should have a formal system for certifying their trainers to ensure they provide high-quality instruction to new implementers. This process usually includes a certain number of days spent training the trainers as well as a "probation period" when new trainers are observed leading training workshops of their own. Surprisingly, research on factors that contribute to effective training processes is limited (Fixsen *et al.*, 2005). However, there is some evidence that training which utilizes active forms of learning, like role modeling and role playing, leads to better skill acquisition and increased self-confidence (Dufrene *et al.*, 2005; Elliott and Mihalic, 2004). Similarly, adequate time must be devoted to practice and potential implementers should receive specific feedback on their performance.

While there is consensus that training is essential for successful implementation, Fixsen *et al.* (2005) conclude that training *by itself*, no matter how well done, cannot ensure high-quality implementation. Training alone will not produce all the organizational change required to fully and faithfully implement a new program, practice, or policy. It is also critical to monitor implementation processes and provide implementers with regular feedback on their performance. TA from program developers and/or their trainers can help ensure that implementation proceeds smoothly (Wells *et al.*, 2000).

When problems occur with the delivery of the intervention, implementers or other program staff should seek TA to help remedy the difficulty. Research confirms that monitoring the delivery of the intervention from the start, asking for TA at the first sign of difficulty and re-training providers when necessary has a significant effect on the fidelity of the implementation and the targeted outcome(s) (Durlak and DuPre, 2008). In one study, monitoring and re-training staff who were having difficulties implementing a tutoring program doubled their adherence to the implementation requirements (Dufrene *et al.*, 2005; Greenwood *et al.*, 2003). Other research has shown that staff retention is higher when implementers receive feedback about their performance (Aarons *et al.*, 2009).

Monitoring staff performance and implementation processes is critical for ensuring **implementation fidelity**, as we discussed in Chapter 10. Doing so helps ensure that program delivery closely corresponds to the program as it was originally designed, evaluated and found to be effective, and it will help ensure that these outcomes are replicated in new sites. An evaluation of the Early Alliance program found that high levels of fidelity were attributed to implementation monitoring (Dumas *et al.*, 2001).

Although many replications of effective crime prevention programs have resulted in low levels of implementation fidelity (Durlak, 2013; Gottfredson *et al.*, 2000; Lipsey, 2009), some larger scale dissemination trials have demonstrated relatively high fidelity. For example, when implemented in over 400 schools as part of the Blueprints project, the **Life Skills Training (LST)** program had adherence rates of 86% and 71% of instructors taught all the required lessons (Mihalic, Fagan, and Argamaso, 2008). Likewise, communities implementing school-based and family interventions as part of the **PROSPER** project had average adherence rates of 90% (Spoth, Guyll, *et al.*, 2007). Sites implementing school-based, afterschool, and family-focused programs also showed very high levels of fidelity in an evaluation of the **Communities That Care** system (Fagan, Hanson, *et al.*, 2009). Although none of these studies involved random assignment of sites to a condition in which fidelity was monitored and a condition in which it was not, all three projects involved detailed monitoring systems. It is also true, however, that all three projects were research studies, and that research staff played an active role in setting up the processes by which implementation was monitored. Outside of research projects, communities typically do not engage in routine implementation monitoring (Mihalic, 2004). Thus, it is critical that large-scale dissemination efforts include attention to implementation monitoring and that user-friendly methods for doing so are created and tested (Spoth, Rohrbach, *et al.*, 2013).

Monitoring systems are especially important in understanding the degree to which **adaptations** are being made during replication. As discussed in Chapter 10, local agencies often make changes to crime prevention programs' content, methods of delivery, or dosage requirements. When interventions begin to be implemented more widely and in the "real world," the adaptation/fidelity debate becomes even more important, especially given the uncertain but nonetheless very real likelihood that adaptations can undermine program effectiveness.

We previously discussed some of the reasons why local communities change program protocols. However, we did not describe in detail what Morrison *et al.* (2009) refer to as **scientifically motivated adaptations**: cases in which program developers make deliberate and careful changes to a program and then test the effectiveness of the new model. Unlike reactive adaptations made in local communities, such projects involve planned adaptation. Developers pay explicit attention to program logic models, often hold focus groups with targeted populations to better understand their needs, design the new intervention based on these considerations and then thoroughly evaluate the new intervention. These types of adaptations are especially relevant to the discussion of dissemination, because they are often undertaken with the goal of fostering the spread of crime prevention efforts to new populations and/or settings.

Consider how the following examples have allowed program developers to be responsive to requests by local implementers to make programs more culturally relevant or geographically specific, while also evaluating the effectiveness of the new version(s) of the program. Importantly, these examples also show how planned adaptation efforts can increase the spread of effective interventions to new populations and to new countries, which is important given that the majority of effective interventions have been developed and tested in the USA. In the first example, the **Strengthening Families Program (SFP) for Parents and Youth 10–14**, originally designed and tested with White, rural families in Iowa, was adapted by researchers at the University of Georgia to increase its relevance for African American families in the rural South. The result was the **Strong African American Families (SAAF)** program, which is similar in dosage to SFP 10–14 but with added content related to racial discrimination and socialization. As discussed in Chapter 7, SAAF has been shown to reduce adolescent substance use. In the second example, **Parent Management Training-Oregon (PMTO)**, first created and tested with Caucasian families in Oregon, was revised to be relevant for Norwegian families. Subsequent evaluations showed that the new version, like the original version, was effective in improving the family context and reducing children's conduct problems (see Chapter 7).

In other cases, developers have altered key features of prevention programs in order to identify the core components of the intervention most strongly linked to outcomes. These types of projects allow for a very rigorous test of a program's logic model and can provide important information regarding the parts of the intervention that must be implemented with fidelity and the parts which may be dropped during replication. One of the first substance abuse prevention programs to be tested in this manner involved an evaluation of the Adolescent Alcohol Prevention Trial (Donaldson, Graham, and Hansen, 1994). The original version of this school-based curriculum involved teaching students skills to resist peer influences to use drugs and normative education to correct students' impressions regarding the number of their peers who actually use illegal substances. Adapted versions were also created in which each component (peer resistance skills and normative education) was delivered as a separate program. When the effectiveness of the three versions was compared, normative education alone reduced middle school students' drug use but peer resistance skills alone did not. In addition, the combined version was the most effective in reducing substance use, leading the authors to recommend dissemination of the full version of the program.

Another example involved an evaluation comparing two versions of the **Nurse–Family Partnership (NFP)** home visitation program. The first was delivered by registered nurses (RNs) and represented the model originally tested and shown to be effective. The second version was delivered by paraprofessionals, a common adaptation made by communities with limited applicant pools or resources to hire RNs (Olds *et al.*, 2002). The evaluation showed weaker effects among families visited by paraprofessionals compared to those visited by RNs, indicating that the RN staffing requirement is a critical element of program success and should not be altered by communities.

These types of evaluations provide information of both theoretical and practical value. Unfortunately, such research is rare; few program developers have used experimental research to identify their programs' core components. In most cases, they rely on theories and hypotheses to describe how and why their programs produce outcomes. A more explicit testing of the unique effect of each component of a program can provide a much more complete understanding of effectiveness and give communities more specific guidance on how to implement programs with fidelity. Although some claim that local adaptations will increase community support for interventions and the likelihood of program sustainability (Backer, 2001), there is little evidence to support this view. But it is also true that unless effective crime prevention programs can be sustained in the long term, the reach and impact of prevention efforts will be very limited.

Sustainability of effective crime prevention programs, practices, and policies

The effort to implement effective crime prevention programs, practices, and policies on a scale that will have a significant impact on community and national rates of crime must involve attention to **sustainability**. Sustainability of prevention programs refers to their ongoing implementation. As Scheirer and Dearing (2011: 2060) state, sustainability is *"the continued use of program components and activities for the continued achievement of desirable program and population outcomes."* This definition calls explicit attention to the importance of sustainability in producing widespread, long-term positive changes.

A relatively small but growing body of research has investigated factors that can facilitate and impede efforts to sustain interventions (Aarons, Hurlburt, and Horwitz, 2011; Altman, 1995; Scheirer, 2005). Not surprisingly, having adequate and stable funding is one of the most critical elements needed for sustainability. In most cases, however, the main source of funding for crime prevention programs is a time-limited "seed" grant from a local, state, or federal agency. When programs are tested, developers typically receive a 3-to-5-year grant to test the intervention in one or more agencies or communities. Funding for implementation is rarely continued after this initial period, even if the evaluation continues to assess the long-term effects of the program on participants (Bumbarger, Perkins, and Greenberg, 2010). Similarly, many communities obtain their own grants to pay for program implementation, but these funds almost always have a short expiration date.

The solution to this short-term funding problem is to integrate effective crime prevention programs and practices into existing justice, education and/or health systems. These systems provide most of the resources for prevention and treatment, and many of these are stable funding streams that can be drawn on year after year. The integration of programs, practices, and policies into primary social institutions is referred to as **institutionalization**. The goal is to ensure that effective prevention interventions become part of systems' routine operations and that funding is included in annual and projected budgets.

What do we know about how to secure long-term funding for crime prevention programs on a scale that can impact community and national rates of crime? Research on this topic is relatively limited, in part due to the small number of large-scale, long-term projects that can study such issues (Cooper, Bumbarger, and Moore, 2015; Greenwood and Welsh, 2012). Nonetheless, a key factor appears to be starting early in planning for long-term funding (Bumbarger *et al.*, 2010). As soon as an agency or community decides to adopt a new intervention, it is critical to develop a sustainability plan (Johnson *et al.*, 2004). Ideally, local communities and program developers and TA providers should partner in this effort. For example, in the randomized evaluation of the **PROSPER** project (see Chapter 7), TA providers worked extensively with coalitions to support and encourage team planning for sustained funding early in the project, and this early planning predicted levels of funding secured (Greenberg *et al.*, 2015).

Both **financial planning** and **alignment planning** should be done (Tibbits *et al.*, 2010). The former involves identification of the amount of resources needed to sustain interventions and possible sources of funds, while the latter entails an assessment of how the prevention program's goals and outcomes fit with those of the implementing organization's or with those of the larger system or community in which the intervention is implemented. The logic is that it will be easier to convince funders to invest in a particular strategy if they can easily see its benefits for their organization/system. For example, when seeking long-term funds for a school-based program, it is helpful to identify how the program content aligns with the state or national educational standards that must be met by the school district. Completing this work can lead to a "win/win" situation: the program receives funding and the school(s) can meet its educational goals (Fagan, Brooke-Weiss, *et al.*, 2009). As another example, a review of 19 US and Canadian health programs indicating that aligning the program goals and outcomes with those of the implementing organization helped to foster ongoing support in two-thirds of the cases examined (Scheirer, 2005). Planning efforts should always include all important stakeholders, especially those in a position to influence funding decisions in the implementing organization and in other community agencies (Fagen and Flay, 2009; Hahn *et al.*, 2002).

In addition to long-term funding, organizational capacity and support have been linked to program sustainability (Cooper *et al.*, 2015). We noted in Chapter 10 that organizational support and "buy-in" is associated with greater levels of program adoption and better implementation fidelity, and it has also been linked to success in achieving sustainability (Rohrbach *et al.*, 2006). To best ensure sustainability, it is good to have high levels of support from the community, agency administrators, and program staff (Fagen and Flay, 2009). One way to foster widespread community support is to establish formal community coalitions or informal partnerships between agencies. Doing so creates shared responsibility and accountability for prevention efforts, such that individual agencies may be less likely to withdraw their support and more likely to show how their efforts are contributing to the larger effort (Bumbarger and Perkins, 2008; Fagan *et al.*, 2008).

The third general factor shown to predict sustainability involves the program implementers and characteristics of the program (Cooper *et al.*, 2015). When interventions are relatively easy to implement, involve minimal resources, are consistent with the goals and mission of the organization and appear to be working, support will be greater and sustainability more likely (Fixsen *et al.*, 2005; Gregory, Henry, and Schoeny, 2007). To illustrate, a study of school-based programs (Han and Weiss, 2005) found that the feasibility of implementing the program, teachers' and administrators' belief that the program was achieving its intended positive outcomes and their support for the intervention were all associated with sustainability.

There is no doubt that some effective crime prevention programs are easier to implement than others, require fewer resources and have quicker and/or more dramatic effects. These interventions are probably going to be easiest to sustain. With this in mind, in Table 11.3, we outline what we

Table 11.3   The "ideal" crime prevention program for dissemination and sustainability.

- It addresses the major risk and protective factors related to crime that can be manipulated with significant and meaningfully large effect sizes
- It is relatively easy to implement with fidelity and requires few adaptations no matter where it is implemented
- Its logic model and services are consistent with the values of staff implementers and agency administrators
- It targets easily identified types or dimensions of crime
- It is inexpensive and/or has positive cost–benefit ratios
- It can influence many persons or have large effects on some lives

Source: Based on Shadish *et al.*, 1991.

consider to be the "ideal" effective crime prevention program. Note that we base these recommendations on our own experiences and interpretation of research on program implementation and sustainability.

What are the chances of achieving sustainability of crime prevention programs and practices? Efforts to institutionalize interventions will take time and long-term support and dedication will be needed to achieve sustainability. Simply "starting up" a new effective prevention program typically requires 2–4 years (Elliott and Mihalic, 2004; Fixsen *et al.*, 2005). Sustainability requires continued implementation and funding beyond this period. As a result, in order to achieve state, national, and international reductions in rates of crime, programs must be embedded in ongoing systems and their operating budgets. However, because the status quo is so entrenched in these systems, it is likely to take at least 5–10 years to overcome resistance and change the features of these systems that present obstacles to adopting and implementing effective prevention programs, practices, and policies. For example, many public systems currently have incentive systems based on numbers served rather than outcomes achieved, meaning that the more people who are served, even with ineffective services, the more successful the agency appears to be. Most agencies have a practitioner-centered rather than a program or practice-centered philosophy, such that staff are considered as experts who know what is most needed by clients, which can lead to use of ineffective, un-evaluated and/or uncoordinated services. Likewise, decisions about which programs and practices should be implemented may be based on personal preferences or on political connections and pressures, rather than on reliable and valid evidence. These and other barriers impeding large-scale dissemination and sustainability are summarized in Table 11.4.

Changing these attitudes and practices presents a major challenge to dissemination and sustainability efforts. However, we have some research-based guidelines and success stories for how to achieve such outcomes and can build upon these examples in future efforts. In the next sections, we

> *It is unreasonable to expect that people will change their behavior easily when so many forces in the social, cultural and physical environment conspire against such change.*
>
> National Research Council, 2000: 4

Table 11.4 Barriers to widespread dissemination of effective crime prevention programs, practices, and policies.

- It is more difficult to "sell" prevention because the public views after-the-fact responses to crime as more urgent and necessary
- Current incentives for public systems are based on the number of clients served, not demonstrated reductions in criminal or antisocial behavior
- It is difficult to change the status quo; no matter how attractive a new intervention, current services always have the advantage
- Politics and personal opinion often take precedence over research
- There is much confusion about the level of evidence needed for programs to be considered "effective" or "evidence-based" and about why different programs are identified as effective on different lists of what works
- Few agency administrators are trained to understand the value of using effective prevention programs and practices
- The "credentialed practitioner model," which assumes that service providers with certain credentials know best how to work with clients, is entrenched in professional associations, unions, human resource policies, state laws/regulations and funding requirements (Fixsen et al., 2005)
- There is increasing professional resistance to using crime prevention programs shown in scientific studies to reduce crime (Farabee, 2013)
- There are real costs associated with discontinuing ineffective programs, practices, and policies and with initiating new effective interventions. These include: a change in the philosophy and normal operating procedures of an agency, re-training of staff, high start-up costs, potentially intrusive methods of program monitoring and supervision, and the possibility of job loss

identify additional examples of successful large-scale dissemination strategies. But, first, we offer a few words of caution about the dangers of going to scale too fast.

Going to Scale, Implementation Quality, and Crime Prevention Outcomes

It is well established that when effective programs and practices are "scaled-up" and disseminated more widely, their level of effectiveness typically drops, sometimes dramatically (Dodge, 2001; Welsh, Sullivan, and Olds, 2010). Research on the impact of large-scale dissemination of criminal justice interventions has estimated a decrease in effectiveness ranging from 33% to 75% (Lipsey, 2003; Lipsey and Landenberger, 2006). The primary reason for this decline is a loss in implementation fidelity (Lipsey, 1999). As discussed in Chapter 10, outside of research trials, programs are often not well implemented. Another explanation is that clients served in the community may represent a lower risk population than those targeted in evaluation studies, given that high-risk participants are usually more difficult to reach with community services (Welsh et al., 2010). As described in earlier sections, community agencies may also have less capacity to implement programs effectively and weaker levels of support and commitment for the new interventions (Elliott and Mihalic, 2004; Welsh *et al.*, 2010).

Several strategies have been recommended to counter these obstacles and take programs to scale without this loss of effectiveness. *First*, we need more replications and evaluations of particular interventions, because the greater the number of high-quality evaluations, the more we will know about what to expect when taking the program to scale. This is one of the reasons that Blueprints, but few other registries, requires a replication before identifying an intervention as a Model program and recommending that it be taken to scale. It is also the reason why prevention scientists advocate for **effectiveness evaluations** (Flay *et al.*, 2005; Spoth, Rohrbach, *et al.*, 2013) that test programs under "real world" conditions, ideally by investigators other than the original developer of the program. Multiple evaluations allow for some variation in the risk levels of clients, the quality of the service infrastructure, capacity of the implementing agency, and levels of fidelity. These factors all allow assessment of the **external validity** or generalizability of a program's effectiveness (see Chapter 4). Given all the variables that can affect program effectiveness, a good rule of thumb is that *no program with a single evaluation should ever be taken to scale*.

Second, the better the overall quality of the implementation, the greater the likelihood of realizing the expected outcome of a preventive intervention (Durlak and DuPre, 2008). As emphasized in Chapter 10, it is essential that sites engage in careful needs assessments and planning prior to selecting and implementing a new intervention. This work will increase the chances of successful implementation, sustainability, and positive effects. *Third*, adaptations can either increase or decrease the likelihood of achieving the expected effects. More planned adaptations and rigorous evaluation of new models can help increase our understanding of programs' generalizability and core components, thus providing guidance about what could or should not be adapted. At the same time, local adaptations made without the consent of the program developer and undertaken in a reactive manner with no regard to the program's logic model can undermine program effectiveness and should be avoided.

Examples of Successful Community-, System-, and State-Level Dissemination Projects

Communities that Care (CTC)

The CTC prevention system was identified in Chapter 7 as an effective community-based model which prevents adolescent substance use, delinquency, and violence. Relevant to this chapter's focus, a major goal of CTC is to build local communities' capacity to select, implement with fidelity and sustain effective prevention programs. CTC also advocates the implementation of multiple interventions that target multiple local needs, which are to be delivered in a coordinated fashion to a large enough segment of the population to significantly alter local rates of crime. CTC provides tools and guidance to help communities realize these goals.

A key feature of CTC is the activation of a broad-based coalition of local stakeholders to initiate and oversee program implementation. CTC does not prescribe the specific types of individuals who should comprise the coalition but recommends that it include all key leaders, service providers and individual stakeholders in the community who wish to prevent crime and related antisocial behaviors. Representation will definitely be needed by agencies who can fund and/or deliver services, as well as individuals who can serve as champions and solicit the support and resources needed for successful intervention. Once coalitions are activated, CTC provides them with training and TA to assist in needs assessments and identification of prevention priorities. Following this step, community coalitions jointly decide on interventions that can address these needs. They may already have some services in place to target risk and protective factors, but services may need to be expanded to reach additional participants or improved because implementation fidelity is poor. The coalition may also choose to implement new programs. In this case, they are guided to select interventions listed on the Blueprints website. Finally, CTC provides support on how to set up implementation monitoring procedures and emphasizes the need for local agencies to receive TA from program developers to ensure programs are implemented with fidelity (Fagan, Hanson, *et al.*, 2009; Fagan and Hawkins, 2013).

A randomized trial conducted in 24 communities indicated that use of the CTC system increased program dissemination, high-quality implementation, and sustainability. According to data collected from service providers in both intervention and control communities, at the start of the study, communities in both conditions were implementing a similar number of effective school-based, after-school and parent training interventions. However, 3.5 years after CTC began in intervention communities, they reported greater use of effective services, implementing a total of 44 effective prevention programs compared to 19 in control communities (Fagan *et al.*, 2011). In addition, participation was higher in CTC communities, with about four times as many youth and families reached by programs in CTC versus control sites. More programs and better participation rates were also reported by teachers and other service providers 6.5 years after CTC began (Fagan *et al.*, 2012). In addition, CTC communities were more likely to sustain effective prevention programs at this time.

An examination of implementation fidelity in the CTC communities showed that all sites replicated programs with high levels of adherence, dosage, quality of delivery, and participant responsiveness. Averaging implementation fidelity results across the four years in which research staff provided local communities with TA to monitor implementation, overall adherence rates ranged from 91% to 94%. Implementers reported teaching most of the required objectives and achieving the majority of core components in all programs, and these results were verified using information from independent observers. Dosage levels averaged 94%, indicating that nearly all sessions were taught each year, and both quality of delivery and participant responsiveness were rated by observers to be about a 4.5 on a 5-point scale (Fagan, Hanson, *et al.*, 2009).

These implementation fidelity levels far exceed what is typically demonstrated in community replications. As noted earlier in this chapter, the successful outcomes in this project were likely due to CTC's emphasis on implementation fidelity and monitoring. Having a coalition oversee implementation activities and the TA provided by research staff likely also contributed to the positive results. It is generally understood that communities will struggle with implementation and that outside support and TA can help them avoid or solve such problems so they do not threaten implementation (Bumbarger and Perkins, 2008).

PROmoting School-community-university Partnerships to Enhance Resilience (PROSPER)

CTC is not the only community-based model that has helped communities effectively replicate prevention programs. Similar to CTC, PROSPER (also described in Chapter 7) is not a prevention *program*, but rather is an evidence-based program delivery *system*. It provides a structured approach intended to increase communities' use and sustainability of effective youth- and family-focused programs. Similar to CTC, it involves collaboration among multiple partners, but this model involves a three-tiered partnership that links (i) university prevention experts with (ii) local community teams and (iii) a prevention coordinator team led by a prevention expert from the state land-grant university Cooperative Extension System (CES). Having staff and consultants from university settings provides expertise in prevention science and evaluation and lends stability to community efforts, all of which tend to be missing in most coalition-based prevention efforts (Spoth, Redmond, et al., 2007).

The PROSPER community team allows for local input and decision-making in prevention activities. It is jointly led by CES staff persons and a representative from the public elementary or secondary school system. Team members include staff from local human service agencies, other relevant school personnel and service providers and other community stakeholders such as youths and parents. The team is directly responsible for selecting, implementing and sustaining effective prevention programs, which should include at least one effective, universal family-focused program and one program implemented in middle schools. Over time, PROSPER team members seek participation and support from other community members to help recruit, fund and/or monitor these efforts. The local teams receive proactive TA from the university scientists and CES staff in the form of frequent (weekly or biweekly) meetings and phone calls to assist with program implementation (Spoth and Greenberg, 2005; Spoth et al., 2004).

PROSPER has been evaluated in a RCT involving 28 school districts located in rural areas of Pennsylvania and Iowa. This study showed that two years following the start of PROSPER in intervention communities, all sites had implemented their chosen parent training and school-based programs with high levels of implementation fidelity. Adherence rates averaged about 90% across programs, program staff were rated as highly competent and student engagement was high (Spoth, Guyll, et al., 2007). Based on reports from over 12,000 students in both PROSPER and control communities, the intervention was also shown to significantly delay the initiation of substance use and to reduce current substance use. At the five-year follow-up, when youth were in 12th grade, reductions in drunkenness, marijuana, and hard drug use ranged from 3% to 31% lower for those in the intervention compared to control conditions (Spoth, Redmond, et al., 2013).

PROSPER communities were able to sustain funding for their community teams and prevention programs through the six-year follow-up, a few years after the initial seed-grant period (Greenberg et al., 2015). As mentioned earlier, TA was provided to help communities plan early for the end of study funding, and resources were gradually phased out so that funding did not end suddenly. According to interviews with community members, teams from all 14 PROSPER sites were still functioning at the six-year follow-up. All were successful in raising funds for their prevention activities, although there was substantial variation in the level of funding secured. Across sites, the majority of funding support was generated from school boards, local foundations, United Way agencies, and state agencies. The study evaluators attributed this success to the fact that PROSPER is intentionally designed to support dissemination and sustainability of prevention programs via community teams and proactive TA from prevention experts.

Washington State Juvenile Justice Initiative

The Washington State Juvenile Justice Initiative provides a very useful model for how states can enhance the dissemination of effective crime prevention programs and practices. In 1997, the Washington State legislature passed the Community Juvenile Accountability Act (CJAA) (see: http://apps.leg.wa.gov/rcw/default.aspx?cite=13.40.500.) The primary goal of the Act was to reduce juvenile crime and to do so cost effectively by increasing the use of effective programs in the state's juvenile courts (Barnoski, 2004). According to the Washington State Institute for Public Policy (WSIPP), this Act led to the "first statewide experiment of research-based programs for juvenile justice" (Barnoski, 2004: 1). Indeed, the approach was very innovative for its time: the State wished to determine if juvenile justice programs shown to be effective in small-scale evaluation studies could be well implemented across the state, affect state-wide levels of juvenile recidivism *and* result in cost savings.

In the first step of the initiative, WSIPP identified programs previously proven effective in reducing recidivism which they determined could realistically be implemented in WA State's juvenile courts. Four programs (**Functional Family Therapy**, **Multisystemic Therapy**, **Aggression Replacement Training (ART)**, and **Coordination of Services**) were identified, and juvenile courts across the state were required to select one of these programs and were provided funds for implementation. Importantly, the CJAA also eliminated funding for any existing program found to be ineffective in reducing recidivism. The state's Juvenile Rehabilitation Administration (JRA) was charged with helping juvenile courts select and implement their programs, with the assistance of program developers. JRA and developers worked together to provide state-wide training and TA to ensure implementation fidelity (Barnoski, 1999, 2004). Ultimately, ART was implemented in 26 courts, FFT in 14 courts, MST in 3 courts, and COS in 1 court.

An evaluation of the impact of these programs revealed significant reductions in recidivism ranging from 10% to 57% and cost–benefit ratios of $3 to $8, meaning that for every dollar invested in these interventions, $3 to $8 was saved. The evaluation also demonstrated that when the quality of implementation was high, recidivism reductions increased, from 24% to 58%, and the cost–benefit ratios increased from $8 to $12 (Barnoski, 2004; Drake *et al.*, 2009). As these findings demonstrated, the quality of implementation mattered. The evaluators concluded that when "competently delivered," interventions found effective in small-scale projects could reduce recidivism when implemented at scale. The evaluators emphasized that "*These findings affirm the merit of the legislature's investment in research-based programs for juvenile offenders*" (Barnoski, 2004: 1).

Based on the successful reductions in recidivism shown in this initiative, the WA State legislature decided to expand their efforts. It instructed WSIPP to conduct a more comprehensive search for programs and practices shown in high-quality studies to impact outcomes related to education, child welfare, mental health, substance abuse, juvenile crime, and adult offending. The results of this research, which is ongoing, are reported throughout Section III of this book, and WA State continues to invest its funds in evidence-based interventions targeting crime and other outcomes. The project has also led to a national initiative, **Results First** (http://www.pewtrusts.org/en/projects/pew-macarthur-results-first-initiative) in which the Pew Charitable Trust Foundation and the MacArthur Foundation are providing states across the USA with TA to conduct similar reviews of their use of evidence-based programs and analysis of the cost benefits of their practices.

State of Florida Redirection project

Another state-level effort designed to increase the use of effective juvenile crime prevention programs was begun in Florida in 2004. Its goal was to: (i) divert youth offenders from the juvenile justice system who would otherwise be committed to residential facilities for non-law violations of probation or misdemeanor offenses, and (ii) ensure that they received effective family therapeutic, community-based interventions (Office of Program Policy Analysis and Government Accountability (OPPAGA), 2010). Initially, the state selected **FFT** and **MST** to be used state-wide. In 2008 the project added **Brief Strategic Family Therapy**, a therapeutic intervention intended for Latino and African American families, to its list of funded programs.

The initial project, implemented in five judicial circuits, indicated that youth diverted to the community-based programs had lower recidivism rates than youth in state residential facilities and that state costs for these services were substantially lower. Based on these early successes, the project expanded to 18 of the state's 20 judicial circuits. Since it began in 2004, the Redirection project has trained 21 service provider teams and 60 therapists in the family therapy programs, provided services to over 1,000 youth and families annually and reached more than 8,800 delinquent youth and their families (OPPAGA, 2010; Winokur, Hand, and Blankenship, 2013).

An evaluation of the project indicated that during 2010–2011, re-arrest rates among youth diverted to the family therapy programs were reduced by 8% and felony re-arrests by 24% compared to offenders sent to traditional state residential facilities. In addition, re-conviction rates were 38% less and re-commitment rates were 33% lower (The Justice Research Center, 2013). A summary of these and other results are shown in Figure 11.2. Comparable reductions in recidivism were reported in earlier years of the project (Hand *et al.*, 2011). Given that the community-based services also cost much less than residential placement, Florida taxpayers saved $124 million during the initiative (The Justice Research Center, 2013).

The state of Florida provided $9 million in funds to its judicial circuits during 2010–2011. The project was awarded the Prudential-Davis Productivity Award for innovations in case processing and the 2008 Science and Service Award from the Substance Abuse and Mental Health Services Administration for its success in helping local communities successfully adopt and implement effective programs. This type of initiative is now being implemented in Georgia with **FFT**, **ART**, and the **Strengthening Families Program (SFP) 10–14** being disseminated at scale.

> *If we keep doing what we're doing, we're going to keep getting what we're getting.*
>
> Stephen Covey, author of *The Seven Habits of Highly Effective People*

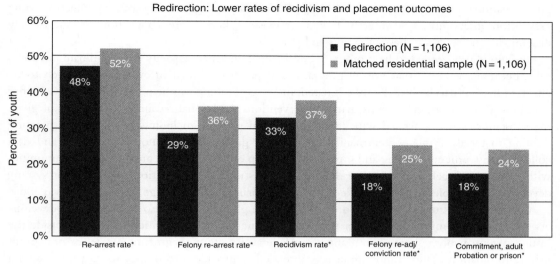

Figure 11.2 Reductions in arrest, conviction, and incarceration rates found in the Redirection Project. Source: The Justice Research Center, 2013.

Next Steps: Building The National Capacity for Effective Crime Prevention

Now that we have some examples of successful community and state-level crime prevention efforts, what do we need to do to create a successful national crime prevention initiative? Do we have any hope of reducing rates of violence by 20%, a rate close to that achieved in Washington State's Juvenile Justice Initiative and Florida's Redirection Project? What types of actions are needed to build federal capacity to implement and sustain multiple effective programs, practices, and policies so that such outcomes can be reached?

At this point, many prevention interventions exist, but taking them to scale on a national level requires changes in funding mechanisms, creation of independent centers to help local communities build their capacity for implementation and dissemination and more consistency in the standards needed in order to designate a program, practice, or policy as "effective" and/or "evidence-based." We describe these issues and provide recommendations for overcoming these obstacles in this last section of the chapter.

Funding effective crime prevention on a national scale

We noted earlier in the chapter that a relatively small proportion of funding for prevention is invested in research on dissemination and implementation and that our body of knowledge in implementation science is quite limited. Funding implementation research should thus become a greater national priority (Glasgow *et al.*, 2012). The ability to significantly scale-up effective crime prevention interventions is directly linked to existing knowledge about how to successfully disseminate and replicate these programs and practices.

Funding is also needed to help program developers build their capacity to disseminate interventions because we know that not all programs and practices shown in evaluation research to be effective are ready to be broadly disseminated. Increased funding can help developers and/or other commercial organizations to mass market interventions. Additional resources are important given the substantial costs associated with taking a program to scale, including: finalizing and printing training materials, implementer manuals, participant guides, fidelity monitoring tools and data collection instruments; training and supervising a group of staff who will provide local communities with training and technical assistance; designing and testing a data collection and evaluation system; developing and implementing a marketing plan; and hiring staff to manage the dissemination effort.

A greater level of investment and longer term funding streams must also be provided to developers and to local communities. The primary funding mechanism for crime prevention outside the justice system involves short-term grants from federal or state government agencies or non-profit private foundations. These funds are usually intended to provide seed money to start the program and, if given to program developers, to evaluate its effectiveness in the short term. As mentioned, the average start-up time required for a crime prevention program is 2–4 years (Fixsen *et al.*, 2005). It takes this long to hire and train staff, recruit eligible participants, develop and implement an implementation monitoring system, address unanticipated problems, make necessary adjustments, and assess outcomes. The typical federal grant for a crime prevention program has a three-year duration. Funding can sometimes be extended if the intervention has some preliminary evidence of success, but rarely are prevention programs supported by grants for longer than 5–6 years.

Given that most funding mechanisms are barely long enough to support the initial start-up of a program, they clearly cannot sustain implementation over the long term. Likewise, they are not substantial or long enough to fund dissemination at a level that can produce a significant impact on community-level crime rates. Grants are important for getting prevention programs developed and evaluated, but they are not a reasonable funding source if the goal is to broadly disseminate programs in communities and ensure their long-term sustainability. To meet these goals, programs must be institutionalized; embedded in a justice, public health or educational system; and included in annual operating budgets.

Social Impact Bonds (SIBs) represent an innovative mechanism for funding prevention at scale. Sometime referred to as **Pay for Success** initiatives, their goal is to allow local and state governments to take effective programs to scale without having to assume financial risk, as they use funding from private investors to pay for government-sponsored programs (Costa, 2014). In these public–private partnerships, a government agency specifies a measurable outcome(s) it hopes to achieve – for example, a 20% reduction in recidivism – and agrees to pay an external organization a certain amount of money if it is able to produce the identified outcome. Private investors provide the financial capital to the external organization, and that agency works with a local community(ies) to implement and monitor effective prevention programs and practices. An independent evaluator determines if the outcome is achieved, and if this is the case, the government pays the external organization, which re-pays its investors along with a profit since they have assumed a financial risk. If the external organization fails to achieve the designated outcome, the government does not pay for the intervention and the investors lose their initial investment. Figure 11.3 provides a diagram of how these relationships work.

SIBs were first used in the UK and have now been implemented across the USA. For example, in Massachusetts, investors provided $18 million to reduce recidivism among approximately 1,000 young men exiting the juvenile justice system or on probation. Goldman Sachs provided half of the funding and will receive 5% interest annually if targeted reductions in recidivism are achieved; other backers will receive 2% interest. The Social Impact Bond Act is currently a Congressional bill intended to provide $300 million to pay for SIB projects. These examples underscore the strong interest in the use of SIBs which will hopefully continue in the future and provide sustainable funding for effective crime prevention programs and practices. From a scientific standpoint, SIBs are very useful because they involve rigorous evaluations to assess effectiveness; findings from these studies can then be added to the evidence base for the particular intervention(s) being implemented.

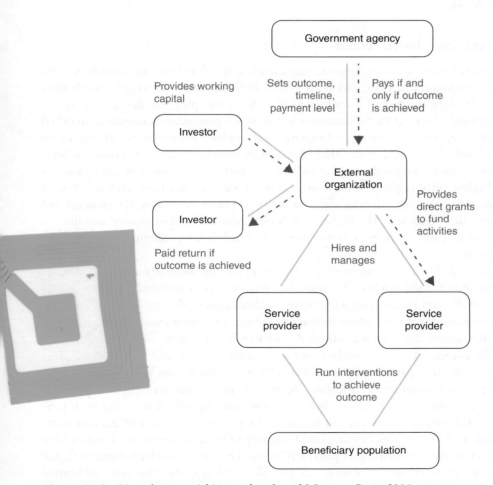

Figure 11.3   How does a social impact bond work? Source: Costa, 2014.

Although they represent a very promising way to pay for crime prevention, they may not work for all interventions. In fact, there have been notable SIB failures where the investors lost their money, likely due to the selection of a program with little or no evidence of effectiveness or the failure to implement the program with fidelity. One example is the recent failure of the Rikers Island, NY SIB, in which an employment program for ex-prisoners selected by the City of New York was not an evidence-based program (Roman, 2015; Vera Institute of Justice, 2015). Implementation of this intervention did not lead to the expected reductions in recidivism, no profits were generated and the initiative was discontinued. These and other findings have suggested that SIBs are most appropriate and should be most effective when government officials are more open to changing the status quo, when desired outcomes can be clearly defined and measured, when programs to be implemented have a demonstrated cost effectiveness compared to existing services *and* when interventions have prior, credible evidence of effectiveness in producing outcomes (Costa, 2014).

Creating more evidence-based centers

One of the important lessons from implementation science is that local communities need help selecting effective programs, practices, and policies and building their capacity to implement interventions that fit their needs and resources. Given that some program developers have a limited ability to provide TA to assist communities in this work, prevention scientists have called for the creation of independent agencies to facilitate local implementation efforts (Greenwood and Welsh, 2012; Spoth, Rohrbach, *et al.*, 2013). Sometimes referred to as "purveyors" or "evidence-based centers," such independent agencies have as their primary mission increased dissemination and high-quality implementation of effective programs, practices, and policies. In their study of state-level dissemination of effective juvenile justice programs, Greenwood and Welsh (2012) found that states with the highest levels of dissemination had created and funded these types of resource centers to help local providers select and monitor the implementation of effective interventions.

Elliott and Mihalic (2004) also recommend that an agency or organization independent of the program developer monitor the fidelity of community replications of prevention programs and provide TA when challenges threaten to undermine implementation fidelity. In the Blueprints project, program implementers were often slow to recognize implementation problems and to contact program developers for help. State-funded evidence-based centers could likely provide more proactive TA compared to that available through developers. In addition, such services could be more cost effective, particularly when multiple interventions are being implemented by multiple agencies or communities in a state. Being able to provide training and TA via a "one-stop" state-level center, rather than each local community/agency contracting with program developers, would reduce the travel and fees typically incurred. Center staff are also more likely to be familiar with the culture, resources, and capacity of local communities. Centers have the added benefit of creating a network of providers across the state all implementing the same intervention or type of intervention, which can provide local communities with additional sources of support.

There are currently only a few agencies of this type in the USA (Greenwood and Welsh, 2012). As one example, the Pennsylvania Commission on Crime and Delinquency funds the **Evidence-based Prevention and Intervention Support Center** (EPISCenter; see www.episcenter.psu.edu) to support community selection and implementation of effective crime prevention programs throughout that state (Bumbarger and Campbell, 2012). Because it is located at Penn State University, Center staff are prevention experts with detailed knowledge of implementation science and with expertise in the 11 prevention programs funded by the state. They provide proactive TA via phone calls, site visits, and occasional state-wide meetings of providers to assist with implementation monitoring and program evaluation.

Reducing inconsistencies in "what works" lists

A major challenge to be overcome before we can hope for widespread dissemination of effective crime prevention programs, practices, and policies is to clarify exactly what it means for an intervention to be effective. Research indicates that lists or registries of "what works," which are intended to assist practitioners and funders in identifying programs recommended for dissemination, are not well understood (Bridgeland, 2015; Burkhardt *et al.*, 2015). For example, a 2005 survey of state education directors found that, although these administrators consulted federal registries to identify drug prevention programs, they made no distinction between levels of evidence within lists or between lists when making recommendations for adoption (Hallfors, Pankratz, and Hartman, 2007). In other words, as long as a program appeared on a list, they considered it "effective," and all such programs were considered equally effective even if the lists ranked some as more effective than others.

How can we improve understanding of these lists among those who should be making use of them? *First*, as discussed in detail in Chapter 5, there needs to be greater consensus among scientists about the standards that should be met in order to certify an intervention as effective. It is confusing for practitioners, funders and the general public when nearly 80% of programs certified as evidence-based on one of 15 different registries are found on *only one list*. Likewise, when such programs are found on multiple lists, they are rated differently over 40% of the time (Means *et al.*, 2015). If prevention scientists cannot agree on the type and level of evidence needed to determine if a program, practice, or policy is effective and ready to be widely disseminated, the discipline will lose its credibility.

Second, it is important that registries identify programs for which high-quality evaluations have found no significant impact on criminal behavior or have had an iatrogenic effect. Given the current state of crime prevention knowledge, knowing what does not work may be just as important as knowing what does work if justice system reform is to be successful. *Third*, none of the currently maintained registries reports on evidence-based policies. In part, this is due to the fact that far fewer policies can be certified as effective, as the scientific design standards applied to programs and practices are very difficult to apply to crime prevention policies. However, there is growing interest in expanding the list of effective policies and recognition that certain quasi-experimental and non-experimental designs, which do not require control groups, as well as some archival data can be used to evaluate policies (Glasgow *et al.*, 2012). The next step is for prevention scientists to agree on scientific standards for certifying policies as effective and to ensure that identified policies are added to registries.

We are hopeful that development of each of the areas outlined in this section can lead to an expansion in the dissemination, high-quality implementation and sustainability of effective crime prevention programs, practices, and policies. In the concluding chapter of the book, we will provide a few more recommendations to help advance crime prevention and our ability to significantly impact rates of crime nationally and internationally.

Three principles for improving government's services to children, youth, and families

- *Build evidence about the programs, practices, and policies that will achieve the most effective and efficient results*
- *Invest limited taxpayer dollars in what works*
- *Direct funds away from programs, practices, and policies that consistently fail to achieve measureable outcomes.*

Nussle and Orszag, 2014

Summary

In previous chapters we identified a number of effective crime prevention programs, practices and, to a lesser degree, policies. In this chapter we reviewed the extent to which these interventions are being widely disseminated and sustained over time. At present, there is little evidence that these interventions are being disseminated, implemented and sustained on a scale that can impact community, state, or national rates of crime. More knowledge is needed about how to disseminate programs, encourage their adoption, implement them with fidelity and sustain their funding over long periods if we are to substantially reduce crime.

The goal of implementation science is to advance understanding about these issues. We described this emerging field of study and recent research findings related to the dissemination, implementation and sustainability of prevention interventions. The chapter reviewed challenges facing developers in taking their programs to scale, the importance of community support and planning for successful implementation and the advantages and disadvantages of adaptations. We also discussed ways to increase the sustainability of effective interventions in the long term, including the importance of institutionalizing programs into systems and their operating budgets.

In the last sections of the chapter, we identified some current and planned initiatives that can help scale-up effective interventions in communities, states, and nations. We also identified some important next steps that will be necessary to achieve significant reductions in crime nationally and internationally.

Critical Thinking Questions and Practice Activities

1. When reading the first section of this chapter, were you surprised to learn that effective crime prevention programs, practices, and policies are not widely implemented? Describe your reaction to this information. What do you think is the most significant challenge to dissemination?

2. This chapter discussed reasons why many program developers are not well equipped to disseminate their interventions. Why do you think developers lack this capacity? What do you think is a better solution: to provide more funding to developers to help them improve their dissemination capacity or to entrust dissemination and technical assistance to other organizations? Defend your answer based on the information you have read in this chapter.

3. What features of effective interventions do you think make them most appealing to the justice system? What features make them unappealing and/or less feasible for the justice system to adopt?

4. Which of the community- and state-initiatives described in this chapter do you think has the best chance of increasing the dissemination and high-quality implementation of effective interventions? Defend your position.

5. What do you think about using social impact bonds to scale-up crime prevention programs, practices, and policies? Would you invest in SIBs? Why or why not?

Endnotes

1. LST is probably the most widely used Blueprint evidence-based program. Ringwalt *et al.* (2011) note it was being used in about 19% of schools in 2008. It is currently implemented by schools in all 50 states, plus Washington DC, Puerto Rico, and the Virgin Islands. Globally it is implemented in 37 countries, with approximately 50,000 teachers trained to deliver it in 10,000 schools/sites involving 3 million students (www.lifeskillstraining.com/global-reach.php).

2. As mentioned in Chapter 5, some lists contain programs that were evaluated many years ago and are not available for *any* dissemination, even in one site. In some cases, these programs may never have been intended to be replicated outside of a scientific trial.

Helpful Websites (last accessed August 9, 2016)

- http://moneyballforgov.com/
  This website provides recommendations for how government can make policy and funding decisions that take into account scientific evidence about what works.
- http://www.violenceprevention@cdc.org/
  The **CDC Division of Violence Prevention** *summarizes the types of violence prevention programs, practices, and policies being used in the United States and around the world.*
- http://www.crime-prevention-intl.org/
  The **International Centre for the Prevention of Crime** *provides information and tools to help local authorities, governments, and international organizations implement successful crime prevention programs and policies.*

- http://www.pewtrusts.org/en/projects/pew-macarthur-results-first-initiative
  The **Results First Initiative** *website describes efforts to assist US states with identifying their current use and cost benefits of effective prevention programs.*

Further Reading

- Fixsen, D. L., Naoom, S. F., Blase, K. A., Friedman, R. M., and Wallace, F. 2005. Implementation research: A synthesis of the literature. Tampa, FL: University of South Florida, Louis de la Parte Florida Mental Health Institute, The National Implementation Research Network.
  This monograph provides a very thorough review of implementation and dissemination literature across diverse fields.
- Nussle, J., and Orszag, P. (eds). 2014. *Moneyball for Government*. Disruption Books.
  An edited book emphasizing the need for government to invest in effective interventions.
- Pew-MacArthur Results First Initiative. (2015). Legislating evidence-based policymaking. Washington, DC: The Pew Charitable Trusts, MacArthur Foundation.
  This brief identifies various state-level policies designed to increase dissemination of effective prevention programs and practices in the United States. It can be downloaded at: http://www.pewtrusts.org/en/research-and-analysis/issue-briefs/2015/03/legislating-evidence-based-policymaking.
- Rabin, B., Brownson, R. C., Haire-Joshu, D., Kreuter, M. W., and Weaver, N. L. 2008. A glossary for dissemination and implementation research in health. *Journal of Public Health Management and Practice*, 14:117–123.
  This article provides an easy-to-understand overview of key terms and concepts related to dissemination and implementation.

References

Aarons, G. A., Hurlburt, M., and Horwitz, S. M. 2011. Advancing a conceptual model of evidence-based practice implementation in public service sectors. *Administration and Policy in Mental Health*, 38:4–23.

Aarons, G. A., Sommerfeld, D. H., Hecht, D. B., Silovsky, J. F., and Chaffin, M. J. 2009. The impact of evidence-based practice implementation and fidelity monitoring on staff turnover: Evidence for a protective effect. *Journal of Consulting and Clinical Psychology*, 77:270–280. doi: 10.1037/a0013223

Altman, D. G. 1995. Sustaining interventions in community systems: On the relationship between researchers and communities. *Health Psychology*, 14:526–536.

Azocar, F., Cuffel, B., Goldman, W., and McCarter, L. 2003. The impact of evidence-based guideline dissemination for the assessment and treatment of major depression in a managed behavioral health care organization. *The Journal of Behavioral Health Services & Research*, 30:109–118. doi: 10.1097/00075484-200301000-00008

Backer, T. E. 2001. Finding the balance: Programme fidelity in substance abuse prevention: A state-of-the-art review. Rockville, MD: Substance Abuse and Mental Health Services Administration, Center for Substance Abuse Prevention.

Barnoski, R. 1999. The Community Juvenile Accountability Act: Research-proven interventions for juvenile courts. Olympia, WA: Washington State Institute for Public Policy.

Barnoski, R. 2004. Outcome evaluation of Washington State's research-based programs for juvenile offenders. Olympia, WA: Washington State Institute for Public Policy.

Bjorklund, R.W., Monroe-DeVita, M., Reed, D., Toulon, A., and Morse, G. 2009. Washington State's initiative to disseminate and implement high-fidelity ACT teams. *Psychiatric Services*, 60:24–27. doi: 10.1176/ps.2009.60.1.24

Bridgeland, J. 2015. Testimony before the US House of Representatives Committee on Ways and Means, Subcommittee on Human Resources (March 17, 2015 ed.). Washington, DC.

Bumbarger, B. K., and Campbell, E. M. 2012. A state agency–university partnership for translational research and dissemination of evidence-based prevention and intervention. *Administration and Policy in Mental Health*, 39, 268–277. doi: 10.1007/s10488-011-0372-x

Bumbarger, B. K., and Perkins, D. F. 2008. After randomised trials: Issues related to dissemination of evidence-based interventions. *Journal of Children's Services*, 3:53–61.

Bumbarger, B. K., Perkins, D. F., and Greenberg, M. T. 2010. Taking effective prevention to scale. In: B. Doll, W. Pfohl, and J. Yoon (eds), *Handbook of Youth Prevention Science*, pp. 433–444. New York, NY: Routledge.

Burkhardt, J. T., Schroter, D. C., Magura, S., Means, S. N., and Coryn, C. L. S. 2015. An overview of evidence-based program registers (EBPRs) for behavioral health. *Evaluation and Program Planning*, 48:92–99. doi: 10.1016/j.evalprogplan.2014.09.006

Connell, D., Turner, R., and Mason, E. 1985. Summary of findings of the School Health Education Evaluation: Health promotion effectiveness, implementation, and costs. *Journal of School Health*, 55:316–321.

Cooper, B. R., Bumbarger, B. K., and Moore, J. E. 2015. Sustaining evidence-based prevention programs: Correlates in a large-scale dissemination initiative. *Prevention Science*, 16:145–157. doi: 10.1007/s11121-013-0427-1

Costa, K. 2014. Social impact bonds in the United States. Washington, DC: Center for American Progress.

Dodge, K. A. 2001. The science of youth violence prevention: Progressing from developmental epidemiology to efficacy to effectiveness to public policy. *American Journal of Preventive Medicine*, 20:63–70.

Donaldson, S. I., Graham, J. W., and Hansen, W. B. 1994. Testing the generalizability of intervening mechanism theories: Understanding the effects of adolescent drug use prevention interventions. *Journal of Behavioral Medicine*, 17:195–216.

Drake, E. K., Aos, S., and Miller, M. G. 2009. Evidence-based public policy options to reduce crime and criminal justice costs: Implications in Washington State. *Victims and Offenders*, 4:170–196.

Dufrene, B. A., Noell, G. H., Gilbertson, D. N., and Duhon, G. J. 2005. Monitoring implementation of reciprocal peer tutoring: Identifying and intervening with students who do not maintain accurate implementation. *School Psychology Review*, 34:74–86.

Dumas, J. E., Lynch, A. M., Laughlin, J. E., Smith, E. P., and Printz, R. J. 2001. Promoting intervention fidelity: Conceptual issues, methods, and preliminary results from the Early Alliance Prevention Trial. *American Journal of Preventive Medicine*, 20:38–47.

Durlak, J. A. 2013. The importance of quality implementation for research, practice, and policy *ASPE Research Brief*. Washington, DC: Office of the Assistant Secretary for Planning and Evaluation, Office of Human Services Policy, US Department of Health and Human Services.

Durlak, J. A., and DuPre, E. P. 2008. Implementation matters: A review of the research on the influence of implementation on program outcomes and the factors affecting implementation. *American Journal of Community Psychology*, 41:327–350.

Elliott, D. S., and Mihalic, S. 2004. Issues in disseminating and replicating effective prevention programs. *Prevention Science*, 5:47–53. doi: 10.1023/B:PREV.0000013981.28071.52

Fagan, A. A., and Hawkins, J. D. 2013. Preventing substance use, delinquency, violence, and other problem behaviors over the life-course using the Communities That Care system. In: C. L. Gibson and M. D. Krohn (eds), *Handbook of Life-Course Criminology*, pp. 277–296. New York, NY: Springer-Verlag.

Fagan, A. A., Brooke-Weiss, B., Cady, R., and Hawkins, J. D. 2009. If at first you don't succeed … keep trying: Strategies to enhance coalition/school partnerships to implement school-based prevention programming. *Australian and New Zealand Journal of Criminology*, 42:387–405.

Fagan, A. A., Hanson, K., Briney, J. S., and Hawkins, J. D. 2012. Sustaining the utilization and high quality implementation of tested and effective prevention programs using the Communities That Care prevention system. *American Journal of Community Psychology*, 49:365–377.

Fagan, A. A., Hanson, K., Hawkins, J. D., and Arthur, M. W. 2008. Bridging science to practice: Achieving prevention program fidelity in the Community Youth Development Study. *American Journal of Community Psychology*, 41:235–249.

Fagan, A. A., Hanson, K., Hawkins, J. D., and Arthur, M. W. 2009. Translational research in action: Implementation of the Communities That Care prevention system in 12 communities. *Journal of Community Psychology*, 37:809–829.

Fagan, A. A., Arthur, M. W., Hanson, K., Briney, J. S., and Hawkins, J. D. 2011. Effects of Communities That Care on the adoption and implementation fidelity of evidence-based prevention programs in communities: Results from a randomized controlled trial. *Prevention Science*, 12:223–234.

Fagen, M. C., and Flay, B. R. 2009. Comments on challenges in sustaining public health interventions. *Health Education and Behavior*, 36:29–30. doi: 10.1177/1090198107299789

Farabee, D. 2013. The fallacy of "what works" in offender rehabilitation. *Offender Programs Report*, 16:83–86.

Fine, M. J., Stone, R. A., Lave, J. R., *et al.* 2003. Implementation of an evidence-based guideline to reduce duration of intravenous antibiotic therapy and length of stay for patients hospitalized with community-acquired pneumonia: A randomized controlled trial. *The American Journal of Medicine*, 115:343–351. doi: http://dx.doi.org/ 10.1016/S0002-9343(03)00395-4

Fixsen, D. L., Naoom, S. F., Blase, K. A., Friedman, R. M., and Wallace, F. 2005. Implementation research: A synthesis of the literature. Tampa, FL: University of South Florida, Louis de la Parte Florida Mental Health Institute, The National Implementation Research Network (FMHI Publication #231).

Flay, B. R., Biglan, A., Boruch, R. F., *et al.* 2005. Standards of evidence: Criteria for efficacy, effectiveness, and dissemination. *Prevention Science*, 6:151–175. doi: 10.1007/s11121-005-5553-y

Fors, S. W., and Doster, M. E. 1985. Implication of results: Factors for success. *Journal of School Health*, 55:332–334.

Glasgow, R. E., Vinson, C., Chambers, D., *et al.* 2012. National Institutes of Health approaches to dissemination and implementation science: Current and future directions. *American Journal of Public Health*, 102:1274–1281.

Gottfredson, G. D., Gottfredson, D. C., Czeh, E. R., *et al.* 2000. Summary: National study of delinquency prevention in schools. Ellicott City, MD: Gottfredson Associates, Inc.

Greenberg, M. T., Feinberg, M. E., Johnson, L. E., *et al.* 2015. Factors that predict financial sustainability of community coalitions: Five years of findings from the PROSPER Partnership Project. *Prevention Science*, 16:158–167. doi: 10.1007/s11121-014-0483-1

Greenwood, C. R., Tapia, Y., Abbott, M., and Walton, C. 2003. A building-based case study of evidence-based literacy practices: Implementation, reading behavior, and growth in reading fluency, K-4. *The Journal of Special Education*, 37:95–110.

Greenwood, P. W. 2006. *Changing Lives: Delinquency Prevention as Crime-Control Policy*. Chicago, IL: University of Chicago Press.

Greenwood, P. W., and Welsh, B. C. 2012. Promoting evidence-based practice in delinquency prevention at the state level: Principles, progress, and policy directions. *Criminology and Public Policy*, 11:493–513.

Greenwood, P. W., Welsh, B. C., and Rocque, M. 2012. Implementing proven programs for juvenile offenders: Assessing state progress. Downington, PA: Association for the Advancement of Evidence-based Practice.

Gregory, A., Henry, D. B., and Schoeny, M. 2007. School climate and implementation of a preventive intervention. *American Journal of Community Psychology*, 40:250–260.

Hahn, E. J., Powers Noland, M., Rayens, M. K., and Myers Christie, D. 2002. Efficacy of training and fidelity of implementation of the Life Skills Training Program. *Journal of School Health*, 72:282–287.

Hallfors, D., Pankratz, M., and Hartman, S. 2007. Does federal policy support the use of scientific evidence in school-based prevention programs? *Prevention Science*, 8:75–81. doi: 10.1007/s11121-006-0058-x

Han, S. S., and Weiss, B. 2005. Sustainability of teacher implementation of school-based mental health programs. *Journal of Abnormal Child Psychology*, 33:665–679.

Hand, G., Winokur Early, K., Chapman, S., and Blankenship, J. L. 2011. Redirection continues to save money and reduce recidivism: Methodology appendix. Tallahassee, FL: Justice Research Center.

Harris, J. R., Cheadle, A., Hannon, P. A., *et al.* 2012. A framework for disseminating evidence-based health promotion practices. *Preventing Chronic Disease*, 9:1–8.

Henderson, J. L., MacKay, S., and Peterson-Badali, M. 2006. Closing the research–practice gap: Factors affecting adoption and implementation of a children's mental health program. *Journal of Clinical Child & Adolescent Psychology*, 35:2–12. doi: 10.1207/s15374424jccp3501_1

Hoagwood, K. 2003. Evidence-based practices in child and adolescent mental health: Its meaning, application, and limitations. *NAMI Beginnings*, pp. 3–7. Arlington, VA: National Alliance on Mental Illness.

Hoagwood, K., and Olin, S. 2002. The NIMH Blueprint for Change report: Research priorities in child and adolescent mental health. *Journal of the American Academy of Child and Adolescent Psychiatry*, 41:760–767.

Institute of Medicine. 2001. *Crossing the Quality Chasm: A New Health System for the 21st Century*. Washington, DC: The National Academies Press.

Johnson, K., Hays, C., Center, H., and Daley, C. 2004. Building capacity and sustainable prevention innovations: A sustainability planning model. *Evaluation and Program Planning*, 27:135–149.

Joyce, B., and Showers, B. 2002. *Student Achievement Through Staff Development*. Alexandria, VA: Association for Supervision and Curriculum Development.

Kelly, B., and Perkins, D. F. (eds). 2014. *Handbook of Implementation Science for Psychology in Education*. New York, NY: Cambridge University Press.

Kristof, N., and WuDunn, S. 2014. The way to beat poverty. September 12, 2014. *The New York Times, Sunday Review*. Retrieved from http://www.nytimes.com/2014/09/14/opinion/sunday/nicholas-kristof-the-way-to-beat-poverty.html (accessed August 9, 2016).

Kumpfer, K., and Alvarado, R. 2003. Family-strengthening approaches for the prevention of youth problem behaviors. *American Psychologist*, 58:457–465.

Lipsey, M. 2003. Those confounded moderators in meta-analysis: Good, bad and ugly. *Annals of the American Academy of Political and Social Science*, 587:69–81.

Lipsey, M. W. 1999. Can intervention rehabilitate serious delinquents? *Annals of the American Academy of Political and Social Science*, 564:142–166.

Lipsey, M. W. 2009. The primary factors that characterize effective interventions with juvenile offenders: A meta-analytic overview. *Victims and Offenders*, 4:124–147.

Lipsey, M. W., and Landenberger, N. A. 2006. Cognitive-behavioral interventions. In: B. C. Welsh and D. P. Farrington (eds), *Preventing Crime: What Works for Children, Offenders, Victims and Places*, pp. 57–72. New York, NY: Springer.

McCormick, L. K., Steckler, A. B., and McLeroy, K. R. 1995. Diffusion of innovations in schools: A study of adoption and implementation of school-based tobacco prevention curricula. *American Journal of Health Promotion*, 9:210–219.

McCullough, D. 1977. *The Path Between the Seas*. New York, NY: Simon and Schuster.

Means, S., Magura, S., Burkhart, B. R., Schroter, D. C., and Coryn, C. L. S. 2015. Comparing rating paradigms for evidence-based program registers in behavioral health: Evidentiary criteria and implications for assessing programs. *Evaluation and Program Planning*, 48:100–116.

Mihalic, S. 2004. The importance of implementation fidelity. *Emotional and Behavioral Disorders in Youth*, 4:83–105.

Mihalic, S., Fagan, A. A., and Argamaso, S. 2008. Implementing the Life Skills Training drug prevention program: Factors related to implementation fidelity. *Implementation Science*, 3:5.

Mihalic, S., Irwin, K., Fagan, A. A., Ballard, D., and Elliott, D. S. 2004. Successful program implementation: Lessons from Blueprints. Washington, DC: Office of Juvenile Justice and Delinquency Prevention, US Department of Justice.

Morrison, D. M., Hoppe, M., Gillmore, M. R., *et al.* 2009. Replicating an intervention: The tension between fidelity and adaptation. *AIDS Education and Prevention*, 21:128–140.

National Research Council. 2000. *Promoting Health: Intervention Strategies from Social and Behavioral Research.* Washington, DC: The National Academies Press.

Nussle, J., and Orszag, P. (eds). 2014. *Moneyball for Government.* Washington, DC: Disruption Books.

Office of Program Policy Analysis and Government Accountability (OPPAGA). 2010. Redirection saves $51.2 million and continues to reduce recidivism. Tallahassee, FL: Florida State Legislature.

Olds, D. L., Robinson, J., O'Brien, R., *et al.* 2002. Home visiting by paraprofessionals and by nurses: A randomized, controlled trial. *Pediatrics*, 110:486–496.

Parcel, G. S., Ross, J. G., Lavin, A. T., *et al.* 1991. Enhancing implementation of the Teenage Health Teaching Modules. *Journal of School Health*, 61:35–38.

Rabin, B. A., Brownson, R. C., Haire-Joshu, D., Kreuter, M. W., and Weaver, N. L. 2008. A glossary for dissemination and implementation research in health. *Journal of Public Health Management and Practice*, 14:117–123. doi: 10.1097/01.PHH.0000311888.06252.bb

Ringwalt, C., Hanley, S., Vincus, A. A., *et al.* 2008. The prevalence of effective substance use prevention curricula in the Nation's high schools. *The Journal of Primary Prevention*, 29:479–488.

Ringwalt, C., Vincus, A. A., Hanley, S., *et al.* 2011. The prevalence of evidence-based drug use prevention curricula in U.S. middle schools in 2008. *Prevention Science*, 12:63–69.

Rohrbach, L. A., Grana, R., Sussman, S., and Valente, T. W. 2006. Type II Translation: Transporting prevention interventions from research to real-world settings. *Evaluation and the Health Professions*, 29:302–333.

Roman, J. 2015. Putting Evidence First: Learning From the Rikers Island Social Impact Bond. www. huffingtonpost.com/john-roman-phd/putting-evidence-first-le_b_7738994.html (accessed August 9, 2016).

Ross, J. G., Luepker, R. V., Nelson, G. D., Saavedra, P., and Hubbard, B. M. 1991. Teenage Health Teaching Modules: Impact of teacher training on implementation and student outcomes. *Journal of School Health*, 61:31–35.

Schectman, J. M., Shroth, W. S., Verme, D., and Voss, J. D. 2003. Randomized controlled trial of education and feedback for implementation of guidelines for acute low back pain. *Journal of General Internal Medicine*, 18:773–780.

Scheirer, M. A. 2005. Is sustainability possible? A review and commentary on empirical studies of program sustainability. *American Journal of Evaluation*, 26:320–347.

Scheirer, M. A., and Dearing, J. W. 2011. An agenda for research on the sustainability of public health programs. *American Journal of Public Health*, 101:2059–2067.

Shadish, W. R., Cook, T. D., and Leviton, L. C. 1991. *Foundations of Program Evaluation: Theories of Practice.* Newbury Park, CA: Sage.

Spoth, R., Redmond, C., Shin, C., *et al.* 2013. PROSPER Community–University Partnership delivery system effects on substance misuse through 6 1/2 years past baseline from a cluster randomized controlled intervention trial. *Preventive Medicine*, 56:190–196. doi: 10.1016/j.ypmed.2012.12.013

Spoth, R. L., and Greenberg, M. T. 2005. Toward a comprehensive strategy for effective practitioner-scientist partnerships and larger-scale community health and well-being. *American Journal of Community Psychology*, 35:107–126.

Spoth, R. L., Greenberg, M. T., Bierman, K. L., and Redmond, C. 2004. PROSPER Community–University Partnership model for public education systems: Capacity-building for evidence-based, competence-building prevention. *Prevention Science*, 5:31–39.

Spoth, R. L., Guyll, M., Lillehoj, C. J., Redmond, C., and Greenberg, M. T. 2007. PROSPER study of evidence-based intervention implementation quality by community-university partnerships. *Journal of Community Psychology*, 35:981–999.

Spoth, R. L., Redmond, C., Shin, C., *et al.* 2007. Substance use outcomes at eighteen months past baseline from the PROSPER Community–University Partnership trial. *American Journal of Preventive Medicine*, 32:395–402.

Spoth, R. L., Rohrbach, L. A., Greenberg, M. T., *et al.*; Society for Prevention Research Type 2 Translational Task Force. 2013. Addressing core challenges for the next generation of Type 2 translation research and systems: The translation science to population impact (TSci impact) framework. *Prevention Science*, 14:319–351.

The Justice Research Center. 2013. Redirection: Consistently reducing juvenile crime in Florida. Tallahassee, FL: The Justice Research Center.

Tibbits, M. K., Bumbarger, B., Kyler, S., and Perkins, D. F. 2010. Sustaining evidence-based interventions under real-world conditions: Results from a large-scale diffusion project. *Prevention Science*, 11:252–262.

Vera Institute of Justice. 2015. Impact evaluation of the Adolescent Behavioral Learning Experience (ABLE) program at Rikers Island: Summary of findings. New York, NY: Vera Institute of Justice.

Wells, K. B., Sherbourne, C., Schoenbaum, M., *et al.* 2000. Impact of disseminating quality improvement programs for depression in managed primary care. *Journal of the American Medical Association*, 283:212–220.

Welsh, B. C., Sullivan, C. J., and Olds, D. L. 2010. When early crime prevention goes to scale: A new look at the evidence. *Prevention Science*, 11:115–125.

Winokur, K., Hand, G., and Blankenship, J. 2013. Florida Redirection cost-effectiveness evaluation. Tallahassee, FL: Justice Research Center.

World Health Organization. 2014. Global status report on violence prevention 2014. Geneva, Switzerland.

12

The Future of Crime Prevention

Introduction

The main conclusion of the 1997 *What Works* report to the US Department of Justice was that it was possible to identify some effective and ineffective crime prevention programs but that "most programs have not yet been evaluated with enough scientific evidence to draw conclusions" (Sherman *et al.*, 1998: 1). While it is still true that much of what occurs in communities and in correctional settings to prevent crime remains unevaluated, and many more high-quality evaluation studies are needed to investigate the effectiveness of current and yet-to-be-developed interventions, we know far more about crime prevention now than we did in the

> *Imprisonment has become the response of first resort to far too many of our social problems.*
>
> Angela Davis, political activist

The Prevention of Crime, First Edition. Delbert Elliott and Abigail Fagan.
© 2017 John Wiley & Sons, Inc. Published 2017 by John Wiley & Sons, Inc.
Companion website: www.wiley.com/go/elliott/prevention_of_crime

late 1990s. We now have a varied and growing list of *effective* crime prevention programs, practices, and policies. We also have scientifically valid information about some interventions that *do not work*.

Our philosophy and knowledge about how to undertake crime prevention have also changed substantially in the past few decades. Historically, crime prevention has been guided by **deterrence theories**, which consider the threat and/or receipt of punishment enough to deter offenders and potential offenders from breaking the law. Given this orientation, prevention has traditionally been considered the responsibility of the police and criminal justice system and has often relied on harsh punishments to deter offending. Although these views still guide much crime prevention, it has become increasingly clear that deterrence-based approaches are not very effective and sometimes can *increase* offending.

One of the most significant advances in our understanding of how to prevent crime over the last few decades has been the emergence of the **life course developmental paradigm**. This perspective emphasizes that crime is affected by many factors, including individual characteristics and attitudes, as well as family, peer, school, work, and community experiences. To successfully prevent crime, then, we can use a variety of approaches targeting different aspects of the individual, his/her social context and the environmental opportunities for crime. Most of these efforts will be implemented by individuals and agencies outside of the criminal justice system. The life course perspective provides us with many more options for crime prevention.

The life course paradigm also notes that different influences will affect individuals in different ways and at different points in their lives. From the **criminal career framework**, we understand that some factors provide opportunities for individuals to initiate offending, others may affect escalation and persistence in offending and still others help individuals desist from crime. Together, these insights suggest that we should use different strategies depending on the type of offending we wish to prevent and that interventions should target factors that are most relevant for the developmental stage (i.e., age) of the offender. We also know that individuals who initiate criminal behavior in late childhood will face a greater likelihood of engaging in crime during adulthood compared to those who initiate at later ages and that, on average, the prevalence of crime peaks during adolescence and begins to lessen in early adulthood. These insights emphasize the importance of offering prevention in the early years of life.

The goal of this concluding chapter is to review what we have learned in the past few decades regarding crime prevention and consider where we must go in the future. We begin by summarizing the types of interventions we can say with some confidence work as well as those that do not work. We also identify gaps in our knowledge of how to prevent crime – the areas for which effective models of crime prevention are lacking. We know that addressing these gaps requires more rigorous evaluations, as well as greater awareness and agreement among criminologists, policy-makers and the public as to how such evaluations should be conducted. We provide a set of recommendations to achieve these goals. Finally, we identify actions needed to increase the dissemination of effective programs, practice, and policies and minimize the use of ineffective strategies.

What Works to Reduce Crime

Following any highly publicized criminal event, the first question usually asked by the public is: *how could this crime have been prevented*? After reading this textbook, you should be able to answer this challenging question. In fact, you should be able to offer a variety of options to those seeking to implement effective prevention programs, practices, and policies. *So, what really does work to prevent crime?*

Scanning the information provided in Section III, we can point to evidence that state and federal policies regarding the **legal age at which minors can drink alcohol**, **raising taxes on alcohol** and **setting and enforcing laws that minimize alcohol use by drivers** all reduce under-age drinking and/or driving while intoxicated (see Chapter 6). Considering various law enforcement strategies, **hot spots policing** is currently the only practice with strong evidence of effectiveness in reducing crime.

In Chapter 7's review of social context interventions, the family setting emerged as the area with the greatest number of effective programs and practices and with interventions targeting families and children in each stage of the life course. We identified two effective **home visitation** programs in which trained facilitators provide pregnant women and parents of very young children with one-on-one consultation and support. These interventions were shown to reduce child maltreatment by caregivers and children's antisocial behavior. Many effective **parent training** programs, developed and tested in the USA and in other countries, were discussed. These can be used with universal or selective populations to teach caregivers how to effectively manage children's and adolescents' behavior, better communicate with them and provide them with social support and affection. Several intensive **family therapy** programs were also identified as effective in reducing recidivism and out-of-home placement for teenagers already involved in the criminal justice system.

In the school setting, **bullying prevention** interventions which change school-wide policies and practices have been shown to reduce bullying and other delinquent behaviors. In Chapter 8, we also identified **early childhood education** programs and **classroom-based** interventions which can delay the onset of drug use, aggression and/or violence. These curricula rely mostly on teachers to provide instruction as they would any academic subject, using both lecture and interactive methods to foster academic achievement and help students learn to avoid or better cope with risk factors related to delinquency. Some **multi-component** programs have been shown to reduce the initiation of delinquency and substance use, particularly interventions which combine parent training with teacher training and/or classroom curricula. Compared to school-based interventions, there are far fewer effective community-based interventions. Nonetheless, both **Communities That Care** and **PROSPER** have shown that it is possible to build support from community members to prevent crime and related problem behaviors and to implement effective prevention strategies (see Chapter 7). In terms of afterschool programming, **mentoring** has been demonstrated in high-quality evaluations as an effective prevention practice (see Chapter 8).

Even the most successful interventions will not prevent every crime, and we must also implement indicated interventions with those who have already broken the law in order to reduce recidivism. As described in Chapter 9, effective correctional practices for juvenile and adult offenders include **drug treatment** programs and interventions which use a **cognitive behavioral therapeutic (CBT)** approach. For adult offenders, interventions which use a **risk, need, and responsivity (RNR)** model have shown reductions in recidivism by offering services to address offenders' malleable risk factors.

To summarize "what works," we conclude that universal and selective interventions, which target for change risk and protective factors that affect individual involvement in offending, have greater evidence of effectiveness in preventing crime compared to indicated interventions offered in correctional settings and to situational crime prevention which focuses on environmental opportunities for offending. Although additional models are needed, we are encouraged by the diverse list of effective family-focused interventions, as well as the number of classroom-based programs that have been shown to reduce youth externalizing behaviors, adolescent substance use, delinquency and/or adult crime.

What Does Not Work to Reduce Crime

After reading this text, you should have a good understanding that many strategies implemented by the criminal justice system, especially deterrence-based strategies and those meant to "get tough on crime," are unsuccessful in reducing crime. Many have been shown in well-conducted evaluations to have no impact on crime and some have been shown to actually *increase* rates of offending among participants. It is just as important to identify these programs, practices, and policies as it is to understand what is effective in preventing crime.

In Chapter 6, we identified both **mandatory arrest policies for perpetrators of domestic violence** and **processing juvenile offenders in the adult criminal justice system** as ineffective in reducing recidivism. As discussed in Chapter 9, even the most basic criminal justice strategy of **incarceration** does not reduce future recidivism among adult offenders. In fact, official statistics in the USA indicate that nearly 80% of all offenders are re-arrested within five years of their release from prison (Durose, Cooper, and Snyder, 2014). Multiple studies have shown **Scared Straight** programs increase offending among the at-risk juveniles who participate in such interventions and that **boot camps** have no impact on juvenile or adult recidivism.

When considering universal and selective programs, several studies have shown that when interventions intentionally or unintentionally bring together high-risk and/or delinquent youth, they can increase rather than decrease offending. Evaluations of the **Adolescent Transitions Program (ATP)**, the **Cambridge-Somerville Youth Study**, and **Reconnecting Youth** (see Chapters 7 and 8) have all attributed iatrogenic effects to **deviancy training**, which occurs when youth spend unsupervised time with deviant peers who reinforce delinquent behavior, as hypothesized by social learning theory. Many afterschool programs have also failed to reduce crime, perhaps because they often bring together large groups of adolescents, some of whom may be engaging in delinquency, and adequate adult supervision is not always provided.

Although in Chapter 8 we identified many effective classroom-based curricula, several programs have been shown in multiple studies to be ineffective in reducing substance use and/or crime. Examples include **G.R.E.A.T.**, **Project Alert**, and **D.A.R.E.**, all of which are widely used in the USA and in some other countries. The most recent evaluation of D.A.R.E. has shown that it *increases* substance use (Sloboda *et al.*, 2009). Why these interventions fail to reduce crime is not clear, but given evidence of ineffectiveness from multiple studies, we recommend that these interventions be discontinued and resources re-allocated to effective crime prevention strategies.

What We Do Not Know About Crime Prevention

While we are not quite as pessimistic as Sherman *et al.* (1997) about the lack of good evaluation of crime prevention efforts, it is true that many strategies require much more rigorous evaluation to learn if they increase, decrease or have no impact on rates of offending. This need is especially true in the area of **situational crime prevention**. Although strategies like **target hardening, increasing guardianship and surveillance** and **Crime Prevention Through Environmental Design (CPTED)** have been used for several decades, most have not been subject to rigorous evaluation (see Chapter 6). These interventions make sense and are appealing because they can be widely implemented, oftentimes by private citizens, but few have been subject to RCTs or rigorous QEDs. As also discussed in Chapter 6, we also need more systematic evaluation of law enforcement practices such as **problem-oriented policing, pulling levers**, and **community-oriented policing (COP)**. Given that these are general strategies that can take various forms in different agencies, evaluations must include detailed process evaluations to study implementation procedures, as well as to study the impact of these practices on crime.

As discussed in Chapter 7, there is a definite lack of information about how to reduce crime by altering peer relationships. Very few interventions have attempted to promote positive peer interactions and some have inadvertently led to deviancy training by bringing together delinquent peers. To be more effective in this context requires more knowledge of exactly how peers influence each other and how program implementers can better monitor peer interactions and create positive peer cultures. We also need more effective **gang prevention** programs. Although some federal agencies in the USA advocate the use of multi-component gang interventions that involve a coordinated delivery of universal, selective, and indicated interventions, these strategies require better evaluation to understand whether or not they reduce gang-joining and gang-related crime.

Knowledge of how to effectively change school and community settings to reduce crime must also be enhanced. Few policies and practices designed to change school rules, norms or climate have been well evaluated (see Chapter 7). Many of these interventions have not been evaluated to assess their impact on crime, and some studies have shown inconclusive evidence of effectiveness. As a result, it is currently unknown if commonly used interventions like having **zero-tolerance policies** and **placing armed guards or police officers in schools** actually reduce crime. Similarly, many **community mobilization** approaches, as well as community/police partnerships like **neighborhood watch groups** and **community-oriented policing** have not yet shown credible evidence of effectiveness in reducing crime.

Changing the norms and interactions occurring in school and neighborhood settings is likely to be challenging, given the number of people who must support such efforts, but the potential pay-off is large. Improving the school environment may not only help to reduce crime among all students in the school, but also improve students' academic success and increase healthy interactions with peers and teachers. Creating more supportive communities is also likely to have benefits in multiple areas and has the potential to create positive change in both youth and adult members of the population.

More evaluation of correctional practices is also needed. Although Lipsey (2009; Lipsey and Cullen, 2007) has conducted meta-analyses of findings from numerous evaluations of correctional interventions (see Chapter 9), many of the programs and practices he has reviewed had a single evaluation, were not evaluated using RCTs, were poorly implemented and were evaluated only by the program developer. All of these factors reduce the ability to draw strong conclusions regarding intervention effectiveness of any individual program. To remedy this problem, correctional interventions must be subject to more high-quality independent evaluations. More evaluation is also needed to understand the effectiveness of newly emerging justice reinvestment and diversion initiatives which seek to increase the use of evidence-based indicated programs and practices, reduce the prison population and increase investments in effective, community-based interventions.

> *Finding ways to stimulate more production of rigorous studies will be the most critical step in the next generation of prevention research, school-based or otherwise.*
>
> Petrosino, 2003: 201

More generally, we noted in every chapter in Section III that there are fewer effective prevention **policies** and **practices** compared to **programs**. Policies are very challenging to evaluate, particularly because they are typically enacted across an entire school district, community, state or country, making it difficult to establish an appropriate control or comparison group (Nagin and Weisburd, 2013). Effective practices are also difficult to identify because doing so requires a comparison of information from multiple studies all testing the same technique or strategy, but true replication is very difficult to determine (Aos, Cook, et al., 2011; Valentine et al., 2011). Because policies and practices are often thought to be easier to implement compared to programs with stricter requirements (Embry, 2004; Lipsey and Howell, 2012), there have been increasing calls for their use in communities, but this call to action is premature without more evaluation of their impact on crime.

It is also true that far more of the effective crime prevention efforts have been developed and tested in the USA compared to other countries. Progress has been made in Canada, Australia, New Zealand, the UK, and some other European and Scandinavian countries, but evaluation has been particularly lacking in less developed countries (World Health Organization, 2014). The lack of progress is likely related to more limited funding for prevention and evaluation in these countries, as well as a lack of systematic training for professionals in evaluation methods (Catalano et al., 2012). This disparity is troubling, especially given that according to the World Health Organization (2014), rates of homicide are highest in low- and middle-income countries and these areas have not seen the same reductions in crime as found in high-income countries over the past decade.

Ensuring High-quality Evaluations of Crime Prevention Efforts

In order to increase our knowledge of effective and ineffective crime prevention strategies, it is essential that more evaluations of existing and yet-to-be created interventions occur. It is equally important that these evaluations use the rigorous methods and criteria we discussed in Chapters 4 and 5. Yet, we also know that there is some disagreement among criminologists regarding the feasibility and usefulness of such methods and that policy-makers and funders do not always require such standards when adopting and funding research projects or interventions. How can we overcome these challenges? We offered some possible solutions in Chapter 11 and make additional recommendations here. Before doing so, however, we first note that there is reason to be optimistic about our ability to increase the use of high-quality evaluations.

Building on progress

We have seen much progress in criminological research in recent years, including increased use of RCTs in program evaluation (Farrington and Welsh, 2005). Not all of these advances have been made in criminology, but the discipline has benefitted from efforts by prevention scientists working in related fields of education, medicine, psychology, public health, and social work. As discussed in Chapter 3, risk and protective factors associated with criminal behavior have also been linked to outcomes of interest to these other disciplines, such that interventions designed to change other outcomes – by targeting risk and protective factors – have often been shown to affect crime as well. For example, the early childhood education **Perry Preschool** program (see Chapter 8), intended to enhance academic performance among low-income, African American youth, was shown to reduce crime in adolescence and adulthood (Heckman *et al.*, 2010; Schweinhart, 2005, 2013). Similarly, **Nurse–Family Partnership (NFP)** (see Chapter 7) was initially designed to reduce the number of low birth-weight infants but was shown to be effective in reducing child abuse and crime by mothers and delinquency by their children, as well as reduced welfare dependency and maternal unemployment. As prevention scientists expand the list of "what works," criminology will also benefit (Catalano *et al.*, 2012).

To provide a few specific examples of progress in criminology, we noted in Chapter 5 that the international Campbell Collaboration was begun in 2000 to identify crime and justice programs demonstrated as effective in rigorous scientific studies. Around the same time, the Academy of Experimental Criminology (AEC) was founded to recognize notable crime prevention scholars. Most of its members also became involved in the Division of Experimental Criminology (DEC), an academic society within the American Society of Criminology established in 2010 "to promote and improve the use and development of experimental evidence and methods in the advancement of criminological theory and evidence-based crime policy" (http://expcrim.org/). The *Journal of Experimental Criminology*, launched in 2005, is the official journal of the DEC dedicated to publishing high-quality experimental and quasi-experimental evaluations as well as systematic reviews of crime prevention literature.

Having organized groups promoting standards of scientific evaluation will no doubt advance the use of such methods in criminology. It is also encouraging that in recent years, the National Institute of Justice, the federal agency charged with overseeing and funding much crime research in the USA, lists as one of its strategic goals: "fostering science-based criminal justice practice." NIJ funding announcements now commonly include the following statement to encourage rigorous evaluation methods: "*If an application includes an evaluation research component … the application is expected to propose the use of random selection and assignment of participants to experimental and control conditions, if feasible. Applications that include evaluation research but do not propose the use of randomization should explain clearly why randomization is not feasible, and should propose a strong quasi-experimental design that can address the risk of selection bias.*" This statement explicitly calls for RCTs in crime prevention evaluation and requires justification for failure to utilize this methodology. Presumably, evaluations that lack rigorous design will not receive funding. Addressing the question of feasibility, a recent systematic review of deterrence-based program evaluations concluded that even large, area-based deterrence-based interventions can and should be subjected to rigorous RCT and QED evaluations (Braga and Weisburd, 2014).

Another indicator of progress discussed in Chapter 5 is the emergence in the last decade of various lists or registries intended to identify effective interventions based on evaluation criteria and outcomes. Although there is much variation in these criteria, there is also significant overlap. For example, there is agreement that RCT evaluation designs provide the strongest evidence for program effectiveness and that having a control or comparison groups is a minimum requirement for a "well-conducted" evaluation. In most cases, this means that lists judge evaluations according to their ability to demonstrate strong internal validity including, for example, reliable and valid measures, baseline comparability, minimal attrition, an intent-to-treat analysis, and use of appropriate statistical techniques.

Reducing disparity in lists of effective crime prevention programs, practices, and policies

So, if various lists use similar criteria, why is there so much disparity in the programs rated effective on different lists? There are a number of reasons. *First*, while there is general agreement across lists regarding the quality of evaluation designs, there is little agreement about standards related to replication, sustainability and independence of the evaluator. Although replication is generally acknowledged as an important criterion for determining effectiveness, it is not a required condition on many lists; most lists require only a single, high-quality evaluation. In Chapters 4 and 11, we identified many reasons why replication is important, most notably because it provides additional information about the program's feasibility, helps avoid inflated effect sizes and increases the external validity and generalizability of effects. Sustainability of program outcomes is a criterion on only two lists, and the independence of the evaluator is not included as a standard on any list. As noted in Chapter 5, all three of these criteria were included in the standards created by the Federal Collaboration on What Works (2005) and, in our opinion, all lists should adopt these criteria.

Second, we believe part of the explanation for the inconsistency across lists is the variation in how, exactly, the evidence is reviewed and criteria are applied (Biglan and Ogden, 2008; Institute of Medicine, 2008). As discussed in Chapter 5, different lists utilize different review processes and reviewers differ in their expertise with research methods. We strongly believe in the value of a systematic review process which takes into account *all* evaluations of a particular intervention and which is updated periodically to take new findings into account. Moreover, we recommend that interventions be reviewed by multiple parties who are well trained in research methods, have no vested interest in particular programs and who must reach consensus on whether or not standards are achieved. The value of having an Advisory Board comprised of independent evaluation experts and program developers who meet and discuss the evidence cannot be understated. Although requiring all of these parties to agree as to whether or not standards have been met likely results in a very rigorous review process and a smaller number of programs rated as effective, it significantly reduces the chances of recommending an intervention that is not effective.

As we argued in Chapter 5, our position is that high standards are critical for making determinations of program effectiveness, *especially* when such determinations are linked to calls for widespread dissemination of these interventions. *To significantly impact crime rates, we must ensure that communities are implementing well-evaluated, effective programs.* If programs that do not have a strong likelihood of success are promoted, changes in crime rates are unlikely to occur and confidence in prevention science and criminology will be shaken. For this reason, we have outlined in Chapter 5 a set of criteria similar to that used in the Blueprints review process that we hope will become the norm in crime prevention. For example, Blueprints, but not all lists, require the use of RCTs, a replication of program effects and evidence of sustained effects for at least one year post-intervention for all Model programs, those recommended for widespread dissemination. Intervention specificity and system readiness also must be met for a program to be rated as effective.

An alternative strategy to adopting evidence-based programs like those on Blueprints or CrimeSolutions has been proposed by Lipsey and colleagues (Lipsey, 2009; Lipsey *et al.*, 2010; Lipsey and Howell, 2012). Lipsey's approach is based upon his meta-analyses identifying effective types of juvenile justice *practices*. In addition to calculating the average effect of the programs using a given type of practice, his analyses identified specific program characteristics that were associated with more positive program effects, specifically therapeutic type of program (e.g., counseling or skill-building programs rather than deterrence or discipline-based programs), targeting high risk offenders, high dosage, and quality implementation. As noted earlier, not all programs using an evidence-based practice have positive effects and some may even be harmful, but his analysis showed that the use of these identified characteristics helped to distinguish between programs with and without positive effects. Lipsey then argued that the use of an evidence-based general practice (one of the therapeutic types) together with the other three program implementation characteristics or "components" qualifies a program as evidence-based.

Lipsey and colleagues have created a practical application of these findings, the **Standardized Program Evaluation Protocol (SPEP)** (Lipsey *et al.,* 2010; Lipsey and Howell, 2012). SPEP is a rating system or fidelity assessment tool for measuring the extent to which a juvenile justice program is implementing an effective program as measured by these four characteristics or components. Using SPEP guidelines, juvenile justice agencies are encouraged to modify or adjust their existing programs to incorporate the characteristics associated with positive effects on recidivism. Doing so transforms these interventions into evidence-based practices using Lipsey's criteria. Lipsey promotes SPEP as an alternative to adopting the "brand name" programs found on Blueprints , CrimeSolutions, and other lists (also see Greenwood and Welsh, 2012). It allows existing juvenile justice programs (many of which are likely to be ineffective) to be certified as evidence-based with relatively "modest" adaptations and without having to make fundamental and more difficult changes to the content of existing services or to conduct rigorous and expensive evaluations to determine the effectiveness of their programs. Lipsey does note that the adoption of a new brand-name program that addresses targeted risk and protective factors, particular types of offenders, or certain types of crimes is appropriate when existing justice system services are not available to address these needs.

> *Few policies are approved that call for more than marginal changes in the status quo: few widely implemented social change efforts are conceptually bold.*
>
> Shadish *et al.*, 1991: 442

We believe there is merit in Lipsey's effective component-based approach and that it could be applied to criminal justice services in the not too distant future. However, there are a number of concerns that suggest it is premature to advocate for widespread use of SPEP. Most critically, there is no *experimental evidence* that the set of implementation components identified by Lipsey actually do account for variation in program effectiveness. Instead, these secondary findings from the meta-analyses provide only *correlational evidence*, a type of evidence that cannot justify a causal interpretation of the relationship between these characteristics and program effectiveness. Correlational evidence is particularly weak when there is no theoretical basis and no identified causal mechanism underlying the components' relationship to effectiveness. At best, the analyses identify some hypotheses about the types of program characteristics that *might* be causally related to an impact on crime. But some mechanism that explains this relationship is needed along with an experimental study to validate these hypothesized relationships. Sampson, Winship, and Knight (2013) warn of the danger in basing criminal justice policy and practice on research when causal mechanisms are unknown and we agree.

To date, SPEP has not been rigorously evaluated; no QED or RCT has been conducted to determine if offenders in correctional agencies that use this approach have lower rates of recidivism compared to those in agencies that do not use this approach. Just as no "brand name" program would be rated as effective on any of the lists reviewed in this book without some experimental evidence of positive results, a program with a high score on the SPEP cannot currently be considered evidence-based. Nonetheless, SPEP is currently being implemented in agencies across the USA (Lipsey *et al.*, 2010), perhaps because it claims to meet the standard for evidence-based and because it often requires only modest changes to correctional practices. Given that many of the interventions used in the correctional setting are deterrence-based, and these approaches have been shown to be generally ineffective, we believe more radical, not more modest, changes are needed to improve justice system practices.

It is possible that, at some point in the future, SPEP will have evidence of effectiveness from rigorous evaluation studies. Prevention science does advance, and we believe that criteria for determining effectiveness should be adjusted as new methods and knowledge are accumulated. Doing so will likely involve the application of even more rigorous standards in order to best ensure the identification and promotion of truly effective interventions. For example, in Spring 2015, Blueprints expanded its classification system to include a "Model+" designation. Model+ programs must meet all the criteria required for Model programs *and* have been evaluated by a scientist independent from the program developer. Adding this classification means that Blueprints now has the same criteria as the Federal Collaboration on What Works Standards (2005). Independent evaluations are still rare, but requiring independent evaluations should motivate researchers to conduct this type of study and funders to support them. Doing so will also improve evaluation standards and increase our confidence that programs which meet these standards are truly effective. Similarly, with increased replication and evaluation, we are better able to assess the external validity of programs and perhaps require that interventions be tested in multiple settings and/or with different types of populations prior to their promotion, as also advocated by Sampson and colleagues (2013).

Utilizing new methods of evaluation

Our last major recommendation is that program evaluations capitalize on advances in research design and analysis. One of the main critiques of the RCT is that it is not always feasible to employ (Biglan, Ary, and Wagenaar, 2000; Hough, 2010; Mears, 2007). For example, it can be difficult to randomly assign groups to enact policies, which could explain why the list of effective crime prevention policies is relatively small. However, policies and other efforts to change social contexts can be well evaluated using certain quasi-experimental designs (Cook and Campbell, 1979). They could also be evaluated using "adaptive" intervention designs which stagger the implementation of a particular policy or program such that some areas enact the intervention first and others do so at a later time (Brown, Mason, and Brown, 2014).

Adaptive designs have also been recommended when evaluating complex, multi-component interventions, such as the CTC and PROSPER community-based systems reviewed in Chapter 7, which is important given that few effective interventions of this type currently exist. These designs can involve implementation of a different service or set of services to different individuals/groups depending on their need for intervention (Collins, Murphy, and Bierman, 2004). For example, the **Raising Healthy Children** intervention described in Chapter 8 included the delivery of universal school- and family-based interventions to teachers, students, and families, and tutoring services to a selective group of students who had poor academic performance. An adaptive research design provides a rigorous method for examining effects across groups who received a different set or dosage of service.

Increased use of new and more rigorous statistical analytic methods can also help to increase the number of effective interventions and to better understand how they produce their effects. We noted in Chapter 7 the lack of effective peer-, gang-, and community coalition-based prevention models. Social network analysis (SNA) is one type of statistical methodology that could help address these gaps in knowledge. SNA is designed to evaluate relationships between and among individuals and/ or groups, including how these actors affect one another's decision-making processes and behaviors (Hassmiller Lich *et al.*, 2013). By focusing on social relationships, SNA could allow researchers to pinpoint more specifically how peers may have positive and negative effects on each other's behavior (e.g., Osgood *et al.*, 2013) or how differential participation by community stakeholders can affect the impact of a coalition-driven prevention approach (e.g., Valente, Chou, and Pentz, 2007). Statistical methods for analyzing mediating and moderating effects, as well as estimating interventions' cost effectiveness, have also advanced in recent years (e.g., Crowley *et al.*, 2014; Fairchild and MacKinnon, 2014). We hope this progress will lead to increased use of these techniques and, eventually, more rigorous standards requiring that interventions identified as "evidence-based" conduct such analyses.

Our recommendations for increasing the use of rigorous, scientific evaluations of interventions are listed in Table 12.1. We expect that it will take time for these goals to be realized, particularly in developing nations in which funding for prevention/evaluation and training in evaluation methods is often minimal (Catalano *et al.*, 2012). Nonetheless, given the advances in prevention science and crime prevention in the USA and some other high-income countries in the last few decades, we are hopeful that progress will be made.

Increasing the Dissemination of Effective Crime Prevention Strategies

We know that to significantly impact crime rates, we must ensure that communities are implementing well-evaluated, effective programs correctly and at scale. Although we have already made some progress towards this goal, we must continue our efforts to convince the public: (a) that prevention is a good investment, (b) to choose to implement effective strategies and avoid strategies known to be ineffective, and (c) to implement effective interventions widely and with fidelity. We discussed

Table 12.1 Recommendations for increasing the use and rigor of evaluation methods in crime prevention.

Goal	Recommendation
Reducing differences in lists of "What Works"	• Use systematic review processes • Require rigorous evaluation standards • Require consensus on evaluation standards by multiple experts • Regularly update lists and evaluation standards
Increasing the number of effective interventions	• Employ rigorous quasi-experimental designs when randomized control trials are not feasible • Use "adaptive" research designs to evaluate multi-component interventions and policies • Use emerging methods such as Social Network Analysis to evaluate social context interventions

ways to improve dissemination and implementation in Chapters 10 and 11. In this section, we summarize the challenges faced in each of these areas and the critical actions needed to ensure that these outcomes are achieved.

Until the public is convinced that prevention works, there will be little incentive to invest in these types of efforts and to scale back the use of deterrence-, punishment-, and criminal justice-oriented strategies. How can we change the current mindset? Most importantly, we must take the actions reviewed in the prior section and expand the number of effective, well-evaluated crime prevention strategies available for use. At the same time, we must

> *In the absence of a radical shift towards prevention and public health, we will not be successful in containing medical costs or improving the health of the American people.*
> Barrack Obama

promote these interventions to the public, emphasize the degree to which they have been shown to reduce crime in the short- and long term and indicate their cost effectiveness.

Biglan and Taylor (2000) provide some useful advice for helping us think about how to make gains in crime prevention. They contrast the advances made in tobacco prevention to the lack of progress in violence prevention during the late twentieth century. They argue that widespread support of anti-smoking initiatives followed a very public campaign that emphasized the harms of smoking, the risk factors associated with smoking and the actions needed to reduce these risk factors, all of which were communicated in ways that the public could easily understand. In contrast, they note that there is a lack of consensus among scientists as to what predicts violence and how to best prevent it, which likely hinders a coordinated effort to change public views about violence and violence prevention. They also state that few organizations or agencies consider violence *prevention* to be their primary focus, but that there is a well-established and well-funded network of law enforcement and correctional agencies dedicated to *reactive* crime control strategies, such that preventing the onset of crime or eliminating crime altogether is not in their interest.

Biglan and Taylor (2000) emphasize that a culture shift is needed to significantly alter public perceptions of crime and violence. We agree. Criminologists must help initiate this change, given that they are the experts with knowledge of what causes crime and how to prevent it. It is also true, however, that criminologists disagree as to whether or not they should make policy recommendations about crime and crime prevention and exactly what they would recommend if they were to do so (Blomberg, Mestre, and Mann, 2013; Dodge and Mandel, 2012). Despite these debates, there are signs of progress. The American Society of Criminology now oversees a journal dedicated to public policy (*Criminology and Public Policy*) and regularly convenes meetings with policy-makers to discuss policy-relevant issues (such as those organized by the Consortium of Social Science Associations, or COSSA, see: www.cossa.org/). In addition, US academics have taken leadership roles in public agencies such as the National Institute of Justice and the Bureau of Justice Statistics.

Biglan and Taylor (2000) suggest that there are few organizations dedicated to violence prevention but, in fact, a number of public and private agencies have a stake in reducing crime. Many of these organizations have also begun to lobby for increased use of effective crime prevention and decreased use of ineffective and harmful practices. For example, based on research indicating iatrogenic effects of Scared Straight programs (Petrosino, Turpin-Petrosino, and Buehler, 2003), the Assistant Attorney General for the Office of Justice Programs (Laurie O. Robinson) and OJJDP's Acting Administrator (Jeff Slowikowski) stated in an article in the *Baltimore Sun* that because these programs are ineffective and harmful "*the U.S. Department of Justice discourages the[ir] funding [and] … States that operate such programs could have their federal funding reduced*" (Robinson and Slowikowski, 2011). The willingness of officials in two of the federal agencies responsible for crime prevention in the USA to speak out against a widely used intervention is notable. As another example, the Centers for Disease Control has promoted effective crime prevention through its Guide to Community Preventive Services (www.thecommunityguide.org/) and its Preventing Youth Violence: Opportunities for Action initiative (David-Ferdon and Simon, 2014). The CDC has also helped communities implement effective youth violence prevention strategies by funding Academic Centers for Excellence (ACE) (http://www.cdc.gov/ViolencePrevention/ACE/program_eval.html).

Also in the USA, many private foundations have made crime and crime prevention an area of concern and have funded large-scale evaluation research. These include, to name a few, the Ford Foundation, MacArthur Foundation, Pew Charitable Trusts, and the John and Laura Arnold and Annie E. Casey Foundations, which currently fund the Blueprints for Healthy Youth Development initiative. The Coalition for Evidence-Based Policy is also an important private organization whose mission is to increase government effectiveness by using evidence-based interventions, including crime prevention strategies. The Coalition's identification of effective home visitation programs played a key role in the development of the US Maternal, Infant, and Early Childhood Home Visiting (MIECHV) initiative, which has provided $1.5 billion to states since 2011 to implement such interventions (http://mchb. hrsa.gov/programs/homevisiting/index.html). As a last example, a unique public–private partnership involving the Council of State Governments, MacArthur Foundation, and the Bureau of Justice Assistance in the USA recently issued a joint report recommending actions needed to reduce recidivism and improve other outcomes for youth in the juvenile justice system (Seigle, Walsh, and Weber, 2014). The agencies called for increased use of validated risk and needs assessments to guide services (consistent with the **RNR** approach described in Chapter 9), greater implementation of programs proven effective in reducing recidivism, more coordination across service systems and more attention to the developmental needs of youth when designing interventions and policies.

We are encouraged by the number of organizations dedicated to crime prevention but take seriously Biglan and Taylor's (2000) recommendation that academics and agencies must promote the same message regarding the benefits of crime prevention if the public is to get behind this effort. We recommend a focus on the economic benefits of prevention approaches, given the nearly universal concerns regarding the costs of crime and incarceration. Analyses by the Washington State Institute for Public Policy (www.wsipp.wa.gov) have indicated that the majority of crime prevention programs and practices identified as effective in Section III of this book are cost effective and save money in the long term. As discussed in Chapter 11, such information led the state of Washington to increase its use of effective interventions and, as a result, the state has seen reductions in crime rates *and* financial savings (Aos, Lee, *et al.*, 2011). Hoping to replicate this success, the Pew–MacArthur **Results First** initiative (http://www.pewtrusts.org/en/projects/pew-macarthur-results-first-initiative) is currently providing funds and training to states across the country to help them conduct cost-benefit analyses, increase their investments in effective interventions and reduce the use of ineffective interventions.

Although widespread dissemination of effective crime prevention programs, practices, and policies will take time, many seeds have been planted and we are hopeful they will grow and flourish in the next decade. As one last indicator of progress, the Results First initiative identified over 100 statutes passed in the USA in the last decade requiring agencies to assess their use of effective interventions, providing incentives or mandates to increase use of effective interventions and/or eliminating funds for ineffective interventions (Pew–MacArthur Results First Initiative, 2015). For example, in Oregon, five state agencies, including the Department of Corrections, have been mandated to increase the amount of funding spent on programs that meet standards of effectiveness. Beginning in 2005, agencies had to spend at least 25% of their funds on evidence-based interventions, but that proportion grew to 75% in 2009. Such laws provide increased accountability for the use of effective crime prevention and we hope to see even more states and countries passing such statutes in the years to come.

The Future of Crime Prevention

As emphasized throughout this text, achieving significant reductions in crime rests on our ability to increase the use of effective crime prevention programs, practices, and policies. We hope a number of you who are reading this text will become program practitioners implementing effective crime prevention interventions or researchers evaluating the effectiveness of crime prevention programs, practices, and policies. We hope this text has provided a useful framework for working in the field of crime prevention. To send you on your way, we provide a few last recommendations for you to consider as you embark on your careers in criminology, criminal justice, and related fields of study.

For Practitioners (including system/agency administrators, implementers, and other staff):

- Develop and utilize a user-friendly system to collect, store, and analyze data on clients, services and outcomes and use these data to guide decision-making and implementation. The commitment to use data to inform decisions regarding intervention implementation and sustainability is the most critical step in creating a culture that encourages evidence-based crime prevention. Use of the data/system also provides accountability for human and financial investments in these interventions.

- To select a new intervention, find a program or practice that: fits your need(s), has been proven effective for preventing your specific problem with the type of clients you serve, requires resources that you have available, fits your budget and is acceptable to your community. If multiple interventions meet these criteria, pick the one with the strongest evidence of effectiveness (based on its effect size). If there are no evidence-based programs or practices that fit your need(s), work with a developer to create a new intervention; be sure it is based on a strong theory of crime and existing evidence about what works, then evaluate it to determine if it is effective. Do not launch an untested program without a commitment to evaluate it.
- Prior to or in the early stages of implementation, work with the program developer to determine how to make local adaptations to the selected program if needed. Make sure adaptations are consistent with the intervention's logic model and existing research.
- Monitor implementation fidelity on an ongoing basis. Realize that implementation challenges will occur at the start of most programs and practices and that the quality of implementation tends to decline over time, resulting in a decreased level of effectiveness. Engage in quality improvement practices to correct implementation problems as needed.

For Program Evaluators:

- Work with the program developer(s) and current implementers to determine the specific research question(s) to be addressed by the evaluation. The evaluation design, data collection and analysis will vary based on the questions to be answered.
- Utilize the strongest research design the situation allows. Do not be scared to use a randomized controlled trial. They are often possible, though they may sometimes require "creative" sample selection strategies. RCTs can also be easier to implement than other designs, such as when the pool of eligible participants is much larger than can be treated with existing resources or personnel; randomization can be the fairest strategy for deciding who can receive services and who cannot.
- No matter what research design you have selected, pay close attention to implementation processes and all the threats to internal validity. Be transparent in reporting how your evaluation was carried out and how you addressed any threats to internal validity. Use guidance such as that recommended by the Consolidated Standards of Reporting Trials (**CONSORT**; see www. consort-statement.org) to both plan your evaluation and ensure that you are reporting all necessary information to allow adequate assessment of the merit of your intervention.[1]

Conclusion

The goal of this textbook is to provide a comprehensive and current review of crime prevention. Much progress has been made in the last few decades in this area, with crime prevention moving from a nearly exclusive focus on deterrence- and punishment-based interventions implemented by law enforcement to a more developmentally informed, public health approach that allows for a wider range of prevention activities. In addition, more of the recently developed crime prevention programs and practices have much stronger evidence of effectiveness than the earlier, deterrence-based efforts.

Although much work remains to be done to increase the number and use of effective interventions, we fully expect that future editions of this book will include more examples of effective programs, practices, and policies. We are also optimistic that dissemination and sustainability of these interventions will increase as policy-makers and the public become more aware of the benefits of crime prevention. Finally, we believe that you, the readers of this text, are critical to the future development of crime prevention. We hope that you put your new knowledge of "what works" into practice as you begin your careers in criminology, criminal justice, and related fields.

Critical Thinking Questions and Practice Activities

1. What do you think is the best way to prevent crime? Base your answer on the strategies reviewed in Section III of this book, as well as considerations related to implementation fidelity, cost, dissemination, and sustainability discussed in Section IV.
2. What types of interventions do we need to know more about in order to more effectively prevent crime?
3. What do you think is the biggest challenge we will face in increasing the number of effective crime prevention strategies and their widespread dissemination?
4. What are your future career goals? How will the information covered in this book be of use to you in your chosen field(s) of study?

Endnote

1. We have not previously discussed the CONSORT guidelines, but these recommendations are well known in the fields of medicine and public health. They were designed in order to ensure complete, accurate, and consistent reporting of randomized controlled trials, including information on the sample selection and attrition, randomization procedures, statistical methods, and results (Schultz *et al.*, 2010). Some journals will only publish studies that report on all the elements specified in the CONSORT guidelines (http://www.consort-statement.org/checklists/view/32-consort/66-title). Researchers are currently discussing ways to create a similar set of recommendations to guide the methodology and reporting of evaluations in criminology and other social sciences (Grant *et al.*, 2013).

Helpful Websites

*   http://cbkb.org/about/
    The **Cost–Benefit Knowledge Bank (CBKB)** *provides information about cost-benefit studies in crime prevention.*
*   http://www.pewtrusts.org/en/projects/pew-macarthur-results-first-initiative
    This website describes the Pew-MacArthur **Results First** *initiative in the United States and provides examples of state statutes passed to increase the dissemination of effective crime prevention programs, practices, and policies.*
*   http://www.cdc.gov/ViolencePrevention/ACE/program_eval.html
    The **Centers for Disease Control** *website describes the Academic Center for Excellence initiative to prevent youth violence.*

Further Reading

- National Research Council. 2012. *Reforming Juvenile Justice: A Developmental Approach.* Washington, DC: The National Academies Press.
  This report provides recommendations for reforms to the juvenile justice system in the United States, including the use of more effective prevention and treatment services.
- Pew-MacArthur Results First Initiative. 2015. *Legislating evidence-based policymaking.* Washington, DC: The Pew Charitable Trusts, MacArthur Foundation.
  This brief discusses progress made in "evidence-based policymaking," or using research to guide government policies and decisions.

References

Aos, S., Cook, T. D., Elliott, D. S., *et al.* 2011. Commentary on Valentine, Jeffrey, *et al. Prevention Science,* 12:121–122.

Aos, S., Lee, S., Drake, E. K., *et al.* 2011. Return on investment: Evidence-based options to improve statewide outcomes (Document No. 11-07-1201). Olympia, WA: Washington State Institute for Public Policy.

Biglan, A., Ary, D.V., and Wagenaar, A. C. 2000. The value of interrupted time-series experiments for community intervention research. *Prevention Science,* 1:31–49.

Biglan, A., and Ogden, T. 2008. The evolution of evidence-based practices. *European Journal of Behavior Analysis,* 9:81–95.

Biglan, A., and Taylor, T. K. 2000. Why have we been more successful at reducing tobacco use than violent crime? *American Journal of Community Psychology,* 28:269–302.

Blomberg, T. G., Mestre, J., and Mann, K. 2013. Criminology and public policy: Establishing causality, providing best available knowledge, or both? *Criminology and Public Policy,* 12:571–584.

Braga, A. A., and Weisburd, D. L. 2014. Must we settle for less rigorous evaluations in large area-based crime prevention programs? Lessons from a Campbell review of focused deterrence. *Journal of Experimental Criminology,* 10:573–597. doi: 10.1007/s11292-014-9205-8

Brown, C. H., Mason, W. A., and Brown, E. C. 2014. Translating the intervention approach into an appropriate research design: The next-generation adaptive designs for effectiveness and implementation research. In: Z. Sloboda and H. Petras (eds), *Defining Prevention Science,* pp. 363–388. New York, NY: Springer-Verlag.

Catalano, R. F., Fagan, A. A., Gavin, L. E., *et al.* 2012. Worldwide application of prevention science in adolescent health. *The Lancet,* 379:1653–1664.

Collins, L. M., Murphy, S., and Bierman, K. L. 2004. A conceptual framework for adaptive preventive interventions. *Prevention Science,* 5:185–196.

Cook, T. D., and Campbell, D. T. 1979. *Quasi-experimentation: Design and Analysis Issues for Field Settings.* Boston, MA: Houghton Mifflin.

Crowley, D. M., Griner Hill, L., Kuklinski, M. R., and Jones, D. E. 2014. Research priorities for economic analyses of prevention: Current issues and future directions. *Prevention Science,* 15:789–798.

David-Ferdon, C., and Simon, T. R. 2014. Preventing youth violence: Opportunities for action. Atlanta, GA: National Center for Injury Prevention and Control, Centers for Disease Control and Prevention.

Dodge, K. A., and Mandel, A. D. 2012. Building evidence for evidence-based policy-making. *Criminology and Public Policy,* 11:525–534.

Durose, M. R., Cooper, A. D., and Snyder, H. N. 2014. Recidivism of prisoners released in 30 states in 2005: Patterns from 2005 to 2010. Washington, DC: Bureau of Justice Statistics, US Department of Justice.

Embry, D. D. 2004. Community-based prevention using simple, low-cost, evidence-based kernels and behavior vaccines. *Journal of Community Psychology*, 32:575–591.

Fairchild, A. J., and MacKinnon, D. P. 2014. Using mediation and moderation analyses to enhance prevention research. In: Z. Sloboda and H. Petras (eds), *Defining Prevention Science*, pp. 537–556. New York, NY: Springer-Verlag.

Farrington, D. P., and Welsh, B. C. 2005. Randomized experiments in criminology: What have we learned in the last two decades? *Journal of Experimental Criminology*, 1:9–38. doi: 10.1007/s11292-004-6460-0

Grant, S., Mayo-Wilson, E., Hopewell, S., *et al.* 2013. Developing a reporting guideline for social and psychological intervention trials. *Journal of Experimental Criminology*, 9:355–367.

Greenwood, P., and Welsh, B. C. 2012. Promoting evidence-based practice in delinquency prevention at the state level: Principles, progress, and policy directions. *Criminology and Public Policy*, 11:493–513.

Hassmiller Lich, K., Ginexi, E. M., Osgood, N. D., and Mabry, P. L. 2013. A call to address complexity in prevention science research. *Prevention Science*, 14:279–289.

Heckman, J. J., Moon, S. H., Pinto, R., Savelyev, P. A., and Yavitz, A. 2010. Analyzing social experiments as implemented: A reexamination of the evidence from the HighScope Perry Preschool Program. *Quantitative Economics*, 1:1–46.

Hough, M. 2010. Gold standard or fool's gold? The pursuit of certainty in experimental criminology. *Criminology and Criminal Justice*, 10:11–22.

Institute of Medicine. 2008. *Knowing What Works in Health Care: A Roadmap for the Nation*. Washington, DC: The National Academies Press.

Lipsey, M. W. 2009. The primary factors that characterize effective interventions with juvenile offenders: A meta-analytic overview. *Victims and Offenders*, 4:124–147.

Lipsey, M. W., and Cullen, F. T. 2007. The effectiveness of correctional rehabilitation: A review of systematic reviews. *Annual Review of Law and Social Science*, 3:297–320.

Lipsey, M. W., and Howell, J. C. 2012. A broader view of evidence-based programs reveals more options for state juvenile justice systems. *Criminology and Public Policy*, 11:515–523.

Lipsey, M. W., Howell, J. C., Kelly, M. R., Chapman, G., and Carver, D. 2010. Improving the effectiveness of juvenile justice programs: A new perspective on evidence-based practice. Washington, DC: Center for Juvenile Justice Reform, Georgetown University.

Mears, D. P. 2007. Towards rational and evidence-based crime policy. *Journal of Criminal Justice*, 35:667–682. doi: 10.1016/j.jcrimjus.2007.09.003

Nagin, D. S., and Weisburd, D. 2013. Evidence and public policy: The example of evaluation research in policing. *Criminology and Public Policy*, 12:651–679.

Osgood, D. W., Feinberg, M. E., Gest, S. D., *et al.* 2013. Effects of PROSPER on the influence potential of prosocial versus antisocial youth in adolescent friendship networks. *Journal of Adolescent Health*, 53:174–179.

Petrosino, A. 2003. Standards for evidence and evidence for standards: The case of school-based drug prevention. *Annals of the American Academy of Political and Social Science*, 587:180–207.

Petrosino, A., Turpin-Petrosino, C., and Buehler, J. 2003. "Scared Straight" and other juvenile awareness programs for preventing juvenile delinquency *The Campbell Collaboration Reviews of Intervention and Policy Evaluations (C2-RIPE)*. Philadelphia, PA: Campbell Collaboration.

Pew-MacArthur Results First Initiative. 2015. Legislating evidence-based policymaking. Washington, DC: The Pew Charitable Trusts, MacArthur Foundation.

Robinson, L. O., and Slowikowski, J. 2011. Scary – and ineffective. *The Baltimore Sun,* January 31, 2011.

Sampson, R. J., Winship, C., and Knight, C. 2013. Translating causal claims: Principles and strategies for policy-relevant criminology. *Criminology and Public Policy*, 12:587–616.

Schultz, K. F., Altman, D. G., and Moher, D. 2010. CONSORT 2010 Statement: Updated guidelines for reporting parallel group randomised trials. *Journal of Clinical Epidemiology*, 63:834–840.

Schweinhart, L. J. 2005. *Lifetime Effects: The High/Scope Perry Preschool Study Through Age 40*. Ypsilanti, MI: High/Scope Press.

Schweinhart, L. J. 2013. Long-term follow-up of a preschool experiment. *Journal of Experimental Criminology*, 9:389–409. doi: 10.1007/s11292-013-9190-3

Seigle, E., Walsh, N., and Weber, J. 2014. Core principles for reducing recidivism and improving other outcomes for youth in the juvenile justice system. New York, NY: Council of State Governments Justice Center.

Shadish, W. R., Cook, T. D., and Leviton, L. C. 1991. *Foundations of Program Evaluation: Theories of Practice*. Newbury Park, CA: Sage.

Sherman, L. W., Gottfredson, D. C., MacKenzie, D., et al. (eds). 1997. Preventing Crime: What Works, What Doesn't, What's Promising: A Report to the United States Congress. Washington, DC: US Department of Justice, Office of Justice Programs.

Sherman, L. W., Gottfredson, D. C., MacKenzie, D. L., et al. 1998. *Preventing Crime: What Works, What Doesn't, What's Promising*. Washington, DC: National Institute of Justice.

Sloboda, Z., Stephens, R. C., Stephens, P., et al. 2009. The Adolescent Substance Abuse Prevention Study: A randomized field trial of a universal substance abuse prevention program. *Drug and Alcohol Dependence*, 102:1–10. doi: 10.1016/j.drugalcdep.2009.01.015

Valente, T. W., Chou, C. P., and Pentz, M. A. 2007. Community coalitions as a system: Effects of network change on adoption of evidence-based substance abuse prevention. *American Journal of Public Health*, 97:880–886.

Valentine, J. C., Biglan, A., Boruch, R. F., et al. 2011. Replication in prevention science. *Prevention Science*, 12:103–117.

Working Group of the Federal Collaboration on What Works. 2005. The OJP what works repository. Rockville, MD: Office of Justice Programs.

World Health Organization. 2014. Global status report on violence prevention 2014. Geneva, Switzerland.

Glossary★

Absolute Deterrent Effects Effects estimated from an evaluation of an intervention in which the control condition was one in which participants received no specific treatment or service.

Adaptation A modification of an intervention's components or protocols.

Adherence The extent to which all essential components of the intervention are delivered using the recommended methods and materials and to the intended population.

Adolescent Limited Offenders Offenders who limit their involvement in crime to their adolescent years.

Anomie A condition of societies during the transition from primarily rural to urban forms of social organization and solidarity when the traditional norms, values, and shared understandings of rural society break down and are no longer effective in regulating behavior.

Atavism A less evolved form of humanity; a subhuman, primitive, or savage species.

Attrition The loss of participants from the treatment and/or comparison groups during the implementation of the intervention or during the evaluation's follow-up periods.

Blueprints for Healthy Youth Development An online registry of evidence-based, experimentally proven programs maintained by the Center for the Study and Prevention of Violence at the University of Colorado, Boulder. See Table 5.5.

British Crime Survey A self-report victimization survey administered in the United Kingdom.

Campbell Collaboration An independent non-profit organization that conducts systematic reviews of crime and justice other health-related interventions.

Classical School of Criminology A criminal justice reform movement, based largely on the work of Jeremy Bentham and Cesare Beccaria, who argued for more just and reasonable criminal sanctions for offenders, believing they would be more effective in deterring criminal behavior because the public would view these punishments as more reasonable and fair.

★ *Definition of terms as used in this text and related specifically to usage in a crime prevention context.*

The Prevention of Crime, First Edition. Delbert Elliott and Abigail Fagan.
© 2017 John Wiley & Sons, Inc. Published 2017 by John Wiley & Sons, Inc.
Companion website: www.wiley.com/go/elliott/prevention_of_crime

Coalition for Evidence-Based Policy An online registry of evidence-based, experimentally proven programs maintained by this non-profit organization. See Table 5.5.

Code of Hammurabi A code created in the eighteenth century BC by the Babylonian ruler Hammurabi defining conduct that was prohibited and the specific punishments for a violation of each prohibited act; an early criminal code relying primarily on retribution as the prevention strategy.

Construct Validity An assessment of how well a measure accurately reflects the construct it is intended to represent in an evaluation of an intervention; how well it captures the essence of the risk or protective factor or crime outcome it is intended to represent.

Crime Behavior that violates a local, state, or federal criminal code or ordinance; unlawful behavior.

Crime Prevention Any program, practice, or policy that reduces the likelihood of future involvement in criminal behavior from what is expected without this intervention.

CrimeSolutions.gov An online registry of evidence-based crime prevention programs and practices maintained by the Office of Justice Programs in the US Department of Justice. See Table 5.5.

Crime Victimization Survey An Australian survey of persons aged 15 years or older asking them to self-report any criminal victimization they experienced over the past year.

Crimes Known to the Police A count of all the crimes reported to the police regardless of what was done by the police about this reported crime. One of the measures available in the annual FBI Uniform Crime Report (UCR).

Criminal Career Framework Criminological perspective conceptualizing involvement in crime as a job or career and identifying a set of concepts that describe different types, levels, and stages of involvement in crime, from the first to the last offense in an individual offender's life. See Table 3.1.

Criminal Ordinance A law passed by a city or county that prohibits specific behaviors in that city or county; a law limited in jurisdiction to a given city or county.

Cyber Crime Crimes committed on or through the Internet.

Developer Bias Situations in which evaluations conducted by an intervention's developer report higher effect sizes than evaluations by other independent investigators, resulting in an inflated effect size; when all or most evaluations of an intervention are conducted by the developer or his/her close colleagues.

Differential Association Theory Criminological theory stating that criminal behavior is the result of high levels of exposure to or intimate associations with criminal role models.

Differential Attrition A condition in which there is a difference between the treatment and comparison groups in the attrition rate or the type of participants that drop out of an evaluation; one of the major threats to the internal validity of an evaluation.

Dissemination The promotion, delivery, and adoption of interventions outside of research evaluations.

Diversion Programs Programs designed to keep persons apprehended or arrested for a crime out of the formal justice system, providing alternatives such as fines, community service or treatment in a community program; programs that are designed to minimize the stigma of having an official arrest or conviction record.

Dosage The amount of programming delivered by implementers; the number, length, frequency, and duration of programming sessions or services delivered to program participants.

Effect Size A measure of the relative strength and substantive significance of the intervention's main effect.

Experimental Evaluation An assessment of the effects of the intervention on criminal behavior that involves a matched or very similar group of intervention and control or comparison groups; an evaluation design that can provide the strongest evidence of an intervention's effect on crime.

External Validity An assessment of the extent to which the findings from an evaluation or set of evaluations can be generalized to other settings and populations.

Fear of Crime The psychological and emotional costs associated with worry or anxiety about one's own victimization or victimization occurring to friends or relatives.

Felony Crime A class of serious crimes that involve a sentence of confinement for more than a year in a state or federal prison if convicted. See Table 1.1.

Environmental Crime Prevention A type of crime prevention that attempts to change the physical features of places in which crimes are likely to occur or reduce the personal and contextual interactions that provide opportunities for crime, making crimes more difficult to commit, easier to detect and more likely to result in an arrest.

Fit Assessment A review of potential evidence-based interventions to determine which one best addresses a local community's or agency's targeted risk and protective factors, type of clients or participants and available local resources and which is most consistent with community values and philosophy of treatment; matching available interventions to local needs and resources.

General Deterrence A strategy for reducing crime that calls for increasing public awareness about certainty and severity of punishments for crime, assuming that the punishment is severe enough to deter a rational person from engaging in that behavior.

Going-to-Scale The wide dissemination, adoption, and implementation of an intervention; implementation on a state-wide or national level. Sometimes referred to as "scaling-up."

Hot Spot Policing A policing strategy that increases law enforcement activities such as patrol and surveillance at geographical areas where the rates of crime are particularly and consistently elevated.

Ignition Interlock Device A device that disables an automobile until the driver takes and passes a breath alcohol content test; the device may also require testing at random intervals while the car is in use.

Implementation Monitoring Tracking the implementation of an intervention to insure that it is being delivered as specified by the intervention developer; that is, with fidelity.

Implementation Science The study of how to effectively disseminate and successfully implement effective programs, practices, and policies at a level that can impact community, state, and national levels of crime.

Indicated Prevention Intervention An intervention intended for individuals who have already engaged in criminal behavior to deter them from any further criminal behavior.

Intangible Costs Non-financial costs of crime related to the physical and emotional pain and suffering of victims.

Integrated Theory A theoretical explanation created by Del Elliott and colleagues that combines elements of Strain, Social Control, and Social Learning Theories. Identifying two primary pathways leading to involvement in criminal behavior.

Integrated Theories Theories that combine the central hypotheses from earlier theoretical explanations into a single coherent, more complex and comprehensive explanation. For specific examples, see Integrated Theory, Interaction Theory, and the Social Development Model.

Intent-to-Treat Analysis A type of evaluation data analysis in which all those assigned to the treatment and control conditions are included in the pre-test and follow-up data collection points and analysis regardless of whether they complete the treatment or drop out of the treatment or control groups.

Interaction Theory An integrated theoretical explanation that combines elements of Social Control and Social Learning theories. This explanation claims that the relationships between causal variables are likely to be reciprocal rather than unidirectional.

Internal Validity An assessment of the extent to which an evaluation has eliminated potential alternative explanations for an intervention's effectiveness; that is, explanations other than an effect of the intervention.

Justice Reinvestment Initiatives (JRI) An initiative by the US Bureau of Justice Assistance (BJA) to reduce prison populations and costs by using evidence-based interventions and then using the savings generated by lower recidivism rates and corrections costs to provide funding for community-based crime prevention programs, practices, and policies.

Life Course Developmental Paradigm A conceptual framework describing personal growth and development over time and in response to changing social and physical environments. In criminology, this paradigm is used to explain individuals' likelihood of engaging in crime at different ages and in different contexts.

Life Course Persistent Offenders Offenders who initiated offending during childhood and continue offending through adolescence and adulthood.

Logic Model The underlying rationale for a program's content, operation, and expected effect on criminal behavior; the theoretical model and behavioral change model guiding the development of the program and explaining why and how it should work.

Macro Theory A theory explaining the variation in rates of crime in societies or communities, such as why one society has higher rates of crime than another society.

Marginal Deterrent Effect Effects estimated from an evaluation of an intervention in which the control condition was one in which the participants received an alternative treatment or service, often the typical treatment or service offered to offenders in correctional facilities.

Mechanical Solidarity A form of solidarity found in pre-literate and pre-industrial societies where families were self-sufficient and larger groups were homogeneous and functioned independently of one another, providing all their own needs.

Mediation Analysis A statistical analysis to determine if the change in crime attributed to the intervention was the result, at least in part, of a change in the targeted risk and or protective factors; a test of the validity of the intervention's logic model.

Meta-Analysis A method for combining evaluation results from different studies of a given program or of a general type of program or intervention strategy, to obtain an average effect size for the program or practice.

Micro Theory A theory explaining variation in individuals' participation in crime; for example, why this individual rather than that individual engages in crime.

Misdemeanor Crimes Less serious offenses that typically involve sentences of up to a year in a county jail and/or monetary fines or community service if convicted. See Table 1.1.

Mobilization for Youth A delinquency prevention initiative implemented in 1962 in Manhattan, New York based on Strain Theory; an intervention designed to increase opportunities for disadvantaged youth and establish a more equitable distribution of resources in low-income neighborhoods.

Model Programs Guide An online registry of evidence-based programs maintained by the Office of Juvenile Justice and Delinquency Prevention in the US Department of Justice. See Table 5.5.

Moderation Analysis An evaluation analysis to identify factors that may influence the strength or direction of intervention effects; for example, participants' age, sex, or race/ethnicity.

Monitoring the Future Study A self-report survey of victimization and offending administered annually to a nationally representative sample of 8th, 10th, and 12th grade students in the United States, best known for its reported rates of substance use.

Mosaic Law A set of commandments and regulations given to Moses and the Israelite Tribes around the twelfth century BC. The Ten Commandments were a central feature of this set of laws. The laws represent primarily a threat of retribution prevention strategy.

Motivational Interviewing (MI) A non-confrontational, non-judgmental, one-on-one therapeutic practice allowing clients to reflect on their own behaviors and decide on the future actions they will take to reduce problem behaviors.

National Crime Victimization Survey The largest national victimization study in the United States, administered every six months by the US Census Bureau to a representative national sample of persons aged 10 years and older. Respondents self-report their victimization on a set of specific offenses including most UCR Part I crimes.

National Incident-Based Reporting System An official measure of crime incidents in the United States based on law enforcement reports of crime events and arrests for crimes known to the police; part of the annual FBI Uniform Crime Reports (UCR).

National Registry of Evidence-Based Programs and Practices (NREPP) An online registry of evidence-based programs and practices to prevent substance use/abuse and mental health problems maintained by the Substance Abuse and Mental Health Services Administration in the US Department of Health and Human Services. See Table 5.5.

National Survey of Children's Exposure to Violence A nationally representative self-report survey conducted in 2008 and 2011 in the United States asking parent and children aged 0 to 17 years old about youth victimization occurring in their homes, schools, and neighborhoods in the past year and in their lifetimes.

National Youth Survey A longitudinal self-report survey of offending and victimization of a national representative panel of individuals. The study was begun in 1976 when youth were aged 11–17 and involved 11 surveys over their life course until 2003, when they were aged 38–44. All Part I and most of Part II offenses are included in reports of both offending and victimization. Reports by parents and children of the original sample are included in specific years. Data on risk and protective factors are also collected at each of the 11 surveys.

Needs Assessment A survey and review of local data on (i) the types of crimes occurring, where and when they occur and characteristics of offenders, and (ii) the risk and protective factors contributing to these crimes; together, these data are used to identify the types of intervention needed in a community.

Official Measures of Crime Law enforcement agency records of crimes, including crimes known to the police, arrests, court convictions, crimes cleared by arrest, and crime incidents.

Organic Solidarity A type of solidarity found in larger, more complex, post-industrial societies where families and larger groups are no longer self-sufficient, there is a high division of labor and individuals have specialized roles and tasks.

Paradigm A worldview or tradition within a scientific discipline.

Parens Patriae A British doctrine in which the government assumes the role of parent, providing for children's basic needs and protection when their natural parents are not doing so. A philosophy adopted by US juvenile courts in the early years of the courts' operation.

Part I Offenses A set of serious personal and property offenses included in the FBI's Uniform Crime Reports (UCR) including: homicide, rape, robbery, aggravated assault, burglary, larceny-theft, motor vehicle theft, and arson. See Table 1.1.

Part II Offenses A set of less serious crimes included in the FBI's Uniform Crime Reports (UCR). Only arrest data are reported for Part II Offenses. See Table 1.1.

Personal Crimes Offenses that involve physical or mental harm to an individual.

Positivism A movement calling for the use of the scientific method to determine if hypothesized causes of crime could be demonstrated empirically and if crime interventions had any demonstrable effect.

Pre-Post Outcome Evaluation A non-experimental assessment of the effects of an intervention on the criminal involvement of clients or population being served; there are no control or comparison groups and decisions regarding effectiveness are based on information collected before the intervention begins and after it ends.

Prevention Science The study and accumulated body of knowledge about interventions that are developed to minimize the risk factors and enhance the protective factors identified in established theory to explain criminal behavior and other forms of health-compromising behaviors and to promote a healthy, positive course of development for individuals.

Prevention Policy A regulation or law enacted by local, state, or federal governmental agencies designed to prevent involvement in criminal behavior on the part of the population under their jurisdiction.

Prevention Practice A general strategy, approach or procedure that utilizes similar, but not necessarily the same specific interventions to reduce crime; a generic class of interventions like bullying or parent training interventions.

Prevention Program A package of services, including a specific set of activities, protocols, and procedures, designed to address specific risk and protective factors in a specific population of clients or eligible persons, typically with training, technical assistance, and implementation fidelity requirements.

Primary Prevention Program Used in older classifications of prevention interventions to indicate an intervention designed to prevent the onset of criminal behavior.

Process Evaluation An assessment of the intervention's logic model, implementation fidelity, integration into the local agency network, and community acceptance.

Property Crimes Offenses that interfere with another person's right to use or enjoy his/her property.

Protective Factor A condition or trait that buffers the negative effects of a risk condition; it eliminates or weakens the expected effect of a risk factor.

Publication Bias A tendency for academic journals to favor evaluation studies that find positive effects over those that find negative effects, resulting in an inflated estimate of an intervention's effect size.

Purveyors Individuals or agencies certified by a program developer to deliver the program or provide specific program services like training and technical assistance.

Quasi-Experimental Design A type of experimental evaluation that involves matching intervention and comparison groups on factors thought to affect the outcome of the intervention; the design most frequently used in the evaluations of interventions.

Randomized Control Trial (RCT) A type of experimental evaluation that involves assigning individuals or groups to a treatment group and a control group before the intervention begins using a random selection process; a type of study that provides the strongest evidence of internal validity and the effectiveness of an intervention; the "gold standard" in evaluation.

Rational Choice Theory A variation of deterrence theory which states that individuals make rational choices regarding whether or not to engage in crime based on maximizing their profits or rewards and minimizing their losses or costs; people act according to their own self-interest. The crime prevention focus is primarily on how to influence individual perceived risks and anticipated rewards of crime.

Recidivism Re-offending after release from some correctional or justice program; crimes committed after the end of a planned intervention or after one has dropped out of an intervention.

Resource Assessment A survey of local agencies and/or community resource guides to determine the crime prevention programs, practices, and policies currently available in a community.

Restorative Justice An intervention strategy designed to minimize the stigma associated with treatment in the justice system and facilitate re-integration into the community. It typically requires the offender to admit his/her guilt and hear from and respond to victim(s) in a meeting with a trained mediator.

Return on Investment An estimate of the societal financial benefit of investing in a particular intervention; the extent to which the financial returns or benefits outweigh the costs of investing in a given intervention.

Risk Factor A condition or trait that increases the likelihood that one will engage in criminal behavior; it predicts future criminal behavior.

Roman Twelve Tablets An early set of laws enacted by the Romans around 451 BC. The laws rely on retribution as the primary crime prevention strategy but include some provisions that influenced contemporary US criminal law, such as establishing due process, grace periods for paying a debt, and recognition of extenuating circumstances.

Routine Activities Theory A theoretical explanation which considers both the environmental context and individual decision-making as primary causes of crime; the more exposed to crime and criminal opportunities in one's everyday routine activities, the greater the chances of becoming a perpetrator and a victim of crime.

Secondary Prevention Intervention Used in older classifications of prevention interventions to refer to programs or practices designed to reduce criminal behavior on the part of those who are already offenders.

Selective Prevention Intervention An intervention intended for individuals or groups known to have experienced one or more risk factors for crime.

Self-Reported Measures of Crime A measure of criminal activity based on personal reports of offenses in a written survey or personal interview. These reports allow for the identification of the number of crimes committed (frequency), number of persons committing crimes (prevalence), number of crimes per person (personal crime rate), number of specific types or seriousness of crimes and other types of criminal involvement (arrests, convictions, placement in a correctional facility, etc.).

Situational Prevention Intervention A type of intervention that attempts to change the physical features of places in which crimes are likely to occur or reduce the personal and contextual interactions that provide opportunities for crime, making crimes more difficult to commit, easier to detect and more likely to result in an arrest. See also **Environmental Crime Prevention**.

Social Control Theory A criminological theory stating that crime is the result of a failure to develop and/or sustain internal (personal) normative controls on behavior and conflict or inconsistency in external controls (family, peer group, neighborhood, and community norms) that serve to regulate behavior.

Social Impact Bonds (SIBs) A funding mechanism where private investors pay for government-sponsored programs and realize a profit if the interventions produce a pre-specified level of reduction in recidivism or sustain a loss if the goal is not met.

Social Learning Theory A criminological theory stating that crime is the result of basic learning processes; criminal onset is the result of imitation and persistence is the result of positive social reinforcement for criminal behaviors.

Somatotypes A typology of body types based on observed clusters of physiological body characteristics developed by William Sheldon.

Specific Deterrence A prevention strategy based on providing offenders with a level of punishment that is severe enough to prevent a rational offender from committing another crime.

Stigmata Physical signs or indicators of atavism – a subhuman, primitive, or less evolved form of humanity.

Strain Theory A criminological theory stating that the basic motivation for crime is the strain or frustration experienced by those facing limited opportunities to achieve conventional goals and aspirations.

Sustainability The ability of an intervention to have a prolonged effect on crime that is demonstrated after the end of the intervention, typically for a year or longer; or, the continued implementation of an intervention over time.

System Readiness An assessment of the dissemination capacity of an intervention; the extent to which the intervention developer can provide training, tools, manuals and ongoing support to agencies wanting to implement the intervention.

Systematic Review A rigorous approach for summarizing the results from multiple evaluations of an intervention or set of interventions that involves a formal set of procedures that guide the search, selection, evaluation and analysis of findings.

Tangible Costs Financial costs related to crime victims' medical bills and lost productivity at work, law enforcement operations, court processing and correctional facilities expenses incurred to house offenders in jails and prisons or supervise them when released back to the community.

Target Hardening Crime prevention practices designed to make places more difficult to vandalize, burglarize or enter for unlawful purposes; examples include locks, metal detectors, fencing, and surveillance cameras.

Technical Assistance Advice and support provided by program developers or purveyors intended to ensure that staff are delivering interventions with fidelity.

Tertiary Prevention Interventions Used in older classifications of prevention interventions to refer to treatment services for those with a substance abuse or mental health disorder.

The Social Development Model A type of integrated theory that combines elements from social control and social learning theories. The theory describes what is necessary to create strong positive relationships and social bonds that serve to prevent involvement in criminal behavior.

Three Strikes Laws Laws mandating long sentences, sometimes life in prison without parole, for offenders convicted of their third crime, usually a felony.

Uniform Crime Reports The FBI-generated reports of crimes and law enforcement activity in the United States; data obtained from law enforcement agencies including counts of crimes known to the police, crimes cleared, arrest rates, crime incidents, and law enforcement officers killed and assaulted.

Universal Prevention Intervention An intervention intended for the general public or all individuals in a given setting without regard for their involvement in crime or levels of risk or protection.

Validity A method of judging the merit of an evaluation design and measures of risk, protection, and crime outcomes; the greater the validity, the more confidence can be placed in the evaluation's findings. See Table 4.2.

Youth Risk Behavior Survey A self-reported survey of public school students in Grades 9–12 in the United States conducted by the Centers for Disease Control and Prevention every other year since 1991. Both offender and victimization data are collected as well as information on risk and protective factors.

Vicarious Victimization Personal stress, trauma or fear resulting from witnessing or hearing about crimes perpetrated against others.

Zero-Tolerance Policy Typically a school policy that requires relatively severe and certain punishment for each and every violation of the policy without exception, such as a policy requiring expulsion for any student who carries a gun onto school property.

Author Index

Page numbers in *italics* refer to figures; page numbers in **bold** refer to Tables.

Subject Index

Page numbers in *italics* refer to Figures; page numbers in **bold** refer to Tables

The Prevention of Crime, First Edition. Delbert Elliott and Abigail Fagan.
© 2017 John Wiley & Sons, Inc. Published 2017 by John Wiley & Sons, Inc.
Companion website: www.wiley.com/go/elliott/prevention_of_crime